D0070480

Urban Government

VAN NOSTRAND POLITICAL SCIENCE SERIES

Editor

FRANKLIN L. BURDETTE
University of Maryland

GODSHALL, W. L. (Editor)—*Principles and Functions of Government in the United States*

LONDON, K.—*How Foreign Policy Is Made*

PLISCHKE, E.—*Conduct of American Diplomacy*

DIXON, R. G., JR. and PLISCHKE, ELMER—*American Government: Basic Documents and Materials*

SPROUT, HAROLD and MARGARET—*Foundations of National Power,* 2nd Ed.

LANCASTER, LANE W.—*Government in Rural America,* 2nd Ed.

JORRIN, M.—*Governments of Latin America*

TORPEY, WILLIAM G.—*Public Personnel Management*

PLISCHKE, ELMER—*International Relations: Basic Documents*

GOODMAN, WILLIAM—*The Two-Party System in the United States*

WATKINS, J. T., IV and ROBINSON, J. W.—*General International Organization: A Source Book*

BAKER, BENJAMIN—*Urban Government*

SWARTZ, WILLIS G.—*American Government Problems*

Urban Government

by

BENJAMIN BAKER
Rutgers University

D. VAN NOSTRAND COMPANY, INC.
PRINCETON, NEW JERSEY
TORONTO LONDON
NEW YORK

To

Sophie, Milton, and Harvey

D. VAN NOSTRAND COMPANY, INC.

120 Alexander St., Princeton, New Jersey
257 Fourth Avenue, New York 10, New York
25 Hollinger Rd., Toronto 16, Canada

All correspondence should be addressed to the principal office of the company at Princeton, N. J.

Library of Congress Catalogue Card No. 57-9696

Published simultaneously in Canada by
D. VAN NOSTRAND COMPANY (Canada), LTD.

PRINTED IN THE UNITED STATES OF AMERICA

Preface

This book is designed for those students and readers interested in the study of municipal political institutions and their development. Stress is placed upon the dynamic character of these institutions. The municipality and its functions are presented as being in a constant state of flux, and its authority and responsibility as being highly sensitive to the changes in the society of which it is now a significant part. Hence the traditional emphasis on form and structure in the study of urban government has been supplemented in this book and given vitality by a new ingredient—an examination of the forces that have shaped the course of city development over the years. An understanding of these forces will supply the student with the rationale underlying the functioning of municipal political institutions, in addition to giving him a familiarity with the institutions themselves.

Among the many factors influencing the development of the city, of major importance are the divorce of men from the soil and the use of energy in the form of steam, electricity, and the internal combustion engine. The concentration of people in the city in response to these factors created a virtual revolution in our thinking concerning the role of municipal government. Conceptions of individual liberty common to rural areas were modified and changed. The city found itself compelled to take an interest in the activities of the individual and to guide them with a view to the welfare of the whole community. Municipal government, confronted by problems that required expert attention, began to look beyond the impractical amateur to the fulltime professional for help. At the same time, problems of its accountability to the citizen arose.

In recent years, a centrifugal force has operated on the city, causing the dispersal of plants and people. The automobile and the truck, together with widespread use of electricity, have transformed, almost overnight, rural areas into urban ones. The explosion of cities, in brief, has resulted in the movement of plant and people to peripheral areas while at the same time the nexus to the central city has been maintained. The creation of these vast, amorphous economic regions has brought a crisis in municipal political institutions. Problems common to an area are dealt with on a fragmented basis by many cities, with no common governmental instrumentality. How to broaden the legal instrument to make it correspond to social and economic fact has emerged as one of the most fundamental problems of municipal government.

Thus it can be seen that the factors affecting the growth and development of municipal institutions are a necessary part of the study of urban government. Until some measure of understanding is gained about the phenomena affecting the course of city development, our knowledge of the subject will remain inadequate.

ACKNOWLEDGMENT

This book owes a great deal to many people who have stimulated my interest in municipal government. Dr. Luther H. Gulick, now president of the Institute of Public Administration and formerly of Columbia University, did much to awaken my initial appreciation of the importance of municipal government. Needless to say his many stimulating articles in professional journals have constantly broadened my knowledge of the subject.

My colleagues at Rutgers University—Professors Bennett M. Rich, Norman L. Stamps, and Ardath W. Burks—have aided me greatly by their constructive criticisms of portions of the manuscript. I am also especially indebted to Professor Edward McNall Burns of Rutgers University. His comments on the manuscript have been very helpful and his encouragement has been so great that, without it, this book might never have been written.

The Research Council of Rutgers University kindly made available the services of Walter Volkomer, who was very helpful in some of the research and in the proofreading and indexing of the book.

The responsibility for any errors in the book is, of course, my own, and any corrections and suggestions for improvement of the presentation will be highly welcome.

BENJAMIN BAKER

Rutgers University
New Brunswick, N. J.

Contents

Part Five—Conclusion

PART ONE

The City as a Social Fact

Chapter One

The Changing City

The Role of the City

The city looms large upon the horizon of civilization. Scarcely a civilization has existed which has not been based upon the city. The progress of the arts and sciences, the development of the essentials of civilized life, and, indeed, the spread of civilization over the globe are, in large part, the result of the cultural leaven provided by the city. World history, wrote Spengler, "is the history of civic man. Peoples, states, politics, all arts and all sciences rest upon *one* prime phenomenon of human being, the town." [1]

In the city are found the division of labor, the specialization of talent, the productive apparatus, the wealth and leisure, and the constant contact of man and mind that make for intellectual advance. It is the city that, in Victor Hugo's graphic phrase, contains the vital juices of society. City life "creates new economic activities, new political ideas and ideals, new forms of social intercourse, new possibilities of interchange of ideas." [2]

It is the city that provides the precondition for intellectual activity. Freedom and democracy, city-born in ancient Greece, have become part and parcel of Western civilization. In the Middle Ages the municipalities fought—and won—the battle for local self-government.[3] Today, and yesterday, the constant stimulus of man in the mass has catapulted the city into the forefront of advancing civilization. The change in the condition of man from agricultural to civilized existence has been proportionate to the degree of urban development.

---

1 O. Spengler, *The Decline of the West,* trans, C. F. Atkinson (New York: Alfred Knopf Co., 1928), II, pp. 90-91. Italics in the text. Spengler regards cosmopolis as the endpoint of culture. For a refutation of his point of view see C. Tunnard, *The City of Man* (New York: Charles Scribner's Sons, 1953), pp. 45-46.

2 L. S. Rowe, *Problems of City Government* (New York: D. Appleton and Company, 1915), p. 13.

3 E. W. Burgess, ed., *The Urban Community* (Chicago: University of Chicago Press, 1926), pp. 60-61.

In our society, the city is the central fact of our existence. More than two-thirds of our people live in cities. If one adds the rural nonfarm population, approximately 85 percent of our population is urban in character.[4] Within our cities, too, are those life processes of production, distribution, commerce and finance that provide the wherewithal of our national existence. Most of our industrial capacity is located within the city. Urban areas contain a major part of our work force, and most of the goods and services so essential to modern living originate in the city. Our cities, as the National Resources Committee has pointed out so correctly, are "the workshop of our industrial society and the nerve center of our vast and delicate commercial mechanism." [5]

From a governmental standpoint, the city is the unit that touches us most closely, and most often. In its corporate capacity it performs those tasks which we are unable to do ourselves. Thus health, education, protection, housing, and a multitude of other functions become the object of its concern. Indeed, most of our problems sooner or later come to "city hall." Life under urban conditions can hardly exist without the presence of urban government. The city, in its political form, may be regarded as the key to human life in large aggregates.

THE MEANING OF THE CITY

Since the city plays such a significant role in our daily lives, it becomes extremely important for us to understand the meaning of the term "city." A city may be defined in several ways: as a population aggregate; as a community; and as a political entity. While our major concern will be centered on the governing instrumentality, it is, nevertheless, necessary to discuss the city as a sociological concept in order that we may more fully understand the consequences that follow from the existence of the city as a social unit.

---

[4] U. S. Dept. of Commerce, Bureau of the Census, *U. S. Census, 1950, Census of Population,* II, 105.

[5] National Resources Committee, Report of the Urbanism Committee, *Our Cities —Their Role in the National Economy* (Washington, D. C.: U. S. Government Printing Office, 1947), Foreword, p. v. In 1947 American cities contained 240,881 factories with an annual employment of 14.3 million workers. U. S. Bureau of Census, *Census of Manufactures* (Washington, D. C.: U. S. Government Printing Office, 1947), I, p. 23. In 1948 retail trade in areas with a population of 2,500 or more amounted to $131 billions. In that same year 501 cities of 25,000 or more did 57.6 percent of the retail sales. U. S. Bureau of Census, *Retail Trade—General Statistics* (Washington, D. C.: U. S. Government Printing Office, 1952) 1, Part I, p. 14.

The Census Bureau employs population concentration as the measure of urbanization. Urban population, in its view, includes the following: all persons living in places of 2,500 or more inhabitants incorporated as cities, boroughs, and villages; those residing in incorporated towns of 2,500 or more, except in New England, New York, and Wisconsin, where towns are considered minor civil divisions of the county; those located in densely settled urban fringes, including both incorporated and unincorporated areas surrounding cities of 50,000 or more people; and those unincorporated areas of 2,500 or more inhabitants outside of the urban fringe. An urban place, according to this definition, is a population of 2,500 or more persons regardless of legally prescribed limits.[6]

Urbanized areas were first defined in 1950 in order to distinguish more carefully the urban and rural populations. Each urbanized area contains at least one city with 50,000 or more people in 1940, or according to a special census taken between 1940 and 1950. Such areas are considered to be the physical city as distinguished from both the legal city and the metropolitan community. In general, the urbanized areas represent the thickly settled core of the standard metropolitan areas.[7]

The remainder of the population is considered rural. All persons living on farms, regardless of occupation, are considered a part of the farm population. In 1950, as compared with the previous census, persons living on what might be regarded as farm land were classified as nonfarm population if they paid rent for their homes and yards.[8]

Ever since the advent of the motor car it has been recognized that the city is not complete as a unit unless the people living on its outskirts are considered an integral part of the urban unit. Suburbs and rural areas in the process of urbanization reflect the drift away from the core city, and yet, economically and socially, they are still part of a single urban community. Bureau of Census efforts to measure this fundamental change have been reflected in two classifications, the metropolitan district and the standard metropolitan area.

---

[6] U. S. Dept. of Commerce, Bureau of the Census, *U. S. Census, 1950, Census of Population,* II, 105. The 1940 census definition limited the classification of urban population to *incorporated areas* containing 2,500 or more inhabitants. Author's italics.

[7] *Ibid.,* p. x.

[8] Rural nonfarm population, another category based upon population density, consists of all persons living outside urban areas who do not live on farms.

The former, employed until 1950, was based upon minor civil divisions. The latter, except for New England, uses the county as its basis of measurement.[9]

A classification of urban areas on the basis of population density is important for it clearly differentiates urban from rural areas. Population concentration, of necessity, means more governmental control, and this, in itself, measures the difference between rural and urban areas.

If we go beyond the mere classification of people in terms of numbers, we can view the city as a social fact. The city is a conglomerate of people living together in a multifaceted relationship. Its people are social beings bound together in a community of purpose with a common body of customs and ideals. It is here that the sociologist views the city as a "functional unit" that is "closely identified with the lives of the people." [10] The city is a "state of mind . . . a product of nature and particularly human nature." [11] Perhaps the more comprehensive definition of the city in the social sense was given by Elihu Root in a speech before the Russell Sage Foundation. In his words,

> A city is a growth. It is not the result of political decrees or control. You may draw all the lines you please between counties and states; a city is a growth responding to forces not at all political, quite disregarding political lines. It is a growth like that of a crystal responding to forces inherent in the atoms that make it up.[12]

---

[9] See chapter 18 for further elaboration of the definition of metropolitan areas. A standard metropolitan area is a county or group of counties (except in New England) which contain at least one city of 50,000 or more inhabitants. Contiguous counties are also included if they are metropolitan in character. Criteria of a metropolitan character relating to the county are the following: (1) The county must contain (a) 10,000 nonagricultural workers or (b) 10 percent of the nonagricultural workers employed in the metropolitan area or (c) have at least one-half of the population residing in minor civil divisions with a population density of 150 or more per square mile and contiguous to the central city and (2) nonagricultural workers must constitute two-thirds of the total number of employed persons of the county.

[10] J. A. Kinneman, *The Community in American Society* (New York: Appleton-Century-Crofts, Inc., 1947), p. 403. Also R. M. MacIver, *Society* (New York: Farrar and Rinehart, Inc., 1937), p. 8 "The mark of a community is that one's life may be lived wholly within it, that all one's social relationships may be found in it." Also R. M. MacIver, *Community, A Sociological Study* (London: Macmillan and Co., 1917), p. 23.

[11] R. E. Park, E. W. Burgess, and R. D. McKenzie, *The City* (Chicago: University of Chicago Press, 1925), pp. 1, 4.

[12] Quoted by H. W. Zorbaugh, "The Natural Areas of Cities" in E. W. Burgess, ed., *The Urban Community* (Chicago: University of Chicago Press, 1926), p. 221. Copyright 1926 by the University of Chicago. Root is not, of course, a sociologist.

With his concept of the community, the sociologist examines the social structure of the city and seeks to determine whether it is functionally adequate. The impact of the city upon the individual, the deterioration of social controls, and the erosion of a coherence of purpose become the object of his inquiry. A study of the community within this framework of reference is beyond the limits of this book, yet it is important, nonetheless, for it is in the breakdown of the community that the city is brought face to face with many of the problems with which it must deal in its political capacity.

While a city is composed of people and exists as a community, it is also more than this. It is a governmental entity, representing the politically organized expression of the community; a corporate being which in its collective capacity performs those functions which the individual cannot carry out for himself. The city acts for the public. It is, in Fairlie's words, "an organized public authority."[13] The city, in brief, holds governmental powers to deal with the needs of society resulting from the concentration of people within a given area.

The city may be defined as an urban place with territorial limits, possessing a legal instrumentality which, in large measure, guides the conduct and behavior of its people. City government is urban government—the means through which the community in its organized political form attempts to solve its problems on the basis of mutual interest.

URBAN GROWTH

Depopulation of the countryside, a concomitant of industrialization, is a factor of profound importance. As long as the city was minor in its significance, the conditions of rural life dominated the thought of the nation. Extreme individualism, suspicion of government, and "independence of the farmer" were the hallmarks of rural society. The drift of people to the city, however, meant a changed conception of government. Independence was replaced by interdependence, and the expansion of governmental functions occurred. As the cities grew in size and population density increased, it was they who determined the political and cultural values of the nation. The imposition of new standards took place, although it resulted in a moral protest against city life. Today the values of our

---

[13] J. A. Fairlie, *Municipal Administration* (New York: Macmillan Co., 1906), Preface, p. vi.

society are urban-oriented. Rural depopulation, therefore, has had a profound effect upon our society.[14]

The relatively rapid rate of urbanization of this country is revealed by Fig. 1. In 1790, the population of this country was predominantly rural in composition with approximately 95 percent

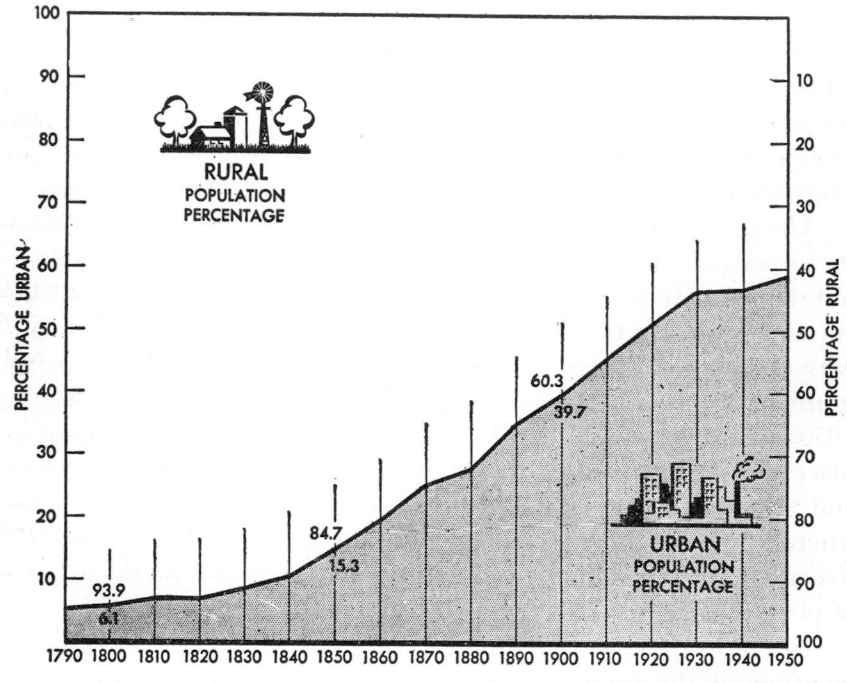

Fig. 1. Percentage of Urban and Rural Population, 1790-1950.

of the people gainfully employed in agriculture. A half century later the number of people in urban areas had approximately doubled (10.8 percent). By 1860, 20 percent were living in cities.

The urbanization trend was intensified in the decades following the Civil War. By the turn of the century, 39.7 percent of the people were living in urban areas.[15] By 1920 the urban population exceeded the rural population for the first time. A decade later, 56.5 percent of the population was to be found in the cities. According to the census of 1950, urban population has progressed to the point

[14] Rowe, *op. cit.*, Chapters IV, V. Also Burgess, *op. cit.*, pp. 55-56.

[15] U. S. Bureau of Census, *Statistical Abstract of the United States* (Washington, D. C.: U. S. Government Printing Office, 1953), p. 26.

where approximately three out of every five persons are living in urban territory.[16]

The rate of growth in the decade 1940–1950 is of special significance. If one compares the 1940 urban population with that of the old urban definition for 1950, one finds an increase in urban population of approximately 14.5 million within a single decade. A comparison of rural populations on the same basis for the decade 1940–1950 reveals a decline of approximately 7 million in the rural population.[17] The gain in urban population was second only to the increase in the decade 1920–1930 and marked the seventh consecutive decade in which the numerical increase in the urban population exceeded that of the rural population.

Urban places, the measure of urban growth, began to appear in increasing numbers at the time of the Civil War. In 1860 the number of such places was 392. The number steadily increased until, at the turn of the century, there were 1,737 urban as compared with 8,931 rural places of 2,500 or less in population. By 1940 the number of urban places was approximately double that of 1900. In 1950, according to the old urban definition, there were 4,023 urban places.[18] Five urban places had a population of a million or more, and a total of 106 cities had a population of 100,000 or more, whereas in 1940 there were only 92 cities of this size. In these cities live 44,311,617 persons, an increase of 16.6 percent over the number of people living in cities of 100,000 or more in 1940.[19]

No measurement of urban growth is complete without some mention of the growth of suburban and what John Perkins has called "rururban" areas. The suburb differs from the city only in degree but not in kind. It is composed largely of persons who have sought surcease from the cares and confusions of city life. Finding life in the city difficult and having the means, either in the form of mass transportation or private motor, people forsook the city in droves. A peaceful countryside soon became a thriving municipality, a result duplicated, over and over again, throughout the land. Some

[16] *U. S. Census, 1950, Census of Population,* I, xv.

[17] *Ibid.* The census definition of urban population was changed in 1940. Comparisons, therefore, can be made only on the basis of the 1940 definition. The 1940 urban population, according to the old urban definition, was 74,423,702; that of 1950, 88,927,464.

[18] *Statistical Abstract, 1953,* p. 27. In 1790 this nation did not have a single town with a population of 50,000 people. New York in 1880 became the first city with a population of 1 million. *U. S. Census, 1950 Census of Population,* I, xv.

[19] *U. S. Census, 1950, Census of Population,* I, xxix.

who came to the country might have become disillusioned and moved farther away from the environs of the central city, but the migration from the city of others who have sought the benefits, real or imagined, of suburban living continued. Population statistics of the 1950 census reveal the extent of this trend. While the central cities experienced a population increase of 14 percent, the suburbs grew at a rate approximately three times as great.[20] The trend, which began in 1900, is still with us and promises to continue to be a dominant one for some time to come.

The proliferation of suburban areas is a development of tremendous import. People left the central city. So did the plants. Rural areas were transformed almost overnight into urban ones. What were once hardly more than place names became municipalities. But while the outskirts grew rapidly they retained their nexus to the central city, largely because of the relative ease of access. As a consequence, there arose what the Bureau of Census has termed the standard metropolitan area, a community of interest and people but without any common governing instrumentality. In other words, while the metropolitan area has economic and social reality, it has not, as yet, come of age politically. Each municipality, whether central city or suburb, has its own governing body, its own functions and separate fiscal authority. How to broaden the legal instrumentality to make it correspond to economic and social fact constitutes one of the fundamental problems of municipal government.

LIFE IN THE CITY

The city, in the words of the Urbanism Committee of the National Resources Committee, is "the heart of cultural activity." Within its boundaries are found "the institutions, the facilities, the personnel, the atmosphere and the conditions . . . from which a rich intellectual and cultural life can spring and through it can be promoted and diffused." [21] Because of its dominance of the cultural apparatus, the city molds the thoughts and attitudes of the nation. Thus, what happens in the city is of tremendous importance for all of us.[22]

---

20 *Ibid.*, xxxii.

21 Report of the Urbanism Committee, *op. cit.*, p. 2.

22 E. Peterson, ed., *Cities are Abnormal* (Normal Oklahoma: The University of Oklahoma Press, 1946), Foreword, p. 5. Speaking of the period after 1870 the author remarks, "The forms and folklore of city living began to set the modes of our thoughts and aspirations."

An interdependent mechanism. The city, in the words of one authority, is a "huge mechanism for interdependence. . . ."[23] In contrast to the countryside, it is a highly integrated society largely devoted to the production of goods and services for the market place. The network of relationships that enables large numbers of persons to concentrate in one place is an important consideration for people in the city.

For one thing, this network means that the city dweller is more dependent than his country brother. The latter lives largely off the land. The farmer is the jack of all trades. His scale of living is determined both by his efforts and by the vagaries of climate and soil. He *makes* his living. In contrast, the urban dweller sells either goods or services and with its proceeds he purchases the necessities of life. He *buys* his living. In the city, the individual is dependent not only upon his job but upon others to supply him with the comforts of life. Loss of income or economic disorganization within the city has an almost immediate impact upon him.[24]

The danger of specialization. In the city, the individual is constantly exposed to the dangers of specialization. He pays for goods and services which he would otherwise have to provide for himself. Concern with the job tends to produce people who know more about their work than the society in which they live. Over a century ago, De Tocqueville wrote persuasively on this point.

> When a workman is unceasingly and exclusively engaged in the fabrication of one thing, he ultimately does his work with singular dexterity; but at the same time he loses the general faculty of applying his mind. . . . What can be expected of a man who has spent twenty years of his life making heads for pins? And to what can the mighty human intelligence which has so often stirred the world be applied in him except it be to investigate the best method of making pins' heads? When a workman has spent a considerable portion of his existence in this manner, his thoughts are forever set upon the object of his daily toils . . . he no longer belongs to himself, but to the calling he has chosen.[25]

---

[23] *Ibid.*, p. 10.

[24] According to the Census of 1950, 78.9 percent of the urban grouping were private wage and salary workers; 10.6 percent were government workers; 10.2 percent were self-employed. In contrast, the rural farm category showed 32.6 percent as private wage and salary persons; 54.2 percent were self-employed. *U. S. Census, 1950, Census of Population,* I, 101.

[25] A. De Tocqueville, *Democracy in America* (New York: Alfred A. Knopf Inc., Vintage Books, 1954), II, 168-169.

Despite the many improvements of the past century, it is still fair to say that city life tends to produce vocational types.[26]

The anonymity of city life. Depersonalization of human relationships is another facet of city life. The modern city is probably the most impersonal collection of individuals ever found on the face of this earth. "In our own life," said Cooley, "the intimacy of the neighborhood has been broken up by the growth of an intricate mesh of wider contacts which leaves us strangers to the people who live in the same house.[27] Its population is held together by the job nexus, but what James Bryce called the "social cement" is almost nonexistent. Thus relationships among individuals are casual and fleeting. "The principal institutions of the American city," says Mumford, "are merely distractions that take our eyes off the environment. . . ." [28] Men come together in the city but are not united in a spiritual unity. Institutions that can bind the individual to the community and make it meaningful to him are in a semideveloped state.[29] It was this spiritual and institutional impoverishment that made Mumford ask: "We have created cities, but have we created civilization?" [30] The city of today is inchoate and anonymous. It lacks both form and design. Despite the improvements in city life, we can, to a large extent, still agree with Bryce who described the city as "an aggregation of human atoms, like grains of desert sand which the wind sweeps hither and thither." [31] Unless we rewrite our institutions in terms of coherent purpose, the condition noted by Bryce will continue.[32]

Proximity of existence makes its impact upon the city dweller. Poverty, crime, health, and a multitude of other problems acquire new dimensions within the city. The dangers to public health and welfare are multiplied. As "the balance of nature" is destroyed, human development becomes more difficult.[33] The anonymity, the dependence upon the job, and the tensions of city life are reflected

---

[26] Park, Burgess, and McKenzie, *op. cit.*, pp. 14-17.

[27] C. H. Cooley, *Social Organization* (New York: Charles Scribner's Sons, 1929), pp. 24-25.

[28] L. Mumford, *City Development* (New York: Harcourt, Brace and Co., 1945), p. 13.

[29] L. Mumford, *The Culture of Cities* (New York: Harcourt, Brace and Co., 1938), p. 6.

[30] L. Mumford, City Development, *op. cit.*, p. 5.

[31] J. Bryce, *Modern Democracies* (New York: The Macmillan Co., 1924), pp. 109-110.

[32] Cf. The brilliant comments of R. S. Lynd, *Knowledge for What* (Princeton: Princeton University Press, 1939), Chapter III.

[33] Peterson, *op. cit.*, p. viii.

in the vital life process of birth. Urban birth rates have been so low that without migration from the farm and overseas, the population of the cities would have decreased. In the years 1930–1935, the net reproduction rate was 747 and for the succeeding five years it fell to a low of 726. In 1949, for the first time in forty years, the net reproduction rate climbed to 1186. In contrast, for the same year the rural rate was 1,628 and had remained fairly stable for the past fifty years. Thus, it is only recently that the city has been able to reproduce itself. Whether this is a reflection of the high level of employment or a permanent characteristic remains to be seen.[34]

One final comment remains to be made. The dangers incident to life in the city are not intrinsic weaknesses of the city. The city is the condition of the good life as the ancients have demonstrated. Democracy, respect for the dignity of man and his aspirations—these are the guide posts of city life. In modern times it is essential that we seek the means of achieving these goals, for unless we do so, the city and the nation will suffer. As Frank Gervasi has remarked in a somewhat different connection:

> The danger to the democratic life comes when government—the instrument man created for the achievement of his political, economic and social aspirations—breaks down. . . . At that point the disillusioned turn to new prophets, as did the people of Italy and Germany, and, before them, of Russia.[35]

---

[34] *Statistical Abstract,* 1953, p. 48. A net reproduction rate of 1,000 means that each generation would just about replace itself, if birth and death rates of a specified period were to continue indefinitely. See also Milbank Memorial Fund, *Postwar Problems of Migration* (New York: Milbank Memorial Fund, 1947), pp. 125, 163, 167. Burgess, *op. cit.,* 126-127. New York in 1790 had a population of 49,401. In 1920 it had risen to 5.6 million. If reproduction had been limited to those residing in 1790, its population in 1920 would have been 190,000.

[35] F. Gervasi, *Big Government* (New York: McGraw-Hill Book Co., Inc., copyright 1949), p. 6. See also the bitter comment of R. S. Allen, ed., *Our Fair City* (New York: The Vanguard Press, Inc., copyright 1947), p. 3.

> "We are a mighty nation, we Americans. Industrially and financially we are without equal. . . . But, ironically, while our victorious Armies are imposing democracy on millions in Europe and the Far East, local government here at home is a reeking shambles of corruption, incompetence, waste and misrule. There was scarcely a city in Nazi Germany or jingoist Japan that was not managed more efficiently and intelligently than comparable communities in the United States. Yet there is nothing in the principles and practices of democracy which prohibits efficient and intelligent administration of civic affairs."

Also, A. De Tocqueville, *American Institutions,* H. Reeves, Trans., revised by F. Brown (Boston: John Allyn Publisher, 1847), p. 76. ". . . municipal institutions constitute the strength of free nations."

Conversely, to the extent that the city realizes these ideals, our nation will be strong.

CONSEQUENCES OF CITY GROWTH

Intellectual stimulus. Writing about municipal government approximately a half century ago, a noted authority remarked that city life "creates new economic activities, new political ideas and ideals, new forms of social intercourse, new possibilities of interchanges in ideas." [36]

In the city the concentration of the labor force makes possible the division of labor and a consequent rise in labor productivity. Today the machine, in contrast to the slave of ancient Greece, has brought leisure time within the compass of all classes. While this development focuses attention upon the importance of municipal institutions, it also provides the preconditions of the intellectual growth. In the city there is opportunity for contact with others, there is competition in various fields of endeavor, and there is social imitation of those who occupy positions of prominence and importance. All these facets are stimuli for intellectual growth, and although it may well be argued that the city dweller has not made much of his opportunity, it is also a fact that the great civilizations of the world are predominantly urban in their composition.[37]

Changed concept of liberty. Life in the city has as its end-product a changed conception of individual liberty. In the intricate maze of human relationships that constitute the modern city, the points of contact between the individual and the community are multiplied. Opportunities for the violation of property rights and the danger to the health of others are ever present. Under such circumstances the city has a legitimate interest in the range of choices undertaken by the individual and it may intervene at the point where it feels that individual action may constitute a source of potential danger to the community. In brief, the city is, or at least should be, an organic whole. The price of survival in the city consists of the acceptance of the principle that the individual must subordinate his selfish interests to the community as a whole.

The drift of people to the city, as described in previous pages, is largely responsible for the changed concept of individual liberty.

---

[36] Rowe, *op. cit.*, p. 13.

[37] *Ibid.*, Chapter 3. For a contrary view, see Peterson, *op. cit.*, Chapters 2, 9. This study contains most of the arguments against the city by the "back to the farm group."

Although we take great pride in the fact that government is the guarantor of rights, the city has had to interfere in areas which, in the country, would be regarded as matters of individual concern. A few examples may be cited. The disposal of sewage and refuse in the country may be carried out as the farmer sees fit, but, in the city, action of this sort may menace society as a whole. In the city some businesses may be prohibited, and still others may be allowed to operate with a minimum of control. Similarly, safety of food supply and building construction must be guaranteed. In these and other instances individual impulse is curbed and the permanent interest of the community is recognized.

Increase in functions. This becomes almost self-evident when we examine the increase in the number and kinds of functions performed by the city. A case study of Detroit during the period 1824–1930 revealed an increase in municipal activities from 23 to 306.[38] In the 40-year period 1890–1930 the number of cities doubled, but their expenditures tripled. Nationally the outlay of major cities, those with a population of 100,000 or more, for the performance of municipal functions rose from $221 millions in 1902 to $1.7 billions in 1935. By 1940 major cities disbursed $2.0 billions.[39] The cost of city government still is on the rise. In 1951 the 481 cities with 25,000 or more inhabitants spent $4,797 millions for such purposes as police and fire protection, highways, sanitation, public assistance, education, health and hospitals, recreation, and a host of other functions.[40] Over 1 million people, exclusive of school employees, with a monthly payroll of $253.9 million, were required for the performance of these activities.[41]

These relatively large expenditures point to the enormously important role played by law as the politically organized expression of the community. The shift from primary to secondary relationships and the deterioration of group controls have meant that law

[38] L. D. Upson, *The Growth of a City Government* (Detroit: Detroit Bureau of Governmental Research, 1931).

[39] U. S. Dept. of Commerce, U. S. Bureau of Census, *Historical Studies of the United States, 1789–1945* (Washington, D. C.: U. S. Government Printing Office, 1949).

[40] *Statistical Abstract,* 1953, p. 407. The total of all municipal expenditures was $6.2 billions for 1951.

[41] *Ibid.,* p. 393. By October, 1953, the number of municipal employees had risen to 1,382,000 with a monthly payroll of $367.6 millions. See U. S. Department of Commerce, Bureau of Census, *City Employment in 1953* (Washington, D. C.: U. S. Government Printing Office, 1954).

must increasingly replace the restraints previously vested in the primary group.[42]

Changing attitudes toward governmental structure. City growth has been accompanied by a paradox, the survival of rural traits under urban conditions. This phenomenon resulted largely from the fact that urban areas in America, unable to reproduce themselves, have drawn heavily on the countryside. Farm elements migrating to the city have brought with them rural attitudes toward the economic and social problems faced by the city. Although these "survivals" have never become dominant, their presence in the city has had a wholesome effect tempering the tendency toward paternalism upon the part of the city dweller.[43]

Industrialism, largely responsible for the rise of cities, was also instrumental in revising our concepts of governmental structure. Government in agrarian America was characterized by a fear of a strong executive, as well as a disposition to the division of power and responsibility among a mayor, committees, and boards. The spurt of industrial development in the post-Civil War period, the gravitation of people to the cities, and the evils of city government so graphically described by Lincoln Steffens in his *The Shame of the Cities,* all led to the search for more fundamental principles. Gradually, as the need for more technical and continuous administration made itself evident, there was the slow acceptance of the idea of concentration of power with its corollary, accountability to the people. The fact that business had so successfully applied the science of administration made a distinct impact upon its public counterpart, the municipal corporation.

As a consequence there was a perceptible change in the locus of power in municipal governments. At the turn of the century, governmental power was gradually assumed by a strong municipal executive, either a mayor or a city manager. Boards and independent commissions steadily lost favor, and in general, distrust of governmental authority waned. The doctrine of distrust began to yield to the principle of coordination and cooperation.

---

42 Park, Burgess and McKenzie, *op. cit.,* pp. 23-31.

43 A. S. Tomars, "Rural Survivals in American Urban Life," *Rural Sociology,* viii (December, 1943), pp. 378-386.

CONCLUSION

The modern nation, in the words of the Urbanism Committee, finds the city "the focal point of much that is threatening and much that is promising in the life of its people."[44] The city is the workshop of the nation providing the goods and services essential for modern living. Our vast and delicate commercial mechanism is centered in the city. In the city are to be found the centers of culture and learning and most of the media of information and communication.

The concentration of people in the city, in response to the almost insatiable demand of the machine, created a host of problems. It also revolutionized our way of life and our attitudes toward government. Urban governments perform services without which people under conditions of mass living cannot exist. A safe water supply, adequate disposal of sewage and waste, protection of life and property, regulation of trade and industry, provision for education—these are the minimal services which the city provides. Of late the pressures of population have caused a further stretching of the boundaries of governmental power. Regulation of individual relationships has been supplemented by service for the individual. Recreation, health education, welfare, and housing have appeared as added functions of the city.

Since ours is an urban civilization, the future of our nation will depend less upon man's ability to escape the city and more upon his ability to master the forces within the city. The challenge to America today is to employ the governmental instrumentality to establish those conditions which will make the city a better place in which to live.

BIBLIOGRAPHY

Books:

Allen, R. S. (ed.). *Our Fair City.* New York: The Vanguard Press, Inc., 1947.

Bryce, J. *Modern Democracies.* New York: The Macmillan Co., 1924.

Burgess, E. W. (ed.). *The Urban Community.* Chicago: University of Chicago Press, 1926.

Cooley, C. H. *Social Organization.* New York: Charles Scribner's Sons, 1929.

---

44 National Resources Committee, Report of the Urbanism Committee, *op. cit.,* Foreword, p. 5.

De Tocqueville, A. *American Institutions.* H. Reeves translator. Revised by F. Brown. Boston: John Allyn Publisher, 1847.

———. *Democracy in America.* 2 Vols. New York: Alfred A. Knopf Inc., Vintage Books, 1954.

Fairlie, J. A. *Municipal Administration.* New York: The Macmillan Co., 1906.

Kinneman, J. A. *The Community in American Society.* New York: Appleton-Century-Crofts, Inc., 1947.

Lynd, R. S. *Knowledge for What.* Princeton: Princeton University Press, 1939.

MacIver, R. M. *Community, A Sociological Study.* London: Macmillan Co., 1917.

———. *Society.* New York: Farrar and Rinehart, Inc., 1937.

Milbank Memorial Fund. *Postwar Problems of Migration.* New York: Milbank Memorial Fund, 1947.

Mumford, L. *City Development.* New York: Harcourt, Brace and Co., 1945.

———. *The Culture of Cities.* New York: Harcourt, Brace and Co., 1932.

National Resources Committee, Report of the Urbanism Committee, *Our Cities—Their Role in the National Economy.* Washington, D. C.: U. S. Government Printing Office, 1947.

Park, R. E., Burgess, E. W., and McKenzie, R. D. *The City.* Chicago: University Press, 1925.

Peterson, E. (ed.). *Cities Are Abnormal.* Norman, Oklahoma: The University of Oklahoma Press, 1946.

Rowe, L. S. *Problems of City Government.* New York: D. Appleton and Co., 1915.

Spengler, O. *The Decline of the West.* Translated by C. F. Atkinson. New York: Alfred A. Knopf Inc., 1928.

Tunnard, C. *The City of Man.* New York: Charles Scribner's Sons, 1953.

Upson, L. D. *The Growth of a City Government.* Detroit: Detroit Bureau of Governmental Research, 1931.

United States Department of Commerce, Bureau of Census, *Census of Manufacturers.* Washington, D. C.: U. S. Government Printing Office, 1947.

———. *1950, Census of Population.* Vols. I and II. Washington, D. C.: U. S. Government Printing Office, 1952 and 1953.

———. *City Employment in 1953.* Washington, D. C.: U. S. Government Printing Office, 1954.

———. *Historical Studies of the United States, 1789–1945.* Washington, D. C.: U. S. Government Printing Office, 1949.

———. *Statistical Abstract of the United States, 1953* (seventy third edition). Washington, D. C.: U. S. Government Printing Office, 1953.

Periodicals and Other Material:

Tomars, A. S. "Rural Survivals in American Urban Life," *Rural Sociology,* December, 1943, pp. 378-386.

Chapter Two

The Growth of the City

The city is an economic, social, and political organism. It is a product of need, man's need when he lives in close proximity to his fellow man. Its institutions are man-made, and like man, the city has a life cycle of birth, renewal, and decay. The city has meant different things to men at different stages in history, but it has always embodied the higher aspirations of civilization. The city *is* civilization.

In previous pages, the consequences for America of urban growth were noted. It is now essential to isolate those factors that were the prime movers in the origin of the city. Since the city is part and parcel of civilization, an analysis of its genesis can be expected to reveal those causes that have been instrumental in the shaping of our way of life.

Causes of City Growth

The city is an agglomeration of people residing within a relatively confined area. Why do people concentrate within the city? What causes them to reside permanently in a given locality? What factors enable them to continue in close association? The answers to these questions are as old as the city itself.

Divorce of man from the soil. It is a common conception that commerce and industry are responsible for the growth and development of the city. Although there is considerable merit in this viewpoint, it is necessary to point out that both production and distribution are operations that are characterized by intricate division and specialization of labor. Both processes require a work force which, if it is to devote its time fully to commercial pursuits, must have a means of sustenance. Thus, a revolution in agriculture is a necessary precedent to the industrial and commercial revolutions.

One basic reason, therefore, for the congregation of people in the city is the divorce of men from the soil. In early times agriculture was an all-embracing occupation. The farmer produced the foodstuffs needed for his own sustenance and, in his spare moments, he made whatever else was needed. Gradually, however, human wants multiplied and could not be supplied by food alone. Specialization was introduced, and the business of supplying newer wants was separated from agriculture. In the village, the clothier and the weaver devoted full time to their occupation, but this was made possible not by diminishing the importance of bread and butter, but rather by a rise in agricultural productivity.

City growth, then, is dependent upon the presence of an adequate supply of food, for cities are composed of people who do not cultivate the soil. The existence of the city, therefore, presupposes a surplus food supply; this, in turn, assumes either great natural fertility of the soil or an advanced stage of agricultural output. In both instances, either nearness to the countryside or an effective means of transportation is a further requisite to city existence.[1] All of these conditions are present when cities begin to grow.[2]

In brief, people cannot exist in the city if they are required to devote the major part of their efforts to food production. Therefore, as long as agriculture remained in a rudimentary stage and consumed all that was produced, the city remained relatively undeveloped. However, when agricultural output rose sufficiently to provide both food surpluses and the release of a significant portion of the agricultural labor force, the city began to develop. As Mumford has pointed out, "The thriving of towns has its origin in the agricultural improvement of the countryside. . . ." [3]

The presence of surplus agricultural commodities permitted the rise of large cities in both Greece and Rome. In the Orient, highly developed agriculture enabled cities with populations as high as 100,000 inhabitants to exist. In our country the vast improvements in agricultural methods during the past 150 years undoubtedly quickened the pace of urbanization, although the tremendous advances have been overshadowed by the attention paid to the impact of the Industrial Revolution.[4]

---

[1] A. Weber, *The Growth of Cities* (New York: The Macmillan Co., 1899), p. 162.

[2] The first cities on the Nile and Tigris-Euphrates rivers—Thebes, Memphis, Babylon, and Nineveh—arose mainly in response to these factors.

[3] L. Mumford, *The Culture of Cities* (New York: Harcourt, Brace and Co., 1938), p. 24.

[4] A farm population of 23.3 million provides the foodstuffs for a nation of 150.6 millions. U. S. Bureau of the Census, *U. S. Census of Population: 1950.* II, *Characteristics of the Population,* Part 1, United States Summary, Chapter B, pp. 1-105.

While it is true that high agricultural output is an essential prerequisite for the growth of cities, it is not correct to infer that only those nations with food surpluses can develop urban concentrations. In modern times a highly developed transportation system is fully as important as agricultural sufficiency. Indeed, because of this factor the rate of urbanization of any nation has become dependent upon the status of the world's food supplies. England, one of the most highly urbanized areas in the world, is a case in point. Forced to rely upon other nations for a substantial part of its food supplies, she has, nevertheless, been able to evolve into an urban society because transportation brought the foodstuffs of other lands to her doorsteps. Thus, both an advanced stage of the agricultural arts and an effective means of transportation are essential if cities are to come into being.

Commerce and trade. These are also active ferments in the growth of the city. Professor Weber has pointed out, "In point of time, the earliest economic force working for the concentration of the release of agricultural population was trade." [5] When an increase in agricultural output enabled a portion of the agricultural population to abandon farming and to obtain, in turn, their food in exchange for the product of their labor, the foundation of trade was laid. Specialization of labor in the broad sense began. Exchange of goods and services took in ever-widening circles. Commercial centers arose and agricultural areas were gradually transformed into urban places.[6]

Without trade and commerce the city could not come into being, for its existence assumed a nonagricultural population that bought its foodstuffs. The appearance of outlets for surplus agricultural foodstuffs resulted in a further stimulation of production, and the by-product of this development was the migration of surplus rural population to the town and the city.

Within the city, in response to the needs of its inhabitants, primitive hand industries developed. The revival of city life following the Dark Ages saw the grouping of crafts into guilds, an association designed to protect both the producer and the consumer. "In its essentials," wrote Pirenne, "the medieval crafts may be defined as an industrial corporation enjoying the monopoly of practicing a par-

[5] Weber, *op. cit.,* p. 170.
[6] Mumford, *op. cit.,* p. 6.

ticular profession in accordance with regulation sanctioned by the public authority." [7]

The city became a glorified market place where the barter of goods and services occurred. Trade became a town monopoly and outsiders were subjected to discriminatory action. In medieval times the economic aspects of city life became so important that a fusion of economic and political power occurred. Those who held the reins of economic power, the merchants and the men of money, emerged as the actual governors of the city. Gradually, as transportation improved and protection was assured, trade between town and country yielded to trade between towns. The town monopoly was broken and cities became trading centers of economic regions. Ultimately, as political conditions bettered, the town economy was transformed into a national economy.

Factory system and technology. Wider markets meant an increased emphasis on production. The concentration of people in the city and the division of labor, already in existence, were brought to a climax when the factory system was introduced. It was when this industrial revolution occurred that the city as we know it today came into being.

The city is the product of the factory system, and the latter owes its existence to many scientific discoveries, of which perhaps the most significant was the use of steam, both as a source of energy and as a means of transportation. Steam, like its predecessor water power, had a centripetal effect upon the city. Power from the steam engine must be transmitted directly to the machine through a system of pulleys and shafts. Steam power can be extended only over limited distances. Factories, as Warren Thompson once put it, were built around boiler rooms.[8] Factories in the age of steam grew larger and larger. Since in its early phases transportation was in a semi-developed state, the work force tended to live close to the industrial center. Poor housing and slums in many a factory town are a grim reminder of the concentrative power of steam.

Steam in the form of rail transport also caused a concentration of urban population. The coming of the railroad meant a widening of market outlets and the tapping of new sources of raw materials.

---

[7] H. Pirenne, *Economic and Social History of Medieval Europe* (New York: Harcourt, Brace and Co., 1936), p. 184.

[8] W. S. Thompson, "It Was Not Always So," in E. Peterson, ed., *Cities Are Abnormal* (Norman, Oklahoma: University of Oklahoma Press, 1946), p. 60.

People as well as material came to the centralized city. The well-established industrial and commercial city through volume transportation and favorable rates found steam transportation a real asset to its growth, for these advantages enhanced its market position. More industry was attracted, more managerial and distributive activities arose, and an ever-larger population settled in the city. The large city grew by leaps and bounds, and many of the structural and physical aspects of the modern city can be traced to the dependence of the city upon steam as a source of energy and motive power.

It was only with the coming of newer forms of power, electricity and the internal combustion engine, that the possibility of reversing the trend toward concentration became a likelihood. Both permitted the dispersal of plants and people. Electricity, since it could be transmitted economically over long distances, enabled industry to locate outside of the central city. Automotive transport also had a centrifugal effect, making it possible for the work force to live at a considerable distance from its jobs. The trend toward deconcentration, first noted in 1920, became more pronounced in the succeeding three decades and has not as yet run its course. It is evident that the central city is not growing as rapidly as its peripheral areas,[9] but it is yet too early to predict the ultimate impact of electricity and the internal combustion engine. It is certain that continued dispersal of industry will have widespread effects upon the governmental instrumentality. Economic regions will tend to replace political jurisdictions and thus inhibit the ability of governmental power to deal with the problems that arise.

Transportation. The sociologist, C. H. Cooley, has given us another reason for the growth of cities, the "break in transportation" theory. The diffusion of power resources, he argues, cannot alone cause the dispersion of industry. Energy is merely the first part of the industrial process. It must be accompanied by specialization of labor, raw materials, and machinery. These can be brought together only by transportation.[10] Transportation is, therefore, one of the most important reasons for the rise of cities.

Cooley's concept may be stated in his own words, "Populations and wealth tend to collect wherever there is a break in transporta-

---

[9] See Chapter 1.

[10] C. H. Cooley, *Sociological Theory and Social Research* (New York: Henry Holt and Co., 1930), p. 64.

tion. . . . By a break is meant an interruption of the movement at least sufficient to cause a transfer of goods and their temporary storage."[11] Two kinds of "breaks" were identified by Cooley: a mechanical break where the physical movement of goods is temporarily stopped; and a commercial break where the ownership of goods changes hands.

The physical break necessitates machinery for the transfer and storage of goods. Facilities for unloading and loading are required. Warehouses are necessary. As a consequence, provision must be made for specialized personnel who conduct these operations. As people concentrate for the performance of these tasks, secondary services develop such as agriculture, housing, stores, food, and other necessities of organized living. Aside from the fact that more highly specialized personnel are needed when a commercial break occurs, the conditions for the growth of the city are substantially the same. Concentrations of people take place whenever a change in the form of transportation becomes necessary.[12]

Public health. Modern sanitation is also a necessary prerequisite for the existence of a large city. Before the advent of modern public health methods, the rate of deaths in cities often was greater than the number of births. Under congested conditions epidemics spread like wildfire. In ancient and medieval times pestilence and disease were the lot of the urban dweller, and H. W. Haggard, the medical historian, has described them vividly. In 164 A.D. the bubonic plague struck Rome for the third time, and for the next decade and a half it continued almost unabated. At its peak, it carried off about 16,000 people a day. In the fourteenth century, 24 million people perished, a third of the population of Europe. In London of the 17th century the ravages of the Black Death were so great that only one governmental representative, the Duke of Albemarle, remained in the city. Before the plague ran its course, many thousands had died. Streets were empty and houses were closed. So inadequate was the state of medical knowledge that not until the great fire of 1666 were the rats which had borne the disease destroyed.

Health hazards are still present in the modern city, but the risks to the city dweller have been cut to a minimum by the perfection

---

11 *Ibid.*, p. 76.

12 Pirenne, *op. cit.*, p. 42, points out that towns arose at the junction of two rivers or where a river was no longer navigable. Those "became places of passage and sojourn for merchants. . . ."

of central sewers and waste disposal systems, by the assurance of a safe water supply, by the public control of communicable diseases, and by countless other public health measures. The dependence of the modern city upon medical knowledge has been well stated by Haggard in these words: "Modern urban civilization is founded on preventive medicine. . . . If preventive measures were relaxed, the pestilences would quickly return and even the most civilized countries would be ravaged now as they were in the Middle Ages." [13]

FACTORS AFFECTING THE LOCATION OF CITIES

The site of a city has an important bearing upon its development. City growth must accommodate itself to the demands of topography. Expansion is often inhibited and congestion occurs. Seaports and cities on lakes and rivers follow a pattern of semicircular development because the water location blocks their expansion. Developers and builders take advantage of the natural configuration of the land and influence street and transportation development. Rivers running through cities, although they may not prevent the dispersal of people, may divide the city into distinctive neighborhoods. In a city such as New York, the fact that Manhattan Island is the center of activity necessitated vast expenditures for tunnels, bridges, and ferries. Since the factors affecting the situation of a city are intimately bound up with the functions of the city, a consideration of these elements will aid in understanding the problems a city must face.[14]

Defense sites. A number of reasons suggest themselves as explanations for the location of cities. There is, first of all, the need for a defense site. "In an age," says Pirenne, "when pillage formed one of the means of existence . . . ," protection against invaders and marauders was essential.[15] In early times settled areas were subject to constant attack and pillaging. The student of history is familiar with the incursions of the Huns under Attila, and the periodic forays of the Saracens and Norsemen who terrorized both the southern and northern coasts of Europe. In medieval times the first public works expenditures were for the construction of walls, moats,

---

[13] H. W. Haggard, *Devils, Drugs and Doctors* (New York: Pocket Books, Inc., 1946), p. 196.

[14] For a general description of the geographic factors affecting the location of cities see C. Bridenbaugh, *Cities in the Wilderness* (New York: The Ronald Press, 1938), pp. 1-30.

[15] Pirenne, *op. cit.*, p. 41.

and castles. The countryside was a place of danger and, as long as this condition existed, the dominance of the medieval town was assured. When law and order were established, the town lost its preeminence.[16] To ward off the attacker, fortified sites were necessary.

For purposes of defense, many of the early cities were located on hilltops, or within easy reach of water, or perhaps in areas where both were combined. These natural features often served as bastions against the aggressor. It is interesting to note that Athens was located in the center of a fertile valley almost entirely surrounded by hills except in the south where access to the sea was easily available. Rome, too, was a hill city with a rich plain area sufficient to attract and maintain a large population. Like Athens, it was encompassed by mountains and, through the Tiber River, it had easy access to the sea. Both cities were strong citadels for warding off the attacker.[17]

Where hills were unavailable, open water was employed as a buffer against hostile forces. Insular cities afforded a means of keeping the invader at bay. In the fifth and sixth centuries when Italy was overrun by the Huns and Lombards, only Venice and other island cities managed to hold off the raiders. Before Paris spread across the banks of the Seine, it was also an island city. When the Roman Empire collapsed and Paris was preyed upon by the Norsemen, it receded once more to its original insular environs.

In brief, defense considerations determined the location of the early towns. With the coming of gunpowder and advanced assault methods, the hilltop and water sites were no longer impregnable against assault. Many cities, however, which were founded for protective purposes continued to exist.

Changes in transportation. Factors of topography also influence the location of cities. Towns arise where a change in the type of transportation becomes necessary. Such changes occur at the junction of land transportation with water transportation, the junction of one kind of water transportation with another, or the junction of one kind of land transportation with another.[18]

Seaport towns were usually located at the junction of land and

---

16 Mumford, *op. cit.*, p. 65.

17 L. S. Rowe, *Problems of City Government* (New York: D. Appleton and Co., 1915), pp. 16, 20; also, N. Carpenter, *The Sociology of City Life* (New York: Longmans, Green and Co., 1932), Ch. 2. The latter contains an excellent description of the factors influencing the location of cities.

18 Cooley, *op. cit.*, p. 77.

water transportation. To the seaport came goods from overseas for distribution to the interior. Land transportation in turn brought goods to the city, either for use within the city or for export overseas. The early towns, such as Boston, Philadelphia, Baltimore, and New Orleans, used ocean voyages as a means of shipping goods to one another. As transportation to the interior developed, the resources of the area surrounding the city were tapped and each city became the center of an economic region.

New York City provides perhaps the best illustration of a seaport city. Blessed with excellent harbor facilities, it soon became a convenient transfer point for exports from inland. A network of roads and railroads facilitated access to the city, and as rates became lower because of volume transportation, merchants, bankers, and shippers were attracted to the city. Hamburg, Antwerp, and London follow a similar pattern of growth because of their location on or near the sea.

Lake cities show a growth pattern resembling that of the seaboard city. Cities arose on the Great Lakes because lake shipment permitted the economical movement of bulk products such as wheat, iron ore, and lumber to a central point where these items could be stored or processed for subsequent shipment further eastward. Duluth, Chicago, Cleveland, and Buffalo are but a few of the many cities that fall into this category. Chicago has acquired its huge network of railroads, its processing plants, and its grain elevators because it was strategically located in the Great Lakes region with excellent transshipment facilities.[19]

A navigable stream or an artificial body of water such as the Erie Barge Canal frequently affect both the location and the growth of cities. From time immemorial, water has been the cheapest form of transportation. The cities on the Hudson, Delaware, Susquehanna, Missouri, and Mississippi rivers owe their existence mainly to their physical location. Goods from the interior were brought to shipping points and floated down the river. New Orleans, at the mouth of the Mississippi, grew because of the necessity for a change from river to ocean-going vessels. "The break was between two varieties of water transportation. . . ." [20]

---

[19] Carpenter, *op. cit.*, Chapter 2, has an excellent description of the rise of Duluth as a great transfer point. For a brief review of Cooley's transportation theory, see N. F. Gist and L. A. Halbert, *Urban Society*, (New York: Thomas Y. Crowell Co., 1933), pp. 57-68.

[20] Cooley, *op. cit.*, p. 78.

The building of the Erie Barge Canal gave tremendous impetus to the growth of the city of New York. "The Erie Canal opened the first and only direct route to and from the East by water." [21] When the canal was completed, the cost of transporting goods from Buffalo to New York City was reduced from $80 or $100 per ton between 1830–1850 to an average of less than $9 per ton. The canal also tapped the large wheat growing area of western New York, and Rochester, located in the center of the region, emerged as a large flour-milling city.[22] The canal enabled New York to profit at the expense of its sister seaports. When the canal was superseded by the railroads, the latter continued to bring goods to New York City and thus assured its continuous commercial dominance. Buffalo, a collecting point for the great lakes traffic, also experienced a similar resurgence.

Cooley's "break in transportation" theory yields another reason for the location of cities, the change from one kind of transportation to another. Vehicles employed in mountainous areas frequently differ from those used on the plains, and when a transportation "break" occurred, a city arose.[23] Denver, originally a gold mining camp in a mountainous area, became an important gateway to the whole Rocky Mountain area. Again, the necessity for a shift from short-haul to long-haul vehicles was an important reason for the location of a city. Cities served both as markets and points of assembly for the subsequent distribution of goods on a wider basis.

Mineral resources. An abundance of mineral deposits was frequently responsible for the location of cities. Coal, iron ore, and oil reserves were consumed in ever-larger quantities by the almost insatiable demands of our rapidly evolving economy. Science and technology showed new uses for these items. Not only was coal the chief fuel used for domestic heating during the 1830s, but it also became the mainstay of steam power, electrical energy, and rail transport. With the invention of the internal combustion engine an era of a nation on wheels was ushered in, causing a huge demand for petroleum and its by-products. The development of the railroad absorbed additional amounts of iron and steel and, at the same time,

---

21 G. Soule, *Economic Forces in American History* (New York: William Sloan Associates, 1952), p. 195.

22 C. W. Wright, *Economic History of the United States* (New York: McGraw-Hill Book Co., Inc., 1949), p. 274.

23 Cooley, *op. cit.*, pp. 79-80.

provided the means for bringing coal and iron ore together. To satisfy the appetite of our expanding economy, a feverish search for mineral resources took place.

Mining and other extractive industries produced towns and villages in areas that were formerly uninhabitable. People gravitated to these places to mine coal, dig iron ore, and drill oil wells. Auxiliary services appeared in support of them. Commerce and industry followed in their wake, and soon full-fledged cities arose. The coal towns of Pennsylvania and the oil cities of Oklahoma and Texas owe their existence to this phenomenon. Birmingham, Alabama, in the center of a coal and iron region of the South, can trace its evolution to the presence of these products. Large-scale operations, necessitated by increased demand, were paralleled by a revolution in transport which permitted the concentration of processing facilities in the cities. Pittsburgh, close to coal resources and located strategically on the junction of the Allegheny and Monongahela rivers, benefited greatly from the existence of efficient transportation which gave it relatively easy access to the cheap ores of the Mesabi range. The coming of the machine age caused a specialization in both production and processing.

Noneconomic factors. City location is not solely caused by transportation and economic relationships. Various noneconomic factors —religion, politics, education—also affect the choice of a city site. Shrines, the symbolic religious expressions of people within a given area, have witnessed the growth of cities around them. Holy places, such as Mecca, Rome, and Jerusalem, are good examples of this phenomenon. Sometimes cities arose as a result of their designation as political centers. Many state capitals and our national capital were a product of political considerations. Washington, D. C., now a large thriving city, was hardly more than a wooded tract about a century and a half ago. Since it was the center of political authority, it attracted large numbers of people, some as visitors and others as part of the work force assisting in the transaction of public business. Educational centers have also served as nuclei around which a pattern of urbanization developed. The great state universities and many private institutions are the centers of university towns.

Religion, politics, and education are secondary factors in the life of the city. Although these may have caused the rise of the city or may have given it a unique character, their importance tends to recede as the city grows. The existence of the city is, in the final analysis, dependent on the more basic economic relationships.

THE ECONOMIC BASE OF THE CITY

An excursion into economic relationships almost inevitably leads the student of political science to ask: Of what value is such an inquiry? To this a brief reply may be made. Economic factors have important political and social consequences.

The importance of these causal factors lies in the fact that they stress a fundamental point. The growth of every city is "related to what may be called its 'economic base,' that is, to the source or sources from which it derives the means of livelihood for its people." [24] The economic base also, in large measure, determines the income of the city and its ability to provide for its people. Good times, high levels of industrial production, full employment, and mass purchasing power are reflected in the continued growth of the city. This was amply demonstrated during the boom of World War II and the relatively stable economic pattern of the post-war years. Conversely, dips in the business cycle cause a contraction of the economic base and, paradoxically, an increase in the problems faced by the city.

Not all cities are equally affected by the vagaries of the business cycle. Some can weather economic storms better than others. In some instances, cities may enter a period of decline even though the economic health of the country remains unimpaired. A shift in industry from north to south is causing economic hardship in Lowell, Massachusetts, and other textile towns; or a change in the use of different and competing forms of energy, such as the shift from coal to oil, may have a marked effect upon a city. Undoubtedly the gradual exhaustion of the ore deposits of the Mesabi range will have an impact upon cities in the immediate vicinity. The construction of the St. Lawrence Seaway will have significant economic consequences for many cities in the northeastern part of the United States.

Classification of cities. The predominance of one or more major economic characteristics enables one to classify cities. McKenzie distinguishes four main categories of cities: (1) "the primary service

[24] W. B. Munro, "The City," in E. R. A. Seligman and A. Johnson, eds., *Encyclopaedia of the Social Sciences* (New York: The Macmillan Co., 1935), III, 477.

community," (2) the "commercial community," (3) "the industrial town," and (4) "the community which does not have a specific economic base." Communities in the first category include agriculture, mining, and fishing, those which provide both raw materials and markets. Cities that engage primarily in commerce and trade, the distributive activities, may be grouped under the second heading. Industrial communities may have one or many industries or a combination of industry and commerce. Capital cities, resort areas, and educational centers fall into the fourth grouping.[25] In 1948, four-fifths of the manufacturing cities were located in the Northeast, Middle Atlantic, and East-North Central states. Southern cites, in contrast, were mainly retail or diversified in their economic development. Three-fourths of the residential cities contained less than 25,000 population.[26]

While McKenzie's listing may be open to the charge of oversimplification, it is, nonetheless, valuable for the light it casts on the growth factors of a city. Fixed-site cities, those near water power or those based upon extractive processes, are most vulnerable to technological change. Communities of this sort usually pursue an uncertain existence, since their means of livelihood may be suddenly withdrawn. The current doldrums of the coal towns of Pennsylvania and West Virginia are a good case in point. At the other end of the scale are those cities without any specific economic base. Since their growth or decline is not dependent upon either production or distribution, they have a relatively stable pattern of growth. Commercial cities, on the other hand, are dependent upon the presence of an advantageous site location. A decline in this advantage will produce difficult problems of readjustment. The industrial community may also become a prey to economic forces, for it is largely dependent upon market outlets. If these contract or disappear, growth will cease or decline. A city based upon industry, however, has a greater degree of flexibility since, in most instances, it will have a multiplicity of industries and may even have a large

[25] R. E. Park, E. W. Burgess, and R. D. McKenzie, *The City* (Chicago: University of Chicago Press, 1925), pp. 66-68. For another and more specific classification, see the International City Managers' Association, *The Municipal Yearbook for 1948*, pp. 35-39. Communities are grouped on the basis of one or more economic characteristics as "manufacturing," "industrial," "wholesale," "retail," "diversified," "dormitory," "educational centers," "government centers," "mining towns," "transportation centers," and "amusement or health resorts."

[26] *Ibid.*, pp. 38-39.

amount of trade. Thus a contraction of one area may result in a compensatory expansion in another. But, to repeat, all cities are sensitive to economic conditions. The forces which give rise to the city often determine its resiliency or response to economic change.

CONCLUSION

The city is the product of many forces. Transportation, agriculture, location, manufacturing, and energy resources, all play an important role in the growth of the city. Improvements in agricultural production freed large numbers of people from the soil. The factory provided employment opportunities, and transportation bridged distances in bringing people and markets together. Steam power, electricity, and the internal combustion engine supplied the motive power for the industrial machine. In brief, the city is a complex mechanism affected by many factors, several of which are not the result of governmental action. Yet it is these socio-economic conditions that create problems with which the city as a political instrumentality must deal.

BIBLIOGRAPHY

Books:

Bridenbaugh, C. *Cities in the Wilderness.* New York: The Ronald Press, 1938.

Carpenter, N. *The Sociology of City Life.* New York: Longmans, Green and Co., 1932.

Cooley, C. H. *Sociological Theory and Social Research.* New York: Henry Holt and Co., 1930.

Gist, N. F., and Halbert, L. A. *Urban Society.* New York: Thomas Y. Crowell Co., 1933.

The International City Managers' Association, *The Municipal Yearbook for 1948.* Chicago: 1949.

Pirenne, H. *Economic and Social History of Medieval Europe.* New York: Harcourt, Brace and Co., 1936.

Soule, G. *Economic Forces in American History.* New York: William Sloan Associates, 1952.

Weber, A. *The Growth of Cities.* New York: The Macmillan Co., 1899.

Wright, C. W. *Economic History of the United States.* New York: McGraw-Hill Book Co., Inc., 1949.

Articles:

Encyclopaedia of the Social Sciences. 1st Ed., Vol. III, Article, "The City."

PART
TWO

The City and Its Internal Relationships

Chapter Three

The Municipal Corporation

The Role of the Municipal Corporation

The migration of people in response to the needs of a rapidly evolving industrial and commercial economy was reflected in the growth of cities. As more people congregated in urban centers, the town evolved into the large city and finally into the metropolitan region. For an ever-increasing number of people the city determined the way of life.

Step by step, as the city developed, life for the urban dweller became increasingly complex. Gradually, as the individual found himself incapable of dealing with the problems around him, municipal intervention took place on his behalf. The harshness of sustained and rapid urban growth was modified by the introduction of many municipal services. Protection of health, facilities for education, and provision for the citizen's welfare were assured. So rapidly did these functions develop that today we regard them largely as commonplace.

Today our attention is usually drawn to the physical aspects of the city, its streets and highways, its playgrounds and green space, its schools, hospitals, and other public buildings. We tend to forget that the city is much more than this. It is a public corporation performing essential services for the community, possessing authority to lay and collect taxes and to borrow money. It can sue and be sued. As an artificial person, it is endowed in perpetuity with responsibility for administering local affairs. Although we may be only dimly aware of this facet, without this network of legal relationships the city hardly would be more than a name on a map. To gain an adequate understanding of the role of the municipal corporation, it is essential for us to understand its origins.

Growth of the Municipal Corporation

The word "municipal" has a variety of meanings in our state constitutions and statutes. In some instances, it is employed to designate cities, villages, and incorporated towns; in others it has been applied to any unit of government below the level of the county. But whether used in either the strict or the elastic sense, "municipal" applies to a unit of government which acts as an agent of the state.

The Roman influence. The municipal corporate concept is Roman in origin and its development as a juristic entity stems largely from Roman practice. When Rome extended its sway over most of the world it knew, it found itself face to face with a gigantic problem in administration—how to control the provinces without, at the same time, provoking the displeasure of the local inhabitants. It met this difficulty by making the cities of the provinces its administrative agents. Wherever Rome established its influence, the mother city, which had extensive power over its own inhabitants, granted similar privileges to the *municipia*. Provincial cities enjoyed a large measure of autonomy with respect to local affairs, although in matters of national concern they were subject to the political decisions of the republic. The Romans endowed their cities with corporate status, and it is from the Romans that we have obtained the idea of a municipal corporation.[1]

The collapse of the Roman Empire was followed by a long period of chaos and confusion. Cities could not exist under such circumstances, and urbanism as a phenomenon was brought to a grinding halt. With the gradual restoration of law and order and the revival of trade, municipal development began once more. In the medieval period, the town, largely a commercial enterprise, steadily sought a larger measure of freedom from the restraints of the lord. In common with the pecuniary atmosphere prevailing at that time, the town purchased rights and gradually gained a greater degree of self-government.

The English borough. In England, where town government evolved less rapidly than on the continent, this development was especially marked. Whenever the town gained an exemption, the right was usually embodied in a written instrument. Charters granted by the Crown to budding municipalities crystallized the changed relationship between burgess and lord, town and Crown. Borough government in the five centuries following the Norman

[1] J. S. Reid, *The Municipalities of the Roman Empire* (Cambridge: at the University Press, 1913), Chapter 1.

Conquest was featured by the steady increase in the powers of the borough. In general, corporate independence from feudal authority became the central objective of the town, a tendency that was strengthened by the growth of kingly power.

A description of the evolution of the English borough system is obviously beyond the scope of this volume. However, the main outlines of change may be sketched briefly.[2] Although the pattern of evolutionary development was uneven, almost all borough charters eventually contained three main privileges: freedom from feudal levies, choice of local officers, and a court system separate from the royal courts. Early in their existence, boroughs were able to obtain relief from the irksome burden of feudal tolls and excises by the contribution of an annual lump sum payment. This right, *firma burgi,* led to still another. If the burgesses were to collect the required amounts of money, local collectors armed with the necessary authority were needed. Finally, the fact that royal courts were often not suited to the needs of the local units led to the creation of a special court system. Gradually, whether by accident or design, the boroughs were employed by the central government as units of administration.[3] As municipalities increased in number and size, they gained more privileges. In 1439 the grant of a charter to Kingston-on-the-Hull marks the first formal incorporation of a municipality in the modern sense of the term.[4]

Borough government arose during the period 1200–1500, not only through negotiation with the Crown that led to the purchase of a charter, but also because of a serious weakness in the chain of administration. The Crown, regardless of its intentions, had few technically trained bureaucrats. In matters of administration, particularly those concerned with finance (the borough was essentially a commercial unit), the royal officials were, to say the least, novices. Opportunities for the evasion of royal directives were numerous, but knowledge of whether or not they did occur will have to await fundamental research in the municipal institutions of the period.

In any event, English boroughs enjoyed a large measure of self-

[2] The reader may consult two outstanding historical studies: H. Pirenne, *Economic and Social History of Medieval Europe* (New York: Harcourt, Brace and Co., 1936); C. Stephenson, *Borough and Town* (Cambridge, Mass.: 1933) especially pp. 44-74.

[3] J. A. Fairlie, *Municipal Administration* (New York: The Macmillan Co., 1906), pp. 43-45.

[4] C. W. Tooke, "Municipal Corporation," *Encyclopaedia of Social Sciences* (New York: The Macmillan Co., copyright 1935), XI, p. 87.

government and for awhile they also had democratic government. The officials needed were relatively few in number and were chosen by a constantly expanded electorate. But the increased volume of trade, the rise of guilds, and the general complexity of municipal government were followed by the tendency to vest the reins of community power in the hands of the men of substance who, by prescription, gradually assumed the actual powers of governance. Those who controlled the guilds monopolized political authority. Indeed, one of the main purposes of incorporation was the protection of the guilds.[5] Fairlie has correctly summarized this evolution in these words, "It is not too much to say that what had been the democracy of 1200 had become the oligarchy of 1500." [6]

Borough governments varied in accordance with the specific grants received from the Crown, but one point was indisputable. All boroughs were "closed corporations," dominated by small cliques possessing both the power to perpetuate themselves in office and to name their successors. It was this circumstance that ultimately proved to be the undoing of borough autonomy, for the boroughs soon found themselves caught in the crossfire of battle between King and Parliament. Boroughs, as an outgrowth of the practice of *firma burgi,* had been given representation in Parliament as early as 1295, although the right had not become an accepted fact until the fifteenth century. As corporate entities, boroughs furnished the Crown with a ready-made opportunity to gain control of Parliament. If the Crown could obtain its own people as heads of the municipal corporations, the Crown could also manage the boroughs' representation in Parliament. Thus it was not entirely by accident that the Crown undertook to withdraw charters by *quo warranto* proceedings. It was not entirely coincidence that led it to create new municipal corporations.[7] In time, the boroughs were almost completely demoralized and became the private preserves of the Crown, the lords and ministers, all of whom, at one time or another, laid claim to borough representation.[8]

Thus by the sixteenth century the borough and town system had

---

[5] S. and B. Webb, *English Local Government* (London, New York: Longmans, Green and Co., 1908), II, p. 186.

[6] Fairlie, *op. cit.,* p. 48.

[7] W. B. Munro, *Municipal Government and Administration* (New York: The Macmillan Co., 1925), I, pp. 72-74.

[8] A. Shaw, *Municipal Government in Great Britain* (New York: The Century Co., 1895), p. 23.

become an anachronism. All reason for the continued existence of the "closed corporation" had disappeared. Corruption had reduced the old towns to a state of helplessness. New urban centers, by-products of a rising industrialism and suffering from its backwash, had neither representation in Parliament nor authority to deal with pressing problems. Under pressure from desperate municipal authorities, Parliament passed a variety of special acts, some of which sought to strengthen existing corporations and others which granted power to a variety of independent boards. The net result was a welter of confusion. "Closed corporation" continued to exist until the fundamental reforms of the Municipal Reform Act of 1835.[9]

The municipal corporation in America. At first, American municipal corporations were very similar to their English counterparts.[10] Charters were conferred by the governor instead of by the Crown; the council, consisting of the mayor, recorder, aldermen, and councilmen, was the governing body of the municipality. In one important respect, however, the municipal corporation did differ. "Close" boroughs did not exist except in Philadelphia, Annapolis, and Norfolk.[11]

In colonial times the powers of the municipal corporations were severely circumscribed by the laws of the province and the mother country. Police protection and, in some instances, control over commercial matters were the prime concern of the municipalities. Aside from these minimal responsibilities, the local units were forced to depend upon the provincial legislature for additional authority. Municipalities had no rights to tax, and whenever funds were needed they had to seek a special act. Although the towns constantly received additional prerogatives, the fact that such grants were dependent upon a legislative act tended to make them creatures of the colonial assemblies.[12] This trend was strengthened after the Revolutionary War. The disappearance of the royal governor was followed by the supremacy of the state legislatures. The latter granted and changed charters in the same manner that they enacted any other law. By the first decade of the nineteenth century the sub-

[9] *Ibid.*, pp. 23-24; Fairlie, *op. cit.*, pp. 63-72, gives an interesting account of municipal government after the Reform Act of 1835.

[10] T. H. Reed, *Municipal Government in the United States* (Rev. ed.; New York: Appleton-Century Co., 1934), p. 45.

[11] Fairlie, *op. cit.*, pp. 73-74.

[12] *Ibid.*, p. 76.

ordination of the municipality to the state had become an accomplished fact.

The years since then have been marked by continued attempts by the municipal corporation to free itself from state domination. The constitutional prohibitions against special legislation, the home rule movement, and the growth of optional charter legislation gave greater autonomy to the municipality, but it is still in many respects a creature of the state.

In the light of what has been said, it can be seen that the city as a municipal corporation stands at the end of a long line of evolutionary development. In Roman times when the idea of a corporate personality was first conceived, the corporation served as an agent of the central government. When the city was re-establishing itself after the chaos following the fall of Rome, the corporation symbolized the hard-won gains of the town from the Crown and the lord. Whenever a town was successful in gaining a right, it was quick to incorporate it in a written instrument generally called a charter. Within the medieval community, however, liberty existed only in the corporate sense. The individual had only such privileges as the corporation was willing to grant to him and all individual activity was subject to regulation by the political community. The concept of individual rights did not exist. Indeed, the idea that people could find themselves in opposition to the community was unthinkable.

Following the industrial revolution, the breakdown of the old order ushered in a new period and individualism became the order of the day. Gone was the status concept of the medieval period and in its place came freedom and mobility. Man found himself free to join with others in voluntary associations. With the accent on individualism, the municipal corporation found itself denuded of almost all of its functions with the possible exception of the responsibility for the maintenance of law and order. In the America of the eighteenth and nineteenth century, this trend was very evident. A land of vast unexplored potential, dominated by the rural values of "every man for himself," America had little use for the type of controls symbolized by the municipal corporation.

The growth of commerce and industry described in previous pages gradually compelled a re-evaluation of the role of the individual. The rapid pace of urbanization began to make itself felt after the Civil War, and as the nation neared the turn of the twentieth century, the more somber effects of life in the city became apparent to an ever-larger number of people who were forced to live in the city. More and more, persons began to look to the municipal corporation as an instrument for the attainment of the good life within the city. The municipal corporation, almost neglected in the race toward individual self-betterment, gradually came into its own. Today, we accept the fact that the municipal corporation should perform those functions that we cannot accomplish in our individual capacity.

THE NATURE OF THE MUNICIPAL CORPORATION

Today's cities are generally regarded as municipal corporations. To say this, however, is not sufficient since as a corporation the city has many legal attributes that spring from the very act of incorporation. Unless the nature of the municipal corporation is clearly understood, its place in the constitutional system cannot be adequately comprehended.

Generally speaking, the municipal corporation is the product of an action by a sovereign power, usually the state legislature, and because of this its meaning varies in accordance with the practice of the state in which it is located. In its most elemental sense it is a local public corporation whose main purpose is to govern the affairs of the area under its jurisdiction. It may be distinguished from other public corporations by virtue of the fact that it possesses the power of local legislation. It differs from the private corporation in that the consent of its members is not necessarily required for its incorporation. Unlike its private counterpart, too, the municipal charter is not regarded as a contract and does not receive the same constitutional protection. In more concrete terms, the municipal corporation "is a body politic, created by the incorporation of the people of a prescribed locality and invested with subordinate powers of legislation, for the purpose of assisting in the civil government of the state and of regulating and administering its local and internal affairs." [13]

There are, of course, many other definitions. Some corporations are classified by status either as *de facto* or *de jure*. Others are described according to the manner in which they have been created;

[13] Tooke, *loc. cit.*, XI, p. 86.

those that are a product of general or special law, or those that have been formed in accordance with home rule provisions. The courts, in turn, through their decisions have introduced additional variations. If one allows for all of the differences that exist, there is still accord as to what are considered the essential characteristics of the municipal corporation. They are the following: (1) a formal act of incorporation in conformance with either the constitutional or statutory requirements; (2) a grant of power over the people within a prescribed area in the form of a charter; (3) a corporate name and seal to authenticate the acts of the corporation; (4) the consent of the people to the act of incorporation, although this is not required since in the legal sense the corporation derives its powers from the state and not the people; and (5) the right of local autonomy, although this is not regarded as an absolute right but rather one that arises from the fact that it is more convenient for the state to permit local inhabitants to handle matters of specific concern to them.[14]

Each of these aspects of the corporation may be explained in greater detail. The corporate existence of the municipality, to reiterate, springs from the fact that it is a creature of the state and, largely, a product of its law. Subject to the restrictions contained in either the constitution or the statute, the state legislature has virtually unlimited authority to create such legal entities.[15] Although the power of the legislature to establish such corporations by special act is now generally prohibited by either home rule or optional charter provisions, it still retains the right to specify the conditions under which municipal corporations come into being. When these are observed, a *de jure* corporation is formed with full legal power to act for the community. The statute, in other words, is the test of municipal existence.

This, however, is not the only way in which the legality of a municipality is established. It has sometimes happened that a bona fide attempt has been made to conform with the procedural requirements for incorporation and that mistakes in the process have occurred. In such a case the Supreme Court has held that a *de facto* corporation has been created with full legal responsibility for its

---

[14] E. McQuillin, *The Law of Municipal Corporations* (3rd. ed.; Chicago: Callaghan & Co., 1949), I, sec. 207. Justice Thomas Cooley in *People ex. rel. Le Roy v. Hurlburt,* 24 Mich. 44 (1871) asserted that municipalities had an inherent right of self-government.

[15] *U. S. v. Home Insurance Co.,* 22 Wall. 99 (1877).

actions.[16] Two other departures may be briefly noted. First, municipalities may be recognized by implication. When a statute refers to a specific function of a municipality, it is usually inferred by the courts that the legality of the municipality as a whole is recognized.[17] Second, municipalities may be incorporated by prescription. If a municipality has been in existence for a period of time and has exercised the powers of a corporation, even though it has not availed itself of the opportunity to incorporate under the laws of the state, it is still a municipal corporation in the eyes of the courts.[18]

The municipality, then, is a product of legislation. Its formal articles of incorporation are usually contained in its charter and in the general law passed in amplification of its original grant of authority. The charter is a grant of power from a superior, the state, to a person or group of persons who are authorized to act in a corporate capacity for the people of a given area. It is the constitution of municipality describing the manner in which public authorities discharge their obligations, and because of this it is also the means by which public officials are held accountable for their actions. Although there is a wide variation in the form and substance of the charter from state to state, a charter usually contains the following elements: (1) the powers of the municipality; (2) the form of government; (3) a description of its corporate boundaries; (4) the distribution of powers among the various officers and departments; (5) the manner in which powers may be exercised; and (6) the qualifications of the voter and the procedure for the holding of elections.[19]

The corporate name does not seem to have much significance to the layman; and yet if he will but ponder the matter for a moment, he will soon see that it does have much importance. Like that of a natural person, the name of a corporation is the link between the past and the future. It is the means by which the perpetual succes-

---

16 *Tulare Irrigation District v. Sheppard,* 185 U. S. 1 (1901). Mr. Justice Peckham, speaking for the court, laid down three essential prerequisites for the *de facto* corporation: "(1) a charter or general law under which such corporation as it purports might be lawfully organized; (2) an attempt to organize thereunder; (3) actual user of the corporate franchise."

17 *Jameson v. The People,* 16 Ill. 257 (1885). An act of 1852 authorizing a town to subscribe to the stocks of other corporations was held to be a recognition of the legal existence of the municipality.

18 *Robie v. Sedgwick and Hardenbrook,* 35 Barb. 319 (1861).

19 McQuillin, *op. cit.,* section 9.03. Item (6) is usually considered a matter of state concern, although in a number of instances this has been incorporated in municipal charters.

sion of the corporation is rendered certain. The name of the corporation, in the happy phrase of a court decision, constitutes "the knot of its political existence."[20] Pursuing the analogy somewhat further, the name is the means by which the responsibility of a person, natural or artificial, is guaranteed, and, although the person may be known by many names, he cannot escape his obligations. Great legal weight is attached to the corporate name. It cannot be changed without the consent of the state legislature, and even if assent is given, corporate rights and liabilities remain unaffected.[21]

Municipal corporations must have legally prescribed boundaries or else they cannot exist.[22] This concept is based upon two assumptions: (1) authority, if it is to be exercised, must be over persons or things within a given area, and (2) if limits are to be imposed upon authority, then the area or object of control must be clearly defined. Since municipal corporations are creatures of law, it follows that changes in the legal boundaries of municipalities are determined by the state legislature. Such action is normally not subject to review by the courts unless the legislature has been arbitrary or unreasonable.[23] But once the boundaries have been defined, the rule is that no two municipalities can have identical power and jurisdiction within the same area, for obvious confusion would exist. Of course, the same area may be controlled by other public corporations, but only if each has a separate governmental purpose.

Once a municipal corporation is created, it continues to exist until the sovereign authority, the state legislature that gave it life, decides otherwise. In this respect the procedure for the dissolution of a municipal corporation in this country differs markedly from English practice. In England a municipal corporation can be dissolved by one of four procedures: (1) by an act of Parliament, (2) by loss of an "integral part of the corporation . . . ," (3) by the action of the King who may demand the surrender of the charter, and (4) by forfeiture of the charter by reason of negligence or abuse.[24] In America, however, nullification of incorporation can be accomplished only by the action of the state legislature which, by law, specifies the procedure to be followed. The American equivalent

20 *Clarke v. Potter County,* 1 Pa. St. 159.

21 McQuillin, *op. cit.,* secs. 5.01, 5.06. Also *Sykes v. People,* 132 Ill. 32; *Village of Northbrook v. Sterba,* 318 Ill. 360.

22 McQuillin, *op. cit.,* sec. 7.105.

23 *State v. City of Reno,* 64 Nev. 127.

24 McQuillin, *op. cit.,* sec. 8.03.

of the English loss of an "integral part of the corporation," the failure to elect officers or to use corporate powers, does not result in the dissolution of the corporation since officers are not regarded as an integral part of it.[25] However, state legislatures may conditionally create corporations, and if there is failure to comply, the corporation automatically ceases to exist.[26] Unlike English doctrine, the courts in this country have no inherent right to forfeit charters.[27] In brief, in this country disincorporation is a legislative function. What the legislature grants, it can withdraw.

One final comment may be made about the dissolution of municipal corporations. Only the powers of the corporation disappear. Its liabilities remain because of the constitutional protections against the impairment of a contract, and may either be assigned to a newly created corporation or be subject to disposition either by a court of equity or in some other manner provided by law. But in no event may a municipal corporation avoid its responsibilities for debt merely by going through the process of dissolution.

Governmental vs. proprietary powers. Broadly speaking, the object of a municipal corporation is to provide for the general welfare of its inhabitants. To obtain this end, the municipality is armed with two main kinds of powers: governmental or public, and proprietary or private. When the municipal corporation carries out state functions at the municipal level, it is acting in its governmental capacity. When it exercises its powers for the specific benefit of the citizens of a local area, it is acting in its proprietary capacity. The distinction between the two is somewhat vague, for it rests upon the key words "specific benefit." What is of specific benefit to local inhabitants? It is clear that public health, education, police protection, and election administration are public functions. It is also fairly certain that markets, docks and wharves, airports, and public utility systems are proprietary in character. In between, however, is a twilight zone. For example, which level of government is responsible for the maintenance of parks or public cemeteries? There is no definite answer except to say that there is an uncertainty which must be resolved by what the Supreme Court, in a different connec-

[25] *Hill v. Anderson*, 122 Ky. 87.

[26] McQuillin, *op. cit.*, sec. 8.07.

[27] They may do so only if a statute expressly grants them the right. See *Boone County v. Verona*, 190 Ky. 430.

tion, has called the process of judicial inclusion and exclusion.[28] The matter is, however, of great importance in determining both the liability and the range of municipal authority.

The strict construction rule. Municipalities perform their tasks in a corporate capacity. As indicated previously, they have no inherent powers but instead obtain their jurisdiction from a series of miscellaneous sources such as the state constitution, the general laws of the state, laws of specific application, and their own charter. The scope of municipal authority is determined largely by the legislature of the state and by judicial construction.

Like the federal constitution, the municipality is regarded as a government of enumerated powers. Municipalities, in the words of an important court decision, "are to take nothing from the general sovereignty (the state) except what is expressly granted." [29] Unlike the federal practice, however, such grants are strictly construed and the interpretation of the courts are governed by Dillon's now famous rule of strict construction:

> It is a general and undisputed proposition of law that a municipal corporation possesses and can exercise the following powers, and no others: First, those granted in express words; second, those necessarily or fairly implied in or incident to the powers expressly granted; third, those essential to the declared objects and purposes of the corporation—not simply convenient, but indispensable. Any fair, reasonable, substantial doubt concerning the existence of the power is resolved by the courts against the corporation, and the power is denied.[30]

Judge Dillon's rule has had wide acceptance. In practice it has meant that a valid exercise of municipal power must be based upon some provision, either in the constitution or law creating it. Thus, the right of inspection reasonably implies that a charge may be made for the inspection; but the fact that a municipality has the right to construct or maintain streets does not permit it also to build dikes for the protection of the municipality against floods. Hence, unless specific authorization is contained in the charter or in law, the

---

[28] *Green v. Frazier U. S. 233* (1920). "Courts, as a rule, have attempted no judicial definition of a 'public' as distinguished from a 'private' purpose, but have left each case to be decided by its own peculiar circumstances. . . ."

[29] *Port Huron v. McCall,* 46 Mich. 565.

[30] J. F. Dillon, *Commentaries on the Law of Municipal Corporations* (5th ed.; Boston: Little, Brown & Co., 1911), I, sec. 237. Also McQuillin, *op. cit.,* II, sec, 10.09, which cites a long list of cases supporting this proposition.

municipality cannot assume a power, no matter how great the urgency may be.

One may wonder, recalling the fact that federal courts have expanded the delegated powers of the national government, why the municipality has had its powers so narrowly interpreted. The answer lies in the nature of this corporation and its relation to the state. The corporation, asserted Dillon, exists to protect both the majority and the minority. If it is not confined in its activities to its specific grant of authority, then the minority will be at the mercy of the majority. Thus, whenever the corporation acts in a fashion seemingly beyond its powers, the burden of proof must be assumed by the municipality. Unless it can relate what it is doing to its grant of powers, it cannot act, even though it seems as if it is necessary that it do so to prevent an injustice. Those who uphold the Dillon view argue that this will not necessarily result in injury since ultimate authority rests with the state. Presumably, if the municipality is without power, then it is the duty of the state to undertake the protection of the people.[31] The strict construction doctrine usually is applied only to the exercise of governmental functions. Adherence to it in the same degree does not exist with respect to the proprietary functions, for when a municipal corporation engages in business activities it becomes subject to the general law governing private corporations, and in such instances, adequate protection is afforded the minority.[32]

Several other corollaries spring from the rule of strict construction. The method by which a municipal corporation carries out its responsibilities is usually specified in state law, regardless of whether it exercises governmental or proprietary powers. Municipalities cannot depart from this procedure unless the legislature has failed to act, and where this should occur, the municipality is governed by the principle of reasonableness. Again, since the municipality is a public corporation, it must exercise its powers only for a public purpose. Although this term has a tinge of vagueness, it is subject to court interpretation.[33]

---

[31] Dillon, *op. cit.*, I, p. 48; also *Meday v. Rutherford,* 65 N. J. 645. The same approach has been used by most of the courts of the country, see McQuillin, *op. cit.*, II, sec. 10.21.

[32] Compare *Potts v. Cape May,* 66 N. J. 544 with *Nelson-Johnson and Doudna v. Metropolitan Utilities District,* 137 Neb. 871.

[33] *Green v. Frazier, op. cit.*

Mandatory vs. discretionary power. Finally, the freedom of a corporation and its officers to act is governed by the nature of the powers vested in them. Municipal officials may exercise either mandatory or discretionary authority.[34] Where allowance is made for the use of judgment, a discretionary act occurs. The power of the council to pass ordinances to decide whether streets and other public improvements are to be undertaken, the power to fix the tax rate, or the authority of the mayor to veto ordinances or sign bond resolutions fall into this category and can be utilized only by the office or officer to which the power or authority is assigned by either the charter or the general law. Authority of this sort cannot be delegated. Thus, the council may rely upon engineering reports in making its decision upon a public improvement; it can ask the assistance of the municipal assessor in the fixing of the tax rate; but it, and it alone, must make the decision. Discretionary acts are rarely subject to judicial review for the court is extremely loath to substitute its judgment for that of the municipal agent. However, if discretion is abused or if there is an element of unfairness, the courts will intervene.[35] Mandatory powers, on the other hand, are concerned with the implementation of discretionary authority. These powers may be delegated because they can be defined with such exactness that there is no element of choice involved.

CONCLUSION

In brief, the municipal corporation is a legal entity embodying the organized legal will of the community. Its main justification for existence is that it seeks to provide for the welfare of all of its citizens. Through its officers and agents, it wields an enormous amount of authority. It levies taxes, it can sue or be sued, it has the right of eminent domain, and, in general, it has the right to impose such restraints upon the individual as it deems consistent with the good of the community. The nature of free institutions requires that authority must be made responsible. The network of legal relationships described above is designed to achieve that objective. The legislature, the courts, and ultimately political action, if properly employed, can make the municipal authority compatible with free institutions.

---

[34] Mandatory powers are sometimes called ministerial.

[35] McQuillin, *op. cit.*, II, secs. 10.32-10.37. Also, Munro, *op. cit.*, I, pp. 206-208.

BIBLIOGRAPHY

Books:

Fairlie, J. A. *Municipal Administration.* New York: The Macmillan Co., 1906.

McQuillin, E. *The Law of Municipal Corporations,* 3rd Ed. Vol. I, Sections 1.01—3.65. Chicago: Callaghan & Company, 1949.

Munro, W. B. *Municipal Government and Administration,* Vol. I. New York: The Macmillan Co., 1925.

Reed, T. H. *Municipal Government in the United States.* New York: Appleton-Century Co., 1934 (revised).

Reid, J. S. *The Municipalities of the Roman Empire.* Cambridge, Great Britain: The University Press, 1913.

Shaw, A. *Municipal Government in Great Britain.* New York: The Century Co., 1895.

Stephenson, C. *Borough and Town.* Cambridge, Massachusetts: Harvard University Press, 1933.

Webb, S. and B. *English Local Government.* Vol. II. London and New York: Longmans, Green and Co., 1908.

Periodicals and Other Material:

Encyclopaedia of the Social Sciences. 1st Ed. Vol. XI, Article, "Municipal Corporations."

CHAPTER FOUR

Municipal Tort Liability

INTRODUCTION

Population concentration means an interdependent society. Furthermore, if such a society is to exist and thrive, restrictions or invasions of areas of conduct formerly considered private must occur. That this has taken place is indicated by the large number of people employed by municipalities. The increase both in the municipal work force and in the powers of government, however, poses the possibility that the municipal corporation and its agents may cause damage or injury to the citizen.[1] To protect the individual, the municipality has been made liable for torts, defined as wrongful acts not involving a crime or a breach of contract.[2] Tort liability is one of the most controversial issues, and the need to hammer out a more definitive policy is most important.

Consideration of what is at stake will make this clear. In carrying out its functions, the municipality needs freedom to fulfil the responsibilities vested in it by law. If it is held legally accountable for the acts of its agents, it may be subjected to such complete harassment that it will hesitate to act in order to avoid legal entanglement. Moreover, liability for its actions might very well impair the financial resources of the municipality if damage awards were high. Subjection of municipalities to suits in tort holds forth the prospect of complete paralysis of government action. Yet the grant of immunity to the corporation may mean the possibility of arbitrary exercise of power and possibly irreparable injury to the citizen, unless the agent of the corporation is made individually liable for his actions. This too is not very satisfactory, since it forces the individual employee to assume a burden which logically belongs to the municipal corporation. If it be asserted that the elimination

---

[1] L. T. David, *The Tort Liability of Public Officers* (Chicago: Public Administration Service, 1940), preface, p. 1.

[2] Webster's New International Dictionary, "Tort"; John Bouvier, *Law Dictionary* (Philadelphia: J. B. Lippincott Co., 1891), II, p. 736; *Encyclopaedia of Social Sciences,* "Tort," XIV, pp. 653-657.

of corporate immunity will cause municipal hesitancy, then it is doubly certain that the employee will defer needed action because of the possibility of legal entanglements. Thus, where to draw the line between freedom for the corporation and protection for the citizen is truly a knotty problem.

GOVERNMENTAL AND PROPRIETARY FUNCTIONS

Although Roman law contained the germ of the concept of municipal liability in tort, the liability of municipalities for tort in American jurisprudence stems from the ancient common law doctrine that "the King Can do no Wrong." Consequently, the rule of a superior responsible for the acts of his agents does not apply. If injuries result, it is the servant who is responsible. In municipal law, the liability of the municipal corporation also springs from this distinction. In any challenge of municipal action, the first question is always whether it has acted in its sovereign capacity.

Tort liability of the municipal corporation is governed by the judicial distinction, noted in the previous chapter, between governmental and proprietary functions. In essence this fundamental differentiation is the be-all and end-all of all municipal responsibility.[3] As a general rule, unless a law states otherwise, a municipality is not liable for torts resulting from the performance of its governmental functions. Support for this viewpoint is based upon the reasoning that a municipality is not required to perform such duties. It is simply acting as an agent of the state applying the latter's powers at the local level. As a consequence, it is argued, the municipal corporation, when carrying out governmental acts, is cloaked with sovereign immunity similar to that enjoyed by the state.[4] Although this doctrine of sovereignty is the subject of constant controversy among legal scholars, it is rather widely accepted by the courts.[5] Its general acceptance has meant in effect that the negligence of municipal corporations in their public acts can be corrected only by legislative action or by the indictment of the public official responsible for the wrong committed.

---

[3] Governmental functions may be used interchangeably with the following: public, mandatory, essential, legislative, and discretionary; proprietary functions include: nongovernmental, corporate, nonessential, commercial and permissive, see John S. Repko. "American Legal Commentary on the Doctrines of Municipal Tort Liability," *Law and Contemporary Problems* (Durham: Duke University Press, 1942), IX, p. 219.

[4] McQuillin, *op. cit.*, XVIII, secs. 53.01, 53.06 and 53.24.

[5] *Ibid.*, XVIII, pp. 194-197.

Modifications of sovereign immunity. This immunity of the municipal corporation acting in its governmental capacity must be modified in two respects. First, if property damage results from either municipal trespass or the maintenance of a nuisance, then the prohibitions of the federal constitution against the seizure of property without due compensation come into operation. Neither the municipality nor its agents can avoid their responsibilities in this regard merely because they are engaged in the performance of a public function.[6] It is this condition which has led one observer to remark, "It thus seems that the courts are prone to protect a person more assiduously in his property rights than in the inviolability of his person." [7]

Secondly, since the municipal corporation is a product of law, the legislature may permit individuals to sue a municipal corporation even where it is engaged in carrying out a governmental function. It may also make the liability of a municipality conditional upon adequate notice that injury has been sustained.[8] Thus, although the maintenance of the peace is a governmental function, municipalities have been made answerable for damages to property resulting from riots.[9] In other words, the state, by statutory action, may withdraw the cloak of governmental immunity. Just as it may permit itself to be sued, so the state may make municipal corporations subject to suit.

While municipalities enjoy considerable freedom in their governmental capacity, such is not the case where they engage in proprietary activities. Since the primary criterion of such a function is whether it provides a special pecuniary benefit for the municipal corporation, the courts are prone to consider the public corporation in the same light as a private corporation. Consequently a municipality, subject to the common law of master-servant, may be sued with or without its consent if its actions result in either injuries to persons or damages to their property.

This fundamental distinction between governmental and proprietary acts is the rule in most states of the union, with the possible

[6] McQuillin, *op. cit.,* XVIII, sec. 53.24, 53.27.
[7] Repko, *op. cit.,* p. 218.
[8] McQuillin, *op. cit.,* XVIII, sec. 53.05.
[9] McQuillin, *op. cit.,* sec. 53.45, 53.47. Wisconsin and New York have adopted such laws.

exception of South Carolina and Florida.[10] In practice, the governmental category includes the general function of maintaining the health, welfare, morals and public safety—in short, the application of the police power of the state at the municipal level. It also encompasses all buildings and instrumentalities necessary to carry out these purposes. Thus buildings housing these functions such as schools, jails, hospitals, work houses, police and fire stations, as well as motor vehicles, are covered by this classification. In this area the municipality "can do no wrong." Only its agents and officers are responsible for damages. Indeed, some courts have held that the municipality is not even responsible for the negligent condition of apparatus used by its employees.[11] On the other hand, municipal operation of water works, gas and electricity plants, airports, markets, piers and wharves, ferries, quarries and gravel pits, bus and transportation systems, and a host of other enterprises are generally considered operations of a private or corporate character.

Borderline cases. The distinction between governmental and proprietary functions is fairly obvious. Where an activity falls clearly into either category, the liability of the municipality for torts can easily be determined. But often the matter is not so simple, since borderline cases exist. In the words of one court "the distinction between governmental and proprietary functions has probably been the subject of as much controversy as any other question before the courts." [12] To put the matter somewhat differently; some portion of municipal property is under the tent of municipal immunity; another part is outside, but in between are those kinds of property that are half in and half outside of the tent. It is in this area that controversy exists. The maintenance of parks is a good case in point. In twenty-three states of the union the burden of judicial opinion holds that it is a governmental function and, therefore, the municipality in its administration of this activity is not liable for tortious acts committed by its officers. But in many states the converse of this principle is accepted. Parks are considered to be

---

10 George A. Warp, "Can the 'King' do no Wrong?", XXXI, *National Municipal Review,* (1942), p. 312.

11 *Wild v. Paterson,* 47 N. J. L. 406; *Miller v. Borough of Belmar,* 5 N. J. Misc. 224 (police); *Hammond v. Atlanta,* 25 Ga. App. 259 (fire) *Valentine v. Englewood,* 76 N. J. L. 509 (boards of Health).

12 *City of Pendleton v. Holman,* 177 Oregon 532; also McQuillin, *op. cit.,* sec. 53.28.

a corporate activity with the result that the municipality is made responsible for acts of negligence.[13]

Difficulty also occurs when an instrumentality owned by a municipality serves both governmental and private purposes at the same time. A city hall is a public building and its maintenance is regarded as a governmental function. But suppose that it houses the offices of both the police department and a municipally owned water works. Assume further, that a person entering the elevator of the building is injured as a result either of faulty equipment or the negligence of the operator. Is the city immune from suit because it is engaged in carrying out a public function? The answer to this question must be equivocal. In some jurisdictions, such as New York and Wisconsin, municipalities are not liable, but in Pennsylvania they are.[14] Again, the operation of a municipal lighting plant is considered proprietary in character, but street lighting with electrical energy coming from the same source is considered a governmental function. The operation of a water works poses a similar quandary. If a municipality sells water to consumers, it is acting in a proprietary capacity, but where it supplies water to put out a fire it is acting governmentally.[15] Playgrounds and recreation centers also fall into both the public and the private arenas.[16] Most perplexing of all is the maintenance of sewers. A municipality is not obligated to construct sewers, but if it does, then it is responsible for keeping them in good condition. Its failure to do so will result in the loss of municipal immunity if it can be shown that the municipality was negligent in the performance of its functions.[17]

Ministerial vs. discretionary powers. Aside from the differentiation between public and proprietary functions, municipal tort liability is further entangled in the Gordian knot of several other concepts: the distinction between ministerial and discretionary

---

[13] In the state of Michigan, parks are held by municipalities in their private capacity. Municipalities are, therefore, held liable for negligence. *Detroit v. Park Commissioners,* 44 Mich. 602. Contrariwise, in Massachusetts, maintenance of parks is a public function. See, *Higginson v. Treasurer and School House Commissioners of Boston,* 212 Mass. 583.

[14] McQuillin, *op. cit.,* sec. 53.32; also *Snider v. St. Paul,* 51 Minnesota 466; *Wilcox v. Roberts,* 190 N. Y. 137; *Fox v. Philadelphia,* 208 Pennsylvania 127.

[15] *State v. Barber,* 116 Iowa 96.

[16] *Love v. Buffalo,* 232 App. Div. 334 (governmental); *Epstein v. New Haven,* 104 Conn. 283 (private).

[17] The municipality is immune from suit in New Jersey since construction of sewers is regarded as a public function, *Waters v. Newark,* 56 N. J. L. 361.

powers; the doctrine of *ultra vires;* and the rule of *respondeat superior.* Generally speaking, a municipality is not legally accountable for damages resulting from its failure to exercise its discretionary power. It need not furnish adequate police or fire protection. It is not required to construct roads, nor is it responsible for the lighting of the streets. It is not open to suit when it does not engage in proprietary activities. In these and many other operations it may choose an alternative means of serving its citizens. However, once it has decided to undertake a municipal function, it is incumbent upon the corporation to execute the task in a manner that will not harm the citizen. From then on, negligence upon the part of the municipal corporation exposes it to a legal challenge. In summary, the municipality exercises discretion when it decides whether or not to construct a street. But once the public improvement has been made, it acts ministerially and has no alternative but to maintain the road in a safe condition. In the first instance, municipal failure to act makes it immune from a court suit; in the second, if negligence can be shown by the complainant, it is not immune.[18] In both instances the test of municipal liability for tortious action hinges on the distinction between discretionary and ministerial acts. Indeed, the courts often employ this as an independent test, quite apart from the governmental-proprietary dichotomy

Ultra vires. The doctrine of *ultra vires* also serves as a criterion to determine whether a city may be sued by those affected by its actions. As has been previously pointed out, the powers of the municipal corporation are governed by Dillon's rule of strict construction. The city, therefore, possesses only such authority as it can derive from general law, from ordinances, and from the provisions of its own charter. Consequently, when it goes beyond its assigned authority, the municipality is not responsible for its actions. If it performs a function *ultra vires*—that is, beyond the powers of the corporation—it is not liable for the effect of its actions.

The reasoning behind this theory is that the city cannot confer on its officers and agents that which it does not possess.[19] This principle applies whether the municipality engages in either a governmental or a corporate enterprise. For example, a municipality by the provisions of its charter may be prohibited from changing the

18 *Murrain v. Wilson Line,* 270 App. Div. 372 (police); McQuillin, *op. cit.,* secs. 53, 55.

19 See *Town of Palm Beach v. Vlahos,* 153 Fla. 781.

grade of its streets, except where it enacts an ordinance. It may, however, lay sidewalks which have the incidental effect of changing the grade of the streets. If damage to property occurs even though the action was not authorized by statute, the city cannot be sued.[20] Moreover, even where the city is managing a private enterprise without authority, such as a lighting plant, it again cannot be held accountable for injuries caused by its agents. In summary, therefore, the usual distinction between the public and private roles of the municipal corporation do not apply when it acts in an *ultra vires* fashion. In such instances it is no longer necessary to classify the functions of the municipality in order to determine liability.

Respondeat superior. The rule of *respondeat superior* applies only to the proprietary activities of the municipal corporation. It arose as a result of the general recognition of the fact that when a municipality ventures into the field of proprietary activity it should observe the same standards of conduct as its private business counterpart. As a consequence, the common-law rules of negligence normally governing the business world are also applied to the public corporation. Stated briefly, the rule of *respondeat superior* means that an employer or superior is responsible for the acts of his subordinates if damage or injury occurs. The rule, related to the municipal corporation, declares that it is accountable for the negligence of its officers or agents if two conditions prevail: (1) if a master-servant relationship exists; and (2) if the action taken by the officer is within his lawful authority and is not beyond the power of the corporation.[21] If these criteria are present, then a municipal corporation conducting a proprietary enterprise is liable for wilful wrongdoing and negligence upon the part of its officers or agents. A municipality operating a lighting plant or any other corporate enterprise can be sued in almost all states of the Union, except California, where the doctrine of *respondeat superior* is almost completely absent from the common law of the state.[22]

General rules of judicial construction. The law of tort liability for municipal corporations may be summarized briefly in the following fashion. In American law the doctrine of sovereign im-

[20] McQuillin, *op. cit.*, secs. 53.60-56.61.

[21] G. A. Warp, *op. cit.*, p. 311; also McQuillin, *op. cit.*, sec. 53.65.

[22] *Karpinski v. South River Borough,* 85 N. J. L. 208 (electric lighting utility). David, *op. cit.*, pp. 12-16. David confines his comment to the application of the common law rules to the activities of municipal corporations.

munity enjoyed by both the federal and state governments has been modified somewhat with respect to municipal powers. It is only in its governmental capacity that the municipal corporation is immune from all suits.[23] When it acts in a manner that brings special benefit to the members of the corporation, it loses its pre-eminence and is subjected to legal challenge with or without its consent. In its proprietary activities then, the municipality is expected to observe the same standards of morality as a private corporation. It is here that the rule of *respondeat superior* applies. When acts of negligence occur, the city is fully accountable to the citizen. In the light of what has been said, under no circumstance can the municipality be held responsible for discretionary acts. This much is clear, but the fundamental distinction between governmental and proprietary acts remains beclouded because the lag in judicial decisions sometimes assigns a function in one jurisdiction to the governmental camp and in another to the proprietary side. The consequence of this is that in some municipalities citizens have no remedy, while in others they may obtain legal redress.

CRITICISMS OF THE GOVERNMENTAL-PROPRIETARY RULE

The increase in the number and scope of municipal services accompanied by a corresponding rise in the number of public officials has heightened the likelihood that the citizen may be injured by the action of the agents of the municipal corporation. The wrongs done a citizen can be remedied through litigation in the courts in which both the complainant and the city are represented. To assert that this system enables both parties to obtain justice, however, is to oversimplify the problem.

In recent years the present concept of tort liability has been subject to severe and searching examination.[24] Criticisms leveled against the governmental-proprietary test are many and varied. In the main, the burden of complaint is directed against the immunity of the municipality from suit, but considerable discontent also is evidenced in regard to the conflicting judicial decisions.

---

23 The distinction between governmental and proprietary functions arose in 1842 in the case of *Bailey v. The Mayor of New York,* 3 Hill 53.

24 *Law and Contemporary Problems, op. cit.,* contains a whole series of excellent articles on the subject. See also Murray Seasongood, "Municipal Corporations: Objections to the Governmental and Proprietary Test" *Virginia Law Review,* XXII, p. 910 ff. The best study was made by Edwin Borchard, "Governmental Liability in Tort," *Yale Law Journal,* XXIX, p. 129 ff.

A commonly voiced complaint is that municipal immunity from suit does not provide an adequate remedy for the citizen who is injured, either in person or property. Critics readily will admit that agents of a municipality are liable for their acts to the injured party; but they question whether any real protection exists when such responsibility is enforced. Again, opponents of the prevailing doctrine point out that the public officer may not have sufficient property or other assets to satisfy the claim against him. If, the argument continues, it be asserted that the municipality should reimburse its agent, then, in effect, the corporation becomes a party to the suit and reliance upon municipal immunity becomes meaningless. Moreover, the situation contains an element of unfairness, for very often the officer is not solely responsible for the acts committed. Finally, it is contended that the constant possibility of legal harassment may deter able and courageous people from assuming the duties of office.[25] The view expressed above is well summarized in the strong words of George A. Warp, "The monarchical doctrine that the king can do no wrong and the tyrannical rule that the government can be above the law can scarcely be harmonized with the democratic idea that the law is supreme." [26]

Another attack upon the bifurcated concept asserts that it is outmoded and does not reflect sufficiently the realities of modern municipal life. The legalism that some functions are of major concern to the state as a whole and therefore are governmental and that others give special benefit to the members of the municipality is regarded by critics as a legal fiction that does not correspond to fact. Police, fire, education, to list a few of the activities of the municipality, fall into the governmental category. Yet there are few laymen who will not argue that these are of special interest to the inhabitants of a locality. In reality all functions performed at the local level, regardless of the source of their authority, concern the people living within the jurisdiction of the corporation. Yet prevailing judicial doctrine separates some functions from others. It grants the municipality immunity in the governmental area but subjects it to legal restraint when it carries out a proprietary purpose. The consequence of this judicial distinction is that, in some instances,

---

[25] F. F. Blachly and M. E. Oatman, "Approaches to Government Liability in Tort: A Comparative Survey," *Law and Contemporary Problems, op. cit.*, p. 213; David, *op. cit.*, preface.

[26] Warp, *op. cit.*, p. 311.

the citizen has an opportunity to defend himself but in other cases he is left without legal remedy.[27] It is the continued existence of this false dichotomy that led George Warp to comment, "Discredited in theory and unwarranted in fact, the arbitrary, absurd, and unjust governmental—proprietary rule should be eliminated from municipal law. Liability should be made to depend not upon the nature of the act." [28]

Dissatisfaction with the existing system of tort liability is undoubtedly well-grounded. Judicial decisions are based not upon the nature of the act, but rather upon the purpose of the municipal activity. If, by chance, an officer commits a tort while engaged in a governmental function, he, rather than the municipality, becomes liable. Whether the citizen has an adequate remedy depends largely on whether the agent of the municipality has sufficient assets to reimburse the injured party. The official may not be entirely responsible, and yet, because he is employed by the municipality, he is forced to shoulder the entire blame.

Moreover an aggrieved citizen who presses a claim against the city soon finds himself enmeshed in a skein of legal entanglement. He must file a claim within a given period of time. The city must investigate to establish the validity of the claim. Suits generally are not brought into the courts until other administrative remedies are exhausted. The legal office must decide carefully whether the amount of the claim justifies either the settlement or contest of the suit. Finally, when the case does come to the court, the docket is often crowded.[29] In the meantime the citizen must wait hopefully until his case is decided.

Under modern conditions of interdependent living the governmental proprietary rule has become a legal anachronism. The thinking of responsible authorities on the subject has been well summarized in the words of one commentator, "The present state of things is one of confusion, fears, assumptions and often injustice." [30]

A first glance would seem to indicate that there is considerable merit to the plea that municipal immunity from tort suits should be eliminated. Certainly the experience of some nations indicate that this is at least a possibility. Blachly and Oatman have pointed out

[27] Repko, *op. cit.*, pp. 221-222.
[28] Warp, *op. cit.*, p. 320.
[29] David and French, *op. cit.*, pp. 348-356.
[30] Repko, *op. cit.*, p. 233.

that, "The French system . . . entirely eliminates the doctrine of sovereignty as a reason for nonresponsibility. It eliminates the distinction between public or sovereign acts and proprietary or fiscal acts . . . It does away with the doctrine that the state can do no wrong." [31] In France, all cities are responsible for the acts of their agents and all claims against the city are handled by administrative courts. Under this plan, municipal liability for tort becomes a matter of legal administration. The speed with which such cases are processed is a measure of the justice to the individual.

But whether the French system would work effectively in this country is at least open to conjecture. On the basis of his studies, Warp believes that the waiver of municipal immunity would work well in Virginia. For the fiscal year 1940 the total cost of all claims against selected cities containing most of the population of the state amounted to only $7,500. Most of the suits against a city, he argues, result from injuries received from sidewalks, streets, and utilities. In almost all such instances legislative action already had made municipalities liable for damages. To extend this principle to all governmental functions would not, in his opinion, cause any difficulty.[32] Whether his plan would be feasible for larger states with more populous cities is yet another matter. Available studies show that the city of Los Angeles spends $25,000 annually in handling tort claims. Tort litigation in Boston costs that city an estimated $85,000 annually.[33] Acceptance of such a proposal to abandon completely municipal immunity would require the striking of a balance between the present cost of tort administration and that of the potential claims that might be filed against the municipality were it to waive its sovereignty in the governmental sphere.

A closer look would justify the statement that the step should not be undertaken lightly. To place the municipal corporation on the same footing as its private counterpart would subject it to many disabilities. Its common council, like the board of directors of a private corporation, would be responsible whenever an injury occurred whether or not it had acted. Thus the failure of the governing body to pass an adequate police ordinance would subject it to suit, or if it had enacted a statute and an injury to person or

[31] Blachly and Oatman, *op. cit.*, p. 210.

[32] Warp, *op. cit.*, pp. 314-315.

[33] L. T. David and P. H. French, "Public Tort Liability Administration: Organization, Methods and Expense," *Law and Contemporary Problems, op. cit.*, p. 360.

property resulted, it would still be liable. The action of the council, legislative in nature, could then be overruled by a jury, which might render an award for damages. If this condition prevailed, the entire democratic process would be nullified, for it would mean that the decision of the elected representatives of the people could be overturned.[34] There is a real possibility that the city may be victimized if it is subject to suit on every occasion that it seeks to exercise its powers.

It is evident that what is at issue in the tort liability of a municipality is, in the pertinent words of Professor Borchard, "a societal obligation." [35] As long as the municipality is engaged in the performance of its functions, there is the possibility that harm may be done to the individual. "The burden of the injury," say others, "should be considered a legitimate public expense, incidental to carrying on the complicated public functions.[36] This attitude has gained increasing acceptance.

Legislation has been passed assigning liability to a municipality regardless of the nature of the function carried out. Municipalities in many jurisdictions are now responsible for the negligent operation of motor vehicles by their officers who are engaged in the performance of police and fire protection. Damages caused by mobs and riots are now the subject of suit by the aggrieved party even though the maintenance of the peace is a public function. Municipalities, in other words, are no longer above the law merely because their agents are engaged in public activities.[37] While there is a general hesitancy to throw municipal immunity overboard, these and many other instances that might be cited indicate that in some areas it has been recognized that justice to the individual requires that the burden of injury should be shared by the municipality. It is in this direction that we have a hopeful development. Better and more effective tort statutes will do a great deal to eliminate some of the confusion and fears that exist at the present time.

Similar in some respects to this trend is the view that the liability of "all units of government should be based upon the insurance

---

[34] P. Nichol, "Between the Devil and the Deep Blue Sea," *National Municipal Review,* XXXI (1942) pp. 550-552. Nichol has an illuminating discussion of this point.

[35] E. Borchard, "Proposed State and Local Statutes imposing Public Liability for Tort," *Law and Contemporary Problems, op. cit.,* p. 282.

[36] Blachly and Oatman, *op. cit.,* p. 213.

[37] L. T. David, "Public Tort Liability Administration: Basic Conflicts and Problems," *Law and Contemporary Problems, op. cit.,* p. 339.

principle." [38] The city of San Diego, California seems to have pioneered in this respect. Faced with the fact that it had claims and damage payments of approximately $30,000 and with other claims and losses filed for action of about $1 million, it decided to purchase public liability and property insurance to cover both the city and its employees. The innovation had a twofold effect; (1) it placed the burden of payment on a private insurance company; and (2) it relieved the city officer of liability whether engaged in a public or proprietary activity.[39]

Both of these developments and many other legal innovations yet to come reflect the inadequacy of the governmental-proprietary rule. The dilemmas and contradictions noted above are a consequence of the rapid change of our society and the failure of common law to keep pace with changed conditions. Statute law is gradually supplementing common law, and the freedom enjoyed by the municipal corporation a century ago is a thing of the past. The municipality of today, like its private counterpart, is being saddled with new responsibilities in order to keep pace with its enlarged authority.

SUMMARY

The municipal corporation is a significant feature of our life. It is the sole repository of the legal will of the community, and without its activities, life in the city would be well-nigh intolerable. All of us at one time or another are affected by the operation of this corporate instrumentality. Our health, education, welfare and safety are, to a considerable extent, dependent upon the exercise of powers possessed by the municipality.

The corporation as an instrument of regulation and control did not spring full-blown from the head of man. It was rather the product of a gradual evolution in response to the changes in the condition and character of urban society. Originally its functions were devoted to minimal services such as law and order and fire protection, but as society became more complex, its activities were enlarged to cover a wide variety of services.

It was in the performance of these activities that the problem of municipal liability in tort arose, for the likelihood was increased

[38] Blachly and Oatman, *op. cit.*, p. 213.

[39] S. M. Roberts, "City Buys Liability Insurance from Lowest Bidder," *Public Management* XXVII (March 1945), p. 86.

that harm might be done to the individual. The lag in legal thinking with respect to the older and newer functions often left the citizen without remedy against his municipality. The slow evolution of a more realistic attitude toward municipal liability for tort augurs well for the future. The responsibility of the municipal corporation has matched its increased authority.

BIBLIOGRAPHY

Books:

Bouvier, J. *Law Dictionary*. Vol. II. Philadelphia: J. B. Lippincott Co., 1891.

David, L. T. *The Tort Liability of Public Officers*. Chicago: Public Administration Service, 1940.

McQuillin, E. *The Law of Municipal Corporations*. 3rd Edition. Vol. 18. Sections 52.01–53.171. Chicago: Callaghan and Co., 1950.

Periodicals and Other Material:

Bochard, E. "Governmental Liability in Tort," *Yale Law Journal*, XXXIV (1924–25), 129-143.

Encyclopaedia of the Social Sciences, 1st Edition, Vol. 14. Article, "Tort."

Nichol, P. "Between the Devil and the Deep Blue Sea," *National Municipal Review*, XXXI (1942), 550-552.

Roberts, S. M. "City Buys Liability Insurance from Lowest Bidder," *Public Management*, XXVII (1945), 86-87.

Sanders, P. H. (ed.). "Governmental Tort Liability," *Law and Contemporary Problems*, IX (Spring 1942), 179-370.

Warp, G. A. "Can the 'King' do no Wrong?" *National Municipal Review*, XXXI (1942), 311-315.

Chapter Five

Politics and Public Opinion

The Nature and Meaning of Politics

Within the past half-century or so of our national existence, we have witnessed the steadily widening area of governmental power in response to both the needs and demands of the citizen. For good or ill, the phenomenon of more government is here to stay, a condition that to some holds forth a promise and to others a threat. But regardless of one's particular viewpoint, the trenchant fact that emerges is that the liberty of the individual, whatever the reason or necessity, is in someway being curbed by the government. This is a circumstance of crucial importance since it is the government and those entrusted with its authority who exercise power based upon the collective will of the community. Whether the end product of governmental action is good or evil depends in large measure upon the citizen's awareness of the nature of politics.

Its central meaning. What is the meaning of politics? To some it is low and unprincipled action, evoking images of the ward-heeler and backroom maneuvering. To others it is a form of high-minded unselfish action that is designed to bring about a consensus among different and competing energies in our society. In between, there are many other shades of meaning, almost too numerous to mention. All, however, gloss over the fundamental point that politics is the exercise of political power; that some use the power and that others are affected by it. As Professor V. O. Key has put it, since power runs throughout the political process, the central meaning of politics is to be found in the relationship between the rulers and the ruled.[1] In a democratic society the leaders are responsible to the people; but if the citizens do not take an active part in enforcing this accountability, then public officials may become irresponsible and democratic government may become merely shadow without substance. Recognition of this fact imposes upon all citizens the obligation to

---

[1] V. O. Key, *Politics, Parties and Pressure Groups* (New York: Thomas Y. Crowell Co., 1952), ch. I, especially pp. 3-4.

participate in the politics of their democracy. Politics, as Professor McLean has so aptly put it, is what the citizens make it. Intelligent participation will make for enlightened politics; apathy opens the way for corruption. Indeed, this is one of the main weaknesses of local politics. If a citizen does not participate in politics it does not follow that he is not affected by the political process. It merely means that he is exposed to the exercise of power by persons over whom he has no direct control.[2]

The nature and meaning of politics have been the subject of constant speculation ever since the beginning of recorded history. Aristotle spoke of man as being by nature a political animal. Plato in his *Republic* and *The Laws* sought to structure political power in a manner designed to achieve the stability of the state. Throughout the years others have attempted to probe into the relationship of the governors and the governed and a variety of meanings have attached themselves to the term. As a consequence, the concept has come to mean many things to many men.

The change in political attitudes. At the turn of the century the exposures by the muckrakers and the general comment on the sad state of municipal politics made politics a term of opprobrium. Attention was focused mainly on the interaction of parties and the rise of the boss. Politics soon acquired an invidious connotation denoting the backroom, "the deal," corruption, and the "machine." Behind government was an "invisible government," a boss and those dependent upon him, who were not elected by anyone and therefore not accountable to the people. Very often, as Elihu Root asserted, the "invisible government" was the real government.[3]

In a similar vein Lincoln Steffens, a crusader par excellence, wrote of "paper government" and directed his attention to the men behind the scenes who held the actual reins of political power. Although he expressed an abiding faith in the people, Steffens, nonetheless, characterized politics as a business and politicians as political merchants selling political favors to the highest bidder.[4] Indeed, acceptance of this view was so widespread that reformers devoted their

[2] J. E. McLean, *Politics is What You Make It* (New York: Public Affairs Press, 1952), p. 1.

[3] E. Root, *Addresses in Government and Citizenship* (Cambridge: Harvard University Press, 1916), pp. 201-202.

[4] L. Steffens, *The Shame of Cities* (New York: McClure, Phillips & Co., 1904), pp. 3-5.

efforts to obtaining nonpartisan and nonpolitical reforms in government.

Articulation of group interests. Yet the fact seldom noted by the reformers and others interested in good government was that the steady integration of society since the turn of the century gradually had changed the nature of politics. The growth of an industrial society and the vicissitudes experienced by people led groups to organize either to protect or to represent their interest. In the multigroup society more and more people began to realize that power came from organization, and as this slowly entered the public consciousness, every interest sought to articulate its demands by means of a group.[5] All phenomena of government, as Arthur Bentley perceptively noted at the turn of the century, are a product of group pressures.[6]

The phenomenon of group articulation of interests led many observers to comment upon the oligarchic nature of politics. Munro pointed out that the complexity of modern life made it virtually impossible for "one citizen in a hundred" to spare the time needed to educate himself on the problems of government. Citizens, as a consequence, were forced to rely upon others and he concluded: "It is the essence of all government that the Few shall lead and the Many follow." [7] It was because of this tendency that he believed that the major problem of democracy was to hold "the Few" strictly accountable for their actions.[8]

Michel, too, noted what he termed the oligarchical tendencies in groups and political parties. Organization, to him, meant oligarchy, since the leadership essential to group objectives must, of necessity, be concentrated into relatively few hands. His "iron law of oligarchy" meant that the power of any group was concentrated in relatively few persons, those who were in a directive capacity. Oligarchy existed in every group whether it was a political party or any other association. The supremacy of the leaders was aided by the use of fear, force and the manipulation of public opinion. Leadership, he argued, was incompatible with the tenets of democracy, but

5 R. M. MacIver, "Interests" *Encyclopaedia of Social Science,* VIII, p. 147.

6 A. F. Bentley, *The Process of Government* (Bloomington, Indiana: The Principia Press, 1935), p. 269.

7 W. B. Munro, *The Invisible Government* (New York: The Macmillan Co., 1928), pp. 46-47.

8 *Idem.*

it was, nevertheless, an indispensable feature of social life. But while oligarchy was a necessary by-product of group action, Michel felt that the struggle among leaders would result in changes among them.[9]

In a somewhat similar vein, Lasswell describes politics as the relationship between an elite and the mass. The values available to society—income, deference, and safety—are distributed among various groups. Those who benefit most are considered by Lasswell to be the most influential. Politics, in his view, is the competition for power; its manipulation by skill groups determines "Who gets What, When, How." [10]

As society grew more interrelated and independent, the articulation of multigroup demands upon government increased in intensity. Gradually there arose an awareness that politics was more than the mere interaction of parties. It was power in all its organized forms and it encompassed all of human behavior. Politics was policy, the determination or settlement of a definite course of action by the government.[11] "No public policy," wrote Schattschneider, "could ever be the mere sum of the demands of organized special interests." [12] Government, it was recognized, functioned as an arbitrator. Its politics or policies were nothing more than the choice of alternative courses of action in response to the anticipated reactions of groups.[13] Politics involves the high art of compromise. As William S. White has said, "At its infrequent very best, politics makes a sensible and tolerable amalgam of the wishes and desires and prejudices of a great many people." [14] It is, it might be added, an amalgam of organized wishes.

In summary, therefore, the nature and significance of politics can best be comprehended if one grasps the fact that politics, in its broadest sense, is concerned with the formulation of policy. Politics

---

[9] E. and C. Paul (trans.), R. Michel's *Political Parties* (New York: Heart's International Library Co., 1915), pp. 26, 37, 40, 177, 377. For a criticism of Michel, see Lipson, *The Great Issues of Politics* (New York: Prentice-Hall, Inc., 1954), pp. 262-263.

[10] H. D. Lasswell, *Politics: Who gets What, When, How* (New York: McGraw-Hill Book Co., Inc., 1936), pp. 3, 20.

[11] For a present day restatement of this viewpoint, see E. Latham, *The Group Basis of Politics* (Ithaca, New York: Cornell University Press, 1952), pp. 12-16.

[12] E. E. Schattschneider, *Party Government* (New York: Farrar and Rinehart, 1952), p. 31.

[13] J. Dickinson, "Democratic Realities and Democratic Dogma," *American Political Science Review,* XXIV (1930), pp. 283-309, especially p. 291.

[14] W. S. White, "The Eighth Lively Art—Politics," *New York Times,* Magazine Section, October 3, 1954.

is decision-making, the choice of alternative courses of action. It may involve a decision to pave a street or build a school or, something as momentous as the declaration of war, but, regardless of the significance of the issue, it represents a regulation of the citizen by his government. The powers of governance, however, are never exercised in a vacuum. They are always employed in the light of the anticipated response of those affected by governmental policy. It is here that group demands, if they affect policy, also become an important part of the political process. Politics, to paraphrase William Penn, is the "motion" that men give to government.

THE GROUP BASIS OF POLITICS

Citizens' obligation. The citizen in a democratic society shoulders an important burden. According to the postulates of democracy, it is he who is ultimately responsible for the policy decisions that are made as well as the quality of politics, regardless of the level of government, federal, state, or local. As Professor Miller has so ably stated, *"So far as individuals are concerned the art of democracy is the art of thinking and discussion independently and together."* [15] Two things in the quotation should be stressed, "thinking . . . independently and together. . . ." To think independently, an individual must have the facts essential to arrive at some intelligent decision. The channels of information are open to him. As a citizen, it is his task to avail himself of these. He must learn not only to ask questions but also the right questions. He must also know where to get the answers to his queries. In short, he needs a knowledge of the municipal facts of life before he can adequately fulfil his duties as a citizen.

To be intelligent and well-informed is not enough. Politics in a democracy implies a knowledge of how to bring one's views to the attention of the policy makers within the government. Political power results from organization, and the citizen must realize that only by participating in a group or party will his information become an ingredient in the political decisions undertaken in his community. Thus it may be said that democracy is not self-executing. Although the pre-conditions of freedom exist, it is only by thinking and acting together that the government can be made responsible to

[15] A. M. Lee and E. B. Lee, *The Fine Art of Propaganda* (New York: Harcourt, Brace and Co., 1939), foreword, p. viii. The italics are Professor Miller's in his introduction to the book.

the people. Politics, as Professor McLean has said, requires "the year-round citizen." [16]

It is, of course, no easy task to be well-informed on the whole range of problems facing urban governments today. The following list, admittedly incomplete, will make this evident: better schools, improved roads, snow removal, garbage collection, police and fire services, traffic management, recreation, water supply, health and hospital facilities, inter-governmental relations, archaic forms of local government, civil rights and the treatment of minority groups in housing and other areas, and generally, high taxes and low return for the municipal dollar. The citizen of a municipality will no doubt assert—and with good reason—that it is virtually impossible to be intelligently informed on these matters. But what he fails to realize is that virtually every community, if polled, will prove to have experts who know about the major problems of the municipality. If the citizen will pool his resources, enthusiasm and energy with others, he will find that he can be adequately briefed on the major problems facing his local government. Politics requires year around participation. Intelligent evaluation of the issues of policy on the local level can be obtained if one is willing to act in committee fashion with others.[17]

The role of the group. A consideration of politics at the local level, therefore, involves a discussion of the role of the group. The American political system, because of its emphasis on the rights of freedom of discussion and petition, tolerates group activity.[18] Williams maintained that the rapid pace of urbanization destroyed the older forms of social organization and introduced anonymity into our modern society. Despite this, however, the need for the personalization of relationships continued and new group relationships replaced the older forms of association.[19] This development explains why the Beards, commenting on the proliferation of groups in American life, were able to remark, "The tendency of Americans to unite with their fellows—a tendency noted a hundred years earlier

---

[16] McLean, *op. cit.*, p. 22.

[17] C. King, *Your Committee in Community Action* (New York: Harper & Brothers, 1952), especially pp. 5-6.

[18] R. M. Williams, Jr., *American Society* (New York: Alfred A. Knopf Inc., 1951), p. 469.

[19] Williams, *op. cit.*, p. 470.

by de Tocqueville—now became a general mania." [20] Fergusson, in common with Williams, asserted that an integrated economic order inevitably caused the growth of interest groups. The rationale underlying the formation and utilization of groups was ably summarized by Fergusson, "All power is organization and all organization is power." [21] He derides the role in politics of the independent and the unorganized. The former is a political nullity who places his destiny in the hands of those who are organized, and the latter, he scathingly remarks, "is truly a political body in search of a head because it has no head of its own." [22] To Fergusson the boss and the crime syndicate are ample demonstrations of this thesis, since both of these, he points out, derive most of their power from organization.[23]

It is, of course, difficult to trace the interaction of the forces that exert pressures on government, but it is obvious that the mere existence of organization means power. Thus the political boss who is unopposed may be supreme and may have nothing to fear; but where he is faced with an organized opposition, either within or without his party, he may be in for a real challenge if he abuses his powers. Impressed with the importance of organization, Fergusson proposes as an antidote for the tyranny of the organized minority, the greater organization of the unorganized majority. It was only in this manner that Fergusson felt that a balanced society could be created.[24]

Fergusson's viewpoint has a great deal of merit. In many respects it is merely the echo of a phenomenon expressed much earlier in the century by Arthur Bentley. Groups are not only part of the social process but are also a vital part of the political process. Group interaction produces public opinion and this is the environment in which the political instrumentality operates. It is only when public opinion is organized that it can make an imprint on policy.[25] "Public opinion," Bentley noted, "is also a phenomenon of the group process. There is no public opinion that is not a voice reflecting the activity of a group or set of groups." [26] The group basis of politics

[20] C. A. Beard and M. Beard, *The Rise of American Civilization* (New York: The Macmillan Co., 1927), II. pp. 730-731.

[21] H. Fergusson, *People and Power, Political Behavior in America* (New York: William Morrow and Co., copyright 1947), p. 101.

[22] *Ibid.*, p. 142.

[23] *Ibid.*, p. 112.

[24] Fergusson, *op. cit.*, p. 119.

[25] Bentley, *op. cit.*, p. 236, 238.

[26] Bentley, *op. cit.*, p. 223.

operates at all levels of government. Indeed, the very fact that the citizen feels impelled to organize is an indication of the measure of his concern, and very often the difference between organization and the lack of it is the index of citizen interest.[27]

Kinds of groups. Thus the raw ingredients of politics, whether on the level of the national, state, or local government, are the individual and the group. The role of the individual has been dealt with briefly. Now let us examine the part played by the group. In any municipality the number of organized groups is so numerous as almost to defy description. Warner and Lunt found that in a city of 17,000 there were approximately 900 associations.[28] Hunter found approximately the same situation in Regional City.[29] Any issue of the *World Almanac* or the *Statistical Abstract of the United States* will show that the formation of associations is not an isolated phenomenon. As the Beards have said, Americans are joiners.

Obviously all groups are not organized to the same degree. Some are loosely knit and others are so tightly structured that they are almost monolithic in character. Nor do they all occupy the same position on the prestige ladder. The Negroes in Regional City, for example, rated twenty-two out of their 250 organizations as being the most powerful.[30] But all groups, regardless of their level in the community, do seek to influence policy wherever and whenever the interests of their membership are affected. Their power and pressure will vary according to the community in which they are located.

Broadly speaking, most municipalities contain the following significant associations: racial and national origin minorities; religious groups; business and allied interests; labor organizations; educational and reform elements; and "fringe" groups. While these are not directly engaged in politics, the fact that they represent specific interest and are organized presents a factor with which the political party, either in control of government or seeking power, must reckon. While the party may be seeking office, the groups are very much interested in how the office holders will exercise their power.[31]

---

27 E. E. Schattschneider, *op. cit.,* p. 21.

28 W. L. Warner and P. Lunt, *The Social Life of a Modern Community* (New Haven: Yale University Press, 1941), p. 303.

29 F. Hunter, *Community Power Structure* (Chapel Hill: The University of North Carolina Press, 1953), introduction, pp. 1-2.

30 Hunter, *op. cit.,* p. 115.

31 Hunter, *op. cit.,* p. 158.

As such, the action or reaction of the group becomes a factor in the political decision.

The city as a melting pot. The cities of America are polyglot in composition. Because its net rèproduction rate has been low, the city has been forced to draw on either the countryside or other nations for additional population. As a consequence, almost every large American city is a hodgepodge of people of many nationalities, races, and religions. In 1910 thc total foreign white stock in this country was 32.0 million and thirty years later it had risen to 35.0 million.[32] The number of foreign born in our cities can be gathered from Table 1. The fact that these minorities exist has exerted a powerful pull on the politics of the city.

Table 1—URBAN FOREIGN-BORN WHITE POPULATION, BY COUNTRY OF BIRTH (1950)

Country of Birth	*Urban Population*	*Country of Birth*	*Urban Population*
England and Wales	480,012	U.S.S.R.	820,512
Scotland	211,019	Lithuania	130,245
Northern Ireland	13,769	Finland	57,468
Ireland	464,043	Rumania	78,555
Norway	136,495	Greece	157,786
Sweden	242,920	Italy	1,301,875
Denmark	74,088	Spain	38,712
Netherlands	69,270	Portugal	44,933
Belgium	41,232	Other Europe	66,502
Switzerland	49,008	Asia	162,570
France	88,893	Canada—French	191,818
Germany	776,525	Canada—Other	599,390
Poland	762,289	Mexico	309,630
Czechoslovakia	217,315	Other America	109,335
Austria	346,102	All Other	51,462
Hungary	228,984	Not Reported	50,927
Yugoslavia	115,181	Total	8,488,865

U. S. Bureau of the Census, *Statistical Abstract of the United States:* 1954 (Seventy-fifth edition), Washington, D. C. 1954, p. 43, Table 34.

New York City has a population of diverse races, religions and nationalities. Its eight million people include Jews, Negroes, Italians, Irish and virtually every national or racial minority under the

[32] U. S. Bureau of Census, *Statistical Abstract of the United States* (Washington, D. C.: U. S. Government Printing Office, 1954), p. 40.

sun. Yet, as the municipally owned station WNYC has often remarked, "they live in peace and harmony." Like New York City, Chicago has a polyglot complexion. It boasts proudly that it has the "sixth-largest German city, the second-largest Bohemian city, the second-largest Swedish city, the second-largest Norwegian, and the second-largest Polish city in the world." [33] Its three hundred thousand Negroes also make up a significant portion of the city's population.[34] Boston is principally Irish and Catholic. Miami Beach, whose white population is half-Jewish and half-Gentile, also has a large Negro population. Detroit has a variety of nationalities and races, with the Negroes, approximately 17% of the population, largely restricted to "Paradise Valley." [35] Moving further westward we find that Milwaukee's 630,000 people are mainly early native white stock on to which was later grafted Germans, Poles, and Jews.[36] St. Louis has a large German population with Irish and French Catholic elements also prominent.[37] So it is with almost every city in America.

The presence of racial and religious groups is reflected in the politics of the city in many ways. Public acceptance of the religion of candidates for office seems to be a primary prerequisite for political success. Political parties, in making nominations, tend to recognize all ethnic and religious groups if they constitute a significant portion of the voting population of the city. In San Francisco membership on the board of education is a matter of rotation among various religious groups.[38] And a similar situation applies in regard to the appointments to both the Board of Education and the Board of Higher Education in the city of New York. It is probable that a religious factor is present in almost all appointments of this kind regardless of the city that one considers.

In the make-up of the political ticket, races and faiths are given recognition. The late Edward J. Flynn, "boss" of Bronx County in New York, in explaining how nominations were made for city-wide and county-wide offices, stressed the fact that since Jews, Italians,

---

[33] R. S. Allen, ed., *Our Fair City* (New York: The Vanguard Press, Inc., copyright 1947), p. 169.

[34] *Ibid.*, p. 187.

[35] *Ibid.*, pp. 27, 92, 158, 167.

[36] H. Hansen, editor, *The World Almanac and Book of Facts* (New York: The World Telegram and the Sun, 1952), p. 433; also Allen, *op. cit.*, p. 202.

[37] Allen, *op. cit.*, p. 245.

[38] Allen, *op. cit.*, p. 353.

and Irish made up a large part of the population, it was essential that they be recognized politically. A well-rounded ticket presented by his county committee contained two Irish, two Jewish, and two Italian candidates.[39] In Seattle a Scandinavian name, wrote Neuberger, was considered to be worth at least thirty thousand votes.[40]

In Boston the predominance of Catholic and Irish elements led to a long line of Irish political bosses. The influence of Boss Hague in Jersey City cannot be considered apart from the influence of the dominant religious groups in the city. Through careful distribution of patronage in the form of well-paid city chaplains and the granting of favors and dispensations to favored religions, the resistance to the political machinations of the dominant party was weakened.[41] In both Boston and Jersey City, the opposition could have done much to check the abuse of political power.

The career of Anthony Cermak, the Czechoslovakian who became mayor of the city of Chicago, demonstrated the influence of national minorities. His rise to power was based upon the fusion of such elements as the Poles, Czechs, Lithuanians, Greeks, and Irish.[42] When the Kelly-Nash machine came to power following Cermak's death, only one county judge was able to defy them, and his ability in this respect was largely because of his popularity with the Polish population.[43]

Zink's penetrating study of city bosses in the United States has suggested that, "There seems to be some relationship between the racial stock of municipal bosses and the dominant racial group of foreign origin in their cities." [44] The premium placed by the party on religion and/or national origin was also noted by Zink who pointed out that of the twenty municipal bosses studied, ten were Catholic, nine were Protestant and one was Jewish. Many of the bosses of America were Irish and only one, "Doc" Ames, seems to have been of native American stock. Although generalizations are risky because of the absence of sufficient empirical data, it can be

---

[39] E. J. Flynn, *You're the Boss* (New York: The Viking Press, 1947), pp. 221-223.

[40] Allen, *op. cit.*, p. 338.

[41] C. Van Devander, *The Big Bosses* (New York: Howell, Soskin, Publishers, 1944), pp. 99-100; also D. D. McKean, *The Boss, The Hague Machine in Action* (Boston: Houghton Mifflin Co., 1940).

[42] *Ibid.*, pp. 267-268.

[43] *Ibid.*, p. 275.

[44] H. Zink, *City Bosses in the United States* (Durham, North Carolina: The Duke University Press, 1930), pp. 4-5. Zink is confused in his terminology. His study concerned itself with religious and national-origin groups rather than racial groups.

said that the political leaders of any municipality are generally representative of the significant racial, religious, or national origin elements.

The ethnic and religious composition of the city becomes especially significant as the regulatory function of the city and the nation expands. The flood tide of immigration before World War I resulted in the presence in the city of large numbers of the foreign born. When the flow of immigration was halted during World War I and thereafter, the Negro and the Southern White replaced the immigrant as a source of cheap labor.[45] The general tendency of these groups was to join the dominant party of the city in which they were located.[46] As these groups became amalgamated, they sought political recognition from the party in control and there arose what Lubell called the "Jacob's Ladder" of political opportunity.[47] Although at first they received minor posts from the party in power, allocation of candidates to higher posts became an accomplished fact when the minority contained enough votes to influence significantly the decision at the polls.

Of even greater significance was the attitude toward governmental power of the descendants of the generation who came to these shores during the second decade of this century. Having come of age during the period when government was expanding its functions and having experienced the trauma of a nation-wide depression during the years 1929–1933, they tended to feel that their salvation was dependent upon governmental action. This change in attitude was of great importance, for it meant that those who lived in the cities had a different attitude from the country dweller. The city elements, noted Lubell, had a different view from their country cousins. "Never having known anything but city life, this new generation was bound to develop a different attitude toward the role of government than that of Americans born on farms or in small towns." [48]

The natural and almost inevitable result of at least a generation of city life has been that significant elements have come to think of government in positive terms. Having been accustomed to look

---

[45] S. Lubell, *The Future of American Politics* (New York: Harper & Bros., 1951), pp. 28, 30.

[46] A. W. Macmahon, "Political Parties: United States," *Encyclopaedia of Social Sciences,* XI, p. 600.

[47] Lubell, *op. cit.,* p. 77.

[48] *Ibid.,* p. 32.

to government for their welfare, they were not suspicious of governmental power. Indeed, the general tendency was to seek to use governmental power for their own purposes. Thus Negroes, through the legal and political means of such organizations as the National Association for the Advancement of Colored People or the Urban League, seek to abolish segregation in schools and housing, although this by no means includes all their efforts. Civil rights, in their view, is an acute matter of governmental concern. Religious groups, on the other hand, demand "released time" for religious training, and in general, they are to be found among the ranks of those who wish to raise the tone and morality of government.

The "melting pot" of the city thus contains the elements of political brew, but the degree to which ethnic and religious elements become important depends in large measure on whether they are organized. The inarticulate mass is not an effective political instrument, although it does provide a sounding board for the rather strident tones of political warfare.

Business in politics. Another significant force in the municipality is the complex of interests generally called business. These interests, although numerically small, occupy a position of strategic influence since the municipality, in large measure, is dependent upon them for many essential services. The production and distribution of goods, the size of the labor force, and especially in the one-industry town, the economic welfare of the municipality are, to a considerable degree, reflected by the kinds of business located in the city. Mainly because of its central economic position, business has a real opportunity to exercise leadership.

Although business is not directly engaged in party activity, it is, nevertheless, interested in *how* political power is exercised. Because it has a legitimate interest in the politics of the municipality, it has organized itself, but it is not a unified interest. The views of business generally vary with that segment of the economy of which they are a part. Local Chambers of Commerce, seeking to improve the conditions under which business operate, will usually reflect a general view seeking to incorporate the consensus of business. Utilities, however, are more dependent upon local government. They may desire a franchise or they may wish to escape regulation but, in either event, they may be willing to work out a modus vivendi with the dominant political leadership, since their continuance may very well depend upon how the political winds blow. Such at least was the characteristic of municipal politics in the past when "boodling," the granting of privileges and rights of cities to private interests without adequate compensation, was the common practice.[49] Although such conduct in this day and age is regarded as reprehensible, it is still true that utilities have a vital stake in the politics of the municipality.

Industries have a variety of needs which the municipality must provide. They are concerned about the conditions of roads, the adequacy of police and fire protection, water supply, sewage and waste disposal, to mention but a few municipal functions. They desire these services but may object to higher taxes on the grounds that they are being forced to shoulder more of the burden than the rest of the community. In such cases they may threaten to move out of a municipality, and the threat is often enough acted upon to bring about a "moderate" attitude on the part of the municipal authorities.[50] Taxpayers' groups may insist upon economy in government, the elimination of archaic governmental practices, and even the institution of a sales tax. Retail merchants will be found in the ranks of those who oppose the sales tax, but they will want more adequate parking facilities and more favorable tax treatment of the downtown area. Real estate interests may protest against zoning ordinances or be opposed to public housing.[51]

All of this indicates that on specific issues business will divide into general groups; but on such matters as economy in government and opposition to higher taxes and labor, the business community is in substantial agreement. The homogeneity of the business interest is further enhanced by the network of economic relationships that tie all business interests together. While it is difficult to trace these, it is almost obvious that there are all kinds of situations where some segments are more independent than others. A retail merchant may be dependent upon a bank for credit or a bank may desire to expand its functions. In all of the multitudinous business activities there are some interests that occupy a dominant position and others a subordinate one. Those on a secondary footing may behave as mavericks, but there is always a point beyond which they may not go for fear of retaliation by their more fortunate brothers.

The web of interrelationships is brilliantly portrayed by Floyd

---

49 Steffens, *op. cit.*, pp. 32, 108, 165.

50 The recent case of an industry in the city of Yonkers is a good example.

51 Allen, *op. cit.*, pp. 119, 191.

Hunter in his study of Regional City. "The men of power" within this community were those in charge of the direction of the commercial, industrial and financial enterprises.[52] Policy making was in the hands of approximately forty persons, and entrance into the policy echelons was not generally due to political eminence.[53] In this tightly structured community, policy making seemed to appear suddenly, and the citizen had no idea as to how policies were formulated. But as Hunter pointed out, the policy makers took into consideration both political and economic factors within the community and sought to strike a balance between them. The men of power "use the public power but they also use private economic power to achieve their objectives." [54] Channels of information were controlled and discussion was throttled if it appeared to go contrary to the interest of the dominant group. The ". . . policy makers," reported Hunter, "have a fairly definite set of settled policies which have been historically functional in the community." [55] Although the probable reaction of people and subordinate groups was taken into account, decisions were made at the top level.[56] The fusion of economic and political power led Hunter to conclude, "There appears to be a tenuous line of communication between the governors of our society and the governed. This situation does not square with the concepts of democracy that we have been taught to revere. The line of communication between the leaders and the people needs to be broadened and strengthened. . . ." [57]

Hunter's emphasis on the role of business in Regional City may not be representative of all municipalities.[58] There are signs, however, that business awareness of its position in the municipality is on the increase. The old attitude of the "public be damned" has been replaced by a newer philosophy based upon public relations. Business is taking an increasingly active part in the civic life of the community. Denver's Chamber of Commerce has taken upon itself the task of reviewing the municipal budget annually and making suggestions to the citizens. The Business Men's League and the Cham-

---

[52] Hunter, *op. cit.*, pp. 12-13, 261.
[53] *Ibid.*, p. 81.
[54] *Ibid.*, pp. 158-160.
[55] *Ibid.*, p. 246.
[56] *Ibid.*, pp. 207-208.
[57] *Ibid.*, p. 1.
[58] For an excellent criticism of his thesis, see H. Kaufman and V. Jones, "The Mystery of Power," *Public Administration Review*, XIV, No. 3 (1954), pp. 205-207.

ber of Commerce are prominent in the affairs of St. Louis. In Detroit, the Civic Uplift League was instrumental in mustering popular support for the revision of an antiquated city charter. Milwaukee, Kansas City, and Norfolk (Nebraska), to mention but a few others, tell the same story.[59] The possibility that a business interest might be shown in a bad light has often led it to change policies.[60] Although the unanimity of business interest is often exaggerated, it is a fact that it is a powerful force within the municipality.

Labor. Like business, labor is important because it can dominate strategic sectors of the local economy. Like business, too, labor originally frowned upon state interference in labor-industry relationships. But gradually labor came to realize that if it did not take an active part in politics, it would be subject to punitive action from those who had gained control of the machinery of government or else its enemies would use the power of the state against it.

On the local level, labor may be concerned with the attitude of the city toward collective bargaining, the behavior of the police in strikes, better schools, welfare, recreation, public housing, building codes, and a host of other issues. Labor may express its interest in a variety of ways—by the exercise of economic power, by the attempt to lobby for issues it favors, and, in rare instances, it may engage in politics either by nominating or endorsing candidates for office.

The fact that labor is organized for the protection of its members brings its views to the attention of the policy makers of the municipality. The threat of a strike together with the possibility that it will interrupt a service essential to the life of the city is a factor with which the city must reckon. The city fathers must always anticipate the reaction of labor leaders to its policies. Labor's attitude toward its business counterpart is also an important facet of politics. It may regard itself as a natural enemy of the business interest and seek to counteract the pressures of the latter; or it may take the position that its welfare is dependent upon business with the consequence that it will accommodate itself to the dominant business elements of the community.[61] Labor, itself, may be torn

59 N. Kuhne, "Main Street and City Hall," *Nation's Business,* XXXVIII (October 1950), pp. 39-41 describes the efforts of business groups to get better fire equipment and to reorganize the street department.

60 King, *op. cit.,* pp. 40-41.

61 S. Alinsky, *Reveille for Radicals* (Chicago: University of Chicago Press, 1946), p. 45. Alinsky seems to think that labor believes that its welfare is dependent upon business.

betwixt and between, one side believing in craft and the other in industrial unionism, and the net result might be a series of jurisdictional disputes with the general welfare of the community left hanging in a limbo. In some instances, the labor interest in the community or at least its leadership might be seduced by offers of patronage from the local political machine. Where this does occur, there is very little difference between the dominant political elements and the viewpoint of the labor interest.

The range and variety of activity of local trade unions can be demonstrated by a few examples. Unions are strongly organized in Philadelphia and the labor vote is predominantly Democratic. Detroit's labor unions are very powerful economic groups, but politically they have failed to elect a single one of their number to the municipal council. However labor's reaction to the policies of the city must be taken into account. In Milwaukee, labor unions are a significant political force with both the C.I.O. and the A.F. of L. granting or withholding endorsement of candidates.[62]

The fact that organized labor is a Johnny-Come-Lately on the political scene has aroused the fear and suspicion of other groups. Mayor Hague of Jersey City sought to marshal all of the forces of the city to blunt the organization drives of the C.I.O.[63] Seattle's Dave Beck, leader of the longshoremen, was a powerful figure not because he controlled votes but rather because he represented an alternative to the C.I.O. Although the city recognized that through his union's power to negotiate collective bargaining arrangements the economic life of the community was affected, it was willing to accept him because of his opposition to the C.I.O. In New York City during the latter part of the thirties, labor unions made a strong effort to engage in politics. In 1937 the newly formed American Labor party contributed approximately five hundred thousand votes toward the election of a fusion mayor, and four years later it undoubtedly carried the day for the same candidate giving him an almost equal number of votes.[64] An ideological schism led by the International Ladies Garment Workers was followed by the rise of a second labor party called the Liberal party. Although the American Labor party has disappeared from the scene, the Liberal party

[62] Allen, *op. cit.*, pp. 69, 150.
[63] Van Devander, *op. cit.*, p. 103.
[64] Van Devander, *op. cit.*, p. 52.

is still a potent political voice in the city and its endorsements are sought by the contending political parties.[65]

Rackets and vice. In almost every community there are fringe groups whose members earn their livelihoods from rackets, vice, and other devious sources. Existing largely upon the sufferance of society, they owe their survival to the fact that they are organized, and by virtue of this they are able to gain the cooperation of law enforcement agencies. There has always been an alliance or misalliance between fringe groups and the political elements within the municipality. "Protection," at the turn of the century, Lincoln Steffens noted, was sold in almost all of the municipalities which he surveyed. Steffens[66] pointed to Minneapolis as one of many examples, where an alliance between "Doc" Ames, the political boss, and the police resulted in almost complete freedom for underworld elements. In Chicago during the nineteen twenties, gangland "bought into" both local political parties. One writer, describing this situation, remarked that "Big Bill" Thompson was so busy threatening to punch King George "in the snoot" that he forgot about the underworld personage who gained control of large sections of his party.[67] In the nineteen thirties, Thomas Dewey, then District Attorney, gained fame by his exposure of the racket control of politics in New York City. How deeply the racketeering elements had penetrated the process of politics in our greatest city was demonstrated by the Dewey crime investigations of the thirties. Defeated and discredited, the criminal elements were supposed to have been driven from the city, yet within the short space of less than two decades they were once more a factor to be reckoned with, despite the activities of a reform mayor who constantly threatened to "throw the bums out."

In 1950 the elasticity of the criminal elements and their ability to recover from the shock of exposure were once more brought to the attention of the public. Through the magic of television and the activity of the Kefauver Crime Committee, the alliance between crime and politics was brought into the living room and made a living reality for many persons. For the first time the citizens received

---

[65] The combined Liberal-American Labor Party vote in 1945 was 380,245 or 19% of the total vote cast. In 1949 it was 729,913 or 27% but by 1950 it had declined to 371,571 or 15% of the total vote. See *The World Almanac, op. cit.*, p. 154.

[66] Steffens, *op. cit.*, pp. 70-71.

[67] Van Devander, *op. cit.*, pp. 264-265.

an inkling of the insidious effect of criminal influence on the political process.[68]

As a result of the evolution of syndicated crime and gambling, over $25 billion changed hands annually, a great source of temptation to the local political leaders.[69] Organized crime, the Kefauver Committee pointed out, was not "limited to any single community or to any single state, but occurs all over the country." [70] Party organizations were dominated to a considerable extent by racketeers and many pliant public officials owed their office to gamblers' money.[71] At least two members of the Board of Police Commissioners of Kansas City, Missouri, were acceptable to a local underworld figure who had made substantial contributions. In Philadelphia, according to the Senate Committee, the alliance between the underworld and politicians was so complete in the years 1945–1950 that of the thousands of arrests made for gambling only two convictions were obtained.[72]

In New York City, cited by the same legislative committee as one of the "major centers of organized crime," a leading racketeer had "unquestionably had complete dominance over Tammany Hall." The rackets head had a hand in picking political leaders and even candidates for the judiciary. Van Devander tells of a political leader who refused to knuckle under and was then defeated in a primary fight by the underworld elements.[73] Indeed, so great was the influence of the racket syndicate head that a judge called by phone to thank him for his nomination to office.[74]

As in New York City, so throughout the country. Not only in the large cities was the gambler-political-police alliance invariably present but also in the cities in the medium population range, those with 100,000 inhabitants. To cite but one of the many examples, the head of rackets in one city ". . . has a great deal to say about running the Atlantic City police force. . . ." [75] In Florida racketeers even

[68] "Big rackets spread out; crime-police-politics tie-up," *United States News and World Report,* November 10, 1950, pp. 18-19.

[69] U. S. Senate, 82nd Cong., 1st Sess., *Special Committee to Investigate Organized Crime in Interstate Commerce pursuant to S. Resolution 202, Report no. 141* (Washington, D. C.: U. S. Government Printing Office, 1951), *Second Interim Report,* p. 3.

[70] *Ibid.,* p. 7.

[71] *Ibid., 3rd Report,* p. 4.

[72] *Ibid.,* pp. 4, 47.

[73] *Ibid.,* pp. 33-34.

[74] *Ibid., Third Report,* pp. 121-122.

[75] *Ibid., Final Report,* pp. 37, 40.

went so far as to attempt to control public opinion through the ownership of a newspaper.[76]

To some, the union between political and criminal elements may be considered "old fashioned," and the assertion may be made that gangsters have no proper role in the political process.[77] It is undoubtedly true that old-style methods of crime infiltration no longer exist; but the criminal element, as demonstrated by the Kefauver hearings, has a chameleon-like capacity for changing its color whenever pressures are put upon it by an aroused public. Yesterday its methods may have been crude and "old fashioned," but today crime is syndicated and manned by suave persons who often buy into legitimate businesses. Their understanding of the political process is considerable, and they are often able to manipulate the machine for their own devious purposes.

The consequences for the democratic process of this development were noted by an observer in the thirties: "During the past dozen years this sinister interlocking of bosses, gangsters, rackets, police and the courts has been carried to the point where it gravely imperils the whole fabric of our municipal democracy."[78] This might well apply to the condition of municipal politics today. The criminal elements furnish a graphic demonstration of the power of organization. Unless the citizens bestir themselves and apply the "know how" of organization in a degree equal to that employed by the criminal-political alliance, the underworld elements will continue to be a feature of municipal politics.

Newspapers. The newspaper is central to the activity of organized groups within the city. So important is its role that without it public opinion can hardly be said to exist. All groups are interested in gaining the attention of the public, and for most of them the newspaper is the only medium for making an impact upon the citizen. While one cannot entirely agree with Munro that the newspaper "manufactures the opinions which control all the others . . ."[79] one can say as did Lippmann that the "newspaper is . . . the book out of which a people determines its conduct. It is the

---

[76] *Ibid.*, pp. 74-75.

[77] E. J. Flynn, *op. cit.*, p. 61.

[78] W. B. Munro, *Personality in Politics* (New York: The Macmillan Co., 1934), p. 83.

[79] W. B. Munro, *Invisible Government* (New York: The Macmillan Co., 1928), pp. 87-88.

only book they read every day." [80] In every city the newspaper performs a primary function. It provides the information, news and comment upon which citizens can base their decisions and actions. If it is properly employed, the newspaper "can do more than any other agency to weld the people into a working team." [81]

But the mere existence of a newspaper in a city is not enough. If it is to be a force for the public good it must act in the tradition of responsible journalism. So motivated, it can act as the conscience of the community. It can throw the spotlight of pitiless publicity on all municipal wrongdoing. It can expose corruption and chicanery. It can "keep the fear of the Lord in the machine. . . ." Without the existence of the press and given the general inertia of the citizen, the public would be in a sad state. This implies, of course, that facts will be presented regardless of where the chips will fall. If the newspaper has the facts but does not present them for fear that they will antagonize a vested interest in the community, the public will be less knowledgeable about the affairs of their city, and public opinion will remain a sleeping giant. "A newspaper that does not have a public and an editor dedicated to the public good without thought of personal credit or glory," wrote Tate, "is a newspaper without a soul. It is, in fact, not a newspaper but a business parading under the colors of a free and enlightened press." [82]

Tate's attitude mirrors the role of the newspaper as an opinion medium. Responsible journalism is indispensable to a free society. Some indication of the part played by a free press can be gathered from circulation statistics. Four hundred morning and 1,454 evening dailies, and approximately four hundred Sunday papers reach a total, respectively, of 53.5 million and 43 million readers.[83] In the two decades since 1929 reader circulation has almost doubled. It is probable that at least twice as many people see their daily and Sunday newspapers. As Walter Lippmann has said, the newspaper is the only book that people read every day.

Unfortunately statistics have a way of hiding things. Against the increase in circulation must be placed what Morris Ernst has called "the evaporation of diversity of opinion." [84] Concentration, a fea-

---

[80] W. Lippmann, *Liberty and the News* (New York: The Macmillan Co., 1920), p. 57.

[81] H. C. Tate, *Building a Better Town*, (New York: Harper & Brothers, 1954), p. 34.

[82] Tate, *op. cit.*, p. 37.

[83] *Statistical Abstract for 1953*, p. 507.

[84] M. Ernst, *The First Freedom* (New York: The Macmillan Co., 1946), foreword.

ture of our industrial development, has also penetrated the free marketplace of ideas. The small newspaper with its premium on individuality has been replaced by the large metropolitan daily. Newspaper chains, a symbol of bigness, have appeared on the scene gradually absorbing an ever larger amount of the daily circulation. Wide coverage, human interest and feature stories and dependence upon press associations are now the distinctive characteristics of our press.

Evidence of this change can be found in the statistics of ownership. Since 1909 the number of daily newspapers has decreased by 25 percent.[85] One-fourth of our daily circulation is now controlled by fourteen companies owning eighteen newspapers.[86] More than 90 percent of the cities contain only one newspaper and in only 117 cities does competition exist among dailies. To the diminution of competition should be added the fact that 25 percent of our daily press is controlled by absentee owners.[87] A similar trend is apparent in the weekly press, considered by many to be the backbone of local democracy. Since the turn of the century, thirty-two hundred have suspended publication, and one company with three thousand under its wing dominates almost 50 percent of the weeklies.[88] Truly, as Laski remarked, "The owner-editor is thus a vanishing type. More and more, the chains dominate the scene."[89]

It is this evolution of the press in response to the dictates of economics which poses a fundamental dilemma for the opinion forming processes of our democracy. For a nation which prides itself on diversity of opinion and localism, bigness presents the threat of uniformity. The growth of the nationally syndicated column, the one-newspaper town, and the dependence upon the press associations are danger signs that point to the potential neglect of local issues. Already the independent and crusading newspaper is fast becoming a relic of yesteryear. The community press exists because it can cover local issues more adequately than can the large dailies. But it, too, is in danger of following in the footsteps of its big

[85] "Local Monopoly in the Daily Newspaper Industry," *Yale Law Journal*, LXI (1952), p. 949.

[86] Ernst, *op. cit.*, pp. xii, 289.

[87] Ernst, *op. cit.*, p. xii.

[88] *Ibid., also Statistical Abstract for 1953*, p. 507.

[89] H. Laski, *The American Democracy* (New York: The Viking Press, 1948), p. 647.

brother.[90] "Clearly," said Janowitz, "the integration of the local newspaper with the political party, business interests, and the dominant churches, spells success or failure for the paper, and community editors speak for and to the leaders of these groups." [91] Since the community press tends to be all things to all men, it tends to take a neutral attitude toward the issues of the day. Nonetheless, it does assist in the solution of many problems of the community such as traffic control, schools, water supply, garbage collection and many other matters touched only tangentially by the large metropolitan daily.[92]

Bigness and concentration in newspapers have meant large investments and important economic interests. In the drive for circulation there is always the possibility that the newspaper may hew more to the canons of business than of journalism. And if, as some allege, the newspapers tend to support dominant political and economic interests, then press concentration is a factor of profound political importance.[93] If this be true, then those who control the newspapers of the city occupy a strategic place and those who have its ears are likewise blessed.

To say this, however, is not to sound a note of doom. The concentrative tendency of the press must be placed in perspective. The daily press still plays a significant role in the opinion making processes of the community. Even though the citizen may live in a one-newspaper town, he can still glean the essential knowledge needed for active participation in the life of the community. But the newspaper is more than a mere purveyor of information. By furnishing a channel of communication, it bridges the impersonal gap among the people of the city and contributes greatly to the maintenance of common values and community solidarity. All this is of great importance; but it should not be forgotten that the high role of the newspaper as a sounding board of public opinion has been greatly attenuated by the economics of journalistic endeavor. Unless the present trend is reversed or stopped, the real victim will be public opinion at the local level.

---

[90] M. Janowitz, *The Community Press in an Urban Setting,* (Glencoe, Illinois: The Free Press, 1952), p. 23.

[91] *Ibid.,* p. 86. Janowitz is concerned with the metropolitan area of Chicago.

[92] *Ibid.*

[93] Laski, *op. cit.,* p. 637; also H. L. Ickes, *America's House of Lords,* (New York: Harcourt, Brace and Company, 1939).

CONCLUSION

Enough has been said to indicate that public opinion results from the interaction of groups within the city. The view that the citizen arrives at is, as Laski pointed out, "an equation in which quite literally, an immense number of variables is present." [94] In each city, multiple interests, organized in group form compete for the attention of the citizen. Organization of interest is needed if public opinion is to exist, for as Bentley has pointed out, the "group cannot be called to life by clamor." [95] It is not only in number but in intensity and techniques that the group gains power.[96] All groups employ a series of propaganda devices designed to enlist the support of the public. The Lees list seven of those most commonly employed: name calling, glittering generalities, transfer, testimonial, plain folks, card stacking, and band wagon.[97] The thinking person very often may become confused by the barrage of appeals leveled at him, but once he becomes aware of the propaganda tricks, he can examine each issue on its merits.

But just as leadership exists within a group, so does it exist among groups. Some groups are more prominent and more important than others and therefore, take the lead in community action on given issues. Public opinion is the product of group responses. Groups at the community level represent only a small percentage of the voting public. The unorganized majority is helpless against its pressures, but if it is to protect itself it must take a page from the experience of those already organized. Group interaction is often very complex, and while its responses may not be easily traced, the group basis of politics in the city is so essential that it cannot be ignored, save at the risk of gaining a superficial view of municipal politics.

BIBLIOGRAPHY

Books:

Alinsky, S. *Reveille for Radicals.* Chicago: University of Chicago Press, 1946.

Allen, R. S. (ed.). *Our Fair City*. New York: The Vanguard Press, Inc., 1947.

[94] Laski, *op. cit.*, p. 615.
[95] Bentley, *op. cit.*, p. 227.
[96] *Ibid.*, pp. 215-216.
[97] Lee and Lee, *op. cit.*, pp. 23-24.

Beard, C. and M. *The Rise of American Civilization.* Vol. II, New York: The Macmillan Co., 1927.

Bentley, A. F. *The Process of Government.* Bloomington, Indiana: The Principia Press, 1935.

Ernst, M. *The First Freedom.* New York: The Macmillan Co., 1946.

Fergusson, H. *People and Power, Political Behavior in America.* New York: William Morrow and Co., 1947.

Flynn, E. J. *You're the Boss.* New York: The Viking Press, 1947.

Hunter, F. *Community Power Structure.* Chapel Hill: The University of North Carolina Press, 1953.

Ickes, H. L. *America's House of Lords.* New York: Harcourt, Brace and Co., 1939.

Janowitz, M. *The Community Press in an Urban Setting.* Glencoe, Illinois: The Free Press, 1952.

Key, V. O. *Politics, Parties, and Pressure Groups.* New York: Thomas Y. Crowell Co., 1952.

King, C. *Your Committee in Community Action.* New York: Harper & Brothers, 1952.

Laski, H. *The American Democracy.* New York: The Viking Press, 1948.

Lasswell, H. D. *Politics: Who Gets What, When, How.* New York: McGraw-Hill Book Co., Inc., 1936.

Latham, E. *The Group Basis of Politics.* Ithaca, New York: Cornell University Press, 1952.

Lee, A. and E. *The Fine Art of Propaganda.* New York: Harcourt, Brace and Co., 1939.

Lippmann, W. *Liberty and the News.* New York: Harcourt, Brace and Howe, 1920.

Lipson, L. *The Great Issues of Politics.* New York: Prentice-Hall, Inc., 1954.

Lubell, S. *The Future of American Politics.* New York: Harper & Brothers, 1951.

McKean, D. D. *The Boss, The Hague Machine in Action.* Boston: Houghton-Mifflin Co., 1940.

McLean, J. E. *Politics is What You Make It.* New York: Public Affairs Press, 1952.

Michel, R. *Political Parties.* Translated by Eden and Cedar Paul. New York: Heart's International Library Co., 1915.

Munro, W. B. *The Invisible Government.* New York: The Macmillan Co., 1928.

Root, E. *Addresses on Government and Citizenship.* Cambridge: Harvard University Press, 1916.

Schattschneider, E. E. *Party Government.* New York: Farrar and Rinehart, 1952.

Steffens, L. *The Shame of the Cities.* New York: McClure, Phillips and Co., 1904.

Tate, H. C. *Building a Better Town.* New York: Harper and Brothers, 1954.

U. S. Department of Commerce, Bureau of Census, *Statistical Abstract of the United States: 1954.* (Seventy-fifth edition). Washington, D. C.: 1954.

Van Devander, C. *The Big Bosses.* New York: Howell, Soskin, Publishers, 1944.

Warner, W. L. and Lunt, P. *The Social Life of a Modern Community.* New Haven, Connecticut: Yale University Press, 1941.

Williams, R. M. *American Society.* New York, Alfred A. Knopf, 1951.

Zink, H. *City Bosses in the United States.* Durham, The Duke University Press, 1930.

Periodicals and Other Materials:

"Big Rackets Spread Out, Crime-Police-Politics Trap," *United States News and World Report,* November 10th, 1950, pp. 18-19.

Dickinson, J. "Democratic Realities and Democratic Dogma," *American Political Science Review,* XXIV (1930), 283-309.

82nd Congress, 1st Session. *Special Committee to Investigate Organized Crime in Interstate Commerce Pursuant to Senate Resolution 202.* Second, Third, and Final Reports. Washington, D. C.: U. S. Government Printing Office, 1951.

Encyclopaedia of the Social Sciences. 1st edition. Volume 8, Article. "Interests."

Kaufman, H. and Jones, V. "The Mystery of Power," *Public Administration Review,* XIV (1954), 205-212.

Kuhne, N. "Main Street and City Hall," *Nation's Business,* XXXVIII (1950), 39-41.

"Local Monopoly in the Daily Newspaper Industry," *Yale Law Journal,* LXI (1952), 949-1009.

White, W. S. "The Eighth Lively Art—Politics," *New York Times Magazine,* October 3, 1954, pp. 13+.

The World Almanac and Book of Facts. Harry Hansen ed.; New York: *The World-Telegram and the Sun,* 1952.

Chapter Six

Political Parties and the City

Introduction

Enough has been said in the previous chapter to indicate that the interaction of groups gives rise to public opinion. Each special group has its own axe to grind and will compete with others for the attention of the public. This is a condition that is almost inevitable. As long as there is a democratic society, there will be a free play of interests. Groups will pressure and bedevil the public and the political party. Although group conflict gives rise to public opinion, the latter is not synonymous with policy. "No public policy," wrote Schattschneider, "could ever be the mere sum of the demands of organized special interests." [1] Some reconciliation of these competing energies has to be made on behalf of the community as a whole if a truly public policy is to evolve. To obtain a consensus is the primary function of politics or, more specifically, of the political party.

Although the political party, especially at the local level, has come in for a great deal of criticism, it performs an undeniably essential function. Government could hardly function without it. It picks issues, simplifies alternatives for the voters, and nominates candidates for office. By these means it seeks control of the government. In this respect, it differs from other associations. Because it seeks the privilege of exercising the sovereign power of the community, it generally represents a blending of many interests within the community rather than any special interest. The political party is "one of the parts into which a state or municipality is divided by questions of public policy or the election of public officers." [2]

The essence of the party, as of the special interest, is organization. Its members, workers, and leaders are bound together to

---

[1] E. E. Schattschneider, *Party Government* (New York: Farrar & Rinehart, Inc., 1952), p. 31.

[2] A. Holcombe, "Political Parties: Theory," *Encyclopaedia of Social Science,* II, p. 590.

achieve victory at the polls as a common objective. A chain of authority provides a network of communication and command. Power comes from the top downward and responsibility from the bottom upward. The degree of control exercised by the party over its members will vary with the local political situation. Where a machine is entrenched, unquestioned obedience is demanded from the rank and file. Defiance against discipline is punished by expulsion and ostracism. Where boss control is absent, however, party action is a social process wherein the lower echelons have a considerable voice in decision-making.[3] Nevertheless, at each level of the organization, power and responsibility are commensurate, and generally, the higher the rank, the greater the concentration of power.

American politics is flavored by a strong tradition of localism. The party in the city has insisted upon local independence and, to a large degree, has been successful in this endeavor. The significance of this lies in the fact that the political party can compete for local offices. If successful, it then has its own resources. It need not necessarily be beholden to either the state or the national party. Unlike the parties in England and on the continent, it can if it so chooses, be its own boss.

PARTY ORGANIZATION

Municipal party organization usually coincides with the legal limits of the municipality. At the base of the party pyramid is the election precinct, the smallest unit of the party organization both in terms of population density and area. More than one hundred thousand of these exist, and in each of them there are at least two precinct committees representing the two major parties. It is on the shoulders of these rank and file members that the success or failure of the party rests. Precinct committeemen maintain almost daily contact with the voters in their area and get to know them intimately. To them, come people from all walks of life seeking favors, services, or in some way a simplification of the complexities of government. The party worker seeks to assist everyone, and if he cannot help by himself, he, in turn, reports the matter to those on a higher echelon of party authority. Thus the resources of the entire party are placed at the disposal of the individual seeking assistance, and for

[3] R. L. Morlan, "City Politics: Free Style," *National Municipal Review* XXXVIII (1949), p. 486.

the individual, to all intents and purposes, the precinct leader is the party.

Party organization above the level of the precinct is less uniform in structure. In some cities, precinct committees are grouped into wards; in others, into districts. In New York City the party at this level is the assembly district, which incorporates within it the election districts. Above the district is the county committee. Elected by the precinct committees, it is the real center of all party authority. It selects the captains or chairmen of the precinct committees, the district officers, and the two district leaders, usually a man and woman. Through the appointing power, the precinct is bound to the district organization and the latter, in turn, is made responsible to the county committee.

Actually, however, the organization is more tightly knit than this. District leaders and key people of the county committee are made members of its executive committee, and the latter, in turn, delegates its powers to a chairman who is, in fact, the real political leader in the county. The line of actual authority runs from the chairman of the executive committee to the district leaders, and then downward to the heads of the numerous precinct committees.

Although the power of the county leader is unquestioned, a system of mutual responsibility exists. His power is based upon the supporting units. Both he and they are dependent upon victory at the polls for influence and power. He is always under constraint to "guess right," for this is the usual margin between victory and defeat. It is a mistake to assume that the "boss" is merely a wielder of arbitrary power. To be a successful leader requires a high degree of statesmanship and a perceptive appreciation of the temper of the organization and of the people of the city to whom appeals for support are made.

But "guessing right" enables the leader to become the actual political ruler of the city. He nominates and elects candidates for office; he controls, to a large extent, the policies of the governing body; and he decides, in large measure, the degree and kinds of services that the citizen will receive. His power is enormous, but if it is to be retained he must successfully gauge the response of the people. In him rests the capacity for becoming the uncrowned king of municipal government, the real but invisible government which, like an iceberg, lies beneath the surface and shows its authority only occasionally.

MACHINE METHODS

The political party, like Napoleon's army, marches on its stomach. Active party workers require a means of sustenance, and the political leader is always aware of the fact that their zeal is all too often dependent upon whether they obtain jobs for their loyal supporters. Key people and their families "are taken care of in some way or other."[4] Most political leaders operate on the theory that it is the job nexus that binds the individual to the party organization. Almost everyone, they reason, wants a job. Hence political leaders are careful in staking out claims to the exempt positions which are then allotted on the basis of recommendations emanating from various parts of the organization. Those who are rebellious are denied job opportunities.[5] Indeed the success or failure of the political leader depends upon how he handles this delicate matter. The continued triumphs of an Edward Flynn of Bronx County in New York or of a Boss Crump of Memphis, Tennessee, are eloquent testimony on this point. A former reform mayor was quite correct when he stated that a political machine is unable to stand mass job starvation.[6] While the dispensation of party plums may be a source of strength to the organization, it may also be its Achilles' heel. Passing out the patronage enables the political leader to gain a foothold in local government. Loyal adherents constitute the "staying power" of the party, and this power is one of the principal reasons why the "organization" has been able to withstand the often bitter onslaughts of reform groups.

Once in power, the political leader has a tendency to spread his wings until almost all of city government becomes his own private preserve. The monopoly of the political processes gives him a vantage point from which he can dominate the affairs of the city. Seizure of the legal machinery—the office of the district attorney, the courts, and the police—virtually insure him against prosecution. Not only does he gain freedom from the law but, in all too many instances, he is the law. The reputed remark of Mayor Hague, when he was boss of Jersey City, New Jersey, that "I am the law," was no idle assertion. He was the law; and those who opposed him soon found themselves the victims of trumped-up charges, investigation, litigation, and

---

[4] E. J. Flynn, *You're the Boss* (New York: The Viking Press, 1947), p. 224.

[5] *Ibid.*, pp. 5, 26.

[6] F. H. La Guardia, "Bosses are the Bunk," *The Atlantic Monthly*, CLXXX (1947), p. 23.

prosecution.[7] So efficient was the Hague machine, decrepit though the government of Jersey City might have been, that "Hagueism" became a way of life for the people of the city. "Its agents," wrote Van Devander, "were to be found in every police and fire station, in the hospitals and schools, on the bench and in the jury box, in the bar association, and in the chamber of commerce." [8]

Control of the police usually opens the way for election frauds, ballot stuffing, and the padding of the registration lists, all a means of continuing the leader in power. In the capital city of New York State, for example, the O'Connell machine was noted for this practice. In some elections, an extraordinarily high percentage of their voters seemed to turn out at the polls. In Kansas City, after the political demise of Pendergast, investigations revealed large numbers of ghost names on the registration lists.[9] Very often the tax machinery is employed to win friends and discourage the opposition. Favored adherents are given tax exemptions or tax reductions while foes of the machine are subjected to economic pressure and discrimination. In Hudson County of New Jersey, the stronghold of Boss Hague, the tax board employed this authority with unusual vigor against the opponents of Hague.[10] Similar conditions exist in almost all of the larger cities and in many of the smaller ones. Only an outraged citizenry with aid from either the state or the federal government can loosen the hold of the party organization on the city government.

Once safely ensconced in power, the political leader is in a position to exercise great influence. In the fullest sense of the word he becomes a political merchant whose chief function ". . . is to serve as a broker between those who want public favors and those who are able to give him something in return." [11] All those who need assistance camp on his doorsteps. For the poor and the humble, Martin Lomasney's formula still operates to a considerable degree: "Is somebody out of a job? We do our best to place him, and not necessarily on the public payroll. Does the family run into arrears with

[7] C. Edison, "Lets Quarantine the Boss," *National Municipal Review*, XXXVI (1947), p. 6.

[8] C. Van Devander, *The Big Bosses* (New York: Howell, Soskin, Publishers, 1944), p. 94.

[9] *Ibid.*, pp. 82, 96, 233-234.

[10] Edison, *op. cit.*, p. 6.

[11] W. B. Munro, *Personality in Politics* (New York: The Macmillan Co., 1934), p. 56.

the landlord or the butcher? Then we lend a helping hand." [12] Candidates for office seek his support. Even self-sufficient business and financial interests, while not always in agreement with his politics, seek his "helping hand" since he is certain to simplify the twists and turns of governmental procedure.[13] From all of these the leader obtains tribute which he employs to perpetuate himself in power. As a broker of influence, the leader, because of his power, becomes the great mediator of the city. His is the power to give and the power to take away.

The power of the boss is always subject to abuse. To paraphrase Lord Acton, power corrupts and absolute power means absolute corruption. In a sense this is the life cycle of boss power. From his position of dominance he can usually take what he wants. He can, if he chooses, enrich himself; or he may use his authority to reward his friends and maintain himself in power. He may nominate candidates or seek office for himself. He may become the silent partner in a business firm having dealings with the city, or he may indulge in what Plunkitt euphemistically called "honest graft," that is, use his inside knowledge to buy choice sites in advance of capital improvements by the city. In brief, he can go as far as an apathetic public will permit him, and where citizen inertia has existed, it must be admitted that he has gone very far.[14]

All this represents the extreme. It must be remembered, however, that the power of the boss is tied to fragile moorings. His power as head of the organization entails a great many responsibilities. Above all, he is dependent upon the supporting units. To them he must bring victory and its fruits in the form of patronage. He must obtain money, the sinews of political warfare, and to hold his power he must, as Plunkitt has said, study human nature and act in accordance with its responses. He must pick his way carefully among the thorns of conflicting rivalries within his organization. Although he may be all-powerful and enjoy long tenure, his dominance is subject to challenge at any moment. It is probable that his

[12] H. Zink, *City Bosses in the United States* (Durham, North Carolina: The Duke University Press, 1930), p. 83.

[13] F. R. Kent, *The Great Game of Politics* (New York: Doubleday, Doran & Co., 1930), pp. 90-93.

[14] See H. F. Gosnell, *Machine Politics: Chicago Model* (Chicago: University of Chicago Press, 1937); J. T. Salter, *Boss Rule: Portraits in City Politics* (New York: McGraw-Hill Book Co., 1935); W. Riordan, *Plunkitt of Tammany Hall* (New York: Doubleday, Doran & Co., 1905).

power is much less certain then it appears to the casual onlooker.

An even more dangerous threat to the boss's continuance in power is the elimination of the conditions on which he thrives. The absence of a merit system, the presence of inadequate contract procedures, the general dispersion of power, and the general inefficiency and complexity of municipal government are factors that contribute to his continued importance. As Munro has pointed out, "The more twists and tangles there are in the framework of government, the greater is (his) advantage." [15] To the confused citizen who requires assistance and the perplexed business man desiring short cuts, the political leader is a godsend. He, alone, seems to have the ability and authority to unravel the complexities of governmental structure. In the absence of effectively organized government, it is to him that they come for the solution to their problems. Reform groups, sponsors of merit systems, and modernized forms of government that concentrate authority and responsibility have done much to modify the service function of the political leader. If their objective of more effective municipal administration is reached, it will do much to remove the halo of indispensability from the brow of the boss.

Finally, the power of the boss stems from his control of the primaries, a party election which not only legalizes the party organization but also selects the candidates for office. Through this instrument, the leader determines who will occupy positions of responsibility in the organization. Through it, too, he can restrict the voters' choice. He may make up a ticket composed of men of recognized reputation within the community, or he may leaven it with a sprinkling of party regulars, but in any event, the choice is largely his. Those who vote in the primary merely ratify his selections made in advance by the party caucus.[16] Because of the crucial importance of the primary, it is almost axiomatic to say that the leader cannot afford to lose primary elections.

It is here that we have the Achilles' heel of boss power. Most authorities are agreed that the primary election time is the only time when the party and its leadership may be made more responsive to the voters.[17] It is at the primary that the stewardship of the leader is subject to recall. The late Edward Flynn was correct when he stated, ". . . wherever the majority of the voters work actively in-

[15] Munro, *op. cit.,* p. 48.
[16] Kent, *op. cit.,* pp. 105-106.
[17] Kent, *op. cit.,* p. 7.

side a political machine, you have a machine that represents the voters." [18]

Yet the sad fact is that few voters take advantage of the opportunity afforded them. As low as the voting record has been in general elections, it has been still lower in the primary. Of course it is difficult for the unorganized to override the machine, but if opposition is determined, the boss will have to pay heed to their wishes. Party organization of some kind is necessary, but whether it is "good" or "bad" depends upon the voter.[19] Furthermore, the growth of such innovations as the nonpartisan primary has weakened the hold of the boss on the nominating process and resulted in "city politics; free style." [20] Effective demand for better government will cause the "political merchant" to sell better politics.

POLITICS AT THE MID-CENTURY

It is now a half century since Lincoln Steffens wrote *The Shame of Cities* "to sound the civic pride of an apparently shameless citizenship." In his survey of the status of municipal politics, he found no single group or class at fault but rather that "The misgovernment of the American people is the misgovernment by the American people." [21] In St. Louis, Philadelphia, Minneapolis, Pittsburgh, indeed almost everywhere that he went Steffens found the "boodler" whose "stock in trade . . . (was) the rights, privileges and real property of the city. . . ." [22] To him, "public spirit had become private spirit; public enterprise became private greed." [23] Steffens concluded that, "Wherever anything extraordinary is done in American politics, whether for good or evil, you can trace it invariably to one man." [24]

In the interval since Steffens wrote, the face of the country has undergone considerable change. Urbanization has proceeded at an astonishing pace. Impersonality and mobility are now distinctive characteristics of our society. In the interval between then and now many reformers have labored diligently in the vineyard of municipal

---

[18] Flynn, *op. cit.*, foreword, p. x.

[19] Flynn, *Ibid.*

[20] Morlan, *op. cit.*, p. 486. The spectacular rise of Hubert Humphrey, a novice in politics, is attributed to the nonpartisan primary.

[21] Steffens, *op. cit.*, p. 3.

[22] *Ibid.*, p. 108.

[23] *Ibid.*, p. 30.

[24] *Ibid.*, p. 63.

politics. We are led, therefore, to inquire into the present status of municipal politics.

There is considerable evidence that indicates that we have made considerable progress since the turn of the century. The gradual acceptance of the merit system has put the spoilsmen on the defensive. Election administration has been improved, municipal autonomy vis-a-vis the state legislature has been strengthened, and forms of government concentrating both authority and responsibility have been adopted. Consequently, there is "less direct vote fraud," less "franchise boodling and sale of rights to use the city streets," "less raw sweeping patronage," and "fewer sudden, hidden, crooked deals." [25]

But this is, of course, a difference of degree. As Luther Gulick has pointed out, we still have a long way to go. There are still municipal inefficiency, still "deals," and still "patronage." The boss is still with us and he is still running the government at his own price for the inert citizen.[26] Governmental activity and expenditure have increased tremendously, and the high stakes invite collusion with public officials and evasion of the law. Moreover, this situation is not helped by the virtual disappearance of the crusading press and the generally low tone of "civic morality." [27] Gulick correctly summarizes the half century of development in these words: "Thus we have made important procedural advances in restricting and controlling the shame of cities, we have improved our standards of taste but we have gained no ground in the fundamental moral standards and patterns of behavior." [28]

It is this last point—the need for an ethical approach to political morality—that is undoubtedly the crux of the matter. As long as the standards of political morality are low, very little substantial progress will be made for, as Wilson pointed out, ". . . the record indicates that political morality reflects rather than shapes the society which it operates and that, more pertinently, it is naive in the extreme to expect from the politicians a far different standard from that which prevails throughout the country." [29] If municipal politics

[25] L. Gulick, "The Shame of Cities, 1946," *National Municipal Review*, XXXVI (1947), p. 23.

[26] *Ibid.*, p. 21.

[27] *Ibid.*, p. 24.

[28] *Ibid.*, p. 25.

[29] H. H. Wilson, *Congress, Corruption and Compromise* (New York: Rinehart and Company, Inc., 1951), p. 234.

is to take gigantic strides forward, it is essential that citizen participation in groups organize for effective solicitation of their demands. "We need," as one observer remarked, "to substitute more social for personal objectives and to find satisfactions in life that are not based so extensively on merely the possession of material goods." [30]

CONCLUSION

The political party is one of the many associational groups that exist in our society. Like all groups, its power springs largely from the fact that it has organization, ideology and adherents, and that it can be marshalled to go into political battle at any time. Like all other groups, too, it endeavors to influence public opinion in its favor. Unlike the others, however, it seeks votes and office for its supporters. The stakes sought by it are high—control of office and the right to use the politically organized power of the community for the period that it is in control.

This is a fact of cardinal importance, often overlooked by the citizen who is more concerned about the mundane facts of his existence. Yet it is the political party that, to all intents and purposes, is the government. Through the wide span of authority vested in the municipality for which it speaks, the political party can and does determine the level of municipal services and, indeed, the kind of community in which one lives. Whether he likes it or not, the individual's daily life is affected by the policies of his party. Even if he does not become active politically, he is still affected by the consequences of his inactivity.

The price of political apathy comes high. In the last quarter of the nineteenth century, graft, corruption and the generally low level of political morality led the brilliant Lord Bryce to characterize municipal government as the single most conspicuous failure of our government. The city was wide open for the bosses and political adventurers. We have come a long way since then, but we still have a good way to go before, in the words of the Ephebic oath administered to the young men of Athens, we can say that we will transmit the city more beautiful than it was before. For although outright bribery and graft are gone, in its stead are the influence peddlers who use their skills and techniques to gain special exceptions from the general application of laws. This is a tendency that is becoming

30 M. B. Clinard, "Corruption Runs Far Deeper than Politics," *New York Times*, Magazine Section, August 10, 1952, p. 21.

more accented as the city government increases the scope of its power to deal with the multitudinous problems that it faces.

The remedy is, of course, more effective governmental machinery and the creation of an attitude that recognizes all, and not a special few, should be the beneficiaries of governmental power. But this, in turn, is dependent upon an understanding of the role of government and, further, upon the willingness of the people to become active politically in order that this view might prevail. This seems to be the crux of the matter. The abuse of political power by the uncrowned kings of American politics will not cease until the citizen takes upon himself the task of redirecting the organizational talents of those who presently are in posts of authority.

BIBLIOGRAPHY

Books:

Flynn, E. J. *You're the Boss.* New York: The Viking Press, 1947.

Gosnell, H. F. *Machine Politics: Chicago Model.* Chicago: The University of Chicago Press, 1937.

Kent, F. R. *The Great Game of Politics.* New York: Doubleday-Doran and Co., Inc., 1930.

Munro, W. B. *Personality in Politics.* New York: The Macmillan Co., 1925.

Riordon, W. L. *Plunkitt of Tammany Hall.* New York: Doubleday-Doran and Co., Inc., 1905.

Salter, J. T. *Boss Rule: Portraits in City Politics.* New York, McGraw-Hill Book Company, Inc., 1935.

Schattschneider, E. E. *Party Government.* New York: Farrar and Rinehart, 1952.

Wilson, H. H. *Congress, Corruption and Compromise.* New York: Rinehart and Co., Inc., 1951.

Periodicals and Other Material:

Clinard, M. B. "Corruption Runs Far Deeper than Politics," *New York Times Magazine,* August 10, 1952, pp. 7.

Edison, C. "Lets Quarantine the Boss," *National Municipal Review,* XXXVI (1947), 5-10.

Encyclopaedia of the Social Sciences, 1st edition. Vol. II. Article. "Political Parties: Theory."

Gulick, L. "The Shame of Cities, 1946," *National Municipal Review,* XXXVI (1947), 18-25.

La Guardia, F. H. "Bosses are the Bunk," *The Atlantic Monthly,* CLXXX (1947), 21-24.

Morlan, R. L. "City Politics: Free Style," *National Municipal Review,* XXXVIII (1949), 485-490.

Chapter Seven

The Governing Body of the Municipality

The Council—Its Status and Role

Writing at the turn of the century, Professor Goodnow commented upon the lowered prestige of the council. Some people, he remarked, compared the council "with the vermiform appendix, where pressure in the human organism is liable to cause trouble, without discharging, so far as is known, any useful function." [1] Even for that time this was a feeling indictment of our representative institution at the municipal level. Yet, surprisingly enough, the same charge has considerable validity today. In the public mind the council, at its worst, is a negligible factor; at its best, it is hardly more than a junior partner in municipal government. All eyes are focused on the executive, but the governing body is neglected. This attitude is evidenced in the failure of better men to run for the council, in the feeling that the council is a rubber stamp, in the poor attendance of the public at council meetings, and in the generally low voting response. Yet the powers of the council are not inconsiderable, and their exercise should properly be the concern of the citizen.

One is impelled to ask, in view of the tradition of representative government, how did this situation arise? It is certain that the council did not always occupy a lowly position. In the early days of the republic all powers of municipal government, legislative and administrative, resided in the council. Government by council meant that as a body it would formulate policy and through committees it would administer the affairs of the municipality. As new functions were added, the council increased its powers. The high point in council supremacy, according to Professor Munro, was reached in the decade 1840–1850.[2] Industrialization, population concentra-

[1] F. J. Goodnow, *City Government in the United States* (New York: The Century Company, 1914), p. 139.

[2] W. B. Munro, *The Government of American Cities* (New York: The Macmillan Co. 1913), pp. 180-181.

tion, the appearance of technical problems—in short, emerging urbanism—dealt a death blow to council dominance. State interference, the growth of separate departments, a popularly elected mayor were by-products of the malaise of the council. With attention centered on the executive, the council deteriorated still further. By 1900 when this development had run its course, the council emerged, shorn of most of its administrative powers.

Strangely enough the same fate did not overtake the municipal council in England. Despite the fact that it, too, faced the problems of a growing urbanism, it retained its pre-eminence, even enjoying an expansion of power to meet its heavier responsibilities. The continued success of the municipal council in England may be attributed, in part at least, to the wide-reaching and extensive changes that took place under the Municipal Reform Act of 1835. Apparently Parliament was able to sense the need for strengthening the government of the municipalities.[3] In part, too, council prestige in England was maintained because municipalities did not play the same role in the national politics as in this country. Here control of cities, at least the larger ones, has an important bearing on both national and state politics. Consequently, the cities in general and the council in particular were subjected to the periodic forays of political parties with disastrous results for both.

At the turn of the century the council began gradually to regain some of its lost prestige. While no one desired a return to the earlier period of council dominance, almost everyone was willing to concede that the council was a necessary instrument of free government. Then, too, there were practical reasons for the rehabilitation of the council. The continuance of home rule and the continued growth of local autonomy were dependent largely on a strengthened council. Its powers were mainly legislative in character and by their very nature were not likely to be given either to the municipal executive or to independent departments or boards. If municipalities were to pry functions away from the state legislature, it would be essential to have an effective council. Otherwise, in all likelihood legislative powers would be retained by the state legislature.

Restoration of the council came to pass because of two other factors. The council composed of many individuals was likely to be more representative of community interests than would a single

[3] A. Shaw, *Municipal Government in Great Britain* (New York: The Century Company, 1895), pp. 23-24.

executive, however, well-intentioned he might be. Because of this, moreover, it could be expected that the council would be more deliberative in the formulation of policy. More important, however, was the need of emergent urbanism for a corps of experts, with continuity in office, to discover the solution to technical problems. The intrusion of politics in administration would have disastrous consequences since every position, from the policy maker at the top to the lowly clerk at the bottom of the hierarchy, would become the object of patronage. The existence of a strengthened council permitted the separation of politics from administration. It enabled government to be popular while at the same time it freed the administrative side from political intrusion.

The necessities of local autonomy, the need for more deliberation in the formulation of policy, and the unavoidable necessity to divorce administration from political considerations led to the gradual rejuvenation of council prestige. Today the council, although deprived in most cities of its administrative powers, is a full-fledged member of the municipal team. It possesses most of the powers of the municipal corporation. It forms the policy, establishes departments, and enacts ordinances. Through legislation, it regulates the behavior of both public officials and citizens. Traffic, police and fire protection, health, education, welfare, taxation, and a host of other concerns come within the compass of the council. Though no longer possessing administrative power, the council's legislative prerogatives have been enhanced considerably, perhaps because its attention has been diverted from matters of administration.

THE COMPOSITION OF THE COUNCIL

The large number of city councils, the almost bewildering variety of statutes and charters upon which they rest, and the fact the councils are in various stages of development make the attempt to describe their organization in great detail an exceedingly hazardous enterprise. Fortunately, there are enough elements of similarity among them to enable one to obtain a bird's-eye view of its composition.

Bicameralism. In the years following the adoption of the constitution, most municipalities, following the federal pattern, accepted bicameralism. The presumed justification for the two-house system was that it would impose a brake on hasty action by the council. However, the evils resulting from this arrangement more than outweighed its benefits. The three d's—deadlock, delay, and dispute—and the blurring of responsibility as a result of the division of the legislative into two houses caused much dissatisfaction. Over the years there has been a pronounced trend toward unicameralism. Today only eight cities still have bicameral councils.[4] As a general rule, it may be said that the size of the council has been gradually reduced, although there are still many councils that are large and unwieldy. Cities over 5,000 in size with the mayor-council form of government have the largest governing bodies. Commission governments have the smallest councils; council-manager plans, in size of council, are in between the other two forms.[5] In the various population ranges, the last two forms have uniformly smaller councils than the mayor-council governments.

Partisan and nonpartisan elections. Councilmen are chosen in either partisan or nonpartisan elections. Here again the choice varies in accordance with the form of government. In fifty-five percent of the mayor-council cities, candidates run under a party label, whereas this is true in only thirty-four percent of the commission cities and only sixteen percent of those cities governed by the council-manager plan. When one considers the basis of representation, the trend is reversed. Only thirty-eight percent of the mayor-council cities elect their councilmen at large, but almost all of the commission governments select their councilmen at large, for the self-evident reason that councilmen, in their administrative capacity, are supposed to represent the entire city. At-large election is also the preferred method in most council-manager cities, seventy-five percent of them employing this procedure. A sizable minority of mayor-council and council-manager municipalities have combined ward and at-large representatives. A relatively small number nominate their councilmen by wards but elect them at large.[6]

Basis of representation. The bases of representation are sufficiently widespread and different to justify further comment. There are some who have said, somewhat sarcastically, that the ward system is based upon the somewhat tenuous assumption that provi-

[4] *Municipal Yearbook for 1955,* pp. 58-59. These are Danbury, Connecticut; Augusta and Waterville, Maine; Everett, Malden, Northampton and Springfield, Massachusetts; and New York City.

[5] *Ibid.,* p. 58, table 4. Mayor-council cities have legislative bodies varying from two to fifty members; Commission cities from two to seven; Council-manager cities from two to twenty.

[6] *Ibid.,* pp. 59-60. There are 48 cities that nominate by ward and elect at large.

dence has made a geographical distribution of brains. But putting this comment aside, there are some valid reasons why many cities employ this method. For one thing the ward simplifies the task of selection. There are fewer councilmen, often only one, chosen from the ward and this enables the voter to become more readily acquainted with the qualifications of candidates for the council. Moreover, if large racial or religious minorities are located within a particular section of a city, the ward provides them with an opportunity to gain representation in the council, an advantage that they might not have were the councilmen elected on an at-large basis. The fact that some cities nominate candidates by wards, although they elect them at large, is a further indication of the need to represent minorities.

The fact, however, that a councilman represents a ward rather than the city as a whole may have unfortunate by-products. The aim of ward representation may be to give minorities a greater voice in policy, but the individual councilman may interpret this as "getting things for the district." The councilman, well aware of the importance of reelection, may feel that it is more important to give the public visible evidence of his efforts to represent the ward. He tends to emphasize such public improvements as roads, playgrounds, building, parks, whether or not they are needed. He may engage in "log rolling" and vote trading to gain his end. In so far as he is guided by this objective, the overall interests of the city are apt to be neglected. At-large representation may, on the other hand, give the city better councilmen, since they are elected from any part of the city. But it, too, suffers from the disability of "log rolling," and it is extremely doubtful whether the whole interest of the city will be taken into account. Moreover, it is entirely possible that minorities will not be adequately reflected in the council. Enough has been said to indicate that there is no hard-and-fast rule on a preferred method of representation. In the final analysis, the size of the city, the presence or absence of minorities, and a host of other factors determine whether a given basis of representation is applicable to a city.

Terms and compensation. The terms of office for councilmen are usually two or four years. About one half of the mayor-council cities prefer the two-year term. Council-manager and commission plans in the majority of cases, however, have accepted the longer term of office for their legislators. Most cities over 50,000 in population exhibit a preference for the four-year term; those under that amount choose the shorter term.[7] In general, during the first half of the twentieth century, there has been a pronounced tendency toward a lengthened term of office.

As a general rule, councilmen in commission governments, probably because they have administrative as well as legislative duties, receive higher salaries. Councilmen in cities with more than 500,000 people have an annual stipend that varies from a low of $1800 to a high of $12,000. In the most numerous group of cities those in the 50,000-100,000 class, councilmen in mayor-council plans receive compensation varying from $100 to $2,000 per annum, while those in commissioned-governed cities vary from a low $2,250 to a high of $10,000.[8]

COUNCIL ORGANIZATION AND PROCEDURE

Before the council can begin to function, it must make provision for the formal conduct of its business. This, at a minimum, entails the selection of a presiding officer, a clerk and other minor officers, the parcelling out of committee assignments, and the adoption of rules of procedure.

Shortly after their election, members-elect meet as the council and proceed "to organize." The first order of business is usually the selection of a presiding officer. If he is chosen independently in a city-wide election as in New York City and Kansas City, then, of course, their task is simplified. But if, as in Cincinnati, he is chosen from the membership, then an election is held. Presiding officers may be called mayors or presidents of the council. The clerk of the council may be appointed by the council or he may gain office on the basis of an election.

Committees. Like any other legislative body, most of the work of the council revolves around its committees. The number, kind, and function of committees vary with the form of government. In the commission and weak-mayor plans, the council committees possess both legislative and administrative powers. Leadership usually comes from the committees and, as a consequence, they play a key role. In those governmental plans with a strong executive, the council-manager and strong-mayor forms, council committees are

---

[7] *National Municipal Yearbook for 1952,* p. 49; and the *National Municipal Yearbook for 1955,* p. 60.

[8] *Ibid.,* p. 61.

largely confined to the consideration of legislation. Most of the administrative problems and most of the fact finding are handled for the committees by the executive. Usually, council committees are appointed by the presiding officer subject to confirmation by the council. Seniority and politics are the main considerations in staffing committees. Newcomers are usually put on minor committees at first and, as they gain in experience, they are promoted gradually to more important assignments.[9]

A great part of the work of the council, whether it is concerned with legislation or administration or both, is accomplished through committees. Whether he likes it or not, the freshman councilman soon learns that the council must work as a team and that he is only a tiny cog in a big machine. His first lesson occurs as a member of a committee. In his work with others he soon realizes that he must accommodate his views to those of the majority of the committee and that he "must go along" at council meetings, regardless of his individual opinion. It is the task of the committee chairman to obtain consensus. He must exert leadership without becoming domineering. It is the considered opinion of Professor Bromage that if the work is well done in the committee, it is "fairly well set for passage."[10]

Parliamentary procedure. One other aspect of council organization is worthy of further comment. The council is a decision-making body. Therefore, it must possess rules of parliamentary procedure that will enable it to facilitate both discussion and policy determination. Moreover, since its ordinances and resolutions affect others and are binding upon the community, the council must observe the requirements of adequate notice and hearing. The rules governing council deliberations, however, are different. Consequently, the council has greater freedom with respect to these. Within the limits of the charter and state law, it may accept the procedures of the previous council or it may modify and change them as it sees fit. Ordinances and resolutions, however, establish standards of conduct and behavior. Their enactment, therefore, is rather carefully specified either in the municipal charter or in state law.[11]

The passage of ordinances by the council usually follows a set

---

[9] A. W. Bromage, *A Councilman Speaks* (Ann Arbor, Michigan: The George Wahr Publishing Company, 1951), pp. 22-23.

[10] *Ibid.*, pp. 40-44.

[11] J. B. Fordham, *Local Government Law* (Brooklyn, New York: The Foundation Press, Inc., 1949), p. 387.

pattern. Every ordinance must be introduced in writing in the form in which it is to be passed. In most instances, it undergoes two readings, although in some jurisdictions there are three readings. Finally, the ordinance must be approved by the executive and be properly authenticated.[12] All members of the council may propose ordinances, and it is generally the task of the borough attorney to put suggestions into appropriate legal form. The proposal then becomes the subject of committee action and, following the recommendation of the committee, the council votes either to accept or to reject the advice of the committee. In most instances, discussion in the committee has been so thorough that the action by the governing body is almost a foregone conclusion.

Protecting the public. Most charters and statutes contain requirements to insure that the public is protected. Two such prerequisites may be noted. First, almost without exception, statutes and charters specify that an ordinance must relate only to a single subject. The reason for this mandate is not hard to discover. It is considered desirable not only to achieve clarity but also to prevent the public from being misled.[13] Second, in keeping with the desire to keep the public informed, charters and statutes generally prohibit the passage of an ordinance unless it has been publicly read twice at two sessions of the council on different days.[14] Occasionally by unanimous consent, this procedure may be avoided; but it is rare that this occurs. In the period between introduction and final consideration of the measure, public notice is given of the time and place where final consideration of the ordinance will occur. The objectives of the "layover" are to avert hasty passage and to encourage public discussion.[15] Public hearings are mandatory where ordinances are concerned with zoning, penal offenses, or public improvements. Indeed, failure to observe the prerequisite of adequate notice and hearing invalidates the statutory action.[16]

At the public hearing the proposed ordinance is read in full and

[12] See the suggested procedure in the National Municipal League, 5 ed., *Model City Charter* (New York: 1941), sections 18-20.

[13] E. McQuillin, *The Law of Municipal Corporations,* 3rd ed. (New York: Callaghan & Co., 1949), section 16.17. Appropriation ordinances are not bound by this requirement.

[14] See for example, *Kentucky Revised Statutes,* sec. 85.110 (1942).

[15] McQuillin, *op. cit.,* section 16.30.

[16] *Ibid.,* section 16.10: also *State v. Plainfield,* 38, New Jersey L. 95; and *Model City Charter,* Article II, sections 19-20.

the public is invited to present its views.[17] After the hearing the council may pass the ordinance with or without amendment. If an amendment substantially changes the proposed ordinance, the procedure of notice and hearing must again be observed.

Every measure adopted by the council, properly signed by the presiding officer and the clerks, must be presented to the mayor for his consideration. Most charters give the municipal executive ten days to consider. If he does not act within this period, the bill becomes a law without his signature. Generally, the mayor has the power of veto and can be overridden only by an extraordinary majority of the council, usually either by a two-thirds or three-fourths vote.[18] When passed, the ordinance must be properly validated, published in full, and placed in the custody of an appropriate official. Only when compliance with this procedure takes place can the ordinance go into effect.[19]

Resolutions of the council, since they do not have the same force and effect as ordinances, are not required to conform with the above-described procedure. These are usually directives to administrative officers and, though they are in writing, the requirements of adequate notice and hearing to the public are not necessary. Moreover, since they are not binding upon the community as a whole, the action of the council does not normally require the concurrence of the municipal executive.

POWERS OF THE COUNCIL

Any attempt to describe the powers of the council encounters a practical difficulty. Charters and general laws vary greatly from state to state in the amount of authority granted to the council. Moreover, this diversity is accentuated by a wide variety of court decisions, each of which construes the powers of the council somewhat differently. Although the divergence is great, it is nevertheless possible to isolate a sufficient number of common elements.

To begin with, it may be stated as a general rule that all the powers of the municipal corporation are vested in its governing body unless the charter or general law makes special exceptions. For example, the state legislature, unless forbidden by the constitution, may give ordinance-making authority to local boards of health,

17 Bromage, *op. cit.*, Ch. 5, "Ordinance Making."
18 McQuillin, *op. cit.*, sections 16.42, 16.45.
19 *Ibid.*, section 16.01.

police and fire boards, and public works commissions. But if such agencies have purely administrative duties, they do not enjoy ordinance making power.[20] Thus it may be said that the powers of the council are residual, since it possesses that which is not denied.[21] Furthermore, the council may exercise its authority only in accordance with Dillon's rule of strict construction. Stated somewhat differently, this means that the powers of the council are construed narrowly. They may be employed only for the furtherance of express powers of the corporation or for those that may be reasonably inferred or those that are necessary for the declared objects of the corporation. Finally, the actions of the governing body must serve a public purpose. It cannot employ the power of the corporation for the advantage of a single person or a special few.[22]

Legislative power. These generalizations, then, constitute the broad frame of reference. Within it and subject to the limitations contained in the charter and state law, the council makes provision for the maintenance and operation of the government. Its powers fall roughly into two main categories, legislative and administrative. Externally, the council applies the police power of the state to the local level, regulating the conduct and affairs of the citizen on behalf of the public interest. Internally, it establishes the departments and agencies of government. It provides them with the authority necessary to conduct the affairs of government and thus, in large measure, determines the scope of their activity. The council may investigate the conduct of departments. It votes funds and prescribes the manner in which financial transactions are validated. The council does this, and much more, through ordinances and resolutions.

Since ordinances and resolutions are the means through which the council exercises its powers, it is essential that these should be examined in greater detail. An ordinance, in its broadest meaning, signifies any law, whether passed by a national, state, or local unit of government.[23] More narrowly and perhaps more correctly, as Webster's Encyclopedic Dictionary has defined it, an ordinance is "a law enacted by a municipal government for local application." Stress

---

[20] Goodnow, *op. cit.*, p. 166.

[21] McQuillin, *op. cit.*, sections 15.03, 16.04.

[22] *Ibid.*, section 15.17.

[23] The Northwest Ordinance of 1787 and South Carolina's Nullification Ordinance of 1832 are examples.

must be placed upon the word "law." An ordinance is an enactment of a local governing body which establishes a rule of conduct that is obligatory upon the entire community and is operative only within the jurisdiction of the municipality.[24] It is legislation, and because of its binding character, its validity depends largely upon the observance of the legislative procedure described above.[25]

Administrative power. Resolutions, on the other hand, are much narrower in scope and effect. Normally they deal with administrative questions and, as such, are concerned with matters of a more temporary and transient nature. A resolution may direct an administrative officer to perform a ministerial act required of him by statute. A borough attorney may be directed to institute a suit. Sometimes, however, the charter may be silent on the manner in which the council may exercise its authority. In such instances, it may make a choice of either ordinance or resolution. Thus, rights of way may be granted by resolution. Where the charter is indefinite, the council, by resolution, may vote to abolish offices and may even determine indebtedness.[26] More often, however, the charter denies discretion to the council and specifies the objects of legislation that are to be made the subject of an ordinance.

The distinction between ordinance and resolution is largely one of procedure. Actions of the governing body establishing a norm of conduct for the community must be in accordance with a procedure that requires proper notice and hearing, and validature by the municipal executive. Resolutions, however, only need the concurrence of the governing body. Since a resolution is much narrower in scope and in effect, it is not subject to the requirements of a public hearing or the veto power of the executive. To put the matter somewhat differently, the ordinance, because it governs the conduct of citizens, is surrounded by procedural safeguards. The council cannot accomplish by resolution that which is normally the object of legislation, unless the procedure for the passage of an ordinance is observed. The action of a city council in granting a right of way by resolution was upheld by the courts, but only because the procedural requirements for ordinances were observed.[27] Undoubtedly if such a step had not been taken, the resolution would have been void.

---

[24] McQuillin, *op. cit.*, section 15.01.
[25] *Samuel v. Borough of South Plainfield,* 136 N. J. L. 187.
[26] McQuillin, *op. cit.*, sections 15.06-15.07.
[27] *Sower v. Philadelphia,* 35 Pennsylvania St. 331.

Status of local law. Again both the spirit and the letter of the municipal charter must be observed. Any local law that is contrary to the organic law of the municipality is invalid.[28] If the charter vests the appointment and removal of officers in the council, or if the charter fixes their term of office, the governing body cannot take contrary action.[29]

The council, in passing an ordinance, must observe other legal requirements. The ordinance must have a public purpose. It must be passed in good faith and be in conformity with public policy and common law. Public purpose has been interpreted by the courts to mean that the council cannot employ the ordinance making power to grant privileges to a special few where the many are eligible. Discrimination, in the issuance of a license or the granting of a contract, unless there is a compelling reason, will be outlawed by the court. Good faith is a necessary aspect of all local legislation. The council will face a legal challenge if it attempts to do by indirection what it cannot achieve by direct action. It cannot employ a public health statute to drive a food concern out of business. The courts, however, assume that good faith exists unless the complainants can demonstrate that the ordinance does not bring about the desired result.[30]

Public policy and common law are additional criteria with which the council must conform. If the state, through law, has prohibited the showing of movies on Sunday, or if it has already legislated on the subject of gambling, the municipality is forbidden to pass an ordinance unless authorized to do so.[31] Public policy, in other words, cannot be superseded by a local act. Common-law principles are an added element of restraint. Police power ordinances cannot classify an object or an action as a nuisance unless it has been customary to consider it as such under common law. The council may depart from this prerequisite only when it can demonstrate that it is essential to keep pace with the "felt necessities of time." [32] Finally, although everyone is presumed to have a knowledge of an ordinance and to be bound by it, local enactments, particularly those defining penal offenses, must be drafted in such a manner that they will be under-

[28] *Landis v. Vineland,* 54 N. J. L. 75.
[29] *Idem.*
[30] *Ibid.,* sections 15.16 and 15.23.
[31] *Ibid.,* section 15.20; also *Beirerle v. City of Newport,* 305 Kentucky 447.
[32] *Ibid.,* section 15.22.

stood by men of ordinary intelligence. Although the council is given wide latitude in this regard, it cannot, nevertheless, prescribe punishment for disobedience unless the standards of misconduct are clearly stated. These restrictions are in accordance with the well-known principle that the accused must know the nature of the offense with which he is charged.

THE SCOPE OF MUNICIPAL LAWMAKING

In more specific terms, local legislation covers the following main areas: (1) the health, safety, welfare, and morals of the community; (2) privileges in the form of franchises, contracts, and licenses in which the city is an interested party; (3) public improvements; (4) organization and administration; and (5) the financial affairs of the city. The power of the council to regulate the conduct of citizens emanates from the police power of the state which is applied by the municipality at the local level. Governing bodies, by ordinance, may establish standards of health and safety and prescribe penalties for lack of conformance. Traffic and health codes, building and fire regulations are but a few of the many areas that have been made the subject of municipal regulation.

Again, through ordinances, the council may grant privileges and make contracts that are binding upon the municipal corporation. It may grant licenses for the disposal of refuse and garbage. It may authorize private parties to maintain a bridge over a public way. It may permit a private corporation or utility to use its streets for the conduct of business. It may license restaurants to sell alcoholic beverages. In these and many other areas, the council exercises a wide range of power that may commit the municipality to a course of conduct for years to come.

Through ordinances, city councils may authorize public works programs. The construction of buildings, the paving of streets, the elimination of dangerous street crossings, the development of water and sewage disposal systems, and public improvements generally are the subject of local legislation. City councils may even legislate street improvements that are to be paid for by private parties whose property abuts on the improvement. Public works ordinances may even eliminate a nuisance if a citizen fails to act and levy a charge upon the citizen for noncompliance.

Less sweeping in their effect but important, nonetheless, are a whole host of ordinances regulating the methods by which city officers conduct the affairs of the city. Procedures for the handling and settling of accounts against the city are specified in local law. Offices may be established, their functions defined, and the salaries of officials fixed by statutory action. The council in this area determines the scope and sphere of municipal activity.

Last, but not least, are a whole series of ordinances dealing with the fiscal powers of the municipality. Here the council is not a free agent. It does not have the independent authority either to tax or to incur debts. But once it has been authorized to do so, it can determine through ordinances the amount of money it needs and how it shall be obtained.

Federal restraints upon ordinance making. Since the municipality is a creature of the state, it is subject to the same constitutional restraints that govern the action of the state. Consequently the council, in legislating, must keep in mind the pertinent provisions of the federal constitution. The council is an organic part of the state and, like the latter, it cannot invade the constitutional rights belonging to the citizen.

Both the federal constitution and federal law protect the citizen against arbitrary action by the municipality. The council cannot, by ordinance, impair the obligation of a contract.[33] This does not mean, of course, that the municipality cannot regulate the contractual interests of others in the interest of the general welfare. It can and does do this. But it is prohibited from independently abrogating all agreements to which it is a party. If it grants a franchise, or if it borrows money by pledging the credit of the city, it, thereby, creates an obligation which it must fulfil.[34] Any modification of rights under contract with the city is subject to review in the federal courts.[35]

Similarly, no municipal ordinance can violate the due process clause of the Fourteenth Amendment. To say this, however, is merely to pose the problem. Everyone has the right to conduct a lawful business or to engage in a lawful occupation. But under its police powers emanating from the state the municipality can regulate private conduct in the interest of the community as a whole. In so doing it may trample on personal rights. The line between pri-

[33] *The Federal Constitution*, Article I sec. 10.

[34] *New York v. The Third Avenue Railway Co.*, 33 New York 42, (franchise). *Quincy v. Bull*, 106 Ill. 337 (construction of a waterworks). *State v. Lehman* 100 Florida 1313 (bonds).

[35] McQuillin, *op. cit.*, section 19.43.

vate right and public interest is exceedingly difficult to define. It has always been the subject of constant litigation. As a general rule, it might be said that the ultimate test of the constitutionality of an ordinance is whether or not the municipality has acted in a reasonable manner. It may take property for a public purpose, if it provides proper compensation.[36] For purposes of zoning or the regulation of property generally, it may develop a classification that is impartial. The council, through ordinances, may also regulate police matters, set the tax rate or grant or refuse licenses on a rational basis. But if in its action it is arbitrary and capricious, it will come into conflict with the due process clause of the Fourteenth Amendment. In brief, the council's ordinance making power remains unimpaired as long as it does not discriminate unfairly.[37]

Municipal ordinances cannot invade the civil liberties of the people of the city. Under the Federal Constitution no municipality can deny to any person within its jurisdiction the equal protection of the laws. Ordinances are presumed to treat all alike. Nevertheless, any person who can prove that unrestrained arbitrary power is being vested in a public official will find the federal court a ready listener. Local laws that discriminate unfairly often have been declared invalid.[38] The civil liberty protections of the Bill of Rights have been transferred almost in their entirety to the Fourteenth Amendment. Ordinances granting released time for religious instruction on school premises have been declared invalid.[39] The federal courts have exhibited the same attitude toward attempts by municipalities to prohibit the distribution of religious materials.[40] The rights of free speech, press, and assembly cannot be abrogated by an ordinance.[41]

In brief then, ordinances passed by a city council must conform with both the state and the Federal Constitutions. A city council may apply the police power of the state at the local level, but it must do so in a manner that will satisfy the federal courts that

---

36 *Schwarz Brothers Company v. Jersey City Board of Health,* 84 N. J. L. 735.

37 *In re Russell* 158 N. J. S. 162 (zoning ordinance upheld); *State Board of Equalization v. Young's Market Co.* 299 U. S. 59 (reasonable classification of property upheld); *Mayor of Savannah v. Savannah Distributing Co.,* 202 Ga. 559 (discrimination in granting of a license makes action invalid).

38 McQuillin, *op. cit.,* section 19.13.

39 *Illinois v. Board of Education,* 333 U. S. 203.

40 *Jones v. Opelika,* 316 U. S. 584.

41 *Hague v. C. I. O.* 307 U. S. 496.

its actions, beyond a reasonable doubt, are not arbitrary or discriminatory.

SUMMARY

The authority of the council has undergone many modifications since the founding of the republic. Originally it possessed all the powers of government. Under the pressure of urbanization, however, it began gradually to lose much of its power. The need for full time administration resulted in the rise of a popularly chosen executive and the creation of independent departments and commissions. Soon the executive became the dominant figure in urban government. After the Civil War the council's demonstrated inability to deal with the problems of a technical society further accentuated executive authority. Councils almost lapsed into mediocrity. The low point in council prestige was probably reached at the turn of the century.

Although the council lived in the shadow of the executive, it gradually began to recover some of its lost eminence. There were, as we have seen, cogent reasons for this. It was recognized that much of the onus attached to the council was due, in large measure, to the fact that it had been asked to perform tasks for which it was not suited. The council could not administer. It could legislate. With the council shorn of its administrative powers, the stage was set for a revival of the council's policy making authority. Since the turn of the century, the council has emerged as the body which determines the drift and direction of municipal governmental action. Its powers have been strengthened and its attention redirected. With this retooling still in process, the council is gradually emerging as a vital element in local democracy. It can, to a considerable degree, set the conditions under which the people of a city live. In its effort to do so, however, it is essential that it receive the support of John Doe, the citizen.

BIBLIOGRAPHY

Books:

Bromage, A. W. *A Councilman Speaks.* Ann Arbor, Michigan: The George Wahr Publishing Co., 1951.

Committee on Revision of the Model City Charter. *Model City Charter.* 5th revised edition. New York: National Municipal League, 1941.

Fordham, J. B. *Local Government Law.* Brooklyn, New York: The Foundation Press, Inc., 1949.

Goodnow, F. J. *City Government in the United States.* New York: The Century Co., 1914.

McQuillin, E. *The Law of Municipal Corporations.* Vol. 5. Sections 14:01–19:88. Chicago: Callaghan & Co., 1949.

The Municipal Yearbook for 1952. Chicago: The International City Managers' Association, 1952.

The Municipal Yearbook for 1955. Chicago: The International City Managers' Association, 1955.

Munro, W. B. *The Government of American Cities.* New York: The Macmillan Co., 1913.

CHAPTER EIGHT

Forms of Urban Government

INTRODUCTION

Forms of government as a subject for discussion often evoke much derisive comment. Pope's famous remark, "For forms of government let fool's contest, whate'er is best administered is best," is usually cited. For Pope and those who follow along with him substance is more important than form. Only results count. Governmental forms as means are either neglected or considered incidental. Good administration, it is asserted, can be achieved, regardless of the form of government.

Pope's observation, however, is somewhat unrealistic for several reasons. The judgment "whate'er is best administered is best," is subjective. Those who have labored to establish standards for the measure of municipal performance well know how difficult and unrewarding is the task.[1] But even if an objective conclusion could be drawn, the fact remains that administration is mainly the interaction of men within a framework of structure and authority. An instrument, that is government, is needed as a means to achieve an end. Whether it is crudely or finely drawn will determine the facility with which the government can perform its functions.

Moreover, it is the form of government that very largely determines the competence of its staff. Men of initiative and ability ordinarily are not attracted to a governmental situation that forces them to shoulder responsibility without granting to them a corresponding amount of authority. At the very least, they will want an opportunity to exercise their talents. If such people are repelled, the administrative process is bound to lack momentum and will most certainly languish. In brief, the forms of government are tools designed to facilitate the attainment of an objective. The expert will require good tools and the run of the mine public practitioner, perhaps because of his deficiencies, will need them.

[1] C. E. Ridley and H. Simon, *Measuring Municipal Activities* (Chicago: The International City Managers' Association, 1943).

In fairness to Pope and those who agree with him, it must be conceded that the form of government is not all important. Good government will not be guaranteed by form alone. There is no substitute for ability. Competent officers are needed and must be chosen by the people. Their quality will depend in large measure upon the political intelligence of the voter. Once elected, however, their effectiveness and indeed their responsiveness to the people will depend upon the governmental implements made available to them.

EVOLUTION OF GOVERNMENTAL FORMS

Governmental form and societal needs. Form is merely a function of the object of government. Its effectiveness must be measured in the light of the governmental tasks it must perform. No one form of government is necessarily better or worse than another unless it can be said that it more adequately meets the needs and wants of the people in a given situation. Different circumstances may require different governmental forms. Thus a rural society may well have a part-time government, the impractical amateur, and the dispersion of political power among a large number of individuals, and yet perform the functions required of it reasonably well. But the same governmental arrangement may well become hopelessly inadequate when it has to deal with the problems of a highly complex urban community where continuous attention to the needs of people is required. From this it can be concluded that as the country became more urbanized, as the manner in which people live has changed, the forms of government have been altered to reflect the increased responsibilities imposed upon the governmental instrument. In the succeeding pages we shall attempt to demonstrate the validity of this thesis.

Changes in forms of government, as we have implied, are a product of the changed degree of urbanization of a society. In our country the convergence of people upon the city brought new needs and a proliferation of governmental functions. In such circumstances part-time government by the impractical amateur soon became impossible. The governmental prescriptions for the ills of emerging urbanism were professionalization of the work force and full-time government. A strengthened municipal development was the emergence of the strong executive. As one authority has said, "The actual and the relative importance of the executive office increases with the concentration of population in urban centers." [2] Thus it may be said that population concentration wrought profound changes in municipal political institutions.

Urban government before 1800. Urban forms of government in the period before 1800 reflect the relatively low degree of urbanization. Out of a total of approximately four million people hardly more than 200,000 could be considered as living in urban places.[3] Towns, rather than cities existed. "A genuine urbanization" took place only in New York City, Philadelphia and Charleston, S. C.[4] The authority of the municipality was derived from a charter granted by the provincial governor. In form and in inspiration the local government leaned rather heavily on the English borough.[5] Governmental power was vested in a common council which was composed of the mayor, recorder, alderman and councilmen. The mayor, recorder, alderman were justices of the peace and together they formed the local court of record. Administrative power was limited to those matters that were not in conflict with the law of the province, but even this restricted authority was carried out either by the council as a whole or through council committees.[6]

Most striking of all during this period was the relatively insignificant role of the mayor. In New England he was merely the moderator of the town meeting. Elsewhere he was, at most, first among equals, although in Albany and New York City he was responsible for the issuance of tavern licenses. His powers depended in the main upon his personality. If he was strong and powerful, he could accomplish a great deal. Baltimore, in its charter of 1796, furnished the only departure from this general pattern. Its mayor was chosen indirectly through an electoral college. It empowered him to make legislative recommendations, gave him limited appointive power and armed him with the veto subject to an overriding vote of three-fourths of the council. The Baltimore charter was entirely out of

---

[2] R. M. Story, *The American Municipal Executive* (Urbana, Illinois: University of Illinois Studies in the Social Sciences, 1918), VII, No. 3, p. 12.

[3] U. S. Bureau of Census, *Historical Statistics of the United States, 1789–1945* (Washington, D. C.: 1949), p. 25.

[4] E. S. Griffith, *History of the American City, The Colonial Period* (New York: Oxford University Press, 1938), p. 413.

[5] *Ibid.*, Chapter 1.

[6] J. A. Fairlie, *Municipal Administration* (New York: The Macmillan Co., 1906), pp. 73-76.

consonance with its time, as Story has said it was "a thing born out of due season." [7]

The impact of urban growth. By 1820 urban population had increased considerably having reached almost 700,000. Yet in the whole of the United States there was only one city with more than 100,000 inhabitants. There were only five cities over 25,000 with a combined population of 320,720.[8] Little change in governmental form took place. Municipalities were engaged in little more than the maintenance of law and order. The period 1820–1850 saw a spectacular growth of the cities. In the latter year urban population reached a high of 3.5 million, roughly six times greater than that in 1820. The number of urban places with a population of more than twenty-five thousand increased from five to twenty-six, with a total of 2,070,351 people.[9] The increased pace of urbanization was reflected in the appearance of additional municipal functions and the revitalization of the older ones. The old night watch was supplemented by the addition of day police. School boards and relief offices appointed by the council appeared. New York City began the construction of a municipally owned water supply system.[10] From the standpoint of governmental structure and authority, two important developments took place. The prestige of the mayor's office increased and the demands placed upon the municipality far outran the authority it possessed, thus paving the way for increased state interference through special legislation. In this period the first beginnings of the popular election of the mayor became an established fact, giving him greater prestige, if not power. The foundation of executive dominance over the council was laid, leading one authority to conclude that this "was a development that (had) changed the character of American municipal institutions." [11]

Governmental changes 1850–1870. From 1850 to 1870 the trend toward city growth became even more pronounced. Approximately ten million people, about one third of the nation's population became urban dwellers. More than half of these were located in cities with a population over twenty-five thousand.[12] Again, as in the previous period, there was a definite expansion of municipal func-

[7] Story, *op. cit.*, p. 24.
[8] U. S. Bureau of Census, *op. cit.*, p. 29.
[9] *Ibid.*, pp. 25, 29.
[10] Fairlie, *op. cit.*, p. 83.
[11] Story, *op. cit.*, p. 28.
[12] U. S. Bureau of Census, *op. cit.*, pp. 25, 29.

tions. The uniformed police system appeared in New York. Boston, Chicago and Baltimore embarked upon the construction of water supply systems. Municipalities spent money and went into debt as never before.[13]

It was in this period that the role of the council as an agency of administration suffered an eclipse. The reasons for this decline are not readily apparent. It is argued that the Jacksonian belief that all public offices should be elected resulted in the desire to choose popularly the chief administrative offices. It is also asserted that the council, enmeshed in politics, was incapable of governing. Finally, it is suggested that the barter and sale of public franchises provoked popular reaction against the council.[14] Whatever the real reason, there was a decided movement away from the council during this period. Increasingly there was the tendency to place the administration of many municipal activities in the hands of boards, commissions or departments who were either partially or entirely independent of the council. Most of these newer agencies were chosen by the people.

New York City's 1849 charter made twelve important administrative offices elective. In 1852, Cleveland chose its mayor, engineer, auditor and street commissioners. Similar trends were noticeable in Boston, Detroit and Philadelphia. Indeed, the tendency was widespread to vest the administration of important areas of municipal activity in popularly elected officials.[15] Since the mayor's supervisory powers were feeble, the result was a "headless" municipal government in which all branches could seemingly gallop off in different directions at the same time.

The period 1850–1870 was also marked by extensive state intervention in municipal affairs. Again, the reasons for this are somewhat obscure. Legislative interference, in part at least, may be attributed to the fact that the responsibilities of many municipalities far outran their power. Maladministration of city affairs may also be advanced as a motivation. Fairlie suggests that control of the cities meant spoils, control of the jobs resulting from the increase in municipal functions. This, he feels, became an important aspect

[13] Fairlie, *op. cit.*, p. 87.

[14] E. McQuillin, *The Law of Municipal Corporations* (Chicago: Callaghan and Co., 1950), section 9:09.

[15] *Ibid.*, section 9:09 contains many illustrations of this. See also Fairlie, *op. cit.*, pp. 88-89.

of the national parties in their effort to control the federal government.[16] Few cities were able to avoid state legislative interference. Baltimore in 1860, St. Louis in 1861 and New York City in 1857 lost control of the police functions to their respective states. In New York City, state supervision of local policies had reached the point where only one-sixteenth of its expenditures were under its own control.[17] What happened to the large cities also occurred with respect to the smaller ones. The period 1850–1870 represented the high point of interference and had a marked impact upon the form of government. It was only with the coming of home rule that reform of municipal political institutions could take place.

Further consequences of urban growth. In the first two decades after the Civil War the consequences of urban growth were demonstrated in the constant inability of the governmental structure to adapt itself to the constantly changing urban conditions. The council's prestige dropped almost to a vanishing point. Fragmentation of executive authority among many independent offices and departments continued to exist. Bribery, election frauds, the bartering of public franchise, a general disregard of public trust and a host of other evils were everywhere in evidence. Each addition of a municipal function was the occasion for the further invasion by the spoilsmen. Bryce, in characterizing this condition said of American cities, "they are like the sick man who cannot find rest upon his own bed but seeks to ease his pain by moving from side to side." [18]

The growth in population further accentuated the strain placed upon municipal political institutions. The year 1900 found 30.2 million people in the cities, with more than half of these clustered in 160 urban places, each with a population of more than 25,000.[19] Population pressure caused the reorganization of old functions such as police, fire, public education, transportation. New functions were being organized constantly. The cities underwent a political nightmare best expressed in Bryce's comment that the government of American cities was, "the one conspicuous failure of the United States." [20]

---

[16] Fairlie, *op. cit.*, p. 91.

[17] *Ibid.*, p. 90.

[18] J. Bryce, *The American Commonwealth* (2nd ed.; New York: The Macmillan Co., 1891), I, pp. 618-619.

[19] U. S. Bureau of Census, *op. cit.*, pp. 25, 29.

[20] Bryce, *op. cit.*, p. 608.

Gradually, however, public reaction against these excesses began to make its weight felt. State interference with local affairs was at least partially checked by the growth of municipal home rule. "Good citizens," as John Hamilton has said, "foreseeing that . . . our great cities would dominate the public life of the nation felt that unless the problems of popular government of cities were solved the ultimate subversion of the republic was inevitable." [21] The attempt to solve the "problem" took two main forms: the strengthening of the office of mayor, and the search for new forms of government.

The appearance of the strong executive. In the latter half of the nineteenth century there was the gradual growth of an awareness that the division of political power and responsibility, and the election of large numbers of public officials would not assure either good government or political accountability. The example set by the large industrial corporation began to impress itself more and more upon the public consciousness. "The traditions of concentrated powers developed in business life," said Professor Rowe, "have had a distinct influence upon that portion of our political system which it most closely resembles viz., the organization of city government." [22] From 1870 onward the mood for efficiency and economy in the management of civic affairs was expressed in the centralization of powers in the hands of a municipal executive.

From 1870 onward, too, administrative matters began to receive increasing attention in the city. When the home rule movement began to check state intervention in local affairs, the cities undertook administrative reorganization. The defeat of the corrupt Tweed machine in New York City was followed by a new charter which vested financial planning in a Board of Estimate and Apportionment.[23] The powers of the mayor, primarily because he was popularly elected were also strengthened. He became the acknowledged political head of the city. People came to him for aid in the solution of their problems, regardless of whether he had the necessary authority. The gradual grant of more power to the mayor reached such proportions that he was soon to become a full fledged execu-

[21] J. J. Hamilton, *The Dethronement of the City Boss* (New York: Funk and Wagnalls Company, 1916), p. 16.

[22] L. S. Rowe, *Problems of City Government* (New York: D. Appleton and Co., 1915), p. 104.

[23] Fairlie, *op. cit.*, pp. 92-93.

tive. His powers of appointment were increased greatly. In Philadelphia and Boston the mayor's appointive power was subject to council concurrence. In other cities, as in Brooklyn in 1882 and Greater New York in 1890, his power to appoint was made final. Buffalo and Cleveland followed suit in 1891.[24] Although the removal power of the mayor was not fully developed, here and there, as in New York City and second class cities of the state, the cities were granted final power to remove officials. In this period, too, the veto power, originally designed to protect the executive against legislative encroachment, was expanded as a weapon employed by the mayor to influence legislation. His veto could only be overridden by an extraordinary majority. In some cases the veto power of the mayor was final.[25] The net result of such accretions of authority was that the mayor became the administrative as well as the political head of the city.

In general, these developments were in keeping with the view expressed by Seth Low, mayor of Brooklyn: "A strong executive can accomplish satisfactory results; a weak one can disappoint every hope." [26]

COMMISSION AND COUNCIL-MANAGER GOVERNMENT

Commission government. The general reaction against divided powers in a mayor, departmental heads and independent boards and commissioners was followed by the concentration of administrative powers in the hands of the mayor. This, in its turn, paved the way for the newer forms of government, the commission and council-manager plans. Inherent in both was the belief that efficiency was a by-product of concentrated executive authority.[27] In the commission form, however, power was divided among a small number of departments but no one person was the chief executive.

The precursor of commission government was that of the District of Columbia. In 1878 Congress, by statute, specified that the nation's capital should be governed by a three-man board of commissioners. Two were to be appointed from civilian life and the third was to be a member of the Army Engineer Corps. Although

---

24 Story, *op. cit.*, p. 30. Fairlie, *op. cit.*, p. 96.

25 *Ibid.*, p. 135. In Baltimore, Rochester and San Francisco the mayor had a qualified veto. In New York and Boston it was final.

26 Bryce, *op. cit.*, p. 627 of the chapter written by Seth Low.

27 Story, *op. cit.*, p. 35.

Congress served as the legislature for the District of Columbia, the commissioners were authorized to enforce the statutes and to issue such rules and regulations as were necessary.[28]

It is not clear whether the capital city's model served as a subsequent influence, but commission government which was likened to "the directorate of a bank or a manufacturing or a commercial corporation . . ." can be said to have begun in Galveston, Texas at the turn of the century when flood and calamity revealed the incompetence of the mayor and council to deal with the situation. When a five man commission effected a remarkable transformation of the city, the foundation of the new plan was laid. Soon it spread to Dallas, Fort Worth and many other Texas cities. In 1907 it was adopted by the city of Des Moines which added many features common to the spirit of the time such as initiative, referendum and recall. Aided by the growth of home rule and local option legislation, the new plan spread. By 1917, when the movement was at the height of its popularity, some four hundred cities had adopted it as a form of government. As one commentator has remarked, "it brought optimism to local politics."[29] As time went on, however, popular enthusiasm faded and the movement gradually lost out in competition to the strong-mayor and council and council-manager plans.

Council-manager government. The council-manager plan evolved out of the commission form of government. The latter, in some respects, may be considered an advance over the mayor-council form in that it forsook the traditional doctrine of the separation of powers and concentrated governmental power in the hands of a small popular elected council. Supporters of good government were quick to perceive that the commission plan suffered from a fatal weakness. Although legislative and administrative powers were vested in the council, the power was divided among many councillors. Something more had to be added. Advocates of good government proposed that the authority of the council should be delegated to a single professionally trained administrator. When this idea was accepted, the council-manager plan was born.[30]

The plan took its first halting step in Staunton, Virginia in 1908.

---

28 Rowe, *op. cit.*, p. 183.

29 Hamilton, *op. cit.*, p. 25.

30 H. A. Stone, D. K. Price and K. H. Stone, *City Manager Government in the United States* (Chicago: Public Administration Service, 1940), pp. 5-9.

The city, operating with a bicameral council and numerous standing committees of administration, was constantly plagued with jurisdictional conflicts. Impressed with the need for finding a way out of the administrative morass, the council in 1907 made a study of the commission plan of Galveston and Houston. It found that many features of the Texas experiment were found to be desirable, but since the Virginia Constitution forbade the adoption of the commission form, it recommended the appointment of a general manager. This was done in 1908.[31]

The Staunton experiment was hardly more than a beginning. The manager had no clearly defined authority and was merely superimposed upon the existing form of government. No actual unification of authority had occurred. Indeed, the plan was hardly better than that of those commission cities that had adopted the mayor-commissioner with increased power over his fellow commissioners.[32] In Lockport, New York, in 1911, the council-manager plan took another step forward. There the Board of Trade sponsored a charter that gave considerable administrative power to the manager and was able to obtain the approval of the people. The plan, however, was rejected by the state legislature.

Sumter, South Carolina, represents yet another stage in the evolution of the plan. Both the idea of a trained manager and the short ballot were adopted in 1912, and shortly thereafter the city hired its first administrator. Sumter is regarded as the first municipality to have a genuine city-manager plan of government. Two years later, Dayton, Ohio, after a large flood had reduced the city to a state of virtual helplessness, became the first large city to adopt the "commission-manager plan." [33] The "Dayton Plan" gave the manager full responsibility and authority for the direction of the work of the city departments. Legislative and executive powers were carefully defined, with the council retaining the power to formulate the framework of the policy within which the manager would operate. The progressive features of the commission plan, the merit system, referendum, and recall were embodied in the new governmental instrument. The complete delegation of administrative power to a single nonelective officer was a political innovation of great signifi-

---

31 *Ibid.*, p. 10.

32 Houston, Dallas, Portland, Oregon and St. Paul, Minnesota, were examples. Cf. Story, *op. cit.*, p. 192.

33 Stone, Price and Stone, *op. cit.*, p. 13.

cance. Undoubtedly the acceptance of this principle by both municipalities did much to popularize the merits of the plan.

Once the successful venture was launched, the plan of government received added impetus from the forces of good government. It is interesting to note that many of those who had sponsored the commission form were also responsible for the growth of the council-manager idea. The National Short Ballot Association, while not taking an official position, nonetheless gave the movement wide publicity. Its secretary had drafted the Lockport plan. The National Municipal League, which for years had favored the strong mayor, made a study of the council-manager plan in 1913. Two years later it made the plan part of its Model Charter and placed its not inconsiderable resources behind the campaign to popularize the new form of government. The gradual professionalization of the manager, reflected in the growth of the International City Managers' Association, also assisted in the promotion of the plan.

Since its lowly beginnings in Staunton in 1908, the council-manager plan has demonstrated astonishing vitality, and it has been accepted by an ever-larger number of cities. The present status of

Table 2—PERCENTAGE OF COUNCIL-MANAGER CITIES TO THE TOTAL CITIES IN THE U. S. (1954)

Population Group	*Total Number of Cities*	*Cities with Council-Manager Plans*	
		No.	%
1000–2,500	3,408	100	4.4
2,500–5,000	1,557	195	12.5
5,500–10,000	1,093	283	25.9
10,000–25,000	752	279	37.1
25,000–50,000	249	110	44.1
50,000–100,000	126	56	44.4
100,000–500,000	88	33	37.5
over 500,000	18	1	5.6

Local governments (218) with council-manager plans are omitted because (1) they have less than 1,000 people (2) they are not classified as incorporated urban places or (3) they are outside continental U. S.[34]

adoptions can be gathered from Table 2. In 1954, 41.6% of all the cities in the United States with a population of more than 25,000 are council-manager governed, and 37.1% of the cities between 10,-

[34] Source: *Municipal Yearbook for 1955,* p. 279.

000 and 25,000 people have this form of government. Indeed, in the cities in the population groups, 25,000 to 50,000, 50,000 to 100,-000, and 250,000 to 500,000, the plan is more popular than either the mayor-council or the commission forms.[35]

Much more could be said, of course, about the various forms of municipal government. In the succeeding pages we shall describe the plans in more specific terms. The long-range trend in municipal government in the period of the Civil War was along the path of a strengthened municipal executive. The mayor and the council-manager have been armed with power necessary to carry out their responsibilities. Even commission government, with its centralization of authority in the council, was a step in this direction. The trend toward a strengthened municipal executive is a reflection of the fact that population concentration brings about changes in the structure and function of government.

PRINCIPAL FEATURES OF THE MAYOR-COUNCIL FORM

Fifty-two percent of all cities in the United States with a population of more than 5000 employ the mayor-council plan of government.[36] Although it is most popular, its pattern of development has been rather uneven. In the less urbanized areas, weak-mayor and council government still exists with a structure very similar to that which prevailed during the first half of the nineteenth century. In the larger cities the strong-mayor and council plan has evolved, reflecting no doubt the increased demands placed upon the governmental mechanism. In other instances, particularly in the case of the medium-sized city, the governing instrument has lagged far behind. The semirural, weak-mayor plan continues to be used, despite the fact that an entirely urban condition has been attained.

Weak-mayor and council. The weak-mayor and council form closely approximates the type of government predominant during the first eighty years of the republic. Its most distinctive feature is the "long ballot." The mayor, councilmen, the heads of departments, boards and commissions, and, in some instances, a collector and an assessor are elected by the people. Although the mayor is elected and, in the words of Professor Story, "is marked for respon-

35 *Ibid.*, pp. 278-279.
36 *Ibid.*, p. 57.

sibility," [37] his actual powers of office are attenuated. The following Fig. 2 outlines its organization.

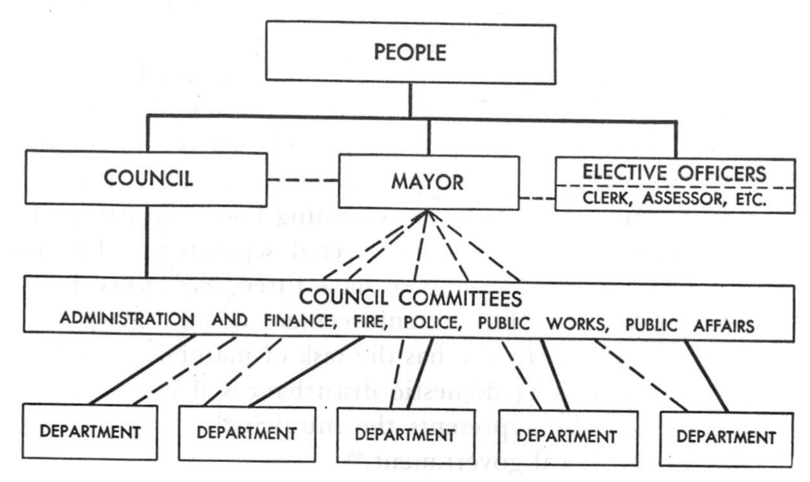

Fig. 2. The Weak-Mayor and Council Form of Government.

In the weak-mayor and council plan the accent is on the council. The latter retains almost all the power over legislation and administration. The mayor is "weak" in the institutional sense, and whatever powers he possesses are largely of a residual nature. His, for example, is the ultimate responsibility for the maintenance of the peace. In the normal course of city government, however, the mayor may recommend legislation and can veto legislation; but the council either can ignore his recommendations or override his veto. He may make appointments, but here again council confirmation is required. It is obvious that the council may have a great voice in determining who shall hold appointive office.

In matters of administration the role of the mayor is advisory. He is the acknowledged political head of the government and consults with the council because people come to him for the solution of their problems. But heads of departments or boards of commissions are chosen popularly and have no reason to follow his lead. If anything, the initiative lies with them rather than with the mayor. Nor does he have any power to remove public officials who are not responsive to his wishes. It is the council that retains the power, through an elaborate committee system, to supervise administration. Indeed, the mayor's power in this respect is proportionate to

[37] Story, *op. cit.*, p. 13.

the degree that he is able to persuade the council of the correctness of his position. To say the least, the weak-mayor and council form violates the administrative principle that power and responsibility must go hand in hand.

A good example of the weak-mayor and council form of government is the municipality of North Plainfield, New Jersey, a community of approximately fourteen thousand people. Today it has virtually the same governmental structure that it had in 1878 when it was first founded. A seven-man governing body consisting of six councilmen and a mayor are each elected separately. The mayor serves for two years and councilmen have three-year terms. Legally, the mayor is responsible for the enforcement of all ordinances approved by the council. He also has the task of maintaining the public peace and suppressing domestic disturbances if and when they occur. The mayor also represents the municipality in its dealings with other units of local government.[38]

In actual practice, however, administration of local activities is carried out through council committees covering the following areas: administration and finance, fire, police, public works, public affairs, and laws and ordinances. Rules of order adopted at each opening session of the council govern the manner in which council committees are selected. The usual practice followed is the nomination of council committees by the mayor subject to confirmation by the council. There have been occasions where the council has denied this authority to the mayor. In any event, if council confirmation is not obtained within thirty days, the council appoints its own committees. Each committee chairman is responsible for the management of his department, although by law the council as a whole has both jurisdiction and authority over the department or activity. All councilmen serve as either chairmen or members of the various committees. The same people in a collective capacity determine the legislative policies of the municipality.[39]

The weaknesses of this form of government were stated in the findings of a charter commission which reported to the citizens in 1954. In their view there was no separation of legislative and administrative power. As a consequence, the same people who established the legislative policies were also responsible for carrying them

---

38 *New Jersey Statutes Annotated,* XL:86-1 *et. seq.*

39 *Report of the Findings and Recommendations of the Charter Commission* (North Plainfield, New Jersey: August 1954), p. 8.

out. No single, full-time person was responsible for the coordination of all administrative activity. The mayor, it was pointed out, was saddled with responsibility but had no commensurate authority. Finally, it was pointed out that the absence of a strong executive made it impossible to plan a long-range coherent program for the municipality.[40]

Strong-mayor and council, New York City. It was the presence of these major defects in almost all municipalities, coupled with the appearance of complex urban problems, that led to widespread dissatisfaction with the council as an agency of administration. The structural changes that occurred were evidence of this mood. In the twentieth century the view soon became widely held that a drastic revision in the distribution of powers between mayor and council was essential if the executive was to attain the full stature needed to direct effectively the affairs of the city.

Since the mayor-council was the traditional pattern of government, the change in mood was first reflected in this instrument. Over a period of years, the strong-mayor and council plan came into being and, as Professor Munro has remarked, it was "the outstanding feature . . . in the evolution of American municipal institutions." [41] The strong-mayor and council form is identified by a popularly chosen executive, the "short ballot," and extensive powers of appointment and removal in the hands of the mayor. Under this plan the authority of the council is up-ended, and executive dominance and leadership are assured.

Unlike its weaker prototype, the strong-mayor and council plan invariably grants the mayor the power to appoint the principal officials subject to confirmation by the council. In some municipalities the appointing power is even more highly developed. The Brooklyn Charter of 1882 permitted the mayor to appoint key personnel without council confirmation. When that city was incorporated as part of New York City, the charter became a standard feature of the latter's form of government. In like manner, removal of officials by the mayor is usually subject to the concurrence of the council, but again, as in some cities, the removal power of the mayor is absolute.

The changed status of the mayor is also reflected in the presence

---

[40] *Ibid.*, pp. 3-4.

[41] W. B. Munro, *The Government of American Cities* (New York: The Macmillan Co., 1913), p. 207.

of both the qualified and absolute veto. In the 1897 Charter of Greater New York, the Board of Estimate and Appointment, consisting of the mayor, comptroller, the president of the board of aldermen, and the five borough presidents, was given the authority to formulate the fiscal program for the city. The power of the council was limited to the reduction of financial items, and even these could be vetoed by the mayor unless overruled by a two-thirds of the council. This arrangement, which continued until a new charter went into effect in 1938, presented the public with a comprehensive program formulated under the direction of the mayor.

With the evolution of the strong-mayor and council type of municipal government, the ghost of Jacksonian democracy in the form of the weak mayor was laid to rest. The conviction that political accountability could be obtained by the correlation of authority in the hands of a single executive was here to stay.

New York City, the world's largest municipality, has one of the most highly developed strong-mayor and council governments. Its more than eight million people are divided into five boroughs whose boundaries are contiguous with its five counties. In a sense the city operates on the federal principle. Representation in the governing body is apportioned on the basis of population and boroughs. City-wide functions are administered from the "central government" at City Hall, but those which are of an essentially local character are under the jurisdiction of borough presidents.[42] An insight into the nature and extent of services provided for the citizens can be gained from the fact that in 1950 the city employed approximately 225,000 people.[43]

New York City's present charter, which went into effect in 1938, is essentially the same in form and structure as that which existed when the Greater New York Charter was adopted in 1897 and revised in 1901.[44] However, the huge mass of legislation, in many cases inconsistent with one charter, was consolidated into an organic whole at the time of charter revision. The powers of the mayor and council were clarified and, for a decade, the council was chosen

[42] *New York City Charter and Administrative Code* (Albany, New York: The Williams Press, 1952), pp. VII-XIII. "Report of the New York Charter Revision Commission."

[43] Griffenhagen and Associates, *Classification and Compensation of the Service of the City of New York* (New York City, 1951), I, p. 123.

[44] *New York Laws of 1897,* Chapter 378; and *Laws 1901,* Chapter 446.

by proportional representation. Under the present form of government the mayor is strong, measured by any standards. He has the absolute power to appoint and remove heads of departments, members of boards and commissioners, municipal court justices and other nonelected officers, except as otherwise provided by law.[45]

In 1950 he appointed 27 departmental heads, the members of 17 boards and commissions, among them the Boards of Education and Higher Education, and immediate assistants, a total of approximately 100 administrative officers.[46]

The mayor has great legislative and fiscal powers. At least once a year he forwards to the council a statement on the government and affairs of the city. He has the power of veto which can be overridden only by a two-thirds majority of the council. He prepares the expense budget, setting forth the operating plan of expenditures for the fiscal year. As a leading member of the Board of Estimate, he also has an important role in deciding the fate of the capital budget as submitted by the City Planning Commission.[47] The Board of Estimate has an ex-officio membership consisting of three city-wide officials, the mayor, comptroller, and president of the city council, as well as the five borough presidents. All except the president of the city council are heads of large departments.[48] Perhaps one index of the mayor's status is his annual salary of forty thousand dollars. But more than this, the measure of the office can be found in his extensive powers over personnel, finance, and planning. He can appoint and remove any official without council confirmation and, through this, achieve the integration of the executive branch. The policies of the city are largely a product of his initiative and he can be held responsible for them. Indeed he is clearly the political as well as the administrative head of his city.

In recent years, particularly in the large cities, the feeling that the mayor should be given assistance in the performance of his administrative duties has led to a further evolution of the strong mayor into what might be called the mayor-administrator form of government.

---

45 *New York City Charter and Administrative Code, op. cit.,* Chapter 1, section 3.

46 R. B. Rankin, *Guide to the Municipal Government of New York* (New York: Record Press, 1950), pp. 25-28.

47 *New York City Charter,* sections 113-114.

48 *Ibid.,* sections 39, 67.

PRINCIPAL FEATURES OF COMMISSION GOVERNMENT

The remarkable success of the Galveston experiment in commission-type of government led to its imitation in Houston, Dallas, and other Texas cities. Later in Des Moines, in 1907, the plan underwent further evolution. To the prototype were added nonpartisan elections, initiative, referendum, and recall. Distribution of powers among the commissioners was made more specific. Five departments were created each dealing with one of the following functions: (1) public affairs, (2) accounts and finance, (3) public safety, (4) streets and public improvements, and (5) parks and public property. The public affairs function was considered most important.[49] In most commission plans the assignment of commissioners to departments is usually made by the commissioners as a body, although in some instances the voters are permitted to choose them as heads of departments.[50] The mayor is chosen from the governing body and is usually the man who has received the most votes. By common agreement he is made the head of the government and given the supervision of the most important department. As a body, the board of commissioners had all the powers of the boards and commissions supplanted by it, except as otherwise provided by law.[51] The following figure portrays the plan's principal features.

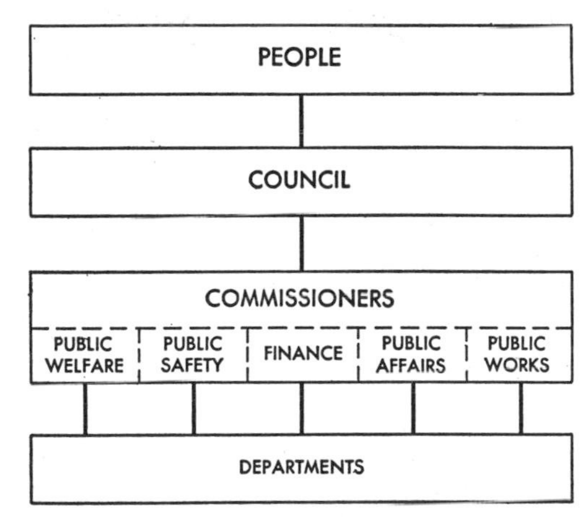

Fig. 3. The Commission Form of Government.

[49] Hamilton, *op. cit.*, pp. 22-23.

[50] The courts will not interfere with the allocation of departmental assignments, regarding these as legislative rather than judicial matters. See, for example, *Moore v. Haddonfield,* 62 N. J. L. 386; *Hendee v. Wildwood, 96* N. J. L. 286.

[51] See, for example, *New Jersey Statutes Annotated,* XL, sec. 71-9.

The "Des Moines plan," as it was popularly called, was subjected to legal attack in many states on the ground that the union of legislative and administrative power was violative of the provisions in various state constitutions which required a separation of these powers.[52] Once the constitutional obstacle was hurdled, the plan spread rapidly throughout the country. Although its influence declined after 1917, it is still employed by 14.1 percent of the cities of the United States.[53]

On the surface, at least, the commission plan seems entirely in accord with the principles of good government. Power is concentrated in relatively few hands and responsibility to the public is established through nonpartisan elections, initiative, referendum, and recall. The general tone of local government would be dependent upon an alert citizenry. As one writer has hopefully suggested, democracy and efficiency are combined "in the greatest practicable degree. . . ." [54] But as one begins to dig below the surface one is inclined to wonder at the optimism expressed. For one thing, the combination of legislative and administrative functions does not necessarily result in efficiency. The people choose legislators, not administrators, yet commissioners discharge both responsibilities. The ability to garner votes is not necessarily the best recommendation for handling the complex and often expensive affairs of the city. In matters of administration, the individual commissioner is an amateur.[55]

The plan is also open to the charge that it fosters personal politics. Commissioners operating on the principle of "reciprocal noninterference" hesitate to oppose projects of their fellow members for fear that their proposals in turn will be attacked.[56] Bitterness among commissioners often results if individual commissioners do not get choice assignments. Unless a modus vivendi exists in the form of the common acceptance of the role of seniority, there is bound to be strife, and this may be heightened where membership in the council is divided among both parties. The division of powers

[52] *State v. Bentley,* 100 Kansas 399; *Cleveland v. Watertown,* 222 N. Y. 159; *Cunningham v. Rockwood,* 225 Mass. 574.

[53] *Municipal Yearbook for 1955,* p. 57.

[54] Hamilton, *op. cit.,* p. 64.

[55] C. M. Fassett, "The Weakness of Commission Government," *National Municipal Review,* IX (1920), pp. 642, 647.

[56] *Preliminary Report of the Newark Charter Commission* (Newark, N. J. 1953), pp. 13-15.

among commissioners is apt to result in a political tug and haul rather than coordination.[57]

It is in precisely this latter aspect that the main defect of commission government is pointed up. Fragmentation of authority invariably results in as many governments as there are departments. When departmental heads are co-equal without an acknowledged superior, coordination is bound to be difficult, if not impossible. Jurisdictional squabbles, waste of time and money, and competition among commissioners for the public eye almost always result.[58] In the scramble for prestige and power among the commissioners, the city is often denied the benefit of the most elementary practices of advanced management.[59] Its fatal weakness, as the New Jersey Commission on Municipal Government has noted, is that it ". . . has no single responsible executive . . . (and) this makes impossible a unified public policy as well as a known and effective responsibility." [60]

Commission government has many other inherent weaknesses. The wonder is that it has survived for so long, in the midst of the constant demand for more services and better municipal performance. Perhaps the key to its survival lies in the memory of the high standards established by the earliest commission governments. Its greatest contribution was the stimulation of civic interest. When enthusiasm for the plan waned, the optimism it generated was transferred to more effective governmental plans. This, in the final analysis, was its real contribution.[61]

PRINCIPAL FEATURES OF COUNCIL-MANAGER GOVERNMENT

Many years ago, Dicey commented on the lack of political inventiveness. Yet in the growth of the council-manager plan we have a unique development in our municipal political institutions. The manager plan is old in the sense that it is based upon the doctrine of councilmanic supremacy. But it is distinctively new and different in its emphasis on the professional management of municipal activity in preference to the use of council committees. The manager plan, in brief, is a genuine political invention.

---

57 *Ibid.*

58 H. G. James, *Applied City Government* (New York: Harper & Bros., 1914), pp. 62-65.

59 Report of Newark Charter Commission, *op. cit.*, p. 15.

60 Final Report of the Commission on Municipal Government, *Local Self Government in New Jersey: A Proposed Optional Charter Plan.* (Trenton, New Jersey, 1949), p. 20.

61 See the comments on this point by Fassett, *ibid.*, above.

Enough has been said in previous pages on the origin of the council-manager plan. It is now necessary to detail its principal features in order that its role as an instrument of government can be clearly understood. The plan rests upon three basic principles. First, there is the idea that the most capable and civic-minded people should serve on the governing body as community representatives to determine municipal policies. Second, there is the concept that municipal administration is the province of a career administrator rather than of a part-time amateur. Finally, there is the principle of the short ballot which enables the voter to hold the council accountable for policy and the supervision of the professional administrator.[62] Fig. 4 gives a diagrammatic description of the plan.

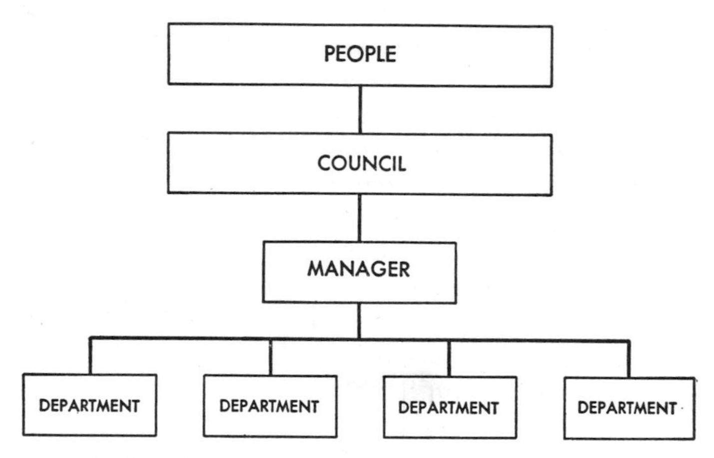

Fig. 4. The Council-Manager Form of Government.

Institutionally, these ideas have been crystallized in the following manner. The council has been restored to its original position of pre-eminence. It is now not only the organ for policy making but it is also the chief judge of the manager's conduct of administration. The Model City Charter of the National Municipal League describes in considerable detail the power and authority of the council. The council consisting of five or more members possesses all the powers of the municipality and is responsible for the determination of all matters of policy.[63] It appoints and removes the manager, establishes departments, approves the budget, and also authorizes

---

[62] Stone, Price and Stone, *op. cit.*, pp. 17, 236.

[63] Committee on Revision of the Model City Charter, *Model City Charter* (New York: National Municipal League, 5th ed., 1941) Article II Section 8.

the issuances of bonds. The council has the authority to inquire into the conduct of any office or department and also has extensive powers of investigation. It must provide for an independent audit.[64]

The council, in brief, is relieved of the burden of administration. Instead, its role as a supervisor of administration and as a policy maker has been heightened. In dealing with the manager, the council must act as a body. Individual councilmen are forbidden either to influence the manager's appointment or to interfere with the performance by the manager or his subordinates of their duties, "publicly or privately." The council, except in case of an inquiry, must deal with the administrative service solely through the manager. Violation of these mandates is considered a misdemeanor. A member convicted is disqualified as a councilman.[65]

It would be overstating the case to say that the mayor under the council-manager plan is merely a figurehead. Strong personalities such as Seasongood of Cincinnati can provide leadership. Generally, however, the mayor's powers are limited.[66] He is chosen by the council as in Cincinnati or elected separately, as in Kansas City. Regardless of how he is chosen, however, the mayor usually is the head of the city government for ceremonial purposes. He may be given special powers by the governor for purposes of military law, but, aside from a crisis situation, he is normally overshadowed by the manager. Under New Jersey's Optional Municipal Charter law of 1950, the mayor has somewhat more power. He appoints trustees of the public library and, in some instances, members of the Board of Education. All bonds, notes, contracts, and written obligations are executed by him on behalf of the municipality. But the law confines his authority to these functions only.[67]

The heart of the plan is the city manager. Here we have a phenomenon that is unique in municipal politics. A career administrator, chosen solely on the basis of his executive ability and his knowledge of accepted municipal practice, is given complete authority and responsibility for the administration of the affairs of the municipality.[68] Residence requirements are waived, but during his years of service he must become a resident of the city. Political con-

64 *Ibid.* above. See also N. J. S. A. 40:69A-91 which paraphrases the Model Municipal Charter.

65 New Jersey Statutes Annotated, XL, 69A-91.

66 Story, *op. cit.,* 203.

67 New Jersey Statutes Annotated XL, 69A-87.

68 Stone, Price and Stone, *op. cit.,* pp. 53, 55.

siderations are noticeably absent in his choice. To repeat, the ability of the manager is the only criterion of availability.

In keeping with the nonpolitical tradition of appointment is the Code of Ethics adopted by the International City Managers' Association. This is the bible of the profession and sets forth in some detail the aims and expectations that the profession requires of its members. Several points are worthy of being stressed. The municipal manager, according to the code, "believes that personal aggrandizement or personal profit secured by confidential information or by misuse of public time is dishonest."[69] The manager is not only enjoined to observe rigorous standards of integrity, but he is also asked to remember that he is in no sense the political head of the community. It is his job to provide the council with the information and advice necessary to intelligent policy making and to encourage "positive decisions on policy by the council instead of passive acceptance of his recommendations."[70] Finally, the manager is reminded that the council must receive full credit for effectuation of municipal policies.[71]

The manager is the link between the council and the administration. He is the municipality's chief executive officer and head of the administrative branch. As such, he is granted sufficient authority to administer the affairs of the city. A fairly detailed statement of the duties and powers of the manager can be found in New Jersey's Optional Charter Law. It is sufficiently specific and representative to be quoted:

> "The municipal manager shall: (a) be the chief executive and administrative official of the municipality; (b) execute all laws and ordinances of the municipality; (c) appoint and remove a deputy manager if one be authorized by the council, all department heads and all other officers, subordinates, and assistants for whose selection or removal no other method is provided . . . except that he may authorize the head of a department to appoint and remove subordinates in such department, supervise and control his appointees and report all appointments or removals at the next meeting thereafter of the municipal council; (d) negotiate contracts for the municipality subject to the approval of the municipal council, make recommenda-

69 Internation City Managers' Association, *Code of Ethics,* drafted in 1924, revised in 1934 and 1938. The latter revision occurred in Boston on September 29, 1938.

70 *Idem.*

71 *Idem.*

tions concerning the nature and location of municipal improvements, and execute municipal improvements as determined by the council; (e) see that all terms and conditions imposed in favor of the municipality or its inhabitants in any statute, public utility franchise or other contract are faithfully kept and performed, and upon knowledge of any violation call the same to the attention of the municipal council; (f) attend all meetings of the municipal council with the right to take part in the discussions but without the right to vote; (g) recommend to the municipal council for adoption such measures as he may deem necessary or expedient, keep the council advised of the financial condition of the municipality, make reports to the council as requested by it, and at least once a year make an annual report of his work for the benefit of the council and the public; (h) investigate at any time the affairs of any officer or department of the municipality; (i) perform such other duties as may be required of the municipal manager by ordinance or resolution of the municipal council." [72]

These powers are, to say the least, enormous in their implications. The wide latitude given to an executive officer not subject to the usual political checks has led to the often repeated charges that the plan is autocratic, undemocratic, and dictatorial.[73] Needless to say, these accusations have been countered with refutations. The key point in the controversy is the tenure of the manager. In San Diego, Sacramento, and other California cities; in Pontiac and Ypsilanti, Michigan; in Phoenix, Arizona and in many others, managers have tenure. They hold office after a probationary period and can be removed only for cause after a hearing. New Jersey's City Manager Act of 1923 contains similar safeguards for the manager.[74] The existence of this provision enables the manager to appeal over the head of the council to the courts.[75] Advocates of the council-manager plan have consistently opposed tenure for the manager.[76] The National Municipal League's Model City Charter contains a provision which authorizes the council by a majority vote to dismiss a manager "after full consideration." [77] In this way, it is asserted, adequate supervision of the manager is insured.

72 New Jersey Statutes Annotated XL, 69A-95.

73 Stone, Price, and Stone, *op. cit.*, pp. 29-30.

74 New Jersey Statutes Annotated, XL, 80-1.

75 *Lohen v. Borough of Keansburg*, overruled in 1950 4 N. J. 489 (1950), wherein it is argued that a manager cannot waive his right to tenure.

76 R. S. Childs, "No Tenure for City Managers," *National Municipal Review*, XXXVIII (1949), pp. 167-170.

77 *Model City Charter, op. cit.*, Article II, section 10.

The manager plan, like its predecessor the commission form, has borrowed heavily from the progressive movement. The Model City Charter calls for nonpartisan elections, proportional representation, initiative, referendum and recall. Most of these appear, to a greater or lesser degree, in the charter of those cities that have accepted the plan.

There seems to be a uniform acceptance of the devices of direct democracy, but some council-manager cities have rejected nonpartisan elections; others have disclaimed an interest in proportional representation; and still others, have repudiated both provisions.

Evaluation of the council-manager plan. The council-manager plan has made a significant impact upon municipal government. In the relatively short time that it has been in existence it has demonstrated astonishing vitality. As of January 1955, the plan has been adopted by 1,275 places. More than half of these adoptions have occurred within the last eight years.[78] Everywhere the plan has been introduced it has resulted in more effective government. In Cambridge, Massachusetts, a city manager, after seven years, transformed an incompetent and dishonest government into one that was stable and efficient.[79] It is, of course, unwise to generalize on one specific example, but there are ample data available in the form of three major studies sponsored by The Social Science Research Council.[80]

Perhaps the best measurement of the viability of the plan is its rate of abandonments once it has been tried. Since 1912 only a total of 53 cities voted to reject the plan. This is, indeed, an excellent performance record and it is even more remarkable when one considers the circumstances under which the plans were repudiated. In a study of twenty-five cities in 1940, Professor Arthur Bromage found three main reasons: (1) defects in charters and failure to adhere to the recommended model; (2) economic circumstances, such as the collapse of real property values, which were blamed on the plan; and (3) too brief a trial period under conditions of weak citizen interest.[81] In a more recent study of four small cities in the mid-

[78] *National Municipal Yearbook for 1955,* p. 277.

[79] H. Stein, editor, *Public Administration and Policy Development, A Case Book* (New York: Harcourt, Brace and Company, 1952), pp. 573-621.

[80] Stone, Price and Stone, *op. cit.,* pp. 259-260: also F. C. Mosher and others, *City Manager Government in Seven Cities* (Chicago: Public Administration Service 1940). H. A. Stone, D. K. Price and K. H. Stone, *City Manager Government in Nine Cities* (Chicago: Public Administration Service 1940).

[81] A. W. Bromage, *Manager Plan Abandonments* (New York: National Municipal League, 1940), pp. 10-13.

west, other reasons for abandonment were cited. In some instances the failure of the city "to keep pace with recent urban growth" was responsible for the defeat of the plan. In two of the cities a retired farmer class formed the core of opposition to the plan. In two cities, too, the merits of the manager plan were confused with the issue of wards or at-large elections. In most instances, the charge of "dictator" seemed to gain considerable currency.[82] None of the reasons stated, however, reflects upon the merits of the plan itself.

The manager. The council-manager plan has introduced the tradition of the professional manager and, by its success, it has pointed the attention of the public to the importance of effective administration. Despite the fact that, in most instances, the manager holds office at the pleasure of the council, the main elements of a career service are gradually emerging. In 1951 four out of every five managers appointed had been managers in other cities, assistant managers, or had held some other governmental position. A similar trend was evident in 1954.[83]

The average term of office for managers in 1954, exclusive of those with less than five years of service, was 7.26 years. For the seventeen managers who either died or retired in 1954 the average term of service was nineteen years. In this group was one who had served thirty-six years, six who had from twenty-five to thirty-five years of experience, six from ten to twenty-five years and four with less than ten years.[84] "The long tenure of managers who either died or were retired during the year gives conclusive evidence of a developing professional group. . . ." [85] This conclusion formulated in 1951 still applies today.

Salaries, too, are an index of the developing status of the profession. In 1951 for the nine city manager cities over 250,000 in population the mean average salary of the manager was $18,627 and the salaries varied from a low of $15,000 to a high of $27,500. The mean average salary of cities in other population ranges are also extremely favorable.[86] The reward for professional training and the opportu-

[82] E. O. Stene and G. K. Floro, *Abandonment of the Manager Plan A Study of Four Small Cities* (University of Kansas Governmental Research Center, 1953), pp. 92-97.

[83] *Municipal Yearbook for 1955*, p. 503.

[84] *Ibid.*, p. 504.

[85] *Municipal Yearbook for 1951*, p. 521.

[86] For cities in 100,000-250,000 class the mean average salary for 1951 was $16,030; for 50,000-100,000 it was $12,172; in 1952 for those between 5,000-10,000 it was $6,273. *Ibid.*, pp. 118-120.

nities for advancement are great. Both should serve to attract additional capable people to the field.

Two other trends are worth while noting. More and more cities are selecting men as managers who have had university training in public administration. In 1955 the profession was able to report, "The trend for some years has been toward the appointment of men with public administration training and experience, partly as a result of careful selection of capable young men and the provisions of graduate training in public administration by a number of universities." [87] Following their training, prospective managers are usually first apprenticed as assistant managers and, as they gain in experience, they become full-fledged managers. Once having attained this status they tend, as their work becomes more widely known, to move from smaller to larger cities. At each stage in their development their reward for effective performance is either promotion or advancement. Emphasis on performance standards is reflected in a second trend. Increasingly, cities tend to waive residence requirements when seeking administrative talents. In the year 1954 residence requirements were waived for seventy-five percent of the managers.[88]

THE MAYOR-ADMINISTRATOR SYSTEM

Within the past twenty years the idea of providing the strong mayor, particularly in the large cities, with managerial assistance has gained considerable favor. It is now widely held that the increasingly complex city mechanism requires greater central direction by the head of the city. Thus, although the tradition of an elected head of government is continued, the concept of professional administrative assistance has been added. The new version of the strong-mayor plan commonly called mayor-administrator form, has now been adopted by eight large cities and many smaller ones.[89]

Why this evolution has taken place is not too clear. The council-manager plan with its strong emphasis on the professionally trained administrator might have been employed, but, strangely enough, the

---

[87] *Municipal Yearbook for 1955,* p. 504.

[88] Municipal Yearbook for 1955, p. 504. This compares favorably with seventy-six and seventy-four percent for the years 1950 and 1951. See also L. White, *The City Manager* (Chicago: The University of Chicago Press, 1927), and C. E. Ridley and O. F. Nolting, *The City Manager Profession* (Chicago: The University of Chicago Press, 1934).

[89] W. S. Sayre, "The General Manager Idea for Large Cities," *Public Administration Review,* XIV (1954), p. 253.

large cities have been exceedingly loath to depart from the principle of the elected municipal executive. Statistics show that the only large city now using the city manager plan is Cincinnati. Cleveland, the only other large city to experiment with council-manager, abandoned it after a decade, and within the last twenty years, no major city has accepted the plan. Eighty percent of the cities with council-manager plans have populations of less than 25,000 people.[90]

The failure of large cities to employ the council-manager plan as a solution to their managerial difficulties indicates a real weakness of the council-manager plan. The latter assumes that the political and administrative processes can be compartmentalized and separated, but this is not the case. The political process is continuous and spills over into administration. Administrative programs inevitably have political ramification. As a special state commission appointed to study the government of the city of New York has said, "The Commission accepts the unity of the governmental process here; it is opposed to trying to divide the indivisible." [91]

The failure of the council-manager plan to accent properly the political aspect may well account for the reluctance of the large city to accept it. Control of the city is a political prize of vast significance, not only in the city itself, but also in the battle for power at the state, and even the federal, level. To assume that a professional manager would keep himself aloof from political strife is to expect the impossible. The manager will need to expect and to solicit support from the citizens. To the extent that he does this, to the degree to which his policies become subject to criticism, the manager is acting in a political capacity. The people of the large cities feel that political decisions should be made by a politically accountable official, the mayor.[92] If this viewpoint is accepted, and there is considerable merit in the argument, then it is logical to keep the elected head at the helm of city government and add to it the necessary managerial assistance.

The assumption can be made, as Professor Sayre had pointed out, that the mayor can choose an administrator as wisely and as well as the council.[93] In contrast to the council-manager plan, the

---

[90] Report of the Temporary State Commission to Study the Organizational Structure of the Government of the City of New York, *Four Steps to Better Government of New York City,* (Albany, N. Y., 1953), p. 33.

[91] *Idem.*

[92] Sayre, *op. cit.*, pp. 257-258.

[93] *Ibid.*, p. 253.

administrator or the manager will be responsible to the political head of the city instead of to the council. Unity of politics and administration, therefore, may be expected to occur.

Apparently this is what the large cities hope to accomplish. They seem to feel that political accountability is a value which should not easily be discarded. Although the mayor-administrator form is in various stages of evolution, certain features have become imbedded in its practice. It is clear that the administrator is responsible to the mayor, and except for the city of San Francisco, is dependent upon him for continuance in office. Almost all are charged with the duty of advising the mayor on matters of administration. Only New Orleans, Los Angeles, and San Francisco make no provision in this regard, although it may be inferred from the nature of the administrator's duties. The administrator's power of appointment and removal is in a state of flux. In San Francisco, the administrator may appoint and remove officers without the consent of the mayor, but in New Orleans and Philadelphia the concurrence of the elected head is required. The city administrator has no authority to appoint and remove, although his power to advise the mayor is magnified.[94]

New Jersey's Optional Municipal Charter Law of 1950, which was revised three years later, contains the most explicit statement of the duties of the administrator. For cities with less than 250,000 people, the administrator under the direction and supervision of the mayor is required to "(a) assist in the preparation of the budget, (b) administer a centralized purchasing system, (c) be responsible for the development and administration of a sound personnel system, and (d) to perform such other duties as council may prescribe." [95] For larger cities in the state, the administrator, again under the direction of the mayor, is granted the power to supervise other departments.[96]

Although there is the inevitable problem of the continuity of administration, it would seem as if the amalgam of politics and administration represented by the mayor-administrator form has taken a strong foothold in American municipal practice. Professor Sayre, in his brilliant article, asserts that it is not only here to stay

---

[94] Sayre, *op. cit.*, 256. Also C. R. Adrian, *Recent Concepts in Large City Administration* (mimeographed). A paper read before the American Political Science Association, Washington, D. C.: September 6, 1956.

[95] *New Jersey Statutes Annotated,* XL, 69A-44.

[96] *Idem.*

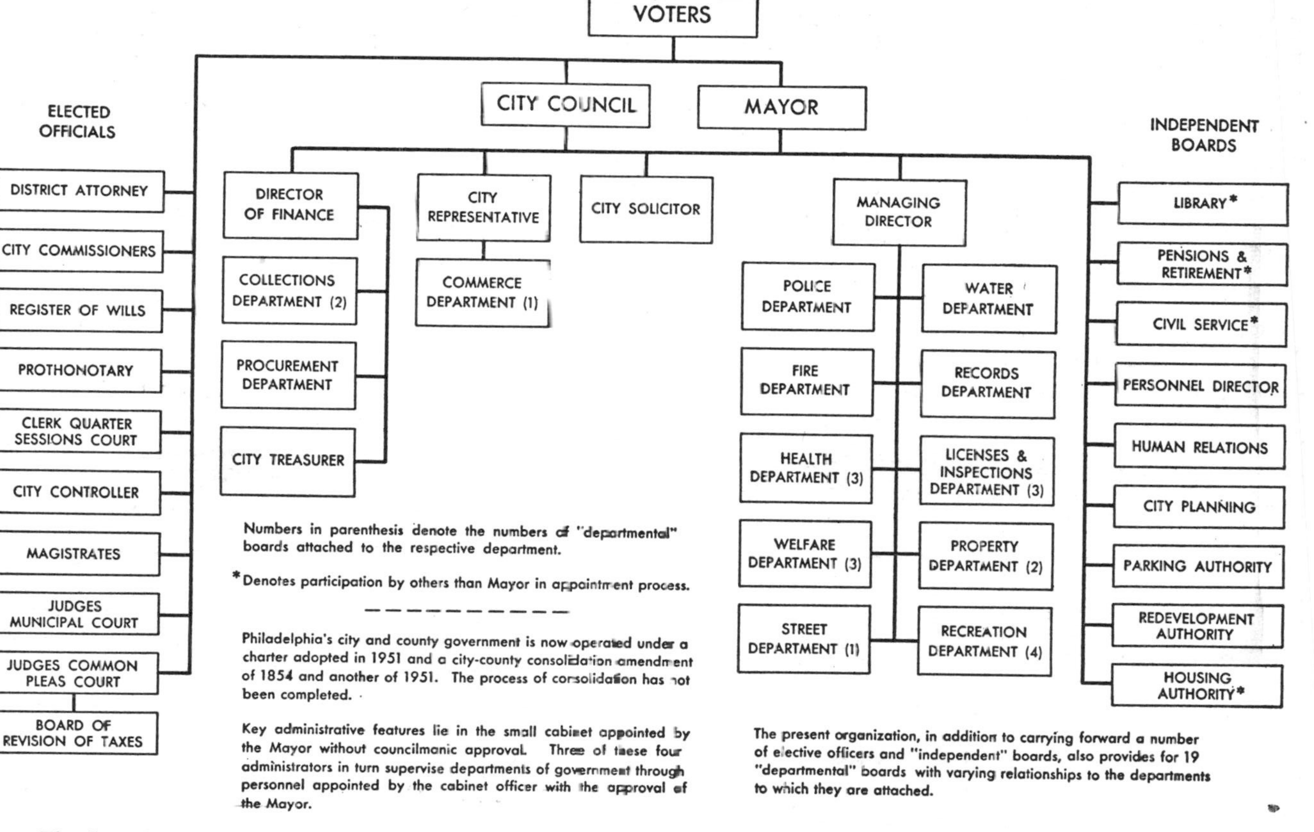

Fig. 5. The Strong-Mayor and Council Plan as Illustrated by the Government of Philadelphia City and County. (Chart prepared by Lennox Moak of the Pennsylvania Economy League.)

but will be accepted increasingly in the years to come. He suggests that, "The mayor-manager plan is likely to dominate the course of large city administrative reorganization for the next several years. The council-manager plan is not likely to break into the large city league, because this plan does not represent an accommodation to either the political or the managerial requirements of the large cities. The emergence of the mayor-manager plan has breached the monopolistic claim of the council-manager plan to the managerial virtues by presenting the new and strong competition of an alternative manager plan." [97]

SUMMARY

Administration may be considered as purposive activity. Goals are established and means are required to obtain an end. The essential ingredients of administration are form, structure, and personnel. Competent people are needed, but their talents cannot be utilized effectively if the instrument of government is weak. Administrative performance is related directly to the tools provided. Form and structure define duties and responsibility and provide the framework of direction. They are the cement that bind the administrative endeavor into an organic whole.

In the early city the form of government was weak, in keeping with the philosophy that the best government was that which governed the least. All the powers were vested in the council, and it was both a legislative and an administrative body. Administration was carried out on a part-time basis.

The burgeoning of the city in the middle of the nineteenth century caused a gradual but distinct change in the form of city government. New demands were followed by an enormous upsurge in city power. The functions of government multiplied rapidly and council-committee administration soon proved unsuitable. The strengthening of the mayor's office was accompanied by the allocation of administrative power to independently elected departmental heads, boards, and commissions. The council lost its position of dominance, but there was no corresponding centralization of authority in the hands of the municipal executive. Instead, administrative authority was divided among many executives each with his own

---

[97] Sayre, *op. cit.*, p. 257. But see also a contrary view by J. E. Bebout, "Management for Large Cities," *Public Administration Review,* XV (1955), pp. 189-195.

source of authority in the people. Supervision of municipal activities rested in the people.

After the Civil War a vast increase in the urban population occurred. People flocked to the city in droves and again its problems multiplied. Divided authority and lack of accountability soon led to misgovernment on a wide scale. Toward the end of the century, civic outrage against those excesses led to changes in governmental structure. Conviction grew that a strong executive, accompanied by the short ballot, could be made fully responsible for his acts. This new mood was reflected in the growth of the strong-mayor form and experimentation with both the commission and council-manager plans.

The strong-mayor was a logical extension of our existing form of government. The tradition of a politically accountable head of government found ready acceptance. Regarded widely as the political head of government, he was made the actual head by the grant of extensive powers. Commission government, which briefly enjoyed wide popularity, was in a similar vein. A small council with wide powers of legislation and administration was thought to be readily accountable to the people, and the people's role was strengthened by the addition of nonpartisan elections, initiative, referendum, and recall. But the concentration of authority soon proved to be an illusion, for there was no central point of decision. Moreover, the problems of government had become so complex as to require expert administration and assurance of continuity which the commission government could not supply.

Out of commission government was born the council-manager plan. The latter went one step further. Centralization of executive power was lodged in the hands of a manager, and the council was made the judge and jury of his performance. The devices of popular government were retained, and to them were added the authority of the council to hire and fire the manager. Emphasis on a single executive who was professionally trained stressed the need for both the impartial and effective administration of the city's services. That the plan was widely adopted is a tribute, not only to the talents of the manager but also to the widespread need for better government. Today it is the chief challenger to the strong mayor-council form.

But the council-manager plan with its stress on trained managerial personnel neglected the relationship between politics and administration. It viewed administration as a separate compartment from politics, whereas, in actuality, politics and administration are joined together in a single process. The manager, in the broad sense of the term, was engaged in making policy, that is, in politics. He made judgments and, through regulations, he determined the scope of the policies laid down by the council. It is perhaps because of this that the plan has made no headway in the large cities. Citizens feel that such judgments should be subjected to political review.

But the council-manager plan did point up the need for expert administration. As a consequence, the large cities with preference for the politically elected head took steps to strengthen the managerial side by providing the mayor with a chief managerial assistant who has been called both administrator and manager. Thus it is that the strong-mayor plan in the large city is gradually becoming the mayor-administrator type. The need for sound administration is universally acknowledged.

The forms of government grew in response to the changed needs of our society. They are not ends in themselves but must be judged by the manner in which they meet the responsibilities of the city.

BIBLIOGRAPHY

Books:

Bromage, A. W. *Manager Plan Abandonments.* New York: National Municipal League, 1940.

Bryce, J. *The American Commonwealth.* 2 Vols. 2nd edition revised. New York: Macmillan and Co., 1891.

Charter Committee of Newark, New Jersey. *Preliminary Report of the Newark Charter Commission.* Newark, 1953.

Final Report of the Commission on Municipal Government. *Local Self Government in New Jersey: A Proposed Optional Charter Plan.* Trenton, New Jersey, 1949.

Griffenhagen and Associates. *Classification and Compensation of the Services of the City of New York.* Mayor's Committee on Administrative Management, 1951.

Griffith, E. S. *History of the American City.* New York: Oxford University Press, 1938.

Hamilton, J. J. *The Dethronement of the City Boss.* New York: Funk and Wagnalls Co., 1916.

James, H. G. *Applied City Government.* New York: Harper & Brothers, 1914.

McQuillan, E. *The Law of Municipal Corporations.* Volume 2. Sections 4:01–10:45. Chicago: Callaghan & Co., 1950.

Mosher, F. C. *et. al. City Manager Government in Seven Cities.* Chicago: Public Administration Service, 1940.

Municipal Yearbook for 1951. Chicago: The International City Managers' Association, 1951.

Municipal Yearbook for 1955. Chicago: The International City Managers' Association, 1955.

New Jersey Statutes Annotated. 1954 Cumulative Annual Pocket Part. Newark, New Jersey: Soney and Sage Co., 1955.

New York City Charter and Administrative Code. Albany, New York: The Williams Press, 1952.

Rankin, R. *Guide to the Municipal Government of New York.* New York: The Record Press, 1950.

Report of the Findings and Recommendation of the Charter Commission. North Plainfield, New Jersey, 1954.

Report of the Temporary State Commission to Study the Organizational Structure of the Government of the City of New York. *Four Steps to Better Government of New York City.* Albany, New York: 1953.

Ridley, C. E. and Nolting, O. F. *The City Manager Profession.* Chicago: University of Chicago Press, 1934.

Simon, H. and Ridley, C. *Measuring Municipal Activities.* Chicago: The International City Managers' Association, 1948.

Stein, H. *Public Administration and Policy Development.* New York: Harcourt, Brace and Co., 1952.

Stene, E. O. and Floro, G. K. *Abandonments of the Manager Plan—A Study of Four Small Cities.* Lawrence, Kansas: Governmental Research Center, 1953.

Stone, H. A., Price, D. K., and Stone, K. H. *City Manager Government in Nine Cities.* Chicago: Public Administration Service, 1940.

———. *City Manager Government in the United States.* Chicago: Public Administration Service, 1940.

Story, R. M. *The American Municipal Executive.* Vol. III. Urbana, Illinois: University of Illinois, 1918.

U. S. Department of Commerce, U. S. Bureau of Census, *Historical Statistics of the United States 1789–1945.* Washington, D. C.: United States Government Printing Office, 1949.

White, L. *The City Manager.* Chicago: University of Chicago Press, 1927.

Periodicals and Other Material:

Bebout, J. E. "Management for Large Cities," *Public Administration Review* XV (1955), 188-195.

Childs, R. S. "No Tenure for City Managers," *National Municipal Review* XXXVIII (1949), 167-170.

Fassett, C. "The Weakness of Commission Government," *National Municipal Review* IX (1920), 642-647.

Sayre, W. S. "The General Manager Idea for Large Cities," *Public Administration Review,* XIV (1954), 253-258.

Chapter Nine

Suffrage, Registration, and Elections

Control by the Electorate

All governments possess sovereignty, the power to make final determinations for the society. A government that cannot do this, that cannot enforce obedience to its will, is in reality no government at all. It is only because its power is supreme that government is distinguished from other social institutions. The power to make decisions may be vested in the hands of one, a few, or many persons. In a rough way we characterize the allotment of prerogative as dictatorial, oligarchical, or democratic. Regardless of the form of government, however, those who control it have the opportunity, if not the right, to use the collective power of the community.

Democratic safeguards. In a democratic society it is axiomatic that the power of government must be made responsible to the people. It is the people, directly or through those whom they have elected, who determine the terms and conditions of the power exerted over them. In other words, it is primarily through the process of nomination and election that the people maintain control of their government.

This channel of control is so important in democratic societies that many safeguards have been built around it. Perhaps the most important have been the methods and procedures for the conduct of elections. The law seeks to insure that the process of selection will be free from fraud. Nothing is more destructive of civic morale than the prevalence of the feeling that elections have been "fixed" and that nothing the citizen can do will affect their outcome. Equally important is the fact that public officials have a fixed term of office. The power of office is fixed by law and its occupant can exercise its prerogatives, only because he has been elected to office. Moreover, by common consent it is generally recognized that political office must be surrendered if an unfavorable verdict is encountered at the polls.

The powers of government as a whole are limited. Civil liberties are protected in order that a healthy atmosphere of free discussion might flourish and a real freedom of choice might exist. It is these pre-conditions that make political accountability something more than a mechanical process. Indeed, only the opportunity to choose freely between rival candidates for office distinguishes a democratic from a dictatorial government. In short, it is primarily through free elections that the governed periodically pronounce judgment on those who have exercised the power of government. As one authority has so aptly put it, "an election is like the morning rollcall in the army; it brings all public officers to attention. . . ."[1]

Special conditions in the city. These, of course, are generalizations that apply to democratic governments everywhere, but it would be unwise to apply them to the government of the city without bearing in mind the fact that there are special conditions, which, to say the least, are not conducive to the effective functioning of the election process. The city, as we have previously noted, is a social as well as a political fact. Large numbers of people of diverse language, race, creed and national origin are grouped together merely by reason of residence rather than of interest. There is a general lack of coherence of purpose and the community fabric is only half formed.

Moreover, conditions of impersonality prevail. People hardly know their next-door neighbor, let alone the candidates for office. Complicating the situation is the presence of rural attitudes toward government that seem to survive in an urban situation. In rural areas the elective system worked fairly well since neighborhoods were fairly stable, administrative tasks were relatively simple, and officers to be chosen were few in number. People were able to acquaint themselves with candidates. City government today, despite many of the advances made, is still based upon the idea that many, if not most, offices shall be filled by elections. The persistence of this attitude actually imperils the democratic process of control since it is virtually impossible for the voter to appraise effectively the performance record of the office holder. Small wonder, then, that the history of municipal politics actually demonstrates that cliques of unscrupulous men have constantly seized control of local governments and used them for their own purpose.

It is not enough to insist that the people of the city should have the right to choose their officers and to determine the direction of

[1] A. DeGrazia, *The Elements of Political Science* (New York: Alfred A. Knopf, Inc., 1952), p. 157.

municipal policy and administration. More of this by way of implementation is necessary if the will of the people is to become more effective. Greater control over the nominating process is essential. The number of public offices should be reduced if the people are to vote more intelligently. The implications of direct democracy for citizen control of legislation and administration demand exploration. Finally, ways and means have to be found to further stimulate citizen interest in local affairs. Concern with these aspects has been the constant preoccupation of the reformer, and in the process of experimentation and change, much progress has been made. This chapter will attempt to summarize the results of their efforts during the past half century.

SUFFRAGE

Its scope. Suffrage is intimately associated with popular elections. It may be defined as "the right or act of voting on some measure or candidate for office." [2] It is in fact the means by which the people control their government. Since government makes final decisions for everyone, it is essential that everyone be given the right to vote, for it is only in this way that people can participate in decisions affecting them. In view of this consideration, it is proper to assert that everyone should have the right to vote unless there are substantial reasons to the contrary.[3] This is true in theory, but in practice the struggle to broaden the suffrage base has been long and arduous. The voter is not yet identical with the people. Barriers to suffrage still exist, and the condition of political equality as yet has not been obtained. But great strides have been made, and full participation seems to be now only a matter of time.

Suffrage is primarily a matter of state concern and definition. The constitution as originally adopted gave the state almost full responsibility, stating that, "the electors in each state shall have the qualifications requisite for electors of the most numerous branch of the state legislature." State standards, in other words, governed the participation of voters, not only in national and state elections, but in local ones as well. Municipal suffrage then is almost inextricably intertwined with that of the state. The voter within the city must

[2] H. F. Gosnell, *Democracy, The Threshold of Freedom* (New York: The Ronald Press, 1948), p. 12.

[3] L. Lipson, *The Great Issues of Politics* (New York: Prentice-Hall Inc., 1955), p. 125. A justification of equal political participation is contained in pages 126-136.

comply with the qualifications established by the state before he can exercise his franchise. As a minimum these requirements include age, evidence of good moral character, citizenship, residence and literacy, to mention the obvious ones.[4] In some instances, the cities are permitted to prescribe additional conditions in order to maintain the integrity of their elections.[5] Thus the citizen who wishes to vote on a bond issue must, in some instances, also qualify as a taxpayer.

Elimination of the property requirement. In matters of suffrage, apart from those measures designed to modify the effect of the Civil War amendments, most states and cities have gradually attained a condition of universal suffrage. The historic barriers of property, race, color, and sex have steadily crumbled. But this was not always so. The earliest and perhaps oldest voting requirement was either the possession of property or the ability to pay taxes on property. At the time of the drafting of the federal constitution and for several decades thereafter all states and most municipalities made wealth, in some form or degree, a necessary prerequisite for voting. The creation of conditions of stability and the opening of the western lands, however, soon combined to make the property requirement meaningless. Land was to be had for the asking, and the new states that were carved out of the western frontier granted suffrage to all. The example of the West served as a leavening influence in the more settled states. By 1830 fourteen of the twenty-four states had adult manhood suffrage and, by the Civil War, almost every state in the Union had done away with the property requirement. Property, as a voting prerequisite, still remains in a vestigial form as the poll tax and as a condition for voting on bond issues and special assessments.[6] The widening of the suffrage base was not without

[4] A detailed statement of the qualifications by states will be found in *The Book of States, 1954–1955* (Chicago, Illinois: The Council of State Governments, 1954), pp. 80-81.

[5] Courts of the states have taken a contradictory stand on this point. In *Carville v. McBride,* 202 Pacific 802 (1922) a provision in the Elko City, Nevada charter requiring voters in bond elections to be taxpayers was upheld but a similar provision in the city charter of Portland, Oregon was declared unconstitutional, *Loe v. Britting,* 132 Ore. 572 (1930). Virginia and Mississippi allow local units to impose added qualifications but in general the practice is frowned upon.

[6] *The Book of States, op. cit.,* p. 82, lists Michigan, Montana, Nevada, Texas and Utah as requiring voters to possess property in elections involving bond issues and special assessments. One state, Mississippi, requires voters to pay all past due taxes before they can vote.

consequence. In the city, it resulted in the shift in political power from the wealthy to the political boss.[7]

Negro suffrage. The Civil War and the passage of the thirteenth, fourteenth, and fifteenth amendments gave the Negro both suffrage and citizenship. As Professor Lipson has so ably put it, "By these amendments the principles of the constitution caught up with the philosophy of the Declaration of Independence." [8] Thereafter, legally at least, the Negro was no longer a second-class citizen. Nevertheless, the political leaders of the South, through the use of a series of ingenious legal restraints, were able to mute the political voice of the Negro.

Literacy and poll tax requirements. One restrictive device employed to disfranchise the Negro was the literacy test which, incidentally, is used in both northern and southern states. The objective of this requirement is laudable, and it is designed to insure a minimum of intellectual competence. The voter is at least required to be able to read and write. In the South, however, "reading and understanding tests" have often been employed in a discriminatory fashion. Administration of this device was placed in the hands of local election boards. Prospective registrants were asked, in some instances, to give a reasonable interpretation of any provision of the state constitution. In others, they were requested to read and explain any article of the federal Constitution. The choice of what was to be read and understood was left to the discretion of local election officials, and in deference to the climate of opinion prevailing in the locality, the literacy test was used as a means of discrimination between Negro and white.[9]

The poll tax, a remnant of the property qualification, is now enforced in six southern states. An annual levy of one to two dollars is imposed on each voter. To vote one must present a poll tax receipt as evidence of payment. The tax originating in the nineties of the last century has had the effect of limiting the vote of both the poor white and the Negro. As a deterrent to voting, the tax has steadily

---

[7] Gosnell, *op. cit.,* p. 45.

[8] Lipson, *op. cit.,* p. 143.

[9] D. O. McGovney, *The American Suffrage Medley* (Chicago: The University of Chicago Press, 1949), pp. 60-62. Only the "grandfather clause" which sought to enfranchise the illiterate whites was declared unconstitutional by the Supreme Court. *Guinn v. U. S.* 238 U. S. 347 (1915).

lost its effectiveness and is being abandoned gradually by the southern states.[10]

White primary. Exclusion of the Negro from participation in the primary of the Democratic party was yet another means devised for nullifying the potential political power of the Negro voter. The real contest for office and power in most southern states has taken place in the Democratic party primary rather than at the election where the results have been usually a foregone conclusion. In the South, therefore, exclusion of the Negro voter from the primaries in effect has deprived him of his power to affect the outcome of the election. With the coming of the direct primary, the possibility arose that the Negro might influence the choice of candidates for office. Southern leaders, on the basis of the Newberry case [11] decision in 1921, assumed that the primary was not part of the election process and proceeded to deny to the Negro the right to participate in the Democratic party primary.

The outcome of such thinking was the white primary. Because of its potentiality for muting the political voice of the Negro, it was not accepted without resistance. Indeed, the white primary was the subject of constant legal challenge for almost three decades. It first received attention in Texas where an especially bitter primary battle between two factions for a local office led both sides to make an active attempt to enlist the support of the Negro voter. This was followed in 1923 by the passage of a statute that stated that "in no event shall a Negro be eligible to participate in a Democratic primary" and furthermore that "should a Negro vote in a Democratic primary, the ballot shall be void." When appealed to the Supreme Court, the law was declared to be a violation of the "equal protection" clause of the fourteenth amendment.[12]

Legal challenges. Faced by this rebuff from the courts, and still desiring to prevent the Negro from voting in the primary, the legislature of Texas passed a new law authorizing "every political party in this State through its State Executive committee . . . to prescribe the qualifications of its own members and shall in its own way determine who shall be qualified to vote or otherwise participate in such a political party." Following this rule, the state committee adopted a

[10] Gosnell, *op. cit.*, pp. 25, 32, 96.

[11] *Newberry v. U. S.*, 356 U. S. 232 (1921). The Supreme Court refused to apply to the primaries a federal law governing expenditures in a general election.

[12] *Nivon v. Herdon*, 273 U. S. 536 (1927).

regulation denying to the Negro the right to vote in the Democratic primary. Again there came a legal challenge and again the law of the state was held to be discriminatory and as such violative of the fourteenth amendment.[13]

Both of these decisions contained the clear intimation that if a state in some way was a party to a discriminatory action against the Negro, the fourteenth amendment could be invoked. Texas, therefore, took no further action, but the state Democratic convention in 1932, acting on its own initiative, limited participation in the Democratic party primary to white citizens. A Negro appeal to the courts resulted in the ruling that there was no denial of rights under either the fourteenth or fifteenth amendments.

In the light of its later decisions, the reasoning of the court in this instance is interesting, if not appealing. The resolution of a party convention, in its view, was merely a refusal of party membership by a private group. Every group had the right to determine the qualifications of its members. This was a matter with which "the state need have no concern" since it was not directly involved.[14] The key to the decision is to be found in the court's conclusion that the political party was not an organ of the state. The attitude of the court may have been myopic, but its consequences were far-reaching. As long as the state was not involved and the political party *itself* undertook discriminatory action, the Negro had no way of gaining the right to vote in the party primary.

The Classic case. Thus matters stood until 1941. The white primary, according to Harold Gosnell, became one of the most effective means for limiting the political power of the Negro.[15] The Negro could vote if he were able to hurdle the various registration barriers, but even if he did, it meant little in view of the fact that victory in the Democratic primary meant that the result in the election would be a foregone conclusion. In that year, however, a suit was brought by the federal government against Classic and other commissioners of elections in the city of New Orleans on the grounds that they had conspired to deprive individuals of their rights "secured by the Constitution," and, more specifically, rights protected by an ancient enforcement statute passed shortly after the end of the Civil War. Classic and his associates had altered and falsely

[13] *Nixon v. Condon,* 286 U. S. 73 (1932).
[14] *Grovey v. Townsend,* 295 U. S. 45 (1935).
[15] Gosnell, *op. cit.,* p. 96.

counted and certified the ballots of voters cast in a primary for a Democratic candidate for Congress. In upholding the conviction, the Supreme Court pointed out that where "the state law has made the primary an integral part of the procedure of choice, or where in fact the primary effectively controls the choice, the right of the elector to have his ballot counted at the primary, is likewise included. . . ."[16] By inference at least, the Supreme Court seemed to say that Congressional primaries were part of the election process and that the federal government, if it desired, could maintain the integrity of the primaries.

Present status of the white primary. The decision in the Classic case introduced an element of uncertainty. It was clear that the dictum handed down was in obvious conflict with its 1935 ruling in the *Grovey v. Townsend* case. But did this mean that the court had decided to outlaw the white primary? In 1944 the attitude of the court was clarified in the *Smith v. Allwright* decision. At issue once more was the same white primary convention resolution that had been upheld by the court as a private action in 1935. This time the court left no doubt as to its stand. It asserted that the political party was acting as an agent of the state, and therefore that the state was involved if discriminatory action took place. It also voiced the opinion that the right to vote in the primary "for the nomination of candidates without discrimination, like the right to vote in a general election, is a right secured by the constitution. . . ."[17] In other words, a political party that was entrusted by Texas law with the power to determine the qualifications of its members could not act in a discriminatory fashion, and if it did, then those affected could invoke the protection of the fifteenth amendment. The previous ruling of *Grovey v. Townsend* was overruled.

Reaction of the Southern States. Space does not permit a detailed account of the various efforts of the southern states to circumvent the effects of the *Smith v. Allwright* decision. Their response, to put the matter succinctly, was varied. In Texas, following the decision, Negro voters who paid their poll taxes were permitted to vote in the Democratic primary "more or less freely in many counties."[18] Where elections were conducted in Texas municipalities on a non-

16 *U. S. v. Classic,* 313 U. S. 300 (1941).

17 *Smith v. Allwright,* 321 U. S. 651 (1944).

18 O. D. Weeks, "The White Primary: 1944–1948," *The American Political Science Review,* XLII (1948), p. 501.

partisan basis, the Negro, of course, was not affected by the white primary. The Negro vote in municipal elections has become significant in Dallas, Fort Worth, San Antonio, Port Arthur and Houston. It is the conviction of one responsible observer that Negro voting on the municipal level "was there to stay." Indeed, he reports, the practice has now received wide acceptance. One reservation, however, was noted. The Negro was rarely a candidate for public office.[19]

In other states, the reaction was somewhat more determined. Louisiana, North Carolina, and Virginia repealed their white primary laws but continued their literacy tests, presumably in somewhat strengthened form. Alabama followed suit, requiring voters in the primary to be able to "understand and explain" provisions of the federal Constitution selected by local officials. Presumably this would have opened the door to discriminatory practices upon the part of registration officials, but despite the fact that neither color nor race was mentioned in the statute, the courts recognized the intent of the requirement and refused to permit it to be used as a means for circumventing the decision in the *Smith v. Allwright* case.[20] Arkansas and Mississippi acknowledged that they could no longer maintain the white primary, but, in its stead, the Democratic party in these states required that party voters be made loyal to party principles. For a while Arkansas even went to the lengths of setting up separate primaries for state and federal offices, hoping to thus maintain its control over the former, but this device was soon repealed. Georgia pursued a hesitant course, first making the party a private organization by removing all references to it in state law, and then, in 1946, deciding to admit Negroes, since the repeal of laws governing primaries opened the way to the possibility of fraud.[21]

South Carolina adopted a tactic similar to that of Georgia, save that it persisted in it. It sought to resurrect the judicial thinking in the *Grovey v. Townsend* case by converting the political party into a private club. If this could be done, then the state could not be accused of discrimination under either the fourteenth or the fifteenth amendments. In accordance with this reasoning, all constitutional and statutory references to the political party were eliminated. Then the Democratic party refused to permit the Negro

---

19 D. S. Strong, "The Rise of Negro Voting in Texas," *American Political Science Review,* XLII (1948), pp. 511, 518, 520-522.

20 *Schnell v. Davis,* 336 U. S. 933 (1949) which reaffirmed a decision of a District Court.

21 Weeks, *op. cit.,* pp. 503-507.

to vote in the primary. But the stratagem of the party was of no avail. The district court, in a decision affirmed by the Supreme Court, held that it did not matter whether the party was a public or private organization. Where the party primary controls the election choice, a vote in the primary was held to be equivalent to that of a vote in the general election and was to be surrounded with the same protections as applied to the latter.[22]

Future trends. It is not too easy to assess the impact of these decisions upon Negro suffrage in the South. One thing seems fairly certain; the political party will no longer be able to practice discrimination upon the ground that it is a private party. Whether new discriminatory election practices will occur remains to be seen. But the concentration of the Negro city vote in such key states as New York, Pennsylvania, Ohio, Michigan and Illinois may have a decisive effect upon the outcome of a presidential election and this, in turn, may have a bearing upon the attitude of the federal government.[23] From what has been said above there is no doubt that the national government has the power to deal with both primary and election violations. Whether it will act or not will depend largely upon the "control function" of the northern Negro.[24] The present status of Negro suffrage in the South seems best summarized by Professor Weeks: "The decision (*Smith v. Allwright*) will not, however, dispose of all remaining suffrage and registration hurdles in the way of the Negro, nor will it insure that his vote, if cast, will always be counted. There will need to be legislation and litigation if these obstacles are to be removed." [25] The legal repeal of discriminatory legislation when combined with the key role of the northern Negro will undoubtedly result in the enhancement of the southern Negro's political power.

REGISTRATION

Meaning and importance. If majority rule is to reflect faithfully the wishes of the people, it is essential that a process exist that eliminates or at least minimizes the possibility of fraud. The votes are not synonymous with the "people." In the previous pages we have

[22] *Elmore v. Rice,* 72 F. Supp. 516 (1947), affirmed by the Supreme Court in *Rice v. Elmore,* 333 U. S. 875 (1948).

[23] H. L. Moon, *Balance of Power: The Negro Vote* (New York: Doubleday & Co., 1948), p. 198 ff.

[24] Gosnell, *op. cit.,* pp. 98-106.

[25] Weeks, *op. cit.,* p. 510.

indicated that only those who meet the requirements established by the state can vote. The rationale behind such action is not hard to ascertain. Maintenance of voter eligibility is essential if voting frauds are to be avoided. This is insured through a practice known as registration, defined as the formal process by which public authorities decide who is entitled to vote.[26] It is the opinion of one of the leading students of the subject that registration is "one of the most important safeguards of the purity of the ballot box." [27]

An urban problem. Registration is primarily the concern of an urban society. In rural areas it was relatively easy for an election official to check voter eligibility since, in most instances, the potential voter was known to him. When the country was rural, therefore, registration was the exception rather than the rule. Massachusetts, which passed a law in 1800, may be considered the pioneer in this respect. Pennsylvania in 1836 and New York in 1840 also adopted similar statutes, although these were limited to Philadelphia and New York City.[28]

In the decades after the Civil War the pattern changed. More and more states adopted registration statutes. The reason for this trend is not hard to find. The stepped-up pace of urbanization brought with it many by-products: the mass migration from farm and overseas to the city; the anonymity and mobility of the city dweller; and the impersonality of city life. Under such conditions, floaters, repeaters, colonization, and the padding of registration lists with nonexistent persons were common. Indeed, there was hardly a city that did not have election irregularities and "many varieties of downright fraud." [29] It was soon obvious to most persons that rural reliance upon the personal knowledge of a voter's qualifications was no longer possible. A system had to be devised for determining voter eligibility. This was done and, although few states have registration statutes that cover the entire state, every state of the union except Arkansas or Texas now has a law governing at least the urban areas. However, both of the latter states have a poll tax requirement which

[26] J. P. Harris, *Registration of Voters in the United States* (Washington, D. C.: The Brookings Institution, 1929), p. 4. He defines registration as the ". . . determination of what persons are qualified to vote."

[27] *Idem.*

[28] *Ibid.*, pp. 65, 72.

[29] Harris, *op. cit.*, pp. 3-4, 8.

compels the voter to disclose the pertinent facts concerning his eligibility.[30]

Despite the passage of registration statutes, frauds continued to occur. Indeed violations were so numerous as to cast doubts upon the efficacy of the entire system. The ineffectiveness of existing arrangements for the determination of voter eligibility was highlighted by a report of the National Municipal League's Committee on Election Administration, which in 1927 pointed out that few states had workable registration systems. In a more comprehensive study published two years later Professor Harris, who was also a member of the League's Committee, reaffirmed its conclusions. Frauds and violations were common in large urban areas. Strangely enough, he found that those systems that were most costly also were most ineffective.[31] The inability of the then existing registration systems to cope with the problem of urban voter eligibility was attributed by him to several factors: (1) use of bipartisan boards, (2) absence of central supervision of the registration process, (3) unwieldly and virtually unusable election records, and (4) ineffective procedures for checking and correcting registration lists.[32] Since the publication of these pioneering studies, a great deal of progress has been made. Voter identification by signature has been adopted in slightly less than half of the states of the Union, but this is a substantial advance over what it was originally.[33] Effective and relatively inexpensive registration systems have been adopted by approximately three-fourths of the states.[34] Thirty-three states have state-wide permanent registration systems: twelve have systems in partial form, mainly in the urban areas.

Systems of registration. Registration systems employed in this country are of several kinds—personal or nonpersonal, compulsory or noncompulsory, permanent or periodic, or finally, some combination of these. When the voter is required to appear at the polling place, registration is personal. Where the election official makes up the voting list independently of the voter, registration is nonper-

---

30 J. P. Harris, "Registration of Voters," *Encyclopaedia of Social Sciences,* XIII, p. 219.

31 Harris, *op. cit.,* p. 16.

32 Harris, *op. cit.,* pp. 24-25.

33 National Municipal League, *Model Voter Registration System* (New York: The National Municipal League, 1954), pp. 10-11. Twenty-one states now use this method of identification.

34 *The Book of States,* 1954–1955, p. 83.

sonal. Contrary to what seems to be the popular impression, nonpersonal registration still exists in this country, although it is confined to the rural areas.[35] Registration is usually compulsory, that is, a person is required to register before he can vote. This arrangement is almost universal, but situations do exist that permit voters to vote if their qualifications are vouched for by two other voters.[36]

Permanent and periodic registration. Registration may be either permanent or periodic. The chief difference between the two is implicit in their names. Under periodic registration voters are required to register each year during a stated time before the election. When the election is over the lists are discarded, and the following year a new registration list must be made up again. Many large cities employ this method, even though it has been repeatedly criticized as being both costly and ineffective. The chief justification for the continuance of the system apparently lies in the fact that its adherents believe that re-registration is an effective device for purging the election rolls each year.

Yet a careful scrutiny of the procedures employed would indicate that the contrary is actually the case, for the system places major stress on the compilation of a list of eligibles with little or no attempt to determine actually whether those who appear are actually entitled to vote.[37] With so little time between registration and election, hardly more than a cursory check can be made of the registrant's statements to the polling officials. The phantom voter and the "colony" are an ever-present menace to the periodic registration system. Indeed, at one time or another it has been a feature of all such arrangements.

Permanent registration, in its most elemental form, is simply a procedure which enables a voter, once registered, to continue his eligibility without the necessity for further application to the registrar. As such, it is hardly more than the system prevalent in most rural areas, where either the election officials make up the voter roster or the individual makes application. The danger of padded registration lists and the lack of a means for systematically purging the voter rolls are not eliminated. This type of permanent registration exists in forty-four states, either in whole or in part.

---

[35] In New York, nonpersonal registration exists in towns and villages with a population of less than five thousand persons.

[36] Harris, *op. cit.*, pp. 110-111, said that seven states have this requirement.

[37] *Ibid.*, pp. 99-100.

Permanent personal registration is a modern system for determining voter eligibility. It combines many of the features common to other systems. The voter must appear in person to register, and once registered he remains upon the voter rolls as long as he remains at the same address. But the similarity ends at this point. Unlike the other methods, permanent personal registration employs a permanent staff chosen on a nonpartisan, merit basis. Registration is no longer a bipartisan operation where honesty was to be ensured by the check of one party against another. Instead, the new system operates on a full-time professional basis and seeks to facilitate both ease of registration and the purging of voter rolls. Under it, the voter can register at a central office throughout the year and at stated times prior to the election. Precinct registration is eliminated. When the voter moves, a simple procedure, usually the mailing of his identification card to the central office, is sufficient to re-establish his eligibility.

It is obvious that permanence of registration rolls implies the necessity of a means for keeping the list accurate and up to date. Without some provision along this line the system would be virtually worthless. It is not surprising, therefore, that means have been devised to make the system in this respect almost foolproof. The methods are almost too numerous to be described. A few might be mentioned briefly. Boston employs its police to make a house-to-house canvass of adults and compares its census with that of the voting roster. In some municipal jurisdictions, lodging houses are required to list their occupants. In some cities, election officials use death notices and public utility reports listing requests for changes in service. In all modern registration systems there is a continuous check on voter eligibility throughout the year instead of the hurried process of the periodic system where a short interval between registration and election places major reliance upon the fact that a new list is made up each year. Finally, almost all permanent personal registration systems stipulate that registration will be automatically canceled unless the voter exercises his franchise within a given period of time.[38]

Evaluation of permanent personal registration. When compared with the periodic registration system, its chief competitor,

[38] Harris, *op. cit.*, p. 224. St. Paul, Denver and Salt Lake City cancel registration if votes are not cast within a two year period. Philadelphia compels the voter to re-register if he has not voted at least once in four years.

permanent personal registration, in the opinion of many qualified observers, has many features that represent a distinct advance. Its proponents claim the following advantages for it: It simplifies the task of the voter; it prevents frauds; and it is economical to operate.[39] Supporters also have accumulated considerable data to buttress their assertions. On the score of voter convenience, they point to the fact that the voter can register at any time during the year and, once having registered, he remains on the voting roster. They are willing to concede the fact that registration at a central office instead of a precinct, as is possible under the periodic system, does represent a slight inconvenience, but they argue that if the voter values his franchise he will register anyway.[40]

Most objections to permanent personal registration center around the fear that it will result in padded registration lists and inflated voter rolls. Those who argue in this vein point out that, whatever demerits inherent in the periodic system, at least it has the virtue of automatically purging the voting lists each year. From this they conclude that, in large urban centers where mobility and impersonality exist, only periodic registration can cope with the situation. That there is ground for such a belief can be gauged from a brief review of statistics. In a single year, 1950, twenty-two percent of the names were removed from the voting rolls in Los Angeles.[41] In Philadelphia where the registration system had been under intense scrutiny by both state and federal agencies in the period 1937–1941, it was estimated that the padding of the rolls ranged from 9.2 to 11.8 percent of the total registration.[42] The concern of the opponents of permanent personal registration is real only if an effective means for revising the voter roster does not exist, for as Professor Harris has remarked, "an unsound permanent system is more dangerous than an unsound periodic system." [43] The fact is, however, that the system of permanent personal registration with its great stress on the purging of the rolls has shown that it can cope effectively with this problem. It is at least as competent as the

---

39 *Model Voter Registration System, op. cit.*, pp. 17-24. The proponents are members of the Committee on Model Voter Registration of the National Municipal League.

40 When permanent personal registration systems are installed, the first registration is usually on a precinct basis in order to avoid overburdening the central office. Once the lists are complete, registration is then on a central office basis.

41 *Ibid.*, p. 26.

42 J. P. Horlacher, "The Administration of Permanent Registration in Philadelphia," *American Political Science Review*, XXXVII, No. 5 (October 1943), pp. 830-831.

43 Harris, *op. cit.*, p. 19.

periodic system. Indeed, the experience of larger cities has been uniformly good in this respect.[44]

On the matter of cost, supporters of permanent personal registration maintain that their system is more economical. Statistical data have been mustered to show that, with few exceptions, the cost per registrant under the permanent system is less than that under the periodic system. A study in 1929 by Professor Harris led to the conclusion that, although there was a wide variation in registration expenses, the cost of the permanent system was one half to one tenth that of the periodic system. A similar conclusion was reached by him in a survey conducted in 1954. Permanent personal registration costs in nine cities and counties ranged from a low of 10.5 cents for Detroit to highs of 53.8 and 55.1 cents in Boston and Philadelphia respectively. The average annual cost per registrant was 32.0 cents.[45] New York City, which uses the periodic system, had a higher cost per registrant than Los Angeles, San Francisco, Seattle, Detroit, and Milwaukee. Its costs, however, were roughly equal to that of Chicago, and lower than Philadelphia and Boston.[46]

Aside from statistics, the administrative situation under which periodic registration operates makes for great waste. Each year, annual registration must hurdle such obstacles as: the rental of polling booths; the bipartisan choice of precinct officials; the printing of registration books. All of these are expensive items. In 1952 New York City employed four officials for each precinct at a city-wide cost of $778,441. For the same period publication costs were approximately $270,000.[47] These items—personnel, rentals, and printing—are costly under any periodic system. They exist also under the permanent system, but by the use of a full-time operation and the professionalization of staff, these expense items are kept at a reasonable level.

Since its adoption by Boston in 1896, permanent personal registration has made great strides. Almost all the large urban centers except those in the South have made provision for its use on a state-

---

44 Philadelphia during the early period of permanent personal registration may be considered an exception to the general rule; see Horlacher, *op. cit.*, pp. 829-837. But he does make the point that the system must be free from political interference if it is to work. Boston, Chicago, Detroit, Cleveland, Cincinnati and San Francisco are some of the large cities that have been able to conduct their registration without fraud.

45 *Model Voter Registration Systems*, p. 18.

46 *Ibid.*, p. 20.

47 *Ibid.*, pp. 20-21

wide basis.[48] The prospect is that there will be further adoptions of the plan.

ELECTIONS

Election administration, like registration systems, is a primary concern of urban communities, although rural areas are not without their problems in this regard. But it is different in the city where impersonality makes voter identification difficult. When this is combined with the high stakes involved in the control of municipal government, a potentially dangerous situation is created, a fact unfortunately demonstrated by the political history of the city during the second half of the nineteenth century. The temptation to engage in fraud, needless to say, was great and irregularities occurred with astonishing frequency. As the country became more highly urbanized, the maintenance of the integrity of elections became the concern of an increasing number of municipalities. Many election improvements have occurred since the founding of the country, but many more will be required before the reformer and the interested citizen will be satisfied.

Early elections. Early voting methods were rather primitive. Officials were chosen by either a voice vote or a show of hands. In the second quarter of the nineteenth century, as the country began to feel the dim stirring of urbanization, the paper ballot was added. Party organizations and candidates began to print their own tickets, and these were then marked with the voter's choice. None of these methods was acceptable, and all were open to abuses. Both the voice vote and the show of hands deprived the voter of the secrecy of choice, subjecting him to intimidation. Originally it was thought that the paper ballot would remedy these weaknesses, but it, too, was subverted by the necessities of politics. Ballots were printed on paper of various colors, thus identifying the party supporting the candidate. Soon the practice of voting the straight ticket became a standard procedure. State actions prescribing a uniform color for the ballots of all parties were nullified by the use of paper of varying thicknesses. In addition, the private printing of ballots gave corrupt politicians an opportunity to stuff the ballot boxes, since two votes could often be as easily cast as one.[49]

48 *The Book of States 1954–1955,* pp. 80-81. In New York (1954) the adoption of the system has been made optional by counties.

49 J. P. Harris, *Election Administration in the United States* (Washington, D. C.: The Brookings Institution, 1934), Ch. 4.

The Australian ballot. In the post Civil War period the rapid growth of cities, accompanied by a rising tide of immigration, made the system described above almost unworkable. Manipulation of both ballots and recently arrived minorities, together with a host of other factors, not only led to the growth and perpetuation of corrupt machines but also threatened to make a mockery out of the election process. In the last quarter of the nineteenth century as the situation threatened to get out of hand, the Australian ballot was introduced into this country. First to adopt it on a state-wide basis was Massachusetts in 1888, although the city of Louisville was also authorized to use it during the same year. A year later the state of New York followed suit. Thereafter, although attacked by city machines as "unfair," it gained wide acceptance. It is now used in almost every state of the Union.[50]

The Australian ballot differed from its predecessor in many respects. First, it was printed at public expense. In elections where it was used there was only one ballot and that ballot could be obtained only from an appropriate election official. Custody of the ballot, in other words, remained in the hands of election officials before, during, and after the vote was cast. Fraud and ballot stuffing might continue, but the blame for irregularities would rest upon the heads of election officials. Secondly, because of the uniformity of the ballot, voter secrecy was protected. Finally, since ballots were printed at public expense they could only contain the names of authorized candidates. All of these features represented a distinct advance over the previous system of balloting.

Although the central idea of the Australian ballot was accepted, there were many modifications made to fit American practice. While the Australian ballot listed candidates for each office with party designations, our version reflected the needs of party politics. Party labels or symbols and other means of identification were employed to indicate the candidates' affiliation. Ultimately two main kinds of ballots were developed: the office block and party column types. The former, employed by Massachusetts and approximately a dozen other states, lists the names of candidates under the title of the office to be filled. Straight ticket voting is more difficult with this ballot. The party column type, as its name implies, lists candidates according to party designation or, more correctly, in party columns.[51] Per-

[50] The exceptions are Georgia, Delaware and South Carolina.
[51] H. F. Gosnell, "Ballots," *Encyclopaedia of Social Sciences,* II, pp. 411-412.

haps because it facilitates party voting, it has been adopted by thirty-five states. When these changes are coupled with the long ballot so prevalent in this country, the Australian ballot may be characterized as a mere shadow of its former self.

The short ballot. It was the belief that the long ballot was largely responsible for voter ignorance that led to yet another reform of the ballot, the short ballot. The movement, fathered by Richard S. Childs in 1909, had as its objective heightened voter intelligence. In his study, *Short Ballot Principles,* he compared a ballot of Los Angeles measuring twenty-three by thirty-two inches with one in England, the latter, one inch by two inches in size. "The ballot," he asserted, "must be kept short. How short? Short enough. . . ." [52] Its principles, as stated by Childs, were "First—that only those offices should be elective which are important enough to attract *and deserve* public scrutiny. Second—that very few offices should be filled by election at one time, so as to permit adequate and unconfused scrutiny of the candidates by the public, and *so as to facilitate the full and intelligent making of original tickets by any voter for himself unaided by political specialists.*" [53] The idea soon received nation-wide attention. In the period 1910–1914 it was accepted in California, Oregon, and Pennsylvania. Charles Evans Hughes urged its adoption in New York. Soon it was made part of the commission form of government and benefited from its popularity.

At the beginning of World War I it was made part of the program of the National Municipal League and, as such, it received added support. The trend toward greater concentration of authority in the strong-mayor and council-manager forms of government, as well as the growth of the merit system, led to a still further advancement of the idea.[54] Childs cites several major developments: the reduction in the size of the city council of New York City in 1937 from 70 to 25; that of Philadelphia from a bicameral body of 145 to a unicameral unit of 21; the general adoption of strong executives and small councils in such widely separated cities as San Francisco, Boston, Detroit, and Pittsburgh.[55] He might well have employed a host of other illustrations to buttress his record of accomplishment. Another by-product of the short ballot was the movement to separate

52 R. S. Childs, *Short Ballot Principles* (Boston: Houghton Mifflin, 1911), pp. 1, 30.

53 R. S. Childs, *Civic Victories* (New York: Harper and Bros., 1952), p. 84. Italics in text.

54 *Ibid.,* pp. 80-90.

55 *Ibid.,* p. 189.

national, state and local elections by holding them in alternate years. Thus, in the relatively short span of fifty years, there has been an almost complete reversal in our thinking about accountability of our public officers. Today, in principle at least, the idea of the short ballot to check on the performance of our officials is almost universally acknowledged.[56]

Nonpartisan election officials. The actual mechanics for recording the will of the people is yet another area where reform was, and is still, needed, despite the many improvements made within the last twenty years. On the surface, the election process seems rather simple. The voter on Election Day enters the polling place, establishes his eligibility to vote, and then casts his ballot.

Behind the scenes, however, a vast number of arrangements have been made even before the voter arrives. Election districts or precincts have been laid out and voters have been assigned on the basis of residence. Each election precinct is manned by a precinct election committee, and it, in turn, has been made subject to some type of central supervision, usually a city-wide election board. The latter, subject to the state law, not only issues regulations and directives for the conduct of elections, but is also responsible for such housekeeping functions as the selection of polling places, supplies, paper ballots or voting machines, and the preparation of voting lists for purposes of voter identification. Both the central and the local units occupy key positions and the integrity of elections rests largely on their shoulders.

The counting of votes usually begins some time during the voting day. Although the citizen may assume in good faith that the votes will be honestly counted, the law leaves nothing to chance. Very properly, and in great detail, it specifies the manner in which the count will be conducted by appropriate officials. If paper ballots are employed, they are opened and tallied in the presence of accredited watchers from the major parties. If voting machines are used, the results on the voting machine counter are read aloud and the returns are recorded. Election returns are then certified by the appropriate official. In either instance, paper ballots or voting machines, ballot boxes or machines are sealed until a specified statutory period, usually sixty days, has passed. Local returns are then consolidated at a central place and the results are then announced.[57]

---

[56] This does not mean, of course, that we do not still have the long ballot.
[57] Harris, *op. cit.*, pp. 207-209, 213-215.

Inadequacy of election procedures. On the face of it at least, the procedure seems to be reasonably efficient, but as one examines the procedures more closely, there are a number of weaknesses that soon become apparent. For one thing, the system of election administration is based almost entirely on bipartisanship. Both the central and the local election boards, presumably on the theory that one party will act as a check on the other, are usually bipartisan in composition. In theory, at least, the central unit is supposed to appoint the local election units and supervise their activities. Actually local election boards are composed of party workers who are nominated by the party organizations. Since the political complexion of the central office parallels that at the local level, precinct election committees have a minimum of supervision.

Moreover, since appointments are made invariably with political considerations in mind, there is a decided lack of professionalization. The corrosive impact of the political factor upon the quality of the work force was demonstrated by the experience of New York City. There the employees of the election boards for years were appointed upon the basis of a mock examination where answers to questions were supplied in advance to prospective employees. A two-year inquiry into election administration by the Commissioner of Investigations revealed evidence of widespread incompetence among election personnel. In a properly administered test, it was found that only 12.3 percent of the 1,790 individuals were able to get a grade of 60 percent.[58] The role of political employees on election boards has been significantly noted by an eminent authority in the following words: "The precinct officer determines the character of elections." [59]

The remedy for this fundamental weakness is the appointment on a nonpartisan basis of qualified personnel selected upon the basis of a competitive examination. It is only in this manner that the ties to the political organization can be broken. Citing the trend in this direction in the cities of Minnesota and Wisconsin, Professor Harris hails the selection of precinct officers by competitive examination as "the most important development in election administration for many years." [60] He predicted that it would be widely adopted, par-

---

[58] J. P. Harris, "Election Developments in 1940," *The National Municipal Yearbook for 1941,* p. 533.

[59] Harris, *op. cit.,* p. 126.

[60] *Ibid.*

ticularly in the larger cities and, as a result, would bring great improvements in election administration.

Cost of elections. Significantly, the ineffective utilization of election personnel is reflected in the high cost of elections. The nation's bill for the conduct of elections in the thirties was estimated at approximately $40 million. In view of the upward trend of costs, expenditures for the conduct of elections is much higher today. For the cities during the same period, measured by a four-year span, the cost per vote varied from 37 cents per vote in Minneapolis and Salt Lake City, to roughly twice that amount in Omaha and Denver. In large cities such as New York City, San Francisco, Chicago, and Kansas City the cost per vote was more than four times the minimum figure.[61] Reduction in costs may be obtained by intelligent utilization of voting machines, but the merits of this device are debatable, although it does assist in the honesty and accuracy of returns.[62] Economy also may be obtained by the adoption of the central count where the tally of returns is made by clerks in the central election office.[63] Professor Harris, however, argues that personnel expenditures constitute three-fourths of the election costs. Election officers are paid salaries that are far in excess of the responsibilities and duties required of them. He has estimated that the annual cost for conducting elections could be reduced to a quarter of what they presently are. One may, of course, argue that honesty and accuracy of election returns are the prime consideration, but this assertion cannot gainsay the fact that effective methods of election administration have a direct bearing upon the attainment of this objective.[64]

CONCLUSION

The roots of political behavior are deep in the American culture. Apathy, low voter interest, and, in some instances, corruption and fraud may be found in almost any city of the United States. Despite the presence of these factors in politics, the American people possess a deep and abiding faith in majority rule.

It is true that the faith of the people has been shaken by many

---

[61] Harris, *op. cit.*, pp. 386-387.

[62] Harris, *op. cit.*, pp. 62-63, 259-260, lists the cost factor, the increase in distance to the polls, high cost of maintenance, initial expenditure of $1,000 or more per machine and the rapid rate of obsolescence as some of the deterrents.

[63] San Francisco and the cities of Indiana have tried this method.

[64] Harris, *op. cit.*, pp. 385, 420.

political abuses brought to light by investigations, but it has not resulted in cynicism. Since the founding of the republic, Americans have persistently sought to improve the processes through which they express their approval or disapproval of the acts of their government. First there was the battle to widen the suffrage base in order that all might participate in the process of decision making. When urbanization made the problem of voter identification difficult, efforts were made to improve the system of registration. Political machine domination, especially in the cities, led reformers to demand and obtain such reforms as the direct primary, initiative, referendum, and recall. Preferential voting schemes and proportional representation were proposed in a similar vein. That many of these increased the burden of the voter and, in some instances, actually compounded the evils they sought to remedy is most certainly true. But, nevertheless, they still were a graphic demonstration of a belief in the capacity of the people to govern themselves. Until recently very little attention was paid to the election machinery, the means through which the people registered their choice at the polls. Here again a start has been made. One can predict that a complete overhaul, in the interest of both honesty and efficiency, will take place because the reforming zeal of the American public is not likely to fade away.

BIBLIOGRAPHY

Books:

Book of States, 1954–1955. Chicago: The Council of State Governments, 1954.

Childs, R. S. *Short Ballot Principles*. Boston: Houghton-Mifflin, 1911.

DeGrazia, A. *The Elements of Political Science*. New York: Alfred A. Knopf, Inc., 1952.

Encyclopaedia of the Social Sciences. Volume 2. 1st edition. Article. "Ballots."

Encyclopaedia of the Social Sciences. Volume 13. 1st edition. Article. "Registration of Votes."

Gosnell, H. F. *Democracy, the Threshold of Freedom*. New York: The Ronald Press, 1948.

Harris, J. P. *Election Administration in the United States*. Washington. D. C.: The Brookings Institute, 1934.

———. *Registration of Voters in the United States*. Washington, D. C.: The Brookings Institute, 1929.

McGovney, D. O. *The American Suffrage Medley.* Chicago: University of Chicago Press, 1949.

Moon, H. L. *Balance of Power: The Negro Vote.* New York: Doubleday and Co., 1948.

National Municipal League, *Model Vote Registration System.* New York: The National Municipal League, 1954. 4th edition.

National Municipal Yearbook for 1941. Chicago: The International City Managers' Association, 1941.

Periodicals and Other Material:

Horlacher, J. P. "The Administration of Permanent Registration in Philadelphia," *American Political Science Review,* XXXVII (1943), 829-837.

Strong, D. S. "The Rise of Negro Voting in Texas," *American Political Science Review,* XXXXII (1948), 510-522.

Weeks, O. D. "The White Primary: 1944–1948," *American Political Science Review,* XLII (1948), 500-509.

CHAPTER TEN

Devices of Direct Democracy

The American people display an ambivalent attitude in their politics. On substantive issues, except on rare occasions, they are almost apathetic, accepting abuses of power by their politicians with relative indifference. This is a tendency once described by a former governor of New Jersey, Charles A. Edison, in the following fashion: the American people, he asserted, were willing to send their sons overseas to fight dictators on foreign soil, but at home they permit individuals of similar inclination to fasten themselves on the body politic with little or no dissent.

Yet on matters concerned with the mechanics of election, Americans have demonstrated marked interest and ingenuity. Reforms of this nature have been accepted with enthusiasm, even where the practicality of such measures is often in doubt. This should not be taken to imply that there were no fundamental reasons for the adoption of various electoral devices. In fact, many of them came into being or were given prominence at the turn of the century when a tidal wave of protest swept the country. All the many reforms that originated during the progressive era had one fundamental objective: to increase the power of the people to manage their political affairs. Direct primaries, the Grand Junction or Bucklin plan, preferential voting, proportional representation, initiative, referendum, recall, all were efforts along this line. In the years that have gone by since that hopeful time, many of the dreams of the reformers have not materialized. None of the devices has seriously inconvenienced the "old pros," but these reforms do function as the "gun behind the door"; they are a means for checking arbitrary exercise of power.

NOMINATING METHODS

The evils of the caucus system. Like registration, the nominating process was forced to accommodate itself to the conditions of city life. Originally candidates for municipal office were nominated in a highly informal manner. A group of citizens met together and named a candidate for office. As cities grew in size, and as political parties became more highly developed, this arrangement no longer proved satisfactory. Party caucuses at the ward and district levels and city-wide conventions were employed in its stead. With minor modifications this was the procedure employed for a good part of the 19th century.

There were, however, a number of potential evils inherent in this scheme of things. Population concentration and closeness of living resulted in a rapid increase in the number of municipal functions. With the prevalence of the relatively immature administrative thinking—the belief that public officers could be controlled solely by the election process—the tendency was to create new offices whenever a new function was added. The consequent dispersal of power among a great many municipal agencies enabled the party to assume the role of centralizer. Nominations and elections, as a consequence, were often controlled by relatively few individuals within the party.[1]

Perhaps more important than this, however, was the fact that the entire nominating process was not subject to legal supervision. The abuses that developed undoubtedly contributed to the folklore of American municipal politics. Snap caucuses and conventions called without notice were the order of the day in many cities. Party leaders would pack a hall with their adherents and exclude their rivals. Strong-arm tactics, the use of thugs, the stuffing of ballot boxes at the convention, and a whole host of other frauds were sanctioned by the more unscrupulous political leaders. Control of political office yielded such lucrative rewards that there were few who were willing to surrender their authority without resort to every weapon at their command. Even those who were not inclined to engage in election malpractices were forced, by a sort of Gresham's law of politics, to conform in the fight for survival. Thus the law of the jungle, with no holds barred, prevailed in the political arena.

The seeming indifference of legally constituted authorities continued until at least the Civil War period. Then, beginning with New York in 1866, bribery, fraud, and intimidation in both nominations and elections were gradually outlawed. By the turn of the

[1] C. E. Merrian and L. Overacker, *Primary Elections* (Chicago: The University of Chicago Press, 1928), pp. 3-4, 278.

century the law of nominations and elections had been greatly improved.[2]

Early development of the primary. The primary is not a new political invention. It is at least a century old having originated in Crawford County, Pennsylvania where convention and caucus abuses led to its adoption.[3] Its acceptance on a wider scale did not occur until after the Civil War. The general mood of dissatisfaction with the then existing electoral system coupled with the coming of the Australian ballot in 1883 undoubtedly hastened the process of nominating reform.[4] The political party was given legal status and, with the adoption of a ballot printed at public expense, increased state regulation was bound to follow, and it did. By the turn of the nineteenth century the steps taken to safeguard the integrity of the election process were also applied to nominating procedures in most of the large cities with "varying degrees of severity." [5]

Reform of the nominating process received added impetus from the general movement for civic betterment current during the last quarter of the nineteenth century. Muckrakers and reformers exposed graft and corruption. The description of city government that emerged from their reform tracts was, in essence, the same as that noted by Lord Bryce; namely, that municipal government was the one conspicuous failure of America. Civic leaders in this country were appalled at what they saw and were stirred to action. Symptomatic of this feeling was the attitude of Brand Whitlock who wrote that ". . . the moral atmosphere of politics was foul and heavy with the feculence of all the debauchery that is inseparable from privilege." [6]

The reformers were not only indignant but they were also inspired to think and do something about the condition that they had

---

[2] Numerous studies of this phase of American politics exist. Of a general nature the most important are J. Bryce, *Modern Democracies,* 2 volumes (New York: The Macmillan Co., 1921), and M. Ostrogorski, *Democracy and the Organization of Political Parties,* 2 volumes (New York: The Macmillan Co., 1908). A few studies of a more specialized nature include, W. Riordan, *Plunkitt of Tammany Hall* (New York: Doubleday, Doran & Co., 1905), J. Bright, *Hizzoner Big Bill Thompson* (New York: J. Cape and H. Smith, 1930), and W. B. Munro, *Personality in Politics* (New York: The Macmillan Co., 1934).

[3] J. H. Booser, "Origin of the Direct Primary," *National Municipal Review,* XXIV (1935), pp. 222-223.

[4] T. H. Reed, *Municipal Government in the United States* (New York: D. Appleton-Century Co., Revised edition, 1934), pp. 237-238.

[5] Merriam and Overacker, *op. cit.,* pp. 26-27.

[6] B. Whitlock, *Forty Years of It* (New York: D. Appleton and Company, 1913), p. 95.

noted. Convinced that many of the abuses were a result of the fact that the people had not been given enough direct participation in government, they joined in the sponsorship of measures designed to permit people to select their own candidates for office. The voice of La Follette was representative of this spirit: "Abolish the caucus and convention. Go back to the first principles of democracy; go back to the people. Substitute for both the caucus and the convention a primary election—held under the sanctions of law which prevail at the general elections. . . . The nomination of the party will not be the result of 'compromise' or impulse, or evil design—the 'barrel' and the machine—but the candidates of the majority honestly and fairly nominated." [7]

La Follette's clarion call for greater participation by the people was put into practice in 1903 when Wisconsin adopted the first statewide primary law. Thereafter, despite the initial opposition, the primary gained wide acceptance. By 1917 all but four of the states had the direct primary in some form or other.[8] Today a similar use of the primary has spread to every state of the union.[9]

A primary is a party election to select its candidates for office.[10] It is, in La Follette's words, "a system where the citizen may cast his vote directly to nominate the candidate of the party with which he affiliates and have it returned just as he cast it. . . ." [11] It may also be described, perhaps more realistically, in these words: "The direct primary nominating procedure may be regarded . . . as a formal procedure superimposed over a pre-existing informal organization." [12] It is, in brief, a means by which the voter is given a greater voice than was formerly the case in the nomination of candidates for office. The primary, however, does not eliminate party caucusing prior to the primary election, nor does it outlaw the presentation of a party slate to the party voter.

Acknowledgement of the principle of voter choice in the nomination as well as the election of candidates meant increasing state

---

7 R. M. La Follette, *La Follette's Autobiography,* (4th edition; Madison, Wisconsin: R. M. La Follette Co., 1920), pp. 197-198.

8 L. Overacker, "Primaries, Political," *Encyclopaedia of Social Sciences,* XII, p. 396.

9 *Book of States, 1952–1953,* p. 78. Forty-three states have a statewide primary, while four employ it on an optional basis. In 1955 Connecticut adopted the primary which will go into effect on January, 1956.

10 Overacker, *op. cit.*

11 La Follette, *op. cit.*

12 V. O. Key, Jr., "The Direct Primary and Party Structure: A Study of State Legislative Nominations," *American Political Science Review,* XVIII (March 1950), p. 2.

supervision to insure the integrity of the nominating process. The terms and conditions under which primaries are held in municipalities are a matter of state election law. Although the political parties have a hand in the enactment of such statutes, once they are adopted, they govern the actions and behavior of all political parties. Primaries, for example, are mandatory in most states. Majority parties, or those polling a specified number of votes in the last preceding election, are required to make their nominations through the primary in accordance with the procedure specified in state law. In Rhode Island any party that polls five percent of the total vote cast for governor in the last election must employ the primary.[13] Voter qualifications for the primary are also spelled out in state law and, aside from the question of party allegiance, are the same as those for the general election. In brief, the conduct of nominations under public auspices has meant that the safeguards protecting the integrity of elections were also applied to the nominating process.

Types of primaries. Primary elections are of two main kinds: partisan and nonpartisan. The former category, most widely used, may be subdivided into the closed and open primary. In the thirty-six states that employ the closed primary, the party voter must, by some overt act, indicate his affiliation with the party in whose primary he seeks to cast his vote. This is usually accomplished at registration time when the voter can declare that he is in accord with the principles of the party by signing a statement to that effect.[14] In some states the challenge method is employed. Usually this means merely that provision is made for the voter to affirm under oath that he is a party member if his eligibility is questioned at the time he is about to cast his vote in the primary. The closed primary gives the party voter little choice. When he appears at the polling place, he is given a ballot printed at public expense which contains the names of members of his party who are candidates. He may write in names, but he cannot "cross vote" or show his independence in any other way.

Contrariwise, in the open primary no effort is made to determine party loyalty. The voter who appears at the polls on primary day

[13] *Book of States, 1952–1953, op. cit.*, p. 78. In Tennessee the primary is compulsory unless a party does not receive ten percent of the votes. A somewhat similar provision exists in Indiana.

[14] New York City is a good example of a municipality employing this method. In addition to the state of New York, some eighteen other states use this method of determining party loyalty.

receives the ballots of all parties. He may vote for the candidates of one party but cannot split his vote among the ballots of all parties. After voting, the voter places both marked and unmarked ballots in different receptacles. In this manner the secrecy of his choice is protected. It is possible for him to participate in the primary of either party without fear of detection. The open primary, used in eleven states, has not received as wide acceptance as the closed primary.[15]

Somewhat similar in principle to the open primary, although it goes far beyond it in practice, is the state of Washington system of "cross voting" or "blanket primary" adopted in that state in 1935. Under the provisions of this law the voter receives a single-column ballot arranged in office-column style. Voting is carried out in the same fashion as the general election. The objective, however, is to nominate rather than to elect candidates.[16]

The nonpartisan primary. The nonpartisan primary, and indeed the nonpartisan election, is based upon the assumption that national and local issues are distinct and separate. It assumes, further, that many local questions have no connection whatsoever with the national questions which the voter is called upon to decide when he ballots for the President or members of Congress. Whether this separation really exists is a moot point.[17] But it is a fact that the nonpartisan primary has gained fairly wide acceptance. In a study made in 1946 of 2,033 cities with a population of more than 5,000 it was found that approximately 57 percent of these employed the nonpartisan primary in the choice of councilmanic candidates. When one examines the uses of this device in different forms of government, its popularity is even more remarkable. Seventy-six percent of the commission government and 83.5 percent of the council-manager cities employ this device. Even more extraordinary is the fact that 43.6 percent of the mayor-council cities have adopted nonpartisan elections.[18]

The nonpartisan primary may be characterized as nomination by

[15] *Book of States, 1952–1953, op. cit.*, p. 78.

[16] D. M. Ogden, Jr., "Parties Survive Cross Voting," *National Municipal Review*, XXXIX (1952), pp. 237-238.

[17] Compare W. Wilson, *Constitutional Government in the United States* (New York: Columbia University Press, 1921), pp. 207-208 with C. A. Beard, "Politics and City Government," *National Municipal Review*, VI (1917), p. 202.

[18] The International City Managers' Association, *The Municipal Yearbook* (Chicago: 1946), pp. 45-46. Also C. R. Adrian, "Some General Characteristics of Nonpartisan Elections," *American Political Science Review*, XLVI (1952), pp. 766-775.

petition. Ballots are printed at public expense as in the partisan primaries, but, unlike the latter, party designations or emblems are absent. Candidates gain their place on the ballot as a result of a petition signed by a requisite number of voters and are listed on the ballot either in alphabetical order or in a position chosen by lot. The two candidates with the most votes oppose one another in the general election. Nonpartisan primaries are usually employed to choose judges and members of city councils.

The nonpartisan primary has been the object of considerable criticism largely on the ground that it has not fulfilled the expectations of its sponsors. For one thing, it is asserted that nonpartisanship, while admirable in theory, cannot be achieved in practice. Certainly the mere elimination of party designations will not by itself remove the party from the political arena. As Professor Munro has pointed out, this "does not mean that party organizations go out of business." [19] The party will always be on the scene as long as there is a contest for political office. Indeed, wherever nonpartisan nominations prevail, in Chicago or Jersey City for example, they are that in name only and the voter in the primary is fully aware of the fact that the party is behind a given slate.

The nonpartisan primary is also open to attack on the ground that it violates the basic premise upon which our political system is based, namely, that the political party is the principal means of enforcing political responsibility. It is the party that recruits and sponsors candidates. It publicizes their virtues and provides them with the resources for a successful campaign. The party enables a candidate to gain the support of all members of the party, regardless of whether he is financially capable of waging a campaign. In the absence of party assistance, the candidate is faced with a considerable outlay of money which must be marshalled either by himself or by his friends. It is true that the city may contribute slightly toward publicity by permitting all aspirants to send the voter campaign material printed at public expense, but thus far, at least, the trend in this direction has not been marked. It is at least debatable whether it is more desirable to have a candidate indebted to the party or to invisible interests. In the absence of party support, it would seem as if the aspirant would be free to campaign for office

[19] W. B. Munro, *Municipal Government and Administration* (New York: The Macmillian Co., 1925), I, p. 264.

only if he were independently wealthy or could gain the assistance of those who are well off financially.

Aside from this, the nonpartisan primary may well foster factionalism. In the absence of group responsibility for candidates, the tendency is to focus on individuals. Unless there are important issues which cause a large turnout of voters, the tendency will be to vote the man rather than the issue. Fractionalization of the political process into small groups tends to hinder the process of political accountability.

Finally, it is at least arguable whether the nonpartisan primary has resulted in the nomination of better candidates. The absence of party designations leaves the voter with little information as to the qualities of the candidates. The voter may use the place of the aspirant on the ballot or his name as a clue to his race or religion; but in most instances, knowledge of the candidate's position on important issues is almost nonexistent. A condition of this sort may lead the voter to favor a candidate who is smooth or who is publicly prominent; or it may result in political apathy as a tacit admission of the voter's inability to appraise the qualities of potential office seekers. None of these will assure a well-qualified candidate.

The nonpartisan nomination does have one advantage over the other primaries. It makes city politics "free style." The political hopeful is not beholden to the party for his nomination. If he is able to muster sufficient help, he may become an "unbossed" candidate, winning the nomination and even the election. The experience of former Mayor Hubert Humphrey in the city of Minneapolis is a good case in point. Running twice with citizen support, he was defeated. On the third try, he was successful, winning not only the nomination but the election.[20]

Open and closed primaries. Both the open and the closed primaries are party primaries. The former attempts to draw a line of demarcation between party responsibility and voter independence. Since the voter's choice remains secret, he may vote in the ranks of any party without fear that his defection will be disclosed. In theory, the principle of secrecy enables the party voter to punish his party by casting his ballot in the primary of the opposition. Where neither party holds the upper hand, the vote in the hand of the dissident may turn out to be a potent weapon. But where a party is in a posi-

[20] R. Morlan, "City Politics: Free Style," *National Municipal Review,* XXXVIII (1949), pp. 485-490.

tion of dominance, the open primary, paradoxically, may enable it to control the primaries of both parties. It permits a party, certain of the nomination of its own candidates, to "raid" the primary of a rival party by transferring a sufficient number of votes, either to force the nomination of a weak candidate or to obtain the nomination of its own candidate in the opposing party's primary. The practice of "raiding" and "cross-filing" by a dominant party may make a mockery of the general election, since either a weak candidate or the same candidate will appear on the ballot of both parties.[21] It is fortunate that party leaders are hesitant to use these practices fearing that it would encourage independent voting in the election. Otherwise, their extensive use might well negate whatever merit the open primary possesses.

In contrast, the closed primary has one rather simple virtue. It prevents "raids" and fosters party responsibility. There is little room for independence in this kind of primary. On primary day the party voter cannot "cross over" by voting in the primary of the opposition. Indeed, he receives only the ballot of the party with whom he is affiliated. Avenues of protest are closed to the dissident who may express his discontent either by a refusal to vote in the primary or by casting his ballot on election day for the candidates of the rival party. Needless to say, the closed primary is an effective weapon in the hands of those who control the party. The act of voter affiliation in this kind of primary voting gives the party workers a list of party members who may be tapped as a source of party support; when to this is coupled the pre-primary caucus which selects the organization slate, the continuance of those who control the party is virtually assured. Irregulars are isolated, and the very fact that they are forced to "buck" those who are in power places them at a marked disadvantage.

Thus the closed primary places an almost intolerable burden on the rank and file member of the party. He must work within the party. Every effort on his part to challenge the leadership or to make it more responsive to membership is under duress, since it is almost immediately met with the charge of insurgency. But even if the rank and filer is willing to risk the possibility of being labeled, he still is

[21] "Cross-filing" has occurred frequently in California. Designation by both parties of a single candidate occurs in about two-thirds of the contest. See Report of the Committee on the Direct Primary, *A Model Direct Primary Election System* (New York: The National Municipal League, 1951), pp. 34-35.

faced with a formidable task. He will need to select an opposition slate, he will require a means of reaching the voter, and he will have to counteract the apathy and fear of those who regard the primary results as a foregone conclusion.

Nominations in New York County. The nomination of candidates for office and key positions in New York County, home of Tammany Hall, may be an extreme example, but it is nevertheless instructive of the difficulties facing the well-intentioned party voter. The county leadership is divided among district leaders, each of whom is chosen by the members of the county committee from his district. Each district is in turn broken down into election districts. There are, on the average, some thirty of these, although in one instance the number of election districts is as high as 105. To run for district leadership or to challenge such leadership makes it necessary for an aspirant to sponsor a slate of county committeemen pledged to him. Since there are an average of four committeemen to each election district, this means that, on the average, one hundred and twenty persons, supported by the requisite petitions, must be placed in the running. Petitions may be thrown out because they are improperly filed, and furthermore the county committee can overrule the results of the primary in so far as it affects candidates for key positions in the party. A series of truly formidable obstacles must be hurdled. Yet this is the principal means for enforcing party responsibility. Small wonder then that Tammany is able to control so effectively. It is noteworthy, however, that the difficulties have been minimized to some extent by legislation which permits the party, at its option, to permit the direct election of district leaders. A rule to this effect has been adopted, but, it may be added, this was done mainly because of the Kefauver Crime Investigating Committee revelations that disclosed widespread gangster infiltration and resulted in public clamor for a change.[22]

The primary system—an appraisal. The primary, democratic in motivation and sincere as an attempt to strengthen the rank and file, has been the subject of constant appraisal.[23] Comment has centered largely on both the respective merits and demerits of the various kinds of primaries, and on the system as a whole.

[22] J. N. Feldman, "How Tammany Holds Power," *National Municipal Review,* XXXIX (1950), pp. 330-334; also R. S. C., "Tammany Hall Moves Toward More Democracy," *National Municipal Review,* XLIV (1955), p. 258.

[23] Two of the most comprehensive evaluations are Merriam and Overacker, *op. cit.,* and Report of the Committee on the Direct Primary, *op. cit.,* pp. 1-44.

As to the general value of the primary, one can well agree with two outstanding authorities that its working "reveals the fact that many of the predictions made by the friends and foes of the direct primary have not been realized, and that many tendencies unforeseen either by friend or foe have appeared." [24] Contrary to the expectations of its proponents, it has not weakened the hold of the party over nominations. Nor, indeed, has it resulted in greater participation of the voter in the all-important choice of candidates. Party leaders still caucus in advance of the primary at which time an organization slate of candidates and officers for key party posts is adopted. Aside from an occasional rebellion, their suggestions are accepted with almost astonishing regularity by the party faithful. The use of the preprimary caucus was unexpected. Its consequences were soon realized by Charles Evans Hughes, who, as governor of New York, sought to give it legal status by authorizing the party to formulate a slate for the consideration of voters within the primary. His efforts to institute the system, however, were unsucessful. It is not at all surprising that bosses and machines, originally fearful of the innovation, have learned to live with the primary. Indeed, in some respects it has actually strengthened their position, for the very fact that their choices receive legal ratification gives their recommendations even greater weight.

Another development completely unforeseen by primary proponents was the tremendous financial burden placed upon the individual candidate. Some of this has been alluded to in previous pages, but it is necessary to re-emphasize the point. The primary is, to all intents and purposes, an election, with the cost of campaigning borne by the candidate until he wins the nomination. In even a medium-sized city, the amount required for success may be considerable. Freedom to run for public office may often depend upon the resources an aspirant is able to muster. Of course, it must be added in fairness to the primary that the cost of convention nominations are not inconsiderable. Perhaps the principal difference between the two is the fact that there is greater participation in the primary.

The primary may well add to the power of the individual party member, but also it almost inevitably imposes additional responsibilities. The multiplicity of elective offices is such that it entails a

[24] Merriam and Overacker, *op. cit.,* p. 209.

specialized knowledge of the qualities of aspirants. This the partisan possesses, but the rank and filer does not. Because of this, the few rather than the many actually participate in the nomination of candidates for office. Absence of detailed information has undoubtedly strengthened the hand of the party leader, and a realization of this may, in part at least, explain the general apathy of the voter in primaries.[25] Unless a means is devised to reduce the span of attention of the voter, the primary will have lost much of its merit. It was the existence of this condition that led some to propose the addition of the short ballot principle, although this by itself is no final solution.[26]

Finally there is no assurance that the primary will actually provide a better candidate. The qualities of candidates are subjective, to say the least. He who appears to be a "good" candidate in the eyes of one well-intentioned voter may actually be a poor one in the view of other equally honest persons. Even if an objective yardstick could be established to rate candidates, the imponderable still remains: Is it the issue, the times, or the system that brings forth the best candidate? [27]

The shortcomings of the primary system are largely operational in nature. Most of these could be remedied by the adoption of sounder objectives for the primary. These have been carefully set forth in the recommendations of the National Municipal League: (1) the cost of nominating elections should not be such as to eliminate the person without means; (2) the voter should have the opportunity to choose "between qualified candidates *who stand for distinct and different public policies*"; (3) the short ballot should be employed; and (4) the primary should permit the nomination of qualified candidates regardless of party support.[28]

Regardless of the many faults ascribed to it, the primary does represent one real advance over the caucus and convention methods. It has brought the nominating process into the open by introducing a measure of legal supervision that has not previously existed. The real and lasting value of the primary has been most ably stated by Charles Evans Hughes:

---

25 Merriam and Overacker, *op. cit.*, pp. 276-277.

26 *Ibid.*, p. 281.

27 See the comments of Merriam and Overacker, *op. cit.*, pp. 226-227; Report of the Committee on the Direct Primary, *op. cit.*, pp. 14-15.

28 Report of the Committee on the Direct Primary, *op. cit.*, pp. 11-12. Italics in the text.

"First: It places a weapon in the hands of the party voters which they can use with effect in case of need. They are no longer helpless. This fact puts the party leaders on their best behavior. It is a safeguard to the astute and unselfish leader who is endeavoring to maintain good standards in line with sound public sentiment. It favors a disposition not to create situations which are likely to challenge and test.

"Second: The fact of this control gives to the voters a consciousness of power and responsibility. If things do not go right, they know the trouble lies with them. The importance of this assurance should not be overlooked in any discussion of the apathy of the electorate." [29]

These two factors—a weapon of last resort and the lodging of power and responsibility in the hands of the voter—are great steps. Any discussion of the direct primary must bear in mind that it is part of the great movement of protest designed to give the people a greater share in their government. It is, despite the criticisms noted, a flexible device that can be modified to meet the changing needs of the political process.

ELECTION DEVICES

Since it is always premised on majority rule, a democratic society is constantly faced with the need for obtaining a government that is representative of the will of the people. Traditionally, this condition is attained when the people go to the polls to express their wishes. When candidates receive a majority of the votes, it is assumed that they are representative of the people, but, as Hazlitt has pointed out, this is not necessarily so.[30] Our traditional election system in many respects is cumbersome and does not always gain its intended objective, majority rule. Candidates may be, and often are, elected by a plurality instead of a majority. Especially in a three-cornered race, the victor may gain the most votes and be declared elected, regardless of whether he is the choice of the majority. Indeed, it is possible that a thirty or forty percent plurality may be sufficient to put a candidate in office. This is a far cry from the con-

[29] C. E. Hughes, "The Fate of the Direct Primary," *National Municipal Review*, X (January 1921), p. 25.

[30] H. Hazlitt, *A New Constitution Now* (New York: McGraw-Hill Book Co., Inc., 1942), pp. 189-194.

cept of majority rule.[31] Even where an aspirant has a clear-cut majority, it is not certain that he is representative of the wishes of the people. In all too many instances votes are cast for a majority because of the fear that otherwise they would be wasted on a minority candidate.

This condition highlights a basic weakness of the existing election system, namely, its failure to give sufficient consideration to the viewpoint of the minority. When the election returns are in, the votes of the minority are, to all intents and purposes, squandered, even though some have argued that it is the possibility that the minority may sometime become a majority that acts as a brake upon action by the latter. In large part, this voter hesitancy is due to the fact that the traditional system does not discriminate sufficiently between the methods employed for the selection of candidates for the executive as compared with the legislative branch. In the former, majorities and even pluralities are desirable, but in the latter, adequate representation of minorities is necessary, since the aim is to obtain a policy-making body reflecting all shades of opinion.[32]

Limited and cumulative voting. It was out of the conviction that the election system did not reflect voter sentiment adequately that many of the new election devices were born. Prominent among these were limited and cumulative voting, the Grand Junction plan with its Nanson and Ware variations, and last but not least, the Hare system of proportional representation. Space does not permit a detailed discussion of these, but they all are deserving of some treatment since they attempt to strengthen voter choice by giving him a wide range of preference.

Limited and cumulative voting are designed to give the minority greater representation in the legislative branch by making it practically certain that no single party will capture all of the seats. In limited voting this is accomplished by restricting a voter's choice to a number of candidates that is somewhat less than the number of offices to be filled. Hence, if a five-man council is to be chosen, a voter is prohibited from casting his ballot for more than three candidates. This may insure two seats for the minority unless a landslide majority is obtained. Conversely, under the cumulative voting sys-

---

[31] G. Hallett, Jr., *Proportional Representation—The Key to Democracy* (Washington, D. C.: The National Home Library Foundation, 1937), pp. 14-15.

[32] See the discussion of C. G. Hoag and G. H. Hallett, Jr., *Proportional Representation* (New York: The Macmillan Co., 1926), pp. 1-2.

tem the voter choice is considerably wider. He has as many votes as there are offices to be filled and he may give his vote to one candidate or divide them among several. The system presently is in vogue in Illinois where three members of the lower house of the state legislature are elected from each senatorial district. In practice, the scheme has made it exceedingly difficult for one party to monopolize representation. It is probable that the political cleavages existing in northern and southern Illinois were minimized by the use of the device.[33]

Somewhat similar to the cumulative voting system in procedure but not objective is the Grand Junction or Bucklin plan named, respectively, after the city where it was first used and its founder. The plan was used in the parent city from 1909 to 1923. It may be best characterized as a preferential voting scheme designed to obtain a clear majority for the successful candidate. Because the voter could indicate more than one choice, it was hoped that the expense of an additional run-off election could be avoided.[34]

Unlike the traditional system where the voter indicates his intent by placing an X at the appropriate place on the ballot, the elector votes by numbers 1,2,3, etc., in separate columns. If, after the first total no candidate has a clear-cut majority, then the second choices are added to the first. If this does not suffice, then the third choices are counted. Ballot transfers continue until either a majority or, on the last ballot, a plurality is obtained. The preferential system was usually employed to elect a candidate to a single office.[35]

At the height of its popularity the Bucklin plan was adopted by approximately sixty or seventy municipalities, half of which were in New Jersey. In the latter state it was widely heralded as a means for eliminating the expense of a primary election.[36] It was even prescribed by Congress for the election of six of the directors of the Federal Reserve system.[37] Some of the cities employing the plan—San Francisco, Newark, Jersey City, Cleveland, Denver, and Toledo—had substantial populations, but the plan did not seem to be attractive to most cities.

---

33 H. R. Penniman, *Sait's American Parties and Elections* (5th ed.; New York: Appleton-Century-Crofts, Inc., 1952), p. 535.

34 Gosnell, *op. cit.*, p. 169.

35 A good description of preferential voting plans can be found in Hoag and Hallett, *op. cit.*, Appendix, Ch. X, pp. 485-491.

36 Penniman, *op. cit.*, p. 543.

37 Hoag and Hallett, *op. cit.*, pp. 486-487.

The plan failed to gain more adherents mainly because it had a fatal weakness. It was subject to manipulation by party machines. All votes, regardless of whether they were first, second, or other choices, were weighted the same. Political parties soon realized that a concentration on first choices would increase the possibility of victory. The independent vote with second and other choices could be transferred to the party choices while the party vote, because of instructions to the party faithful to vote only a first choice, could make no contribution to their rivals. Of course, as soon as all became aware of this and merely cast a first choice, the system was no different than that which had prevailed before the adoption of the plan. It was the prevalence of this condition that led two outstanding authorities to conclude, "The Bucklin plan may do more harm than good." [38] The experience of Cleveland presented eloquent testimony on this point. In the period 1913–1921 when the city operated under the system, not a single independent candidate for mayor was elected.[39] In 1921 an independent was elected as mayor, but this was largely a result of a temporary rebellion against party organizations which gave the candidate an overwhelming number of first choices.

Two attempts were made to remedy the above-noted defect. The Nansen system, invented by a professor of mathematics at the University of Melbourne, sought to reduce the value of the second and other choices. It was adopted by the city of Marquette, Michigan but was not used elsewhere.[40] The Ware system also sought to minimize the worth of the second and other choices by means of the transfer principle. Unlike the Bucklin plan, after the first total the candidate with the lowest number of votes was declared to be defeated, and his votes were redistributed among the other candidates in accordances with the indicated choices.

Proportional representation. Preferential voting had as its objective the attainment of an absolute majority. Proportional representation, sometimes termed by its proponents the "key to democracy," believes that the minority also has an important role to fulfil, that "justice to minorities is vital." [41] "What is needed," they argue, "is not a system of dividing voters into winners and losers but a system

[38] Hoag and Hallett, *op. cit.,* p. 490.

[39] C. C. Maxey, "The Cleveland Election and the New Charter," *American Political Science Review,* XVI (1922), pp. 83-86.

[40] Hoag and Hallett, *op. cit.,* pp. 491-494.

[41] Hallett, *op. cit.,* p. 5.

of *condensing* them in the right proportions into their chosen leaders." [42]

Proportional representation seeks this objective by the use of a single transferable vote. Candidates in proportional representation elections are listed on the ballot in alphabetical order, usually without party designation. Like the Bucklin plan, the voter has first, second, and other choices. Indeed, he has as many choices as there are candidates. The standard instructions given to the voters usually are stated in the following language:

"Mark your choices with *numbers* only. (Do not use X marks.)

"Put the number 1 in the square opposite the name of your first choice.

"Put the number 2 opposite your second choice, the number 3 opposite your third choice, and so on. You may make as many choices as you please.

"Do not put the same number opposite more than one name.

"To vote for a person whose name is not printed on the ballot, write his name on a blank line under the names of the candidates, and put a number in the square opposite to show which choice you wish to give him.

"If you tear or deface or wrongly mark this ballot, return it and obtain another." [43]

The quota under "P.R." is not a majority. It is the smallest number of votes required to elect a candidate. Quotas are determined in one of two ways: (1) mathematically it is calculated for each office on the basis of the number of votes cast divided by one plus the number of offices to be filled and adding one to the quotient; and (2) legislatively, by either a clause in the city charter or an enabling ordinance which specifies the number of votes necessary to elect a councilman. In New York City, for example, the quota for each member of the city council was fixed at 75,000 votes. In either event, the quota is mathematically calculated in such a fashion as to assure either a majority or minority representation in the council on the basis of the votes cast.

The counting of votes also follows a standard procedure. First

[42] *Ibid.*, p. 8. Italics in quote.
[43] Hallett, *op. cit.*, p. 43.

choices are totaled and those with the quota are declared elected. Next those with less than the quota are considered defeated, and their votes are then transferred in accordance with the indicated second choice. Again those with the quota are elected and those without it are announced as losers. A transfer of votes again takes place and the process continues until the required number of candidates equals the number of offices to be filled.

The case for "P.R." The Hare system of proportional representation, hailed by John Stuart Mill as an outstanding contribution to the theory and practice of government, has been shrouded in controversy ever since its inception. It has been defended and it has been attacked. The case for proportional representation rests largely upon what its proponents regard as the inadequacies of the present election system. Wasted votes, inadequate representation of minorities, voter apathy and minority rule are oft-mentioned weaknesses which they feel must be remedied. All of these, in their view, combine to give the citizen the impression that the election system is "geared" against him and that his voice is heard only when popular discontent reaches a boiling point. Lest these be considered as theoretical objections, the proponents of "P.R." cite illustrations from the election experience of New York City, Cincinnati, Sacramento, Toledo, and many other cities.[44]

According to its advocates, proportional representation would either eliminate or modify many of the weaknesses noted above. It would assure the minority a fairer portion of legislative strength since representation would be proportionate to the votes cast. Thus 66.4 percent of the votes, as in New York City, would not enable the victorious party to obtain 95.4 percent of the representation on the Board of Alderman. Instead, it would give the minority roughly two-fifths of the representation. The prospect that the minority will gain a greater share of power, it is argued, will do away with electoral indifference. Machine rule will then be subject to the constant review of an alert citizenry.[45] Lastly, it is urged that the wide range of choice offered the voter does away with the need for primaries. "It

---

[44] Hallett, *op. cit.*, Ch. 2. "The Old Systems Fail"; Hoag and Hallett, *op. cit.*, pp. 90-111. In 1935 in New York City, for example, 66.4 percent of the Democratic vote was able to gain 95.4 percent of the representation on the Board of Alderman.

[45] O. Reichler, "The Politician Hates P. R.," *National Municipal Review*, XXXVI (1947), pp. 316-320.

does everything that a primary can do, and much more without its disadvantages." [46]

The weaknesses of "P.R." Much credit must be given to the proponents of proportional representation for noting many of the shortcomings of the single-vote system. Whether these are inherent in the system or whether indeed they can be remedied by the substitution of another political device is debatable. Certainly the fact that, in American cities, the movement with few exceptions has been confined to council-manager and commission governed cities indicates that many people are dubious. Moreover, proportional representation is a complex system that suffers from almost all of the weaknesses of the long ballot. There are a large number of candidates, and the voter, forced to make judgments in terms of the relative excellence of candidates to an infinite degree, has imposed upon him an almost impossible burden. Ballot counting, manually or by voting machines, is an expensive and costly operation, although it is argued that the cost of proportional representation election is less than the primary which it makes unnecessary.

Still other criticisms can be noted. It is limited in its use to the choice of members of the council or to those situations where a multiplicity of public officers are to be chosen. It cannot be employed where a single vacancy is to be filled. Even where it is adopted by the voters it is still subject to legal challenge. The courts of Michigan, California, and Rhode Island have declared it unconstitutional. A contrary view, however, has been taken by the courts in New York, Ohio, and Massachusetts. The divergence in legal viewpoint results largely from the presence or absence in the state constitution of a clause which states that qualified persons shall have either the right to vote "at all elections" or "for all officers." Where the clause is present, the courts have taken the position that proportional representation impairs the voters' franchise.[47]

The most telling argument against proportional representation, however, relates to the general question of whether the governing process can function where the power of the majority is fraction-

[46] Hallett, *op. cit.*, p. 72.

[47] *Wattles v. Upjohn,* 211 Mich. 514 (1920), *People v. Elkus,* 59 California App. 396 (1922). Proportional representation has been upheld as constitutional in *Johnson v. City of New York,* 247 N. Y. 411 (1937). See also G. H. Hallett, Jr., "Notes," *National Municipal Review,* XXVIII (1939), p. 400 ff and *National Municipal Review,* XXX (1941), pp. 548-550.

alized, sometimes to the point of virtual helplessness. The leading proponent of this view, Professor Hermens, asks whether it is possible for the will of the people to function where there are many wills instead of one.[48] Government by coalition seems to be the outcome of proportional representation. Where it is in use, the process of political accountability is present but in an atrophied form.[49]

Experience with "P.R." throughout the country. A glance about the country reveals that the system has not found much favor with American cities. Ashtabula, in 1915, was the first city to adopt it. Since then it has been used in other Ohio cities, notably Cleveland, Cincinnati, Hamilton, and Toledo. It was also employed in other cities, a few of which are the following: Cambridge, Massachusetts; Wheeling, West Virginia; Boulder, Colorado; Kalamazoo, Michigan; West Hartford, Connecticut; and both Yonkers and New York City in the State of New York.[50] Adverse action by the legislature, the courts, or the people has caused the abandonment of the plan in many cities.[51] Cincinnati is the largest city which still employs the plan. Although it has been under almost constant political attack, it has managed to survive the successive onslaughts.

New York City, the largest municipality ever to use proportional representation, furnishes a good case study of the difficulties encountered by the system. Adopted mainly as a consequence of popular revulsion arising from the disclosures in the 1930's of the Seabury committee, it functioned for a period of ten years. On the whole, the New York experience indicates that the operation of the system justified the hopes of its sponsors. It did away with Democratic dominance of the city council. It improved the quality of the councilmen and it "deprived (the party organizations) of control over the nominations." [52] But it failed to eliminate the appeal to minority groups, one of the major charges made against it. Indeed, it emphasized this factor with almost mathematical certainty.

Largely, however, it was the failure of the party organization to control nominations that aroused the bitter resentment and opposi-

---

48 F. A. Hermens, *Europe between Democracy and Anarchy* (South Bend, Indiana: The University of Notre Dame Press, 1951), pp. 11-13.

49 Hallett, *op. cit.,* ch. 5 contains both a refutation and an analysis of this viewpoint.

50 Hallett, *op. cit.,* ch. 6, pp. 105-146; also Gosnell, *op. cit.,* pp. 186-187.

51 California and Michigan cities were faced with unfavorable court decisions. West Hartford's plan met a similar fate at the hands of the legislature. In Cleveland and New York City voters rejected the plan after a trial period.

52 B. Zeller and H. A. Bone, "The Repeal of P.R. in New York City—Ten Years in Retrospect," *American Political Science Review,* XLII (1948), p. 1137.

tion of both Democratic and Republican parties. In 1938 and 1940 both sponsored efforts to ban the use of "P.R." but these moves proved unsuccessful. Nevertheless, opposition persisted. The fact that the system gave so much representation to minority groups ultimately proved to be its Achilles' heel. After World War II the effort to repeal "P.R." was renewed. It gained momentum because international "cold war" tensions spotlighted the presence of two communist members on the city council. In the opinion of two responsible observers ". . . the one issue above all others responsible for the repeal of P.R. in 1947 was Communism." [53] Proportional representation was subjected to a labeling campaign. Its opponents castigated it in such terms as "this Stalin Frankenstein" and "a foreign political theory." It mattered little that the system seemed to function effectively, despite the presence of communists on the council; or that the system was supported by many responsible persons of both Democratic and Republican persuasion. The labels stuck and "P.R." was defeated. In the 1949 elections held once more under the 25 single-member district system, the Democratic party once more gained a predominant position, obtaining twenty-four of the seats.[54]

Proportional representation is based upon the proposition that the minority should be given a greater voice in the formulation of governmental policy. This, of course, is a highly laudable objective. Whether we can have this and majority rule, too, seems largely an unanswered question. One thing is certain: the American public is either not ready or unwilling to accept the solution that it proposes.

INITIATIVE, REFERENDUM AND RECALL

"Direct legislation," like so many of the devices of the progressive period, owes its origin largely to the public reaction against the corruption and general lack of responsiveness of state legislatures at the turn of the century. Much of this discontent was caught up in the wave of progressivism that swept the country at the time. South Dakota, in 1898, was the first state to use initiative and referendum on a regularized basis. In the next thirty years it spread to Utah,

[53] *Ibid.*, p. 1133.

[54] R. S. Childs, *Civic Victories* (New York: Harper and Brothers, 1952), p. 247. This should be compared with the 1947 election where the dominant party with 46.9 percent of the votes got 50 percent of the representation on the council.

Oregon, California, and seventeen other states.[55] The use of both initiative and referendum has been confined largely to the western states.

On the city level the development of these instruments paralleled that of the states. Since they were a distinct departure from the usual methods of law-making, it was necessary for the cities to find authorization in either the state constitutions or general law. Otherwise, the legal presumption would be against the validity of these measures. In brief, the spread of these devices in the city was largely dependent upon action by the states.

Nebraska municipalities in 1897 pioneered in the adoption of initiative and referendum. In keeping with the mood of the time, it soon became part of a general movement to give people a greater share of participation in their government. It was soon made part of both the Des Moines Plan and the council-manager forms of government. The demand in many areas for more effective governmental machinery and the popularity of both of these plans led to the passage by many of the states of enabling legislation permitting the use of initiative and referendum. Thirteen states permit their cities to use direct legislation.[56]

Initiative. Initiative is a procedure that enables a required percentage of the voters to propose formally changes in constitutions, charters, or the ordinary laws of the municipality. If their petition is not granted, the petitioners may demand that their proposal be submitted to the people at either a general or a special election.[57] This is a wide grant of powers to the voters and were it not for the fact that it has been hedged in somewhat by various restrictions, a determined group of people could virtually supersede the powers assigned to the legislative branch.

It is worth while to note some of the practices that have developed. For one thing, many charters exempt emergency action from

[55] W. B. Munro, "Initiative and Referendum," *Encyclopaedia of Social Sciences,* VIII, p. 51. The referendum was used in Massachusetts as early as 1778. Initiative was employed by Georgia in 1777. Neither state, however, used these devices on a regularized basis.

[56] See the informative article by W. W. Crouch, "The Initiative and Referendum in Cities," *American Political Science Review,* XXXVII (1943), pp. 491, 493-494. The twelve states listed in the article are: Arizona, Arkansas, California, Colorado, Maine, Maryland, Nevada, Ohio, Oklahoma, Oregon, South Dakota, and Utah. In 1947 New Jersey authorized the use of such procedures.

[57] W. B. Munro, editor, *The Initiative, Referendum and Recall* (New York: D. Appleton and Co., 1912), p. 1.

initiative if such measures have been passed by an extraordinary majority of the council. In some cases, appropriations cannot be made the subject of direct legislation. In still other instances, resolutions concerned with administrative matters are not ordinarily the subject of direct action by the people. Finally, the council retains the power to amend proposals submitted to it, and a measure is rarely referred to the people in the form that it has been submitted to the governing body.[58]

Referendum. Referendum, on the other hand, is the right of a given percentage of the voters to order the submission of a measure to the people already passed by the legislature or city council.[59] Referenda are compulsory, advisory, or protestant in character. Under the first of these, municipal governments have no alternative. Bond issuances or changes in form of government—to cite but two illustrations—must automatically be referred to the people. The advisory referendum is employed where the council is undecided about an ordinance or where it refuses to take a stand on a measure. In such cases, the council voluntarily hands the matter to the people for their decision. San Francisco, for years, has followed a standard procedure in such instances. Its ordinance specifies that where a legislative impasse occurs, either the mayor or the council may submit a broadly phrased proposition to the voters. In a ten-year period only three questions were referred to the people.

The petition or protest referendum imposes the greatest restraint upon the action of the council. Cities employing this variety of the referendum usually have a proviso in their charter depriving all ordinances, except those in the category of emergency legislation, of their legal effect until a period of thirty or sixty days has elapsed. During this time a stated percentage of the voters may protest the enactment of a law and may force its referral to the people at either a special or general election.[60]

Initiative and referendum procedure. The institution of an initiative or referendum hinges on the phrase "a stated percentage" or a "given percentage" of the voters. Propositions for the consideration of the people, in the case of initiative, must be written up in

---

[58] In Detroit, San Francisco and Los Angeles by far the largest number of proposals referred to the people were concerned with charter amendments, see Crouch, *op. cit.*, pp. 499-501.

[59] Munro, *op. cit.*, p. 1.

[60] Crouch, *op. cit.*, pp. 492-493; also W. W. Crouch and D. McHenry, *California Government* (Berkeley, California: University of California Press, 1945), p. 51.

the form of a law. Signatures must be solicited in support of the petition. Although the signature requirements in the states range from 5 to 8 percent, the percentage in the cities is usually much higher, ranging from 15 to 25 percent of the qualified voters or of the total vote in the last preceding election.

Signatures are usually sought on a door-to-door basis by interested parties, although in some instances "petition pushers," commercial signature-collecting firms, will conduct the solicitation on a fee basis. Indeed in some cities a single company will qualify most of the petitions.[61] The prevalence of this practice has led to the demand in some quarters for a change in the method of solicitation, since it is obvious that those groups that can afford to hire such firms have a decided advantage over those that cannot. In Pennsylvania's third-class cities, one hundred voters are permitted to request the municipal clerk to prepare a petition which is then kept at City Hall, where, after public notice, interested parties may affix their signatures.[62]

Once the requisite number of signatures have been obtained, the petition is reviewed by an appropriate person, usually the city clerk. An interesting question that sometimes arises is whether a person is permitted to withdraw his signature after having once affixed it to the petition. It is generally considered that the initiative remains with the signer until the petition has been submitted to the council.[63] Once the petition is certified to the council, the proposition is reduced to a simple form and placed on a ballot for consideration by the people. The procedure for the referendum is quite similar, except that it is unnecessary to frame the proposition, since the law was already enacted by the council.

Justification of "direct legislation." Initiative and referendum were designed to strengthen popular government by giving added power to the unorganized majority. The theoretical justification for these devices rests upon three main grounds: (1) it heightens voter interest since it provides an added avenue of expression; (2) it increases voter information, since, presumably, both sides of an issue will be presented; and (3) it makes the legislative body more responsive to the people. Whether these objectives are actually attained is

---

[61] In San Francisco 95 percent of the initiative and referendum measures were qualified by a single firm. See A. H. Smith, "Can We Afford the Initiative," *National Municipal Review,* XXXVIII (1949), pp. 439-440.

[62] Crouch, *op. cit.,* pp. 496-497.

[63] Crouch, *op. cit.,* p. 497; also *Ford v. Gilbert,* 89 N. J. L. 482 (1916).

debatable. No evidence is available to support the notion that voter participation is greater. On the contrary, an initiative or referendum measure rarely brings out more than 25 to 30 percent of the voters.[64] Available data also indicate that voter information is meager. Moreover, some measures are poorly drafted; others are either unsound or prohibitive in cost and still others are extremely complex. Voters have often approved measures that they do not understand.[65]

Criticisms of initiative and referendum. Studies also show that, far from giving the unorganized majority an opportunity to make its voice heard, it has in fact had a contrary result. Organized minorities instead have been given added avenues of expression. Defeated at the polls and in the legislature they may still sponsor pet measures through both of these devices. The real influence in initiative and referendum proceedings is exerted, not by the voter but by the special-interest group.[66] One thoroughgoing study has concluded that the initiators of proposals in the State of California were groups that were well-organized and well-financed. To require a larger number of signatures to qualify a proposal for the ballot did not diminish their influence. Indeed, it merely gave them a greater advantage over those groups that were loosely or spontaneously formed since the latter could not so easily obtain signatures.[67] The cure for this condition was to require a smaller number of signatures.[68]

Opinion on this point is divided. Some authorities conclude that "direct legislation has neither encouraged or discouraged the formation of pressure or interest groups." [69] But this, of course, does not mean that existing groups do not have a wider platform for appealing to the public than was formerly the case. Moreover, it does miss the main point—that it is not the organized group but rather those spontaneously formed that are seriously disadvantaged. Petition requirements and campaign costs place a premium on the well-financed groups. Others have asserted that initiative and referendum

---

[64] Munro, *op. cit.*, p. 52.

[65] J. G. La Palombara and C. B. Hagen, "Direct Legislation: An Appraisal and A Suggestion," *American Political Science Review*, XLV, pp. 407-408; also Smith, *op. cit.*, pp. 437-439. Both of these refer to the use of initiative and referendum on the state level but contain instructive lessons for their use in the cities.

[66] Munro, *op. cit.*, pp. 31-35, and ch. 11; J. R. Pollock, *The Initiative and Referendum in Michigan* (Ann Arbor: University of Michigan Press, 1940), ch. 3.

[67] V. O. Key and W. Crouch, *The Initiative and Referendum in California* (Berkeley, California: The University of California Press, 1939), pp. 565-567.

[68] *Ibid.*, pp. 552-554.

[69] La Palombara and Hagen, *op. cit.*, p. 417.

have been used sparingly. This was the case in San Francisco, Los Angeles, and other California cities.[70]

Many other criticisms have been leveled against both devices, but many of these may be remedied by appropriate legislative action. It has been pointed out, for example, that measures adopted as a result of direct legislation are often poorly drafted. This may be avoided by the creation of an office of "direct legislative reference." Low voter participation has also been evident in initiative and referendum campaigns. Other inadequacies might also be noted, but when all is said and done, both pro and con, the real weaknesses—the long ballot and voter ignorance—still remain. About a half century ago a writer summarized the status of direct legislation in these words: "The initiative and referendum, then, while they may at times give the righteous a desirable advantage, will in normal conditions . . . secure the passage of undesirable laws or to defeat good ones and to insist for a time at least that this is 'the judgement of the people.' "[71] The initiative and referendum originally advanced as an aid to popular government may actually result in practice in minority rule.

Recall. Like initiative and referendum, recall was also a part of the tide of protest that swept this country at the turn of the century. Venal and corrupt politicians created a favorable climate of opinion for such an experiment. The short ballot movement and the general idea that a lengthening of the term of office would strengthen the process of political accountability were also factors inducing receptivity to the idea. Recall first appeared as a part of the Los Angeles charter of 1903. Soon hailed by some as the application in the wide sense of the principle of ministerial responsibility to public officers, the movement soon gained adherents. It was made part of the "Des Moines Plan" and rode along on the crest of its popularity. Later it became part of the council-manager plan, and as more cities adopted the plan, it also benefited. The recall movement, aside from Theodore Roosevelt's controversial proposal for the recall of judges, for a while made considerable headway. At the peak of its popularity it was adopted by 12 states and 1000 local units. It has not, however, made much progress since 1920.[72]

---

[70] Crouch and McHenry, *op. cit.*, pp. 87-88.

[71] A. M. Kales, *Unpopular Government in the United States* (Chicago: The University of Chicago Press, 1914), p. 121.

[72] F. L. Bird and F. M. Ryan, *The Recall of Public Officers* (New York: The Macmillan Co., 1930), p. 147.

In recall, unlike initiative and referendum, it is the person rather than the policy that is at issue. Policy is, of course, subject to influence, but this is done through the exposure of the public official to the threat of removal from office. This has been the usual method of making the officeholder accountable to the public, but recall represents a departure from the traditional approach in that it enables the voter to separate a public officer from his job before the expiration of his term of office. Recall may be defined as "a political device designed to enable the electorate, through a special election, to replace a public official before the normal expiration of his term of office." [73]

Recall procedure. In more detail, recall is the means through which a dissatisfied citizenry, or a substantial portion of it, takes action against a public official. Complaints accompanied by a demand for an election are embodied in a petition which must be signed by a designated number of signatures, ranging from 15 to 25 percent of the voters. No matter how sweeping the charges may be, these are not subject to review, either by administrative or judicial authorities, since recall is considered a political device. Sufficiency of charges is determined by the people.[74]

Once the requisite number of signatures has been obtained, it is mandatory that the council or the appropriate official authorize the holding of an election. In effect, the office holder faces a public trial by election. The mechanics for accomplishing this are varied. Three methods are usually employed. First, in some jurisdictions the incumbent, as in a general election, is required to compete with others for his office. If he is victorious, then presumably the charges against him are dropped. The city of Los Angeles employs this procedure. Secondly, in some elections two questions are placed upon the ballot: whether the recall of the public officer should be carried out; and who should be his successor. If the first question is answered in the affirmative, then the second portion of the ballot is counted. Oakland, California conducts its recall elections in this manner. Third, and finally, in Modesto, California, a vote is held solely on the recall question. If the voters decided to remove an elected official, then a special election is held later on to choose his successor.[75]

---

[73] F. L. Bird, "Recall," *Encyclopaedia of Social Science*, XIII, p. 147.

[74] J. B. Fordham, *Local Government Law* (Brooklyn, N. Y.: The Foundation Press, 1949), p. 317.

[75] Munro, *op. cit.*, pp. 44-46.

The value of recall. The recall, like the other devices of direct democracy, demonstrates an astonishing faith in the ability of people to govern. Only the boundless optimism of the progressive era could have given birth to such confidence. The device characterized by Wilson as "the gun behind the door" rests upon the assumption that the people have sufficient information at their command to gauge the performance of their elected officers. Indeed, this is the foundation upon which a justification of the device rests. It is asserted that the people can hold their officials responsible for their stewardship of office. If mistakes are made, the people should have the right to rectify their errors. Moreover, it is argued that the device permits a longer term of office, a shorter ballot, and the attendant possibility that a more informed voter will emerge. Thus, its proponents conclude the recall offers the prospect of a continuous check on the political accountability of public officials.

There can be no quarrel with the fundamental objective of recall. Accountability of public officers is desirable, and any means to attain this end should be welcomed. Unfortunately, the practice of recall does not measure up to its theory. Its operation exposes the officeholder to many dangers. He may at any time be put to the added expense of another campaign. He may be victorious at the polls, but at any time a determined and vindictive minority may continue to harass him to the point where his courage and independence may be undermined. In justice to the advocates of recall, it should be pointed out that this potential danger has been minimized somewhat by the adoption of procedural safeguards. To eliminate the possibility that recall may impose a continuous threat, a requirement has been adopted which specifies that petitions must be obtained within a stated period of time. Moreover, no more than one recall action can be instituted during an official's incumbency. Generally, too, the proceeding cannot be undertaken until the official has been in office for a stipulated period of time, usually six months. Despite the adoption of these measures, the use of the device is open to serious objection on the ground that it does give the minority an added opportunity to nullify decisions reached at the polls in the course of an election.

The recall has been used mainly in California. While no recent data are available, such studies as have been made indicate that the device, on the whole, has been used with admirable restraint. Bird and Ryan, in their basic study, report that in the first twenty-five years of its use, only seventy-two recall elections were held in 952 cities, and of these, only about one-half were successful. In small cities of the state, petitions with the requisite number of signatures were completed in only 29 out of 103 instances. In the large cities such as San Francisco and Los Angeles, recall has had only a limited use. More recent data in the form of studies by Crouch and McHenry completed in 1945 indicate that it is the small city that now uses recall action. They conclude: "The recall of individual municipal officers has not fallen into disuse in California. The 'big stick behind the door,' as Theodore Roosevelt described recall, remains well dusted." [76]

Perhaps any general appraisal of recall must await the collection of more basic data. It is an interesting device and it does enable the citizen to remove the incompetent without waiting for the completion of his term of office. But it is open to abuse. Recall, capriciously used, can often do more harm than good, for it may well discourage competent persons from seeking office.

CONCLUSION

The fight to make government more representative of the wishes of the people has been a constant one throughout history. Our country during the first half of the nineteenth century witnessed the appearance of manhood suffrage and the widespread election of public officers. In the wake of the Civil War came urbanization and interdependence of living. It was soon realized that annual elections, though important, were not sufficient to make government responsive to the popular will; or perhaps more correctly, it might be said that the conditions of city life often made a mockery of the election process. To remove the venality and corruption that seemed to have encrusted itself on the political fabric of the community, reformers experimented with a series of devices, loosely termed "direct democracy."

All of these had a laudable objective; a heightened role for people in the political process. The reforms, unfortunately, had limited value primarily because direct democracy cannot function in a society that is based upon representation, that is, where one person acts upon behalf of others. However, the reforms were important because they do establish a new relationship between the governors

[76] Crouch and McHenry, *op. cit.*, p. 103.

and the governed. They were correct to the extent that they sought a heightened citizen response to the problems of government. Unfortunately by widening the avenues of political expression they gave greater scope to the organized minority groups. This in itself was not a bad feature, provided that counterbalances in the form of other citizen associations existed. Unfortunately the latter are hardly a reality. As a consequence, the by-product of political reform, as well-intentioned as it was, strengthened the role of the minority instead of the majority. To the extent that this occurred, the reformers' efforts shot wide of their intended mark.

BIBLIOGRAPHY

Books:

Bird, F. L. and Ryan, F. M. *The Recall of Public Officers.* New York: The Macmillan Co., 1930.

Book of States 1952–1953. Chicago: The Council of State Governments, 1952.

Bright, J. *Hizzoner Big Bill Thompson.* New York: J. Cape and H. Smith, 1930.

Childs, R. S. *Civic Victories.* New York: Harper and Brothers, 1952.

Crouch, W. W. and McHenry, D. *California Government.* Berkeley, California: University of California Press, 1945.

Encyclopaedia of the Social Sciences. 1st edition. Volume 8. Article. "Initiative and Referendum."

Encyclopaedia of the Social Sciences. 1st edition. Volume 12. Article. "Primaries, Political."

Hermens, F. A. *Europe Between Democracy and Anarchy.* South Bend, Indiana: The University of Notre Dame Press, 1951.

Hallett, G. H. *Proportional Representation—The Key to Democracy.* Washington, D. C.: The National Home Library Foundation, 1937.

Hazlitt, H. *A New Constitution Now.* New York: McGraw-Hill Co., Inc., 1942.

Hoag, C. G. and Hallett, G. H. *Proportional Representation.* New York: The Macmillan Co., 1926.

The International City Managers' Association, *The Municipal Yearbook for 1946.* Chicago: 1946.

Kales, A. M. *Unpopular Government in the United States.* Chicago: The University of Chicago Press, 1914.

Key, V. O. and Crouch, W. W. *The Initiative and Referendum in California.* Berkeley, California: The University of California Press, 1939.

La Follette, R. M. *La Follette's Autobiography.* Madison, Wisconsin, R. M. La Follette Co., 1920. 4th edition.

Merriam, C. E. and Overacker, L. *Primary Elections.* Chicago: The University of Chicago Press, 1928.

Munro, W. B. (ed.). *The Initiative, Referendum and Recall.* New York: D. Appleton and Co., 1912.

Penniman, H. R. *Sait's American Parties and Elections.* New York: Appleton-Century-Crofts, Inc., 1952. 5th edition.

Pollock, J. R. *The Initiative and Referendum in Michigan.* Ann Arbor, Michigan: University of Michigan Press, 1940.

Report of the Committee on the Direct Primary. *A Model Direct Primary Election System.* New York: The National Municipal League, 1951.

Whitlock, B. *Forty Years of It.* New York: D. Appleton and Co., 1913.

Wilson, W. *Constitutional Government in the United States.* New York: The Columbia University Press, 1908.

Periodicals and Other Material:

Adrian, C. R. "Some General Characteristics of Non-Partisan Elections," *American Political Science Review,* XLVI (1952), 766-776.

Beard, C. A. "Politics and City Government," *National Municipal Review,* VI (1917), 201-06.

Booser, J. H. "Origin of the Direct Primary," *National Municipal Review,* XXIV (1935), 222-223.

Childs, R. S. "Tammany Hall Moves Toward More Democracy," *National Municipal Review,* XLIV (1955), 258.

Crouch, W. W. "The Initiative and Referendum in Cities," *American Political Science Review,* XXXVII (1943), 491-504.

Feldman, J. N. "How Tammany Holds Power," *National Municipal Review,* XXXIX (1950), 330-334.

Hallett, G. "Proportional Representation Unconstitutional in Rhode Island," *National Municipal Review,* XXVIII (1939), 400-401.

———. "Proportional Representation," *National Municipal Review,* (1951), XL, 540-541.

Hughes, C. E. "The Fate of the Direct Primary," *National Municipal Review,* X (1921), 23-31.

Key, V. O. "The Direct Primary and Party Structure: A Study of State Legislative Nominations," *American Political Science,* XLVII (1950), 1-26.

La Palombara, J. G. and Hagen, C. B. "Direct Legislation: An Appraisal and a Suggestion," *American Political Science Review,* XLV (1951), 400-421.

Maxey, C. C. "The Cleveland Election and the New Charter," *American Political Science Review,* XVI (1922), 83-86.

Morlan, R. "City Politics: Free Style," *National Municipal Review,* XXXVIII (1949), 485-90.

Ogden, D. M. "Parties Survive Cross Voting," *National Municipal Review,* XXXIX (1950), 237-241.

Reichler, O. "The Politician Hates P.R.," *National Municipal Review,* XXXVI (1947), 316-320.

Smith, A. H. *"Can We Afford the Initiative,"* *National Municipal Review,* XXXVIII (1949), 437-442.

Zeller, B. and Bone, H. "The Repeal of P.R. in New York City—Ten Years in Retrospect," *American Political Science Review,* XLII (1948), 1127-1148.

CHAPTER ELEVEN

Administration of Justice

The place of local courts in the state system. There is a popular belief in America, nurtured by colonial experience, that justice is a local function. The feeling persists that local justice is best because it is closer and more responsive to the needs of the people in a given community. Yet this concept today is entirely out of accord with fact. Legally, the administration of justice is a state function. This is especially so since the recent trend toward a unified state court system. In most states, either by constitution or statute, state courts have been established. Today local courts exist only to the extent that the legislature is willing to grant them authority.

It must be admitted that the state legislature, save in the case of the largest cities, has seen fit to grant precious little authority to the local courts. In the main, jurisdiction of municipal courts is limited to traffic violations, small claims, and minor criminal infractions. The function of local courts, largely, is to help relieve the congestion of the state courts by the adjudication of many minor matters. As a consequence of this attitude, the condition of justice in most municipal courts leaves much to be desired. Local judicial bodies lack prestige and status, their judges are underpaid and overworked, and their jurisdiction is determined by the state legislature and not the city council.

There are, to be sure, other courts in the city in addition to municipal courts, but they are state courts handling local problems. These are often chosen by the electorate of the city and their judges are paid in whole or in part out of the municipal treasury; but, again, the city has little or no control over them.

For most people the myth of local justice has reality to this extent: their first and most frequent contact with justice is at the local court level. How these courts of first instance handle the administration of justice is the measure of justice as far as most citizens are concerned. If the municipal courts are to become a vital and necessary part of the administration of justice, it is essential that their role in the state court system be more properly defined.

EVOLUTION OF THE MUNICIPAL COURT SYSTEM

The municipal court before the Civil War. Local courts are as old as America itself. Indeed, in a sense it might be said that their origin antedates this country since borough courts, developed in England, were brought to this country by the migrating colonists.

In colonial times the court development was rather uneven. Since communication and transportation were rather difficult, the tendency was to grant a large measure of authority to county and local judges. Indeed, the pattern of decentralization was even further pronounced. Borough courts enjoyed considerable freedom from the county supervision, although this highly regarded immunity was generally associated with the privilege of incorporation. The city of Philadelphia had its own courts. In many of the smaller boroughs the burgesses were given the powers of justices of the peace. In some cities, New York, Annapolis, and Norfolk for example, the mayor's court was comparable in authority to the London Lord Mayor's court.[1]

Most evident as a characteristic of the colonial court system was the almost complete fusion of legislative and judicial power. In most instances the governing body of the municipality consisted of the mayor, recorder, alderman, and councillors. The first three sat separately as a court and exercised jurisdiction over a wide range of petty offenses and civil cases which previously the entire governing body had subjected to regulation through local ordinances.[2] Justice in colonial times was a simple affair. It was assumed that disputes could be resolved by a fair-minded person and justices often were chosen with this quality in mind. Courts, in other words, were staffed by laymen whose reputation for fairness was known to the community.

In the post Revolutionary War period, separation of the legislative from the judicial function gradually began to take place. As the volume of legal business increased, the practice of assigning the judicial function to a single person became more pronounced, and this tendency was accentuated by the growing complexity of issues facing

[1] E. S. Griffith, *History of American City Governments* (New York: Oxford University Press, 1938), pp. 79-80, 102-104.
[2] *Ibid.*, pp. 169-170.

judicial bodies. In addition to the justice of the peace, therefore, magistrates, police judges, recorders, and other variously named judicial officers came upon the scene. In most instances they were appointed by the governing body, although in rare cases they were also selected by the governor of the state.[3] Later, in the age of Jackson, popular election of judges was introduced, a practice which even today is prevalent in many cities. Until the Civil War, courts at the municipal level consisted of justice of the peace courts, police and magistrates courts and, in a few cases, municipal courts. Measured by today's standards, the system can be considered crude, even primitive, but on the whole it was well-suited to the needs of an agrarian society.

Courts in the period, 1860–1900. The rapid evolution of America into a nation of cities in the period after the Civil War, however, posed the problem of whether rural institutions of justice could be adapted to the needs of an urban society. City life entailed an infinite variety of detailed regulations of human behavior. Common law was modified by statute law to meet new conditions. Legal issues became too complex to be adjudicated by the laymen. The pressures of city life caused maladjustments which could not be solved merely by the application of sanctions. It is no exaggeration to say that during this period the courts of the city were inadequate to meet the problems of a rapidly evolving society. Rural in structure and orientation, they struggled manfully to keep pace with urbanization, but despite strenuous efforts, local courts lagged far behind the changes in the character of the society.

It is extremely difficult to describe the pattern of municipal court development in the period 1860–1900 because there were so many variations. In some instances the prior court system was expanded; in other cases new courts were created; and here and there specialized courts were introduced. In the main three types of city courts prevailed during this period. In the smaller municipalities justice of the peace courts prevailed for a long time. These were hardly more than minor courts of limited authority. In civil actions, their jurisdiction was limited to small claims not larger than $200. Trials were held without benefit of jury and the decision of the judge was final. Cases involving larger amounts could be appealed

---

[3] *Encyclopaedia of Social Sciences*, VI, p. 96. In a few New England cities magistrates were chosen by the governor.

to a higher court. Criminal matters handled in such courts were similarly relatively inconsequential. Violations of city ordinances were prosecuted before such judicial bodies and where felonies were committed, the justice of the peace acted as a committing magistrate, determining whether an offender should be held for grand jury action.[4]

In the large city the administration of justice by the courts was slightly more advanced. Because of the larger volume of business, the judiciary was generally a police or magistrates' court, consisting of a number of judges. Some handled criminal cases, others civil cases, and some both types. It is extremely difficult to describe their jurisdiction since it was so varied. In some instances these courts, where the justice of the peace was superseded, assumed the latter's criminal jurisdiction. In other cases they were authorized to adjudicate more serious offenses. In general, however, they, too, were petty courts.[5]

Finally, as the cities grew in size and in number, even these courts became inadequate to meet the needs of urban justice. Soon they were superseded by municipal or city courts. These were designed to supplement and in many cases to supplant the more outmoded courts but they, too, were soon to prove hopelessly inadequate to meet the emerging needs of urban justice.

Municipal courts during this period suffered from weaknesses, many of which, incidentally, are still with us today. While the need for justices trained in law was recognized, the methods of selection were inadequate. Popular choice of judges was certainly not the best means for obtaining qualified personnel. The method, James Bryce has pointed out, throws "the choice into the hands of political parties, that is to say, of knots of wire pullers inclined to use every office as a means of rewarding political services, and garrisoning with grateful partisans posts which may conceivably become of political importance." [6] The inability of people to appraise the qualification of judges, when combined with their political selection, often made a mockery of justice.

In the period 1860–1900 faulty structure and conflicting jurisdiction were also characteristic of the municipal courts. In their

---

[4] W. F. Willoughby, *Principles of Judicial Administration* (Washington, D. C.: The Brookings Institution, 1929), p. 243.

[5] *Ibid.*, p. 245.

[6] J. Bryce, *The American Commonwealth* (New York: Macmillan and Co., 1889), I, p. 485.

haste to adjust to immediate conditions, cities failed to develop a coherent court plan. The almost universal retention of justice of the peace courts, side by side with the newer courts, created duplication of jurisdiction. Small claims, for example, might be handled in any one of a half dozen courts within the city. Concurrence of authority among courts meant not only rivalry but also costly and improper use of judicial personnel.

Conversely, where specialized courts were established a fragmentation of judicial authority occurred, making it difficult for courts to function. A single problem such as domestic relations became the province of many courts. Disorderly conduct, for example, might be the responsibility of a criminal court. Reconciliation of parents might belong to a family court. Divorce decrees might be granted by a higher court. Juvenile delinquency was within the purview of one court, yet family discord which may have caused the problem might well be within the jurisdiction of another. Many other examples might be cited, but all would merely underline the inability of the court system to develop a comprehensive approach to a single problem.

The by-products of faulty judicial organization were numerous. Court procedures were antiquated. A large number of uncoordinated and semiautonomous tribunals existed with every judge virtually independent. Court calendars were glutted with cases waiting to be heard. Assignment of cases did not permit specialization. Delay, service costs for attorneys, witnesses, and court fees were often so burdensome as to deny justice to those who could not afford to pay for it.[7] Criminal as well as civil justice was bogged down in a maze of technicalities and threatened to defeat the very purpose for which the courts had been created. To the vast majority of citizens whose only contact with justice was in these minor courts the experience must have been disillusioning.

Unified municipal courts. The appalling state of confusion of our municipal courts did not go unnoticed. Judicial reformers were aware that both legal theory and judicial practice were in need of drastic revision. Reform of the court structure was a necessary precedent, in their view, to the modernization of legal thinking.[8] Early

---

[7] R. H. Smith, *Justice and the Poor* (New York: The Carnegie Foundation for Teaching, 1919), pp. 8-9.

[8] R. Pound, "The Administration of Justice in the Modern City," *Harvard Law Review,* XXVI (February, 1913), p. 310.

in the present century improvement of municipal justice took form in the agitation for a unified municipal court system.

This program was extremely modest in its dimensions. It was hardly more than an attempt to combine in a coherent fashion in a single court the separate courts that had grown up during more than a century of legal development. Obsolete and unneeded courts were to be abolished. Jurisdictional defects were to be eliminated. Antiquated civil and criminal procedure were to be modernized. Responsibility for the administration of the courts was to be vested in a chief justice and his immediate associates. In this manner it was hoped that urban justice would be more effectively administered.

In 1906 the city of Chicago pioneered in the establishment of the first unified municipal court system. Prior to this reorganization, the courts of the city were in a woeful state of confusion. Jurisdiction was divided among a number of different judicial bodies. The court system consisted of the following: a probate court for Cook county; circuit and superior courts; and at the bottom of the judicial ladder approximately fifty-four justices of the peace and police magistrates who were appointed by the mayor and aldermen. The latter had criminal jurisdiction controlling, as Herbert Harley described it, "the gateways to punishment and absolution." [9] Indicative of the general inadequacy of the judicial system were the crowded court calendars where cases were delayed as long as three years.

Unification of the Chicago court system brought many improvements not only in the structure of the judiciary but also in both its operation and outlook. The justice of the peace and magistrate courts were abolished. In their stead a single municipal court was established with criminal jurisdiction over misdemeanors and civil jurisdiction over civil matters not in excess of $1,000. Administration of the new court system was entrusted to a chief justice and associate justices, acting as a judicial council. This unit assigned cases so that the work load of the court was distributed evenly. It also sought to develop more effective rules of procedure in order to speed court consideration of cases.[10]

Indicative of the effect of court reorganization on judicial thinking was the record of the Chicago court during the period, 1911–

[9] Quoted by Willoughby, *op. cit.*, p. 283.
[10] Willoughby, *op. cit.*, pp. 281-284.

1916. Separate courts were established to deal with special problems facing the city. There emerged such courts as the Speeders branch, the "Morals Court," the "Boys Court" and the Small Claims branch, the latter to assist the petty litigant. All of these reflected the increasing degree of specialization that was gradually taking place. Despite its advances, however, there was little improvement in the administration of criminal justice in the circuit and superior courts. These were, of course, beyond the authority of the city, although it did have an effect upon the quality of justice meted out to its citizens. This fault was noted by Willoughby who said of the Chicago experiment, "Its most serious shortcoming is that it does not provide for a single court to have general administration of justice. In this direction its creation did little more than eliminate the old justice of the peace and police magistrate courts."[11]

In spite of this obvious weakness, the Chicago court reorganization plan was copied in varying degrees by other municipalities. In 1912 Cleveland tailored its court structure almost wholly along such lines. A year later the state of Ohio authorized the city of Cincinnati to establish a municipal court which replaced the justice of the peace and the police courts. Similar modernization efforts took place at such widely separated points as Kansas City, Missouri; Buffalo, New York; Pittsburgh and Philadelphia, Pennsylvania; Atlanta, Georgia; and Milwaukee, Wisconsin.[12]

A further step forward took place in Detroit. There, in 1920, a Recorders Court was given unified control over all criminal cases, something rather unique in the history of municipal courts. Like Chicago, it also created special courts to deal with specific types of problems that plagued the city. After a fine start, the court bogged down and its general effectiveness was diminished considerably. Willoughby, a critic of the Chicago experiment, has argued that the system was essentially sound but that inferior personnel hampered its operations considerably. Presumably if this lack were remedied, the court would regain its former efficiency.[13]

The unified municipal court movement received considerable acceptance until the late thirties. In 1938 the American Bar Association, the American Judicature Society, the National Municipal

[11] *Ibid.*, p. 287.

[12] *Ibid.*, pp. 298-299.

[13] *Ibid.*, p. 291; also, *Journal of the American Judicature Society*, XIV (1931), pp. 180-188.

League and many allied groups began to press for an integrated state court system. Legal thinking is agreed on the need for court unification but whether the state wide movement will meet the needs of the large city or metropolitan area is still open to question.

The impact of metropolitan areas. The distinctive nature of the problems facing the courts in the large metropolitan area was noted as early as 1916 when the American Judicature Society proposed that a metropolitan court with unified criminal and civil jurisdiction should be established. Since that time the tremendous shifts in population and the consequent growth of metropolitan areas with a multiplicity of governing units, each with its own authority to create courts, gave the proposal more urgency. If it be asserted that unified municipal courts do not meet the situation, then it can also be said that statewide integration is no answer either.[14]

A few examples of the impact of population dispersion upon the court system of metropolitan areas will make this evident. The Chicago metropolitan area of 1932 had over 500 courts, approximately half of which were in Cook County.[15] Today in Chicago, circuit and superior courts with the same jurisdiction are functions of different units of government even though they serve the same area.[16]

In the Detroit area, the original unified court has also become the victim of the mass exodus of people moving to the suburbs. A recent study revealed a judicial hodgepodge of 145 separate and distinct tribunals. Each of the four hundred and fifty-two governmental units has its own authority to establish independent tribunals. Conflicting and overlapping jurisdiction, and the almost complete lack of cooperation among this varied assortment of courts, constitute a most serious problem.[17]

A recent survey of the courts of Hamilton County, Ohio, in which the city of Cincinnati is located, revealed the following inadequacies: (1) too many judges and court employees; (2) rotation of judges with a consequent lack of specialization; (3) crowded court calendars; and (4) lack of effective court organization. The conduct of trials did not add dignity to the court. "Trials in the municipal

---

[14] M. B. Virtue, "Improving the Structure of Courts," *The Annals of the American Academy of Political and Social Science,* CCLXXXVII (May 1953), pp. 145-146.

[15] A. Lepawsky, *The Judicial System of Metropolitan Chicago* (Chicago: University of Chicago Press, 1932), p. 41.

[16] Virtue, *op. cit.,* p. 143.

[17] Unsigned note, "Administration of Justice in Metropolitan Areas," *Journal of the American Judicature Society,* XXXIV (1950), pp. 111-116.

court," the report concluded, "are conducted in an unjudicial manner. Defendants and witnesses are treated either with rudeness or familiarity."[18] To improve the administration of justice a unified court system was recommended.

The condition of municipal courts in the city of New York, the nation's largest municipality, also leaves much to be desired. Space does not permit a detailed description of the city's court structure, but some idea of its importance can be gleaned from the fact that in the year 1951, New York City spent $20,137,500, or 1.6 percent of its budget, for city and county courts.[19] Briefly there are three major kinds of courts. Civil litigation is handled by a Municipal Court, a City Court and a Supreme Court. A Magistrates Court, a Court of Special Sessions, and county courts have criminal jurisdiction. Surrogate courts and a Domestic Relations Court, as their names indicate, handle special matters. All in all, there are 21 separate and miscellaneous courts each with a large degree of autonomy.[20]

New York City obviously does not have a unified court system. City, county and state courts, within its boundaries, have overlapping jurisdiction. In civil actions the Municipal Court hears cases where the amount is not in excess of $1,000; the City Court where the amount is not larger than $6,000; and the Supreme Court has unlimited jurisdiction in such matters.[21] Some court dockets are crowded while others, because of limited civil jurisdiction, operate on a part-time basis. In such circumstances delay and injustice are almost inevitable. In 1952 there were 7,979 cases in New York County awaiting trial with an expected delay of forty-nine months before hearing.[22] One authority summarized the condition of New York's courts in this manner: "The trouble is that New York City's judicial machinery is largely the result of accident. It is the hodge-

[18] C. O. Porter, "Defects in the Administration of Justice in Hamilton County (Cincinnati) Ohio," *Journal of the American Judicature Society,* XXXII (1938), pp. 14-21.

[19] L. L. Tolman, "The Taxpayers' Stake in the Courts," *The Annals, op. cit.,* p. 129. A detailed description of the courts of the city of New York can be found in R. B. Rankin, *Guide to the Municipal Government* (New York: Record Press Inc., 1952), pp. 156-170.

[20] Rankin, *op. cit.,* pp. 156-170.

[21] E. S. Greenbaum, "Plea for Court Reform Now," *New York Times Magazine,* February 27, 1955, p. 12.

[22] W. C. Hecht, Jr., "Expediting Trial of Cases in New York County," *The Annals, op. cit.,* p. 138. Justice Hecht expressed hope that the log jam would be removed.

podge and product of gradual and unplanned growth, and it has never been properly overhauled." [23]

There is considerable hope that the courts of New York City will be revamped. In 1953 a Temporary State Commission on Courts was established to make a study of the courts of the state. Two years later as part of its study, it recommended what in effect was a uniform court plan for the city. For the present jumble of courts it proposed to substitute three major courts: (1) a Magistrates' Court that would absorb the criminal jurisdiction of the present city magistrates courts; (2) a District Court that would, to a large extent, assume the jurisdiction of the Municipal Court and the Court of Special Sessions; and (3) a Superior Court with unlimited authority to hear in the first instance cases in law and equity both civil and criminal. The Superior Court was designed to eliminate the confusion that presently exists between city and county courts.[24] Whether these recommendations will be accepted by the state legislature remains to be seen.

It is evident from this brief review that court unification at the municipal and metropolitan area is essential; but here, as in so many instances, the cities are not masters of their own fate. Even when municipal court unification was at its height, states granted cities only the power to create unified civil courts. In criminal matters, state legislatures were extremely reluctant to yield such responsibility to the city. The Recorders' Court of Detroit, the single example of unified criminal jurisdiction vested in a city court, is perhaps the exception that proves the point. Municipal court unification seems to have been shelved in favor of a state-wide integrated court system. Further progress in municipal court reforms awaits the realization by states that the distinctive problems of judicial administration in cities, particularly the larger ones, will not be solved by state wide court integration.

Municipal courts today. City courts have a variety of names. There are justice of the peace courts, recorders courts, police courts and magistrates courts. In the nation's largest city there are quite a number of city courts, each with a different name. There is the city Magistrates' Court, the Municipal Court, the City Court, and the Court of Special Sessions. In addition, in New York City, as in most

[23] E. S. Greenbaum, "Red Tape Snarl in our Courts," *New York Times Magazine* (January 28, 1951), p. 10.

[24] *New York Times,* June 21, 1955.

cities, there are a series of special courts whose names are indicative of their function: a Small Claims Court, a Traffic Court, a Domestic Relations Court, a Juvenile Court, a Youth Court, and many others.

City courts are minor courts. Their jurisdiction is limited in both civil and criminal cases. Such courts primarily are courts of the first instance, although in rare cases they are given the right to make final decisions. In small claims actions where the amount at issue is rarely more than $200, they hear cases without a jury trial and have final jurisdiction. Where the sum involved is in excess of this amount, jury trial and the right of appeal to a higher court are preserved. In the area of civil jurisdiction, municipal courts perform the useful function of relieving the high courts of the vast burden of petty litigation.

The criminal jurisdiction of the municipal courts is also restricted. Violations of city ordinances punishable by fines and short terms of imprisonment are its main concern. In the public eye, the city court is primarily an agency for the enforcement of traffic laws but it is actually more than this. It assists in the enforcement of a large variety of rules and regulations concerned with public health, welfare, and safety. It has power, though of a limited nature, over family disputes. It has control over minor criminal offenses ranging from the trivial to the serious. In most cases the court functions as a court for the hearing of common complaints but it also deals with malicious mischief, assault, and larceny. The basic function of the inferior criminal judge is "that of conserving the peace of the community." [25] His ability to handle the various disputes is dependent on "good will, good judgment, the employment of unorthodox techniques, and a judicious combination of moral indignation, threat of punitive sanction and persuasion. . . ." [26]

In the case of felonies, that is, major crimes, there is a division of power between the municipal and county courts. The city magistrate has "binding over authority." It is his function to decide, after a hearing, whether the evidence is sufficient to hold the accused for indictment and subsequent prosecution. The trial of criminals takes place in county courts, usually located within a city.

---

[25] M. Ploscowe, "The Inferior Criminal Courts in Action," *The Annals, op. cit.*, pp. 8-12. The quote can be found on page 11.

[26] *Idem.*

Though their judges are paid in whole or in part from the city treasury, they are not city courts.

Municipal courts, in their attempt to administer justice, occupy an anomalous position. Considered to be one of the major law enforcement agencies within the city, they are daily brought face to face with problems which they cannot solve because of the limited authority that they possess. Both their civil and criminal jurisdiction is shared with state and county courts. Whatever powers they do possess are largely residual in nature. Caught between neglect by the state which usually thinks in terms of state-wide integration and the inability of the city to obtain more complete jurisdiction for it, the city courts are in a difficult situation. The way out is obviously a unified court system with both civil and criminal jurisdiction. The city can insist upon this since it does have a legitimate interest in the quality of justice its citizens receive in the courts. Until the states recognize the special needs of the city, the latter's judicial agencies will have only limited prestige and status.[27]

AGENCIES OF THE COURT

The courts are intimately associated with the problem of law enforcement. They apply the law to a specific situation, but their action is conditional upon the efforts of others. The detection of violators, the determination of whether a crime has been committed, the marshalling of evidence, and the decision to prosecute are the functions of other agencies. In civil cases, a dispute between private parties must be brought to the attention of the court before it can act. Even then the issues of fact brought before the court may be decided by a jury. Thus the action of the court is terminal. It begins to function only after the initiative has been taken by others. No discussion of the municipal court system is complete without some reference being made to the role of the prosecutor, the grand and petit juries, and other agencies of the court.

The public prosecutor. Public control of law enforcement rests largely in the hands of the public prosecutor. In the administration of justice in the modern city, the prosecutor is the citizen "writ large." He is the public complainant. Whenever and wherever violations of the law occur, he speaks in the name of the people. The

[27] See one of the most recent efforts at court reform, R. G. Dixon, "Judicial Administration in Maryland—The Administrative Office of the Courts," *Maryland Law Review*, XVI (1956), pp. 185-218.

police perform the necessary task of apprehension and arrest of suspected criminals. However, the prosecutor on his own also may initiate action. In either event, it is his responsibility to see that infractions of the law do not go unpunished.

In this key role, the prosecutor performs many tasks. He conducts a criminal investigation in order to determine whether facts are sufficient to warrant prosecution. He brings to the attention of the grand jury the evidence gathered by him. If an indictment results the prosecutor prepares the case for the trial court. As solicitor he not only presents the government's case to the jury, but when the decision of the court has been reached, he may advise the judge on the disposition of the case. In brief, as Willoughby has remarked, "From start to finish, the prosecuting attorney influences, if he does not wholly control, the prosecution of crime in his community." [28]

Criticisms of the prosecutor's office. Morally and legally the prosecutor has a heavy obligation. He can, if he chooses, set the tone of law observance in his community, but whether he does often depends upon the manner in which his office is organized, as well as upon his own inclination. In many urban communities the organization of the office has lagged far behind its responsibilities. The need is for efficient law enforcement machinery; but in many instances this is definitely lacking. Cooperation between police and prosecutor is often nonexistent; yet the proper presentation of a criminal case by the latter often depends upon the evidence gathered by the police.[29]

Of more immediate concern, however, is the fact that the office of the prosecutor is poorly organized. In its main essentials it hardly differs from the institution as it functioned in early America. Terms of office are short. Specialization, perhaps because of the precarious conditions of employment, is noticeably absent. There is a general lack of continuity of experience. Each new occupant of the office must learn anew his duties and responsibilities. Above all, there is, in general, no provision for the review of the operations of the prosecutor's office. While such conditions may have been in keeping with the needs of rural America, they are utterly out of harmony with the demands of criminal justice in a modern city. The importance of permanence and professionalization has been demonstrated by re-

[28] Willoughby, *op. cit.,* p. 129.

[29] R. Moley, *Politics and Criminal Prosecution* (New York: Minton Balch and Company, 1929), p. 71.

sults obtained by the hard-working prosecutors of the federal Attorney General's office.[30]

Improper organization of the prosecutor's office, however, is not the only way that its functioning has been impaired. Its efficiency has also been hampered by the intrusion of politics. Largely, this has been because the prosecutor occupies such a key position in the community. As we have previously noted, he stands at the gateways of mercy and absolution. His is the prerogative to enforce or not to enforce the law. He may be harsh or lenient, vigorous or inefficient. But in any event, he is a most important cog in the machinery of criminal justice.

Because of his crucial role in law enforcement, the prosecutor, historically, has been made subject to a variety of political checks. His term of office, and those of his assistants, is short. Traditionally, the office has been an elective one. The theory behind political selection was to keep the prosecutor, as Dean Pound has phrased it, "from doing what he should not." [31] While control of the public prosecutor was a wholly laudable objective, in practice it has many drawbacks. In many instances the post is administered on a part-time basis with the prosecutor, and sometimes his assistants, being permitted to have a private practice as well. Moreover, the office has often been a stepping stone to further political advancement. Many a prosecutor has been catapulted into public prominence by his prosecuting zeal. Although many honorable men have occupied the office, the desire to make a "record" has been a constant source of temptation to men of lesser stature. The stress on the sensational case frequently results in the neglect of the routine day-to-day prosecutions so essential to law enforcement. The need to remain in the public limelight may result in convictions but not necessarily justice. In the drive to make a record, "third degree" and other methods of tough law enforcement are employed. "Justice by compromise," as Raymond Moley has called it—that is, the willingness of the prosecutor to accept a plea of guilty on a lesser offense—is a common feature of criminal justice. In the pressure to make a "record," it is often forgotten that the prosecutor should represent both the public and the accused.

Equally important is the intimate tie-up between the prosecutor and the political party. Both election and advancement to higher

[30] Pound, *op. cit.*, pp. 180-181.
[31] *Ibid.*, p. 185.

office are largely a matter of party support. It is this relationship that is crucial to the administration of justice. Our cities, particularly the larger ones, have spawned organized crime, vice, and law breaking. These fringe elements are subject to attack by the prosecutor. If he cannot destroy them, he can at least make their life uncomfortable. His discretion in these matters is very great. Needless to say, this is a fact that has not escaped the attention of the underworld. By political contributions and actual infiltration of the party organization they have sought to temper the zeal of the prosecutor. "The final stronghold, therefore, of organized crime," wrote Raymond Moley, "is actual control over the processes of popular election. The underworld thus reaches the most vital spot in law enforcement, the means through which law enforcement is controlled by the public." [32] Where the party is either influenced or under the dominance of fringe elements, the spectacle is not an enlightening one. Political administration of justice results in failure to prosecute, in the acceptance of a lesser plea of guilty by hoodlums as a necessary practice, and the known association of "political fixers" with racketeers.[33]

The growth of the political party and syndicated crime have made the election of the public prosecutor an anachronism. Political accountability originally was a weapon to protect the public against the prosecutor. Now, because the political party controls the avenues of election and advancement, political influence in many cities actually interferes with effective prosecution of crime. Election, instead of protecting society from the power of the prosecutor, has actually become a weapon against society.[34] Under the modern conditions of city life there appears to be no valid reason why the office of prosecutor any more than the police department should be "in politics." The obvious solution is to take the office out of politics. Until this is accomplished the machinery of criminal justice will continue to lag behind the requirements of the modern city.

The grand jury. This institution has a long and honorable history and it is part and parcel of our Anglo-Saxon legal tradition. Yet here, too, we may well ask whether its function should not be revamped to meet the requirements of an urban society.

---

[32] Moley, *op. cit.,* p. 13.

[33] See for example, N. Mockridge and R. Prall, *The Big Fix* (New York: Henry Holt and Company, 1954), generally, and especially p. 85; also E. Reid, *Mafia* (New York: Random House, 1952), pp. 50-51.

[34] Pound, *op. cit.,* pp. 185-188.

The grand jury came into existence when law enforcement was a sporadic rather than a continuous process. In the England of Henry II, the king's judges were periodically directed to go to the countryside to ferret out violations of the law. The most usual method of accomplishing this objective was to invite the public to report evidence of wrongdoing. Information obtained in this manner was reviewed as to adequacy by citizen juries. Punishment was imposed by royal justices.[35] This historic role as an appraiser of evidence has now become a function of our grand juries.

This common-law institution, as it functions in our society today, ranges in size from thirteen to twenty-three individuals with the most common number being twenty-one. Broadly speaking, it has two main functions: to accuse and to investigate. As an accusatory body, the grand jury is charged with a dual responsibility. It must see that violations of the law do not go unpunished. It must also protect the innocent. It also may inquire into the behavior of public officials.

Originally the grand jury was a citizen instrument and it met in secret. It gathered evidence without the assistance of a prosecutor and it determined whether the evidence was sufficient to warrant the voting of an indictment.[36] Now circumstances have changed markedly. The grand jury does not have time to discharge its intended function. Statutes have become more complicated. More and more it has had to depend upon the prosecutor. As a result, the accusatory functions of the grand jury have atrophied. Today it is common practice for the prosecutor to select the cases that will be heard by the grand jury. He gathers the facts, presents them to the jury, and advises them as to law. The grand jury rarely investigates matters on its own. Although it still retains the responsibility for voting the indictment, it is a rare event when it disagrees with the prosecutor.[37] Indeed, when it does so it is usually characterized as a "runaway jury."

It is this failure of the grand jury to keep pace with modern conditions that has led many to condemn it as an obsolete instrument. In some quarters it is regarded as a rubber stamp for the prosecutor.[38] Moley, for example, has argued that it causes delay,

---

35 Willoughby, *op. cit.*, pp. 174-175.

36 A. V. Shaw, "The Grand Jury: Use it or Lose it," *Journal of American Judicature Society*, XXXVI (1948), p. 6.

37 *Ibid.*, p. 7.

38 Moley, *op. cit.*, p. 145. Willoughby, *op. cit.*, p. 181. Shaw, *op. cit.*, p. 7.

merely duplicating the preliminary hearing.[39] Willoughby has characterized it as "a secondary agency" and has questioned whether a lay jury has the necessary competence to assess the sufficiency of evidence.[40] Conviction that the grand jury is outmoded is evidenced by the fact that about half of the states have substituted indictment by information without a grand jury. Even England, the mother of our law, abolished the grand jury in 1933, and in 1949 the special jury, similar to New York's "blue ribbon" jury, was also abandoned.[41]

While there is no hesitation to question the accusatory function of the grand jury, there is, nevertheless, a disposition to retain it as a political or investigatory instrument. As a watchdog over the activities of public officials it does perform a useful function. On its own, or at the direction of a court, it can conduct useful inquiries, and since its composition is broadly representative of the community as a whole, its recommendations can carry great weight.[42] To return for a moment to the accusatory function, however, one final point must be made. The decline of the grand jury and the consequent rise in the power and discretion of the prosecutor are compelling reasons to take the office of prosecutor out of politics.

The coroner's office. Another cog in the wheel of criminal justice is the coroner. Like the grand jury, this office may be traced to early English times. The coroner has an important role to fulfill. All deaths that occur under suspicious circumstances come under his scrutiny. On his shoulders rests the burden of deciding whether a homicide, the taking of a life, has been committed. Very largely, this is both a medical and a judicial function. Whether death was due to other than natural causes is determined by an autopsy, either by the coroner himself or by some competent medical person employed by him. Whether wrongdoing has occurred is ascertained through the conduct of a hearing generally known as the coroner's inquest. The coroner may summon witnesses to appear before a jury that he has empanelled for that purpose. If evidence of wrongdoing is revealed, then the matter is usually turned over to the grand jury.

It is commonly agreed that the office has just about outlived its usefulness. Several considerations support this view. The coroner's

---

39 Moley, *op. cit.*, p. 137.

40 *Idem.*

41 B. Hollander, "A Change in the Old Order: England Streamlines Her Jury Systems," *American Bar Association Journal*, XXXVI, pp. 455-457.

42 Shaw, *op. cit.*, pp. 6-7.

office is, in the main, a rural instrument that is unable to meet the needs of a modern urban society. Its occupant is either elected or appointed, and political considerations in his choice are not noticeably absent. Modern law-enforcement is a highly specialized function and homicide is a most serious crime. Yet the qualifications of office are such as to make its determination the province of a rank amateur. The inadequacies of the coroner's office to deal with urban situations were strikingly demonstrated in our cities throughout the nineteenth century. The actions of well-meaning coroners often resulted in the disappearance of witnesses and the loss of valuable evidence.[43] The persistence of abuses soon led to reforms. Massachusetts abandoned the coroner system as early as 1877. New York followed suit in 1915. In 1927 New Jersey adopted the medical examiner system.[44]

Perhaps the most telling argument against the coroner is that the function contained in its office can be more effectively carried out by other law enforcement agencies. The determination of the cause of death is primarily a medical problem requiring the efforts of highly skilled technicians. In New York City, for example, the chief medical examiner must not only be a physician but also a skilled pathologist and microscopist.[45] Indeed, so vital is this aspect to the detection of homicide that a full-time staff of fifty-three persons are required. Moreover, the judicial function of the coroner can be more adequately handled by the magistrates or by the grand jury. Finally the prosecutor, trained in the appraisal of evidence, is present in every phase of law enforcement. The abolition of the coroner's office would do much to modernize the administration of criminal justice.

The petit jury. The petit jury, like the grand jury, also has a long and honorable history. It, too, originated in the reign of Henry II where it served as a substitute for trial by battle or ordeal. As such, it represented a great forward step. In colonial times, the juries often took a hostile stand toward the British government. Later the right to trial by jury in both criminal and civil cases, the latter where the amount in controversy was in excess of twenty dollars, was incorporated in the federal and state constitutions. The jury has

43 Moley, *op. cit.*, pp. 110-115.

44 The office of medical examiner in New York City actually did not come into being until 1918.

45 Rankin, *op. cit.*, p. 174.

been hailed by no less a person than Joseph Choate as "the great palladium of our liberties." The jury, he has urged, is the great training ground of our democracy. While most Americans are not given to such flights of rhetoric, they, nevertheless, regard it as the protector of the little man; as the guarantee that he will get the justice due him. Indeed Americans are so convinced of its value that any attempt to modify or simplify the jury system invariably evokes a loud public outcry.

Criticism of the petit jury. Nonetheless, despite the high esteem in which it is held by laymen and many legalists, it is necessary to examine the institution on its merits in order to determine realistically its utility in this day and age. To say this is not to disparage the role of the jury. It is an important part of the court and it works hand and glove with the judge. Its job is primarily one of deciding points of law. Presumably acting together, they decide both law and justice.[46] This is the theory, but the underlying question in all jury decisions—whether twelve men "tried and true" are either capable or equipped to arrive at a "general verdict"—remains to be answered.

The value of the jury hinges mainly on this point. Its ability to render a fair verdict is in doubt. In pioneer America it was reasonable to assume that twelve fair-minded individuals representative of the community could make an acceptable judgment on matters which they could comprehend. But today the situation is quite different. Cases involving accidents, negligence, property, and contracts are so involved that even competent lawyers are often baffled. If the complexity is such as to perplex the specialist, then the problem of the generalist on the jury is magnified a hundred-fold.

Another factor casting doubt upon the value of the jury as a decider of facts is the method of jury selection. The jury is supposed to be representative of the community at large. It is chosen on a random basis. Jurors are impartial and are not presumed to know either the litigants or the issues. But the caliber of the jury after the selection process leaves much to be desired. Many groups by law are relieved of jury service. Those finally selected are then subjected to elimination by lawyers who seek to seat those jurors who will be emotionally responsive to their appeals. Juries often are "packed" with persons of low caliber.

---

[46] J. Ulman, *A Judge Takes the Stand* (New York: Alfred A. Knopf, Inc., 1933), p. 23.

Judge Frank has asserted that the jury cannot decide facts or comprehend the law. In matters of fact they are asked to suspend judgment until the trial is over, but the adversary proceeding which presents conflicting testimony on different points is confusing to the average juror. Under such circumstances it is not surprising that in damage cases the flipping of a coin or averaging of awards proposed by various jurors is often the method of agreement before the jurors leave the jury room. Nor can the jurors adequately understand the law involved. Although the judge is their legal adviser, he does not instruct them in matters of law until all the evidence is in. Even then it may be argued that legal rules can be grasped only by those who have had legal training. In any event, although the judge charges the jury, they are asked to consider the evidence in the light of the law only after the trial is over.[47]

What has been said above by way of criticism applies to criminal as well as civil cases. In an age of specialization, the jury has been largely by-passed. Despite the need for a high intellect and a detached temperament in the analysis of complex issues, it continues as a body of generalists. Critics of the jury system argue that reforms are needed. The method of jury selection is a sore point. Even the defenders of the jury system agree to this. Some have advocated the English system where the judge chooses the jury.[48] In civil cases, it is urged that the jury either be eliminated or greatly restricted in its powers. Judge David Peck of the New York City courts, for example, has proposed the withdrawal from the courts of automobile cases which clog the court calendars. He would put them in the hands of an administrative agency which would award damages, regardless of fault. In this manner expert judgment would be substituted for that of a lay jury.[49] One study of criminal cases in Ohio revealed that a majority of judges, prosecutors, and lawyers favored the waiver of the right of jury trial in criminal cases.[50] Another study urged three main reforms: (1) better methods of selection, (2) abolition of the general verdict, and (3) "control of the judge over the trial as it existed at common law must be restored." [51]

---

47 J. Frank, *Courts on Trial* (Princeton, N. J.: Princeton University Press, 1949), Ch. VIII, especially pp. 115-118.

48 Willoughby, *op. cit.,* p. 512.

49 D. W. Peck, "Do Juries Delay Justice," *New York Times Magazine,* December 25, p. 8.

50 Unsigned note, *Journal of the American Judicature Society,* XVIII, p. 48.

51 Unsigned note, *Journal of the American Judicature Society,* XXVI (1942), p. 71.

Defense of the petit jury. The defenders of the jury system, while admitting many of the inadequacies noted, are not without their arguments. Their "case" rests upon four main points: (1) juries can examine facts better than judges, (2) juries may modify the effect of special law, (3) juries can overrule incompetent and biased judges, and (4) juries can actually assist the judge in making decisions by acting as a buffer when a public is aroused.[52] One can, of course, debate the pros and cons ad infinitum. What is important, however, is the fact that the controversy over the jury is evidence of grave disquiet within the legal community and among responsible and informed laymen. Whether or not the jury system is adequate depends upon the answers to three main questions: (1) does it permit an objective analysis of the evidence? (2) does it hold the jurors responsible for their acts? and (3) does it make for prompt handling of cases? On none of these questions does the jury system rate highly. Until improvements are made, the jury as an institution will continue to lag far behind the responsibilities imposed upon it by our society.[53]

CONCLUSION

Law is the basis of civilization. Without its presence, organized social living cannot exist. Law provides the norms of conduct and prescribes the methods for the settlement of disputes between individuals or groups. The courts are that part of the community framework whose function it is to make decisions among disputants.

The scope and complexity of both law and the courts vary with the needs of a given society. In a rural society law and court structure are relatively simple. Conversely, in an urban society legal controls become more complex, invading an ever larger area of what, under a rural situation, was considered private conduct. Courts, as a consequence, have to deal with much more complex problems.

Our society, which has moved from a predominantly rural to an urban base, reflects this change. Law and the courts have been forced to bear an increasingly heavy burden. Legal institutions and legal philosophy geared to a rural society have become more and more ill-adopted to the needs of an urban society. Efforts to bring our judicial institutions more in consonance with everyday realities have

---

52 Frank, *op. cit.,* Ch. IX. Judge Frank also has a refutation of each of these arguments.

53 Willoughby, *op. cit.,* 490-491 has an excellent discussion on this point.

taken many forms. Justice of the peace courts have been largely eliminated in the cities and municipal courts have taken their place. Courts of special jurisdiction dealing with the child, the delinquent, the family, and domestic relations have been added. The gradual fragmentation of judicial authority led to the growth of the unified municipal court movement.

In the twentieth century state-wide court integration began. Its general aim was to obtain a unified approach to legal problems within the state as a whole. While this was a laudable endeavor, it neglected almost entirely the needs of metropolitan areas. There is still a great need for urban justice in these rapidly evolving districts.

Although we have made much progress in adapting our legal institutions and philosophy to the needs of an urban society, there is still a cultural lag that is to be overcome. As Dean Pound has so correctly remarked, "The methods of the rural magistrate are out of place without the personal knowledge on the part of the court and the community which they presuppose." [54] Both civil and criminal justice have to be geared more effectively to the needs of an urban society.

BIBLIOGRAPHY

Books:

Frank, J. *Courts on Trial.* Princeton, New Jersey: Princeton University Press, 1949.

Griffith, E. S. *History of American City Government.* New York: Oxford University Press, 1938.

Lepawsky, A. *The Judicial System of Metropolitan Chicago.* Chicago: The University of Chicago Press, 1932.

Mockridge, N. and Prall, R. *The Big Fix.* New York: Henry Holt and Co., 1954.

Moley, R. *Politics and Criminal Prosecution.* New York: Minton Balch and Co., 1929.

Reid, E. *Mafia.* New York: Random House, 1952.

Smith, R. H. *Justice and the Poor.* New York: The Carnegie Foundation for Teaching, 1919.

Ulman, J. *A Judge Takes the Stand,* New York: Alfred A. Knopf, Inc., 1933.

Willoughby, W. F. *Principles of Judicial Administration.* Washington, D. C.: The Brookings Institution, 1929.

---

[54] Pound, *op. cit.,* p. 190.

Articles and Other Material:

"Administration of Justice in Metropolitan Areas." *Journal of the American Judicature Society,* XXXIV (1951), 111-116.

Hecht, W. C. "Exploring the Trial of Cases in New York County," *The Annals,* CCLXXXVII (1953), 134-140.

Hollander, B. "A Change in the Old Order: England Streamlines Her Jury Systems," *American Bar Association Journal,* XXXVI (1950), 455-457.

Ploscowe, M. "The Inferior Criminal Courts in Action," *The Annals,* CCLXXXVII (1953), 8-12.

Porter, C. O. "Defects in the Administration of Justice in Hamilton County (Cincinnati) Ohio," *Journal of the American Judicature Society,* XXXII (1950), 14-21.

Pound R. "The Administration of Justice in the Modern City," *Harvard Law Review,* XXV (1913), 303-315.

Shaw, A. V. "The Grand Jury: Use it or Lose it," *Journal of the American Judicature Society,* XXXII (1948), 6-9.

Chapter Twelve

Special Courts and Special Problems

Introduction

City life subjects our judicial system to severe stresses and strains. Urbanization and industrialization have an erosive effect upon the primary institutions of control, the family, the church, and the neighborhood. At the same time, the impersonality and monotony of specialized work seem to create an urge toward individual self-expression. Thus, while the closeness of city living necessitates infinite and varied regulation, the private agencies no longer seem to operate upon the individual with the same force and effect. Law, which is only one of many institutions of restraint, seems to have been put in the position where it is almost the sole instrument of control.

This, of course, is a condition that has been in birth for at least a half-century. For some time urban justice struggled along on the presumption that legal norms and the imposition of generalized penalties were sufficient. Gradually, however, it was recognized that the vicissitudes of city life exposed the individual to many pressures and that, in many respects, he was no longer the master of his fate. Punishment alone was not a sufficient deterrent. It had to be supplemented by preventive and more specialized treatment. When this viewpoint took root, law was tailored not to the *offense* but to the *offender*. Specialized courts arose to deal with problems of individual maladjustment.[1]

Family Courts

The rise of the family court. One of the first institutions to feel the stress of city life was the family. Urbanization and industrialization, changed ideas of personal freedom, and a host of other factors have subjected the family to increasing pressures.[2] Divorce and

[1] R. Pound, *Criminal Justice in America* (New York: Henry Holt and Co., 1930), ch. 5.

[2] E. L. Koos, "Family Problems and the Courts," *The Annals*, CCLXXXVII (May 1953), p. 27.

broken homes are increasing at an alarming rate. One index of the problem facing the nation are the statistics on marriage and divorce. In 1946 the high point in marriage and divorce was reached. For that year the number of marriages per thousand was 16.4 while the divorce rate was 4.3 per thousand. Six years later the marriage rate was 9.9 per thousand, while the divorce rate had declined to 2.5 per thousand. For the year 1954, however, it is estimated that the number of marriages will be 9.2 per thousand, while the divorce rate will increase to 4.0 per thousand. In other words there will be roughly half as many divorces as there are marriages.[3]

The rising divorce rate is of paramount concern to society, but it is also a problem of the courts. The family, after all, is a legal unit that is created and protected by law. When family discord endangers the legal relationship, it becomes a matter of judicial concern. No court can solve all family problems; but it can serve as a focal point around which the purposive forces of the community can rally. This is, or at least should be, the function of the family court.[4]

Weaknesses of the family courts. Family courts in the city suffer from two fundamental weaknesses: faulty legal training and inadequate jurisdiction. Many courts accept the concept of guilt in dealing with family matters. Marital discord often is regarded as a dispute between two parties, one of whom is innocent and the other guilty. Sanctions are applied against the offending party. Yet family relationships are so interrelated and reciprocal that the choice between contending parties is rarely clear. Moreover, even if it were possible to establish guilt, the aim of such courts should not be to compel people to live together but rather to work out a satisfactory relationship.[5] As the noted authority Paul Alexander has remarked, "the broken family is not the result of divorce; divorce is the result of a broken family." [6] The aim of such courts, he urges, should be to discover the causes of a broken home and to employ not only legal sanctions but also "all possible remedies, such as those afforded by religion, medicine, sociology, education, etc." [7] Family courts, he

---

[3] U. S. Bureau of Census, *Statistical Abstract of the United States 1955* (seventy-sixth edition; Washington, D. C., 1956), p. 59.

[4] Koos, *op. cit.*, pp. 27-28.

[5] Koos, *op. cit.*, p. 28.

[6] P. W. Alexander, "Family Life Conference Suggests New Judicial Procedures Toward Marriage and Divorce," *Journal of American Judicature Society*, XXXII (1948), p. 39.

[7] *Ibid.*, p. 34.

suggests, should be taken out of the area of criminal courts. The judge should be assisted by trained personnel in all areas of human relations.

Not only is a more forward approach to the improvement of divorce law needed but also the jurisdiction of family courts must be changed. New York City courts are fairly indicative of the manner in which such courts function. At least six tribunals handle the problems of the family. The Family Court deals with relations in the home. The Supreme Court presides over divorce proceedings. The Children's Court seeks to protect the child. The Home Term Court intervenes in cases of assault and battery. The Surrogates Court has authority over adoption.[8] It is the considered opinion of a New York City magistrate that inferior courts, because of their limited powers, cannot do a satisfactory job.[9] In Richmond, Virginia six different courts of record grant divorces; but the Domestic Relations Court does not have such authority. A survey of the national scene indicates that jurisdiction over family matters is divided among the following courts: domestic relations court, juvenile court, felony court, police court, trial court and, in some instances, equity and probate courts.[10]

Segmented authority handicaps the court in its attempt to deal with problems of family discord. Inferior courts have inadequate powers, and by the time the family dispute reaches a superior court, matters have hardened to the point where solution is most difficult. Moreover, court facilities vary greatly. Some are merely justice of the peace courts where the judge is hardly more than an informed layman. Others may be courts of superior jurisdiction where every means for rehabilitation, legal and social, may be available to assist the judge. Because of the wide variation in scope and function, justice in family matters is largely a resultant of the type of court handling a given case.

Courts of domestic relations or "family courts" are of relatively recent origin. New York State in 1910 was a pioneer. In that year the Buffalo City Court established a Domestic Relations Court, and Manhattan and Brooklyn soon followed suit. A year later Chicago

---

[8] *New York Times Magazine,* December 20, 1953, p. 16.

[9] M. Ploscowe, "The Inferior Criminal Courts in Action," *The Annals, op. cit.,* p. 9.

[10] P. W. Alexander, "The Family Court of the Future," *Journal of the American Judicature Society,* XXXVI (1952), p. 38.

made such a court part of its municipal court system.[11] By now the need for separate and special courts for family relations is almost universally recognized. Proper and effective organization, however, is still needed. Such courts are handicapped in four main ways: (1) part-time justices who are not specialists in family cases; (2) popular-elected judges; (3) a paucity of social and clinical services; and (4) lack of adequate status and dignity.[12] Integrated courts with unified criminal and civil jurisdiction are also a necessity. In Portland, Oregon, Columbia, South Carolina and eight major cities of Ohio this has already become a reality. Family court organization is being gradually shaped to the idea that the family is a single unit and must be treated as such. The basic features of a family court are: (1) the broadest possible civil and criminal jurisdiction over all family matters; (2) adequate quarters and dignity; (3) a trained staff of specialists and case workers; (4) informal hearings; (5) continuing judicial supervision.[13]

JUVENILE COURTS

The wayward youth and the juvenile delinquent constitute a major problem in almost every city. In 1954 the Federal Bureau of Investigation reported that "juveniles (under 18) represented 57.6 percent of all persons arrested for auto theft. They were also high in burglary and larceny arrests, 49.0 percent and 43.6 percent, respectively, of the persons arrested in each category." [14] In 1954, persons under 21 years of age committed 63 percent of the burglaries, 55 percent of the larcenies, and 73 percent of the auto thefts. One may argue that these statistics are inflated since the inexperience of the youthful offender makes his apprehension easier. Nevertheless, a significant share of the serious crimes is perpetrated by those in the age group of 16 to 21. It is in this area that the courts for youthful offenders are important, for they can do much to prevent juveniles from becoming hardened criminals.

Evolution of juvenile courts. Children have always enjoyed the special protection of the state. The phrase "ward of the state" is perhaps most expressive of this view. The child, in other words, was

[11] W. F. Willoughby, *Principles of Judicial Administration* (Washington, D. C.: The Brookings Institution, 1929), pp. 328-330.

[12] Alexander, *op. cit.*, p. 43.

[13] Alexander, *op. cit.*, p. 45; Willoughby, *op. cit.*, pp. 333-334.

[14] U. S. Federal Bureau of Investigation, *Uniform Crime Reports for the United States*, XXV, No. 2 (1955), p. 111.

regarded as especially vulnerable and the state assumed the role of guardian of his welfare. This concept was demonstrated in many ways. Parents were held responsible for the neglect of their children, and where their inability was shown, the government, through the courts, intervened as a protector of the child. The court, in its procedures, also recognized the special interest of the child. Problems of youthful offenders were segregated from the rest of the court business. Prevention rather than punishment gradually became the objective. Paul Alexander has correctly described the change. "Instead of determining whether the child is guilty of an offense, and if so, sentencing him to a children's prison, the court tried to determine why the child behaves as he does and correct his behavior." [15]

This attitude did not spring full blown from the mind of the judge. It was a century or more in its evolution. As early as 1869 Massachusetts made provision for "visiting agents" whose function it was to sit in on judicial proceedings involving the juvenile. The "agent" was regarded as a special officer to advise the judge on the disposition of the case. Many other states soon followed suit and within the short space of three decades it became the general practice in almost all courts. Separate children's courts, however, were not established until the turn of the century.

In this country, Illinois led the way. Chicago, in 1899, acting under a law of the state legislature, established the first juvenile court. It was soon followed by Denver where the court, under the leadership of Judge Ben Lindsay, became world famous. The distinctive feature of the Chicago court, widely copied by all juvenile courts, was its power to intervene upon behalf of the delinquent before he was convicted. The theory behind such action was that corrective efforts could be undertaken before the child had been branded a criminal. This, indeed, represented an almost radical departure from prior court practices where children were involved.

From these halting steps came many further innovations that were destined to make a reality out of the phrase "ward of the state." Chicago, in 1909, added a child guidance center to its court. On a clinic basis it sought to make available therapy and guidance for the potential delinquent. Many other courts soon followed suit. By 1928 more than 500 such clinics had been established.[16] Courts were

[15] Alexander, *op. cit.*, p. 41.

[16] H. E. Barnes and N. K. Teeters, *New Horizons in Criminology* (rev. ed.; New York: Prentice-Hall, Inc., 1945), p. 930.

organized also to handle the problems of the wayward minor. In 1914 Chicago pioneered again with its Boys' Court for those between 17 and 21 years of age. Wayward minors acts have been enacted in New York, Michigan and many other states. New York City, with its Girls' Term Court, its Youth Term Court, its Probation Court and its Adolescent Courts operates under such laws.[17]

In 1940 a further step was taken, this time to rehabilitate the youth convicted of crimes. In that year the American Law Institute proposed a Model Youth Correction Authority Act. This was patterned after the famous English Boorstal system. Under its terms, unless a suspended sentence on a capital offense was involved, the youth was to be turned over to an authority which would seek to reorient him. The act was adopted by California a year later following a report by Judge Ben Lindsay revealing brutality in the Whittier School for Boys. Wisconsin and Minnesota have adopted similar enabling acts. New York and New Jersey have accepted portions of the law. The effort to remake youths into responsible citizens after they have been convicted has filled in a void in the handling of delinquent youth.

In California following conviction, the youth undergoes six weeks of observation in a diagnostic clinic by specialists, after which a program of rehabilitation is undertaken in the Whittier School for Boys.[18] Because of the need for institutionalization, correction after conviction is largely a state concern, although the city has a vital interest in it since its youth are committed.

Thus in roughly a century of evolution the treatment of the juvenile and adolescent has undergone a startling transformation. Separate courts exist to deal with their problems. Prevention and therapy rather than punishment have emerged as the main themes. From the first beginning in 1899 there has now evolved some three thousand courts. Almost every city in the country has at least one such judicial agency. One authority has characterized this development as the most outstanding contribution in the administration of criminal justice since the Magna Carta of 1215.[19]

---

[17] G. Samuels, "Inner View of the Probation Problem," *New York Times Magazine*, May 14, 1952, p. 17.

[18] G. R. Winters, "Modern Court Services for Youths and Juveniles," *Journal of the American Judicature Society*, XXXIII (1948), pp. 117-118.

[19] N. S. Winnet, "Fifty Years of the Juvenile Court: An Evaluation," *American Bar Association Journal*, XXXVI (1950), p. 363.

Distinctive features of children's courts. Having traced briefly the evolution of such courts, let us now examine their distinctive features. Such courts, to repeat, are guided by one major premise, concern for the child. They seek to help rather than punish. Thus they attempt to get at the causes of maladjustment. This means that the court must be assisted by a staff professionally trained in medicine, probation, case work and a host of other areas. The procedure of the court is informal, the judge seeking to ascertain the facts in order that he might be of assistance to the youthful offender.[20] The ideal juvenile court, according to the National Probation and Parole Association, should have the following features: (1) exclusive jurisdiction over children; (2) a judge who is chosen for his sympathetic attitude toward parents and children; (3) informal noncriminal proceedings; (4) a sufficient number of trained probation workers; (5) adequate facilities for physical examination and psychiatric assistance; (6) well-equipped detention homes or selected boarding homes for temporary care of children; (7) efficient record systems; and (8) cooperation with other social agencies.[21]

These, it should be emphasized, represent the ideal. It is fairly evident that it has not as yet been realized in practice.[22] The contrast between the ideal and the actual has three main facets. First, although much progress has been made, the juvenile court has not as yet freed itself from the criminal courts. Second, courts dealing with the juvenile and the adolescent have not attracted the best qualified persons to serve as judges. Such courts are on the lower rung of the judicial ladder and talented judges do not usually seek such service. Moreover, qualified judges need not only legal training but also a thorough understanding of sociological phenomena. Third, there is some ground for believing that even the more progressive courts have not been willing to acknowledge their own limitations. Many courts continue to play a significant role in child welfare programs which more properly might be the province of the Welfare department. Moreover, in some instances there is the tendency of such courts to assume jurisdiction over minor cases that might well have been settled without them. Conversely, there is also the disposition to accept responsibility for cases beyond their

---

[20] I. B. Cooper, "Judge's Plea to the Bar," *American Bar Association Journal*, XL (1954), pp. 118-120.

[21] Unsigned note, *Journal of the American Judicature Society*, XXXV (1951), p. 51.

[22] See comments of Barnes and Teeters, *op. cit.*, pp. 927-928.

resources. Lastly, there is a real need for these courts to exercise more community leadership and to seek ". . . a more sympathetic and effective relationship with social case workers and social agencies." [23]

SMALL CLAIMS COURTS

Equal justice before the law has been an ideal of American justice ever since its Anglo-Saxon beginnings. In rural America this ideal was readily realizable since the legal system was simple and uncomplicated. Aggrieved parties with petty claims were able to obtain a remedy by simply applying to the justice of the peace courts. Settlement of claims was made promptly. Urbanization, however, brought about a tremendous change. Dean Roscoe Pound, writing in the twentieth century, expressed the belief that small claims procedures in the American city had become so complicated that the well-to-do had an unfair advantage over persons without means.[24] Reginald Heber Smith in his study, *Justice and the Poor,* cited three main evils of urban justice in the settlement of small claims; (1) delay, (2) court cost and fees, and (3) the expense of counsel. These weaknesses were made possible by both faulty court organization and antiquated criminal procedure.[25]

The poor quality of justice at the bottom of the judicial ladder was quite common until judicial reform was undertaken. The prospect of delay and expense either dissuaded people from undertaking suits or forced settlements where the anticipated cost seemed larger than the amount to be gained by the suit. Small tradesmen regularly turned over the collection of debts to collection agencies at a huge discount. Wage earners faced by high costs were loath to sue for wages due. "Justice of the peace law" was insufficient and even the advent of the municipal courts did not essentially remedy the situation. For the little man justice was largely an index of his ability to pay. Small wonder then that he found himself at a disadvantage. Equalization of justice waited upon court reform.[26]

The small claims courts originated in the conviction that an informal mediation procedure which discouraged the use of an attorney and the right of appeal would reduce court costs in the inter-

---

23 Winnet, *op. cit.,* pp. 364-366.
24 Pound, *op. cit.,* pp. 305-315.
25 R. H. Smith, *Justice and the Poor* (New York: The Carnegie Foundation for Teaching, 1919), chs. IV-VI, especially pp. 17-19.
26 Smith, *op. cit.,* pp. 33-39.

est of the petty litigant. Its main features, according to Reginald H. Smith, are "extremely low costs or none at all, no formal pleadings, no lawyers, and direct examination of parties and witnesses without formality by a trained judge who knows and applies the substantive law." [27] In 1913 a minimal step in this direction was taken when three cities in Kansas, Topeka, Leavenworth and Kansas City, pioneered in the creation of small debtors' courts. These were hardly more than a beginning since jurisdiction was limited to claims not exceeding $20. Torts were excluded. Judges had no legal training.[28] A more advanced step was taken in the same year when Cleveland established a conciliation branch as part of its municipal court system. Wide discretionary power was granted to the presiding justice. His aim was to gain agreement of both parties. If he were unable to do so, he might make his own decision although this was subject to immediate appeal in a higher court. Like the Kansas courts, jurisdiction was limited in this instance, however, to $35.[29]

Following these initial experiments were a series of other actions taken by other states. In 1915 the District Court of Multonmah County, Oregon, actually a court for the City of Portland, was given jurisdiction over small claims. Two years later, Minneapolis and New York City took similar action. Spokane, Chicago, and Philadelphia followed suit. A feature of the latter court deserves mention. It was given jurisdiction over amounts as high as $1500.[30] Massachusetts introduced a further innovation in 1920. Prior to that time each municipal court followed its own practice, but thereafter a uniform state-wide procedure for the handling of small claims up to $35 was made mandatory. The practice was copied by California, Nevada, South Dakota and Idaho.[31]

Small claims constitute a major portion of the country's legal business. Nonpayment of rent, back wages, torts, small debts, and even the collection of taxes by the city are covered in such suits. Amounts of money involved may seem trivial, but, nonetheless, they are items of significance to the litigants. In some courts these cases are handled expeditiously. The Baltimore People's Court has four

27 *Ibid.*, p. 56.

28 W. F. Willoughby, *Principles of Judicial Administration* (Washington, D. C.: The Brookings Institution, 1929), p. 311.

29 Smith, *loc. cit.*, pp. 49-50.

30 Willoughby, *op. cit.*, p. 314; Smith, *op. cit.*, pp. 58-63.

31 Willoughby, *op. cit.*, pp. 315-316.

judges who handle 65,000 cases annually.[32] In others, proceedings are still enmeshed in technicalities.

Although much progress has been made since the pioneering studies of Pound and Smith, improvements in small claims procedure have not kept pace with the huge population increase.[33] Public attention seems to be focused on the high courts to the detriment of the lower courts. One may well echo the plaint of Glen R. Winters who has written, "To lavish legal talents on courts of last resort and leave small claims to be heard by untrained, fee-paid laymen is equivalent to a bakery having an expert baker for wedding cakes and letting the odd man bake the bread." [34]

TRAFFIC COURTS

The advent of motor transport has brought many benefits to urban America. It has also compounded many of the problems faced by the city. In a motor age the city is largely dependent upon transportation. Its streets are its arteries. The degree to which the city can function depends to a considerable degree upon the ability of its people to move freely and without hazard from place to place. Narrow streets, inadequate parking facilities, and the vast increase in buses, trucks, and cars have brought in their wake choked roads, frustration, delay, and, even worse, accident and death. The city seeks to deal with this rapidly emerging situation by the prescription of a mass of detailed regulations.

Traffic movement under congested conditions of the modern city constitutes a serious matter for most municipalities. In the year 1952 traffic fatalities across the nation numbered 38,000; nonfatal injuries reached a high of 1.4 million. Property damage rose to $3.5 million.[35] For 1951, 729 cities out of a total of 1,371 cities of a population over 10,000 reported 13 million violations of traffic ordinances, of which approximately one-fourth or 3.2 million eventually became traffic cases.[36] The gravity of the situation can be stressed in yet another

32 A. W. Rhynhart, "Baltimore People's Court Saves the Time of Litigants," *Journal of the American Judicature Society,* XXXIV (1950–1951), pp. 24-25.

33 R. H. Smith, "Legal Offices for Persons of Modest Means," *Journal of the American Judicature Society,* XXXI (1947), pp. 37-39.

34 G. R. Winters, "A Hundred Years of Judicial Administration," *Journal of the American Judicature Society,* XXX (1946), p. 26.

35 J. P. Economas, "The Traffic Problem, Traffic Laws and Traffic Courts," *The Annals, op. cit.,* p. 13.

36 *Ibid.,* p. 14.

way. The total of traffic cases is greater than that of the number of civil and other criminal cases in both the state and federal courts.

Traffic movement is largely the responsibility of the police department. Violations of regulations and ordinances are tried in the courts. Traffic courts are those judicial agencies which have jurisdiction over offenses that result from a failure upon the part of the citizens to conform with the legal norms established by the city. They may be municipal courts, branches of the city court, magistrates courts and even justice of the peace courts. Essentially these are courts of limited jurisdiction with the right of appeal to higher courts. Through their doors flow a constant stream of cases, some trivial, some serious. The great majority of these are parking violations, but a goodly number are concerned with accidents, damages, and even fatalities.

From a judicial standpoint the work of these courts has special significance. For 99 percent of the American people this is their first contact with courts. What they see and hear often gives them an ineradicable impression of urban justice.[37] A proper respect for the judicial process is probably as important as the endeavor to prevent the constant and growing threat to life and limb. Yet the procedure of these courts leaves much to be desired. The major criticisms of traffic courts center around the following: (1) the need for an improved court atmosphere; (2) elimination of ticket fixing; (3) segregation of traffic from other offenses; (4) better education for the judges of traffic courts; [38] and (5) separation of the minor from the more serious offenses. Parking violations, it is agreed, should be handled by violations bureaus, whereas the more serious offenses should be dealt with by a summons or court order compelling the defendant to appear in court. For some individuals, no amount of punishment will constitute corrective action. For these, deprivation of the right to drive a motor vehicle is the only solution. For many "repeaters," however, traffic education serves as a valuable adjunct to improvement. Properly administered, it can do much to reduce the threat to life and property.[39] Education and enforcement are prime objectives of traffic courts.

The beginnings of traffic court reform date from 1938 when the

---

[37] E. W. Frost, "The Traffic Court Improvement Program," *Journal of the American Judicature Society*, XXXIII (1950), p. 167.

[38] *Ibid.*, pp. 169-170.

[39] Economas, *op. cit.*, pp. 14-15; 18-19.

American Bar Association authorized a complete study of the subject. The National Safety Congress also established a committee to deal with the problem. Since that time the fruits of these twin endeavors have been reflected in the constant improvement of traffic enforcement. Better training of judges, more careful separation of offenders, the growing movement toward more integration of traffic courts with the state system, uniform traffic tickets and complaints, all have been by-products of the movement. The mounting toll of death and destruction has not been eliminated, but the resources for dealing with an increasingly grave situation have been improved.

THE COST OF JUSTICE

In previous pages we have noted the growing interdependence of modern city life. This trend has been accentuated by World War II and the seemingly insatiable demands of a viable, high-level economy. Under the impact of these conditions a societal revolution has occurred. Relationships between husband and wife, father and child, employer and employee, to mention but a few, have been drastically altered. Even the concept of property has undergone a severe change.

The governmental by-product of such developments has been the growing intervention of the government into what were formerly considered private areas. Law and social control in the interest of organized living imposed legal obligations upon all individuals, regardless of economic status. But as Dean Pound has pointed out, the machinery of justice which protects all within an urban community often operated to defeat its intended purpose—equal justice for all. The cost of justice has been so great that those who are lower on the economic ladder are often forced to forego many of their rights.[40]

As government becomes more and more a party to litigation, the need for more adequate legal assistance for persons of moderate means becomes more evident. In criminal proceedings the government attorney, armed with the authority of the state and backed by an efficient police force, is a formidable antagonist. The individual who is able to hire a capable defense attorney is reasonably certain that his rights under law will be protected. The poor, friendless defendant who becomes enmeshed in the toils of the law, however, finds himself face to face with a strong opponent against whom he can only muster one resource, the barter of some of the rights to

[40] Pound, "The Administration of Justice in the Modern City," *Harvard Law Review,* XXVI (February 1913), p. 316.

which he is entitled by law. Similarly, in civil cases where private parties are involved in controversy, the person without means is at a decided disadvantage. Attorneys point out that wealthy clients are prone to appeal their cases, using the lower courts merely for record-making purposes.[41] Disparity of income often results in a different brand of justice for rich and poor.

The need to provide adequate legal services for persons of moderate means, as Reginald H. Smith has pointed out, "has emerged as one of the greatest post-war problems." [42] Many millions of Americans do not have sufficient income to obtain legal assistance. Emery Brownell, in his comprehensive survey of the status of legal aid in the United States, asserted that a family of three with an income of $2000 cannot afford a lawyer. At least 16 million people in this category live in urban areas.[43] In criminal cases, according to this study, 60 percent of the defendants are unable to employ counsel.[44] Mayer C. Goldman has asserted that the right to counsel in criminal cases has fallen to the level where it is a privilege of those who can afford it.[45] If a lawyer is essential for the protection of one's rights in a court of law, then justice is being rationed upon the basis of ability to pay for a lawyer rather than need.[46]

The high cost of litigation often operates adversely against the person of moderate means. In all courts, litigants are required to pay at least a part of the cost of maintaining the legal facilities for justice. This is largely a product of statute, but the rationale behind the practice is derived from ancient English practice. In those days fees were charged in some instances to discourage false claims; in others, to obtain revenue for the king's treasury.[47] There does not seem to be any valid reason why the entire burden should not be assumed by the government, but nevertheless, the practice has continued to the disadvantage of the person of moderate means.

Court costs involve many charges. There is usually an entry fee

---

[41] E. Marx, "Justice is Expensive," *Journal of the American Judicature Society,* XXXVI (1952), p. 76.

[42] R. H. Smith, "Legal Services for Persons of Modest Means," *Journal of the American Judicature Society,* XXXI (1937), p. 37.

[43] E. Brownell, *Legal Aid in the United States* (Rochester, N. Y.: The Lawyers' Cooperative Publishing Company, 1951), p. 77.

[44] *Ibid.,* p. 83.

[45] "The Public Defender," *Journal of the American Judicature Society,* XVIII (1924), p. 176.

[46] E. Brownell, "Availability of Low Cost Legal Services," *The Annals, op. cit.,* also estimates that 34.7 families in civil cases do not have adequate legal services.

[47] Smith, *op. cit.,* pp. 20-21.

which is the amount necessary to commence litigation. Then there are jury fees, stenographer fees, and witness fees. If appeal is undertaken, the cost of printing briefs and records must also be added. Printing costs for such records in 1951 ranged from $1.25 per page in Arkansas and Maine to $4.50 in Vermont and averaged $2.41 per page in 28 states.[48] An appeal to a higher tribunal usually costs more than $500. One authority estimates that less than 10 percent of our citizens can afford to spend that much.[49] If one can contend that "better and best justice" is obtained as one goes higher in the judicial hierarchy, then "what the balance of our citizens receive is a hit and miss affair . . . Our best justice is not for them." [50]

Court costs and attorneys' fees, then, are the major obstacles in the path of equal justice for all. These factors have not, of course, escaped the attention of responsible observers. As early as 1919 the Carnegie Foundation sponsored Reginald Heber Smith's monumental study, *Justice and the Poor.* Another survey of legal aid was begun by Emery Brownell and a committee of experts, the results of which were published in 1951. A year prior to this the House of Delegates of the American Bar Association adopted a resolution which expressed devotion to the ideal of equal justice. It urged its members to work for the establishment of adequate legal aid facilities all over the country.[51]

The effort to "equalize justice" has taken several forms. Small claims procedure has been simplified through the elimination of the attorney and an extension in the advisory assistance of the court. Court assignment of counsel, usually in criminal cases, has been a standard practice. More recently, within the past fifty years at least, the defender system and "legal aid" have been employed on an increasingly wide scale.

Assignment of counsel is based upon the assumption that the lawyer has both a professional and public obligation to give legal assistance to the person without adequate means. It is employed mainly in criminal cases. In eight states lawyers are assigned only in capital offenses. In eighteen it is mandatory that counsel be assigned;

---

48 G. E. Brand, "The Impact of the Increased Cost of Litigation," *Journal of the American Judicature Society,* XXXV (1951), pp. 102-105.

49 Marx, *op. cit.,* p. 75.

50 *Ibid.,* also H. D. Nims, "The Biography of a Lawsuit," *American Bar Association Journal,* XL, (1954), pp. 575-577. An action to recover $11,806.55 after almost nine years of litigation cost the public and parties to the suit at least $15,000.

51 Brownell, *op. cit.,* p. XX.

but in the remainder, counsel is assigned, either at the request of the defendant or at the discretion of the court. In some states if the defendant does not request a lawyer, it is presumed that he has waived the right.[52] Compensation is normally provided in capital crimes, but only 23 states grant compensation in cases other than these.[53] The experience with these "voluntary defenders" in general has not been a happy one. The assigned attorney may have but little or no trial experience. The fact that hardly any provision is made for compensation leaves the door open for the unscrupulous attorney to prey upon the relatives and friends of the accused for "expenses." [54] Emery Brownell has summed up the situation admirably in the following words: *"First this country cannot afford to go on permitting thousands of its poorer citizens each year to face criminal prosecution without the minimum protection of representation by competent legal counsel. Second, the long and wistful attempt to meet so large a need by the volunteer assistance of individual lawyers is a complete and abject failure."* [55]

The public defender. The general realization that legal assistance, if it is to be effective, must be put on an organized basis led to the public defender and legal aid system. The public defender is an office designed to assist all persons who cannot afford legal aid and assistance. The defender and his staff are full-time employees of the city or other jurisdiction, chosen on a merit basis. He is the public counterpart of the prosecutor and, generally, has the same kind of assistance in making investigations and gathering evidence. Normally, the defender has jurisdiction only over criminal cases, although in a few instances, Los Angeles for example, he may also handle civil cases.

The public defender system first began in Los Angeles County, California, in 1913. In that year the city of Los Angeles also appointed a police court defender. From there it spread to such widely distant places as Chicago, Columbus, Memphis and the counties of Connecticut. After an initial burst of enthusiasm the movement almost came to a halt in the 1930s. Since that time, Tulsa, Min-

---

[52] Brownell, *op. cit.*, p. 124; W. M. Beaney, *The Right to Counsel in American Courts* (Ann Arbor, Michigan: University of Michigan Press, 1955), ch. 6.

[53] *Ibid.*, pp. 124-125.

[54] Smith, *op. cit.*, p. 114; also H. I. Pollock, "The Voluntary Defender as Counsel for the Defense," *Journal of the American Judicature Society*, XXXII (1949), pp. 174-175.

[55] Brownell, *op. cit.*, pp. 143-144, italics in quote.

neapolis and a few other cities have enacted public defender legislation.[56] By states, it is probable that California has the most cities and counties in the plan. All in all, the present number of public defender offices is 28.[57]

The public defender system has been the subject of approval and criticism for many years.[58] The arguments in favor of the plan are numerous. It is asserted that, in general, it is more economical. The average cost of a case is estimated at $25.[59] When compared with the system of assigned counsel, it has a distinct advantage. In both Tulsa and Oklahoma City, the cost of a full-time defender was much lower than the aggregate cost of assigned counsel in the state of Oklahoma. In 1949, Baltimore paid out approximately $48,000 for assigned counsel, but it was estimated that a public defender office could have saved about one half of this amount.[60] Other benefits cited are these: it allows for a more thorough preparation of the case; it permits the sifting "of the deserving from the nondeserving cases . . ."; it is marked by the absence of "unscrupulous defenses . . . that, though few, do appear in the records"; it takes less time to present a case; and finally, it provides a better defense.[61]

Criticism of the system is varied. Some fear it is an entering wedge in the steadily growing pattern of governmental control. "To put it succinctly," wrote Reginald Smith, "if the government becomes the lawyer's paymaster, it may soon become his master." [62] Others worry about politics and inertia creeping into the system. The foremost critic, William Scott Stewart, and he is not alone, has attacked the quality of justice under the system. "I say," he argues, "a lawyer is no longer a defense lawyer after he becomes a public defender. . . . He is so anxious not to be thought to have helped a fabricated defense that he leans over backward." The defender, he asserts, "must choose between his own interest and that of his

---

[56] J. V. Bennett, "To Secure the Right to Counsel," *Journal of the American Judicature Society,* XXXII (1949), pp. 177-181.

[57] Brownell, *op. cit.*, p. 126.

[58] It is advocated by M. C. Goldman, "Public Defenders in Criminal Cases," *The Annals,* CCV (1939), p. 16. Also Bennett, *op. cit.*, pp. 177-181.

[59] D. Freeman, "The Public Defender System," *Journal of the American Judicature Society,* XXXII (1948), p. 76.

[60] Brownell, *op. cit.*, pp. 144-145.

[61] *Idem.*

[62] Brownell, *op. cit.*, p. xvii, introduction by Reginald H. Smith. Smith is talking of the general need to provide legal assistance to the persons of modest means.

client."[63] There is considerable merit in the argument that the defender may be faced with a conflict of interest, but it has merit only where the defendant can afford adequate counsel. In most instances, however, the choice is between some counsel or none at all.

Legal aid assistance. Another organized approach to the problem of legal services for the person of moderate means is legal aid. Legal aid has been defined by one of the foremost authorities on the subject "as the organized effort of the bar and community to provide the services of lawyers free, or for a token charge, to persons who cannot afford to pay an attorney's fee and where cases are unremunerative on a contingent basis."[64] It is characterized by four main elements: (1) a well-publicized place where assistance is given; (2) well-established office hours; (3) competent attorneys; and (4) a supervisory policy group that directs the aid in the interest of the bar and the community.[65] The fact that it is organized and subject to policy direction sets it off from other kinds of legal assistance.

Legal aid is primarily a city movement. It began in New York City in 1876 but did not become a full-fledged service until 1890. In the meantime, Chicago also had made a minimal beginning. It was not until the turn of the century that it began to spread to other cities. By 1912 the movement had developed sufficient coherence to form a National Alliance of Legal Aid Societies, which was hardly more than a loose confederation. Five years later the number of legal aid societies in cities was 41. In 1922 the American Bar Association recommended that every state and local bar association appoint a committee on legal aid work. By 1949, the number of cities with legal aid societies had more than doubled, reaching 92. Of these 73 were in cities of 100,000 or more in population, while the remainder were in smaller communities.[66]

Today, although the need for legal aid is much more widely recognized than it was fifty years ago, there is much work that has to be done. Legal aid societies have increased in number, but the need has far outrun the service. In a sense, it may be said that legal aid has been running fast but standing still. Brownell has commented on the phenomenon in the following manner: "The ability of the estab-

---

[63] W. S. Stewart, "The Public Defender System is Unsound In Principle," *Journal of the American Judicature Society*, XXXII (1948), pp. 115-116.

[64] Brownell, *op. cit.*, p. 3.

[65] *Idem.*

[66] Brownell, *op. cit.*, p. 26.

lished organizations to meet the full need in the communities has risen only from 51 percent in 1916 to 55 percent in 1947."[67] The comment applies only to communities where legal aid work is organized, but in many other communities there is a need that has not, and is not, being met. If the goal of equal justice for all is to be reached, herculean efforts to provide legal services, regardless of income, will be needed.

CONCLUSION

For almost a half-century the evolution of our legal institutions has lagged far behind the change in our society from a rural to an urban one. Urbanism has had a profound effect upon the controls exercised by our society. It has weakened the hold of the church, the family, and the neighborhood on the individual. It has meant that a greater reliance has been placed upon law as a regulator of human conduct. But law and the instrument for its enforcement, the courts, have only begun to reflect the changed needs. Prevention rather than punishment is becoming a major thread in our legal fabric. Increasingly, it is recognized that the personal guilt theory is inadequate: that in some instances an individual has no control over the circumstances that shape his behavior; and that finally, it is necessary to tailor the remedy to the offense rather than the offender. From this it was but a short step to the creation of specialized courts.

Concomitantly with legal specialization came the whole question of the cost of justice at the urban level. In civil cases and in criminal action it was found that the objective of equal justice for all was not being realized. Institutional arrangements designed to minimize the gap between the well-to-do and those of moderate means took the form of legal aid societies and the public defender systems.

There is still a wide gap between the ideal and the actual system of urban justice. Much progress has been made, but, as has been indicated in previous pages, a giant step forward is still needed.

BIBLIOGRAPHY

Books:

Barnes, H. E. and Teeters, N. K. *New Horizons in Criminology*. New York: Prentice-Hall, 1945. Revised edition.

---

[67] *Ibid.,* p. 33. Italics in the quote.

Beaney, W. M. *The Right to Counsel in American Courts.* Ann Arbor, Michigan: University of Michigan Press, 1955.

Brownell, E. *Legal Aid in the United States.* Rochester, New York: The Lawyers' Cooperative Publishing Co., 1951.

Kahn, A. J. *Police and the Children.* Citizens Committee on Children of New York City, 1490 Broadway, New York.

Pound, R. *Criminal Justice in America.* New York: Henry Holt and Co., 1930.

United States Federal Bureau of Investigation, *Uniform Crime Reports for the United States.* XXV Washington, D. C.: U. S. Government Printing Office, 1955.

Articles and Other Material:

Alexander, P. W. "Family Life Conference Suggests New Judicial Procedures Toward Marriage and Divorce," *Journal of the American Judicature Society,* XXXII (1948), 38-42.

Brand, G. E. "The Impact of the Increased Cost of Litigation," *Journal of the American Judicature Society,* XXXV (1951), 102-105.

Economas, J. P. "The Traffic Problem, Traffic Laws and Traffic Courts," *The Annals,* CCLXXXVII (1953), 13-17.

Frost, E. W. "The Traffic Court Improvement Program," *Journal of the American Judicature Society,* XXXIII (1950), 166-171.

Marx, E. "Justice is Expensive," *Journal of the American Judicature Society,* XXXVI (1952), 75-77.

Smith, R. H. "Legal Services Officers for Persons of Moderate Means," *Journal of the American Judicature Society,* XXXI (1947), 37-39.

Wherry, W. M. "Preventive Law and Justice to Children," *Journal of the American Judicature Society,* XXXVI (1950), 363-366.

Winters, G. R. "A Hundred Years of Judicial Administration," *Journal of the American Judicature Society,* XXX (1946), 22-30.

———. "Modern Court Services for Youths and Juveniles," *Journal of the American Judicature Society,* XXXIII (1949), 112-120.

Chapter Thirteen

Municipal Finance: Revenues

Importance of Municipal Finance

One of the most important phenomena of American municipal government is the steady rise in government cost. Within the last quarter century the expenditures of local government have tripled.[1] Annual reports of the Bureau of Census reveal that the skyrocketing of costs is continuing. Since World War II municipal expenses have risen to hitherto unprecedented heights. The reasons for this vast upsurge will be explained in the next chapter. Here it is sufficient to note that, while municipal income is at an all-time high, the cities are still in dire financial need. To finance their activities, cities have resorted to desperate measures. Existing tax rates have been increased. New revenue sources have been tapped. Yet the cities have gone more deeply in debt. Financial stringency is the dominant theme of most city governments.

Large policy questions are involved in the efforts of the cities to resolve their fiscal difficulties. To begin with there is the general question of the ability of the city to finance the services it requires. Most costs are in the area of service, and if the community cannot pay for its services, it cannot have them; or at least it must establish a priority in which the more basic services will be provided and the "frills" will be discarded. Secondly, the financial capacity of the municipality depends, to a large extent, upon its tax policy. Rigid inflexible taxes that do not either adequately adjust to cyclical change or reflect the betterment of business conditions may leave large areas of wealth untaxed. Moreover, emphasis on regressive taxes, those that are not levied on the basis of ability to pay, may place a heavy burden on those who can least afford it. Ineffective fiscal administration and incompetence in governmental management may prevent a government from getting high mileage from its tax dollar.

[1] U. S. Department of Commerce, Bureau of Census, *Summary of City Finances* (Washington, D. C.: U. S. Government Printing Office, November 1952), pp. 1-2.

From this brief review, it is evident that municipal finance is probably the single most important problem facing the municipality. The future autonomy of the city hinges upon its ability to meet its fiscal needs. If it is unable to do so, then the solution will undoubtedly be undertaken by a higher level of government with a resultant loss of municipal independence.

MUNICIPAL INCOME SOURCES

During the past decade and a half American municipalities have made a valiant effort to keep up with mounting costs. This is fairly evident from a tabular comparison of the trough year 1942 with that of a decade later (Table 3). These statistics indicate that every

Table 3—CITY REVENUE 1942–1952

Millions of Dollars

Item	*1942*	*1952*	*Percent of Change 1942–1952*
Revenue	3,339	6,583	97
General revenue	2,690	5,257	95
Taxes	1,957	3,462	77
property	1,699	2,580	52
sales and gross receipts	124	544	339
license and other	134	338	152
Intergovernmental revenue	461	1,034	124
Intergovernmental revenue from state only	491	912	118
Utility revenue	565	1,118	98
Insurance trust revenue	84	209	149

Source: "Trends in Municipal Finance," *National Municipal Yearbook for 1954,* p. 243.

income source was made to yield substantial gains. That this is a continuing effort is evident from the year 1954. Municipal income totaled $7,533 millions, 6 percent higher than the previous year.[2]

Cities obtain their income from three main sources; (1) the property tax on land and improvements, (2) aid from other levels of government, and (3) sales and gross receipts taxes, license fees, utility charges and miscellaneous revenues. The property tax, as Table 3 indicates, is still the mainstay of local government finance. In 1952,

[2] U. S. Department of Commerce, Bureau of Census, *Compendium of City Government Finances in 1954* (Washington, D. C.: U. S. Government Printing Office, 1955), pp. 1-2.

it produced $2,580 millions more than any other single income source. Its proportion of the total revenue, however, declined from 63.1 percent in 1942 to 48.7 percent ten years later.[3] A similar trend is evident in the fiscal returns for 1953. That other revenue sources have shown a greater rate of increase indicates that the resistance of property owners to increased real property taxes is making itself felt. As the cities are faced with constantly rising costs, it is apparent that they will have to supplement their income with other forms of taxation.

The real property tax. Although new sources of revenue have been developed, the property tax will continue to be the foundation of municipal finance for the simple reason that other areas of taxation have been pre-empted, in the main, by both the federal and state governments. Since municipalities are dependent upon the latter for their tax authority, it is not likely that the condition will change in the very near future. Thus, how the municipalities utilize their property tax will determine in large measure their ability to finance their activities.

Property taxation may be traced to early colonial times when it was employed mainly to finance the needs of the central government. Later it was used for state purposes. When the growth of cities began in the nineteenth century, the state governments, either through constitution or statute, granted local governments, particularly the cities, the almost exclusive right to use the tax for local purposes. There was considerable logic in this. Land and improvements are fixed and cannot be moved from place to place as is the case with intangibles. Enforcement is fairly simple since both property and improvements can be easily noted by the taxing authority. Moreover, municipal services such as sewers, roads, police, and fire protection make an actual contribution to the value of the property located within the tax jurisdiction. Thus, over the years, property was recognized as the basic of municipal taxation.

Originally, the property tax was merely a flat rate on land and "stock." In the middle of the nineteenth century, however, the concept of the tax was broadened. It became an *ad valorem* tax, that is, a tax according to the value of the property. The new approach was based upon the theory that property was a source of income.

[3] L. F. Anderson, "The Search for Money," *National Municipal Review,* XLIII (1955), p. 76.

Therefore, cost of government should be apportioned upon the value of property as shown by ownership. This was a definite advance in tax thinking; but it brought with it a trainload of problems. Both the tax yield and fairness in the distribution depended upon the valuation of property. For reasons that will be set forth in a few moments, the general property tax has been improperly administered.

Real property tax administration. Assessment of property for local tax purposes is primarily a local responsibility. The administrative machinery to accomplish this task is relatively simple. A tax assessor or a board of assessors, usually the former, is required to prepare the annual tax roll. This is a listing of all taxable property within the tax jurisdiction together with an assigned value for each parcel. The form and content of the tax document are usually prescribed by state law. At a stated time prior to the filing of the tax roll with the next highest level of government, the public is given notice through the newspapers that the tax lists are available for inspection. It is at this time that the taxpayer may question the verdict of the assessor.

Supervision of the assessment procedure is usually made by a county board of review. Any of these agents may revise, change, or correct assessments in the interest of fairness and equity. It may summon the tax assessor and question him on the levels of assessment. It may challenge particular assessments. In general, the supervising agent must make certain that all properties are fairly and uniformly assessed.

Once the tax roll has been approved by the supervising agent, it becomes the basis for all property levies, regardless of the level of government. In municipalities, tax levies are calculated upon the basis of the assessed valuation multiplied by the tax rate, usually expressed in terms of "points" per hundred dollars of assessed valuation. The tax rate is established by the governing body in the following manner. The total cost of local government is calculated. Then anticipated revenues from sources other than the property tax are deducted. The balance of the expenditures obviously must come from real property. This remainder is then divided by the assessed value of property in the taxing district and the result is a tax rate. For example, if the funds to be obtained from property total $500,000 and the assessed value of the property in the municipality is $10,000,000, then the tax rate "per hundred" is $5.00. When the assessor determines the value of a parcel of property, and the tax rate "per hundred" is applied, a tax bill for the property owner results. In summary, the assessor values the property, the council sets the tax rate, and the municipality bills the taxpayer. Figure 6 is a schematic description of the assessment and collection process.

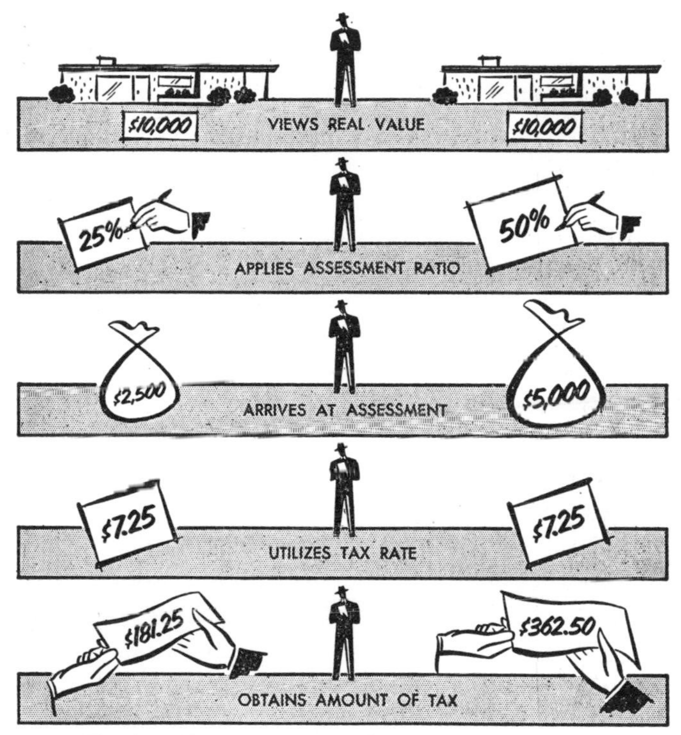

Fig. 6. The Calculation of a Real Property Tax.

The assessment of property is a highly technical job. To determine the value of property the assessor needs to know not only the present but the future worth of the properties in his jurisdiction. He may use the current sales price of similar properties, formulae based upon front-foot values, reproduction cost less depreciation, potential income from property, and a host of other criteria. In the final analysis, however, "a high degree of individual judgment is required." [4]

[4] C. Shoup, R. Blough, and M. Newcomer, *Facing the Tax Problem* (New York: The Twentieth Century Fund, 1937), p. 298.

In the endeavor to counteract the discretion of the assessors, most tax jurisdictions require uniformity of assessments. The assessor is directed to determine the "full and fair value" or the "true value" of all property within his tax district.[5] The almost uniform disregard of this provision is perhaps sufficient commentary upon the adequacy of our tax assessment machinery. Property is rarely assessed at true value. It is estimated that the value of real property in the United States is somewhere in the neighborhood of $600 to $700 billion. Yet assessments total about $200 billion.[6]

The percentage of assessment to full value is termed as assessment ratio. Thus if a property has a value of $10,000 and for tax purposes it is valued at $2,500, the assessment ratio is 25 percent. The practice of undervaluation is justified on the ground that property values are inflated. While there is some merit in this argument, it is also true that the assessed valuation of property has lagged far behind the general rise in the price level. Moreover, the practice of undervaluation has resulted in gross inequalities between communities. Underassessment enables a municipality to minimize its contribution to the county. At the same time the allocation of grants-in-aid by the state to the locality upon the basis of property valuation means that the community which is underassessed will receive a larger proportion of the grants.[7] The present system with its failure to value property at "true value" places a premium upon those municipalities that have low assessment ratios.

Despite the fact that the property tax supplies the major part of municipal income, it has been subject to constant and searching criticism. Objections to the tax rests upon two major premises: (1) it is not considered a good tax according to accepted canons of taxation, and (2) it cannot be administered equitably and adequately.

Philosophical objectives. Most taxes have three main characteristics: (1) they are compulsory; (2) they are levied for the support of the politically organized community; and (3) they are paid without regard to the benefit received.[8] The real property tax has these attributes, but its validity rests upon the twofold assumption: (1) that the tax is levied upon the basis of ability to pay and, further, (2)

---

[5] See for example *Administrative Code of the City of New York*, sections 151-173.

[6] R. A. Freeman, "What Ails the Property Tax," *National Municipal Review*, XLIV (1955), pp. 507-508.

[7] Freeman, *ibid.*, p. 508.

[8] F. B. Carver and A. H. Hansen, *Principles of Economics* (rev. ed.; New York: Ginn and Co., 1938), p. 581.

that land is the measure of income. Neither of these concepts applies to the real property tax of today.

Critics of the property tax point out that the tax is a relic of a bygone era. In colonial and revolutionary times, indeed as late as the middle of the 19th century, a man's wealth came mainly from land or income from land. Since that time, however, new forms of wealth have arisen. Property has become more corporate in character. Stocks, bonds, and securities have become important sources of income. Moreover, as urbanization developed and more and more people left the land and came to the city, salaries and wages, rather than the ownership of property, became the measure of man's ability to pay. Government ignores the changes that have taken place in our society and continues, at least at the city level, to tax land as the main source of wealth. Those whose wealth is in other forms escape their fair share of the municipal tax burden. Continued reliance upon the property tax weighs heavily on those who can least afford the tax.[9]

Moreover, even if it is correct to assume that land is a measure of wealth, the property tax fails to distinguish properly between that land which is a source of income and that which is not. In multiple dwelling units, tenements, or apartment houses the incidence of the property tax, to a large degree, is shifted to the tenants or the ultimate user. But such is not true of the single family dwelling. The owner-occupier cannot pass the tax on and, instead, must bear the entire brunt of the tax. Here again, the person who derives his income from rentals contributes a proportionally smaller share of the total property tax. To the extent that the property tax does not take this difference into account, it is rigid and inequitable.

Even the architects of the tax recognize its inequities and provide exceptions to it. At least sixteen states grant exemptions to veterans ranging from $500 to $5000. A quarter of the states permit new industrial property to receive exemption benefits. Homestead exemptions for owner-occupied homes also exist. Under such laws a tax exemption up to a designated amount of the assessed value of the house is granted. Florida, for example, grants owner-occupied homes an exemption up to $5000. It is extremely doubtful whether this is a sound practice, for exemptions of this sort usually encourage underassessment. In that state, homes with a market value of $25,000 were

[9] H. L. Lutz, *Public Finance* (New York: D. Appleton and Company, 1929), pp. 348-349.

assessed at $5000, thus entirely escaping the tax.[10] Furthermore, where such exemptions exist a correspondingly heavier burden is thrust upon the shoulders of the remaining property owners.

Finally, it should be noted that one third to one half of all property taxes are derived from real estate. A large part of this income comes from the owner-occupier, where, as we have noted, the incidence of the tax cannot be shifted. Moreover, the tax falls most heavily upon housing, an important consumption item. Since the real property tax is not sufficiently related to the principle of ability to pay, the tax may be considered regressive.[11]

Difficulties of administration. Thus at least on the score of tax philosophy, the property tax ranks rather low. But it is on the matter of administration that the property tax comes in for severest criticism. Compared with the more modern forms of taxation the property tax is very difficult to administer and perhaps even more difficult to "sell" to the taxpayer. An income tax is based upon a wage or earning which is known to the taxpayer. A sales tax is based upon the price of an item. But a property tax is a different matter. It rests upon the valuation of property, something which is difficult to comprehend. The taxpayer and the evaluator of property may come to altogether different conclusions as to the value of property for tax purposes.

It is the consensus among students of public finance that faulty valuation of property represents one of the major shortcomings of the property tax. Many factors may be assigned as explanations, but the condition stems mainly from the retention of a rural tax practice long after the country was urbanized. In rural communities it was felt that the local taxing officer should be chosen by the people whose property he assessed.[12] A similar feeling has persisted in the cities. Popular choice of an assessor prevails in most cities, although the appointed assessor is slowly gaining in favor.

Valuation of property is a complex task. The tax assessor is expected to list and assign valuations to all property within his tax district. He may be conscientious and endeavor to view all the property. More often than not, in urban areas this becomes an almost physically impossible task because of the large number of parcels

10 *National Municipal Yearbook for 1942,* p. 275.

11 A. Hansen and H. S. Perloff, *State and Local Finance in National Economy* (New York: W. W. Norton and Company, Inc., 1944), pp. 35-39.

12 F. J. Goodnow, *City Government in the United States* (New York: The Century Co., 1904), p. 291.

of property. But even if the assessor is diligent, viewing is not enough. The constant increase in the tax rate tempts the residential home owner to hide improvements made within the home. The valuation of industrial property requires an examination of stocks and merchandise at the plant. Even if the assessor has the time and the energy to investigate, his inquisitiveness will be curbed with an eye toward re-election or reappointment.

But even if the assessor is zealous, he may be deficient in his knowledge of assessing techniques. If he is unable to make a personal inspection, he must be able, at least, to do "book work," that is, calculate the value of construction from building plans and other paper records. Tax maps, land value maps, market data, permanent property records, and appraisal cards—in short, training in assessment methods—are required by the assessor if he is to make a proper valuation of property.[13] Assessing techniques require a high degree of competence. While there are many able assessors, in many instances the sole qualification possessed by many of them is their ability to get elected. Thus while more training is necessary to improve present-day practice, the uncertainties of office induce hesitation to acquire needed technical knowledge.

In brief then, the *ad valorem* character of the property tax has made the present method of assessment inadequate. Viewing and the shrewd guess are not enough. Valuation and appraisal of real property are needed. Professionalization of assessors and the consequent elimination of the political consideration are required. Failure to observe these principles has, in the past, resulted in many inequities, although of late there has been a consistent attempt upon the part of many responsible officials to remedy the evils.[14]

One of the most obvious faults of the present methods of tax administration is the tendency to rely very largely upon the original assessment. Urban assessing today, in view of the large number of parcels to be assessed, makes a mockery of the requirement that the assessor shall annually make a personal examination of each and every property within his district.[15] Reed has pointed out that the assessment of 230,000 parcels of property in Toledo would require

[13] R. B. Welch, "Better Assessment Administration Increases Revenue," *Municipal Finance,* XXVII (1954), pp. 70-74.

[14] Recently Illinois and New Jersey have made efforts along this line; see A. Noonan, "Assessment Administration," *National Municipal Yearbook for 1954,* pp. 231-232.

[15] See for example *Administration Code of the City of New York,* section 155b-1.0.

five years if two assessors worked on a forty-hour week.[16] The same condition that exists in any medium-sized city makes compliance with the legal mandate a virtual impossibility. One direct outgrowth of this condition is the prevailing tendency to rely upon the initial assessment.

This practice, however, results in serious inequalities. Property already valued is kept on the tax rolls and new construction is merely added as it occurs. In general, therefore, the value of old property remains static, failing to reflect changes in property values. Moreover, since it is likely that the older homes will be modernized, any accretions in value will not be reflected when so heavy a reliance is placed upon the initial assessment. Conversely, since new construction is more closely related to current market values, it is likely that it will be assessed at a higher value. The law may require the assessor to certify that he has personally viewed each parcel of property, but if he does so he merely adds the sin of perjury to that of undervaluation.

The undervaluation of property is quite common. With the passage of time, this situation tended to operate in the fashion of Gresham's monetary law. Undervaluation of property in one municipality was followed by a similar practice in another, a tendency that was heightened by the fact that assessed value determined the contribution made by a municipality to the county and the state. Undoubtedly competent assessors were aware of this condition, but in fairness to the property holders within their district, they swam with the tide.[17] As a result, the ratio of assessed to full value was not only low, but percentage of full value for the same kind of property varied according to the district in which it was located. Thus it was that the same kinds of property often made different tax contributions to higher levels of government. In Pennsylvania, the ratio of assessed to full value ranged from 20 to 78 percent; in Washington from 13 to 38 percent.[18] Similar situations exist in other states.

One final weakness of the property tax ought to be noted. The low valuation of property for tax purposes impairs the borrowing and tax powers of the municipality. Most states limit the property

---

[16] T. H. Reed, *Municipal Management* (New York: McGraw-Hill Book Co., Inc., 1941), p. 177.

[17] Lutz, *op. cit.*, p. 364.

[18] Freeman, *op. cit.*, p. 509.

tax to a percentage of the assessed valuation. If, as in New York, property is valued at half of its real value, the yield from the tax will be correspondingly reduced.[19] If costs are inflated and the yield, because of undervaluation remains the same, then the real income of the municipality will decline. A tax geared to the purchasing power of the 1939 tax dollar does not have much validity in the present inflationary period. Thus undervaluation, where fixed in practice, makes the property tax even more rigid and relatively unresponsive to the changes in the price level.

Improvements in property tax administration. There is no doubt that the property tax suffers from many inadequacies. Yet it is still the largest producer of municipal revenue. With the current tax policies of both the state and the federal governments remaining as they are, it will undoubtedly continue to be so. Consequently the solution to the financial woes of municipalities seems to lie largely in the direction of improved tax administration. This, of course, is not a new concern, but it has acquired more important dimensions in the post-war years in view of the pressing financial difficulties of our cities.

Several steps have been taken to modernize our real property tax machinery. Professor Lutz has noted three main approaches: (1) the growth of local boards of review, (2) state equalization, and (3) use of state commissions.[20] Local boards of review are now common practice. Equalization of the assessment ratio among the various tax districts, which is their principal function, has been, however, impaired to a large degree. Errors in the individual assessment, which usually are the fault of the assessor, cannot be remedied because, in most instances, the reviewing authority does not possess sufficient data. State boards of equalization, a development that took place during the last half of the nineteenth century, were also employed in the endeavor to equalize assessments. They too failed, again largely because their ex-officio composition gave them little time to collect the information needed to perform their assigned task. In time they came to depend largely upon the county boards of review who appeared before the state to justify their assessments.

---

19 R. Baldwin, "Property Tax Updated," *National Municipal Review*, XLIV (1955), p. 512.

20 Lutz, *op. cit.*, pp. 365-368; also his earlier work, *The State Tax Commission* (Cambridge, Massachusetts: Harvard University Press, 1918).

"This meant in reality," remarked Lutz, "a demonstration of the strength of the local political forces. . . ." [21]

More helpful in the general movement to improve the equity of assessments was the rise of the state tax commission, a body appointed for the specific purpose of making changes in assessment ratios. Today some forty states have such bodies with varying degrees of authority. In general they have the following functions: (1) making studies of property tax administration and policy; (2) assessing certain kinds of property such as railroads and utilities, a task normally beyond the competence of the local tax assessor; and (3) supervising local assessments. The effectiveness of this device can be demonstrated by the experience of the State of New York. Although the law required assessment at full value, the general assessment of property for a long time was at half that rate. When costs began to rise, municipalities found that both their taxing and borrowing power was limited to two percent of a five-year average of assessed valuation.[22] To remedy this a state tax committee appointed by the comptroller recommended that tax and debt limits should be based upon the full value of property as measured by a state-established equalization rate. When this was approved by the voters, the State Board of Equalization undertook a revision of the equalization rates. Now, as a result of this change, municipalities are faced with one of two alternatives: (1) they can revalue property in accordance with the revised equalization rates or (2) they may seek other sources of revenue.[23] Since the latter course of action is dependent upon the state legislature, it is likely that municipalities will seek to revalue their property for tax purposes.

Another helpful sign is the growth of state programs of assistance to the local assessor. In the past decade there has been a growing awareness of the need to improve the original assessment. Most tax officials are agreed that, once a mistake is made, it is exceedingly difficult to rectify the error. Consequently, state tax agencies have embarked upon programs designed to improve both the training and assessment practices of the local assessor. It is difficult to give a capsule description of all these programs. Kentucky may be considered as a prototype of the action undertaken. A local assessment

---

21 *Ibid.*, p. 367. State boards were composed of tax officials who had other full time duties.

22 *New York State Constitution,* Article 8, Section 10.

23 Baldwin, *op. cit.*, pp. 512-514.

section was created within the state department of revenue. Field men from this unit worked with local assessors, assisting them in the improvement of assessment techniques. Assessment manuals were developed and pilot revaluation programs were undertaken.[24]

On a national basis efforts to improve the training and technical qualifications gradually are bearing fruit. Elimination of the elected part-time assessor, enlargement of the tax district to justify a full-time assessor, and the intensification of state programs of assistance to the local tax assessor are still greatly needed. The financial stringencies that have caused the cities to intensify their search for additional revenues thus have proved a blessing in disguise.

Other tax sources. While the property tax will continue as the principal source of municipal income, other forms of revenue are also being explored. In 1951 about one half of the 1228 cities with a population of 10,000 or more were using one or more of nine different nonproperty taxes. In no case, however, was a single city using all nine taxes, although in one instance a city did use eight.[25] It is entirely possible that such revenue sources, although they will not supplant the real property tax, will have to be exploited more intensively if the cities are to meet their current and future obligations.

Several considerations support this conclusion. First, it is obvious from our previous discussion that more income from the property tax can be obtained in one of two ways: either by a revaluation upward of existing property assessments or by an increase in the tax rate. Either of these alternatives is bound to provoke opposition from both organized citizen groups and the general taxpayer. Hence, it can be expected that municipalities will handle this problem gingerly, and if the rise in property valuations or tax rates should occur, it will proceed slowly.

But even if the municipalities do take a more determined stand, a second obstacle presents itself. It will be recalled that a single tax roll served as the basis of tax levies by all units of government. Revaluation of property upward means that the municipality will have to share its tax resources with other jurisdictions.[26] Finally, there is

---

24 A. Noonan, "Assessment Administration," *National Municipal Yearbook for 1952*, pp. 184-185. Oregon, Maryland, Idaho, California, Colorado, Illinois, Maine, Minnesota, Virginia and Washington are other states that have a similar program.

25 Municipal Finance Officers' Association, *Where Cities Get Their Money, 1951 Supplement* (Chicago: 1951), p. 5.

26 L. J. Quinto, *Municipal Income Taxation in the United States* (New York City: Mayor's Committee on Management Survey of the City of New York, May, 1952), pp. 4-5.

the widespread feeling that in the interest of city autonomy municipalities should be forced to "sink or swim" upon the basis of their own resources and their ability to utilize them effectively.[27] Because of these factors there has been a dual tendency: a trend toward granting wider tax powers to the municipality, and an effort by municipalities to exploit nonproperty tax sources.[28]

Income taxation. In their search for additional money, the cities have sought to supplement their income by the use of income taxes, general and selective sales taxes, gross receipts taxes, and even taxes on hotel and room occupancy. That these are important is evidenced by the fact they are the fastest growing sources of revenue. Income from sources other than the property tax including intergovernmental revenue in 1942 was $719 million or 21.5 percent of the total city income. Ten years later the amount received from these sources was more than two and one half times as great, although the proportion of the total income only rose by 10 percent.[29] The yield from such sources has not slackened, for the year 1954 saw a further rise to $2,155 millions.[30]

Municipal income taxation is relatively recent in origin. Its use had been considered in Philadelphia as early as 1932 when the city's income was threatened by the general collapse of real property values. The so-called "Sterling Act," named after its author, had empowered the city to tax those areas that had not been subject to state levies.[31] However, the generally low level of income and the fact that it might contribute to further tax delinquencies led to the rejection of the measure. In 1934 New York City, by ordinance, adopted an income tax, but it was withdrawn a year later as a result of an agreement with the state legislature. In 1939 only Philadelphia and the District of Columbia had income taxes.[32]

The period after World War II saw a much wider use of income taxes. In Pennsylvania the provisions of the "Sterling Act" were ex-

---

27 M. N. Davisson and W. Schmelzle, "General Problems of Municipal Revenue," *National Tax Journal,* VI (1953), p. 142.

28 C. F. Snider, "What Can Cities Tax Next?," *National Municipal Review,* XXXVIII (1949), pp. 212-216.

29 Statistics derived from table 3.

30 *Compendium of City Government Finances in 1954,* Table II.

31 Quinto, *op. cit.,* p. 6.

32 "Municipal Income Taxes Increasingly Popular," *The American City,* LXVI (December 1952), p. 162.

tended in 1947 to school districts, boroughs, townships and cities.[33] About 252 localities as of 1952 availed themselves of this authority, 17 of which were cities.[34] Ohio, which also has a home rule provision similar to that of Pennsylvania, also permitted its municipalities to levy income taxes. Toledo started the income tax parade in that state and it was soon followed by eight other municipalities.[35] Four municipalities in Kentucky, Louisville in 1948, Paducah in 1950, and Newport and Lexington in 1952, also adopted a similar levy after appropriate enabling legislation.

St. Louis, Missouri had considerable difficulty in imposing an income tax levy. In 1946, faced with the prospect of mounting deficits and a constitutional limit on the tax yield from real property, the city passed an income tax ordinance modeled after that of Toledo. The ordinance was declared unconstitutional by the State Supreme Court.[36] In 1948, following the passage of additional enabling legislation, the city re-enacted the tax levy. The authority of the city was extended by a state act of 1952 for a period of two more years, but whether the city will be permitted to continue the tax is still in doubt.[37] In 1947 an attempt to adopt an income tax levy in Minneapolis was defeated in referendum. Saginaw, Michigan passed an income tax ordinance only to have the State Supreme Court declare it unconstitutional in 1952.[38]

Space does not permit a detailed description of municipal income levies. Almost all such taxes are "payroll levies" which use wages, salaries, and net profits from professional activities or unincorporated businesses as a base. Tax rates, except in the case of the District of Columbia, are "flat" and range from ½ of one percent to 1½ percent. They are not graduated according to income. Taxes are collected either through withholding at the source or through the filing of individual returns or both. In some instances, as in the case

33 *Laws of Pennsylvania, Act 481,* 1947; *Where Cities Get Their Money, op. cit.,* p. 5, contains a detailed description of the law.

34 *The American City, op. cit.,* p. 162.

35 Quinto, *op. cit.,* p. 3; Anderson, *op. cit.,* p. 77, state that ten municipalities have passed income tax ordinances. It is probable that the city of Portsmouth, Ohio, which adopted an income tax and later withdrew it when the citizens accepted a rise in the real property tax, explains the discrepancy.

36 *Carter Carburetor Corporation v. City of St. Louis,* 356 Mo. 646 (1947).

37 Quinto, *op. cit.,* pp. 75-79.

38 Quinto, *op. cit.,* p. 3. See also A. M. Wisehart, "The Legal Basis for Municipal Income Taxes in Michigan," *Michigan Law Review,* LII (March 1954), p. 710. The author concludes, "Michigan decisions, as well as those from other jurisdictions, offer good authority for such a tax." Apparently the court thought otherwise.

of Philadelphia, it is extremely difficult to check the income of residents whose earnings are obtained outside of the municipality.[39] Only the District of Columbia and the City of Warren, Ohio, provide exemptions for low income groups.[40]

The per capita yield from the income tax ranges from a low of $7.08 in the case of St. Louis, Missouri, to a high of $19.79 in the case of Toledo, Ohio. In between are such cities as Philadelphia with $15 per capita, Louisville with $13.53, and Dayton with $12.09.[41] More important is the fact that the use of the tax has helped many cities stave off financial disaster. An authorized study has concluded "that all of the cities have obtained rich yields, while tax rates have been low and tax bases restricted." [42]

Despite its potential, the income tax has been adopted by only thirty-three cities with a population of more than 10,000 inhabitants. The tax has several principal merits: (1) it yields a relatively rich harvest; (2) it fixes local responsibility, forcing municipalities to live within their means; and (3) it is fairly simple to administer, for it is based upon wages and these are easily verified by a check of the earnings statement of the individual. This, largely, is a clerical and investigative function and does not require the degree of technical competence expected of the assessor. Moreover, with the present outward movement of people beyond the limits of the central city, it furnishes a means by which the suburbanite who works in the city can be made to contribute for the benefits he derives.

It suffers, however, from several weaknesses. On the score of tax philosophy it is not, despite its name, a progressive tax. Its rate is not graduated according to income. Moreover, in the absence of a more comprehensive approach to taxation by both the state and federal governments, it may result in duplication and unfairness.[43] Further-

---

[39] Quinto, *op. cit.*, pp. 27-28.

[40] Warren, for example, exempts the first $1,200 from taxable income, Springfield, Ohio, while it exempts income under $1,040, provides that, if income is in excess of this, the entire income shall be taxed.

[41] *Ibid.*, pp. 39, 53, 61, 73, 81 and 113; unsigned note, "Dayton Adopts an Income Tax," *Public Management*, XXXI (1949), p. 82.

[42] *Ibid.*, p. 114. I am greatly indebted to Mr. Quinto's study for much of the information that appears above.

[43] W. G. Willis and W. M. Bayer, Jr., "The Income Tax Puzzle in the Pittsburgh Area," *Municipal Finance*, XXVII (1955), pp. 140-144. In the area around Pittsburgh, there were 33 first-class cities, 78 boroughs, 23 first-class townships and 24 second-class townships. Only the latter had no authority to levy an income tax. However, 177 school districts were also empowered to levy the tax.

more, if the income tax is levied by some municipalities and not by others, an unhealthy competitive situation may be created. Artificial diversion and relocation of industry may take place. Taxpayers, while continuing to use the facilities of the municipality, may move beyond its jurisdiction. It is probable that the hesitation of many states to authorize income taxation may indicate sincere reservations. In a cogent article, Anderson has suggested that the states should first formulate a long-range policy with respect to the kinds of tax authority that should be given to municipalities. In his view it is only when state tax policy has crystallized that a proper evaluation of the type of taxes required by a municipality can take place.[44]

Sales and other taxes. In addition to the income tax, cities are turning to other nonproperty tax sources. These fall into two main categories: (1) sales taxes, both general and selective, and (2) gross receipts taxes. Over the years the yield from these sources has been appreciable. Income from sales and gross receipts has risen from $124 million in 1942 to $544 million a decade later, a gain of 339 percent. In 1952 municipal income from licenses and other taxes was $338 million, more than twice the amount received ten years earlier. In 1954 revenues from sales, gross receipts, licenses and other taxes were $602 million and $415 million respectively.[45]

The general sales tax, as compared with its selective counterparts, while used less widely, on the whole has brought in more money. Four large cities, New York City, Washington, D.C., New Orleans, and Denver are largely responsible for this.[46] The general sales tax is in use in 114 cities with a population of 10,000 or more people. Eighty-five of these cities are located in the State of California. Selective sales taxes on admissions, alcoholic beverages, tobacco, gasoline and motor vehicles are levied by many municipalities. In terms of the number of cities employing these levies, taxes on admissions and motor vehicles seem to be most popular.[47] Gross receipts based on

---

44 Anderson, *op. cit.*, pp. 80-81.

45 See table 3 of this chapter. Also *Compendium of City Government Finances in 1954,* table II.

46 R. W. Cass, "The Denver Retail Sales Tax," *Municipal Finance,* XXVII (February 1955), pp. 128-131. Revenues during the first year, 1948, totaled $2.9 million; in 1954, $4.2 million.

47 The number of cities of 10,000 or more people using selective taxes are: admissions, 202; motor vehicles, 137; tobacco, 76; alcoholic beverages, 40. See Anderson, *op. cit.*, pp. 77-78. Unsigned note, "Cities Adopt Income, Admissions and Sales Taxes," *Public Management,* XXX (1948), p. 107.

either a percentage of the customers bill or the right to do business have also become important revenue producers.[48]

In recent years the shared tax has also appeared. This is a tax that is collected by the state but shared by the municipality. Railroads, bus lines, utilities, gasoline, motor vehicles and alcoholic beverages are but a few of the revenue sources subject to taxation in this fashion. Under the shared tax, municipalities receive money from the state in accordance with a formula that varies from state to state. In some, money may be allocated in proportion to the amount of business or property located within the municipality. In others, it may be on the basis of mileage. In general, it might be said that the amount received by the city varies in accordance with the purpose of the levy. Shared taxes are open to one major objection. They do not benefit the state as a whole. The wealthier community on the basis of property or business within its borders may obtain a greater portion of the money which it may not need, while the poorer one may receive much less.[49]

Criticisms of indirect taxes. Indirect taxes of this kind have come in for severe criticism. Retail merchants, feeling that it hurts their business, have consistently opposed such levies. Added to this is the fact that such taxes are easier to evade and consequently more difficult to enforce than alternative types of taxation. The same rate of taxation, if applied through an income tax, would not only bring a larger yield but also would minimize the difficulty of enforcement.[50] Again, the use of the sales tax may be inhibited by state adherence to the pre-emption doctrine. In Ohio and other states where this principle is observed, the passage of a state sales tax automatically bars a municipality from adopting a similar measure.[51] The sales tax as a source of municipal revenue remains untapped unless the state is willing to make an exception by passing enabling legislation. There are sound reasons for the pre-emption doctrine. In California and Mississippi, where the doctrine is not observed, the municipal levy is added to the state tax. The addition makes for duplication in both administration and taxation. For the retailer or the wholesaler,

[48] Approximately 285 cities use the percentage levy and 201 use the business license, Anderson, *ibid.*, above; also *Where Cities Get Their Money*, *op. cit.*, pp. 1-2.

[49] The state may insist that the money received on a shared basis should be used only for specific purposes. Where this occurs the shared tax is quite similar to a grant-in-aid.

[50] Davisson and Schmelzle, *op. cit.*, p. 142.

[51] *Zielonka v. Carroll*, 99 Ohio, 220 (1919).

two sets of reports for separate jurisdictions must be maintained. For the taxpayer the additional levy may become burdensome. Finally, in light of the fact that the tax is being used on a wider scale, it should be pointed out that such taxes violate the basic principle of tax equity.[52]

Sales taxes, whatever the type, are levies on consumption items. Since the low income person tends to use the greater portion of his income for necessities, he is forced to bear a correspondingly higher part of the tax burden than the more well-to-do groups. In a word, since these taxes violate the principle of ability to pay, they are regressive in character.[53]

Intergovernmental receipts. Like the sales and gross receipts taxes, aid from other levels of government is rapidly becoming a valuable supplement to the real property tax. In the decade 1942–1952 intergovernmental revenue jumped from $461 million to $1,034 million. This is a substantial amount and yet it was increased still further in 1954 to $1,138 million, a gain of 5 percent above the previous year.[54] That assistance from other governmental levels looms large on the horizon of municipal finance, can be gathered from the fact that in 1954 19 percent of municipal income came from this source.[55]

If these statistics have significance, they mean that municipalities in the past decade have become increasingly dependent upon aid from other levels of government, particularly the states. The consequence of this trend for local autonomy have been noted by Professor Rowland Egger. We have, he asserts, "maintained doctrinal adherence to local self-government and continued almost exclusively to utilize local governments as operating instrumentalities." [56] At the same time, however, the responsibility for policy and standards for five main programs have been shifted to higher levels of government.[57] "When it comes to budgetary matters," he remarks, "most

[52] *Where Cities Get Their Money, op. cit.,* p. 12, contains a justification of the tax. The argument is that the tax is not regressive because it contains exemptions for food and other necessities.

[53] Hansen and Perloff, *op. cit.,* p. 35.

[54] See table 3 of this chapter.

[55] *Compendium of City Government Finances in 1954,* table 11, p. 4. Total city revenue exclusive of utility and employee retirement income amounted to $5,968 million.

[56] R. Egger, "Nature Over Art: No More Local Finance," *American Political Science Review,* XLVII (1953), p. 469.

[57] These are (1) education (2) safety (3) sanitation, health and hospitals (4) welfare and (5) highways and public works.

local governing bodies are currently little more than trustees in bankruptcy for a small group of residual local functions. The major decisions have already been made in the light of the compelling argument not of local community needs, but of optimum possibilities in securing matching state and federal grants."[58] Most state grants, he argues, because they have not insisted upon effective performance have merely condoned outmoded procedures and outworn governmental structure. The measures of the grant often have been "standards of money matched, not mission accomplished."[59]

If state aid to local governments is to be fairly administered, then the higher level must do two things: (1) it must make certain that taxes at the local level are fairly administered; and (2) it must insist that municipal revenues are utilized effectively through adherence to sound management principles. If the states do not demand adherence to these standards before grants are made to the local units, then it will merely compound archaic practices and thus actually sap the administrative vitality of the municipality. The remedy for the existing and almost haphazard system of aid to localities and municipal governments, as Egger has viewed it, is "no more local finance" until (1) the state sets performance standards for statewide activities carried out at the local level and (2) the state through technical assistance is assured that municipalities are effectively managed. Once these conditions were met, he would permit local units to tax at a specified percentage of a state income tax levy. Blocked grants based upon standards of efficiency, in his judgment, would be necessary only if the municipality could not meet its financial obligations.[60]

CONCLUSION

Belief in local autonomy is strong in this country. Most Americans believe that the government which is closest to the people is more responsive to its needs. This feeling stems largely from the realization that the purpose of local government is to deal with special circumstances that are not the immediate concern of higher levels of government. But if this concept is to remain meaningful, it must be accompanied by sufficient fiscal authority to carry out the local responsibility.

---

[58] *Ibid.*, p. 496.
[59] *Ibid.*, p. 475.
[60] *Ibid.*, p. 477.

In this respect the municipality is in a position similar to other units of local government. Its reason for existence rests almost solely on the belief that it is desirable to administer local functions at the local level. Its competence to make its own policy determinations hinges largely upon its ability to finance its own activities. For more than a century and a half, municipal finance has adhered faithfully to these doctrines.

The property tax was based upon the premise that each municipality should be required to live within its own resources. Property benefited from the community. It was visible and it was fixed. It was considered logical that it should contribute to the cost of municipal government. The tax, as we have seen, was badly administered. Property was undervalued. Administration was mainly on an elected part-time basis. Assessment training and techniques lagged far behind the advances in the field. Although many inequities existed, the tax was the principal, if not the sole, revenue producer.

As long as there was no great drain on municipal moneys, the system seemed reasonable to most people. The coming of the great depression, however, strained municipal resources to the utmost. The collapse of real property values came at a time when the municipality was saddled with huge welfare expenditures. Needed capital improvements were postponed, and aid in increasing amounts was sought from higher levels of government. Gradually, as need lessened and real property values were restored, municipal finances came back on an even keel. It was not until the post World War II period that the municipalities were once more shocked into action.

Confronted with the need to balance their budgets in an inflationary period, municipalities embarked upon dual programs. An effort was made to increase the yield from the real property tax, by improving assessment methods and by a planned program for revaluation of property in the light of current market values. A search for nonproperty taxes was conducted. General and special sales taxes were introduced. Pennsylvania, Ohio, Kentucky, and Missouri allowed their municipalities to impose income taxes. But still those measures were not enough. Aid from other levels of government and borrowing, carryovers from the depression era, reappeared as municipalities obtained wider taxing authority and grants from the state legislature.

The desperate measures undertaken by the municipalities, while encouraging to those who believe in local responsibility, have actually precipitated a crisis in tax policy. The already confused pattern of national, state and local taxes has become even more so. The use of nonproperty taxes by municipalities contains the elements of duplication and potential unfairness.[61] Aid from other levels of government has encouraged the continuance of archaic structures and practices, a condition that fosters administrative incompetence and poses a threat to local autonomy.

If the municipalities are at the crossroads, the states are even more so. The cities can be rescued from their present entanglements only by the formulation of long-range state-local fiscal policies.[62] A good part of the task facing the states has already been brilliantly charted by Rowland Egger in an article previously mentioned. It is also necessary to determine those areas of taxation most properly belonging to the state and those most properly belonging to the municipality. The state tax commissions that have hitherto concentrated their energies on the modernization of the real property tax should be induced to make a more comprehensive study of the entire tax structure.

A period of soul searching is also required of the municipalities. Those in charge of municipal fiscal policy should not use the current emphasis on nonproperty tax sources to divert them from the modernization of their property tax administration, even though diversification of their revenue sources may well be in order. Instead, the cities should seek improvement of their local real property administration and relate it not only to the needs of the community but also to the use and function of their nonproperty taxes. "The municipal revenue system must be tailored to the special character of the city concerned." [63] Formulation of tax policy, in other words, involves a close scrutiny of the main characteristics of the city. If it is small and its needs are not great, it is entirely probable that the real property tax may suffice, but if the converse be true, that is, it is large in size and its needs are great, then it undoubtedly will have to search for new revenues.

Location of the city and the general character of its economy also have a direct bearing on its tax policy. Nearness to a central city may result in a rise of property values in the suburb. Correspondingly,

61 W. G. Willis and W. M. Bayer, Jr., *op. cit.,* pp. 140-144. About one hundred units levied income taxes. Enforcement difficulties occurred because a person living in one jurisdiction was not liable for taxes in the jurisdiction where he worked.

62 Davisson and Schmelzle, *op. cit.,* pp. 141-142.

63 *Where Cities Get Their Money, 1951 supplement, op. cit.,* p. 10.

the outward movement of people may cause a decline in property valuations within the central city. Thus the latter may require nonproperty taxes, but the former may not. Again if cities have intangibles as the main kind of wealth, a tax policy is in order to make property of this sort bear its fair share of community cost. Many other criteria might be added, but what is mainly needed is a comprehensive tax policy based upon a total evaluation of all the factors in a given situation. Once this is accepted, municipalities may accommodate themselves to the tax policies of the state in some logical and coherent fashion.

The need and consequences of such an approach have been ably summarized by two authorities in these words: "During the last decade municipal finance has often been characterized by hand-to-mouth operations with little or no consideration of long range of objectives. Perhaps this may have appeared to be the only feasible course at the time; but developments . . . suggest the urgent need for formulation of long range objectives before revenue patterns become so frozen that desirable adjustments in terms of such objectives become virtually impossible." [64]

BIBLIOGRAPHY

Books:

Garver, F. B. and Hansen, A. *Principles of Economics.* New York: Ginn and Co., 1937. Revised edition.

Hansen, A. and Perloff, H. S. *State and Local Finance in the National Economy.* New York: W. W. Norton and Co., Inc., 1944.

Lutz, H. L. *Public Finance.* New York: D. Appleton-Century Co., Inc., 1947. 4th Edition.

Municipal Finance Officers Association, *Where Cities Get Their Money.* Chicago, 1951.

Quinto, L. J. *Municipal Income Taxation in the United States.* New York: Mayor's Committee on Management Survey of the City of New York, 1952.

Shoup, C., Blough, R. and Newcomer, M. *Facing the Tax Problem.* New York: The Twentieth Century Fund, 1937.

State of New Jersey, Sixth Report on State Tax Policy, *The General Property Tax in New Jersey.* Trenton, New Jersey: 1953.

Articles and Other Material:

Anderson, L. F. "The Search for Money," *National Municipal Review,* XLIV (1955), 76-82.

[64] Davisson and Schmelzle, *op. cit.,* pp. 141-142.

Baldwin, R. "Property Tax Updated," *National Municipal Review,* XLIV (1955), 512-514.

Davisson, M. N. and Schmelzle, W. "General Problem of Municipal Revenue," *National Tax Journal,* VI (1953), 129-142.

Egger, R. "Nature over Art: No More Local Finance," *American Political Science Review,* XLVII (1953), 461-478.

Freeman, R. A. "What Ails the Property Tax," *National Municipal Review,* XXLIV (1955), 507-509.

Snider, C. F. "What Can Cities Tax Next," *National Municipal Review,* XXXVIII (1949), 212-216.

Willis, W. G. and Bayer, W. M. "The Income Tax Puzzle in the Pittsburgh Area," *Municipal Finance,* XXVII (1955), 140-144.

Chapter Fourteen

Municipal Finance: Expenditures and Debt

The Financial Plight of the American City

The financial plight of American cities is a product of many causes, some of which have recently appeared and others of which are of much longer duration. Urban growth, two world wars, a major depression, and inflation have combined to form a chain reaction that has given a rude jolt to the finances of many an American city. These trends, not yet at their peak, hold forth the prospect of still further cost increases. When and where the curve of increased spending will slough off is a matter of conjecture, but the fact that expenditures threaten to surpass available resources is not. It is evident that the management of city finances is a "must" if the city is to retain its autonomy.

Casual factors. By far the most important single factor responsible for the financial difficulties of the city is the fundamental change in the character of our society. In the five decades since the turn of the century urban population rose from 30.2 million to 88.9 million, more than two and one half times.[1] Not only has the population increased in size, but its character has changed. There are more older people and there are more younger people. Since 1941, in the city for the first time, births exceeded deaths, a fact that signifies a potentially growing population. The concentration of people in the cities has meant the increase of existing services. Moreover, the changed character of the population also has caused a demand for services. Under such conditions costs are bound to rise.

From a cost standpoint, too, the depression of the thirties set in motion a chain of circumstances that still plague the city. Widespread unemployment meant huge expenditures for relief and welfare. Capital improvements were either kept at a minimum or neglected entirely. When normal conditions were about to be at-

[1] U. S. Bureau of Census, *Statistical Abstract for 1953* (74th ed.; Washington, D. C.: 1953), p. 26. The old urban definition for the year 1950 was employed for purposes of comparison. Full title has been cited earlier.

tained, the second world war broke out. Again a shortage of materials kept capital construction at a minimum. Cities during World War II unfortunately did not avail themselves of the opportunity to pay off their debts. The war, too, brought population shifts in response to the needs for industrial mobilization. Long-standing deficiencies in water supply, sewage, sanitation, health, and education were aggravated,[2] and newer ones appeared.

When the war was over, contrary to the expectations of many, a flourishing high level economy was maintained. The rise in the cost of living meant that the city—a consumer of materials, labor, and equipment—would also have to pay more for the capital programs and services required by its population. Replacement of worn-out capital equipment and the construction of new facilities cost many times more than before the war.

The cities struggled with their financial problems. Complicating their ability to "catch up" was the essential rigidity of the property tax upon which most of them depended for a major part of their income. Not only was property poorly assessed but it was also under-assessed. Real property values did not keep pace with the rise in the market value of property. As Hansen and Perloff have remarked, the cities failed to "maintain tax rates consistent with national and state economy." [3] As a consequence, in the decade after World War II the cities had to meet the inflated costs of the fifties in terms of a municipal tax dollar that was based upon the relatively stable pre-war period.

Recent trends in city finances. What these trends meant to the finances of the city can be stated statistically in Table 4.

It is evident from Table 4 that almost every function, with the exception of general control, more than doubled during the ten-year period, 1942-1952. Highlighting the emergent needs was education with an expenditure of $902 millions. Close on its heels in the order of cost were such functions as highways, police, sanitation, health and hospitals, and welfare. Only general control—the expenditure for the executive, legislative and judicial branches—remained fairly stable.

When one examines the trend for the year 1954 the expenditure pattern is not very different. The largest single municipal function,

---

2 A. Hansen and H. S. Perloff, *State and Local Finance in the National Economy* (New York: W. W. Norton and Company, Inc., 1944), p. 203.

3 *Ibid.*, p. 7.

Table 4—CITY EXPENDITURES FOR VARIOUS FUNCTIONS: 1942–1952

Functions	*1942 (millions)*	*1952 (millions)*	*% Gain 1942–1952*
Police	257	538	109
Fire	190	407	114
Welfare	264	424	61
Education	462	902	95
Libraries	30	80	167
Highways	227	587	159
Health and hospitals	156	454	191
Sanitation	164	534	226
Recreation	89	234	163
General control	144	260	81

Source: *National Municipal Yearbook for 1954,* table 3, p. 243.

as measured by cost, was still education for which $1,027 million was spent. Indeed, education accounted for approximately 17 percent of all general expenditures of the city. Next in cost was the item for the maintenance and construction of sanitation services and facilities with expenditures totaling $691 million.[4] General control again remained fairly stable as a municipal cost item. When one measures municipal expenditures by character and object, one finds that personal services consumed $3,732 million or three fifths of the municipal budget. Capital outlay totaled $1,920 million.

Further analysis of these data reveals that the major cost factors are the expansion of governmental functions in the response to the demands of a growing population and the building and maintenance of a capital plant. General control is a fairly stable expense item and is a relatively small municipal expenditure. In 1954 general control amounted to only $290 million out of a total of $6,107 million spent.[5] Costs, therefore, can be cut either by a contraction of municipal functions or by a reduction in the rate of capital construction. Neither of these, it would seem, is a likely possibility. Moreover,

[4] U. S. Department of Commerce, Bureau of Census *Compendium of City Government Finances* (Washington, D. C.: U. S. Government Printing Office), p. 2. Following sanitation were highways, $669 million; police protection, $699 million; fire protection, $473 million. These were major expenditures. A full list is contained in table 7 of the Compendium.

[5] *Ibid.,* p. 7.

since capital outlay is for the life of the project, usually thirty-five or forty years, expenditures made now will continue in all likelihood for many years to come.

Thus the cities are on a "forced march." Caught between the upper and nether millstones of rising costs and relatively stable or even rigid revenue sources, the cities are making desperate efforts to "catch up." They are laboring to increase the yield from existing taxes. They are also engaged in the search for new revenues. At stake is the large question of municipal autonomy, for inability to finance needed services will mean ultimately a shift in responsibility to a higher level of government.

Fiscal Authority as a Tool of Administration

Since the financial difficulties of the city result from expanding services and greater capital construction in a era of inflation, it is obvious that effective management of municipal finances is of prime importance.

Money, it may be said, is the handmaiden of administration. It is employed by the administrator to supervise the affairs of the municipality. Without the regulation of the use of moneys, no effective administrative performance can take place. Conversely, without adequate fiscal machinery, the council cannot appraise work of either the administrator or his principal subordinates. Sound thinking in regard to the use of finance as a tool of administration is relatively recent in origin.

As late as the beginning of the twentieth century responsibility for this important function was divided among many officials: the mayor, the assessor, collector, treasurer, accountant or comptroller, and the auditor. Most of these were elected, although some were appointed. Because of the method of their selection, almost all were independent of each other. Few owed their allegiance to a central executive. Indeed, the theory was that the division of authority would permit each agent to act as a check upon the other. Coordination, when it did exist, was achieved largely through the dominance of personality or the in-group feeling of the government family. Control over expenditures was accomplished through accounting procedure. Whatever fiscal machinery existed was mainly for the purpose of insuring that expenditures were made in accordance with the law. Little or no effort was made to obtain the most efficient utilization of the tax dollar. In brief, central direction of municipal money was a concept that had not as yet taken root.

TRENDS IN FISCAL ADMINISTRATION

In the half-century, 1900–1950, forces were at work which gradually but certainly compelled a re-evaluation of the role of fiscal machinery. The successful example set by business, the growth in the nature and extent of municipal services, the need for full time direction and control, and the consequent changes in form of government were leavening influences. The coming of the strong-mayor meant that increased attention was to be paid to the fiscal function. If the mayor was to be "strong" in any respect at all it was essential that he be given authority not only to plan municipal expenditures but also, once the council had given its approval, to be armed with the necessary power to see that its directives were carried out. Effective coordination by the mayor could only take place if the fiscal officers and line departments were required to look to him for their moneys. Only by binding them to him could he in turn be properly held accountable to the governing body.

The coming of commission government also focused attention on financial administration. A commissioner of revenue and finance was made responsible for the supervision of a department under which were grouped the functions of collection, disbursement and audit. Although responsibility was centralized, authority was not. The commissioner was merely the head of one department. His fellow commissioners enjoyed equal status and were not subject to his direction in their expenditure or use of public money. As a consequence, the managerial aspects of fiscal administration largely were neglected unless by chance the personal magnetism or party position of the revenue commissioner gave him dominance.

Under the council-manager plan, however, full integration of the finance function was obtained. The Model City Charter of the National Municipal League is perhaps the best example of this. A single department of finance is vested with the responsibility for the supervision of the administrative affairs of the municipality. Budgeting, accounting, assessment, custody and investment of funds, and purchasing are assigned to the department. A post-audit, however, is made by an agency independent of the department. Depending upon the size of the city, the head of the department of finance may be either the manager or an officer appointed by him. In either event, central direction of the city's finances is obtained by this arrangement.[6]

Decentralized administration. Through the years three main facets of finance administration have developed. In some cities this function is completely decentralized; in others it is partially decentralized; and in many it is completely integrated. In general those cities with a weak executive, the weak-mayor council or the commission form fall into the first category. In weak-mayor cities the function usually is divided among an assessor and a treasurer, both elected, and a council. There is no centralized purchasing system. Estimates of departmental needs are prepared by individual councilmen who collectively vote the budget for the municipality. To say the least, the fiscal position in this instance is in the embryonic state of development. Commission government, although it has a department of revenue and finance, is hardly more advanced.

The disadvantages of such a system are fairly obvious. When a council legislates and administers for government it has no time to propose a comprehensive financial plan for the municipality as a whole. Each councilman intent upon fulfilling the needs of his department is reluctant to question the requests of his fellow councilmen. There are no unit cost studies, no evaluations of departmental performance and, indeed, no data that permit adequate decisions regarding the budget. From the standpoint of budget execution, there is no prior approval of expenditures. Finally, since the assessment books are kept by the treasurer, the ability of an individual councilman to control his department is impaired.

The partially integrated system. New York City is a good illustration of the partially integrated system of finance. Most of the financial functions are under the control of the mayor. He appoints the budget director, a seven-man tax commission, and a treasurer who does much of the accounting. However, there is a significant omission. The comptroller, who is the principal auditor, is elected by the people for a term that runs concurrently with that of the mayor. A large part of the fiscal authority of the municipality is vested in this officer. He investigates all matters relating to the finances of the city, reviews all vouchers for compliance with the statue and the budget, prescribes accounting systems for the city, manages the sinking fund, fixes the rates for short term borrowing,

[6] National Municipal League, *Model City Charter* (New York: 1951), sections 86-90.

and at the beginning of the fiscal year he determines the amount of revenues available for expenditures by the city. But this is not all. Through his membership on the board of estimate, an ex-officio body, he may cast three votes on the budget. Many, if not most of these functions are more properly within the ken of the municipal executive.

With such large powers vested in an officer independent of the executive, cooperation or lack of it, often may decide the fate of a mayor's financial program. A case in point occurred in January 1956. The mayor of New York City had sent a bill to the state capital urging the revocation of the city's power to impose an auto-use tax on the condition that the state would allow the city to share in the gasoline and auto taxes, a privilege enjoyed by fifty-seven up-state counties. The ostensible reason for this request was that the city would need more money. At the same time, the comptroller announced that a 50 percent increase in the staff of his excise tax division would enable the city to garner an added $15 or $20 million in its sales tax receipts. The increase in revenue, he asserted, would make it possible for the city to drop its auto-use tax and perhaps even its admissions tax. Coming at a time when the mayor was pressing for a change in the city's tax authority, the remark imperiled the chief executive's program. Needless to say, the statement caused consternation at City Hall.[7] Had the comptroller been under the direction of the mayor, it is unlikely that the event would have occurred.

Highly integrated finance departments. Two Ohio municipalities furnish examples of highly integrated finance departments. Cleveland has a director of finance who is appointed by the mayor and responsible to him. Within the finance department are four main divisions concerned with accounts, treasury, purchases and supplies, and assessment and licenses. Its director, under the supervision of the municipal chief executive, prepares the municipal budget and supervises the custody and distribution of municipal funds. Toledo's city-manager plan employs a similar organization except that the maintenance of the accounts in accordance with Ohio state law is vested in a city auditor.[8] Oakland and Long Beach, California have highly integrated finance departments. In the latter,

[7] *New York Times,* January 12, 1945, p. 1.

[8] International City Managers' Association, *Municipal Finance Administration* (3rd ed.; Chicago, Illinois: 1946), pp. 44-45.

a department of central services combines under a director of finance the following divisions: assessor, tax collector, purchasing, treasurer, and accountant. The former is similar in organization except that the budget officer is located in the office of the city manager.[9]

The merits of fiscal integration. The idea of an integrated finance department has much to commend it. It is the key to executive management for, in essence, it means that all the officers dealing with finance or fiscal matters are bound together in a chain of command, subject to the direction of the chief executive of the municipality. They are *his* agents and as such assist him in the use of money as a tool of administration. In a properly organized finance department there is no doubt at any time that the mayor or manager is the actual head of the government.

Central control of municipal accounts by the municipal chief executive through his director of finance makes possible a continuing review of the entire administrative process with a view toward pruning nonessential or wasteful expenditures. Properly kept accounts give the municipal executive a clear picture of the current status of municipal spending. Unit cost studies, a natural product of accounting, furnish an index of the relative efficiency of departments and enable an executive to change program emphasis where in his judgment such action is needed. Moreover, accounts furnish the basic data upon which budgets are based and implemented. Preaudit or prior approval compel departments and agencies to justify in advance their decision to undertake a given program.

The elected comptroller or accountant does violence to this theory. It places on an independent basis the very tools of control required by the municipal chief executive. The tug and haul between the executive and the comptroller, witness the previously cited example of the City of New York, introduces elements of dissonance which are likely to have disastrous consequences for the administration of the city. In brief, power and responsibility must be commensurate with one another. If the municipal chief executive is to be made truly accountable, it is essential that he be given adequate authority to deal with the financial aspects of city government.

Similar considerations argue for the inclusion of the assessment

[9] Unsigned note, *Public Management*, XXXI (1949), p. 132.

function in a department of finance. Expenditures must be related to revenues. If the real property tax does not yield sufficient revenue, then the municipality must seek additional tax authority or borrow, both of which are subject to state regulation and control. The municipal chief executive who has sought additional revenue will, in all likelihood, be required to demonstrate that existing revenues have been exploited to the fullest extent. This he cannot do unless the function of assessment is closely under his direction. It is entirely probable that much of the inefficiency in real property tax administration, noted in a previous chapter, may be traced to the independently elected assessor who has remained outside of the executive's chain of command. It is true that the assessor in a sense has been subject to supervision by the next higher level of government, the county, but this is probably due to the void left by the failure of the municipal government to exercise control over this most important office.

Again, a central purchase system enables the municipal chief executive to control the largest single item of expense, aside from the cost of personal services. Such a system enables a municipality to buy on a volume basis in accordance with standards and specifications. Departments must come to the chief executive to justify both their requests and their purchases. Dispersion of the purchase function can result not only in loose and costly buying practices but also in a lack of control.

Of all the fiscal activities, only the budget function may justifiably lay claim to location outside the department of finance. The view has merit only to the extent that it can be said that it is difficult to apply the same blueprint of organization to all municipalities. As a general rule, it is more convenient to locate the budget function in the same unit that maintains the accounts for the simple reason that accounts are basic to both budget formulation and execution. Special considerations, however, may dictate the location of the budget function in the office of the chief executive. It is possible that the department of finance may be too cost conscious and thus may act as a deterrent to effective future planning. Again, since the budget is so closely related to the tax rate, the municipal chief executive may desire to have close supervision of the budget because of its possible political repercussions. If this budget function is located outside the department of finance, then it is essential that the budget officer be armed with power and prestige sufficient to enable him to serve as a principal aide to the chief administrator. Failure to do so could conceivably result in the subordination of the budget office to the director of finance. Should this occur, then it is better to recognize administrative reality and lodge the budget function within the finance department.

Above all, organization of an integrated department of finance forces full-time administration and specialization. An elected comptroller or assessor does not insure that the occupant of the office will be properly qualified to perform adequately the duties entrusted to him. Nor is it likely that even if he were competent the politics of the office would permit him to do so. An integrated finance department would obviate these difficulties.

Thus an integrated department of finance has several main virtues: (1) it can provide a blueprint of municipal expenditures and revenues; (2) it can establish priorities with respect to municipal programs on the basis of cost, necessity and administrative feasibility; (3) it can relate revenues and borrowing; (4) it will assist in charting a sounder fiscal policy; (5) it will aid the chief administrator in introducing economies and achieving the maximum possible utilization of the tax dollar; and (6) finally it will bring about more responsible government since it will provide both the council and the taxpayer with the data necessary to make effective decisions.

BUDGET FORMULATION AND EXECUTION

The role of the budget. Most householders are familiar with the word "budget." To them it means the utilization of family income in such a way as to contribute best to the welfare of the group. The budget of a municipality serves a similar purpose; but because its formulation and execution are the responsibilities of a governmental authority, it is much more elaborate and involves the consent of a much larger group not bound by family ties. Furthermore, the municipal budget is much more concerned with the effective use of the tax dollar since the municipality, in a sense, is engaged in the management and expenditure of other people's money.

The budget is not only a financial program. It is political as well. It is the means through which those in charge of the municipal government determine the policies that will be followed during the fiscal year. "Budgets are not affairs of arithmetic," wrote Gladstone, "but in a thousand ways go to the root of prosperity of individuals, the relations of classes, and the strength of kingdoms."[10] Budgets are political, too, in the sense that the expenditure pattern set has a direct effect upon the political nerve center of the community, the tax rate. The rise and fall of the "points" per hundred is an annual event that is carefully watched by citizens and no one is more aware of this than those engaged in the preparation and voting of the budget.

But the budget is even more than this. It is an opportunity for the executive to use money as a tool of administration. Through the formulation and execution of the budget, he can examine expenditures of the previous year in order to ascertain the degree to which his departmental heads have fulfilled the goals established by him. He may also set his administrative sights higher and thus tighten the standards of effective performance. Moreover, what the chief executive does for the municipality as a whole, each departmental head does for the area under his immediate supervision. Both in the aggregate and in its separate parts, the administrative process is subjected annually to a searching scrutiny.

More specifically, the budget is a plan for the monetary requirements of a municipality.[11] The economic resources of the community must be balanced against its total needs. If the latter is in excess of the ability of the community to pay for needed services, either expenses must be trimmed or borrowing undertaken. The budget must be balanced at the end of each fiscal year. In most municipalities the budget contains as a minimum (1) a statement of revenues and expenditures for a specified period, usually two years before the current budget; (2) a progress report on the current status of income and outgo; and (3) a projection of anticipated revenues and needs for the ensuing budget year. Budgets in the larger cities often are much more elaborate. Justifications and explanatory statements usually are included. Fixed charges are described in great detail.

Revenue statements are generally subdivided to show the major sources from which funds are derived. Such items as property revenue, receipts from delinquent taxes and miscellaneous revenues, other than property taxes, and aid from other levels of government are specified. Estimates of income from taxes are usually made either on a cash basis or accrual system. In the former, anticipation of

---

[10] Quote in A. E. Buck, *The Budgets in Governments of Today* (New York: The Macmillan Co., 1934), p. 70.

[11] *Idem.*

revenue is limited to a percentage of the levy measured by an average experience of the two preceding years. To this may also be added the sum that might be realized from delinquent tax collections measured by the same experience factor.[12] The accrual revenue system is based upon the assumption that taxes actually levied constitute the basis of revenue.[13] Expenditures are classified as to personal services and supplies and fixed charges such as debt administration and capital improvements. They may also be grouped under major headings such as purpose and sub-purposes, such as education and supervision; or by major expense items, such as supplies, equipment; or again by organizational unit such as the department of education. When grouped in this fashion they give the council and the citizen a comprehensive view of the major types of expenditure. As in revenues, expenditures are accounted for either on a cash or accrual basis. Both methods are employed by different municipalities, the sole consideration being the element of comparability, since revenue and expenditures must correspond.

Budget formulation. Budget formulation and execution follow three main procedural steps: (1) preparation of the budget; (2) presentation to the council; and (3) execution of the budget by responsible officers. Budget preparation may be simple or complex, depending both upon the size and form of government and the role assigned to it as an agency of administration. In almost all cities the budget must be formulated in advance of the end of the fiscal year. Observance of this requirement is usually a matter of general law amplified by local ordinance. It makes certain that there will be sufficient time for both the formulation of the budget by local officers and its subsequent consideration by the council after a public hearing. This process is usually called the budget timetable. In all cities, the end of the fiscal year is the due date for the budget.[14]

[12] Committee on a Program of Model Fiscal Legislation for Local Government, *Model Cash Basis Budget Law* (New York: National Municipal League, 1946), p. xii.

[13] Committee on a Program for Model Fiscal Legislation for Local Governments, *Model Accrual Budget Law* (New York: National Municipal League, 1946), p. xi.

[14] In New York City the budget is scheduled in the following manner: (1) February first, departmental estimates are submitted to the budget director; (2) February 15th, the comptroller presents an estimate of city resources for the budget years; (3) March 1, the president of the tax commission gives his estimate of the value of real property for tax purposes; (4) April 1, the mayor sends his budget to the board of estimate and the city council; (5) April 7 to 17th public hearings are held; (6) April 27, the board of estimate takes final action; (7) May 20 the mayor certifies the budget to the city council; (8) May 22 final action by the city council must take place; (9) June 1, the mayor may veto items; and (10) June 15, the budget must be adopted. By the charter, no deviation from these time dates is permissible.

In the small city or the city with a decentralized department of finance, the responsibility for budget preparation is vested in a fiscal officer who may have either real or nominal power. In the strong-mayor or manager city, the executive shoulders the burden of budget making. He obtains the various estimates from the accountant or treasurer and balances against it, the expenditure estimates of department heads. Where a commission or weak-mayor form exists, the budget is hardly more than a totaling of revenues and expenditures. Actual decisions on monetary policy are made by the council as a whole.

In the large cities the process of budget formulation is much more elaborate, the aim being to use the budget as a managerial device. There is the call by the chief executive for estimates from departmental heads. The latter must not only state their financial needs but also indicate alternative policies for adoption by the executive. Any expansion in services must be justified. At the same time or perhaps prior to the call for estimates, the financial limits within which departmental heads can function are made known to them. In large part the preparation of the budget and the conduct of hearings are the responsibilities either of a head budget officer, if an integrated department of finance exists, or the director of finance. At appropriate times the municipal chief executive is consulted on major policy decisions. If expenditures exceed revenues, then costs must be pared or additional borrowing may be needed. It is here that the budget justifications are of signal importance, for they are the guide posts to probable alternatives. When the review of executive expenditures is completed, the chief executive will send the budget together with a summary statement to the council.

Budget approval. Executive action on the budget is usually completed a few weeks before the end of the fiscal year. Here again the kind of budget the municipal council receives will depend upon the degree to which the finance function has evolved. If the executive is the center of administration, the council will receive a well-conceived plan, adequately documented with both a summary and detailed estimates. Decisions as to alternative courses of action already will have been outlined, and the council's role will be to choose among them on the basis of well-established criteria. However, if a weak executive and a decentralized finance department exist, the council will need to make its choice on the basis of the shrewd guess on the "tax rate." In such jurisdictions great reliance is placed upon the record of previous years and if these should include error of judgment or undesirable program emphasis, these are compounded. The old saying that five heads (in whom both legislature and administrative powers are vested) are better than one cannot have much merit unless cooperative judgment is based upon substantial fact. Municipalities with weak executives suffer from a loss of managerial direction.

Once the council obtains the budget, the document is, or should be, given the widest possible publicity. The council represents the people. It should provide an independent review and check upon the executive branch. From this it is apparent that the weak-mayor council and even the commission form cannot perform this function effectively since in reality they are passing judgment on themselves. However, where a strong executive exists, the separation of legislation from administration permits a proper appraisal of executive proposals. The council may query the executive on a variety of aspects of his financial program. It may be concerned about the impact of the tax rate upon its constituents. Whether the citizen will "buy" a budget is uppermost in its mind. Whether citizens can afford the proposed programs is another factor that enters into its deliberations. Finally, it must determine whether it has the necessary data to criticize constructively. Professor Bromage has said that the judgment of the council "can only be as good as the facts and figures which are presented to them." [15] More often than not, the council in a government with a decentralized system of finance is not provided with sufficient data for the proper evaluation of municipal expenditures.

Before the action of the council is concluded in the form of an appropriation ordinance, a public hearing is held. It is perhaps no overstatement to say that such meetings are dismal affairs. Although council chambers are small, there rarely is the danger of overcrowding. Few people attend and those that do generally have a special axe to grind. For most, if not all of these citizens, the budget is a meaningless jumble of statistics. Citizens are not able to obtain sufficient information in advance of the hearings and as a consequence, even if they do appear, they do not have a well-thought-out program. Small wonder that most decide that they can spend their time

[15] A. W. Bromage, *On the City Council* (Ann Arbor, Michigan: The George Wahr Publishing Co., 1950), p. 1.

more profitably elsewhere. Thus it is that an important link between the citizen and his government has been broken.

Yet surprisingly enough, a little thought given to the matter could easily result in the revitalization of the public hearing. Initiative in this regard, however, must come from the council and the responsible head of the municipality. In New Jersey an interesting effort has been undertaken along this line. Acting in response to the requests of interested citizen groups, the State Division of Local Government in July 1955 has directed municipalities to supply their citizens with budget information grouped under four main headings: (1) salaries and wages of all personnel by title and wage rate; (2) operating expenditures other than in (1); (3) consolidation by agency and department; and (4) a similar grouping of operating expenditures. This information must be made available upon request of the citizen or an appeal may be made to the State Division of Local Government.

In Metuchen, New Jersey, without prodding from the State Division of Local Government and at the suggestion of the mayor, department heads distribute their work sheets listing their budget requests to the citizens and the council. At the hearing conducted by the governing body, questions may be asked either by citizens or the councilmen. For the convenience of the citizens four evening meetings are held on different portions of the budget. Contrary to the common practice where the governing body first makes its own tentative conclusions and submits them to the people, the process of budget-making in Metuchen is a community affair.

Once the public hearing has been concluded, the council adopts an appropriation ordinance in accordance with the procedure specified for all legislation. Appropriations may be either on a line item or a lump sum basis, or sometimes a combination of both. In the former, expenditures are specified line by line and the spending agency is limited to the indicated amounts, except for a stated period at the end of the year when transfers of money may be made. The lump sum appropriation only specifies the amounts for major purposes. Within this framework the department may use its discretion provided that it does not exceed the amounts voted by the council. In most instances, the itemized appropriation is employed despite its inherent rigidity. It is preferred by many because it enhances council control over administration. In general, lump sum appropriations are voted only when the council is convinced that strong accounting controls exist.[16]

The implementation of the budget. Budget execution has a dual obligation; (1) to see that money is spent in accordance with the interest of the council; and (2) to enable the executive to supervise more efficiently the operation of the executive departments. In those jurisdictions where the finance function is relatively undeveloped, accounts are established for each agency. Fiscal control is limited to the approval of a voucher and supporting documents by the monthly action of the council, usually by resolution.

In the highly developed finance system, controls are more elaborate. The chief financial officer under the direction of the municipal chief executive is made responsible for budget administration. Not only are separate accounts established, but also the devices of allotment, work programs and pre-audit are employed. The allotment system is a method of preventing the expenditure of the entire appropriation before the fiscal year is concluded. Where such a procedure is in effect, a department is authorized to spend only a quarter or a twelfth of an appropriated amount depending upon the allotment period. If this control is to be made effective, it is essential that each account should show the amount of the appropriation, the expenditures made against it, the unpaid obligations and the unencumbered balance.[17]

The work program is a departmental plan which shows what the unit proposes to do with the money allotted to it. Properly employed, the device stimulates the advance thinking of the department and also enables the municipal chief executive to orient his plans more closely to his concept of administration.[18] Finally, the pre-audit when combined with an adequate accounting system not only keeps departments within the limits of their appropriations but also stimulates economy by forcing them to justify their expenditures.[19]

---

[16] The power of the governing body to appropriate is often limited in some fashion. In some cities it has the power either to increase or decrease appropriation items. In New York City it can only reduce items by a simple majority. Appropriation increases may be made only by an extraordinary majority.

[17] *Model Accrual Budget Law, op. cit.*, p. v; also *Model Cash Basis Budget Law, op. cit.*, pp. xvii-xix.

[18] A. E. Buck, "Technique of Budget Execution," *Municipal Finance,* XXI (1948), pp. 8-11.

[19] International City Managers' Association, *Municipal Finance Administration* (Chicago, Illinois: 1949). Ch. 5 contains a detailed description of budget execution.

Budget formulation and execution vary greatly in theory and practice. A budget, to repeat, is a plan of expenditure. If it is to be more than this, it is necessary that the plan be carefully implemented. To make a plan a reality requires careful implementation. It is only where a strong executive and a highly developed finance system exist that the objective can be realized.

DEBT ADMINISTRATION

The relationship of borrowing to municipal finance. Borrowing for capital improvements has been the experience at one time or another of most cities. In recent years the rigidity of the tax structure of most municipalities when combined with rising costs has forced municipalities into debt at an ever-increasing rate. In the year 1954 American cities borrowed $1,542 million, a gain of 26 percent over the previous year. Although municipalities redeemed some of their outstanding obligations, the city debt rose to $12,162 million in 1954.[20] Expenditures for interest and amortization have become an increasingly important part of municipal finance.

Borrowing is intimately related to the tax structure of the municipality. The debt of a municipality is secured by taxes rather than by collateral as is the case with private debt.[21] Bond holders have the right to force tax rates upward, at least until the tax limit is reached, to pay the interest and amortization of the debt. Taxes not only provide the income to pay off debts; they also are an index of the ability of a municipality to incur debts. If the tax rate is low, or the municipality uses its funds improvidently, or its government is inefficient, the credit of the municipality will be poor. Inability of a city to meet its obligations will result in a failure to market its bonds, for prospective purchasers will either hesitate to buy or insist upon higher rates of interest because of the increased risks. Borrowing and taxation are related in yet another way. Charges for the use of money may consume a significant portion of the current revenues of a municipality. In 1951, for example, New York City spent $265.4 million or 18.3 percent of its total budget for debt service. Diversion of large amounts of money from the city treasury to amortize its debts may cause it to postpone needed current activities. It is evi-

[20] *Compendium of City Government Finances in 1954, op. cit.*, p. 1.

[21] G. G. Munn, *Encyclopaedia of Banking and Finance* (New York: The Bankers Publishing Co., 1937), p. 513.

dent, then, that the wise use of municipal funds has a direct bearing on both the tax rates and the level of municipal services.

Restrictions on borrowing. In the past, wasteful and even profligate borrowing practices have thrown cities into default and have caused acute financial stringency. Starting with the Civil War period, the states have taken several steps to curb the borrowing powers of municipalities: (1) constitutional or statutory debt limts; (2) procedural requirements; (3) restrictions on borrowing purposes; (4) time limits on bond issues; and (5) administrative supervision. The traditional form of control, used rather widely today, is the constitutional or statutory limit on the amount of indebtedness that may be incurred. Municipal borrowing usually is limited to a percentage of the assessed value of real property.[22] In several states a maximum percentage of assessed property valuation is set on local indebtedness by state law. The most common percentage is 7 percent.

Most states through statutory action establish a special procedure which must be observed if bonds are to be issued. Normally a public hearing is required and in some cases bond issuances must be approved by a vote of the people. Limitations on debt also exist as to purpose. In most instances, in accordance with Dillon's rule of strict construction, borrowing is limited to the declared objects of the corporation. Normally expenditures for capital equipment may only be made from current revenues. New York municipalities are limited in their indebtedness, except for capital improvements, to 1/10 of 1 percent of their assessed real property subject to taxation.[23] Again, most states have debt service laws which specify that the annual tax levy must include a sum sufficient to cover both principal and interest on outstanding debt.

Finally, most states limit the term of bonded indebtedness to the life time of the project. This usually ranges from thirty to forty years. New Hampshire in 1953 passed a law requiring bonds to be repaid in 30 years.[24] The reasons for such limitations become evident when one cites an extreme example. In 1870, 7 percent noncallable bonds were issued by the city of New York in order that planks might be laid across a road in the West Farms section of the city. The last of these bonds will not mature until March 1, 2147. In

[22] C. H. Chatters and A. M. Hillhouse, *Local Government Debt Administration* (New York: Prentice-Hall, Inc., copyright 1939), pp. 11-12.

[23] *New York State Constitution,* Article 8, section 7.

[24] J. Clark, "Finance Administration," *National Municipal Yearbook for 1954,* p. 225.

1947 the outstanding debt on this construction was $198,000 and cost the city $14,000 annually in interest.[25]

Regulation of municipal borrowing either by constitution or statute has not been very satisfactory in practice. The key to its failure as a form of control is the requirement that borrowing should be limited to a percentage of assessed valuation. If the municipality raises the assessed valuation of its real property, its ability to borrow is increased correspondingly. Thus if property is assessed at a million dollars and the municipality is limited in its borrowing to 7 percent, it can borrow up to a maximum of $70,000. However, if property is revalued upward to $2 million, then the city can issue bonds for twice that amount.

Even if the city does not increase the value of its assessed property, it may achieve the same objective in another way. Limitations upon borrowing apply separately to single units of government. Hence, if a municipality has $5 million of bonded indebtedness, half of which has been incurred for the construction of sewers, it may create a sewer authority. Almost immediately its ability to borrow has been increased because the bonds have become an obligation of the authority instead of the municipality. Through the creation of a multiplicity of overlapping jurisdictions municipal debts may be pushed far beyond their intended limits.

Conversely, if the property valuation is $2 million and if property values should collapse as a result of a severe crisis, the ability of the municipality to borrow may be curtailed precisely at the time when borrowing might very well be a welcome addition to taxes. If none of the above conditions materialize, then constitutional and statutory limitations upon borrowing become a rigid limit preventing the municipality from financing needed capital investments. This, very largely, is what is happening today. Inflated costs of capital construction must be considered in the light of the difficulty in going beyond established debt limits.

The inherent rigidity of maximum limits on borrowing power, the fact that they do not actually prevent a municipality from overtaxing its financial resources, and the further fact that postponed capital improvements are subjecting municipalities to severe financial strain have led to state administrative supervision of municipal

[25] L. Ross, "A Reporter at Large: $1,031,961,754.73," *New Yorker,* XXIII, July 12, 1947, pp. 27-28.

bonding practices. In North Carolina the advisability of bond issuances measured in terms of the financial resources of the municipality and the purpose for which debt will be incurred is subject to review by a local government commission. The state has the power to authorize or disapprove a bond issue. Under no circumstances can bonds be issued unless the voters give their approval in a referendum.[26] In Indiana, somewhat similar authority is vested in a state board of tax commissioners. Bonds in excess of $5000 must be publicized. If ten or more taxpayers protest by a petition to the county auditor, the state board holds a hearing at which the interested parties including the municipality appear. Decisions of the state agency are final.[27]

Borrowing practices. Borrowing by municipalities is either of the short-term or long-range variety. The former is usually undertaken when tax collections are anticipated but are not received when expected. The latter is employed to finance large-scale capital construction beyond the immediate revenue capacity of the municipality. Our concern here is with the latter. The basis of borrowing is a bond, a loan of money by an investor on the basis of a promise by the municipality to repay the loan with interest over a definite period of years, usually the lifetime of the capital project.

Sinking fund and serial type bonds. Bonds may be classified in either of two ways: (1) according to the method of payment, and (2) according to the type of obligation. Sinking fund bonds and serial type bonds fall into the first category. The former requires complete payment with accrued interest at the end of the time when the bonds come due. A $2-million 35-year bond becomes payable at the end of the period with principal and interest. During the life of the bond, the municipality makes annual payments into what is known as a sinking fund which is invested, the proceeds of such operations being devoted to the ultimate amortization of the bond. This method of debt administration has the advantage of being flexible because the failure to make a payment into the fund does not mean that the municipality will be in default of its obligation. However, it is difficult to administer since it involves the computation of actuarial rates and both the accounting and investment of municipal

[26] J. W. Fesler, "North Carolina's Local Government Commission," *National Municipal Review,* XXX (1941), pp. 327-334.

[27] C. R. Dortch, "The Indiana Plan in Action," *National Municipal Review,* XXVIII (1938), pp. 525-529.

funds.[28] The existence of large sums of money in such funds is always a source of temptation. Even if these disadvantages were not present, sinking fund operations could not be conducted by small municipalities since they generally do not have the skills to administer such an operation. As a consequence, authorities recommend the use of serial bonds.[29] These are paid off in annual installments to bond holders. Its advantages are twofold. It avoids the complexities of sinking fund operations and it usually shortens the term of the bond resulting in a saving in debt administration.

General obligation and revenue bonds. Bonds may also be classified according to the type of obligation assumed by the municipality. General obligation bonds are those which are supported by the full faith and credit of the municipality.[30] Such bonds are issued in amounts that usually are not in excess of either the constitutional or statutory tax limits. If revenue is insufficient, taxes may be increased up to the statutory limit in order to meet payments on interest and principal.[31] The use of such bonds is as old as government itself.

Revenue bonds, on the other hand, are a comparatively recent innovation. The era of revenue bonds began in the last decade of the nineteenth century when the State of Washington passed a law enabling its municipalities to sell such issues.[32] It came into full bloom during the depression when most municipalities had reached the limits of their debt-incurring ability. It is still with us in this age of inflated capital costs. "A revenue bond may be defined as an obligation of a revenue-producing enterprise or property, payable solely from the revenues of that enterprise or property." [33] In effect, a revenue bond is secured by the property of the enterprise as collateral. If payments are not met, charges for costs and services must be increased or the property may be in default.

General obligation bonds are protected by a statutory requirement that the annual tax levy must be sufficient to cover the debt service and interest. Of the two types of bonds, the general obligation bonds are considered to be more attractive by the investor for

[28] Chatters and Hillhouse, *op. cit.*, pp. 18-19.
[29] *Ibid.*, ch. V.
[30] Chatters and Hillhouse, *op. cit.*, p. 241.
[31] J. B. Fordham, "Methods of Enforcing Satisfaction of Obligations of Public Corporations," *Columbia Law Rev.*, XXXIII (1933), pp. 28-29.
[32] *Washington Laws 1897*, Ch. 112.
[33] Chatters and Hillhouse, *op. cit.*, p. 241.

the obvious reason that they are backed by the tax authority of the municipality. Consequently, since the risk is less, the interest rate is lower. Municipalities, too, prefer the general obligation bond since the cost is less. However, there are conditions that dictate the use of revenue bonds. Municipalities may have used up their entire borrowing capacity, at least as measured by their constitutional or statutory limit. It is possible too that an enterprise may be so clearly proprietary in character as to justify the use of revenue bonds.

Authorization of bond issuances. Bonding procedures and practices are extremely complex, with considerable variation among municipalities. The general outlines, however, may be sketched rather quickly. Under our system of government, all expenditures are made in accordance with law. Bonds represent a commitment upon the part of the municipality to set aside a portion of its annual revenues for debt service. Therefore, bonds must be authorized in a similar fashion. The issuing authority must have a corporate existence and it must act in accordance with its power and authority. Otherwise, the bond does not constitute a legal obligation.

It is obvious, in view of the nature of a bond, that the procedure is closely regulated by statute. The initial decision to borrow and the determination to use either revenue or general obligation bonds is made by the council. Bonds may be authorized by the council without a referendum vote of the people if a public hearing is granted to the taxpayers. Adequate notice and hearing must be given in order to test adequately the reaction of the affected public. Following this, the governing body by ordinance or resolution may make the formal decision to borrow. This is a fairly simple procedure that does not differ materially from method of enacting local laws. When a vote of the people is required, the process becomes a bit more complicated. Advance notice is given to the public that the question of a bond will be submitted either at a special or general election. Final action is held in abeyance until the results of the vote have been determined.

Because investors will not purchase the bonds unless a binding legal obligation is created, it is essential that all the statutory requirements be observed by the municipality. As a minimum, therefore, the bond issue must be accompanied by the following papers: (1) a certified copy of the council minutes that authorized the issue; (2) a copy of the bond form; (3) legality of the issue as specified by an opinion of a qualified attorney; and (4) a transcript of the entire proceedings that led to the issuance.[34] Since legality is of such primary importance, the services of attorneys well-versed in bonding matters are required. It is common practice for a municipality to employ these specialists to draft all resolutions and ordinances, all public questions, and all procedures governing the borrowing action. This is done even where the resources of a competent municipal attorney are available. The rationale behind such action is that marketability of bond issuances will be enhanced if the attorneys are known to the investors.[35] Finally, bonds cannot be sold without the favorable bond opinion of an attorney or a favorable financial statement.[36]

Loans vs. "pay-as-you-go." Quite apart from fiscal procedure is the matter of financial policy. Municipalities must know the extent of their economic resources and relate it to the nature of the capital improvement to be undertaken. This will almost inevitably determine how they pay for their capital items. Three methods are employed: "pay-as-you-go"; reliance exclusively upon loans; and an intermediate step, part-loan and part "pay-as-you-go." [37]

Most municipalities finance out of current revenues the cost of recovering capital items such as cars, trucks, road scrapers, and other equipment. This may be done either through payments out of the tax levy or through the use of a reserve fund which is built up through annual accumulations to meet anticipated expenditures. A partial "pay-as-you-go" policy means, as its name implies, that a city will finance its capital improvements partly from current revenues and partly from bond issuances. In 1948 of some 633 cities that were polled in regard to their fiscal practices 54.2 percent indicated that they had such a policy.[38] Jackson, Michigan and Norfolk, Virginia are known as "pay-as-you-go" cities.[39]

There is no hard-and-fast rule concerning the merits of one or all of these approaches. A wide variety of policies exists and the fact that this condition is prevalent is an indication that local situations are quite different. "Pay-as-you-go" has much to commend it. In the

---

[34] Munn, *op. cit.,* p. 513; J. B. Fordham, *Local Government Law* (Brooklyn, N. Y.: The Foundation Press, Inc., 1949), pp. 481-524 contains a list of all the documents needed by municipalities in North Carolina.

[35] Chatters and Hillhouse, *op. cit.,* pp. 13-14.

[36] Munn, *op. cit.,* p. 13.

[37] Chatters and Hillhouse, *op. cit.,* p. 375.

[38] C. A. Harrell, "How Cities Can Adopt Pay-As-You-Go Policy," *Public Management,* XXX (1948), pp. 66-70.

[39] *Ibid.,* also unsigned note, *Public Management,* XXXI (1939), p. 148.

long run it is cheaper since it results in the elimination of costly debt service.[40] It also fosters much more careful planning since the cost of the project is immediately reflected in the tax rate. It is probable that taxpayers will protest extravagance or unneeded projects.[41]

The feasibility of "pay-as-you-go" will depend largely upon local circumstances. If the population of a community is stable and if its requirements for capital improvement are relatively slight, then it is undoubtedly the most efficient way to finance capital improvements. But this is indeed a rare situation. In most instances, especially these days, municipalities are faced with mounting capital needs out of all proportion to their ability to pay on the basis of current revenues. Insistence upon such a method of finance would undoubtedly prevent the construction of needed facilities.[42] Consequently, either partial "pay-as-you-go" or complete reliance upon borrowing seems to be the solution for most communities. Like its prototype, partial "pay-as-you-go" has the advantage of forcing sounder borrowing practices but it, too, has its limitations. A new community or a relatively stable community that experiences a sudden rise in population may find itself with a pressing need for schools, hospitals, sewerage systems and the like. In such circumstances, only long-range borrowing can be employed. Though the latter may be more costly, it does permit the expansion of facilities at the time when they are most needed.

In the final analysis, the principal objective to be sought in capital construction is a sound financial policy both as to the amount and as to purpose. Either or all of the above methods can be employed as the local situation warrants. The success of a capital program, like that of an operating one, depends upon the degree of planning undertaken. A necessary prerequisite for any borrowing policy is a master plan and its corollary, a capital budget. Through these devices the long-range capital plans of a municipality can be charted in the light of probable population growth and need. Priorities can be placed on those projects which are most urgent. Nonessential items can be culled from the list and discarded. Those items that can be financed on a "pay-as-you-go," or partial "pay-as-you-go," or on a complete loan basis can be segregated. Planning

---

[40] In Norfolk, Virginia, for example, a school built in 1919 cost one and one half times as much when payments were completed thirty years later.

[41] Chatters and Hillhouse, *op. cit.*, p. 378.

[42] R. E. Brown, "'Pay-As-You-Go' for Local Government," *The Tax Review*, VIII (1947), pp. 28-32.

may be made on a five- or six-year basis. Each year the capital budget may revise the long-range plan in the light of current needs. In brief, it is not the method of payment for improvements but rather *the plan* that is at the heart of sound capital financing.

AUDITING AND PURCHASING

Municipal expenditures are carefully regulated by state statutes and local ordinances. The main concern of city authorities, apart from considerations of efficiency and economy, is to make certain that the municipal dollar is spent in conformance with the law.

Auditing. Fiscal controls, as we have previously noted, vary greatly, depending upon whether the finance system is partially or entirely integrated. In general, however, the procedure for the handling of municipal money is fairly standardized. Accounts for each department or agency are established on the basis of appropriations voted by the council. Expenditures are authorized by departments through vouchers or requisitions. Verification of these documents to determine whether funds are available is made either by the council or by a director of finance. In the partially integrated system this review is limited very largely to a determination of whether compliance with legal technicalities has been observed. However, where the finance function is more highly organized, the municipal chief executive or his director of finance may also inquire into the wisdom of a proposed expenditure before it is made. Finally, the disbursing officer or the treasurer makes payment upon the basis of properly certified vouchers.

Control over municipal expenditures is primarily an executive or administrative responsibility, although in cities with the weak-mayor plan of government this task is discharged by the council. The prior review of all claims and demands upon the municipality is called a pre-audit. It is achieved through a system of accounts which maintains a daily record of all municipal payments and constantly balances them against available funds.

The post-audit—that is, the examination of financial transactions *after* they have been made—is generally regarded as a legislative function. Almost all municipalities are required by law to have annual audits after the fiscal year has ended. Books, accounts, and financial records are examined each year by an agent independent of the executive or administrative branch of the government. The purpose of this investigation is to determine the legality, accuracy, and accountability of all financial transactions concluded by municipal agents. The *Model City Charter* of the National Municipal League recommends that the audit should be made by persons who "have no personal interest, direct or indirect, in the fiscal affairs of the city government or any of its officers."[43] Although no recommendation is made regarding the agency to which the report should be made, in most municipalities the council receives the auditor's statement and takes such action as it deems necessary.

Purchasing. Aside from personnel costs, the purchase of supplies and equipment represents the largest single item of municipal expenditure. It is obvious, therefore, that effective purchasing can mean substantial savings to a city. Conversely, ineffective or even careless administration of purchasing constitutes an open invitation to needless waste, favoritism, low politics, and even corruption.

Purchasing methods employed by municipalities have evolved gradually over the years. In early America where cities were few in number and the range of their activities was limited, purchasing was carried out on a decentralized basis. Each department or agency bought its supplies on a "when, as, and if" basis. Even though the methods were slipshod, such procedures could perhaps be justified on the ground that waste, where it did occur, was only an infinitesimal part of the total municipal budget. Today, however, indifferent and haphazard buying practices can no longer be tolerated. Cities purchase hundreds, and even thousands, of different items at costs that range into millions of dollars. The inflationary impact of rising costs, the consequent decline in the purchasing value of the municipal tax dollar, and the prospect of impending or actual deficits have caused many municipalities to conduct a search for means to get more "mileage" from their tax dollars. In recent years, it is not surprising to find that hundreds of municipalities have discarded traditional buying methods in favor of the widely acclaimed centralized purchase activity.

A centralized purchase system has several main features all designed to obtain economy in buying. In contrast to the earlier decentralized procedures, responsibility for purchasing is vested either in a single person or, if the volume justifies it, in a single agency. Integration of the purchase function almost automatically means the

[43] Committee on Revision of the Model City Charter, *Model City Charter* (5th ed.; New York: The National Municipal League, 1941), Article II, section 23.

combination of small orders and paves the way for volume buying. Elimination of departmental buying means that bureaus and divisions must requisition their supplies from the central purchase unit instead of buying directly from the supplier. To meet promptly the needs of municipal agencies, the purchasing division must also engage in warehousing and storage operations. If this activity is to function effectively, it is essential that purchase records should show not only the location of needed items but also those that are in stock. Finally, consolidation of orders, a characteristic of centralized buying, is accompanied by volume buying on a bid basis in accordance with previously determined specifications.

Centralized purchasing has resulted in lower prices and better quality merchandise. It is estimated that an average saving of 10 to 15 percent can be obtained through such methods.[44] It is now almost universal practice for large cities to have staffs engaged solely in purchase operations. Smaller ones have purchasing agents and even those jurisdictions that do not have sufficient purchases to justify a full-time purchase function often engage in cooperative buying. In Michigan, for example, 70 cities have used this practice extensively.[45]

Savings do not automatically result from the mere adoption of an integrated purchasing system. Much depends upon the skill of purchasing officers and their ability to service the operating divisions. It is essential that such personnel should have an extensive knowledge of supply sources and the standards and prices of items bought for municipal use. Moreover, the needs of operating departments must be anticipated or it will be virtually impossible for them to facilitate the work of the line units. Such information and skill can be acquired by careful recruiting, training, and specialization of personnel. These are obstacles that must be hurdled if the effective utilization of the purchase system is to occur; but a necessary first step in the modernization of purchase practices is the integration of all purchase activities within a single unit.

CONCLUSION

The recent drastic rise in municipal expenditures and the fact that the trend bids fair to be a continuing feature of the city have

---

[44] R. Forbes, *Purchasing for Small Cities* (Chicago: Public Administration Service, 1951), p. 2.

[45] *Idem.*

focused attention on the need for more effective management of municipal finances. It is quite apparent that it is no longer possible merely to make certain that money is spent in accordance with the law. This has always been a consideration. Now it is essential that means be devised to stretch the municipal tax dollar as far as possible.

In other words, sound management is essential. To meet this need comprehensive fiscal organization is required. Taxation and assessment, budgeting, accounting, and treasury must be grouped together and bound to a municipal chief executive through a chain of command. Thus equipped, the chief administrator can marshal his administrative resources to obtain the best possible utilization of municipal money. Recognition of the importance of this development is reflected in the gradual but certain trend toward the creation of integrated finance departments.

In like fashion a new attitude toward debt management is emerging. It is now generally acknowledged that borrowing has a direct relationship to the current revenues and expenditures of municipalities. Wasteful or profligate practices may subject the resources of a city to severe stress. Here, too, the move is in the direction of a more effective administrative organization. Long-range planning in the form of a master plan supplemented by an annual capital budget is now considered essential. Sounder financial programs employing either "pay-as-you-go," or partial "pay-as-you-go," or outright loans are being related to the overall plans for the municipality. Here, too, the value of an integrated finance structure can readily be demonstrated.

Expenditure management is the key to the future of the city as a governmental unit. If it fails to deal effectively with the problem of revenue and finance, then a higher level of government will intervene. If this occurs, as well may happen, the autonomy of the city will be threatened.

BIBLIOGRAPHY

Books:

Bromage, A. W. *On the City Council.* Ann Arbor, Michigan: The George Wahr Publishing Co., 1950.

Buck, A. E. *The Budget in Government Today.* New York: The Macmillan Co., 1934.

Chatters, C. H. and Hillhouse, A. M. *Local Government Debt Administration.* New York: Prentice-Hall, Inc., 1939.

Committee on a Program for Model Fiscal Legislation for Local Governments, *Model Accrual Budget Law*. New York: National Municipal League, 1946.

———. *Model Cash Basis Budget Law*. New York: National Municipal League, 1946.

International City Managers' Association. *Municipal Finance Administration*. Chicago, 1946. 3rd Edition.

Articles and Other Material:

Brown, R. " 'Pay-As-You-Go' for Local Government," *The Tax Review* VIII (1947), 28-32.

Dortch, C. R. "The Indiana Plan in Action," *National Municipal Review,* XXX (1941), 327-334.

Harrell, C. A. "How Cities Can Adopt Pay-As-You-Go Policy," *Public Management,* XXX (1948), 66-70.

PART THREE

The City and Its External Relationships

CHAPTER FIFTEEN

State Control of Cities

THE STRUGGLE FOR MUNICIPAL AUTONOMY

The city is an institutional arrangement, the politically organized section of the community that deals with problems common to it. Its capacity to direct the needs of its inhabitants depends to a large extent upon its own resources; but its ability is also dependent upon its freedom to regulate its internal affairs. To a considerable degree the authority of the city is a matter of legal definition by a higher level of government, the state.

Municipal autonomy has been a bone of contention throughout history. The cities of ancient Greece probably represent the high-water mark in this struggle. City authority was coëxtensive with the state and the state was sovereign. Even under Rome, the city-state that became an empire, towns were able to obtain a large measure of independence with respect to their internal affairs.[1] Indeed, under the aegis of the mother city, the first glimmerings of the idea of municipal incorporation emerged. The virtual disappearance of city life in the age of feudalism was followed by a revival of the demand of the cities to be "free." Cities in north Germany and Italy gained a large measure of autonomy. In the ensuing battle between nationalism and feudalism, the cities cast their lot with the Crown. Corporate entities with powers defined in their charters or articles of incorporation sprang up. Although they were ultimately to become subordinate to the national government, they did obtain considerable control over local affairs.

In this country a similar battle for the right to regulate its local affairs also was waged by the city. At first, lack of adequate communications and relative slowness of transportation forced the isolation of cities. Municipalities were hardly more than urban clots. The problems they faced were restricted chiefly to their own jurisdictional limits. Although the cities were largely dependent upon

[1] J. S. Reid, *The Municipalities of the Roman Empire* (Cambridge: University Press, 1913), ch. 14.

the states, the factors noted above compelled the grant of considerable independence to the cities. In the first half of the nineteenth century, therefore, emergent urbanism was accompanied by a period of relative inaction and interference by the states.

Post Civil War developments, however, once more posed the problem of municipal autonomy. The tremendous upsurge in industrial development caused the rush of people to the city. The nationalizing effects of trade and commerce combined with improvements in transportation and communication began to break down the cultural isolation of the city. It was no longer possible to distinguish local from state affairs. Indeed, the distinction became blurred. Life in the city became inextricably intertwined with that of the state. The city, in brief, became a recognizable part of a larger whole, the state.

A few illustrations will demonstrate the integrating effect of social factors upon city-state relations. Streets and health, to mention two functions, were once matters of local concern and properly so. Only the people of a given city were affected by the presence or absence of regulation in these areas. Transportation advances and improved methods of communication, however, soon brought these within the scope of the state. Streets, for example, were used not only by the residents of the city but also by the people of the state. The condition of city roads, the standards of safety, the enforcement of traffic codes, and a host of other problems affected the citizen outside as well as inside the city. Indeed in the twentieth century with the advent of the motor car a citizen could traverse the roads of many cities. In the interest of uniformity and equality of treatment the state could no longer afford to remain indifferent.

Similarly, a mobile population had an important bearing on the health functions. When cities were relatively remote from one another, the states could afford a hands-off policy. But such was no longer possible when people could move more freely from place to place. Unsanitary or unhealthy conditions in one city could be readily carried to others. Disease, it was found, could not be confined to political boundaries. Again, in the interest of all the citizens, the state was forced to take a hand.

In the United States, evidence of growing state concern over what were formerly local matters coincides with the growing integration and urbanization of our society. The first onrush of industrial development is paralleled by growing state interference in local affairs. It is not entirely accidental that the period 1850–1870 witnessed a rash of special legislation by the states. Although the protests of growing urban centers, partially at least, beat back this attack, it was succeeded by classification devices which permitted general legislation that was special in effect. Still later in the nineteenth century and even today, state legislatures, faced with mounting problems from urban areas that were either technical or which they could not comprehend, resorted to administrative supervision of their cities.

Today the issue is no longer controversial. Serious students admit that the states have a legitimate and continuing interest in the affairs of their cities. What is at stake, however, is the degree and kind of control that should be exercised by the states. State-local relations reduce themselves largely to the distribution of political power. Urban concentration is dominant, but the political structure which defines the area of municipal power remains largely in the state legislature. The matter may be stated somewhat differently. The city is a creature of state law. The extent to which the state legislature will either reflect or appreciate the needs of the city will depend in large measure upon whether the city can gain adequate representation. As long as municipalities remain the victims of under-representation, just so long will they be handicapped in gaining the necessary authority to deal with the problems that plague them daily.

The Legal Status of the City

The legal relationship of the city to the state has an obvious importance. If the state can at any time assume the powers of city government, if it can remove its officers, if it can abolish the municipal corporation, then the right of the city to regulate its internal affairs becomes meaningless. The degree and kind of authority possessed by a municipality constitute the real measure of its self-government.

The inherent right of self-government. In 1871 when the excesses of special legislation were already self-evident, Judge Cooley in the now famous case of the *People ex rel. LeRoy v. Hurlbut* sounded the tocsin of revolt for the cities. Local self-government, he asserted, was "a matter of absolute right; and the state cannot take it away. It would be the boldest mockery to speak of a city as possessing liberty where the state not only shaped its government, but at discretion sent its own agents to administer it; or to call that system one of constitutional freedom under which it should be equally admissible to allow people full control in their local affairs, or no control at all."[2] Arguing from history, he pointed out that the towns and municipalities already had had well-established systems of local government before the constitution. The adoption of the constitution, then, merely confirmed what already had existed. Therefore, the local units had the inherent right to regulate their internal affairs.

In brief, to Cooley the exercise of plenary power by the states over their municipalities was nothing short of calamitous, "a blow aimed at the foundation of our structure of liberty. . . ." If the trend continued, he warned, centralization and despotism would flourish, and the rights gained by cities "through extorted charters and bills of rights" would vanish. To him the alternative was fairly simple: "either an intention that the legislative control should be constant and absolute, or, . . . that there are certain fundamental principles . . . which are within the contemplation of the people when they agree upon the written charter. . . ." The latter he thought to be "too plain for serious controversy."[3]

Dillon's rule. Although some states—Indiana, Michigan, Montana, and Wisconsin—have at one time or another given lip service to the doctrine of Cooley, it has been honored in most states more by breach than observance. The view prevalent among jurists is, that the cities are merely convenient subdivisions for the exercise of powers that belong to the states. Municipalities owe their origin to the state. From this principle there springs a whole legal system in which the city is completely subordinate to the high level of government. The cities are creatures of state law. The extent, duration, and kind of powers they exercise depend upon state law. Those who legislate may grant or withdraw powers, or may assume the powers for themselves, or delegate them to other agencies, boards or commissions.

Since Cooley's doctrine has not been generally accepted, it may be said that the cities have no inherent right of existence. With a single stroke, no matter how unwise the action may seem, the state legislature may strip a city of all of its powers and leave it with merely a name. In the legal view the disappearance of a city will not

[2] 24 Mich. 44, 95 (1871).
[3] *Idem.*

necessarily result in injury to the people since they will still remain under the protection of the state. The state legislature, in short, can take such action as in its discretion it deems necessary, *unless there is a constitutional limitation to the contrary.*[4]

A long line of judicial decisions in which the relationship of the state to the cities has been adjudicated support this view. Indicative of the legal attitude are such characterizations of the cities as "mere tenants at will of the legislature"; as "only auxiliaries of the state, for the purposes of local government"; and as "merely a department of state, and the state may withhold, grant or withdraw powers and privileges as it sees fit." [5] Even the provisions of the federal Constitution do not protect municipalities against the action of the state legislature.[6]

The powers possessed by the city are generally divided into two categories: those that provide for the special needs of its inhabitants, and those in which it administers state functions at the local level for the benefit of the citizens of the state. The distinction, as we have previously noted, is not always clear.[7] Where doubts exist as to either the extent or the nature of the power, the uncertainty must be resolved against the city in accordance with Dillon's rule of strict construction. That legal maxim to which the courts generally give strict adherence states that, "any fair, reasonable substantial doubt concerning the existence of power is resolved by the courts against the corporation, and the power is denied. Of every municipal corporation the charter or statute by which it is created is its organic act. Neither the corporation nor its officers can do any act or make any contract, or incur any liability, not authorized thereby or by some legislative act applicable thereto. *All acts beyond the scope of powers granted are void.* Much less can any power be exercised or any act done which is forbidden by charter or statute." [8] While the courts may be more favorably disposed toward municipalities where a private function is being carried out and grant it more leeway, such is not generally the case where municipalities act as agents of the state. The greater flexibility is probably due to

---

[4] *Barnes v. District of Columbia,* 91 U. S. 540; *Hunter v. Pittsburgh,* 207 U. S. 161.

[5] *City of Clinton v. Cedar Rapids and Missouri Railroad,* 24 Iowa 455; *St. Louis v. Kansas* 191 U. S. 207; *City of Trenton v. New Jersey,* 262 U. S. 182.

[6] *Williams v. Mayor and City Council of Baltimore,* 289 U. S. 36 (1933). A railroad was exempted from a city tax despite the protests of the latter.

[7] See chapter IV on tort liability of the municipal corporation.

[8] J. F. Dillon, *Commentaries on the Law of Municipal Corporations* (5th ed.; Boston: Little Brown & Co., 1911), I, sec. 237. Italics added.

the fact that the municipality is subject to suit where it is engaged in a proprietary activity.

It is evident, then, from this brief review of the legal status of the city, that the authority of the municipality is completely dependent upon the action of the state legislature, unless constitutional limitations exist that impose restrictions upon the higher level of government. Even where the municipality does obtain a measure of autonomy in local affairs, its powers are strictly construed. Small wonder, then, that the city in its struggle to free itself from the state has sought to impose constitutional restraints upon the power of the state legislature.

LOCAL AND SPECIAL LEGISLATION

Legislative definition of municipal power is the oldest form of state control over the cities.[9] Legislative control, as we have already intimated, is a powerful weapon. Used to its fullest extent, it can doom the cities to destruction. Happily for the cities, however, its potentialities have never been fully exploited.

In the early days of the republic the authority of the state over the city remained dormant. Legislative incorporation of the cities was a common practice, but on the whole the towns and municipalities, as Cooley had stated, continued to exercise the powers they had had from time immemorial. Logic and necessity dictated this policy. Large urban concentrations were few and far between. Communication and transportation facilities were primitive. It was not only undesirable but virtually impossible for the state to intervene in the affairs of the city. As a consequence, the relationship between the state and the city was fairly well defined. Municipal affairs were the province of the city. Matters of concern to the state as a whole were the subject of state regulations.

Burgeoning urbanism in the last half of the nineteenth century caused a change. The same factors that caused the rise of cities were ultimately to threaten their relatively autonomous existence. The massing of people in the cities in response to heightened industrial activity brought the city face to face with many problems that could be solved only with the assistance of the state. At the same time, the spread of trade and commerce caused the growth of interrelationships that were much wider than the city. Hence the city could

[9] H. L. MacBain, *The Law and Practice of Municipal Home Rule* (New York: Columbia University Press, 1916), pp. 1-4.

no longer confine its activities to its own inhabitants. Nor, for that matter, could the states avoid a legitimate interest in these developments. Thus the conditions of an emergent urbanism had a profound effect upon the status of municipalities. The distinction between state and local areas of responsibility became blurred. Even if the relationship were more susceptible of definition, the relatively immature thinking on governmental affairs prevented a proper understanding of the problem. State legislatures repeatedly failed to appreciate the difference between state and local affairs. The result was that the state extended its powers to areas that were almost exclusively of special interest to the inhabitants of the city.

Special legislation. The period 1850–1870 witnessed the high point in a phenomenon that may be termed special legislation. State legislatures constantly passed special acts governing the city's internal affairs. State interference became, as Seth Low, Mayor of Brooklyn, has characterized it, "almost a second nature." [10] In the mood that prevailed at the time, state legislatures created independent boards and commissions that determined local policies, prescribed in detail the structure of municipal departments, and forced cities to build streets and construct sewer and water systems.[11] A particularly outrageous example occurred with respect to the city of Philadelphia. In 1870 the state legislature, contending that the city should have new buildings, established a self-perpetuating board of commissioners with authority to incur debts that had to be paid by taxes levied upon the residents of the city. For some two decades thereafter, the city was forced to pay for baroque piles of marble by a decision in which they had no part.

Instances of this sort occurred in different and varying degrees in many states. In 1857 the State of New York created a metropolitan police district covering the city of New York and adjacent territory. A police board, initially appointed by the governor and senate and in 1860 appointed by the state legislature, assumed the responsibility for local police administration.[12] The action of the state legislature was upheld in the courts on the ground that the function was of concern to the people of the state as a whole. Similar

---

[10] Quoted in James Bryce, The American Commonwealth (New York: The Macmillan Co., 1889), I, p. 630.

[11] F. J. Goodnow, *Municipal Home Rule* (New York: Macmillan and Co., 1895), pp. 18-19.

[12] W. F. Willoughby, *Principles of Judicial Administration* (Washington, D. C.: The Brookings Institution, 1929), p. 146.

action took place in Maryland for the city of Baltimore; in Missouri, for Kansas City and St. Louis; in Illinois, for Chicago; in Michigan, for Detroit; in Ohio, for Cleveland; and in many other states. Indeed, so widespread was state interference in the period 1860–1890 that state control of local police systems became the established method of police administration.[13]

State intervention was especially severe in New York. Goodnow paints a graphic picture of municipal subjection to the state. Seemingly no area of municipal activity was considered outside of the scope of state authority. The city of New York, a traditional target of the upstate legislators, found that not only its police but also its health and fire functions were subjected to state control. Aqueduct and rapid transit commissions also were created for the city. The state legislators even attempted to force the pavement of specific streets. In the period 1884–1899, 1284 acts were passed governing 30 cities of the state, of which 390 related to the city of New York.[14] The comment of Goodnow is especially significant in this regard: ". . . in a word the state legislature has attended to a great many matters which are purely local in character; matters which do not affect the people of the state as a whole, and in regard to which there is little excuse for special legislative action."[15] In these and many other instances the abrogation by the state of municipal functions often made local self-government a mockery.[16]

Reasons for state intervention. It is instructive to note the reasons for state intervention. The states were not entirely to blame for the rash of special legislation. In this era the Jacksonian belief in the ability of the people to control their government through the election of officers had unfortunate consequences for the city. The massing of people in the cities, the mixture of people of diverse languages, religions and national origins, when combined with a wide suffrage base and a large number of elective offices, often resulted in incompetence, waste, and corruption. It is not entirely by accident that Lord Bryce characterized our municipal government as our one conspicuous failure. In such circumstances the hope of improving municipal government seemed so remote that many of the "good government" people appealed to the state legislatures for assistance.

[13] *Ibid.*, p. 146.
[14] Goodnow, *op. cit.*, pp. 22-24.
[15] *Ibid.*, p. 23.
[16] See, especially, the comments of J. Bryce, *op. cit.*, pp. 641-642.

The strict construction rule, as propounded by Judge Dillon and applied by the courts, also contributed to state interference in local matters. By implication at least, municipalities possessed only those powers that were enumerated. Even these were strictly construed. Hence municipalities that were either uncertain of their authority or desired new powers invariably applied to the state legislature for new or increased authority. Even where municipalities received broad grants of power they still found themselves handicapped since the means of implementation, that is, their ability to raise money to finance a needed activity, still remained under state control.[17]

Two other factors contributing to state interference in local matters deserve mention. The cities were often made pawns in national politics. The desire for political advantage often led state legislatures under the domination of an opposite political party to attempt to appropriate jobs and positions that normally would belong to the party in power within the city. Aware of the fact that the city contained large numbers of voters, the state administration often would seek to appeal over the head of the municipal government to the people.

Again, rurally dominated state legislatures had neither understanding nor sympathy for local affairs. Even if they did, they had no time to devote to the consideration of such matters since their task was primarily to legislate for the state as a whole. When often this disinterest and neglect became combined with partisan contests, the lot of the cities was a hard one. Before the movement for municipal autonomy finally took root the state legislature had run roughshod over the feelings and needs of municipalities. Much harm was done. State legislatures, as Rodney Mott observed, were turned "into spasmodic city councils." [18] The practice of "legislative courtesy" was no relief, even though it left the leaders of the city delegation in a position of concurrence where matters affecting the city were concerned. With local affairs subject to the whim of the state legislature, civic responsibility was discouraged. Citizens interested either in the reform of local government or in an increase in municipal powers often found that their appeals fell upon deaf ears. In the era of

[17] Goodnow, *op. cit.*, pp. 46-50.

[18] R. L. Mott, *Home Rule for America's Cities* (Chicago: American Municipal Association, 1949), p. 11.

special legislation, confusion, instability and disgust were often the order of the day.

HOME RULE—THE FIGHT FOR MUNICIPAL AUTONOMY

The evils and abuses of special legislation, however, fostered an important reaction. Aroused municipalities bolstered by the teeming masses in the cities staged a rebellion against legislative interference. Home rule was the by-product. "Basically," wrote McGoldrick, "the establishment of municipal home rule implies the complete or partial transfer of a portion of governmental power from the state to the city." [19]

In its ideal form, home rule means that the city in its relationship with the state has the fullest authority to determine its own governmental structure and powers, without either state legislative or administrative supervision.[20] Needless to say, this ideal has never been realized in practice. The cities are still the stepchildren of the state legislatures. They are limited in their powers to those enumerated and even these are strictly construed. Consequently, it is more correct to say that under home rule the state permits the city to form its charter; but in many areas, its powers of government are limited.

Objectives of home rule. Historically the home rule movement has sought to obtain two principal objectives: (1) the prevention of legislation and (2) the attainment of a greater measure of self-government.[21] Both of these have been realized in varying degrees. Under home rule, municipalities may frame their own instrument of government and, to the extent that it is not inconsistent with the general laws or the constitution of the state, may define its own powers over local affairs. It may do so with or without the consent of the state, depending upon the authority contained in either constitution or statute.

A few examples might be cited to illustrate its operation. Missouri, the state which pioneered in the home rule movement, in 1875 gave the city of St. Louis the right to form its own government. California grants its cities the right to adopt a charter with substantive powers relating to municipal affairs, provided that the legisla-

---

19 J. D. McGoldrick, *Law and Practice of Municipal Home Rule, 1916–1930* (New York: Columbia University Press, 1939), p. 2.

20 Mott, *op. cit.*, p. 6.

21 *Ibid.*, pp. 11-12.

ture gives its consent. Approval by the latter has the effect of making the instrument of government a law of the state.[22] Ohio municipalities are not only permitted to frame their own charters but also "have authority to exercise all powers of local self-government and to adopt and enforce within their local limits such local police, sanitary and similar regulations as are not in conflict with general laws." [23] Likewise, in Texas the home rule provision which dates from 1912 allows municipalities to adopt charters and pass ordinances that are not inconsistent with the constitution and laws of the state.[24]

Many other instances might be cited. In general, most home rule provisions allow cities to frame their own charters with or without reference to the state legislature or the governor.

The scope of home rule. Substantive grants of powers to municipalities for self-government are either meaningful or meaningless depending upon the limitations attached to such phrases as "for its own government," "municipal affairs," and ordinances "not inconsistent with the constitution of the state or of the general laws." A narrow interpretation by the courts may leave a home rule city with much shadow but very little substance.[25]

Provisions authorizing municipal changes in forms of government and powers have been bolstered by the adoption in most states of prohibitions against special legislation. The constitution of North Dakota, for example, specifies 35 kinds of local laws that cannot be passed. Similar restrictions exist in the constitutions of Texas, California, and Wyoming.[26] In New Jersey the state legislature is forbidden to pass special laws except upon petition by the governing body and then, only if two thirds of the members of the state legislature concur. Even so the law does not become operative unless it is adopted by a local ordinance or by a referendum of the people.[27]

Unfortunately these restrictions in the interest of home rule were virtually meaningless, for they were not accompanied by any affirmative grant of powers to the cities. This vagueness threatened to create a potentially dangerous situation, for if the states could not act and

22 McGoldrick, *op. cit.*, pp. 5, 49.

23 *Ohio State Constitution,* Article 18, section 3; also McGoldrick, *op. cit.*, p. 211.

24 *Texas Constitution,* Article 11, section 5.

25 W. B. Richland, "Courts Nullify Home Rule," *National Municipal Review,* XLIV (December 1955), pp. 565-570.

26 Mott, *op. cit.*, pp. 15-16.

27 New Jersey Constitution, Article IV, Sec. VII, Par. 10.

the cities had no power, a vacuum would be created where neither could act. To meet constantly changing situations, the legislature was forced to pass acts affecting municipalities, and the courts had no alternative but to sanction such interference.

Classification of cities. Although no one city could be singled out by the state, municipalities could be grouped into categories and be made the subject of state legislation. Whether such laws were considered general or special by the courts depended upon whether the basis of the classification was considered reasonable. Population has been used most often as the basis of classification, even though the constitution may prohibit special legislation. An act of the Pennsylvania legislature applying to cities over 300,000 in population was upheld, although the city of Philadelphia was the only city of this size. In its opinion the court said, "Legislation is intended not only to meet the wants of the present but to provide for the future. It deals not with the past but in theory at least, anticipates the needs of a state, healthy with vigorous development. It is intended to be permanent." [28] The court pointed out that Pittsburgh and other cities might some day reach this size. From this, and many other cases, the rule that may be deduced is this: the states may pass laws applying to a single city classified on the basis of population, provided that other cities may enter the specified population class.[29]

Conversely, closed classification where no other city may enter the class is regarded as special legislation and may be prohibited. Again, and for the same reason, the classification of cities upon the basis of geographical features is unconstitutional because such characteristics are always permanent. A good illustration of the attempt to circumvent the restrictions against special legislation by the use of a geographic classification can be found in a law passed late in the last century by the Pennsylvania state legislature. The statute applied to counties of more than 60,000 inhabitants in which a city of more than 8000 people was located "at a distance of more than twenty-seven miles by the usually traveled public road." A special court was to be held in such municipalities. In deciding that the law was special legislation, the court remarked, "This is classification run mad. . . . There can be no proper classification of cities or counties except by population. The moment we resort to geographical distinctions we enter the domain of special legislation, for the

[28] *Wheeler v. Philadelphia,* 77 Pa. St. 338 (1875).

[29] Goodnow, *op. cit.,* p. 70. Ohio courts have taken a similar stand.

reason that such classification operates upon *certain cities and counties to the perpetual exclusion of others.*"[30]

Thus restraints against special legislation do not mean that cities are free from legislative interference. As Goodnow has said the term "special act" in the constitution of most states "has been so narrowly defined as actually to permit the legislature, at almost any time that it may see fit, to frame a law that it would apply to only one of the cities within the state, and yet be perfectly constitutional."[31] The existence of such strict meaning has led to further attempts to restrict state authority. Procedural restraints and limitations on the number of classes of cities have been incorporated in state constitutions. In New York the state legislature is prevented from interfering with the cities by virtue of the fact that the city itself must request legislation affecting it. Even then the concurrence of two-thirds of the state legislature is required.[32] Chicago has a similar veto over state action which is bolstered by the requirement that special laws must be approved by a referendum vote of the people.

In many states the constitutional restrictions imposed upon state legislatures limited the number of classes into which cities might be grouped. In Pennsylvania the legislature is prohibited from creating more than nine classes of cities. In New York the number of cities is limited to three categories. Country-wide, the most usual restraint is four classes of cities. Hedging the authority of the state in this way, however, carries with it the danger that the state legislature will refuse to act when it is necessary to do so.

AN APPRAISAL OF HOME RULE

Home rule, the freedom of cities from state interference, can be obtained either through legislative enactment or through constitutional provisions. The former is termed legislative home rule, the latter is constitutional home rule.

Legislative and constitutional home rule. Legislative home rule grants the cities the power both to frame their own form of government and to define their powers in relation to the state. Constitutional home rule differs from this only in that the degree of autonomy is more rigid since it is written into the constitution. It is

[30] *Commonwealth ex rel. Fertig v. Patton,* 88 Pa. 258 (1878). Italics in the quotation are the author's.

[31] Goodnow, *op. cit.,* p. 91.

[32] *New York State Constitution,* Article II, sections 11-12.

generally agreed that legislative home rule is undesirable since it leaves the state in the position where it can withdraw authority that it has once granted. The instability and uncertainty of legislative home rule has led one authority to rightly conclude that ". . . no state has obtained satisfactory results from legislative home rule without a constitutional grant to protect the cities. . . . The only safe path to home rule lies through the gateway of the constitution." [33]

Constitutional home rule is, no doubt, an improvement over its legislative counterpart. However, such phrases as "for its own government," "municipal affairs," "local affairs and government," "property, affairs or government," to mention but a few, are terms of uncertain content.[34] Despite the vagueness of meaning, it can be concluded generally that home rule cities do have greater freedom in such areas as streets, sewers, parks, building regulations, and their governmental structures. However, home rule cities do not have appreciably greater powers in matters of education, police control and utility regulation.[35]

Attempts to define local autonomy. It is somewhat astonishing to note that in the years since 1875 when home rule first came of age in Missouri no one has really attempted a coherent definition of home rule phrases in state constitutions. In a major study on the subject, Howard L. MacBain asked "who is to decide whether this or that specific matter is a proper subject for regulation and control by a municipality? And where a state law covers the same subject matter as a charter provision, who shall declare whether this matter is one of state or local concern?" [36] It is in the answer to his questions that one finds the Achilles' heel of the home rule movement. It is exceedingly difficult to distinguish municipal from state functions. If a function is defined in the constitution as belonging to a municipality, then the hands of the state legislature are bound and it cannot act. If changed conditions should make a local function, such as public health or sanitation a concern to the people of the state as a whole, then the state would be helpless to act. It is probable

---

[33] Mott, *op. cit.,* p. 15.

[34] Report of the Committee on State-Local Relations, *State-Local Relations* (Chicago: The Council of State Governments, 1946), p. 164.

[35] *Ibid.,* 165-166.

[36] H. L. MacBain, *American City Progress and the Law* (New York: Columbia University Press, 1918), p. 5.

that a realization of the changing nature of our society led the courts of the various states to construe home rule provisions narrowly in order that the legislatures might remain unfettered in their power to deal with common matters of concern to the entire state.[37]

Uncertainty in the distinction between municipal and state affairs when combined with narrow construction by the courts has had an unhappy effect upon home rule cities. A case in point is the city of New York. Presumably it was protected by constitutional provisions which allowed it to legislate on matters dealing with the property and affairs of the city. Furthermore, no special legislation could be passed affecting the city without the consent of two thirds of the legislature. Yet the city has found that court interpretations have held that sewers, water supply systems, and municipally owned transit systems were matters of state concern. Hence the restrictions noted above did not apply to the state legislature.[38] Indeed, state interference in 1953 went even still further despite the constitutional restraint. When the voters approved a constitutional increase in the realty tax from 2 to 2½ percent of the average assessed value, the city found that it could not avail itself of the new taxing authority unless it agreed to turn over its $1.3 billion transit system to a state authority. The latter, in the legislation which authorized its existence, was empowered also to increase the indebtedness of the system by $565 million over a ten-year period without the consent of the city authorities.[39]

Nor is New York City alone in this respect. In St. Louis, the original home rule city, the mayor, faced with the possibility that the city's earnings tax with a yield of $8 million might be repealed by the state legislature, was forced to travel 18,000 miles and hold eleven meetings with legislators from one end of the state to the other before the tax authority was saved.[40] The moral of these cases is obvious: if the large cities with home rule protections in their constitutions are so dependent upon the state for authority, then the safeguards in their fundamental laws are, indeed, thin.

One can conclude that home rule, if it is not to be a meaningless phrase, must grant the city adequate authority to administer its

---

37 Goodnow, *op. cit.*, p. 95; *McGoldrick, op. cit.*, pp. 299-300.

38 Richland, *op. cit.*, pp. 565-568.

39 *Ibid.*, p. 569; also *New York Times*, April 7, 1953.

40 W. O. Winter, "Mayor Stumps the State," *National Municipal Review*, XLIV (1955), pp. 301-306.

purely local affairs. Yet, as we have noted, if the city is granted complete freedom from the state, the latter is powerless to regulate where uniformity of treatment in the interest of all the people is needed. Obviously, the crux of the matter is the need for an adequate demarcation line between the area of state and purely local concern.

Proposals for a definition of home rule powers. Recognition of this fact has led two leading organizations to seek to define the scope and range of municipal affairs. In its *Model State Constitution,* the National Municipal League has proposed that municipalities be given a broad grant of authority to administer their internal affairs. For the benefit of its inhabitants, cities are to be permitted to pass local ordinances on the following matters: police, sanitary and other regulations; assessment and collection of taxes; local public services; location and maintenance of streets; operation of public utilities; bonded indebtedness; and slum clearance.[41] These substantive grants are subject to the provision that local ordinances are consistent with state law. One leading advocate asserts that this arrangement is most practical "in the light of legislative and judicial history in an area of continual conflict, namely substantive home rule powers." [42] Here again is found a major weakness of the home rule movement. Consistency with state law means that the line between state and local power is definable in the courts. To many of the cities, the previously noted case of New York City may be considered a portent of what might happen to them.

In a similar vein, the American Municipal Association has proposed that municipalities be given a grant of substantive powers that may be exercised without enabling legislation by the state.[43] But, since the traditional distinction between state and local affairs has been eliminated, it appears that state legislative definition of local powers has been guaranteed. Professor Fordham, who was largely responsible for the draft of this proposal, is well aware of this difficulty. Nonetheless, he argues that it is not essential to have "constitutional self-determination." Home rule, he asserts, "must depend

[41] Committee on State Government, *Model State Constitution* (4th Ed.; New York: National Municipal League, 1941), section 804, paragraphs (a)-(z) incl.

[42] A. W. Bromage, "Home Rule—NML Model," *National Municipal Review,* XLIV (1955), p. 135.

[43] Committee on Home Rule, *Model Constitutional Provisions for Municipal Home Rule,* (Chicago: The American Municipal Association, 1953), p. 6.

upon a favorable climate of legislative, judicial and community opinion." [44]

Both of these viewpoints recognize, in different degrees, the paramount interest of the state. Both would grant municipalities considerable autonomy in local affairs. However, their approaches to the problem are somewhat different. One favors partial self-determination, that is, an enumeration of municipal powers in the form of a constitutional grant subject to general legislation by the state. The other, trusting to the climate of opinion, would permit municipalities to have wide powers without state enabling legislation but would permit the states to interfere.

Contributions of home rule. The home rule movement which began in Missouri in 1875 experienced a brief period of popularity. With all its limitations it was accepted by only 17 states. Since 1924 the following have joined the ranks of the home rule states: Utah in 1932; West Virginia in 1936; Rhode Island in 1951; and Maryland in 1954. It appears that the movement has just about run its course for the very evident reason that the integration of the state requires a jurisdictional unit that is somewhat larger than the city.

But while home rule has withered on the vine, it has made some valuable contributions to the practice of municipal government. It encouraged experiments in forms of municipal government such as the council-manager, the commission, and strong-mayor plans. It fostered local initiative and the growth of a civic responsibility. It brought special legislation to a virtual standstill. It gained for the city the right to determine its own form of government. Although it did not make any appreciable additions to the powers to be given to the city, it was successful in halting further state incursions into administration of city affairs, at least to the extent of confining state action to the realm of general legislation. Essentially, therefore, home rule contributed to the growth of local autonomy.

Rural Dominance of Legislatures

It is fairly evident that it is no longer possible to confine the scope of governmental power to either the state or local sphere. Of necessity, the responsibilities of both the state and the city are not only increasing but they also overlap. However, as a result of the centralizing effects of transportation and communication, the powers

---

[44] J. B. Fordham, "Home Rule—AMA Model," *National Municipal Review*, XLIV (1955), p. 137.

of the state are being increased at the expense of the city. Indeed, so rapid is the growth of state power that no one at the present time can foresee when the trend will level off. But the drive, and even the need, for uniformity threatens one of our most cherished institutions, local self-government. State primacy and local self-determination are seemingly at war with one another.

Since the boundary lines of state and local power are in flux, one may well ask how the proper distribution of powers may be obtained. It is obvious that there can be no return to legislative control, since the evils of special legislation are almost self-evident. Nor can a major reliance be placed upon the courts, for their awareness of the rapidly changing situation has impelled them to construe municipal powers narrowly in order to give the states greater flexibility. Nor is the constitutional self determination, of either the National Municipal League or the American Municipal Association variety, much of a solution. Home rule will become a reality only when the state legislature becomes more appreciative of urban needs.

Unfortunately this condition will not occur unless the cities are given greater representation in the state legislatures. The situation at present does not augur well for the "favorable climate of opinion" which Professor Fordham hopes to obtain. City dwellers are in a majority. Yet in most states the rural interests are overwhelmingly in control of at least one legislature house "and overweighted, if not dominant, in the other." [45] Urban areas pay 90 percent of the taxes but receive only 25 percent of the representation in the state legislatures.[46] The largest city in a state usually is under-represented. The populations of New York, Chicago, St. Louis, Detroit, Baltimore, Los Angeles and many other cities are not adequately reflected at the state level.[47] A presidential commission commenting on this condition remarks, "Paradoxically enough the interests of urban areas are often more effectively represented in the national legislature than in their own state legislatures." [48]

The imbalance of representation in favor of the rural interest is

---

[45] The Commission on Intergovernmental Relations, *A Report to the President for Transmittal to Congress* (Washington, D. C.: U. S. Government Printing Office, 1955), pp. 38-39.

[46] G. E. Baker, "Cities Resent Stepchild Lot," *National Municipal Review,* XLII (1953), p. 387.

[47] G. E. Baker, *Rural Versus Urban Power* (Garden City, N. Y.: Doubleday and Co., Inc., 1955), p. 18.

[48] Commission on Intergovernmental Relations, *op. cit.,* p. 40.

a product of many factors. The most frequent reason is the use of a unit of government, a county or town, rather than population as the basis of representation. In New York, New Jersey and California, for example, county representation is so apportioned in the upper house that the dominance of the rural interest is assured. One authority asserts that only 12 states are free from such restrictive device.[49] The height of such injustice can be found in California where the county of Los Angeles with a population of 4.2 million has the same representation as another senate district of only 14,000 people.[50] Even where state constitutions provide for legislative reapportionment, the state legislature has failed to follow the constitutional mandate for the rather obvious reason that state legislators have a vested right in keeping things as they are.[51]

The failure of the states to reapportion their representation is further compounded by the attitude of the courts and the practice of "trading." Courts generally refuse to compel reapportionment by the state legislature when the constitution so specifies on the ground that the matter is a political question.[52] Frequently, too, rural interests are willing to sanction greater representation for the city in the lower house in return for their continued dominance of the upper house. A particularly illuminating instance of rural insistence on its dominance occurred in New Jersey. Constitutional revision was sanctioned by the state legislature on the condition that the existing system of reapportionment remain unimpaired.

Efforts have been made to put teeth in the constitutional mandate which requires reapportionment by state legislatures after each decennial census. In Texas, South Dakota and California provision is made for an executive commission to act if the legislature does not. In 1952 Oregon voters through initiative forced through a measure which insured constant reapportionment in the light of continued shifts in population. Henceforth, in that state the secretary will reapportion when legislative inaction occurs.[53]

---

49 Baker, *op. cit.*, p. 12.

50 *Idem.* Also pp. 33-59.

51 C. F. Norton, "Home Rule Fight Fails," *National Municipal Review*, XLIV (1955), pp. 242-247. No reapportionment of representation in the Indiana state legislature has taken place since 1941, even though 60 percent of the people live in the cities.

52 C. W. Shull, "Reapportionment: A Chronic Problem," *National Municipal Review*, XXX (1941), pp. 73-79.

53 Baker, *op. cit.*, pp. 61-63; Texas also provides for automatic reapportionment. See R. H. McClain, Jr., "Compulsory Reapportionment," *National Municipal Review*, XL (1951), pp. 305-307.

The issue of legislative reapportionment has also arisen in the State of New York in 1955. Charging that "misapportionment" and glaring distortions existed in legislative representation, the governor sent a special message to the state legislature urging that seats in both the senate and assembly be apportioned solely upon the basis of population. Significantly, this would give New York City a majority of the seats in the upper house. The suggested change would require the concurrence of both houses and a referendum vote by the people. It is doubtful whether the measure will be able to run the gauntlet of the legislature under the control of an opposition party. But the fact that it has been brought up at this time underscores the inequities in the present system of representation.[54]

Most interesting of all of the devices to insure continuous reapportionment is the provision contained in the Missouri constitution of 1945. A bipartisan commission appointed by the governor within 90 days after the federal decennial census is required to delineate the senatorial districts. An elective secretary of state then apportions the representation among the counties. Initiative for reapportionment is no longer the province of the state legislature. By gearing representation more closely to population distribution, the interests of urban areas will be more adequately reflected in the legislative body.[55] The experience of Missouri may well be copied by other states.

STATE ADMINISTRATIVE SUPERVISION

Growth of state administrative supervision. The intensity of urban development, which originally served as a plea for local self-government, created a real uncertainty "whether under present circumstances, it [home rule] is a technique adapted to the governmental needs of modern society." [56] The steady growth of an integrated society raises the general question of whether the city, even if its special needs are recognized, can deal adequately with the multitude of problems it faces. Interdependence carries with it the connotation that there are matters beyond the control or concern of a single community. Health, education, welfare and law enforcement are inextricably intertwined with the welfare of the state as a

---

[54] *New York Times,* February 24, 1956. New York City and Erie County with 58.6 percent of the population of the state have only 48.3 percent of the membership.

[55] V. D. Branson, "Missouri's Apportionment Key," *National Municipal Review,* XXXV (1946), pp. 177-181.

[56] G. C. S. Benson, *The New Centralization* (New York: Rinehart and Co., Inc., 1941), p. 120.

whole. Moreover, special problems require technical knowledge and a corps of trained specialists, a competence often beyond the possibilities of many cities.[57] Even if the state is confined to general legislation, the limits of the legislative ability either to anticipate needs or to supply technical direction are almost self-evident. Some type of centralization is necessary and almost inevitable. In the past fifty years there has been a pronounced tendency to move away from legislative control, either of the special or general variety, in the direction of state administrative supervision of cities.[58]

Administrative supervision—its meaning. State administrative supervision may be defined as the technical direction of municipal affairs by state administrative authorities. It has many advantages over the previous system of legislative and judicial control. In the first place, administrative supervision speaks with a single voice for the state as a whole. It is not the will of either the state legislature or city delegations within that body. Secondly, it is a much more flexible means of control. The legislature acts through laws, and these laws come into operation only after a law has been violated. Administrative action by its very nature tends to prevent actions before they occur. Again laws are rigid. To change them requires another statute, and this is often time-consuming when the need is for swiftness and dispatch. A debt limit, for example, can be changed more easily by a state administrative agency which establishes a rational standard for borrowing, and yet at the same time it can prevent unwise borrowing practices. Thirdly, emphasis on the technical aspects tends to reduce the political factor. Fourthly, administrative supervision provides more effective protection for the individual since he can appeal over the head of the local officer when maladministration occurs without resort to costly legal action in the form of a taxpayers' suit. Finally, through the use of grants-in-aid, state administrative authorities can equalize the quality of services regardless of the ability of the community to pay.[59]

Forms of state administrative supervision. State administrative supervision over the cities takes many different forms. Broadly speaking, these fall into two main categories: (1) information and persuasion and (2) direction and control. Under the first of these come

57 D. Pontius, *State Supervision of Local Government: Its Development in Massachusetts* (Washington, D. C.: Public Affairs Press, 1942), pp. 2-3.

58 S. C. Wallace, *State Administrative Supervision over Cities in the United States* (New York: Columbia University Press, 1928), p. 1.

59 Report of the Committee on State-Local Relations, *op. cit.*, pp. 11-21.

such devices as reports, inspection, advice and even grants-in-aid. The second category, differing in degree of coercion exercised, consists of prior approvals, orders, appointment and removal, and finally substitute administration.

Reports required by the state of municipal authorities are perhaps the oldest, and yet the most fundamental, of all controls. Requests for information may seem inconsequential, but when one realizes that data so gathered may form the basis of comprehensive action, requests of this sort soon assume a bolder perspective. The state department can gain an objective view of how a function is being performed in all areas of the state. The health function illustrates this form of supervision. Reports on vital statistics, communicable disease, sanitary conditions and the other phases of health work are often required. Reports may result not only in a measurement of municipal performance but also in the prescription of more uniform standards. Even if no other steps were taken by the state, the fact that reports are required may very well place cities in competition with one another.[60]

Inspection is more positive in its approach. By definition it means a review to observe whether prescribed standards are being met. Inspection offers the state a first-hand view of the manner in which the city adheres to its prescriptions. As Professor Wallace has remarked, "much may go on in municipalities without reaching the public." [61] The process of inspection may be periodic or continuous. It may be at the initiative of either the state or the city. In New York State, for example, the State Commission of Investigation and the Department of Audits and Accounts maintain a continuing review of municipal activity. New Jersey prescribes uniform systems of accounting for its local units and cities. The Director of the State Division of Local Government may make inspections at any time to determine whether its standards are being observed.[62] Country-wide, the audit and inspection of accounts exist in 40 states.[63]

Advice and information usually result from the absence of technical abilities in municipalities. Smaller municipalities, and even larger ones, do not have facilities or personnel to deal with many

60 Pontius, *op. cit.*, p. 5.
61 Wallace, *op. cit.*, p. 43.
62 New Jersey Statutes Annotated, LII, section 27, p. 32.
63 Benson, *op. cit.*, p. 127.

technical matters. Training programs for policemen and firemen, crime and fingerprint laboratories, civil service assistance are a few examples of the kind of assistance provided. Conferences and correspondence bulletins are also means of making the technical information of the state available to the community.[64]

Many grants by the states furnish them with an excellent opportunity to supervise the work of municipalities. Grants-in-aid usually have a dual objective: efficiency of performance and equalization of service. Money may be allocated to the city on the condition that a given level of service is maintained. The standard set is, or at least should be, the basis of supervision. Equalization of quality of service is usually obtained through grant formulae. This phase of supervision usually occurs in the fields of roads, schools, welfare, and health. It is generally agreed that adequate supervision in this area is conspicuous by its absence, although in those instances where state funds are obtained from a federal bureau, the latter is more insistent that standards should be met. For example, in welfare, the activities of municipal authorities are rather rigidly audited by the state because the latter is subject to penalties by the federal government if its use of federal grants is abused.[65]

More direct control of municipal officials is obtained through the device of prior approval. Before a municipality can act, it must obtain the consent of state authorities. Plans and designs for school buildings, water works, or sewage disposal plants are examples that fall into this approval category. A control of this sort is negative. It is designed to prevent a municipality from carrying out a given act that is not in conformity with the intention of state law.

More positive is the procedure by which a state agency directs municipal agents to carry out a function vested in them by law. These directives may be enforced by mandamus, injunction, or suit in equity. Municipal officers who refuse to comply with an order may be guilty of a misdemeanor and subject to fine and/or imprisonment, and may even forfeit their office.[66] "It is the function of the ordinance-making power," Professor Wallace states, "to prescribe

64 Wallace, *op. cit.*, pp. 43-46.

65 Benson, *op. cit.*, p. 126.

66 See, for example, the power of the director of New Jersey's Division of Local Government, *New Jersey Statutes Annotated*, LII, section 27BB-52. Also J. W. Fesler, "North Carolina's Local Government Commission," *National Municipal Review*, XXX (1941), pp. 327-334.

general rules of conduct for municipal officials to follow. The mechanism is, in fact, an exercise of legislative power by supervising authorities." [67]

States may also exercise appointment and removal powers over municipal officers. In New York under the Moreland Act, the governor's removal power extends to all instances where the public welfare is jeopardy. In almost all states incompetence or maladministration is sufficient cause for removal of local officers, although the degree of interference is conditional upon seriousness of the official act. It is, in the main, a negative power since municipal authorities may retain the power to appoint a successor. In some cases the state may make appointments where two or more municipalities are involved. In New Jersey, municipal magistrates, where two municipalities share a single court, are appointed by the governor. A civil service system, when adopted by a municipality, governs both appointment and removal. Local authorities must observe civil service regulations, and their failure to do so may result in an appeal over the heads of municipal agents to the state.

Finally, the state may supersede the system of local administration in case of emergency or where the incompetence of the city is demonstrated. Presumably this was the reason why the State of New York in 1857 assumed the police function of New York City. Failure of a municipality to perform the health function also may result in the state stepping in. Under the provisions of the social security act, some states have authorized the county to assume charge of public assistance where the municipality does not comply with established requirements as stated by both the state and the federal government. Normally, when the reason for state assumption of local authority no longer exists, the power usually reverts back to the municipality. However, substitute administration, if it continues for any long period, may very well become direct state administration. North Carolina and Virginia have accepted responsibility for all roads. Delaware and North Carolina have a state-administered school system. Substitute administration under normal conditions is regarded as a measure of last resort, to be employed when the municipality for one reason or another is found to be incapable of meeting state standards. However, even as a temporary expedient, it still is a

---

[67] Wallace, *op. cit.*, pp. 54-55.

potent weapon that can be wielded with devastating effect should conditions so warrant.[68]

Recent developments. Within the past fifty years the contacts between state and local authorities have multiplied to the point where it has been suggested that all administrative supervision should be centralized in a single state department of local government. This would give the municipalities a central point of reference and would permit the state to develop a uniform attitude toward the local units. New Jersey's Division of Local Government with its local government board might be considered a step in this direction. Although primarily concerned with fiscal supervision, the agency has broadened its activities in recent years to include conservation, health, housing and a host of other functions. This has come about not on the basis of its own volition but rather because debts limits for municipalities and schools have forced local units to seek permission to exceed the present limitations on their borrowing capacity. Pennsylvania has a somewhat similar arrangement, and the local government commission of North Carolina and the Indiana Tax Board are other attempts at centralized supervision.[69] More recently, the former lieutenant governor of New York has proposed a similar arrangement to aid the municipalities of his state in meeting their problems.[70]

All of these attempts, it should be noted, are primarily in the field of fiscal administration. Strong arguments support the need for centralization in this area, but whether they apply with equal force and effect in other fields is another matter. The manner in which municipalities have handled problems of municipal finance leaves no doubt that they should be more effectively controlled by the state. Even if one ignores this unhappy experience, it is still desirable that all technical agencies concentrate their effort through a central point. Municipalities would have a single point of referral, and conflicting and often contradicting directives would be reduced to a minimum. Centralization of state supervision also would pave the way toward a more considered approach to the problems of the municipality.

[68] R. H. Wells, *American Local Government* (New York: McGraw-Hill Book Co., Inc., 1939), pp. 129-130.

[69] Committee on State-Local Relations, *op. cit.*, pp. 48-50. Also Fesler, *op. cit.*, p. 327 ff.

[70] *New York Times,* February 24, 1956.

On the other hand, winning the concurrence of state administrative agencies to the idea of centralized supervision seems an almost insurmountable barrier. From an institutional standpoint, each state department exists on a coordinate basis. The very fact that such agencies have equal status with one another implies that each has a special concern over a given aspect of municipal affairs. Having dealt with municipalities on relatively independent basis for almost a half century, they would undoubtedly feel that their responsibilities would be curtailed if they were required to submit their directives through a central department of local government. If they were so inclined, the relatively slow progress of the governor as administrative chief would allow them to resist integration. In those states where the governor is a strong administrator, the installation of a single department of local government at the state level would still force it to compete for gubernatorial support. If state departments were successful in their resistance, then the department of local government would hardly be more than a referral agency. If this state of affairs should come to pass, then there would be little point in integrating administrative direction at the state level.

Inadequacies of state supervision. While state administrative supervision has many worthwhile aspects as it is presently constituted, it also has several drawbacks. Perhaps the foremost objection to it is the possibility that such supervision may become so severe that local self-government may become an empty phrase. The prescription of uniform accounting systems may be justified but when the state begins to decide whether the municipality can borrow it is, in effect, substituting its decision for that of local policy. Health activities may be performed by the municipality, but when a state agency prescribes the health program in minutest detail, very little in the way of discretion is left to the municipality. Even where state supervision is not fully developed, its exercise may often cause friction between state and local authorities.

Moreover, state supervision is based upon the premise that state agencies are equipped with the necessary administrative skills to direct the performance of state functions at the local level. This may be true of the small city, but it is most definitely not the case with respect to a large city. To the extent that state agencies regard all cities as being alike, direct interference in policy areas of large cities is at least open to question. The large urban area, as in the case of New York and Chicago, often has a budget that is larger than the state itself. Yet the latter is supposed to offer technical advice to its urban counterpart. It may be argued that uniformity may be desirable, but it is also true that the problems of the large metropolitan city are so different as to require diversity of approach.[71] In the light of this it is fortunate, indeed, that the administrative practices of many states are weak.

Although statutory control is still the primary means of state control over the cities, state administrative direction during the past half century has made astonishing gains. One must echo the comments of an authority on the subject when he said that "state administrative supervision is making rapid headway. Administrative officers are everywhere being called upon as a supplementary means of control." [72] The statement made in 1928 is even more true in today's world where the city is being asked to perform ever so many more functions. The intensification of administrative regulation, like its legislative predecessor, raises once more the fundamental question: which level of government shall perform a given governmental task. This is a question that merits continuous study. Even after a differentiation of duties has been made, there is still the need for flexibility since technological changes continually cause changes in the relationships between the two units of government.

CONCLUSION

Writing on the general problem of state-local relations, a prominent state senator expressed the view that the adjustment between the two levels constituted a "major problem of government." [73] There is much merit in his contention. The city is a legal and social fact. It is an agglomeration of people with special needs. It is a community of interdependence, distinguished by the fact that it seeks to meet its common problems through a political instrumentality, a municipal government. At the same time the city is part of a larger totality, the state. Its desires must be curbed in the interest of the greater whole. Consequently, state-local relations have been characterized by a constant clash between the interest of the city and the state. The line between the city and the state is not clearly drawn. Perhaps it can never be, but whether the strength and vigor of local

---

[71] Benson, *op. cit.*, p. 129.

[72] Wallace, *op. cit.*, p. 272.

[73] T. C. Desmond, "The States Eclipse the Cities," *National Municipal Review*, XLIV (1956), pp. 296-300, 306.

institutions can survive will depend in a large measure on the degree of adjustment that takes place between the two levels of government.

The struggle of the city to gain a greater measure of freedom is the heart of state-local relations. The resistance of the city to the centralization of authority has met with varying degrees of success. In the early years of this country the cities, or rather the towns, were relatively free from state interference, but as urbanism began to burgeon the cities were increasingly subjected to state intervention. The reasons for this have already been noted. For a time it appeared as if the city would become engulfed in a torrent of special legislation.

Before the movement had run its course the city countered with a demand for home rule and the right to greater freedom over their internal affairs. In this they were, at least, partially successful. The city received the right to structure its own government in the light of its own needs. But this soon became an empty illusion for the restrictions against special legislation caused the state legislature to pass general laws that were special in effect. Moreover, this tendency was heightened by the strict construction rule of the courts which sought to keep the hands of the state unfettered to deal with constantly changing situations. The net result was that what the state had given with one hand was withdrawn with the other. The city could determine its structure but its authority to deal with its own problems was severely restricted.

At the turn of the century, while legislative control was the primary means of regulation, state administrative supervision began gradually to make its appearance. State agencies equipped with technical skills and functioning on a year-around basis began to exhibit increasing interest in the problems of the city that were rapidly becoming a concern of the state. As the society became more integrated, their scope of activity widened to the point where today many municipal officials are subject to state direction and control. Today the centers of policy and decision making, despite the fact that many cities have budgets larger than the state in which they are located, have shifted to the state level.

That the states have sought to increase their control over local units has often been as much a desire for insuring a minimum standard of performance as it has been a struggle to obtain more political power. Highways, health, education, police protection and public welfare must be administered on the basis of uniform standards for all. Local units cannot, and should not, be permitted to plead fiscal inadequacy in these areas. Local self-government per se, it should be added, has no inherent virtue, unless, of course, it is accompanied by adequate services for its inhabitants.

City-state relations in the final analysis represent a process of slow adjustment based upon the respective needs of both levels of government. It is not a problem of whether the state or the city should pre-empt given areas. Rather, it is one of working out cooperative relationships in which both units will function most effectively. It is in this connection that we come once more to the distribution of political power within the states. The definition of jurisdiction is largely a political matter. Whether or not the city will gain greater recognition will depend upon whether the growing urban majorities will be reflected in the state legislature. City autonomy or city-state cooperative relationships rest upon the degree to which the rural imbalance in the state legislature is removed. Fundamentally, therefore, a fairer representation is the only real method for protecting the city against either rural incursion or inaction.

BIBLIOGRAPHY

Books:

Baker, G. E. *Rural v. Urban Power.* Garden City, New York: Doubleday and Co., Inc., 1955.

Benson, G. C. S. *The New Centralization.* New York: Rinehart and Co., Inc., 1941.

Goodnow, F. J. *Municipal Home Rule.* New York: Macmillan and Co., 1895.

MacBain, H. L. *American City Progress and the Law.* New York: Columbia University Press, 1918.

———. *The Law and Practice of Municipal Home Rule.* New York: Columbia University Press, 1916.

McGoldrick, J. D. *Law and Practice of Municipal Home Rule, 1916–1930.* New York: Columbia University Press, 1939.

Mott, R. L. *Home Rule for America's Cities.* Chicago: American Municipal Association, 1949.

Pontuis, D. *State Supervision of Local Government: Its Development in Massachusetts.* Washington, D. C.: Public Affairs Press, 1942.

Report of the Committee on State-Local Relations. *State-Local Relations.* Chicago: The Council of State Governments, 1946.

Wallace, S. C. *State Administrative Supervision Over Cities.* New York: Columbia University Press, 1928.

Wells, R. H. *American Local Government.* New York: McGraw-Hill Book Co., Inc., 1939.

Articles and Other Material:

Richland, W. B. "Courts Nullify Home Rule," *National Municipal Review,* XLIV (1955), 565-570.

Winter, W. O. "Mayor Stumps the State," *National Municipal Review,* XLIV (1955), 301-306.

CHAPTER SIXTEEN

Federal-City Relations

THE NATION, THE STATES, AND THE CITIES

The language of the federal Constitution completely ignores the cities. No mention is made of them and, to all intents and purposes, they are nonexistent entities. Surprisingly, a federal system which recognizes the need for both unity and diversity divides the power of government only between the nation and the states. Nowhere, to repeat, does our fundamental law make any reference to the city.

The states and the city. Yet as is so often the case, the logic of history often acts to destroy the legal fiction. Since the founding of this country, the nation has been almost completely urbanized. Cities are a part of the states but they have also become a part of the nation. City problems no longer are special and cannot be confined to their boundaries. Increasing interdependence has forced the states repeatedly to intervene in areas considered the special province of the city. Moreover, the incapacity or unwillingness of the states to help the cities, the fact that the former are frequently encumbered by outmoded and inept administrative machinery, led to a shift in emphasis to a higher level of government, the nation. But even where the states were willing and able to aid the cities, the federal government, of necessity, must have an interest in the well-being of people in the cities.[1]

The provisions of the federal Constitution. Furthermore, since the cities are creatures of the state, they are subject to the same restraints in the fundamental law as apply to their creator. Federal constitutional provisions prohibiting impairment of obligation of contract and the denial of equal protection of the laws and granting due process of law apply with equal force and effect to the cities as well as the states. Thus, the attempt of cities to restrict the freedom of their citizens to assemble or to use the constitutional guarantees of free speech and press will invariably provoke an appeal to the fed-

[1] G. C. S. Benson, *The New Centralization* (New York: Rinehart and Company, 1941), pp. 88-89.

eral government. Similarly, cities cannot default their obligations. Nor, for that matter, can they adopt ordinances that discriminate in favor of one person as against another, for such actions may be challenged as a denial of equal protection of the law. On the whole, this represents a negative approach, an appeal to federal courts to apply the federal constitution to municipal action in the interest of uniformity and justice.

The impact of federal powers. More positively, the federal government possesses a whole battery of enumerated and delegated powers, stated or implied, that affect the cities in many ways. Federal law is the supreme law of the land. Federal officers [2] and federal instrumentalities may operate freely in the states and cities without hindrance. Federal facilities are immune from taxation.[3] Indeed, the presence of large numbers of federal buildings within a city may have an exceedingly adverse effect upon the latter's tax base. The federal government may lay and collect taxes and provide for the general welfare. Generally speaking, while it cannot use its taxing power to regulate, it does have a superior financial position. From its vantage point of fiscal autonomy it may undertake independent action that may have a great bearing upon the cities. It may attract highly qualified personnel. It may build a vast storehouse of information on health, safety, welfare, nursing, education and many other areas of municipal responsibility. Through its skilful use of such data in the form of information and advice it may significantly control municipal actions and programs. Loans, grants and offers of assistance by the federal government may be so attractive that cities may make many policy decisions in the light of probable federal aid.

Federal commerce and war power also offer significant areas of intervention in the affairs of the city. River and harbor improvements, navigable streams, airports and air traffic, regulation of utility companies which are interstate in character, these are but a few of the innumerable areas that come within the scope of federal authority.[4]

To sum the matter up, although the Constitution does not mention the cities, the way was open, by reason of federal power of both a negative and positive nature, for many contacts with the cities.

---

[2] *In re Neagle,* 135 U. S. 1 (1890).

[3] *McCulloch v. Md.* 4 L. *ed.* 579 (1819).

[4] W. Anderson "The Federal Government and the Cities," *National Municipal Review,* XIII (1924), pp. 288-293.

Until the thirties of this century, however, federal-city relations were peripheral in nature. That this was so is perhaps best illustrated by the experience of American delegates to the International Congress of Cities in London in 1932. Our American delegates were surprised and perplexed to find their European colleagues worried about the encroachments of the central government.[5] Yet it was not long before they, too, were deeply immersed in this issue. Unlike their European cousins, however, American municipal executives actively sought federal intervention. Whatever fears they may have had on this score were erased by the crisis situation in which they found themselves.

Writing in 1924, Professor William Anderson prophetically remarked, "The time has come in the United States for those interested in the progress of our institutions to consider the relations existing between national and municipal authorities." [6] Yet it was not until the coming of the great depression and the consequent inability of the states to furnish positive assistance that the cities demanded federal aid. When the crisis and emergency disappeared, the scope and dimension of federal interest and power were irrevocably broadened. Since the depression federal-city relations have been fundamentally altered. In the pages that follow, a discussion of work relief, public works, and financial assistance will show the impact in the thirties of federal programs on federal-city relationships.

WORK RELIEF

Relief in the pre-New Deal period. The change in relationships between the city and the national government from a peripheral to a direct contact is highlighted by the administration of work relief programs. Until the crash of 1929, relief was considered a local responsibility. Charity was dispensed by the municipality and private organizations in the city. Indeed, the latter shouldered the major part of the burden. In the thirties, economic paralysis and consequent mass unemployment soon made it evident that these resources were inadequate to deal with the situation. Property values were deflated and municipal income was reduced correspondingly. In a time of increasing need, municipal treasuries were being drained rapidly despite drastic cuts in services and salaries. Faced with a hitherto

[5] P. V. Betters, J. K. Williams and S. L. Reeder, *Recent Federal-City Relations* (Washington, D. C.: U. S. Conference of Mayors, 1936), p. 3.

[6] Anderson, *op. cit.*, p. 288.

unprecedented situation, municipalities appealed first to the states, and finding that they, too, were in dire straits, they turned to the federal government as their savior.

Despite the desperate condition of the cities and the states, the federal government in its early efforts was exceedingly cautious. Loans instead of direct grants were employed and these were made available to the states and the cities on two bases: (1) $300 million in loans were made to the states and the cities subject to the restriction that no state should receive more than 15 percent of the sum; (2) $1.5 billion in loans were provided for self-liquidating projects.[7] By 1933 almost the entire $300 million loan was exhausted, but very little of the $1.5 billion ever found its way into the coffers, either of the state or the city. Largely this was because of political and legal obstacles that could not be easily hurdled. Loans in the second category were to be secured either by a pledge of repayment out of future road grants or from the sale of municipal goods and services. None of the states was willing to accept the first alternative, and the cities found themselves without power to issue revenue bonds. Nevertheless despite the admitted inadequacy of the act, it does mark an important departure in principle from what had previously prevailed. As some have remarked, ". . . for the first time in our history the federal government went so far as to allow cities to borrow federal money to carry on what had been generally held to constitute a local function. It was the forerunner of the federal government's later acceptance of direct responsibility for relieving the distress and destitution existing in urban centers." [8]

Early federal-city relationships. When the Roosevelt administration came to power in 1933 a more determined approach to the problem of work and work relief was undertaken. In May of that year a Federal Emergency Relief Administration was established with an initial appropriation of $500 million. The program was marked by the absence of the self-liquidating provision of the previous year, and grants replaced loans as a means of alleviating widespread distress. Half of the fund was to be allotted to the states in amounts equal to one third of the money spent by the states and its subdivisions for relief purposes. The balance was to be applied by

[7] 47 *Stat. L.*, 709-724, especially section 1 (a). This was an amendment to the Reconstruction Finance Act passed somewhat earlier in the year.

[8] Betters, Williams and Reeder, *op. cit.*, p. 5.

the Federal Emergency Relief Administrator to supplement those grants where the need was evident and not being met.[9]

The principle of state and local responsibility for relief was still maintained. Federal supervision of its grants to the states largely were limited to the requirement of monthly reports, although an effort was made to stimulate work relief instead of the dole.[10] Grants were made to the states and the cities received incidental benefits only to the extent that the funds from state relief administration were spent within the borders of the municipalities.

In the fall of 1933 it was evident that the F.E.R.A. grants were not sufficient to alleviate the distress of widespread unemployment. The prospect of an oncoming winter during which many millions would be without assistance, a rising relief load, the failure of the Public Works Administration to get its public works projects under way more rapidly, and the feeling that even if it were done more employment would not be immediately provided, underlined the need for a new program. In November, 1933 the Civil Works Administration was established after a national conference of governors, mayors and other officials had highlighted the urgency of the situation.

The Civil Works Administration was similar in philosophy to the F.E.R.A. It believed in desirable and useful public works programs. State and local units were asked to sponsor projects, and if these met with the approval of the C.W.A., it bore the labor costs while the sponsor provided the materials and supervision. Under this short-lived program 180,000 projects were undertaken and approximately half of the four millions who benefited were employables.[11] Although widespread criticism forced the abandonment of the program in March 1934, it did represent a partial commitment to the idea that the federal government was responsible for the employables who were on relief rolls.

The creation of the Civil Works Administration marks the beginning of change in the status of the cities vis-a-vis the federal government. Under the crisis of mass unemployment, they were rec-

---

[9] *Public Law, no. 15,* 73d Congress (May 12, 1933) sections 4 (a), 4 (b), and 4 (c). A public works program was also authorized under the provisions of the National Industrial Recovery Act. This will be discussed in a later section of this chapter.

[10] A. W. MacMahon, J. D. Millett and G. Ogden, *The Administration of Federal Work Relief* (Chicago: Public Administration Service, 1941), p. 18.

[11] R. H. Wells, *American Local Government* (New York: McGraw-Hill Book Co., Inc., 1939), pp. 151-152.

ognized as a new partner in the national attack upon the problems arising from the depression. It was due in part to the efforts of the cities under the aegis of the National Conference of Mayors meeting in Chicago in 1933 that impetus was given to the establishment of the new agency. It was their insistence, too, that resulted in the earmarking of $250 million for use within municipalities.[12] Cities also benefited greatly from the various projects undertaken under C.W.A. auspices. Studies of urban tax delinquency, local employment trends, transit and housing, heightened immeasurably the ability of the cities to cope with urgent local situations. The building of parks, playgrounds, airports, beaches, swimming pools and innumerable other projects was a direct contribution to the physical plants of the cities. Moreover, the constant interchange of information and effort among federal and local units led to the development of new relationships with many federal agencies.

A federalized relief program. The discontinuance of C.W.A. did not mean the cessation of federal aid for relief. The F.E.R.A. continued to make grants for this purpose. For the years 1933, 1934 and 1935 the percentage of total relief costs borne by the national government was 60.6 percent, 72.3 percent, and 71.2 percent respectively. The city and county share of total relief costs for these years averaged 16.5 percent.[13] Directly and indirectly the condition of the cities was greatly improved through grants and the general betterment of economic conditions. Work relief, either the C.W.A. or F.E.R.A. version, represented an advance over the previous efforts to deal with what seemingly had become a persistent problem. Both programs contained the essential elements for a coordinated approach. The former, even for the short time that it had been in existence, had sought to distinguish between aid for the able-bodied employables and the unemployables. The latter through grants to the states had stimulated the need for useful work relief projects. Presumably a program of expanded aid could reasonably have utilized the elements of both and yet there were compelling reasons why this was not done.

Four main factors might be noted in this regard. For one thing, federal relief administration was undergoing a pronounced change. Responsibilities of the various federal agencies were being more carefully defined and there was a definite but growing feeling that

12 Betters, Williams and Reeder, *op. cit.*, pp. 80-82.
13 *Ibid.*, p. 75.

the unemployables should be a state and local responsibility. Secondly, the F.E.R.A. was a temporary agency with what some authorities called a habit for improvisation. Yet it was evident that unemployment relief would be for some time at least a continuing part of the American scene and, therefore, constant attention and a long range approach would be needed. Third, there was the political factor; the possibility that under the grant system irregularities in the administration of relief by the states might redound to the detriment of the federal government. This was undoubtedly one of the factors behind the decision of the President to federalize the relief program. Finally, it was the need for new types of programs that pointed up the unsuitability of continuing the existing method of operation. Public support for work relief projects was not enough in the opinion of many members of the Administration. The energy and skills of America should be devoted to programs of permanent benefit to the nation. Some of this might be absorbed by the Public Works Administration, but what was needed was a program that would take more of the able-bodied people off relief roles.[14]

The Works Progress Administration. These factors considered in combination with one another caused the federal government in 1935 to embark upon the third and final phase of work relief. In that year after considerable discussion in the higher levels of the government, the Works Progress Administration was created with the stated objective of removing "from the relief rolls to work on such projects or in private employment the maximum number of persons in the shortest time possible." [15] When this was combined with an expenditure of $4.8 billion "to provide relief work, relief and to increase employment . . ." a change of momentous import occurred.[16]

For the first time in American history, the national government took the position that the collapse of the economic system was its concern; that those who were employable had the right to a job. While the federal government naturally would not employ everyone, it would seek to moderate the side effects of a depression by spending and seeking to stimulate employment. The "new look," which

[14] MacMahon, Millett and Ogden, *op. cit.*, pp. 19-24.

[15] Executive Order no. 7034 (May 6, 1935), section (c).

[16] Public Resolution no. 11, 49 *Stat. L.* 115-119 (1935). The original appropriation of $4 billion was supplemented by $880 million in transfers from prior relief appropriations.

had been in a process of evaluation for two years, has been aptly described by outstanding authorities as "a national commitment to an ideal: the right to work." [17]

How great the federal commitment was can be gathered from a glance at the overall operations of the W.P.A. In the five-year period 1935–1940, approximately $14 billion were spent to return people to an active work status. During this same period 7.8 million individuals were given work. In February 1936, 4 millions were employed on W.P.A. projects. Even as late as October, 1938 some 3.8 million persons were still being maintained with W.P.A. funds.[18]

Like its predecessor, the W.P.A. was a completely federal program. Its operation was nationwide, but the states and districts were the active units of administration. Although federal in operation, the sponsorship pattern of the earlier C.W.A. was retained. Local units made applications to the W.P.A. and agreed that as a condition of receiving the aid they would bear the nonlabor cost of the project. Labor cost was borne by the federal government. While the local government was relieved of the burden of administration, it was still responsible for many aspects of the project and this led to a multitude of relationships with many federal agencies. Airport construction, for example, required the approval of the Bureau of Air Commerce. Local projects concerned with sanitation, health, and mine sealing were cleared with the United States Public Health Service. Investigation of those persons on relief was carried out by state and local relief agencies. Employables were also certified by the United States Employment Service. Thus while W.P.A. administered the vast program, local units were asked to play a significant role.[19]

The federal work relief program was designed to supplement rather than supplant municipal activities. Federal expenditures were not intended as a means to reduce local budgets; while the distinction between normal and substitute activities was difficult to maintain, a determined effort, nonetheless, was made.[20] In New York City out of a total of $698 million in city funds, only about 18% of W.P.A. money was spent for city purposes. On the other hand,

17 MacMahon, Millett and Ogden, *op. cit.*, pp. 2-3.

18 *Idem.*

19 *Ibid.*, pp. 303-311.

20 J. D. Millett, *The Works Progress Administration in New York City* (Chicago: Public Administration Service, 1938), p. 203.

of the $409 million spent on work relief by the W.P.A., four fifths came from federal money.[21]

Consequences of federal relief programs. Needless to say, all federal aid programs, and especially the W.P.A., gave an enormous impetus to federal-city relations. In the two-year period ending in 1937, 45 percent of the W.P.A. projects were sponsored by municipalities.[22] In San Diego the amount of W.P.A. money spent in the city was equal to its annual cost of operation. In Cleveland relationships with federal agencies had become so numerous and important that a "Commissioner of Federal Relations" was established to deal with such activities. One commentator in 1938 summarized the status of federal-city relations in these words: "Today we find the work of practically every federal agency in some way touching municipal government." [23]

The wide net of federal operations can be judged from the following statistical review: "In urban areas 12,797 miles of high type surface streets and 32,248 miles of low type surface streets had been built. The W.P.A. had newly contracted 4,383 school buildings, while making improvements and additions to 30,511 existing school buildings. It built 132 hospitals and made improvements for 1,670 others. . . . The W.P.A. had laid 17,977 miles of new storm and sanitary sewers, while improving 3,422 miles of sewers. It had built 197 aviation landing fields, improved 317, and made additions to fifty others. In order to protect community water supplies, the W.P.A. had sealed 211,000 abandoned mine openings. Thirty-nine electric power plants had been built and 144 others improved." [24] Cushioning the effects of a depression, in brief, had a leavening effect upon city-national relations. No longer was the state an interstitial partner. Direct relationships with the federal government had become a possibility for most cities.

PUBLIC WORKS

Early in 1930 Franklin D. Roosevelt, then Governor of the State of New York, noted a prime paradox in our society; in the midst of a housing shortage, poor roads and inadequate sewer systems there existed relief rolls crowded with the names of millions of construc-

---

[21] *Ibid.*, p. 204.

[22] MacMahon, Millett and Ogden, *op. cit.*, p. 307.

[23] P. V. Betters, "The Federal Government and the Cities: A Problem in Adjustment," *The Annals*, CXCIX (1938), pp. 191-192, especially p. 191.

[24] MacMahon, Millett and Ogden, *op. cit.*, pp. 3-6.

tion workers whose skills could be devoted to the elimination of these major deficiencies.[25] Under the Emergency Relief Appropriation Act of 1932 an effort had been made to bring man and construction job together, but the self-liquidation provision in the law served as an effective deterrent to any full-scale program. Cities simply did not have the means to make loans on this basis. It was not until Roosevelt became President in 1933 that he had an opportunity to implement his ideas.

The Public Works Administration. The economic disorganization of the country which we have previously noted compelled rapid and even drastic action. In 1933 the National Industrial Recovery Act appropriated $3.3 billions to bring this country out of the depression trough.[26] Part of the omnibus measure provided for a Federal Emergency Administration of Public Works headed by an administrator who was to prepare "a comprehensive program of public works." [27] The basis for resolving the paradox, the construction of useful projects to bring man and job together, was thus established.[28]

The administration of this program had great significance for the city. Not only would it benefit from expenditures and public works improvements but also it could enter into direct negotiations with the federal government. The kingpin clause in the statute, section 203, permitted the Secretary of Interior, who was appointed administrator of the new agency, "to make grants to states, municipalities and other public bodies" . . . for the "construction, improvement or repair" of public works projects. Outright grants could be made to the applicants to a maximum of 30 percent of the cost of labor and materials used on approved projects.[29] Loans for the remaining cost of construction could also be obtained at a 4 percent rate of interest if secured by adequate collateral.[30]

Impact upon federal-city relationships. The way was opened for direct federal-city relationships. Cities requiring assistance made direct application to the state P.W.A. offices where their plans were

---

25 H. Ickes, *Pack to Work, The Story of the P.W.A.* (New York: The Macmillan Co., 1935), p. 4.

26 *Public Law no. 67,* 73d Congress, 1st Session (1933), section 220.

27 *Ibid.,* sections 201-202.

28 J. K. Williams, *Grants-in-Aid Under the Public Works Administration* (New York: Columbia University Press, 1939), p. 41.

29 *Idem.*

30 *Ibid.,* p. 49.

reviewed for conformance with federally prescribed standards. At the Washington level, two agencies assisted the administrator, the National Planning Board and the Special Advisory Board. The former, although it had no veto power, maintained a current list of all projects and sought to weave them into a national plan. The latter formulated the criteria for the evaluation of the projects submitted. Four main governing policies were laid down: social desirability; conformance with coordinated national planning; engineering feasibility and financial soundness.[31] Cities entering into contracts with the national government were required to observe federally prescribed standards. Inspection and audit by the P.W.A. were common features of such arrangements.

By the simple device of a city-federal contract the city gained new status and profited in many ways. P.W.A. applications and contracts were made at the initiative of the city.[32] Although there was a great need for funds, the decision as to whether the city would or would not come within the purview of federal supervision lay with the city itself. For its part, the federal government scrupulously avoided interference with local autonomy. It insisted upon compliance with all laws and regulations.

The attitude of P.W.A. led in many instances to the passage of state enabling legislation of immeasurable benefit to the cities. Cities that had reached the limit of their bonded indebtedness found themselves ineligible for loans over and above the outright P.W.A. 30 percent grant unless they had the power to issue revenue bonds as collateral. Similarly, eligibility for P.W.A. housing grants was held up until municipalities were given the power to establish local housing authorities. In both cases aided by P.W.A.'s legal division model laws were adopted by many states.[33] How effective this was can be gathered from a brief summary of the situation, ". . . the total of all revenue bond issues received by P.W.A. as of August 23, 1937, numbered 1,170 or about 43 percent of the total number of all loans made by the P.W.A. by that date, and 42 percent of the dollar volume of such loans." [34]

In fact, in some respects the federal government showed itself

---

[31] Ickes, *op. cit.*, pp. 48-49.

[32] J. K. Williams, "The Status of Cities under Recent Federal Legislation," *American Political Science Review*, XXX (1936), p. 1112.

[33] Wells, *op. cit.*, p. 53.

[34] Williams, *op. cit.*, p. 239.

more sensitive than the states to the needs of the city. When several state highway departments proposed to spend their share of the $400 million N.I.R.A. highway grant for rural instead of city highways, a ruling of the Special Advisory Board to the P.W.A. administrator held that not less than 25 percent of the allotment had to be spent for federal roads within the city.[35] Under the Emergency Relief Appropriation Act of 1935 the amount available for roads within the city was increased by an additional 5 percent. Moreover, appropriations for public works were not required to observe quotas based upon either states or population. Money was allotted on the basis of need, and since the cities had greater numbers and more necessity, they tended on the whole to gain a great deal.

From an economic standpoint the cities were, to a considerable extent, beneficiaries of the public works program. Public works expenditures increased employment and spendable income within the city. Construction of needed projects also enhanced the physical plant of the city. By 1936 P.W.A. had assisted in the building of municipal power projects, sewerage systems, schools, water supply systems, hospitals, and numerous other projects. In more specific terms, in that year the P.W.A. had spent $800 million on 3,804 projects.[36] The P.W.A. administrator estimated that his agency had placed two million people on construction jobs but asserted that at least five times that number had actually benefited.[37] From 1933 to 1938, P.W.A. had made allotments to 16,700 nonfederal projects. P.W.A. loans and grants to public bodies during the same period totaled $2.4 billion. In the same period, too, 17,800 federal projects received $1.8 billion in allotments.[38] Despite the economic betterment in the condition of the country, P.W.A. continued to function until 1939. Its role had been so effective that in some quarters there was talk of creating a permanent public works department.[39] The by-product of this speculation was reorganization plan I which made P.W.A. part of the Federal Works Agency.[40]

The public works experience of the cities demonstrated once again a widened area for federal-municipal cooperation. The cities

35 Ickes, *op. cit.*, p. 83; also Betters, Williams and Reeder, *op. cit.*, pp. 66-67.
36 MacMahon, Millett and Ogden, *op. cit.*, p. 11.
37 Ickes, *op. cit.*, p. 256.
38 Williams, *op. cit.*, pp. 56-57.
39 *Ibid.*, p. 285.
40 The latter agency was abolished in 1949 when its functions were transferred to the General Services Administration, 63 Stat. 378 (1949).

showed that they were able to assume responsibility for their people if they were given the necessary financial assistance. The growth of a corps of trained persons in response to the demands of federal programs meant that henceforth the cities would have a new status in the eyes of the national government.

HOUSING PROGRAMS

Adequate housing for low income families, always a chronic city problem, took on new dimensions during the years of the depression. Public concern for low cost housing was essentially a new idea for the federal government and, indeed, even for the states and cities. Yet under the stress of emergency it became a permanent part of the American governmental scene.

In its early phases, the housing program was regarded primarily as a phase of the public works program. The Emergency Relief and Construction Act of 1932 empowered the Reconstruction Finance Corporation to make loans to corporations whose object it was to provide for low cost housing and slum clearance.[41] Those projects, following the pattern set for the R.F.C., contained a self-liquidating proviso which presented almost insuperable obstacles, considering both the financial condition of states and cities. As a consequence R.F.C. provided little or nothing to the solution of the problem.

The stimulus of P.W.A. In the following year a more determined effort was undertaken. More housing as a means of increasing employment became the dominant theme. Like P.W.A. grants for public works construction there was an outright subsidy of 30 percent for labor and materials. The balance, however, was secured by loans supported by adequate collateral. Unlike nonfederal P.W.A. allotments, however, financial assistance was made to the project itself and not to the city, even though the latter made application.[42] Loans were to be repaid with interest to the federal government over a sixty year period.

Emphasis on the project character of the loan posed a legal obstacle. States, cities, and other public bodies needed laws to give the project a legal status in order that they might borrow and administer the project. In the summer of 1933, only Milwaukee and Los Angeles were legally empowered to take advantage of P.W.A.

---

41 48 *Stat.* 200 (1933).

42 Betters, Williams and Reeder, *op. cit.*, p. 58.

housing loans and grants. The void was filled by a period of intensive activity which had as its end-product the legal creation of local housing authorities.

Under the stimulation of P.W.A., model laws authorizing state and local housing agencies were introduced and passed in many states of the union. While many modifications occurred in their form, in the main they were fairly uniform in pattern. Local housing agencies were created by the municipalities. Indebtedness was assigned to the agency and amortization of the loan was made from rent and revenues. All in all, by 1937 some thirty states took action along these lines.[43]

The passage of enabling legislation, however, took time. In varying degrees state and local housing authorities either were not organized or lacking in experience. In the interim P.W.A. undertook construction of projects in those cities where a fair prospect existed that local units would be able to assume responsibility when they were ready. Some of the projects were designed to demonstrate what could be done with low cost housing developments. Others were devoted to slum clearance. By 1937, P.W.A. found itself in the housing business by virtue of the fact that it had built 51 projects in 36 cities with a total of 21,500 dwelling units.[44]

Although the achievement was small when compared with the actual need for adequate shelter by people of low income, the experience with the program is significant. The partnership principle, either federal-state or federal-municipal cooperation, was accepted. Nonfederal units, particularly the cities, were expected to share not only in cost but also in the operation of housing projects. At the same time the federal government assumed a responsibility for what had hitherto been regarded as a local function. It was this dual aspect that laid the groundwork of a more permanent housing program.

The United States Housing Act. The passage in 1937 of the United States Housing Act represented a culmination of trends prevalent in the years 1932–1937.[45] Housing was shifted in emphasis from a program of work relief to one of aid for low income families. The previous emphasis on the need to increase employment became

[43] E. Longan, "The Present Status of Municipal Housing and Slum Clearance in the United States," *American Political Science Review,* XXXI (1937), pp. 1126, 1129.
[44] *Ibid.,* p. 1128.
[45] 50 *Stat.* 888 (1937).

secondary to the major objective of providing decent housing standards for all Americans, regardless of income. Housing, in brief, was henceforth to be considered on par with all other federal functions concerned with the general welfare.

The pattern of decentralized operations which had its germinal beginnings in the P.W.A. era came to full fruition under the new law. The projects built by P.W.A. as rapidly as feasible were turned over to state and local housing authorities. The new act made a sum of $800 million available at a long-term low interest to assist states and political subdivisions in remedying unsafe and unsanitary housing conditions and the acute housing shortage for low income families.[46] Local housing authorities, created by the cities and yet not a part of them, were permitted to borrow up to 90% of the cost of the project. For purposes of construction costs, cities were classified upon the basis of population, those with more and those with less than 500,000 inhabitants.[47] In the former expenditures per dwelling unit was limited to $5,000 and in the latter to $4,000.

Slum clearance and low rent were made part of the arrangement. For each dwelling unit constructed an equal number of unsafe and insanitary units were to be demolished, closed, or substantially repaired. To assure the use of premises by low income familes, a 5:1 income-rent ratio was to be maintained. In other words, tenant income could not exceed five times the annual rent of the dwelling unit.[48] Finally, to insure rents at a level that low income families could afford, the federal government through the United States Housing Authority agreed to make an annual subsidy to defray the cost of the project.

A brief glance at the gradual evolution of the housing program reveals that something new was added, if one compares it with work relief or public works. While the federal government acknowledged the need for local management and responsibility, it dealt not with the city but rather with a local housing authority that was created by the city. It was the housing agency that accepted the contractual restrictions imposed by the national government. As such it was at best merely a quasi-public body. Thus not only was the city involved but also the state since it was the latter that had endowed the city with the power to establish such an agency. A pattern of

46 *Idem.*
47 *Ibid.*, section 14 (a).
48 *Public Law no. 837,* 74th Congress (1937).

semi-autonomous housing authorities, looking to both the national and city governments, was established. One can well agree with one commentator who has remarked, "Irrespective of the future role of the states in public housing, there is little doubt that a new and permanent federal-local link has been forged."[49]

FEDERAL FINANCIAL ASSISTANCE

In 1933 the financial distress of American cities was almost self-evident. Tax strikes, deflation of real property values and the sudden onrush of relief expenditures reduced the municipal tax dollar almost to the vanishing point. Highly indicative of the straitened circumstances of the city was their debt status. In 1933 from 1,000 to 3,000 cities and towns were in default either of principal or interest in amount variously estimated as ranging from one to two billion dollars.[50] To add to all this, federal measures in the years prior to 1933 were designed merely to aid distressed but not insolvent cities. Those cities that had reached the maximum in the borrowing capacity found themselves in desperate need for financial assistance. Indeed, the debt crisis of local units was of such magnitude that Congress gave considerable thought to the possibility of a debt moratorium.[51]

Insolvent municipalities or those approaching that condition received a great deal of indirect aid through the various public works and relief programs of the national government. Indirectly, as we have seen, gaps in the municipal services were filled in and serious deterioration of valuable public properties was prevented. Of the $4.5 billion expended for relief from January 1933 through August 1936, 66 percent came from the federal government and only 16 percent from the cities. The balance was supplied by the states. From 1934 to 1936 federal expenditures for local government purposes as distinct from its total outlays amounted to $6.8 billion. This was regarded by one authority as either a substitute for local expenditures or it "directly affected functions normally paid for locally."[52] All federal relief and construction "assumed the status of

---

49 Wells, *op. cit.*, p. 173.

50 Betters, Williams and Reeder, *op. cit.*, p. 13.

51 W. Kilpatrick, "Federal Regulation of Local Debt," *National Municipal Review*, XXVI (1937), p. 283.

52 W. Kilpatrick, "Federal Assistance to Municipal Recovery," *National Municipal Review*, XXVI (1937), pp. 337-338.

programs, based upon appraisal of projects, local needs and capacities." [53]

The Home Owners Loan Corporation. More directly, federal legislation proved a tremendous boon to the cities. In 1933 the Home Owners Loan Corporation with authority to issue bonds up to a maximum of $2 billion (later to an amount twice as great) was authorized to make loans to the distressed taxpayer for taxes and repairs in an amount not to exceed 80 percent of the value of the property. The home owner was also permitted to exchange his mortgage for H.O.L.C. bonds. The full impact of this assistance has been told by Paul Betters and his associates. In Westchester County the federal government through tax loans paid $2.7 million into local treasuries. Maryland cities received back taxes to the extent of $2.2 million. In all, the H.O.L.C. Act enabled municipalities through 1935 to obtain $190 million in taxes which otherwise might have been lost through default.[54] The sums obtained in this manner were of incalculable benefit to the cities. Not only were their treasuries at least partially replenished, but also because of this their credit and borrowing capacity were enhanced.

Municipal debt readjustment. For those municipalities who were in default on either interest or principal on outstanding bonds, the federal government undertook to devise a means to rescue them. No direct payments were made to the cities, but efforts were made to facilitate the ability of cities to scale down their debt payments in a manner that was mutually satisfactory to both the municipality and its security holders. In 1934, municipalities were given the same privilege as railroads and other public corporations as a result of the passage of a municipal debt readjustment law.[55] Prior to that time, the consent of one hundred percent of the creditors was required before reorganization could be effected. Recalcitrant security holders through a mandamus proceeding could force municipalities to give their demands priority over other essential services.

After 1934, only the consent of the state and slightly less than one third of the creditors was needed to refund municipal debts. The debt readjustment act, however, was declared unconstitutional. The Supreme Court apparently felt that the federal statute represented an encroachment upon the sovereign fiscal authority of the

[53] *Ibid.*, p. 351.
[54] Betters, Williams and Reeder, *op. cit.*, pp. 19-20.
[55] 48 *Stat.* 789 (1934).

state, even though the latter was required to give its consent.[56] In 1936, amidst doubts as to constitutionality, a new municipal bankruptcy act was passed which differed very little from its predecessor. However, it did require the consent of more than a majority of the stockholders to a reorganization plan. Then, if two thirds of the creditors agreed, the municipalities were freed from the bothersome mandamus proceeding. This new law was upheld.[57] This time, as Professor Fordham has remarked, "State action authorizing local units to proceed under the statute was characterized as cooperation, not abdication." However, as he has also noted the cooperation theory was also applicable to the earlier statute.[58] Apparently the difference in the two decisions was largely in the number of creditors whose consent was required for any refunding operation.

RECENT FEDERAL-CITY RELATIONS

The administrative relations during the period of economic crisis gave a new dimension to federal-city relationships. Peripheral contacts prior to 1932 were intensified. New far-reaching direct contacts between city and nation were developed as a by-product of the national effort to cope with the depression. World War II and the Korean involvement saw a further strengthening of these bonds. Today there is hardly an area of municipal activity that is not in some way affected by the action of the federal government.

It would be almost impossible to detail the multitudinous facets of federal-city relationships. A report of the National Resources Committee devotes about twenty pages to a discussion of these aspects.[59] A summary of the American Municipal Association listing federal services to cities and towns contains seventy-four pages.[60] The Commission on Intergovernmental Relationships notes twenty-three major areas of federal-local governmental contact.[61] Federal payments, perhaps the best index, may be classified into four main

---

[56] *Ashton v. Cameron County Water Improvement District,* 298 U. S. 513 (1936).

[57] *United States v. Bekins,* 304 U. S. 27 (1938).

[58] J. B. Fordham, *Local Government Law* (Brooklyn, N. Y.: The Foundation Press, 1949), p. 682.

[59] National Resources Committee, *Urban Government: Volume I of the Supplementary Report of the Urbanism Committee* (Washington, D. C.: United States Government Printing Office, 1939), pp. 50-77.

[60] R. H. Blundred and D. W. Hanks, Jr., *Federal Services to Cities and Towns* (Washington, D. C.: American Municipal Association, 1950), pp. 1-74 incl.

[61] Commission on Intergovernmental Relations, *Advisory Committee Report on Local Government* (Washington, D. C.: U. S. Government Printing Office, June 1955), p. 15.

areas: (1) primarily for local government; (2) for combined state and local programs; (3) state programs which involve municipalities indirectly; and (4) welfare programs, both state and locally administered. For the fiscal year 1953 payments for these amounted respectively in millions of dollars to 495.6, 651.1, 244.3 and 1,362, or a grand total of approximately $2.8 billions.[62] Yet even these statistics do not by any means describe the multi-faceted contacts that have been developed over the years, since the expenditures do not include federal services that have both a direct and an indirect bearing upon municipal government.

Research and reporting. Federal activities in all their aspects run a wide gamut and almost inevitably have a strong bearing upon the policy and decision-making processes of the city. One of the most important areas is in the field of research and reporting where, because of its superior economic resources and highly competent personnel, it is in a position to make available to the city a veritable mine of information concerning the general trends of life in the metropolis. The Bureau of Census is one of the most important of the innumerable fact-gathering agencies. Its census of government contains national totals on debt and revenue for each type of government, forty-eight states, and cities of over 25,000 inhabitants. Its decennial census contains data on population characteristics, family characteristics, internal migration of population, housing, income and almost every other facet of life. The Bureau of Labor Statistics reports on payrolls, statistics and the work force generally. The National Bureau of Standards provides information on fire inspection and regulations designed to assist in fire prevention work.[63]

Technical services. A multitude of technical services are also made available to municipalities at the latters' request. The Civil Aeronautics Authority provides consulting and advisory assistance on airport planning, design and construction. It develops and recommends principles for incorporation in state and local legislation designed to facilitate airport development. The Bureau of Standards develops purchase specifications for use by state and local units. It works with local jurisdictions in programs designed to promote more effective local and state weights and measures enforcement. It contributes model building, fire, plumbing, masonry and other codes for use by municipal authorities. The Federal Bureau of Investiga-

---

62 *Ibid.*, pp. 16-17.
63 Blundred and Hanks, *op. cit.*, pp. 25, 29.

tion trains municipal police officers in three annual twelve week courses at the National Police Academy. On request of any municipality the FBI will identify and analyze criminal evidence submitted. Microscopic, spectographic, ballistic and other specialized equipment is made available. Indeed, almost all of the national crime facilities are open to use by the local police. The passage of the federal fugitive felon act, the kidnapping law and the national motor vehicle theft acts have brought municipal police forces into extensive contact with the national police unit.

In matters of sanitation the United States Public Health Service at the request of the state health departments will make investigations and surveys of health conditions in localities. The same agency prepares model ordinances covering milk control, food standards and water supply. Advice and assistance in the field of education are contributed by the United States Office of Education. Advice on problems of school organization, teaching aids, and the status of school need constantly flows to the other governmental jurisdictions.

CONCLUSION

Historically, it is evident that the failure of the states to assist the cities in the time of crisis and unemployment in the thirties was the single most important factor responsible for the changed relationship between cities and the national government.[64] Since a viable economy has been restored, the states are once more insisting that they are the channel of communication between the federal government and the city. At the same time the cities, having tasted the fruits of federal aid, are not disposed to sit idly by and permit the states to dictate to them.

There is thus a large issue of public policy that has to be resolved: Shall the federal government continue to deal directly with the cities or should it seek to employ the states as an intermediary? This is a large question to which no final and immediate answer can be given. The definition of relationships is almost inevitably intertwined with the whole matter of city-state relationships. Having gained a measure of freedom, the cities do not want to be excluded from direct dealings with the national government. They are patently aware of the rural imbalance in the state legislatures and the consequent indifference to the needs of the city. States have not ob-

[64] Commission on Intergovernmental Relations, *op. cit.*, p. 27.

tained highway funds for city purposes because no matching money was provided. Civil defense costs fall more heavily on the city, even though the states are the channel of communication with the federal government. Cities remember the House-Senate deadlock on a badly needed Federal Airport Aid Act of 1946. In that case the issue was whether grants-in-aid should be negotiated by the Civil Aeronautics Authority through the states or directly through local sponsors. The attitude of the cities has been summed up rather strongly by one of its supporters. "The question is whether the states will wake up to the facts of municipal life and displace the new, close federal-municipal relationship by considering and providing for the needs of their political subdivisions. . . . If the states cannot or will not heed the cities' pleas and warnings we know that Congress will." [65]

The pressure of the cities for greater federal cooperation can be minimized only if the states undertake to give the cities a greater measure of freedom over their local affairs. Such state actions should include: more equitable city representation in the state legislatures; wider fiscal authority for municipalities consistent with the needs of the state; more local participation in federal grants-in-aid channeled through the state; recognition of joint federal-state and local interest in matters before Congress that affect local governments; more state-local cooperation on programs of interest and need.

Federal aid to state and local governments has become a reality. Whether it strengthens local government or assumes powers that belong to the municipality will depend in large measure on whether the local units are compelled to seek financial assistance from the federal government. In the final analysis city-nation relationships will depend upon the degree to which the state is sympathetic to the needs of the local units.

BIBLIOGRAPHY

Books:

Betters, P., Williams, J. K., and Reeder, S. *Recent Federal-City Relations.* Washington, D. C.: United States Conference of Mayors, 1936.

Blundred, R. H. and Hanks, D. W. *Federal Services to Cities and Towns.* Washington, D. C.: American Municipal Association, 1950.

Commission on Intergovernmental Relations. *Advisory Committee Report on Local Government.* Washington, D. C.: United States Government Printing Office, 1955.

[65] D. W. Hanks, Jr., "Neglected Cities Turn to United States," *National Municipal Review,* XXXV (April 1946), pp. 172-173.

Ickes, H. *Back to Work, The Story of the PWA.* New York: The Macmillan Co., 1935.

MacMahon, A. W., Millett, J. D., and Ogden, G. *The Administration of Federal Works Relief.* Chicago: Public Administration Service, 1941.

Millett, J. D. *The Works Progress Administration in New York City.* Chicago: Public Administration Service, 1938.

Williams, J. K. *Grants-in-Aid Under the Public Works Administration.* New York: Columbia University Press, 1939.

Articles and Other Material:

Anderson, W. "The Federal Government and the Cities," *National Municipal Review,* XIII (1924), 288-293.

Betters, P. "The Federal Government and the Cities: A Problem in Adjustment," *The Annals,* CXCIX (1938), 190-198.

Kilpatrick, W. "Federal Regulation of Local Debt," *National Municipal Review,* XXVI (1937), 283-290.

Williams, J. K. "Federal Aid Due to Continue," *National Municipal Review,* XXXVII (1948), 86-90.

Chapter Seventeen

Metropolitan Area Relationships

The Change in Inter-Area Relationships

American urban life since the start of the twentieth century has been characterized by the tendency of cities to outrun their legal limits. As a consequence we have had the growth of metropolitan complexes in which the central city was merely the core of a larger economic aggregate. It is these units that we called metropolitan areas.

Factors making for change. Metropolitan areas are now a commonplace feature of our society, but needless to say it was not always so. The reasons for their development are not hard to isolate. Technological factors, largely responsible for the rise of the city, were also determinants in its subsequent evolution. In the nineteenth century the requirements of technology exerted a confining influence upon the city. Steam, the main source of energy, had to be used close to its source if it was to be employed efficiently. Factories, in a sense, were built over the boiler rooms. At the same time the work force because of the rudimentary forms of transportation was compelled to live fairly close to their place of employment. There were of course some forms of surface transport but these existed mainly within the municipality. Indeed, it was easier to go from city to city than from city to the countryside. In the last quarter of the nineteenth century by reason of these fundamental factors, urban areas were fairly well-defined, and quite distinct and separate from the countryside.

From the beginning of the twentieth century onward, however, these circumstances began gradually to change. The coming of newer forms of energy, the use of electricity and the internal combustion engine, the latter mainly in the form of motor transport, caused a virtual revolution in city life. It was no longer necessary for either industry or people to locate within the city. The widespread use of electrical energy permitted the dispersal of plants to areas adjacent to the central city. Even where steam was employed as a source of power, it was still possible for plants to locate outside of the central city since ease of transportation permitted ready access to markets.

Of prime importance as a stimulant in the outward movement of people were the coming of motor transport and the vast networks of highways associated with it. In particular, the automobile was an important catalyst in fostering the dispersal of people. Its advent sounded the death knell of the old "railroad-and-horse geography" which sought to place trading and commercial centers at an hour's driving distance or six miles from the people. The use of the motor vehicle meant that people could go five or six times as far in a similar time span.[1] Distance became a factor of time. People no longer felt compelled to live within the city. They could live either in outlying areas and commute to the city or could follow the industrial plants as they left the city. It is not clear whether the plants or the people left the central city first. One thing is certain, however, the technological advance during the twentieth century did significantly modify the social and economic structure of the central city and its environs.

By-products of the change. One basic by-product of what McKenzie has termed "urban disaggregation" [2] has been the gradual disappearance of the distinction between urban and rural areas. The city dweller moved to the country for a variety of reasons but the very fact that he came there in large numbers meant that the easy-going existence of the countryside was impaired at least to some extent. Moreover, the dweller of the city, while moving outside of its limits, still remained a city dweller. His habits and attitudes were essentially urban, and for culture and entertainment, the suburbanite looked to and was influenced by the central city. Even though the population of the central city grew, that of the area around it increased still more rapidly. The disappearance of the countryside meant that it was no longer possible to think of cities as entities in themselves. Instead it was necessary to think of them as related to the satellite centers outside of their immediate environs.

In short, in the economic or even the sociological sense the metropolitan area was an economic region in which a central city

---

[1] P. D. Converse and R. J. Russell, "Why City Workers Live in Agricultural Villages," *Current Economic Comment,* XII (1950), pp. 37-47; also P. D. Converse, "The Automobile and the Village Merchant," *Bureau of Business Research* (Urbana, Illinois: University of Illinois, 1928).

[2] R. D. McKenzie, *The Metropolitan Community* (New York: McGraw-Hill Book Co., Inc., 1933), p. 30.

played a dominant role. In the political sense, however, the metropolitan area had no existence. There was no single government for the area as a whole. As Professor Burgess had described it many years ago: "It has no constitution, no officials, no boundaries. And yet it has a reality which is being grappled for by widely separated persons and groups." [3] It is thus that common problems have to be met not by a single but by many diverse and autonomous political entities; that is, in the absence of a single legal instrument a coordinated approach to pressing situations that face people within the confines of the metropolitan area is virtually impossible. Thus the rise of metropolitan areas poses a fundamental question; namely, whether fragmented political power can deal effectively with the governmental problems of a metropolitan complex.

THE GROWTH OF METROPOLITAN AREAS

The migration of people to the suburbs was uneven. Some areas were more thickly settled than others. Here and there, as Mumford phrased it, "urban clottings" occurred. Population configurations were usually in conformance with economic and social considerations. Population, in brief, did not proceed outward from the center in convenient concentric circles and indeed, it was no respecter of legal boundaries.

The meaning of metropolitan areas. It was this spread of people that led many to feel that any effective appraisal of metropolitan growth would have to consider as a whole unit the people in and around the city. Prior to 1950, the Census Bureau had attempted to measure the continued drift of people from the central city to the suburbs by a classification which it had termed the metropolitan district. This concept was built up upon the basis of minor civil divisions. In the census of 1930 it was defined as an area with a central city or cities together with contiguous and adjacent districts with a population density of not less than 150 persons per square mile.[4]

Use of this concept revealed that metropolitan districts had experienced marked growth, both in size and number, in the first three decades of the twentieth century. The census of 1930 revealed the

[3] E. W. Burgess, *The Urban Community* (Chicago: University of Chicago Press, 1926), p. 191.

[4] U. S. Department of Commerce, Bureau of Census, *U. S. Census, 1930, Metropolitan Districts* (Washington, D. C.: U. S. Government Printing Office, 1932), p. 5.

existence of 96 such districts with central cities of 100,000 or more people. While the population of the central cities for the decade measured grew at the rate of 23.3 percent, it is significant to note that the contiguous areas around the central city reflecting the changes in technology and transport, had population increases that were almost twice as great.[5]

In 1950 the Census Bureau once more refined its yardstick of metropolitan growth. In place of the metropolitan district it substituted the standard metropolitan area with the county as its basic component. The standard metropolitan area includes a larger territory than the corresponding metropolitan district and is defined in the following fashion: a county or group of counties (except in New England) which contain at least one city of 50,000 or more inhabitants. Contiguous counties also are included in the metropolitan area, if according to certain criteria they are sufficiently metropolitan in character and again, sufficiently integrated with the central city.[6] In New England, the city and town, since they are administratively more important than the county, were used as units for defining standard metropolitan areas. The criteria employed for the county could not be used, and in their stead population density of 150 or more persons per square mile was chosen.[7]

The drift away from the city. Measured by the criteria contained in this definition it is evident that the drift away from the central city had become more pronounced in the decade 1940–1950. By the latter year, 168 standard metropolitan areas in continental United States contained an aggregate of 85.4 million people, an increase of 22 percent over the number of inhabitants who live in those areas.[8] Fourteen standard metropolitan areas had a total population of 44.4 million people. Standard metropolitan areas ranged in size from Laredo, Texas with a population of 56,141 to the New York-New Jersey metropolitan area with approximately 13 million people.[9]

---

5 W. S. Thompson, "It Was Not Always So," in Elmer Peterson, ed., *Cities Are Abnormal* (Norman, Oklahoma: University of Oklahoma Press, 1946), p. 62.

6 U. S. Department of Commerce, Bureau of Census, *U. S. Census, 1950, Census of Population,* p. 7.

7 *Idem.* The standard metropolitan areas and metropolitan districts are not comparable.

8 U. S. Census, 1950, *Census of Population,* I, xxxiii; also U. S. Bureau of Census, *County and City Data Book, 1952* (Washington, D. C.: U. S. Government Printing Office, 1953), p. 10. In 1940 69.3 million people lived in metropolitan areas. In 1955 the number of standard metropolitan areas had increased to 172.

9 *Idem.*

Even more noteworthy than the growth of metropolitan areas is the persistent population trend to the suburbs. For the decade ending 1950 the population of the central cities increased by 13.9 percent, slightly less than that of the country as a whole. In the outlying parts of the standard metropolitan area, however, a gain of 35.5 percent of the 1940 population in those areas occurred.[10] "More than 9 million, or nearly half of the country's total population gain," concluded one authoritative study, "took place in the suburbs and outlying parts of these 168 standard metropolitan areas (determined by the Census Bureau)." [11] Equally significant is the fact that the rate of population increase was highest in those standard metropolitan areas that ranged in size from 500,000 to 1,000,000.[12]

CHARACTERISTICS AND CONSEQUENCES OF METROPOLITAN GROWTH

The prime characteristic of metropolitan growth is the spread of people beyond the legal limits of the city. At the same time people in the outlying areas remained attached to the central city in both the economic and the cultural sense. Because of the particular manner in which such areas have developed, they have become important foci of economic and political activity. It is the central city that is the heart of the metropolitan areas. From it radiate arteries of commerce and industry, and the area as a whole is bound together in a community of interest. Politically, however, the same measure of integration has not been achieved. A metropolitan area as Professor Anderson has remarked, "is politically amorphous, without structure or unity. It is not a corporate person. In the eye of public law, it does not exist; even in the field of politics, it speaks with many contradictory voices. It is a place of divided loyalties and conflicting allegiances." [13] The absence of a common governing instrumentality means that a wide variety of *ad hoc* relationships with all levels of government have been created. The metropolitan area is a common greeting ground for all levels of government.

Bewildering variety of units of local government. Although the

10 *Idem.*

11 J. F. Dewhurst, *America's Needs and Resources* (New York: The Twentieth Century Fund, 1955), p. 73.

12 *U. S. Census, 1950, Census of Population,* I, xxxii.

13 W. Anderson, "Political Influence of the Metropolis," R. M. Fisher, ed., *The Metropolis in Modern Life* (Garden City, New York: Doubleday and Co., Inc., 1955), pp. 57-58. Copyright by the Trustees of Columbia University.

metropolitan area is held together in a semblance of unity by reason of economics, a similar binding effect has not been achieved in the political sphere. In the latter there exists a confused jumble of many governmental units, often with independent fiscal powers, separate governing bodies, and a variety of special *ad hoc* districts. The number and bewildering variety of local governmental units furnish eloquent testimony in support of the assertion that political fragmentation has occurred. Indeed, it is the key to the fact that effective government in a metropolitan area is difficult, if not impossible, to achieve.

It would belabor the point to list all of the units of government within the standard metropolitan areas but a few statistics will suffice to describe the picture. Metropolitan areas contain 12 percent of all school districts, and 17 percent of the 8,346 other units of local government. Twenty-one percent of all of the special districts are located in such areas.[14] The pattern and number of local government units are extremely varied. On one end of the scale are to be found 17 metropolitan areas with less than ten units of government while at the other extreme are to be found 11 metropolitan areas with 250 or more units of local government. Foremost among the latter in number of units are Pittsburgh, 616; Philadelphia, 702; Chicago, 960; and New York, 1,071.[15] Table 5 gives a more detailed description.

Further evidence of the proliferation of governmental units may be cited. In counties, where a central city of more than fifty thousand inhabitants exist, there is generally a multiplicity of governmental units. Cook County (Chicago) contains 422 units of local government with the following jurisdictions: a single county, 164 school districts, 99 municipalities, 30 townships, and 129 special districts. A somewhat similar distribution of governmental units can be found in Los Angeles County with 198; in Wayne County (Detroit) with 107; Cuyahoga County (Cleveland) with 101; and Hamilton County (Cincinnati) with 88.[16] Thirteen cities in as many metropolitan areas are completely or substantially surrounded by other cities. Both Hamtramck and Highland Park, for example, are within the heart of the city of Detroit and yet have their own gov-

[14] U. S. Department of Commerce, Bureau of Census, *Local Government in Metropolitan Areas* (Washington, D. C.: U. S. Government Printing Office, 1954), p. 2.

[15] *Ibid.*, p. 4.

[16] *Ibid.*, table 3. This statistic does not include federal units and state agencies. It is limited to counties. A metropolitan area may include more than one county.

Table 5—METROPOLITAN AREAS WITH 250 OR MORE UNITS OF LOCAL GOVERNMENT (1953)

Metropolitan area	*Local governments*		*Population*		*Land area*	
	Number	*Per cent*	*Number (000)*	*Per cent*	*Square miles*	*Per cent*
All metropolitan areas	16,210	100.0	84,671	100.0	214,762	100.0
11-area total	5,716	35.3	37,588	44.4	33,392	15.5
New York-Northeastern New Jersey	1,071	6.6	12,912	15.2	3,939	1.8
Chicago (Ill.)	960	5.9	5,495	6.5	3,617	1.7
Philadelphia (Pa.)	702	4.3	3,671	4.3	3,550	1.7
Pittsburgh (Pa.)	616	3.8	2,213	3.6	3,053	1.4
St. Louis (Mo.)	420	2.6	1,681	2.0	2,520	1.2
San Francisco-Oakland (Calif.)	372	2.3	2,241	2.6	3,314	1.5
Detroit (Mich.)	355	2.2	3,016	3.6	1,965	0.9
Minneapolis-St. Paul (Minn.)	316	1.9	1,117	1.3	1,721	0.8
Portland (Oregon)	314	1.9	705	0.8	3,663	1.7
Los Angeles (Calif.)	298	1.8	4,368	5.2	4,853	2.3
Madison (Wis.)	292	1.8	169	0.2	1,197	0.6

Source: U. S. Department of Commerce, Bureau of Census, *Local Government in Metropolitan Areas* (1954), p. 2.

ernments.[17] Multiplicity of governmental units is further complicated by the presence of state lines. Twenty-three metropolitan areas extend across state lines and twenty-eight reach to a state line.[18] Finally, within the metropolitan area are to be found numerous federal units, each of which in the exercise of their powers has a significant impact upon life in the region.

Lack of concerted action. The number of governmental units is not as important as the consequences that flow from it. The data

17 R. C. Spenser, "Twenty-nine Cities Within Cities," *National Municipal Review*, XXXVII (1948), p. 257.

18 Commission on Intergovernmental Relations, *A Report to the President for Transmittal to Congress* (Washington, D. C.: U. S. Government Printing Office, 1955), pp. 47-55.

becomes meaningful when one recalls that metropolitan areas are the meeting grounds for a wide variety of governmental agencies, local, state and federal. These should be bound together in common and concerted action. Yet each considers itself sovereign with respect to its functions and each, to say the least, is parochial in its outlook toward the region as a whole. Some sense of the difficulty of metropolitan government can be gained by an overstatement; metropolitan areas in microcosm face the same kinds of problems as the United Nations Organization. There is no overall authority that all can or will acknowledge. Whatever action is undertaken is the product of compromise and conciliation. What emerges, largely because of necessity, is a patchwork arrangement that achieves a temporary kind of stability. It might be added that unlike its international counterpart, the organization of the metropolitan region is politically amorphous. The heart of metropolitan government is intergovernmental relations.

Overlap and duplication. Moreover, even if a common authority were acknowledged, the presence of so many different jurisdictions represents an open invitation to overlapping, duplication, waste, and inefficiency. This condition springs not so much from the desire of individuals as it does from the difficulty inherent in the situation. The circumstances will not permit economies. In overhead services such as budgeting, personnel and planning, there are as many units as there are levels of government. Integration would make for economies but it cannot be obtained because legal units insist upon the maintenance of their autonomy. Again cities, school districts, counties and special authorities each have their own purchase units. Yet a single staff with a centralized purchasing office could obtain the benefits of volume buying.

Inefficiency and a general lack of coordination also occur as a by-product of political disintegration. Chicago's metropolitan area has one hundred and three different police jurisdictions, each with its own police force. It is difficult even to know where the authority of one ends and another begins. Movement of a violator across a mythical line removes him from the jurisdiction of the apprehending authority. Moreover, coordination and communication are gained only through the sheriff's office. In Atlanta, Georgia, prior to the reorganization, the city and county police forces were not only separate but often duplicated one another's activities. Separate crime identification laboratories in police administration, duplication of fire equipment and overlapping of road units are also frequent occurrences. Frequently the fragmentation of political subdivision is carried to the point where expensive equipment such as road graders and machinery are employed only part of the time. Finally, layer cake government means that there are as many governing bodies, police and fire departments, indeed as many line services as there are governmental units. Consolidation and rationalization of governmental units undoubtedly would effect many economies. Yet here again, the polarization of political loyalties both in the communities and levels of government act to oppose either the modernization or the dissolution of outmoded units of government.

The impact of governmental units upon each other. The multiplicity of government units, above all, means that no unit of government can fail to be affected and, to a degree, controlled by other units. A central city may effect economic dominance of the region; but the satellite centers may influence the tax base of the city by serving as a center for industrial relocation. Authorities serving both central and satellite areas may, because of independent sources of revenue, be removed from control by either area. The listing might be continued indefinitely.

A few examples may make this point more concrete. Some 5.5 million people live in the Chicago metropolitan area, a region that covers Lake County, Indiana, as well as a host of incorporated areas outside the city limits. In addition to the city of Chicago, there is the county that controls the health districts; special districts such as the housing authority, the park district, the sanitary district, the transit authority, and the Chicago Medical Commission, a state agency.[19] Federal-city relations are highly developed. The three major airfields of the city, especially the Midway airport, were projects to which the federal government contributed heavily. Other activities in which the national government is interested include the diversion of water from Lake Erie, the regulation of water-borne traffic, the previously mentioned housing agency, the medical center and urban slum clearance and redevelopment.[20] Lake County, Indiana, is, of course, beyond the jurisdiction of the city of Chicago. It is here that many of the great steel industries who draw so heavily on the facilities of the central city are located. Yet the central city cannot tax them for benefits received. Indeed, a similar condition

[19] U. S. Department of Commerce, Bureau of Census, *op. cit.*, p. 15.
[20] Commission on Intergovernmental Relations, *op. cit.*, p. 25.

exists with respect to most of the industry and people who have moved into areas outside of the major city. It is almost self-evident, from what has been noted, that in many important aspects the city of Chicago has lost control over many matters that vitally affect it.

Surrounding Los Angeles is a county, with government agencies at that level concerned with air pollution, flood control, public library, and county improvement districts. There are in addition, 258 districts concerned with such vital matters as fire protection, garbage disposal, lighting, park, recreation, sewers and waterworks. There is hardly a major municipal function that is not in some way a concern of the city and yet is beyond its control.

Similar conditions exist in almost every metropolitan area. In the Dallas metropolitan area overlapping jurisdictions have caused considerable friction in many fields. In law enforcement, the sheriff's office functioned in both city and county. But the city, despite the fact that it spent almost $700,000 on its police department, had no authority to make arrests beyond the city line.[21] In the matter of libraries, highway construction, and traffic control there was considerable city-county conflict in Los Angeles.[22] Detroit, girdled by twenty-one cities, twenty-three townships and twenty-four villages, is constantly beset by varying standards and tax rates which in the existing competitive situation generally means that there is a tendency to depreciate the levels of governance to that of the laxest municipality. Try as it might the city cannot, except through the county, control the activities of the units outside of its legal limits.[23]

Like tendencies are evident even in the largest metropolitan area. Thirteen million people reside in the New York-New Jersey-Connecticut metropolitan complex, a 7,500 square mile region. Three states, seventeen counties, at least 500 separate units of local government and a multitude of federal agencies are encompassed within its limits.[24] In the vital areas of traffic and transport, both the central city and the peripheral units alone or in concert with one another have been helpless. For thirty years, roughly the period paralleling the vast expansion of motor transport, a pronounced population drift to the suburbs has taken place, although for many the central city remained as the place of business and work. To ac-

21 National Municipal League, *City Growing Pains* (New York City: 1941), p. 42.
22 *Ibid.*, p. 71.
23 *Ibid.*, p. 49.
24 P. Windels, "Metropolis at the Crossroads," *National Municipal Review*, XXXVII (1948), p. 371.

commodate this condition a vast network of highways has been built binding the entire area together in an economic whole. In spite of these improvements the area has been saturated by vehicles and people, a circumstance that was complicated by the fact that the Hudson River is a natural barrier to the entrance to New York City. Since it is only through tunnels and bridges that people can enter the city, it is not uncommon for congestion to occur. Daily, approximately 850,000 motor vehicles converge upon the city. The number of city-bound commuters each day is estimated to be between 350 and 400 thousand.[25] Vital arteries of transport are choked and the condition is not limited only to the roads leading to the central city. At the periphery between points at the outer edge of the region transportation is also overloaded and strained.

Here again there is patent evidence that there is no single plan that all units within the area are willing to accept. In its absence the region has "muddled through," although the continuance of such conditions is estimated to have cost the area approximately $2 billion.[26] The need is for a single metropolitan government for the entire complex in all of its aspects.

Avoidance of taxation. Metropolitan areas also enable those living outside of the central city to enjoy the benefits of city life without paying for them. The fringe dweller came to the countryside to avoid the confusion and noise of the city. Pleasant surroundings, low taxes and moderate land values were attractive to him. The coming of the automobile gave him ready access to his job in the city and provided him with ease and mobility while at home. The suburbanite worked inside of the central city and lived outside of it. He used it as a place of work, he contributed to its traffic conditions and he was protected by its police. But he was not taxed. When the day was over he left the dust of the city and returned to his pattern of graceful living in the country.[27]

Industry, too, tends to move outside of the central city because of lower taxes and less congestion. Its use of motor trucks and the highway networks surrounding the central city give it easy access to the markets without again bearing any of the share of central city government cost. In the period 1946–1950 the New York-New Jersey-

25 *New York Times,* March 22, 1954, p. 15.

26 *Idem.*

27 C. R. Cherington, "Pattern for Greater Boston," *National Municipal Review,* XXXVIII (1949), p. 70.

Connecticut metropolitan area witnessed the addition of 2,658 plants, three-fourths of which were outside the city of New York but within a twenty-four mile radius of the city.[28] Similarly, shopping centers and suburban branches of large department stores were established outside of the central city. Needless to say the distribution of professional and office personnel followed a similar pattern.

Suburban dependence on the central city. Movement of people in large numbers to the suburbs meant the transformation almost overnight of a rural into an urban area. Closeness of living required city services similar to those which existed in the core city, for the suburbanite soon found that he could not exist upon his own resources.[29] Fire and police protection, schools, sanitation, water supply, garbage and refuse disposal and a host of other functions became necessities. The suburbanite may have shed the worries of the central city; but he had also assumed some of his own. Indeed, the costs of government were just as high as in the central city and, in many instances, the demand for additional governmental programs far outran the ability of his community to finance them.[30]

Moreover, the migration to the suburbs frequently was so rapid that suddenly urbanized areas found themselves without facilities to meet the influx of people. The central city had to provide water, sewers, fire protection, hospitals and other services at cost. In some cases it was forced to furnish such services without any compensation, since the entire area was considered a part of the state. Metropolitan counties also accepted responsibility for health and welfare functions, thus relieving the central city of some of its burden. New York and Chicago, for example, furnish water to cities near their aqueducts.[31] Often the cost of such services is at such a level as to amount in effect to a grant-in-aid to the suburbs.

The shrinking tax base. It is in the area of finance that the movement of people to the suburbs has had most serious consequences for the central city. Unable to control population trends, central cities have been forced to watch helplessly while their revenue sources and tax bases have gradually but certainly trekked off beyond the city

---

28 *New York Times,* March 22, 1954, p. 15.

29 T. H. Reed, "Progress in Metropolitan Integration," *Public Administration Review,* IX (Winter 1949), p. 2.

30 V. Roterus and I. H. Hughes, Jr., "Governmental Problems of Fringe Areas," *Public Management,* XXX (1948), pp. 94-96.

31 V. Jones, "Local Government Organization in Metropolitan Areas," C. Woodbury, ed., *The Future of Cities and Urban Redevelopment* (Chicago, Ill.: The University of Chicago Press), p. 531.

lines. In the process the cities are losing many of their upper and middle income groups to the countryside, thus forcing the burden of city government upon those who are less able to pay.

Moreover, the movement of industry and wholesale and retail services beyond the limits of the city means that ratables that were an important part of the tax base are lost to the city. The city of Highland Park, Michigan, for example, lost 25 percent of its assessed valuation when the Ford Motor Company moved its offices to Dearborn, Michigan. And as we have previously noted, the great steel industries in the Chicago area escape the burden of urban taxes because they, too, are located beyond the boundaries of the city and in another state.[32] These phenomena are associated with almost every metropolitan area of the country. The lower tax rates in the areas that have not been built up often act as an inducement to move from the more settled places.

Not only is the tax base of the central city shrinking but also, what is even more distressing, the city as part of the county is forced to pay taxes to the county to finance governmental functions needed in the unincorporated areas. Kansas City is a good example of this condition. In 1954 it contributed 83 percent of the total property taxes of the county. Yet it was forced to spend approximately $4 million for hospital and medical care for its own needy because the county had ruled that only residents outside of the city could be treated in county hospitals.[33]

Los Angeles in 1948–1949 expended $9.2 million for the direct benefit of people in the unincorporated areas. Since the city contributed a substantial amount of this and at the same time could not tax its environs, the mayor proposed that the unincorporated areas should pay their own way for the services they required.[34] Atlanta, Georgia is another case in point. Its taxpayers not only maintained the city government but also contributed five-sixths of the Fulton County expenses. Added to this was the fact that the central city was forced to contribute more than its fair share to the county because of the consistent practice in the outlying areas to undervalue their property for tax purposes. Yet some of the functions, such as health

---

[32] Commission on Intergovernmental Relations, Advisory Committee Report, *Local Government* (Washington, D. C.: U. S. Government Printing Office, 1955), pp. 25, 46.

[33] *Kansas City Star,* November 8, 1954, p. 1.

[34] E. Mauck, "California Cities Discuss City-County Relations," *National Municipal Review,* XL (1951), p. 44.

and police, were administered separately for the city and county.[35]

It is evident that the metropolitan community encompasses areas and activities beyond the limits of the central city. The suburb may consider itself as being politically detached from the central city but it is inextricably intertwined with the latter. For basic services it is forced to look to the central city. Whether it is willing to admit it or not, the solution to its problems largely involves service contracts. The interaction of governmental units is part of the process of politics, whether or not the suburbanite is aware of it. However a buyer-seller arrangement is not very conducive to the formulation of fundamental policy.

Divided loyalties and lack of political accountability. The presence of numerous legal subdivisions within the area makes for divided loyalties and weakened political accountability. Each governmental unit, it must be presumed, will seek to act upon behalf of

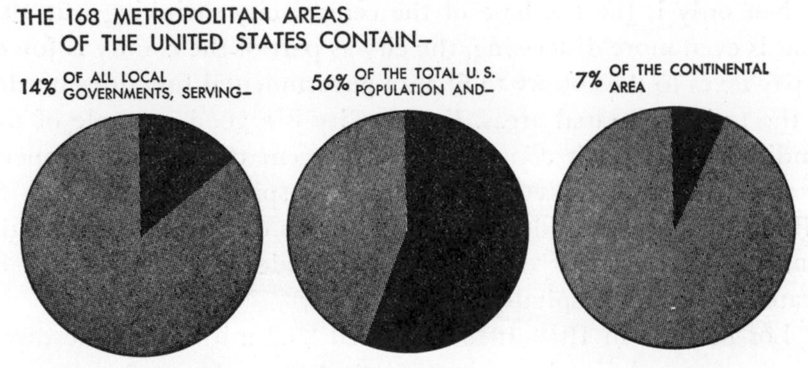

Fig. 7. The Composition of Metropolitan Areas in 1955.

the people within its jurisdiction. Each will have its own structure. The attachment of people will be to their own municipality and their view of the larger problems of the region is apt to be myopic. But even if these were not so, the diffusion of power among many units of government is likely to mean either that a large number of governmental officials are chosen or that dispersal of responsibility is so widespread that no one can be truly held accountable. Voter ignorance or apathy is bound to result from such a condition. Conversely, even if the voters are not apathetic, they may find it difficult to gain control of all the islands of power at one time. Indeed, some of these are either extensions of state and federal agencies, or

[35] National Municipal League, *City Growing Pains*, pp. 17-18. This was eliminated in the subsequent consolidation of the two units.

are semiautonomous authorities and as such are beyond local political control. But even where local political units exist, the prospect of storming individual political battlements again and again to gain control is a task that would dishearten even the most zealous political reformers.

One may conclude that the failure of political and legal lines to coincide is a matter of great consequence to the urban life of America. The municipality as a unit of government is, in many respects, inadequate to perform the tasks required of it. One may well echo the words of Gulick: "We must admit . . . that the basic political institutions of our society were not designed for great and changing metropolitan areas. Nor do they meet certain of the most important metropolitan needs. In fact, many of our institutions stand squarely athwart the dynamic flow of social, economic and political life in the great cities."[36] The size of the problem is suggested in Fig. 7.

EFFORTS AT POLITICAL INTEGRATION

Some form of comprehensive integration will be needed if a metropolitan area is to be governed effectively. Piecemeal arrangements will not suffice, even though this seems to be the prevailing pattern. The resident of the suburb may not feel that he belongs to the central city and may insist upon the autonomy of his suburb. Yet, when all is said and done, his municipality could not function if the central city ceased to provide necessary services. On the other hand, the residents of the central city may well wish they were rid of the suburbs and yet, in a multitude of ways, they are tied to the periphery. Not the least of these is the provision of services for the outlying areas. Thus, regardless of feelings of the core or the rim, a single community exists and is a factor compelling gradual political integration of the area.

Informal cooperation. Many attempts have been made at a unified governmental approach to metropolitan area problems. Broadly speaking, these fall into two main categories: those requiring little or no change in governmental structure, and those that do.[37] The former, because it does not seriously disturb the existing political structure, has been most popular. On its simplest level it consists mainly of informal administrative arrangements that grow out of normal everyday contacts between officials of adjacent municipalities.

[36] L. H. Gulick, "Metropolitan Political Developments," Fisher, *op. cit.*, p. 79.
[37] Jones, *op. cit.*, p. 550.

Commonly in matters of police and fire protection local cooperative agreements are concluded. It may be the creation of regional police and traffic plans as in Cincinnati, or it may be that one municipality will "cover" another if a designated percentage of its equipment is engaged in fighting a fire.[38] Again it may be concerned purely with the exchange of technical information. In Hamilton County, Ohio a coordinated purchasing committee was established consisting of all those engaged in buying either for the city of Cincinnati, the county school board, the university and the public library. In effect the committee acted as a central clearing house on all information concerned with either materials or specifications.[39]

In a somewhat similar vein are efforts, either on a formal or informal basis, to explore the common problems of a region. The work of the state leagues of municipalities which sponsor annual meetings of municipal officials to discuss common matters falls into this category. Area-wide consideration of mutual problems such as the monthly joint meetings of the Milwaukee City Land Commission and the Milwaukee County Park Board is another illustration.[40] Most significant along this line are the publicly and privately sponsored regional planning groups. These devote themselves to the collection of factual data about all aspects of metropolitan development. Such public groups are the Baltimore Metropolitan District Planning and Coordinating Committee, the Tri-County Planning Commission adjacent to Denver, and the Detroit Metropolitan Planning Commission; and such private groups as the Regional Plan Association (New York-New Jersey-Connecticut), Regional Association of Cleveland, and the San Francisco Bay Area Council have done a great deal to awaken the metropolitan consciousness.[41] Indeed, much of the stimulus for action has been provided by the activities of such groups.

Contractual arrangements. Somewhat more formal are the previously mentioned contractual arrangements between central city and suburb to supply sewers, water, schools and a variety of other essential services. Chattanooga can furnish sewers to other cities. In California it is common practice for one city to supply water on a

---

[38] R. H. Wells, *American Local Government* (New York: McGraw-Hill Book Co., Inc., 1939), pp. 95-96.

[39] Jones, *op. cit.*, p. 533.

[40] J. C. Bollens, "Metropolitan and Fringe Area Developments in 1951," *National Municipal Yearbook for 1952*, p. 33.

[41] *Municipal Yearbook for 1951*, pp. 36-37.

contract basis to a large number of others. A "sending school" may send its children to a nearby school district, paying a given amount of tuition per child. A host of such agreements exist, indicative of the rapid changes in population and the inability of municipalities to provide needed services. In general, such forms of cooperation seek to obtain the benefit of volume operation over a large area. While it has the advantage of not interfering with the autonomy of individual political units, it is seriously disadvantaged in that such contracts are subject to change in the light of new conditions. Central cities, hard pressed by the demands of their own people, may, and often do, insist that the peripheral cities take up their share of the burden.

Annexation. Annexation, unlike the above service and informational arrangements, involves the absorption of fringe areas within the legal boundaries of the central city. In this way those who flee to the suburbs and expect city services are brought within the tax jurisdiction of the central city and are compelled to share the burden. Although theoretically it is possible through this device to reunite into one government the population that has spilled beyond the limits of the central city, in practice this end cannot be achieved very simply for a variety of reasons. For one thing annexation cannot take place very easily unless there are areas that are unincorporated adjacent to the city. Unfortunately as time passes the built-up fringes are gradually assuming corporate identity. This development has two by-products. First, it means that the incorporated units cannot be annexed without their own consent and indeed the prospect of annexation has caused many built-up areas to incorporate in order to preserve their suburban identity. In 1948 the prospect that Miami and Dade county would be consolidated led to a proposal for the creation of eighteen new towns.[42] It is not entirely accidental that both Minneapolis and Chicago are ringed by a whole series of incorporated municipalities. A second consequence of the existence of incorporated areas is that they can and do compete with the central city for the available unincorporated areas. The competition between Kansas City and North Kansas City for the unincorporated areas of Clay County is but one example of what may happen on a larger scale.

Secondly, where the fringes outside of the central city contain a

---

[42] J. C. Bollens, *The States and the Metropolitan Problem* (Chicago: The Council of State Governments, 1956), pp. 25-33. Also Jones, *op. cit.*, p. 554.

large number of incorporated areas, the probability is that if reliance is placed upon the wishes of these units, they would never seek amalgamation with the central city unless there were compelling reasons for such a move. In other words, annexation by referendum does not facilitate the process of incorporation within the major city. Consequently it is fair to say that the value of annexation will depend largely upon the kind of annexation statutes that have been enacted in the various states.

If annexation is to be an effective device for metropolitan integration, then it is probable that Virginia has the most practical method. In that state the entire matter is a judicial proceeding. Cities desiring to annex adjacent territory bring suit against it before a special three-judge annexation tribunal whose decisions are subject to review by the Virginia Supreme Court of Appeals. To annex additional areas the city must conform with a number of criteria: it must demonstrate that it will need the added territory for its proper expansion; it must show that the services needed by the citizens of the area are not being provided and that these constitute a hazard to the citizens of the central city; and finally that the rest of the county will not suffer from the loss of ratables. The annexing city by statute is forbidden to plead that it needs the added territory to increase its property valuations.

The Virginia statute is unique in that it does not directly take into account the wishes of the people of the area to be annexed. The court may take cognizance of citizen viewpoints. It may, and does, hear the testimony of planners, engineers and public administrators but these merely become part of the litigation. The decision, however, is made by the court in the light of all of the aspects of litigation.[43]

Under the Virginia statute, Norfolk, Richmond and Roanoke annexed large amounts of land adjacent to them. Indeed, the experience of Virginia with its annexation law was so favorable to the first and second class cities that the state legislature in 1950 voted to stay any further action until its Commission to Study Urban Growth had had a chance to study the situation. Two years later a report of the commission recommended that the law be continued in substantially the same condition.

Both California and Texas cities have benefited from liberal

[43] R. B. Pinchbeck, "City-County Separation in Virginia," *National Municipal Review*, XXIX (1940), pp. 467-472, also Bollens, *op. cit.*, pp. 40-49.

annexation laws. In the former, the residents of the unincorporated territory rather than those of the city must initiate annexation laws. The governing body of the annexing city then votes on whether or not it will accept the petitioning area.[44] In Texas where home rule cities have been given the right to annex fringe areas by council ordinance, annexation is fairly simple. Through this means Dallas and Forth Worth, in 1949, acquired large areas. The largest annexation was carried out by Houston which in the same year added 79 square miles, approximately 100,000 new residents and $2 million in ratables.[45]

In 1951 one of the most significant annexation moves took place in Georgia where the city of Atlanta, acting under a state law, annexed 82 square miles of adjacent land on its outskirts, an action that tripled the size of the city and added 100,000 people in five densely populated sections. Fulton County, from which the land was annexed, once more became rural with only scattered urban clusters. But the action was more than merely physical integration. The rather extensive duplication of city and county functions was eliminated when municipal-type functions such as police and fire protection, water supply and sewer systems were transferred to the city. Thirty-nine schools were brought under the jurisdiction of the city. Only the health services in the area remained a county responsibility.[46] A joint performance committee was established to supervise the transfer of personnel between the two jurisdictions in such a fashion as to protect pension and seniority rights of public employees.[47] It was estimated that savings from the elimination of overlap would result in the gradual elimination of approximately 1500 jobs. Further extension of the city's boundaries was to take place in accordance with judicial proceedings similar to that of the state of Virginia. Finally, future planning for the area as a whole was guaranteed by an agreement for joint city-county action.[48]

Not all the results of annexation are so coherent in purpose or

---

[44] J. C. Bollens, "Elements of Successful Annexations," *Public Management,* XXX (1948), pp. 98-99.

[45] J. C. Bollens, "Metropolitan Area Developments, 1940–50," *National Municipal Yearbook for 1951,* p. 33.

[46] P. V. T. Hedden, "Atlanta Breaks Through its Boundaries," *The American City,* LXI (1951), pp. 106-107.

[47] E. A. Mauck, "Atlanta, Fulton County Get Some Consolidation," *National Municipal Review,* XL (1951), p. 215.

[48] M. C. Hughes, "Annexation and Reallocation of Functions," *Public Management,* XXXIV (1952), pp. 29-30; also Hedden, *op. cit.,* p. 107.

so dramatic in result. Annexation by major city of the fringe area is often a product of mixed motives. In many instances it is due to the fact that the core city has its hand forced by developments adjacent to it. It may not want to incur added obligations by the acquisition of additional land. Yet at the same time the presence of substandard conditions on the fringe does have an adverse effect upon its own position. In such circumstances annexation may seem to be the only way out of a dilemma. The central city hopes that the added property values will pay for the additional services that it will have to provide. On the other hand there are in some cases specific reasons why either the fringe or the core city may desire to institute annexation proceedings. Usually deficiencies in such services as sewers, fire protection, water and police prompt such action.[49] Both the annexing unit and the area to be annexed hope to benefit from the arrangement. Finally a large city may want to acquire large areas in order to avoid piecemeal annexation.

Although annexation is essentially a fragmented approach to what is essentially a comprehensive problem, its use by cities has been appreciable. From 1946 to 1951 the number of municipalities making land acquisitions has risen from 152 to 309, an increase of approximately 100 percent.[50] Aside from Texas, Virginia and Georgia, however, no annexation of any significance has taken place in the last quarter of a century.[51] Yet the fact that they have taken place at a *greater rate* is indicative of the concern felt by many cities in regard to the dispersal of people beyond the city limits.

City-county consolidation. The flight of people to the suburbs has acted as a constant stimulus to unify the governmental authority in metropolitan areas. A major complaint of the city has been that it has been forced, either through contractual arrangements or through tax contributions to the county, to finance or even, in a sense, subsidize the city-type services required by the unincorporated areas at the fringes of the city.

Primarily the aim of urban places has been to force the areas without formal governments to pay their fair share of the burden. Secondarily the objective also has been to eliminate overlap and duplication. Conceivably these objectives could be accomplished by

[49] Bollens, *op. cit.*, pp. 37-38. See also *The States and the Metropolitan Problems*, pp. 49-53.

[50] Bollens, *op. cit.*, p. 35.

[51] T. H. Reed, "Progress in Metropolitan Integration," *Public Administration Review*, IX (1949), p. 5.

annexation; but they have also been sought through either city-county consolidation, city-county separation, or, finally, through what is termed functional consolidation, that is, a form of inter-municipal cooperation where responsibility for one or more governmental services is centralized in a single unit.

City-county consolidation is regarded generally as one of the best answers to the governmental difficulties of metropolitan areas. Logically it is an outgrowth of the expanded functions of both units. The county serves as the basic administrative unit of the state in matters of tax collection, law enforcement, the judicial system, roads, public assistance and, in ever so many instances, health and welfare. Although at one time the county was exceedingly low in prestige, the recent outflow of people has given it a new lease on life.

At the same time the cities, under the intensified pattern of urban living that has emerged during the last three decades, have been given new responsibilities by the state. Education, sanitation, sewers, and public works are provided not only for the residents of the city but also for those outside its jurisdiction. At many points, city and county functions overlap, and, at all times, the city contributes to the operation of county government. Many evidences of the effect of resurgence and growth of the city can easily be found. Within the same county, the citizen may be subject to control by at least three governmental units, the city, the county and the school district. In some instances there are many more than these. In the interest of eliminating duplication and more equitable sharing of the governmental burden, consolidation of governmental units was sought.

City-county consolidation has proceeded gradually over the years. Whenever a county becomes metropolitan or highly urbanized, the tendency is to combine city and county functions. There are at present approximately 36 consolidated city-counties in the United States and, in addition, 271 first class cities in Virginia where according to state law they are classified as counties.[52] Two most recent successful efforts at consolidation were in Baton Rouge and Philadelphia. In the former, the city of Baton Rouge and East Baton Rouge Parish were united in 1949. Four zones were created by the plan: one residential, two industrial, and a very large rural area of

[52] Jones, *op. cit.*, p. 543. See also J. C. Bollens, *The States and the Metropolitan Problem*, ch. V for a record of the consolidation movement.

approximately 500 square miles. Taxes were apportioned among the areas in accordance with the services rendered.[53]

In Philadelphia intermittent agitation for consolidation with the county had taken place since 1854. Finally the hopes became a reality in 1951. All county officers were merged with those of the city, and large segments of authority that had been beyond the control of the city were now brought within its jurisdiction.[54] Perhaps the ultimate in consolidation was a proposal by Professor William Anderson to create 200 city-counties, each with a central city of at least 50,000 people, 2,000 rural counties and 15,000 incorporated places. If the aim were to reduce the number of layers of government, about three-fourths of the people of the country would be under a single legal unit.[55]

City-county consolidation, while popular with many people, is by no means the answer to the problem posed by metropolitan area development. It is difficult to put into effect. Suburbanites fear they will be swallowed up by the central city, and citizens of the latter often do not relish the assumption of added costs attendant upon consolidation. Some semblance of equality in the relationship between city and county generally must exist or the voters will not approve. For example, Miami's attempted consolidation with Dade County was defeated in 1948 largely because the suburbanites feared that consolidation would mean increased taxes without any corresponding improvement in services.[56]

Moreover, legal obstacles may block consolidation. In Philadelphia a multiple voting arrangement that required approval by two successive legislatures frustrated the people until the recently concluded final successful action.[57] But even if these disabilities are surmounted there still remains the fundamental fact that city-counties are only a temporary solution to the problem of metropolitan areas. As long as people retain their mobility, they will continue to move beyond county lines. Metropolitan government must look to a larger area or unit, if it is to attain a greater measure of success.

City-county separation. Sometimes city-county separation takes

---

[53] Reed, *op. cit.*, pp. 4-5.

[54] E. A. Mauck, "Philadelphia Gets Consolidation," *National Municipal Review*, XL (1951), p. 591.

[55] W. Anderson, *The Units of Government in the United States* (Chicago, Illinois: Public Administration Service, 1949), pp. 46-47.

[56] J. F. Willmott, "Miami-Dade Consolidation Defeated," *National Municipal Review*, XXXVII (1948), p. 399.

[57] Mauck, *op. cit.*, p. 32.

place but this is merely the prelude to further consolidation. What actually occurs is somewhat as follows: the urban portions are first physically detached from the county and then the central city and suburb merge to form a new county. The balance of the older political unit, usually rural, retains its own powers of government. An example is the city of Atlanta, which separated from Fulton County; also St. Louis, Denver, and Boston are other examples of city-county separation.[58]

City-county separation too, has serious weaknesses. Most of the ratables, and hence the tax base, are absorbed by the urban area, leaving the rural segment with little or no financial resources. Again, city-county separation makes it difficult to annex added territory at a later date. Thus years ago Nassau County, the rural segment of Queens County, was detached from New York City. Today Nassau County is highly urbanized largely as a result of the outflow of people from the central city. Only a legal line separates it from New York City and yet it is not a part of it despite its physical proximity.[59] Today, New York City would find it difficult to annex the county.

Functional consolidation. A somewhat different approach to interareal problems comes under the heading of functional consolidation, which retains the idea of consolidation but in terms of combining functions rather than units of government. Arrangements of this kind have merit in that the county is kept as a working partner in the administration of functions that are common to many cities. Functional consolidation depends upon the law of the state. Where, as in California, considerable freedom is given to local units, such cooperation is fruitful. Los Angeles County is empowered to provide services to its cities on a contractual basis. Many municipalities have health, library, assessment and collection of taxes, fire protection, garbage disposal, recreation, parkways, water and many other functions performed for them by the county.[60] Transfers of authority also are made to cities such as Los Angeles.

On the whole, evidence seems to indicate that California cities

---

[58] V. Jones, *Metropolitan Government* (Chicago, Illinois: The University of Chicago Press, 1942), p. 130.

[59] *Ibid.*, pp. 132-133.

[60] H. E. Jones and R. F. Wilcox, *Metropolitan Los Angeles: Its Governments* (Los Angeles, California: The Haynes Foundation, 1949), p. 16.

have participated actively in the functional consolidation of their powers.[61]

Consolidation efforts of this kind has taken place at such widely separate points as Buffalo, Milwaukee, Pittsburgh and Miami. In Buffalo the city ceded to Erie County its probation service, its health and hospital departments and its two libraries.[62] However, comprehensive functional consolidation, where an appreciable number of city-type functions are transferred to the county, is not so easily accomplished. The wholesale transfer of functions is akin to consolidation and subject to the same difficulties.

Metropolitan special districts. Somewhat similar to inter-municipal functional consolidation is the metropolitan authority or, as it is sometimes called, the special districts. These units, however, are not as broadly based as municipal governments. They have their own sources of revenue but in origin at least they are usually single purpose units, although generally they add functions as they develop. In contrast to the municipality, such powers as are exercised by the authorities are on a metropolitan-wide basis. Authorities obviate the need for inter-municipal arrangements since they can bridge jurisdictional barriers.[63] The metropolitan authorities are concerned only with problems of the area and this element enables one to differentiate it from others.

In origin and in motivation most authorities are similar. As functional units, they meet special purposes for which the existing municipal governments are unsuitable. They may be the means for avoiding a constitutional debt limit. They may well be a method for surmounting the legal difficulties inherent in either consolidation or annexation. They may originate because of the general feeling that those who benefit from a service should pay for its costs. Authorities also provide flexibility and ease of administrative action. It is these features that have been mainly responsible for the rather extensive use of such units.

Approximately thirty special metropolitan authorities have now come into being with responsibilities for a variety of functions such as sewerage, water supply, bridges, tunnels and ports.[64] The Chicago Sanitary District created in 1889 is one of the oldest of such districts.

---

61 *Municipal Yearbook for 1951*, p. 35.

62 *Idem.*

63 Bollens, *op. cit.*, ch. 6; also P. Studenski, *The Government of Metropolitan Areas in the United States* (New York: National Municipal League, 1930), p. 256.

64 Bollens, *op. cit.*, pp. 124-126 contain a list of these special agencies.

Its basic purpose is to protect the water supply of the Chicago metropolitan area by keeping Lake Michigan free from sewage contamination. That it has been successful is attested to by the fact that the 185 square miles originally controlled by it has been tripled in area.

Most famous of all is the Boston Metropolitan District Commission which also began in 1889 as a sewerage district. Gradually it added parks, water, public works, planning and rapid transit functions. In 1923 it possessed jurisdiction over 43 towns and cities. The commission is not an agent of local government. It is a state body whose five members are appointed by the governor with the consent of the senate. In outline the commission is a prototype of government for a metropolitan area, but it is not likely that urban suspicion of the motives of a rurally dominated state legislature will permit a comprehensive grant of power to such a unit.[65]

The Boston Metropolitan District Commission has been characterized as the "half-way house to union" (of the region). . . . "It permits unified metropolitan service in the functional areas of water, sewers and parks. It enables several hundred thousand people who refuse to admit they are Bostonians to enjoy the benefits of metropolitan service. . . ." [66] But even this most effective of metropolitan instruments has demonstrated its limited utility by the fact that no comprehensive plan for the great Boston metropolitan area has developed. The approximately 83 communities that surround the central city still maintain their separate identity and there has been no visible sign of a common metropolitan consciousness.[67]

Nevertheless the examples of metropolitan authorities have furnished clues for further inquiry into their advisability as instruments of metropolitan government. In a speech delivered to the National Conference on Government in 1955, Dr. Charlton Chute has provided further food for thought on this subject. He expressed doubt that political integration would function for a single metropolitan area since metropolitan areas are expanding and developing relationships with one another. Since this is so, he has suggested a new concept, the "urban region," that is, an area where two or more standard metropolitan areas are adjacent to one another. On the

[65] Jones, *ibid.*, pp. 94-95.
[66] C. R. Cherrington, "Pattern for Greater Boston," *National Municipal Review*, XXXVIII (1949), p. 70.
[67] *Ibid.*, p. 68.

basis of this definition he has found that nineteen "urban regions" would contain most of the important cities of the country. Since many of the problems facing metropolitan areas are state-wide in character, since many are presently being handled by the state, he advocated a strengthened role for the state with respect to metropolitan area functions.

From the legal standpoint there is much merit in his proposals. Certainly it is correct to say that special authorities owe their existence to the state. Moreover, it is true that many metropolitan areas cross state lines and it is here, too, that the state again would play a signal role. Politically, however, it is at least arguable as to whether or not metropolitan areas would take kindly to the idea of increased state control. It is no argument to say, as he has, that the known will be more attractive than the unknown. The long history of the attempts by cities to make the state more responsive to their needs cannot easily be forgotten.[68]

Moreover, regardless of the control by the states, authorities, by the very condition of their origin, are special purpose units. They can administer special functions or groups of powers on an area-wide basis but precisely because they are limited purpose units they cannot govern a region as a whole. Yet in terms of the loose statutory construction under which they presently operate, it is essential that their purposes should be restricted narrowly. Their activities are not presently subject to annual appropriation review since they have independent income sources. Their officers may be chosen independently of the local units. Yet their policies with respect to transit tolls and service rates may well determine the economic growth of the region.[69]

Metropolitan authorities do have the potential for surmounting legal barriers and bringing about a consonance of political and economic areas. The Golden Gate Bridge and Highway District has provided a coordinated approach to a problem that concerns seven counties in a greater or lesser degree. The Port of New York Authority has helped link New York and New Jersey on many trans-

---

[68] C. F. Chute, "A New Approach to the Problem of Government in Metropolitan Areas," *National Conference on Government* (Mimeographed; Seattle, Washington, 1955). Also, "Todays Urban Regions," *National Municipal Review,* XLV (1956), pp. 274-280.

[69] J. McLean, "The Use and Abuse of Authorities," *National Municipal Review,* XLII (1953), pp. 438-444.

portation matters despite the presence of two states and many local units. These and many others demonstrate the capacity of authorities to administer metropolitan-wide functions. Despite its undoubted advantages, the continued use of authorities may have unpredictable consequences unless through law its governmental structure is made more accountable to the will of the people in the area where it operates.

Municipal federation. None of the above plans to meet the governmental problems of metropolitan areas is without fault. It is perhaps because of the complexity of the problems and of the absence of any final solution that experimentation has continued. One of the most interesting suggestions is a pattern for the metropolitan area that is modeled after that of the federal government. As people spread out over a wider area and suburban units achieve corporate identity, localism tends to develop. Norwood is considered distinct from Cincinnati. Brookline is not regarded by its residents as being part of Boston. Yet both suburbs are part of their respective metropolitan areas and both are concerned with matters that affect the region as a whole. Both the need for local identity and a common approach to the problems of the region are necessary. To meet what is essentially a problem of federalism, some have proposed the application of its main features to the government of metropolitan areas.

New York City is probably the best example of this type of thinking, although it must be admitted that the existing government, which dates from 1898 when Greater New York was founded, was a product of many compromises rather than a rational attempt at a distribution of powers among various units. A mayor, twenty-seven department heads, a municipal council and municipal courts exercise city-wide functions. In each of the five boroughs into which the city is divided, a popularly elected borough president has considerable administrative powers with respect to matters that are of concern only to his borough. Local improvements to streets, sewers and minor public works are the responsibility of the borough president. Local school boards within the borough are appointed by the borough executive.

The boroughs, through their elected presidents, receive representation in the upper house of the legislature where the five of them in conjunction with the president of the council, the comptroller and the mayor, help determine the fiscal policies of the city.[70] In the lower house, commonly called the city council, representation is apportioned on the basis of the number of state senate districts in each borough. All in all, therefore, there is a common approach to matters that affect the city as a whole. Matters considered purely local are handled through the offices of the five borough presidents.

More recently efforts to "federalize" have been attempted in the Oakland, Pittsburgh and St. Louis metropolitan areas. These, however, were largely designed to create metropolitan counties that would assume all the powers of government common to the region as a whole. In an almost similar form were the county executive systems of Nassau and Westchester counties (New York) established in 1936 and 1937, respectively.[71] In both of these counties, functions of concern to the county as a whole were administered by county executives. Incorporated units retained authority over their local functions.

Federation has many advantages over the other plans. Foremost among these is the feature which enables the local units to retain their identity and to a considerable degree their power over purely local matters. Suburbs are not "swallowed up." The federal arrangement permits greater flexibility since no fundamental change has to take place each time the population characteristics of an area are altered. Functions that are local and become metropolitan-wide may be handled as a matter of course by the central unit. But federation has many disabilities. It cannot operate where the metropolitan area crosses state lines. To do so would require ironing out a welter of legal relations not only between states but also among the various units within the metropolitan region. An action of this sort would need a special act of the state legislature and probably action by the people. Implementation of such a plan would encounter the same difficulties noted in connection with annexation and consolidation.

The city-state. Most dramatic of all of the proposals to solve the problems of metropolitan government is the city-state. Periodically, large cities such as Detroit, Chicago and New York, when they become embroiled with their state legislatures over tax or financial authority, incline toward the view that they would be better off

[70] The votes of the borough presidents vary. The presidents of Manhattan and Brooklyn are allowed to cast two votes whereas the remaining three are permitted only one vote each.

[71] *Laws of New York,* 1936, ch. 879; *ibid.,* 1937 ch. 617.

without the yoke of state authority around their necks. Chicago in 1925 and New York in 1919 and in 1949 have explored the possibilities, although no concrete action has been taken.

Separation of the large metropolitan city from the state is attractive for a variety of reasons. It is relieved almost immediately of contributions to the state treasury. It can conduct direct relationships with Washington and be the beneficiary of federal grants of various kinds. Last but by no means least, it has control over its own fiscal policies. However, a constitutional barrier exists in the form of the requirement that no state can be formed within the jurisdiction of another state, except with the consent of the state and the Congress of the United States. Such consent is not likely to be given. Even if this possibility should eventuate, the plan is still open to the serious objection that it would withdraw from a state a substantial portion of its revenues. Finally, metropolitan areas are not static. They continue to grow all the time. If a city-state is created, continuing urban expansion would immediately begin to override the new state boundary and the basic problem would recur. It is probable that no plan of this sort, no matter how desirable it may seem to the individual central city, can be effected unless there is a wholesale revision of governmental boundaries in order to reflect more adequately the needs of metropolitan and rural areas.

CONCLUSION

The growth of metropolitan areas represents an important phase in the life cycle of cities. Technology and industrialization were very largely responsible for the rise of cities. Steam power as a form of energy and rail transport not only brought people to the cities in ever increasing numbers but also was a factor in keeping them there. This concentration of people, however, was not destined to last. Very largely the same forces that created the city within a half-century set in motion population movements that burst the city asunder. People scattered to the suburbs and rural areas, although they still maintained an economic nexus to the core city.

The dispersal of people beyond established city limits was a governmental phenomenon of considerable magnitude. It is a measure of the change to say that it is no longer possible to think of the local unit as merely the city. It is just as essential to consider it as something more, the metropolitan area which is, in fact, a single community with an area larger than the central city, with a common culture, interests, and problems but with no single political voice. Indeed, in the standard metropolitan area the single legal instrument is conspicuous by its absence. In 1950, 87,671,000 people, 56 percent of our population, lived in metropolitan areas. By 1955 the number of such regions increased to 172 and it is becoming increasingly apparent that the motor car, an organized highway system, and possibly even the greater use of air transport will cause further dispersal of the people. How to govern such an area is as yet an unsolved problem in municipal government.

But it is more than the mere governing of the area that is involved. At stake are such questions as: who shall bear the cost of government and the services it provides; and how shall such government be made accountable to the people it serves. The average suburbanite has been characterized as a man who works at the place where he does not want to live and lives at the place where he does not want to work.[72] He does not share the burden of the central city even though he may earn his living there. The urban services that he requires are often provided at cost by the central city. He may benefit from the arrangement but he does not pay for it. On the other hand the central city has no control over the areas on its periphery. Its jurisdiction is limited to its boundaries. Yet it is affected by what happens on its outskirts. Dispersed people means dispersed government and the fragmentation of political power. Since no governmental unit is responsible for the metropolitan community as a whole, it is difficult to maintain the accountability of political officers. Moreover, the recognition of this fact by the people often results in apathy and political disinterest.

It is clear from this brief review that metropolitan areas require metropolitan governments. How to attain this objective, however, is a most difficult question to answer. Each of the various alternatives discussed have their merits and demerits. Each, to some degree, has been employed alone or in conjunction with others. But all solutions are piecemeal in nature. It is necessary to create a new form of government that will conform to the realities of metropolitan life in urban America.

---

[72] E. J. Glade, "Urban and Fringe Area Financial and Operating Problems in a Medium-sized City," *Municipal Finance,* XXVII (1954–1955), p. 87.

BIBLIOGRAPHY

Books:

Anderson, W. *The Units of Government in the United States.* Chicago: Public Administration Service, 1949.

Burgess, E. W. *The Urban Community.* Chicago: University of Chicago Press, 1926.

Commission on Intergovernmental Relations. *A Report to the President for Transmittal to Congress.* Washington, D. C.: United States Government Printing Office, 1955.

Dewhurst, J. F. *America's Needs and Resources.* New York: The Twentieth Century Fund, 1955.

Fisher, R. M. (ed.). *The Metropolis in Modern Life.* Garden City, New York: Doubleday and Co., Inc., 1955.

Jones, H. E. and Wilcox, R. F. *Metropolitan Los Angeles: Its Governments.* Los Angeles: The Haynes Foundation, 1949.

Jones, V. *Metropolitan Government.* Chicago: University of Chicago Press, 1942.

McKenzie, R. D. *The Metropolitan Community.* New York: McGraw-Hill Book Co., Inc., 1933.

Studenski, P. *The Government of Metropolitan Areas in the United States.* New York: National Municipal League, 1930.

United States Department of Commerce, United States Bureau of Census, *Country and City Data Book, 1952.* Washington, D. C.: United States Government Printing Office, 1953.

———. *Local Government in Metropolitan Areas.* Washington, D. C.: United States Government Printing Office, 1954.

———. *Metropolitan Districts.* Washington, D. C.: United States Government Printing Office, 1932.

Wells, R. H. *American Local Government.* New York: McGraw-Hill Book Co., Inc., 1939.

Woodbury, C. (ed.). *The Future of Cities and Urban Redevelopment.* Chicago: The University of Chicago Press, 1953.

Articles and Other Material:

Bollens, J. C. "Elements of Successful Annexations," *Public Management,* XXX (1948), 98-101.

———. *The States and the Metropolitan Problem.* Chicago: The Council of State Governments, 1956.

Cherrington, C. R. "Patterns for Greater Boston," *National Municipal Review,* XXXVIII (1949), 68-72.

Chute, C. F. *"A New Approach to the Problem of Government in Metropolitan Areas,"* (mimeographed), Seattle: National Conference on Government, 1955.

Converse, P. D. "The Automobile and the Village Merchant," *Bureau of Business Research, University of Illinois,* 1928.

———. and Russell, R. J. "Why City Workers Live in Agricultural Villages," *Current Economic Comment,* XXII (1950), 37-47.

Glade, E. J. "Urban and Fringe Area Financial and Operating Problems in a Medium-sized City," *Municipal Finance,* XXVII (1954-55), 87-91.

Hughes, M. C. "Annexation and Reallocation of Functions," *Public Management,* XXXIV (1952), 26-30.

Mauck, E. A. "Atlanta, Fulton County Gets Some Consolidation," *National Municipal Review,* XL (1951), 215.

———. "California Cities Discuss City-Country Relations," *National Municipal Review,* XL (1951), 44-45.

———. "Philadelphia Gets Consolidation," *National Municipal Review,* XL (1951), 591.

McLean, J. "The Use and Abuse of Authorities," *National Municipal Review,* XLII (1953), 438-444.

Pinchbeck, R. B. "City-Country Separation in Virginia," *National Municipal Review,* XXIX (1940), 467-472.

Reed, T. H. "Progress in Metropolitan Integration," *Public Administration Review,* IX (1949), 1-10.

Roterus, V. and Hughes, I. H. "Governmental Problem of Fringe Areas," *Public Management,* XXX (1948), 94-97.

Spenser, R. C. "29 Cities Within Cities," *National Municipal Review,* XXXVII (1948), 256-258.

Van Hedden, P. T. "Atlanta Breaks Through its Boundaries," *The American City,* LXVI (1951), 106-107.

Willmott, J. F. "Miami-Dade Consolidation Defeated," *National Municipal Review,* XXXVII (1948), 399-400.

Windels, P. "Metropolis at the Crossroads," *National Municipal Review,* XXXVII (1948), 371-376.

PART
FOUR

The Problems of the City: the Administration of Municipal Functions

Chapter Eighteen

Municipal Personnel Administration

The Scope of Municipal Employment

The modern city performs many essential services for its citizens. Health, welfare, police and fire protection, water supply and education are but a few of the major functions that the citizen has come to expect of his city. Without these, people could not live in close proximity to one another, save at great risk to life and limb. But the administration of these activities is not carried out by automatons. It is performed by individuals who are employed by their city governments. To obtain the properly trained person, to motivate him, to give him the incentive to make public employment his career—these are the tasks that personnel administration must accomplish. The extent to which it is successful in doing so largely determines the level of effectiveness of municipal government.

Its character and size. The modern city is a large employer of labor. In numbers and size of its payroll, public employment is big business. As of October 1955, municipalities had 1,436 thousand persons employed and a payroll for that month of $414 million.[1] Of this number, 85 percent or 1,218 thousand were full-time employees. When the full-time equivalents of the remainder who are on a part-time basis are calculated, a total of 1,262 thousand are employed by city governments.[2] Expenditures for personal services are now nearly one half of the total cost of municipal government.[3]

Unlike the pattern of federal employment which seems to be leveling off, city employment is rising steadily. Since the end of World War II the number of city employees has jumped from 1,115 thousand to 1,436 in 1955.[4] The prospect is that the continued urbanization and industrialization of the country will cause the

[1] U. S. Bureau of Census, *City Employment in 1955* (Washington, D. C.: March 9, 1956), p. 1.

[2] *Idem.*

[3] U. S. Bureau of Census, *Compendium of City Government Finances in 1955* (Washington, D. C.: U. S. Government Printing Office, 1955), p. 3.

[4] U. S. Bureau of Census, *City Employment in 1955,* p. 6.

cities to assume additional responsibilities and will result in a consequent increase in the size of the municipal payroll. When the plateau in employment will be reached is not easily ascertainable at the present time.

The upward trend of municipal employment is not uniform throughout the United States. A distinction has to be made as to the size of the city. In general it might be said that employment must be correlated with the number of inhabitants. Of the 17,000 municipalities that exist, the vast majority are small; together they account for only a small portion of the municipal work force and payroll. At the other end of the scale are 106 cities of more than 100,000 inhabitants which have more than half of all the municipal employees. New York City alone employs one-sixth of the total of all city employment or as much as the nine next largest municipalities.[5] Part-time employment also shows the effect of city size. In general, the smaller the city, the greater the proportion of part-time personnel. In the cities with 100,000 or more inhabitants, 96 percent of all employees are full-time personnel; in the cities under 5000, only 37 percent are in a similar category. Monthly earnings show a similar variation. City payrolls for common municipal functions are about three times as great in the very large cities as compared with those in cities under 5000 inhabitants.[6]

The relationship of population size and municipal employment. The relationship between municipal employment and population size has a direct bearing on personnel administration. There is an enormous difference in the kind of problem faced by the large as compared with the small city. In both jurisdictions the human equation is the same; in both there is a similar need for highly trained personnel. Yet both are not on an equal footing when it comes to the matter of seeking and keeping capable people. In the small city, salaries are lower, full-time employment is proportionately less, and consequently career opportunities are few and far between. The large city is not so disadvantaged. It usually can install an effective personnel system, and whether it does so depends to a considerable extent on the state of public opinion in the community. For the small jurisdiction, however, it is not a matter of willingness but rather of ability. Ways and means need to be developed that will permit it to obtain qualified personnel.

[5] *Ibid.*, p. 1.
[6] *Ibid.*, p. 3.

City employment, reflecting the rapid increase in both the size and the number of cities, has grown enormously. Not only has there been a sharp rise in the number of employed, but also the caliber of people required has changed. In every branch of the municipal work force, highly trained people, whether policemen, firemen, engineers or public health specialists, are needed. With personnel costs now a substantial part of the municipal budget, the success of municipal governments will, in large part, depend upon the extent to which they effectively utilize their personnel.

EVOLUTION OF PERSONNEL ADMINISTRATION

Municipal personnel administration is part of a larger movement the major concern of which is to obtain general recognition of the merit principle in public employment. As a distinctly urban development it is relatively new, being hardly more than fifty years old. As part of the general growth of personnel administration, however, its antecedents are federal and actually go back to the founding of the republic. Since personnel administration stands at the end of a long line of development, a brief review of its evolution will help give one a better understanding of present-day attitudes toward it.[7]

Early beginnings. From the beginning, efforts to obtain competent personnel were beclouded both by party considerations and the general fear that governmental servants would abuse their powers unless they were subjected to political checks. Our first president, Washington, set high standards for his appointees. Professor Fish writes that the "absolute requirement of capacity seems to have been generally understood and nearly every existing application for office under Washington dwells on the applicant's ability." [8] But even under Washington this was a difficult task.

Succeeding administrations, however, witnessed a gradual in-

---

[7] As used in this chapter, there are four main phases of personnel administration. (1) The spoils system where partisan considerations are dominant; (2) the Civil Service, where the Civil Service Commission is concerned only with recruitment on the basis of examination; (3) the merit system which consists of a much more comprehensive concern for position classification, promotion, and other aspects of personnel administration; and (4) career systems which are a part of the merit system. The latter is essentially an attempt to extend the merit principle upward and outward to all areas of government employment. The aim is primarily to recruit and *keep* capable people through the use of incentives. For more detail, see A. W. Bromage, *Introduction to Municipal Government and Administration* (New York: Appleton-Century-Crofts, 1950), pp. 419-421.

[8] C. R. Fish, *The Civil Service and Patronage* (New York: Longmans, Green and Co., 1905), p. 7.

trusion of party principles. Adams made political appointments, especially to the federal judiciary. Jefferson removed about a fifth of his predecessor's appointees. Party service was recognized as a reason for appointment and party dissent was a cause for removal, but it was not the sole reason. Ability was also a consideration, and on the whole the character of the civil service did not change very much.[9]

In the period until 1829 the national government functioned very efficiently. This is not to imply that partisan considerations were absent. Rather it is to suggest that the long tenure in power of one party created a political-administrative corps that was capable. Jobs were parceled out on the basis of party loyalty, but also it was the party that was able to supply competent personnel.

The spoils system. Party considerations without a merit system, however, paved the way for a spoils system. As William Dudley Foulke, the great reformer, has remarked, "the system of spoils comes about as soon as offices are considered the property, not of the state but of the party." [10] On the state and local level this development had already reached the point where Jefferson's concept of due participation had been expanded into a doctrine of party monopoly. Spoils by that time had become the political way of life for most states.[11] It remained for Jackson to give the spoils system national prominence and to articulate its basic philosophy.

The disappearance of a dominant party and the residual bitterness of the campaign of 1824 led Jackson's party to take a full measure of revenge against their erstwhile opponents. The spoils of office were handed out without regard to ability. But more was at stake than merely passing out the patronage. Jackson, the first genuine representative of the frontier in the White House, had a hearty dislike of bureaucracy. Long tenure in office, he felt, tended to develop in people a vested interest in their job to the point that the general good of the public was neglected. Since the duties and responsibilities of any office were fairly simple, the solution was easy. Short terms of office and frequent rotation of personnel would ensure democratic control.[12] Until the end of the Civil War this philosophy

---

[9] *Ibid.*, p. 51.

[10] W. D. Foulke, *Fighting the Spoilmen* (New York: G. P. Putnam's Sons, 1919), p. 5.

[11] Fish, *op. cit.*, p. 103. Also H. L. MacBain, *De Witt Clinton and the Origin of the Spoils System* (New York: Columbia University Press, 1907).

[12] Fish, *op. cit.*, pp. 111-112.

prevailed. Every four years, in obedience to the demand of the spoils system, the offices of the federal service became prizes to be awarded to faithful adherents by the victorious party.

Civil service reform. Although the Civil War had greatly enhanced the patronage opportunities of the party in power, the movement to introduce the merit system began even before the war was over. In 1864 Senator Sumner introduced a measure calling for competitive entrance into the federal service. Three years later a somewhat similar bill was brought before the House of Representatives by Thomas Janckes.[13] Neither bill received much support, but, nonetheless, the action did lay the groundwork for civil service reform. In 1871 a rider to an appropriation bill authorized the President to prescribe regulations to ascertain the fitness of candidates for admission to the federal service. An advisory board was appointed, but Congress refused to appropriate funds for the enterprise. Under President Hayes, competitive examinations were instituted in New York Post Office and Custom House and in the Department of the Interior.

It was during Hayes's administration that Dorman B. Eaton was sent to England to study the British Civil Service system. His report did much to educate the American public. The assassination of Garfield in 1881 by a disappointed office seeker was an object lesson in the need for a merit system. Two years later the Pendleton Act was passed making civil service a permanent part of the American political scene.[14] While only a mere handful of persons were covered into the civil service, the act was important because it was designed ". . . to remove the incentive to that kind of political corruption which is nourished by the hopes of office." [15]

Civil service in the cities. Conditions in municipalities in the period after the Civil War also led to civil service reform. To say the least, cities were badly mismanaged. Bribery, sale of offices, "boodling" and outright corruption were the order of the day. New York City, in the clutches of the infamous Tweed ring, was shamelessly despoiled. Werner cites data showing that in a two-year period the debt of the city was increased by $50 million. During the same time a city plasterer received $2.9 million. The city's payroll became a source of both power and plunder. It was used to reward friends

[13] *Ibid.*, p. 211.
[14] Foulke, *op. cit.*, pp. 7-9.
[15] *Ibid.*, p. 10.

and to permit ruthless individuals to use public power for private purposes.[16] Although this was a particularly bad example, other cities were not much better. Indeed one authority has asserted, "A comprehensive investigation of conditions in American cities during the late sixties would probably have disclosed a state of affairs no better, and much more difficult to remedy, than those laid bare in the boroughs of England by the Royal Commission of 1833." [17]

It was evident to the thinking citizen that the preoccupation of the substantial elements with their own affairs had left the field to the professional politician and that the latter, if left to himself, would soon make a mockery out of the democratic process. The business men, the reformers, and others began to demand efficiency in government. Convinced that the political jobholder was the source of boss rule, they insisted that the merit principle was the key to the purification of politics. It was thus that the competitive federal system was transferred to the states and cities.

In 1883 New York State passed the first civil service law and a year later it was joined by Massachusetts. After a lapse of approximately two decades, Wisconsin and Illinois followed suit in 1905. Thereafter laws were passed in Colorado in 1907; New Jersey a year later; Connecticut, California and Ohio, in 1913; and Kansas two years later.[18] Most state laws contained provisions authorizing cities to establish civil service systems. Municipal civil service first came into being in New York City in the last decade of the nineteenth century when the legislature forced the installation of civil service commissions in almost every city of the state. The merit principle also was incorporated in the commission and city manager plans and, riding on the crest of the latter's popularity, gained wide acceptance. By 1911 two hundred and eleven cities had adopted the merit principle for some or all of its personnel.[19] Today two-thirds of the cities have formal civil service, but only half of these agencies cover all employees.[20] Approximately 38 percent of the cities under 25,000 in population have no formal civil service at all.

Civil service versus the merit system. Out of the struggle for civil

---

[16] M. R. Werner, *Tammany Hall* (New York: Doubleday and Co.), pp. 160-169.

[17] W. B. Munro, *The Government of American Cities* (New York: The Macmillan Co., 1913), p. 16.

[18] F. M. Stewart, *The National Civil Service Reform League* (Austin, Texas: The University of Texas, 1929), p. 143.

[19] Foulke, *op. cit.*, p. 219.

[20] *National Municipal Yearbook for 1954*, p. 174.

service reform has come two differing concepts of personnel; civil service and the merit system. Civil service was born in an age of suspicion. The reformer, it will be recalled, sought to destroy the power of the boss and the machine by denying him the right to make appointments to administrative positions within the city. To accomplish this, three conditions were needed: (1) acceptance of the principle that entrance into the city service must be on the basis of a competitive examination; (2) protection of the individual on the job by a grant of tenure that prevented his dismissal for political, racial, religious or other reasons not connected with his competence; and (3) an independent agency, usually chosen on a bi-partisan basis with overlapping terms of office, to administer the plan.[21]

This, judged by modern standards, is essentially a negative approach to personnel administration. It seeks to prevent and punish, instead of to promote. It assumes that the administrator will abuse his authority and it attempts to curtail his powers. Vigilance of this sort was needed a half-century or more ago, but today with the increase in professionalization, there is a need for greater emphasis on many other aspects of personnel management.

The merit system. It is because of the continuance of the "policeman approach" that civil service has fallen in disfavor with administrators. They accept the merit principle for appointments but insist that cooperation rather than conflict is the basis of good personnel practice. In their view, a personnel office should function as an assistant to the administrator, aiding him in achieving more effective administrative performance. In many council-manager cities, the manager is either the director of personnel or has the personnel officer as one of his principal assistants.

With a positive approach, the needs of the operating officer for better recruitment, classification, salary and wage plans, and promotion and transfer systems are met more readily. An operating official has summed up the matter in the following words: "The truth of the matter seems to be that, on the one hand, civil service commissions have the legal authority to drive operating officials crazy. And, on the other hand, operating officials have means at their disposal to exasperate, frustrate, and cause both the mental and physical breakdown of any commissioner or personnel director that ever lived.

21 International City Managers' Association, *Municipal Personnel Administration* (3rd ed., Chicago, Illinois, 1942), p. 12.

Why don't both sides give up and start all over again?" [22] In brief, a recognition of the fact that the administrator and the personnel office are partners in a joint enterprise rather than natural enemies characterizes the difference between the merit and the civil service systems.

Personnel management in the small city. With personnel costs now at the point where they absorb approximately half of the municipal budget, personnel administration is not, and cannot, be solely the province of the personnel agency. Everyone from the top down, to some degree, shares in the responsibility for the management of personnel. As we have already indicated, the line officials or administrators have an important role to fulfill. They are on the firing line every day of the week. They know the demands of their units for personnel, training, and all the other aspects of personnel administration. They direct and supervise their subordinates. They know the value of motivation and incentive. In turn, the chief executive of the municipality gives directives to his administrators. The endeavor to get full mileage out of the municipal tax dollar is, or at least should be, the objective of all directing officers.

Finally, the council is an important cog in personnel management. It decides the organizational structure of the municipality and, of course, the personnel office. It formulates policies concerning recruitment, classification, pay plans and retirement systems. Through its appropriation authority, it subjects the administrative effort annually to a critical review. Management of personnel, in brief, is a team effort.

While it is generally agreed that the merit principle is an essential aspect of all employment, progress along this line, particularly in the small city, has been extremely slow. There is a noticeably high correlation between city size and the number of personnel covered by civil service. The small city usually has fewer people appointed on a competitive basis. In 1954, 38 percent of the cities in the population range of 10,000-25,000 had none of their personnel under a formal merit plan.[23] The lag has been due primarily to two factors: (1) a misunderstanding of the role of civil service in the small municipality and (2) the failure to work out cooperative relationships with other levels of government.

---

22 W. L. Johnson, "Let's Untie Operating Officials," *Public Personnel Review,* XI (April 1950), p. 61.

23 *The Municipal Yearbook for 1954,* p. 174.

In many small municipalities the view persists that there is no need for an organized personnel activity since the functions of government are fairly simple. Informal methods of selection, it is asserted, may not be efficient, but it is the price one pays for remaining small. Yet a glance at the services performed by any small city would easily demonstrate that these assertions are not correct. City services, regardless of the size of the municipality, are not only technical but are becoming more so all of the time. Sewage disposal plants, water supply systems, street and lighting maintenance, traffic control, utilities and many other functions require highly trained people. They may not have the opportunity to specialize to the same degree as their counterparts in the large cities, but the protection of the city to a considerable degree hinges on their ability. A haphazard system of selection may enhance the position of the local politician or machine, but it is fraught with danger for the citizen.

Even if it is agreed, however, that the small city has the same need as the larger one, it is still debatable whether the number of people employed and the size of the municipal budget justify a separate personnel agency. Can the municipality afford such a luxury (and a luxury it becomes if it is not fully utilized)? There is considerable agreement that the answer is negative. Some authorities feel that a full-time personnel director is needed only where the number of municipal employees is in excess of 750. Others feel that only cities with more than 50,000 people can justify a full-time personnel director.[24] Generally, the personnel function should be separately organized only if it can fully employ at least one personnel technician. For a great many of the small cities this is a virtual impossibility.

The New Jersey and California plans. Acceptance of this view would leave a great many cities without the benefit of technical personnel assistance. Yet the need exists, regardless of the size of the city. How then can the needs of the small municipality be met? "The solution of the problem," one study reports, "lies in adaptation." [25] There are roughly three "adaptations" that have been made to meet the requirements of the small city. These may be termed: (1) the New Jersey plan and its variants; (2) the Massachusetts plan; and (3) the Michigan Demonstration project. Under the terms of

---

[24] International City Managers' Association, *op. cit.*, p. 27.

[25] Public Administration Service, *Personnel Programs for Smaller Cities* (Chicago, Illinois, 1940), p. 3.

New Jersey law starting as early as 1908, municipalities by referendum may accept civil service assistance from the state. Acceptance by the municipality means that the state civil service commission will perform personnel functions for the municipality at no cost. Once a municipality has voted to join the system, its decision is irrevocable. The plan has proved fairly popular in the state. As of 1954, 87 municipalities representing about 70 percent of the state's population have accepted the plan.[26] In New York State in accordance with the provisions of the constitution requiring that all appointments to any civil division be made upon the basis of fitness, the state civil service commission provides civil service for those municipalities that cannot maintain their own technical staffs.

Somewhat similar to the New Jersey plan is the system in California. There, by law, municipalities are permitted to make contracts either with the state personnel board or with counties or other municipalities for the performance of technical services. California practice is somewhat more flexible than that of New Jersey. In the former, municipalities by virtue of the contract may decide the kind of personnel service that they require and at any time may remove themselves from the civil service provisions. On the other hand, they must pay for the personnel services performed, whereas New Jersey's municipalities receive personnel assistance without any charge. In California, ten small cities have contracted with the Los Angeles County Civil Service Commission which, on a fee basis, charges them for services rendered.[27] The laws of Connecticut, Minnesota, and Alabama also permit contractual relationships of the sort with reasonable reimbursement to the state personnel agency.[28]

The Massachusetts system. Massachusetts civil service law, dating from 1884, entrusts the state civil service commission with the administration of local civil service. In Massachusetts, cities of 100,000 or more in population are required to be under state control. For cities below this number the option system of New Jersey prevails. State administration of local civil service is open to the general charge that it ignores the needs of the municipalities.[29]

---

26 S. H. Friedelbaum, *Municipal Government in New Jersey* (New Brunswick, New Jersey: Rutgers University Press, 1954), p. 48.

27 Public Administration Service, *op. cit.*, p. 4.

28 *National Municipal Yearbook for 1954,* p. 161.

29 G. C. S. Benson, *The Administration of Civil Service in Massachusetts* (Cambridge, Massachusetts: Harvard University Press, 1935), pp. 1-2.

In a valuable study of the Massachusetts plan, Professor Benson concluded that the state agency, by assuming a policeman's role, tended to ignore the positive aspects of personnel administration. An elaborate system of employee protection against removal was developed, but programs for the modernization of recruitment and examination techniques, a more adequate transfer system and, above all, more effective use of state-wide eligibility lists, one of the really important advantages of a state personnel system, languished on the vine.[30]

The Michigan Demonstration Project. One of the most interesting experiments, which also avoids some of the pitfalls of state administration of local civil service, is the Michigan demonstration project. Begun in 1935 under the auspices of the Michigan Municipal League, it demonstrated that the problem of supplying small cities with technical assistance for their merit systems was not insurmountable. Moreover, it was carried out without the assistance of the state civil service system. The project began in 1935 when four cities ranging in population from 50,000 to 150,000 were selected for the program. The Municipal Personnel Service, an affiliate of the League, provided, on a cost basis, the cities with all the technical functions needed in connection with their personnel programs.[31] Since it began, four other Michigan cities have joined the plan. The plan has great value for the small cities. Since only twenty-two states have civil service systems, it is obvious that many cities, particularly the smaller ones, can obtain the benefits of technical personnel assistance from a similar arrangement.

PERSONNEL ORGANIZATION AND MANAGEMENT

In American cities, indeed in the states and the nation, the civil service commission of three or more members is still the most popular form of personnel organization. A total of 714 cities with over 10,000 in population have civil service boards or commissions. Three-member boards are most common, although a number of cities have five-men bodies. In 18 cities, city civil service commissions range in size from two to nine members.[32]

The reasons for the multi-headed instead of the single-headed personnel agency are partly historical and partly administrative.

[30] *Ibid.*, pp. xii, 66, 73-74, 78.
[31] *Personnel Programs for Smaller Cities*, pp. 6-10.
[32] *The Municipal Yearbook for 1954*, p. 176.

The board type organization is a product of the era which gave rise to it. Its accent was on reform. To prevent the predatory politician from using municipal offices as his own private bailiwick, it was considered necessary to detach the personnel function from the administrative process by establishing an independent body whose task was to supervise the hiring and the dismissal of personnel. At the same time to prevent one party from gaining control of the personnel function and subverting its purpose, provision was made for the board to be bipartisan in composition. Reflecting the optimism which gave rise to civil service reform, it was hoped that one party through either publicity or protest would act as a check upon the other. In this way the integrity of the personnel process would be assured.

From an administrative standpoint, there was also a measure of justification in the use of the board type of organization. In its administration, the commission issued rules and regulations which were later the subject of hearings and appeals. Adjudication of disputes between administrator and employee was facilitated by a collective rather than an individual decision. Moreover, the overlapping of terms of office in the interest of checking the administrator also provided an element of continuity that would not be present if a single head of the personnel agency were in control.

A twentieth century example of a personnel function organized on this basis is the city of Dearborn, approximately sixty thousand in population. A three-member board, appointed by the mayor, is vested with full responsibility for the operation of the personnel function. Its powers include the administration of recruitment, the classification plan, the service rating system and other technical functions as well as the hearing of appeals and the investigation of the operation of the personnel system. A chief examiner is given authority only to the extent that the commission deems necessary.[33]

Needless to say, the hopes of reformers have withstood the passage of time rather well. There were some "deals," but on the whole the spoils system was placed on the defensive. A general recognition of the merit principle was obtained. But once these gains have been recorded, the question that persists is this: Does the change in administrative climate justify a change in the role of the personnel agency? On the answer to this question hinge the organization and location of the personnel function.

---

33 *Personnel Programs for Smaller Cities*, pp. 7-8.

If the assumption is made that the merit principle has achieved recognition, and of course this will vary from city to city, then the objective of the personnel program is to facilitate work performance. The personnel agency can no longer afford to stand aloof from the stream of administration. It must act as an aid to management at all levels of municipality. Acceptance of this view means that the traditional organization of the civil service agency would yield to the needs of administration. Responsibility for the personnel function would be fixed. In practice this would mean, then, that the collegiate body would be supplanted by a single director. In a personnel agency headed by a director, the municipal chief executive and departmental heads could get advice and assistance on all matters affecting personnel and work performance.

The logic of this approach has not permeated the thinking of many municipal officials for the simple reason that many of them are not too sanguine about the progress of the merit principle in their cities. Where this uncertainty exists—and it seems all too evident—the change in the role and function of the personnel agency has been approached gingerly. The widespread reliance upon the board type of personnel administration has already been noted. In the council-manager cities, however, there has been a general disposition to accept the more modern view of personnel management. In the city of Tacoma, Washington, the charter provides for a personnel director who is appointed by the city manager and a civil service advisory board with adjudicative powers. In both Toledo and Cincinnati a halfway mark in cooperation has been achieved. The personnel officer functions in the areas of training and employee motivation, where the civil service commissions are not empowered to act.

It can be concluded, therefore, that the organization and location of the personnel function in the administrative hierarchy are determined primarily by its objective. If its purpose is to police the personnel process, then it will lie outside of the chain of command. However, if it is to facilitate work performance, it will need to be incorporated within the administrative process.

THE PERSONNEL PROCESS

The personnel agency in the city is primarily a service unit. It assists the operating units on the basic aspects of personnel administration: position classification, salary and wage administration, recruitment and selection, promotion and service rating systems, employee relations and retirement. In theory, at least, these functions can be performed by the operating departments. In practice, however, it is considered more desirable for reasons of efficiency and specialization to centralize these activities within a single personnel agency.

Position-classification. The keystone in the arch of personnel administration is the position-classification plan. It is of fundamental importance because almost all the other aspects of personnel depend upon it. If properly prepared, a position-classification plan will form the basis of a salary and wage plan based upon the principle of equal pay for equal work. If the jobs are properly described, they will serve as an index of the duties and qualifications of prospective applicants. Tests can be more effectively constructed. Position classification is also the basis of promotion. Finally, a position classification plan furnishes a catalogue description of uniform jobs that can be utilized by operating units for the statement of their personnel needs to both the central personnel agency and the budget division.[34]

What is position-classification? The basic principle underlying the plan is classification; that is, the grouping together of like items on the basis of similar characteristics. These are then identified by a definition and a class description.[35] Just as a supermarket arranges similar food items such as a canned food section, so in personnel *similar positions are grouped together.* A position in personnel "is composed of assignments of work, delegations of accompanying responsibilities by competent authority, requiring the services of one employee." [36] The duties and responsibilities determine the position.

To classify positions, it is necessary to determine beforehand the basis of the classification. Positions are usually grouped on three bases: the kind of work, the level of difficulty and responsibility and the qualifications required. Those positions with substantially similar duties and responsibilities are grouped together under a descriptive class or title. A class is ". . . a group of positions . . . sufficiently similar in respect to the duties, responsibilities and authority thereof, that

[34] I. Baruch, *Facts and Fallacies About Position Classification* (mimeographed, undated), p. 1.

[35] U. S. Civil Service Commission, "Classification in a Nutshell" (Washington, D. C.: U. S. Government Printing Office, July 1951), p. 3.

[36] Baruch, *op. cit.*, p. 3.

the same descriptive title may be used with clarity to designate each position allocated to the class . . ." [37]

Thus the kind of work determines the "class." Hence city clerks who perform one kind of work are a "class." City engineers who are engaged in different kind of work are also a "class." Each class, therefore, performs a similar kind of work and each differs from others in that they carry on a different kind of work. Within each grouping, however, positions will be functionally related and are subject to further classification on the basis of the level and difficulty of the work required. Some jobs will be routine in nature; others will be more responsible. Clerks on the basis of this criterion will be graded into junior clerks, senior clerks, principal clerks and chief clerks. Once this is done, then it becomes obvious that similar jobs will require substantially the same skills and different positions will require different capabilities. Once positions are defined and classes are established they will be the same regardless of the unit in which they are located. Thus a chief clerk, whether in the city's police, fire, or public works department, will have the same duties and responsibilities.[38]

The work of preparing a position classification plan is extremely complex. It involves extensive research. A detailed analysis of each occupational grouping is required and usually ascertained through a standardized questionnaire. The data so gathered are then verified through conferences with supervisors and "desk audits" that observe a representative sample of employees actually performing their daily tasks. Then, as indicated above, positions are grouped as to their level of responsibility and difficulty. A title, the official designation of a class, is determined. Finally, detailed class specifications are written up.[39]

It is obvious that the formulation of a position classification plan requires the services of highly skilled technicians. The small city and the large one are faced with a similar problem in this respect. Indeed, the small city, because of the widespread presence of the generalist who is required to perform a multitude of tasks, has more difficulty in the installation of a position classification plan since the jobs do not easily fall into an easily recognizable pattern. In the large city

---

37 I. Baruch, *Position Classification in the Public Service* (Chicago: Civil Service Assembly, 1941), p. 45.

38 U. S. Civil Service Commission, *op. cit.*, pp. 4-5.

39 *Personnel Programs for Smaller Cities*, pp. 11-15.

jurisdiction, position-classification is the responsibility of a central personnel agency. The smaller jurisdiction, however, must depend upon either the state personnel agency or the type of service rendered by the Michigan demonstration project.

Classification plans must not only be developed but also must be kept up to date. Duties and responsibilities change from time to time for a variety of reasons. Unless changes are made as required, inequities will result. A classic example of the failure of a classification plan to keep pace with changing conditions is contained in a report on the city of New York by the Mayor's Committee on Management Services. It was found after a survey that the duties and responsibilities in the overwhelming number of instances did not conform with the actual work of the individual occupying the position. Indeed, positions had become so divorced from reality that they could not be employed as a means for listing either the personnel or the monetary requirements of many agencies. In some instances, supervisors were paid less than the employees working for them. Suspicion among employees was great, and any attempt to bring positions into line with what was actually being done by the employees was fought by employee organizations. The report concluded with an indictment of the municipal civil service commission. "It treats the classification function as if it were one finger on its left hand." [40]

Salary and wage administration. The success of any personnel program depends very largely upon its ability to recruit and retain competent personnel. This is especially true in the field of municipal personnel administration where a failure to observe this principle invariably means a low level of performance. This has become especially important in an era of expanding municipal functions because municipal governments are forced to compete with private industry for the available manpower.

The quality of people attracted depends greatly upon the incentives offered. In this respect the municipality has many weapons in its arsenal that enables it to compete effectively with private enterprise. It can offer a greater degree of security, more adequate vacation and pension rights and, generally, better working conditions. If salaries are roughly on par with those of corresponding position

[40] Griffenhagen and Associates, *Classification and Compensation of the Service of the City of New York,* I (New York City, 1951), p. 10.

in private industry it is probable that the municipality will find itself in a favorable competitive position.

In the final analysis, a successful personnel program in a municipality will depend upon a judicious mixture of the above factors with an effective compensation plan. It is in this connection that the advantages of an effective pay plan become evident. While it perhaps cannot offer the high salaries of private employment, it can at least offer comparable compensation and relate it to the degree and level of work performed. It can make certain that those positions with similar duties and responsibilities will receive similar pay. "A pay plan may be defined as a plan . . . by which pay scales are specified for each class of positions . . . a pay plan serves to fix the salary for each class, for each position, and the pay for each employee at any given time." [41]

What then should be the objectives of an effective pay plan? Most authorities are agreed that for all levels of government, federal, state and city, three principles should be observed: (1) levels of compensation comparable to those of private industry; (2) rates of pay sufficiently high to attract competent people; and (3) "equal pay for equal work." A compensation scheme must embody all three if it is to be successful.[42]

Here again it must be emphasized that the construction of a pay plan is a challenge to most municipalities, regardless of size, for its formulation is an exceedingly complex process.[43] The constituent elements that form the basis of a pay plan involve a wide variety of social, economic, fiscal and administrative factors. Employees must be paid a decent wage or they will either leave public employment or remain disgruntled on the job, with a resultant lowering of the level of work performance. Hence it is necessary for the personnel agency to determine the cost of living, the wage level of comparable positions in private industry, and the relative level of training and experience required for the various positions in the pay plan. Once this is accomplished, it is the function of the governing body to balance these factors against the fiscal abilities of the municipality and the long range objectives sought. The city council, of course, must act on the basis of data and recommendations of the personnel

41 Baruch, *op. cit.*, p. 11.

42 *Personnel Programs for Smaller Cities*, p. 18.

43 See generally Civil Service Assembly of the United States and Canada, *Classification and Compensation Plans, Their Development, Adoption and Administration*, Technical Bulletin no. 1 (Washington, D. C., November 1928).

agency. Finally, it is the function of the personnel agency to assign salaries and ranges of compensation to the various positions upon the basis of legislative policy.

Salary data are gathered through questionnaires. Private employees and officials of other governmental jurisdictions are polled on a representative basis. Salary scales for positions and classes of positions are developed. Vacation, pensions and other fringe benefits are related to compensation in order to determine the real wage of employees. These data furnish the basis of legislative, and later, administrative decision.[44]

Like classification, the construction of a pay plan places a heavy burden on the personnel agency. Yet it is an exceedingly important aspect of public employment. Glaring deficiencies between public and private employment and between individuals performing the same kind of work within the municipal service are potential threats to the morale of the city employee.

Recruitment and selection. Civil service, from its early reform beginnings, has always insisted that appointments should be made on a merit basis. This has laid great stress on the examining process. However, if the personnel program is to succeed, it must do more than this. It must not only examine the candidates who apply but it must also endeavor to attract highly qualified candidates. Recruitment is a necessary precondition for successful selection. If neglected it will make a mockery of the competitive process.

In both of these phases, the personnel agency is assisted materially by both position classification and pay plans. The operating agency can state its personnel needs in terms of standardized positions that will be understood by the personnel office. Classification and compensation also will determine the type of people required and the salary that can be offered to attract prospective candidates for the available positions. Moreover, on the basis of the job descriptions the personnel agency can more readily construct the examination that will test the capabilities of potential employees.

Recruitment, to borrow a phrase from J. Donald Kingsley, is the "quest for competence." [45] It may be defined as the concerted effort of a personnel agency to elicit the widest possible interest in

---

44 *Personnel Program for Smaller Cities,* pp. 18-20.

45 J. D. Kingsley, "Recruitment—the Quest for Competence, *Public Personnel Review,* II (1941), p. 28. Also by the same author, *Recruiting Applicants for the Public Service* (Chicago: Civil Service Assembly, 1942).

vacancies that exist in the public service. If the procedure is carefully employed, it will make competition a reality; but if carelessly or routinely conducted, it will reduce selection to a process of merely weeding out the unfit from those that apply.

In its quest for the most competent people, municipal personnel agencies face many obstacles. There is, first of all, the almost universal practice of making local residence an eligibility requirement. In most instances this means that cities are limited to the talents and abilities of the persons within its jurisdiction. Obviously the larger the city the greater the choice, and correspondingly, the smaller the city the larger the handicap. Again opportunities for advancement vary in accordance with the size of the city. Only the largest of cities enable the individual to make public employment a career. Consequently, municipal personnel agencies find it difficult to interest those who want to grow on the job. In practice again, recruitment may be restricted to those persons with limited horizons. Finally, in many instances, lack of adequate appropriations hinders municipal personnel agencies in the maintenance of current rosters of eligible candidates. This often serves as excuse for an operating official to insist upon making a provisional or temporary appointment. Where this condition exists recruitment is conducted by the operating official rather than by the personnel agency. A condition of this sort often gives the free wheeling operator a chance to gain relative freedom from the merit process.

But even with the presence of these difficulties, it is evident that much more could be done. The normal recruitment procedure employed is singularly unimaginative. It is limited largely to the posting of routine examination announcements in public buildings, to newspaper advertisements, to publicity in civil service publications and sometimes as in the case of New York City, to radio coverage. Very little of a positive recruitment program exists. Some jurisdictions—California, New Jersey and New York—use a mailing procedure to contact the membership of professional organizations. The California State Personnel Board has a program that has much to commend it. It maintains a list of all persons who have evinced an interest in the public service. When an examination is to be given, it notifies by postcard all who have made an inquiry.[46] The

[46] O. G. Stahl, *Public Personnel Administration* (4th ed., New York: Harper and Brothers, 1956), p. 73.

value of such a system, however, depends upon whether those interested are actually qualified for the vacancy that exists.

It would seem necessary in view of what is at stake with more than a million persons in municipal employ to assign at least one full-time person to poll the community resources in sufficient detail so that a thorough search has been made of those who conceivably would want to work for the city. Then, and only then, can a positive recruitment program be undertaken. Needless to say present efforts fall far short of this mark. It may, of course, be asserted that a plan of this sort is not feasible for small cities. Yet the smaller jurisdictions have been able to recruit competent city managers, and moreover, as we have shown, they may be able to draw upon the resources of personnel agencies outside of their own jurisdiction. Full-time recruitment is in need of a more positive approach.

Selection is both a pre-entry and post-entry process. Initially it consists of a written examination designed to test the competence of individuals to perform the duties of the position to be filled. Usually this is a short answer test since it provides ease of scoring. It is, however, a technical task to construct a test of this sort. This is then supplemented by an oral interview, a character investigation and a medical examination. Following certification and appointment, the successful candidate must undergo a probationary period, during which time his performance on the job is evaluated with a view toward determining his ultimate retention in the service. In Dearborn, Saginaw and Kalamazoo the "working-test period" is six months.[47]

Although much progress has been made, the process of recruitment and selection on the municipal level is still in its infancy. Only 403 cities out of 1,064 with a population of more than 10,000 have entrance tests for all groups of employees. Approximately one third use promotional examinations. Local governments are finding it exceedingly difficult to recruit professionally trained college graduates. When one differentiates on the basis of size, the disparity between the two kinds of jurisdictions becomes even more noticeable. Sixty-two percent of the cities over 50,000 in population use entrance examinations, but only a quarter of the smaller units use this method of selecting their personnel.

Again, as we have noted previously, the smaller jurisdiction is at a decided disadvantage. The latter, even with the best of inten-

[47] *Personnel Programs for Smaller Cities,* pp. 33-34.

tions, simply cannot match the efforts of the larger cities. This again is an argument for the use of outside assistance, either at the county or state levels, or the cooperative activity undertaken by the Michigan demonstration project.

Service ratings and promotions. It is in the rating of personnel on the job that the supervisor and the administrator enter directly into the personnel process. It is their judgment, subject to review for uniformity by the central personnel agency, that determines the advancement and progress of employees.

Promotion is one of the most important and yet one of the most baffling aspects of personnel administration. One of the reasons why an employee is attracted to a job is the possibility of advancement. If the opportunity does not materialize, the morale of the employee either may be lowered or his work performance may suffer. Moreover, if an employee is sufficiently discouraged, he may leave the service. In either event, the service of the city will suffer. Finally, if a high turnover in personnel exists, the city's investment in the training of the individual will be lost and the loss of ambitious people will leave a residual corps of routine and dissatisfied employees. The city's loss will be someone else's gain.

Promotion is a testing and rating process. It may be carried out on an open competitive basis, that is, an examination for which those on the inside and those on the outside of the service will compete; or it may be limited to those already employed by the city in the lower echelons. The former has the undoubted merit of bringing new blood into the city service, but when employment in a city is fairly stable and opportunities to get ahead are few and far between, it may hurt morale since the few vacancies that do occur will be actively sought by those who consider themselves in line for promotion.

It would seem, therefore, that unless conditions of employment are fairly fluid, promotion from within is the most logical policy to pursue. But here one comes face to face with the matter of rating performance.[48] Should seniority be employed as the criterion? Should it be performance on the job as rated by the supervisor? Should examinations be employed? Should the growth capacity of the employee be taken into account? No final answer to these questions can be

48 See generally, American Management Association, *Rating and Training Executives and Employees* (New York, 1946).

given, although it is safe to say that almost all of these enter into the final judgment that results in promotion.

In the city of Detroit, five groups of traits, totaling 35 traits of employees, are rated. Only the fifth group covers supervisory and administrative personnel. Employees are rated by supervisors on the basis of three characteristics, poor, satisfactory and above average. The Detroit Municipal Civil Service Commission takes action on recommendations for promotion after a consideration of the supervisor's evaluation of the employee's efficiency.[49]

Competitive examinations are frequently used for promotion purposes in municipal jurisdictions. They are valuable because they dull the charge that favoritism plays an important part in gaining advancement. However, they do suffer from one important limitation. They may be used only where the vacancies to be filled are numerous and routine. In promotion to positions that involve a large amount of discretion, an approach of this kind depends very heavily on the validity of the test employed. As yet no device for the measurement of human judgment has been developed.[50] Until this void has been filled, reliance will have to be placed upon the decision of the supervisor and administrator.

Employee relations. Trade unionism, now a commonplace feature of private employment, is also fast becoming an aspect of public employment. Originally in the cities, because of the limited scope of their governmental function and the rather widespread subordination of governmental employment to the needs of the party, the employee organization took root rather slowly. At the turn of the century, employee organizations were restricted largely to police and firemen benevolent associations, although there were in a few instances some aggressive teachers' unions. Gradually however, employee groups began to proliferate and assume a wider base. In 1918, the International Association of Fire Fighters, one of the most successful of the public unions, affiliated with the American Federation of Labor. During the New Deal, the stepped-up organizing drive of American labor found a ready sounding board among public employees. Units too numerous to mention came into being. Some were affiliated with organized labor and others had a purely local character. Prominent among these were the State County and

[49] W. G. Torpey, *Public Personnel Management* (New York: D. Van Nostrand Co., Inc., 1953), p. 209.

[50] Stahl, *op. cit.*, pp. 149-159.

Municipal Employees (AFL), and the State, County and Municipal Workers of America (CIO), founded in 1936 and 1937 respectively. The Detroit Municipal Employees' Club and the New York Civil Service Forum are organizations that have a more local interest.

Today, it is evident that these organizations are now a permanent part of the employment pattern at the municipal level and, as such, are a factor that municipal supervisors and administrators must accept as a reality. Employee organizations are found in all of the eighteen cities over 500,000 in population, and in all but ten of the cities of 50,000 in size. Approximately 95 percent of the cities of more than 50,000 and 58 percent of those under that size have one or more organizations of local employees. Overall, of the 1347 cities with more than 10,000 people, 874 had employees in one or more of the following organizations: American Federation of State County and Municipal Employees (AFL); Government and Civic Employees Organizing Committee (CIO); and the International Association of Fire Fighters (AFL). At the end of 1953 the AFL had locals in 60 cities composed entirely of police officers.[51]

The tremendous increase in the number of municipal functions, their shift from a regulatory to a service nature, and the growth of the merit system have posed the problem of the relationship of municipal employees to their government.[52] Employees have come to recognize the advantages of organization for the furtherance of their interests. The issues raised with respect to trade unionism in government employment are twofold in nature: (1) the degree to which employees should have the right to organize and (2) the extent to which public employees should be accorded the privileges now enjoyed by trade unions outside of the government.

The right of public employees to organize is somewhat uncertain, being dependent largely upon whether organization and the strike are considered natural concomitants of one another. In the federal government it is clear from the passage of the Lloyd-La Follette Act of 1912 that federal employees have the freedom to organize into a union of their own choice. Practice on the municipal level, however, is not uniform. Police and other protective services are usually considered a special class of employees who cannot join unions. In

[51] *Municipal Yearbook for 1954,* pp. 181-182.

[52] See generally, Civil Service Assembly, *Employee Relations in the Public Service* (Chicago, 1942). This is still the most important study in the field. Another valuable publication is S. D. Spero, *The Government as Employer* (New York: The Remsen Press, 1948).

Omaha, Nebraska, and Portland, Oregon, employees are forbidden to join unions that require their membership to go on strike, although presumably if unions do not have a strike clause, the prohibition is qualified. San Antonio and Dallas, Texas go even further and forbid employees to join any labor organization.

On the other hand, Hartford, Connecticut; Louisville, Kentucky; Lansing, Michigan; Cincinnati, Ohio; and Philadelphia freely grant employees the right to organize. The courts in many states have held that, in the absence of a statutory prohibition to the contrary, employees have the right to join unions. Contrariwise, if statutes or ordinances deny the right, the courts have not felt that this was an impairment of a constitutional right of freedom of association.[53]

The right of public employees to strike has been outlawed in both legislative and administrative practice, although this does not mean that strikes have not taken place. Almost everyone is familiar with the Boston Police strike of 1919. Indeed, over a long period, about 1100 strikes have occurred, of which, surprisingly enough, 66 were undertaken by police and firemen.[54] Legal prohibitions to the contrary, as Professor Spero has asserted, "It is clear that no mere denial of the right to strike will of itself prevent strikes if workers regard their grievances sufficiently great to assume the risks." [55]

But even though it is certain that the right to strike may be denied to public employees, there is still considerable controversy with respect to the entire matter. In support of the view that the right to strike should be denied to public employees, H. Eliot Kaplan, former director of the National Civil Service League, has argued that the right of the public is paramount. Services essential to the safety and welfare of the community, he asserted, cannot be halted by employees who find themselves in disagreement with their supervisors no matter how arbitrary the latter may have been. "No employee has the right to interfere with the orderly conduct of public affairs or to interrupt the public services without the people's consent." [56] In other words, unless the right to strike has been granted by statute or ordinance, it does not exist.

---

[53] City of New York, Department of Labor, *The Right of Public Employees to Organize—in Theory and Practice* (New York City, March 1955, multilithed), pp. 3-16.

[54] D. Ziskind, *One Thousand Strikes of Government Employees* (New York: Columbia University Press, 1940), p. 3.

[55] S. Spero, "Have Employees the Right to Strike? Maybe," *National Municipal Review,* XXX (1941), p. 528.

[56] H. E. Kaplan, "Have Employees the Right to Strike? No," *National Municipal Review,* XXX (1940), p. 520.

A contrary position also exists. Roger Baldwin, former director of the American Civil Liberties Union, has taken a stand in favor of the right to strike. That strikes may have catastrophic consequences he regards as being beside the point, for action of this sort by both public and private employees may have similar effects. Employees of privately owned public utilities, he has pointed out, have the right to strike and disastrous results for the community may ensue. Yet their right to strike has not been curbed. By analogy, similar privileges should be extended to employees of publicly owned utilities. Probing a bit deeper, Baldwin has argued that the strikes are not against the government but rather are directed against the arbitrary power exerted by both politicians and administrators. Unions, in his view, have the right to counteract such action.[57]

In the middle in this controversy is Professor Spero, who recognizes the dangers involved in the acceptance of the position that employees cannot strike. He feels, however, that the majority of governmental functions are comparable to those on the outside. Only law enforcement is dissimilar and it covers only a relative handful of municipal employees. Moreover, although strikes of government employees have taken place, there "is not a single organization composed entirely of government employees which has a strike policy."[58] As he views it, what is at issue is not so much the policy of labor organizations among government workers as it is the danger to the free labor movement. With government steadily assuming more functions, the spread of the no-strike policy into areas that were formerly considered private tends to handicap the ability of labor to express its demands.[59]

Regardless of the merits involved in these arguments, it is clear that legislative and administrative practice has outlawed the right to strike. Union constitutions of public employees, too, have waived this right. Nevertheless, there is still the need for some channel through which employees can express themselves. Everyone is in agreement that employees should have the privilege to negotiate with administrators on matters of pay and conditions of work. Who shall deal with public employee organizations, and to what extent are such agreements binding upon the municipality? In New York

---

57 R. Baldwin, "Have Employees the Right to Strike? Yes," *National Municipal Review*, XXX (1941), p. 517. Baldwin, however, would deny the right to police and fire department personnel.

58 Spero, *op. cit.*, p. 526.

59 *Ibid.*, pp. 528, 551.

City, the power to deal with wages and other conditions of work is distributed among the mayor, the board of estimate, the council and the municipal civil service commission.[60] In Philadelphia negotiations on behalf of the mayor are undertaken by the personnel director and the city administrator. A similar arrangement exists in Louisville, Kentucky.[61]

In practice, the power of labor organizations and employee groups has resulted in a surprising amount of freedom in their dealings with municipal governments. Negotiations range from discussions of compensation and work conditions to actual agreements with employee representatives. Unilateral statements of policy have been issued by cities after consultation with the union. In other instances, bilateral agreements between municipalities and employee organizations are so wide in scope as to represent an innovation in the labor practices of city governments.

A lack of data prevents one from ascertaining how representative these arrangements are, but a few illustrations will serve to indicate how far some municipalities have gone in meeting the demands of their employees. Fairmount, West Virginia not only recognized the union as the sole collective bargaining agent but also required union membership as a condition of employment. Elective officers, police and firemen, department heads and temporary employees were the only exceptions made. Newcastle, Indiana, in 1938 introduced a maintenance of membership clause in its labor relations policy for its employees. Alexandria, Louisiana in 1941 concluded one of the most comprehensive collective bargaining agreements with its work force. Individual agreements were made, covering engineering, street, park and sewer, health, sanitation, light, water and gas employees. The union was accepted as the sole bargaining agent, and wages were conceded as a legitimate subject of negotiation with the city. Machinery for the handling of grievances was established, and almost every aspect of employment was included. The agreement, however, was subject to the provision that any of its provisions were null and void if they came into conflict with either statute or law.[62] Even such a large city as Philadelphia has recognized the District

---

[60] City of New York, Department of Labor, *Government as Employer in the Collective Bargaining Process* (New York City, October 1955), pp. 4-10.

[61] *Idem.*

[62] M. R. Godine, *The Labor Problem in the Public Service* (Cambridge: Harvard University Press, 1951), pp. 243-244. All of the examples cited were taken from these pages.

Council of the State County and Municipal Employee (AFL) as the bargaining agent for city employees.[63]

The present status of city-employee labor relations can briefly be summed up in this fashion. Some cities allow employees to present their demands to administrators, but act in a unilateral fashion by issuing a memorandum on labor policy. Others merely provide grievance machinery for the handling of disputes. Finally, some municipalities have actually bargained collectively with employees to the point where agreements include maintenance of membership, the closed shop, and a recognition that wages and conditions of work are legitimate subjects of negotiation.[64]

In view of the paucity of data, one hesitates to suggest what this portends for the future. The status of employee-government relations at the municipal level is most certainly in a state of flux. It is probable that the conclusion drawn by Professor Spero in a study that he made ten years ago is still valid today. "Fundamentally," he wrote, "these problems (labor relations) are a phase of the perennial conflict between authority and liberty in a free society. The issue admits of no final solution but only of making relations which leave intact the basic claims of each party." [65]

Retirement. This is also a basic aspect of personnel administration. For the employee simple justice demands that he be given the expectation of income during his nonproductive years following the terminal point of his employment. For the government there can be no profit in having superannuated employees remaining in their jobs beyond their period of usefulness, producing at a lowered level of efficiency and blocking others from advancement.

Like employee organizations, the development of retirement systems was gradual. The earliest retirement system was that covering policemen in the city of New York a century ago in 1857. Cleveland, Dayton, Detroit, Philadelphia and Akron thereafter broadened the coverage to include firemen as well. By 1915 developments had progressed to the point where Philadelphia, Pittsburgh and Scranton had included all of their employees in a retirement system.[66] In 1953

[63] City of New York, Department of Labor, *op. cit.*, pp. 23-24.

[64] Godine, *op. cit.*, pp. 244-245.

[65] Spero, *op. cit.*, p. 487. See also R. B. Posey, "Union Agreements in Municipal Employment," *Public Management*, XXX (1948), pp. 35-40. "It behooves the municipal executive to become acquainted with union aims and methods if the power of employee organization is to be used constructively."

[66] Torpey, *op. cit.*, pp. 346-347.

a total of 1,262 cities over 10,000 in population had pension plans covering some or all of their employees. Ninety-four percent of these cities covered their entire work force.[67] However, it is estimated that approximately one million local employees have no coverage whatsoever.[68] In recent years an effort has been made to include more employees. Agreements by forty-three states under the Social Security Act have been concluded. In general, the trend in retirement systems has been toward either state-administered local plans or federal social security.

Systems of retirement administration have developed slowly. The early systems were financed solely from employee contributions. Later the principle of joint responsibility of the employee and government gained increasing acceptance. Retirement plans are also classified as either cash disbursement or actuarial reserve plans. In the former, the contribution of the employee is made part of the income of the government. When the employee is retired, his pension is then made part of the cost of government. In the latter, money is paid into a fund on an actuarially determined basis which is then managed in the interest of the employees. Payments for pension benefits are then made from the fund.

In general, pension plans suffer from inadequacy of coverage. Most are designed to provide retirement benefits, often in extremely modest amounts. Disability and survivors' insurance, except in the case of police and firemen, are rarely part of the coverage, although affiliation with the social security system will do much to remedy this lack. Furthermore, there is no adequate provision for transfer of pension credits between public and private employment, unless employees of the municipality are again a part of the social security scheme. Finally, annuities do not take into account the rise in the cost of living. A pension that was considered adequate, calculated upon the basis of living standards when an employee entered municipal employ some thirty years ago, is most certainly deficient in terms of present day conditions.

Retirement systems are of mutual benefit to both employees and the government. Recognition of this viewpoint is slowly gaining acceptance, but until it becomes a common everyday practice, the interests of both will suffer.

---

67 *Municipal Yearbook for 1954,* pp. 181-182.
68 Torpey, *op. cit.,* p. 348.

CONCLUSION

"Governments," William Penn is reputed to have remarked, "are like clocks. They go by the motion that men give them." It is this cardinal point, that men give "motion" to government, that is the basic part of enlightened personnel administration. It is in the realm of motivation and incentive of people that a real challenge exists. To spur people to the outward limits of their potential is a task that seems to concern too few municipal administrators. Yet it is only in this way that the end product of group activity, governmental performance, can be heightened.

It is the human equation, in short, that is the foundation of all personnel management, whether in private enterprise or the government. It is evident from the preceding pages that a realization of this point is slowly, but certainly, seeping into the municipal consciousness. Much progress has been made but much more has to be done. Writing several years ago, an authority on personnel administration listed the following areas in which further advances must be made: (1) recruitment particularly for the higher and more important positions; (2) training of administrative personnel; (3) a definition of the areas of collective bargaining; (4) the shift in the functions of the personnel agency from policing to service; (5) a sounder pay plan; and finally (6) a greater effort to increase the prestige of the government service.[69]

In the final analysis, sound administration depends very largely upon the quality of the staff attracted to the public service and the extent to which their talents and capabilities are enlisted in the support of desirable governmental objectives.

BIBLIOGRAPHY

Books:

Benson, G. C. S. *The Administration of the Civil Service in Massachusetts.* Cambridge, Massachusetts: Harvard University Press, 1935.

Foulke, W. D. *Fighting the Spoilmen.* New York: G. P. Putnam's Sons, 1919.

International City Managers' Association, *Municipal Personnel Administration.* Chicago: 1942. 3rd edition.

Public Administration Service, *Personnel Programs for Smaller Cities.* Chicago, 1940.

---

[69] J. M. Mitchell, "Problems of Personnel Administration," *Public Management,* XXX (1948), pp. 322-323.

Stahl, O. G. *Public Personnel Administration.* New York: Harper and Brothers, Publishers, 1956.

Stewart, F. M. *The National Civil Service Reform League.* Austin, Texas: The University of Texas Press, 1929.

Urwick, L. *The Elements of Administration.* New York: Harper and Brothers, Publishers, 1943.

Articles and Other Materials:

Appley, L. A. "Organization for Personnel Administration," *Public Personnel Review,* III (1942), 100-102.

Baldwin, R. "Have Employees the Right to Strike?—Yes," *National Municipal Review,* XXX (1941), 515-517.

Kaplan, H. E. "Have Employees the Right to Strike?—No," *National Municipal Review,* XXX (1941), 518-523.

Spero, S. "Have Public Employees the Right to Strike?—Maybe," *National Municipal Review,* XXX (1941), 524-528.

CHAPTER NINETEEN

Administrative Management and the City

THE MEANING OF ADMINISTRATION

Administrative principles and city government. All cities in varying degrees apply administrative principles to achieve desired governmental objectives. The extent to which they do so depends largely on the forms of government employed by them. As we have noted in a previous chapter, the weak-mayor form fails to concentrate executive direction in the hands of a single individual. Instead it is divided among council committees, the mayor, a large number of elected officials, and a wide variety of boards and commissions. In commission government, too, executive power is shared by five councilmen who serve in a dual capacity as both legislators and heads of departments. (See Chapter 8.) The existence of these varieties of executive pluralism, based as they were on the faulty premise that the people would have a greater voice in their government, had a debilitating effect upon the administrative process. The history of such governments is marked by their failure to develop sound management practices.

The gradual acceptance of the idea of integrated executive power, influenced to a considerable degree by the success of the business corporation, set the stage for many advances in administration within the modern city. Power was concentrated in the hands of a strong mayor or a council-manager. Appointment and removal of department heads, control over budgets and personnel, and other attributes of management were vested in a single executive. The strong mayor was made responsible to the voters and the municipal manager was held accountable for his actions by a popularly elected council. In both cases, power and responsibility were commensurate with one another. In municipalities with integrated executive power, neither the mayor nor the manager could blame others for the improper administration of city affairs. They, and they alone, were answerable for their conduct of office. The centralization of executive authority, in other words, is a necessary precondition for the application of administrative techniques. It is no wonder that most authorities are agreed that cities with the strong executive—mayor or manager—are equipped to give their citizens better government.

The nature of the administrative process. Administration is found wherever the objective sought enlists the energies and capabilities of more than one person. It may exist where there is a relatively simple task as the removal of a building that stands in the way of a public improvement. It may be at the basis of the sale of goods and services in order to gain a profit. It is present where a governmental objective, such as health or welfare, is being pursued. In all of these and many other endeavors, there is a common objective, the mobilization of men, materials, and money—the three m's—to obtain a desired goal. How these elements are interrelated to function in a unified fashion is the heart of the administrative process. In this respect municipal management does not differ, save in objective, from any other form of group activity.

This seems to be a fairly simple concept and yet the process of administration is fairly complex. To understand it more fully, it is necessary to make at least a minimal venture into the realm of administrative theory and practice. It is necessary to remember constantly that administration is a social process in which all members of the group are functionally related to each other in such a fashion that, though they differ in talents and interests, they act as one. Several steps are needed if individuals are to be coordinated. First, the purpose of the activity must be clearly stated and defined. If a long-range objective is sought, then it is conceivable that sub-purposes will have to be developed. Second, principles of work division are needed in order that a logical arrangement may be obtained. Third, there must be a structure of authority to compel adherence to the desired goal. Finally, there must be channels of communication that transmit directions and commands to the work force in order that the purposes of the organization are clearly understood by all who have a share in the common enterprise. In brief, as Urwick has put it, administration is a social process. The aim "pursued by all concerned in the administration of each group is an objective enlisting the interest of the group as a whole, and consistent with the interest of groups of which it is a part. . . ." [1]

[1] L. Urwick, *The Elements of Administration* (New York: Harper and Bros., 1943), p. 8.

Politics and administration. Administration of public activity, as Professor White has defined it, *"consists of all those operations having for their purposes the fulfilment or enforcement of public policy."* [2] Inherent in this definition is a fundamental dichotomy that has characterized American thinking on administrative matters; politics and administration.[3] The former, the choice of goals and objectives, was regarded as the province of the legislative branch of government. The latter consisted of all those processes by which the defined objective was to be carried out. It was assumed, in other words, that the two processes could be differentiated.

Yet the distinction, developed approximately a half-century ago by Goodnow, gradually broke down under the stresses and strains that modern society has imposed upon government. For one thing, questions that presented themselves for decision were exceedingly technical in nature. The legislative branch, composed of generalists, could only lay down the broad policy lines which were filled in by specialists. Moreover, even the formulation of policy guides was dependent to an increasing degree upon the technical information largely in the hands of the administrative branch. It was always a question of whether those who supplied the information or those who acted upon it, actually made the final policy decision.

Again, since many of the service and regulatory functions undertaken by the government were by their very nature experimental and in many cases could not be foreseen by the legislature, the tendency was to delegate broad powers to the administrative branch to insure reasonable flexibility to meet changing conditions. Finally, the very fact that administration was a continuous process, and the further fact that the legislature met for only a part of the year, prompted further delegation to the executive-administrative branch.

In brief, the traditional separation of power into its legislative and administrative phases was no longer applicable. This was evident at the national level where the powers of the President, through rule making and administrative direction, were increased immeasurably. It was also present, though in a lesser degree, in the growth of the strong-mayor and council manager forms of government. It

[2] L. White, *Introduction to the Study of Public Administration,* (4th ed.; New York: The Macmillan Co., 1955), p. 1.

[3] Professor White is aware of the fact that the distinction is no longer clear cut. See generally F. J. Goodnow, *Politics and Administration* (New York: The Macmillan Co., 1900).

was clear, in other words, that policy making occurred on both the legislative and administrative sides of government.

Today administration is regarded as involving both politics and processes. "These are two sides of the same coin. . . ." [4] As a process it is concerned with the internal aspects of administration, that is, how the administrative machine functions. In the political sense, administration has a program that is subject to the constant scrutiny by the organized public and the legislature. The administrator must function in "the social environment outside of his agency that affects or is capable of affecting its operations." [5] While this quotation applies primarily to the national government, it has equal validity for the mayor and manager. Without public support, no administrative program can be a success.

Administration, in the final analysis, may be considered as being concerned with the life cycle of a governmental organism. People of diverse talents and interests are related to one another in such a fashion that the many function as one. Just as the human body consists of many finely divided and highly specialized cells that maintain the life and purpose of the individual, so administration seeks to gear individuals of varying abilities for unified governmental effort. In either case, dysfunction in the individual or the governmental organism may result in the destruction of organic unity.

CHANGES IN THE CONCEPT OF ADMINISTRATION

Rudimentary beginnings. In earlier pages it has been indicated that the functions of government at the municipal level were originally undifferentiated. The council was the legatee of all powers vested in the municipal corporation. Gradually, however, a differentiation of functions began to develop. The press of business and the need for specialization even on a rudimentary level resulted in the separation of the judicial function from the council. Lay justices, termed justices of the peace, began to appear. Soon complexities of legal relationships brought a further blossoming of the judicial function. The lawyer-judge appeared on the scene and the lay judge gradually faded until he became a rarity. While this development first took place on the higher levels, federal and state, it also seeped down to the municipality.

---

[4] H. Stein, editor, *Public Administration and Policy Development* (New York: Harcourt, Brace and Company, 1952), p. xii.

[5] *Ibid.*, p. xv.

The popular check on administrative power. Within the council, rudimentary specialization began with the appearance of council committees, each charged through its chairman with the responsibility for the administration of a given task. Early in the thirties of the last century the separation of executive power was symbolized by the appearance of the independently elected mayor as the head of the municipality. Thus even before the Civil War period, the gradual division of the powers of the municipality into the three main areas—legislative, executive, and judicial—had occurred.

In the post Civil War period the growth of cities, and the consequent increase in their responsibilities, intensified the process of specialization and differentiation. The powers of the municipal chief executive expanded to the point where he became the recognized head of the municipality, even though he was not always given authority commensurate with his responsibility. At the same time the council sought to maintain its position by creating specialized boards and commissions to handle specific tasks, often on an *ad hoc* basis. The consequent tug and haul arising from the dispersion of power among many agencies of government, many often independently elected, not only caused confusion but also signified the need for a re-evaluation of the process by which people controlled their government.

Initially, the control of government had been accomplished primarily through the annual appropriation, a large number of elective officers, rotation of people in office in response to the demands of the party, and council committee administration of specific functions. In the period after the Civil War the application of these principles threatened to make a mockery of the democratic process at the municipal level. A spoils system based upon the theory that governmental duties were obviously simple could not apply in an era that demanded of the city the performance of police, fire, sewage, sanitation and health functions. Specialists were needed. If they were to be obtained and their skills successfully utilized, it was necessary that they be given a reasonable measure of tenure and independence. It is not entirely coincidental that the growth of merit systems occurred in the last quarter of the nineteenth century when municipal morality had reached its nadir.

Moreover the process of political checks through the long ballot and the elective office often resulted in a baffled citizenry which had neither the knowledge nor, in many instances, the ability to hold their officials accountable for their administrative performance. The controls, if any, existed in the council, and there the inroads of the boss were such as to make this a mere formality.

A shift in methods of control. Thus in the last quarter of the nineteenth century the stage was set for a re-examination of the control function by which the citizen held his government responsible. Gradually the shift in the direction of the strong-mayor and council-manager forms of government occurred. The rationale underlying these governmental plans was simple. Concentration of authority in relatively few hands would restore political accountability. A clear separation of the legislative and administrative functions would strengthen the council's function of independent criticism. A merit system would insulate the technical staff from the pressures of politics and at the same time would make only a handful of policy making positions subject to election review. A short ballot would enable the voter to scrutinize more carefully the performance of his officials. In short, accountability would be strengthened through the concentration of power rather than its dispersion through many different agencies and boards.

These theories of municipal management were not accepted by all of the cities. Needless to say, their awakening to these factors has been sporadic and uneven. There are all too many municipalities that even in this day and age have lagged far behind in their awareness of the need for the centralization of authority. Indeed, any attempt to strengthen the role of the executive in the administrative process is viewed with suspicion and even hostility. Where the lag still exists, it may be considered a rural survival in an urban age. Comfort, however, may be drawn from the fact that the need for prompt and effective action will compel the laggards to follow the paths already charted by the strong-mayor and council-manager forms of government.

PRINCIPLES OF DEPARTMENTALIZATION

Work division. Whenever the energies of more than one person are involved, work division has to take place. The reasons for this are almost self-evident. Division of work facilitates direction since it gives an individual an understanding of what is required of him. It enables him to specialize in a given task, thus permitting the municipality or the enterprise to gain an advantage that would otherwise be lacking if each employee were a "jack of all trades." Work division is also a recognition of the fact that the sum of human knowledge has grown to the point where it cannot be the province of any one individual. Hence work division reduces the employee's duties to manageable proportions.

Division of work implies the existence of principles upon which it is based. "Work division," wrote Gulick in a brilliant essay, "is the foundation of organization." [6] Work division is the break-up of the whole into the sum of its parts until the point is reached where the full-time activity of one person is involved. Conversely, this fractionalization means that ultimately the parts have to be put back together into a functionally related whole.

Since the work of city government requires the effort of a considerable number of people, it is necessary that the major functions be isolated and organized upon some logical basis. How is this to be done? In most jurisdictions whether federal, state or local, whether public or private, the work is organized upon the basis of a combination of four main principles: major purpose, process, clientele, and place.

Organization by major purpose. When a department is organized on this basis it is virtually self-contained. Within it are all those functions and skills that are necessary for the accomplishment of a particular mission. Thus a public works department in a city would contain statisticians, engineers, maintenance personnel, lawyers, architects, health specialists where garbage and sewage disposal are involved, and indeed anyone who is in any way related to the public works function. In brief, in a department so organized, all related activities essential to its objective are grouped together.[7]

Organization of a department upon the principle of major purpose has many objectives. It, first of all, fixes responsibility, for the very fact that it is so self-contained means that its administrative head cannot blame other departments for his own failures. It facilitates work performance since a department has complete control over its work schedule. If a public works department is engaged in the construction of a public improvement, it does not have to compete with others for the time of a lawyer or an engineer. It has its

[6] L. H. Gulick, "Notes on the Theory of Organization," L. H. Gulick and L. Urwick, editors, *Papers on the Science of Administration* (New York: Institute of Public Administration, 1937), pp. 6-7.

[7] *Ibid.*, pp. 21-22.

own. If its equipment breaks down, it can repair it immediately without having to take its turn at the city garage. Finally, a department concerned with a single major objective finds that it is easier to give both its own personnel and the affected public an understanding of what it seeks to accomplish.

A self-contained department, however, does have certain marked disadvantages. Integration has its limitations. Specialization of personnel is often hindered. The department of public works may want to have control over its design functions by the employment of engineers and, indeed, may have good reasons for doing so, but if there is an insufficient volume of work, there is a tendency to saddle them with other tasks. Skilled engineers often find that the inspection of buildings and other duties are assigned to them in order to keep them busy. The grouping of engineers in one department would permit specialization that is noticeably absent in a major purpose department. Moreover, if all departments were so organized, there would be the ever present danger of duplication since all will contain engineers. Finally, though self-sufficiency may give a department a feeling of independence, it is this very factor that may make it unresponsive to the general public.

Organization by process. The desire to gain the advantage of specialization often dictates the structuring of departments on a process basis. All skills concerning a particular specialty are grouped together. An engineering department will contain all the engineers employed by the city. A public health department possesses all health personnel. Central service functions such as accounting, budgeting and personnel are other groupings of specialists. The assumption is that such departments will act as service departments when and where their skills are needed by other departments.[8]

The grouping of similar skills and the grant to them of departmental status often foster high morale. It allows people to specialize and grow on the job, and it contains the assurance that their interests and skills will not be subordinated, as indeed might well be the case in a major purpose department. However, a process department also has its limitations. The very fact that people of similar interests are grouped together often insulates them from the main stream of administration. They tend to think primarily in terms of techniques and means, how a given task is to be carried out. They are

[8] *Ibid.*, pp. 23-24.

less concerned with ends. This often brings them into conflict with operating heads. A hard-driving operator desiring to implement his program as rapidly as possible often finds it difficult to comprehend the relative slowness of a process department in meeting his needs. Since administration consists of interrelated functions, the failure of a process department to service adequately the operator's program may jeopardize a much needed result. Finally, specialization, that is, the breakdown of functions upon the basis of skill groups, almost inevitably poses a difficult problem in coordination. In the above-mentioned illustration the head of the municipality may find himself in the position where he is the constant referee between purpose and process departments. Coordination is usually brought about by giving the former a greater measure of control over the services that he requires to achieve his objectives.

Organization by clientele. The multiplicity of governmental services has led to an attempt to simplify the relationships between the citizen and his government. This is achieved by the creation of departments on the basis of the group served. A veterans' department, an old-age division within a welfare department, or even, in a sense, education is organized on this principle.[9]

The advantages of this principle of organization are inherent in the purpose underlying its creation. In popular terms it may be described as a "one stop" service. It provides the citizen with a single place where he can transact his business. A veteran, for example, may find in a veterans' division all activities related to him, whether it be health, education, or pensions. A welfare client can deal with the same department on matters of relief budget, pensions, rehabilitation, and even re-employment. The values of simplicity and convenience, however, are largely canceled by its drawbacks. Unless there is an enormous volume of business, specialization cannot be readily obtained. Personnel who become skilled in many tasks cannot become well-versed in any one. Constant dealing with specific groups, moreover, tends to make such departments more susceptible to their pressures. It is not often that one finds city departments organized on this basis.

Organization by area. Distance and space cause a utilization of this principle. Whenever the functions of government cannot be performed at a central point, necessity dictates the decentralization

[9] *Ibid.*, pp. 25-26.

of functions to the level where it comes into contact with those who are affected by a given governmental activity. Nationally, the country is divided into at least three levels—national, state, and local. Within the states, the cities in their governmental capacity act as administrative agents of the state. In the city, if it is fairly large in area, administrative activity is divided between a central headquarters and field offices.[10] In New York City the welfare functions are carried on through a central office and local offices in each of the boroughs. In most cities the police and fire departments are decentralized on a precinct and fire district basis.

Necessity rather than advantage dictates the use of this principle. It is in many instances the only way in which the function of government can be administered. A fire house is located in a neighborhood because it facilitates the movement of equipment to the scene of the fire. A police precinct enables the patrolmen to get to know the character of the neighborhood more readily. Decentralization, in addition, allows greater conformance to the needs of the locality. However, here again one is brought face to face with several disabilities. There is the difficulty of establishing uniformity of treatment among the various decentralized areas. Also posed is the general problem of what functions should be performed centrally and what should be carried on locally. Supervision of the work force at some distance from the center of authority also becomes progressively more complex. The tendency to conform with local attitudes often operates to frustrate the central purpose of the organization.

From what has been said it is obvious that there is no simple formula for the grouping of governmental activities on a departmental basis. Each organization principle has its value and its limitation. Each must be applied as the situation and circumstance warrant. "The problem of organization," wrote Professor Gulick, "thus becomes the problem of building up between the executive at the center and the subdivision of work on the periphery an effective network of communication and control." [11]

In city governments the building of "an effective network of communication and control" is hampered by many factors. In many instances a central executive with power to make decisions does not even exist. Even where it does, the problem of organization is com-

[10] *Ibid.*, p. 29.

[11] *Ibid.*, p. 7. As is evident, considerable reliance has been placed on the ideas contained in Professor Gulick's essay.

plicated by the fact that general laws of the state have already specified the many details of structure. These are not subject to change by the municipal executive. The head of a municipality also finds that much of the structure of his departments has already been established by charter. Thus, even where the logic of the situation demands conformance with established organizational principles, continuance of an existing pattern is necessary. One may then well ask whether organizational principles have any value. To this one may reply in the affirmative. They serve as guides to determine what is in terms of what ought to be. As such, they are stimuli to progress and change.

ADMINISTRATIVE PRINCIPLES

Organization then determines the position of the individual in the group and the relationship of the latter to the total administrative endeavor.[12] But this is merely the first step in the administrative process. It is necessary to translate policy into action. To do this it is necessary to establish a network of communication and a system of sanctions in order that the principal administrator, whether mayor or manager, can direct the work of his subordinates.

Direction. Once departments exist, the work of direction begins. The administrator, save in the rare case of an exceedingly small jurisdiction, normally depends upon others to implement his policies. It is necessary therefore to both assign the work and see that it is carried out. The concepts underlying direction are four in number: (1) duties, that is, the obligations assumed by the individual when he becomes a member of the organization; (2) responsibility, that is, holding an individual accountable for the duties assigned to him; (3) power, defined by Urwick as "the ability to get things done; that is to say, it is a function of knowledge, skill and personal qualities"; [13] and (4) authority, that is, sanctions to require the performance of assigned duties. It is this last element that is of utmost importance. It is the cement that welds the organization together in an organic unit. Without it an organization can hardly be said to exist.

If these concepts are kept in mind the executive is then in a position to direct those under him. He cannot expect employees to

[12] Urwick, *op. cit.*, pp. 40-41.
[13] *Ibid.*, pp. 41-42.

perform their duties, nor indeed can he hold them accountable, unless their functions are carefully delineated. He must carefully select his subordinates since their skill and knowledge are expected to enlist the efforts of others. Finally, to make certain that his aims and wishes are being carried out, he must obtain authority usually from statutes and ordinances, to direct the action of others. A portion of his authority must then be delegated to others in the form of directives and orders and these must then be supplemented by a system of rewards and incentives.

Unity of command. It is now commonly agreed that an administrator is responsible for the acts of his subordinates. To achieve this adherence and to bind others to the executive, the application of other administrative principles are required. There must be a unity of command. All orders must come from a single source, since it is obvious that no man can have more than one master. The use of committees and boards or commissions violates this principle, although such agencies are a commonplace feature of many municipalities.

From the principal administrator downward at each governmental level there must be a point of authority and decision. At each level, authority given must be commensurate with assigned responsibility. Thus, at each stage of the administrative hierarchy responsibility and authority are fixed, and the entire organization is bound together in a chain of command. Increasingly, as one ascends the hierarchy, authority is concentrated into fewer and fewer hands until one reaches the top of the pyramid. This structure of power gives the executive reasonable assurance the orders issued by him will be carried out. If not, then he is able to ascertain quickly who has failed to observe his commands. The existence of a properly organized department in a municipality is a guarantee that only the most important decisions will come to the department head and the principal administrator.

Delegation. Since the principal executive is dependent primarily on others for the performance of work assignments, it is necessary for him to delegate a portion of his authority to others. This must be done in such a fashion that he does not lose ultimate control. An executive who fails to delegate authority subjects himself to the danger of overwork and preoccupation with detail. On the other hand, if he delegates completely he may abdicate his authority completely. Delegation is usually made in the form of directives, work assignments and follow-ups to insure performance.

Span of control. In his supervisory role the executive is governed by another administrative principle, the span of control. In fact it is because of this that the executive is compelled to delegate a portion of his work load to others. Span of control is a concept that has sprung from a recognition of the psychological limitations to an individual's span of attention. There is, in other words, a limit to the number of individuals that can be supervised by most persons. The normal rule that is followed to indicate the boundaries is this; no man can supervise fewer than three or more than seven persons. Of course, where the work is routine, as in a clerical function, many more can be supervised than where an assignment is complex. In the latter instance it is obvious that others will need to be employed to widen the executive's span of control. In most municipalities the number of persons supervised generally ranges from 10 to 23. Observance of the principle of span of control dictates both the numbers of departments and their size.

Line and staff. If, however, the supervisory span of the individual administrator is limited, it is necessary that he be given additional assistance. Here again administrative theory has pointed out a solution. A distinction is made between line and staff. The former may be roughly defined as the doing functions and the latter may be considered as the thinking and advisory activities. In municipal government, an administrative assistant to a city manager or mayor, a budget officer, or a director of planning performs staff functions. A police or fire department engages in line or operating activities. Staff assistance, properly employed, can widen the span of attention of the administrator. The executive, after a review of his work load, can determine his need for staff services. However, when this is done, "work, not authority, should be passed on to the assistant." [14]

Organization of the administrative structure is the foundation of administrative action. Command or direction superimposed upon the structure makes the administrative organism a living reality. Although the principles noted above may seem remote from the everyday life of a municipality, they are actually the hard, cold facts of an administrator's daily existence.

---

[14] O. F. Nolting, *Management Methods In City Government* (Chicago: The International City Managers' Association, 1942), p. 5.

THE FUNCTIONS OF THE EXECUTIVE

Planning. The activities of the municipal executive have been described in various ways. Orin Nolting, writing about the city manager, although his words have application to all city executives, said that the duties of the executive "are to organize, to plan, to direct, to coordinate, to control and to represent the administration in contacts with the council, with the outside agencies and with the public." [15] In a similar vein, Professor Gulick summarized the functions of the executive by the use of the mnemonic device of POSDCORB, that is, planning, organization, direction, coordinating, reporting, and budgeting. Henri Fayol, the great administrative theorist, identified five main elements of administration as planning, organization, command, coordination and control. There seems to be common agreement among all authorities that, regardless of the level on which the executive operates, he must pursue all of these activities. He must plan the enterprise, furnish it with an objective, give it direction, and finally, hold himself accountable to his many publics, the council, and those affected by the exercise of his authority.

Reference has already been made to *organization* and *direction.* A previous chapter was devoted to *personnel administration* or, as Professor Gulick prefers to call it, staffing. It is now necessary to fill in the rest of the picture with special reference to the administration of municipal activities. Planning is basically a predictive process. It is briefly the application of foresight to the problems of administration. Through planning the municipal executive seeks to peer into the future on the basis of trends derived from investigation of present-day problems. Data are also needed to predict the probable consequences of administrative action and for the formulation of policies for the guidance of both the council and the administrative branch. "Research is basic to planning and planning is basic to administration and management." [16]

In every municipality planning has at least two main facets. It is concerned with the physical growth of the city and its consequences for the future of the community. It is related to the purposes and policies of the administrative organism and as such it is classified as administrative planning. Physical planning, sometimes

---

[15] *Ibid.,* p. 1.
[16] Nolting, *op. cit.,* p. 37.

called city planning, deals very largely with the formulation of community objectives in the light of a vast body of economic and social data on the life of the city. Studies are made of land use, population growth, employment, commercial and industrial activity, transit, building construction, municipal income and a host of other factors related to the city as an economic entity. These are embodied into what is called a master plan which, in essence, is a guide to the long-range planning of the city government.

When implemented, the master plan will result in the crystallization of policies by the municipal government. Capital improvements of the city with respect to its buildings and streets may be programmed in the light of municipal income and need. New York City, for example, programs its capital expenditures over a period of six years with a revision each year in the light of changes. Population and land use may dictate a change in housing, zoning and traffic ordinances. Employment and industrial activity may confront the administrator and city fathers with decisions that will determine whether the city will be primarily industrial, commercial, or residential. Housing trends may indicate areas of urban blight and pose the general question of urban renewal through either federal or state assistance. In brief, the growth of the city as an economic entity has a large bearing on the policies formulated by both the municipal council and its executive.[17]

No municipal executive, mayor or manager, can afford to ignore these long-range trends in the evolution of his municipality. The statement of long-range community objectives, while based upon scientific appraisal, require constant modification in the light of changing conditions. Policies that form the basis of council action must be developed. Priorities must be placed on various projects in the light of relative need and the income ability of the community. If a debt limit is reached, the city may well have to choose between the airport and a school, a street improvement or a firehouse. Once the council has acted, the timing of the various projects will have to be specified. In all of these activities the data gathered by the master plan supplemented by special studies assist the municipal executive in the performance of his duties.

Planning is not the sole province of the planning agency. It occurs at all levels of government and is a continuous process in

[17] International City Managers' Association, *The Technique of Administration* (Chicago, 1945), pp. 303-340.

which virtually every employee participates to some degree. While ultimate decisions are made by the council, the basis of much of the administrative action originates with the executive and his subordinates. Each operating department is brought into daily contact with the immediate problems which concern their area of assigned responsibility. A health department with its control over vital statistics may discover and ascertain the reasons for the existence of communicable diseases. It may study the situation and may make recommendations that call for further action by the executive and the council. A police department in its control of traffic may suggest changes in signal systems. A public works department in its maintenance of the streets may find that some types of road materials are better than others. An infinite number of possibilities for planning exist at the level of the operating department. If departmental heads are worth their salt and are given latitude for independent action, they will do much of the preliminary planning that will also serve as the basis of recommendations made by the municipal executive to the council.

Program review. Administrative planning, while it takes place daily, reaches a high pitch of intensity when the budget is being prepared. Each year the municipal executive must present to the council a statement of his monetary requirements during the ensuing year together with an accounting of the money previously entrusted to his care. Department heads, bound to the municipal executive in the chain of command, find that their policies and actions in turn are subjected to executive scrutiny. The occasion furnishes the opportunity for a thoroughgoing review of administrative activity.

Each department, as it translates its work plan into monetary terms, is faced with the need to examine its operations. When its preliminary thinking reaches the municipal executive, it is subjected to further review. The budget officer may make administrative studies to determine whether economies can be made. He may give the executive an evaluation of departmental effort. The personnel officer may also advise the administrator on personnel matters. The finance officer may assist in the development of financial data relating to the capacity of the municipality to pay for services. The administrative assistant may help by making independent studies as required by the executive. All in all, the fact that the activities of the department are subject to appraisal leads to a tightening of the administrative machine.

Administrative planning, in brief, is concerned with the financial needs of the administrative machine. It is obvious that the process described above will apply in only those municipalities that have a strong municipal executive. Where he is absent, administrative planning, if it takes place at all, is on a rudimentary level.

The executive and council. The municipal executive is dependent upon the council for both money and policies. He may request money. He may propose policies and indeed because of his possession of information he may have a marked effect upon council action. In the final analysis, however, it is the council that provides the framework within which he must operate. Success in administration therefore is largely dependent upon the relationship that is established between the executive and the council.[18]

It is in this area that one must distinguish carefully between the elected and appointed municipal executive. The mayor is the political as well as the administrative head of the city. As political head he is often armed with powers to influence council action which are not possessed by the appointed head. He has the power of appointment subject to council approval, he has the veto and often has removal power. Before a council decision has been made, he can appeal to the public for support of his position. However, after the council has acted, he is required to carry out its policies. Nonetheless, it is possible for an elected executive, who is sincerely convinced of the correctness of his point of view, to seek the election at a later date of a council that is more amenable to his point of view.

The appointed executive, however, does not have the same leeway in administrative direction. He is an agent of the council, and his continuance in office depends upon their good will. Most of the duties and responsibilities of the manager are a matter of legal definition. The council cannot interfere with his administration, but, on the other hand, the manager must be in accord with the council's policies or he must resign from office.

Beyond this, the allocation of duties between the two branches is a matter largely of developing an understanding of how the manager will function. The administrative duties of the manager with respect to the council may be summarized in the following fashion: (1) he has the responsibility for keeping the council informed on all matters concerned with the affairs of the municipality; (2) he

18 T. H. Reed, *Municipal Management* (New York: McGraw-Hill Book Co., Inc., 1941), ch. 5.

may either prepare or review the agenda of council meetings; (3) he has the right to attend council meetings; and (4) he has the sole responsibility for executing the policies laid down by the council. The manager, unlike his political counterpart, cannot afford to be in public disagreement with the council. The relationship of the manager with the council, apart from the legal relationship, is not easily described. The personal equation looms large and each manager has to work out a solution of his own.

The executive and his department heads. Leadership is a compound of many factors, the ability to deal effectively with individuals and groups, and the courage to take and defend positions. The basic prerequisite is that the administrator who leads must know where he is going. It is necessary, in other words, that he establish the objectives and constantly remind himself and others of their existence.[19]

In a small city the process of leadership is relatively less complex than in the larger jurisdiction. The municipal executive can get "through" to his employees through direct supervision. Through discussion of work assignments and through the innumerable daily contacts, a framework of understanding between the executive and his subordinates can be developed. The latter soon learn to appreciate the problems of the executive and he, in turn, can infuse them with a constant desire to improve their work. Relationships are personal and the executive's personal qualities are felt immediately by the employees.

In the medium and larger-sized city, however, where the number of employees range in excess of fifty, relationships become more indirect and impersonal. Leadership becomes an infinitely more complex process. The municipal executive finds that he must rely upon others to translate his wishes "down the line" to the employees. It is here that the doctrine of delegation of authority enters the picture, for it is the extent to which the executive can gain the support of his administrators that determines the success of his leadership.

It is not surprising, therefore, to find that in well-run cities a major part of the executive's time is devoted to dealing with department heads.[20] To enlist the energies of their principal assistants, most executives employ the rule of thumb best described in the

[19] H. G. Pope, "The City Manager As A Leader in the Administrative Organization," *Public Management,* XXX (1941), p. 295.
[20] Nolting, *op. cit.,* p. 2.

phrase of the personnel technician, "wide latitude for independent judgment." Department heads are given authority to make decisions on matters of settled policy. Only important changes are referred to the "top." They are encouraged to think and plan and to submit their recommendations for advice and decision. Their participation is enlisted in every phase of municipal activity.

But leadership is more than this. It consists of a recognition that department heads have defined levels of authority and responsibility. Normally these administrative relationships are reduced to writing so that each individual will know his position in the hierarchy. This practice takes the form of administrative codes and manuals. The former embody the major structure of the organization, the functions and duties of the principal administrators and officers, and the essentials of the more important procedures governing the municipality. When promulgated by the council, they become the chief source of administrative authority.[21] The administrative manuals are much more detailed and are intended primarily for the rank and file employees. Procedures common to all departments such as personnel, purchasing, and accounting are described. The practices of a single department are often published by a departmental head.

There is a distinct value that is gained from the employment of administrative codes and manuals. No one is under any illusion as to the source of authority. Indoctrination of new employees and the direction of old employees are facilitated since both devices can serve as guides for training them in the duties of their positions. Employees can gain an understanding of their relationship to the total enterprise by a careful reading of the manual and the code. Finally, written rules and orders supply continuity to the administrative organization. Employees may come and go, but the procedures remain.

Leadership also involves coordination. The interrelationship of the parts to the whole requires constant attention. Orin Nolting, in his discussion of the best administrative practices in cities, furnishes a graphic illustration of this phase of administrative leadership. The fire department, he points out, has the primary task of fighting fires. But this in turn is dependent upon the existence of an adequate water supply which is the responsibility of the water department. Accessibility of hydrants and adequate water pressure are

---

[21] Nolting, *op. cit.*, p. 25. Cincinnati, New York City and Wheeling, West Virginia, are a few of the cities that have administrative codes.

needed for effective fire fighting. Getting to the scene of the fire requires the action of the police department which must clear traffic for the passage of the fire equipment. Police work must be combined with an adequate signal lighting system and this is the concern of the public works department. In case of injury, ambulances are needed. These may be operated by the police or fire departments or by a city hospital department.

Fire prevention is a function of the fire department, but the structure of buildings may also be the province of the building inspector. Arson investigation is a concern of the fire department, but it also involves cooperation with the police department. The latter may also be brought into the picture where false alarms require the enforcement of city ordinances.[22] The coordination of these many activities and, above all, the inculcation of an overall point of view are the responsibility of leadership. The devices employed by the executive include staff meetings, administrative reports, interviews with department heads and a system of reports that endeavor to see that the wishes of the administrator are being carried out.

Finally, leadership involves equity in personnel transactions. No executive can afford to neglect the principle of equity in the handling of personnel transactions. Matters of training, promotion, and pay must be handled intelligently. The executive who is frank and fair in dealing with his departmental heads can demand that they pursue a similar attitude toward their employees.

The municipal administrator and the public. In a democratic society public officials are accountable for their actions while in office. The steady concentration of power into the hands of a single administrator has made him the object of the public's attention. For them he is the personification of governmental authority, and whether he likes it or not, he is forced to provide guidance and leadership to the community.

The two principal administrators, mayor and manager, though selected differently, nevertheless have an almost identical responsibility to the people. Both are dependent upon the public for the continued support of their programs. Both are faced with the same necessity to elicit public response. However, the mayor, since he is the political as well as the administrative head, has considerably more leeway in dealing with the public. He is not an agent of the

---

[22] Nolting, *op. cit.*, p. 15.

council, although of necessity he must cooperate with it. He need not avoid controversial issues. Indeed, he may even thrive on such situations. The manager, on the other hand, faces a much more delicate situation. He must minister to the wishes of the council and yet at the same time he cannot neglect the general public. He must tread carefully between the council and the people in order not to destroy the delicate relationships that exist between himself and the governing body.

But these differences aside, the handling of public relations follows a similar pattern. Both executives must be accessible to the public. Both must maintain the "open door" to the citizen who has a problem that requires solution. But to say this is not to imply that everyone who wishes to see the executive should have the opportunity to do so. To permit this to take place would mean that the executive would have little or no time to direct the affairs of the municipality. Careful use of the administrative structure and personnel permits both service to the citizen and the saving of executive time.

The principle that is usually observed is that the executive will see only those who cannot be reasonably satisfied by others in the administrative organization. Several measures are employed to accomplish this. The secretary to the executive, by a careful inquiry into the nature of the inquiry, may refer the caller to the appropriate department or agency. An administrative assistant may handle some of the interviews. Some municipalities have a central complaint office where all requests for service are screened carefully and referred to the proper channels. Finally, all executives employ a system of follow ups to make sure that matters which they have not personally handled are handled to the satisfaction of the citizen.[23]

Closely related to the matter of handling specific complaints is the more difficult task of dealing with the general public and with organized groups. Both the mayor and the manager have an obligation to provide leadership to the community by explaining the policies of the government to the council and the public, either in private conversation or by public speeches.[24] But where the mayor has almost complete freedom in these aspects, the role of the city manager is limited by his relationship with the council. There is

[23] Nolting, *op. cit.*, pp. 2-3.

[24] See a good description of the role of the city manager in C. A. Harrell, "The City Manager as a Community Leader," *Public Management*, XXX (1948), pp. 290-294.

common agreement among city managers that they will not speak on matters that have not become settled council policy. Controversial issues are avoided.[25] However, where established policies exist, the manager and the mayor have approximately the same freedom in negotiations to enlist the support of the citizens and the affected public interest groups.[26]

Administrative public relations is at once the most difficult and one of the most time-consuming aspects of administration. An administrator who attempts to gauge public reaction to existing or intended programs embarks upon uncharted seas. Yet he knows full well that a program no matter how well-designed will be still-born unless it receives public support. In the absence of a measurement of public response, he can only hope that his daily contacts with the citizen will build the confidence necessary to help him succeed. Small wonder then that a major part of the time of the administrator is devoted to this very important task.

CONCLUSION

In the last century the powers of city government have expanded enormously in response to the needs of a changing society. Under the stress of interdependent living, areas of activity formerly considered private became the province of the government. Regulatory functions grew rapidly and soon were supplemented by service activities. It is the growth of the administrative apparatus that distinguishes the modern city from the ancient one.

Today the "administrative city" is accepted by almost everyone as an everyday necessity. Hardly anyone is aware that it is the product of the application of rational principles that have been in the process of evolution for almost a century. When the American people were first faced with the prospect of burgeoning urbanism roughly a century ago, there were no guides and precedents to serve them. There was little or no appreciation of the need for an effective organization to meet the needs of the city. The democratic tidal wave that swept the country in the forties of the last century left its mark upon the city. Direct election of officers, rotation in office and the operation of the spoils system were hallmarks of city, as well as national government. The view prevailed that almost anyone could perform the duties of public office and in view of the

[25] Nolting, *op. cit.*, p. 57.
[26] Harrell, *op. cit.*, p. 292.

predominantly rural character of the country, few could controvert this premise.

In the latter half of the nineteenth century, however, conditions of city life soon demonstrated the inherent invalidity of such thinking. There was a need for specialization. The subordination of government to the spoils system and the politician soon made a mockery of the prevailing democratic dogma. Soon government in the city began to reverse its path. A strengthened municipal executive, the rise of the merit system, and a general recognition of the need to concentrate authority for effective action gained increasing acceptance. With these conditions came the rise of the administrative theory that has been described in prior pages. The complex mechanism that is city government became manageable. Efficiency and economy were sought and, to a degree, obtained. Despite the increase in its authority, government in the city was made more accountable and responsive to the wishes of the people.

BIBLIOGRAPHY

Books:

Gulick, L. and Urwick, L. (eds.). *Papers on the Science of Administration.* New York: Institute of Public Administration, 1937.

International City Managers' Association. *The Technique of Municipal Administration.* Chicago, 1949. 2nd edition.

Nolting, O. F. *Management Methods in City Government.* Chicago: International City Managers' Association, 1942.

Reed, T. H. *Municipal Management.* New York: McGraw-Hill Book Co., Inc., 1941.

Articles and Other Material:

Encyclopaedia of the Social Sciences. 1st edition. Volume I. Article. "Administration, Public."

Harrell, C. A. "The City Manager as a Community Leader," *Public Management,* XXX (1930), 290-294.

Pope, H. G. "The City Manager as a leader in Administrative Organization," *Public Management,* XXX (1941), 294-297.

Chapter Twenty

Municipal Police Administration

The Importance of the Police Function

The position of the police in the community. The average citizen is barely aware of the multitudinous concerns of his police force. Squadroom life as portrayed on radio or television may awaken a temporary interest. An accident, a crisis situation, a particularly horrible crime, or even a traffic ticket may arouse a momentary consciousness of the police function. But, in the main, it is limited to the comforting assurance that the police "are there." An appreciation of the key position of the police in the structure of law and order of the community is often lacking.

Yet the police do have a central role in our urban communities. Indeed, it might be said that there is hardly a phase of municipal activity that is left untouched by them. Though primarily concerned with law enforcement, as the years have gone by the police have been saddled with additional responsibilities. Suppression of crime has been followed by crime prevention programs. These, in turn, have led to a wider area of inquiry into the causes of crime.

Regulation of human conduct has been extended to cover a concern for public morals. Police, indeed, have often assumed the role of censors. The coming of motor transport and the emergence of the possibility that the automobile in the hands of the careless or reckless driver might become a lethal weapon brought traffic flow and enforcement as added functions. But the police are not alone in all of these tasks. It is necessary that they constantly cooperate with other municipal agencies with similar areas of concern. Finally, since the very existence of the department depends upon public support, it is in the constant process of interpreting its activities to the community of which it is a part.

Aside from their functions, the role of the police in the community can be measured by the public effort devoted to its support. In October 1955, approximately 200,000 police were employed by the cities making it the nation's largest police force. Urban police constitute 14 percent of the municipal work force and absorb 15 percent of its payroll. Police constitute the largest single *common* municipal function. Only education, among what the Department of Commerce classifies as *variable* municipal functions, with 19 percent of the budget exceeded it in cost, although in terms of numbers of employees, the two were about equal.[1]

The crime rate and the community. Crime statistics, while not as attractive as the headline of the daily newspaper are, nonetheless, an index of what is happening to our society. The sober annual "Uniform Crime Reports" of the FBI reveal a picture and pattern of crime that is truly astounding. Each year since 1950 the number of major crimes has increased. In 1953 the number reached what was then considered an all time high. Yet statistics for the first six months of the succeeding year show a further rise over a comparable period of the previous year.[2] Approximately two million major crimes are committed each year. Murder, rape, robbery, assault, burglary and auto theft are seemingly a common everyday occurrence. Organized crime and rackets flourish. The Senate committee investigating organized crime estimated that twenty billion dollars changed hands yearly as a result of these activities.[3] "Organized crime," it concluded, "today is not limited to any single community or to any single state, but occurs all over the country." [4]

Perhaps the most distressing aspect of this picture is the increasing number of boys and girls who have become delinquents. In the two-year period, 1949–1951, there has been a 20 percent increase in the number of crimes committed by the youthful offender. The stream of children through the nation's juvenile courts has increased from 300,000 in 1948 to 385,000 in 1952. If the present trend continues, the number of juveniles in conflict with the law will have doubled by the year 1960.

The seriousness of the problem is further underlined by the fact that since 1948 a larger number of youths under eighteen years of

[1] U. S. Department of Commerce, Bureau of Census, *City Employment in 1955* (Washington, D. C.: U. S. Government Printing Office, March, 1955), pp. 2-3. A variable function is one that is sometimes carried out by the municipality and at other times by another unit of government. The school district, for example, may be a district larger than the city or it may be coterminous with the city.

[2] *National Municipal Yearbook for 1954,* pp. 423-425. Also, *National Municipal Yearbook for 1955,* p. 404.

[3] U. S. Senate, 82d Cong., 1st Sess., *Special Committee to Investigate Organized Crime in Interstate Commerce, Second Interim Report* (Washington, D. C.: U. S. Government Printing Office, 1951), p. 13.

[4] *Ibid.,* p. 7.

age have been involved in burglaries, robberies, and automobile thefts.[5] In sheer numbers the problem appears to be most acute in our larger metropolitan centers. The tragic waste of human beings and the toll of human suffering are obvious, but often obscured is a fundamental point. The police problem is both a political and social problem that involves the community as well as the police.

The data on crime demonstrate the consequences of a rapidly evolving urban and industrial society. Its product has not been an unmixed blessing. Increased leisure time has given the citizen new chances to improve himself, but it has also exposed him to new temptations. The disappearance of green space has restricted greatly recreational opportunities and has forced the city into new programs. Social disorganization has caused the relaxation of primary controls and a corresponding dependence upon law as an instrument of regulation. The automobile has given the citizen new mobility, but it has also made him rootless. The waves of immigration in response to the needs of the industrial machine have given the city a polyglot character. Group interaction and conflict have caused social tensions of an unheard of magnitude.[6] Rapid flux and change have given the police function new dimensions and added significance.

EVOLUTION OF URBAN POLICE

The problems of urban police are inherent in its evolution. Many of its present-day features are a product of its general development over the years. Hence a brief review of the rise of the urban police system is needed to understand the cross currents that bedevil it today.

Police organization, because it is concerned with the regulation of human behavior, is highly responsive to the changes that take place in society. When relationships are fairly simple the police department is either poorly organized or it does not exist at all. But when relationships become more complex and society more interdependent the police function changes to meet the new situation. In a sense this is a rough sketch of the growth of the municipal police

[5] Senate Judiciary Committee, 83d Cong., 2d Sess., *Juvenile Delinquency*, Report no. 1064 (Washington, D. C.: U. S. Government Printing Office, March 1954), p. 7. Also U. S. Federal Bureau of Investigation, "Uniform Crime Reports for the United States," XXV, no. 2 (1955), p. 111.

[6] For the complexity of the police task see O. W. Wilson, "Progress in Police Administration," *Journal of Criminal Law*, XLII (1951), pp. 141-152.

function. As cities grew in size and number, the police increased the scope of their activities and became highly specialized.

Early beginnings. The police department, as we know it today, is barely a century old. Its beginnings go back even farther to the time when America was predominantly rural. Public protection at that time was of the most rudimentary nature. Law enforcement was in the hands of constables who were vested with rather broad powers. This was supplemented at night by volunteer citizen patrols, popularly termed "the watch." These made the rounds nightly to see that "all was well." The "rattle watch" of New Amsterdam and the "watch and ward" patrol of Boston were fairly common place in the larger towns of the early eighteenth century.[7] In 1704 Philadelphia went even further. The city was divided into 10 precincts each covered by a watch in the charge of a constable.[8]

As the duties imposed upon the citizen became onerous, the character of the watch changed from a volunteer to a paid parttime basis. The conduct of the watch during this period represents one of the tawdriest episodes in American police history. The "watch" became the prey of the spoilsmen. The shiftless and the nondescript migrated to the "watch." Drunkenness, brawling, and abuse of authority were frequent. Small wonder then that it was more often the object of derision rather than respect.

The growth of American cities in the nineteenth century with their increasing complexity of life compelled further changes in police organization. Robbery, murder, and assault were widespread. It was apparent that protection was needed by day as well as at night. To meet this need Boston in 1838 instituted an independent day watch. New York and other large cities soon followed suit. But this did little to improve the effectiveness of the police function. The evils so conspicuous in the night watch were continued during the day. Both forces were impermanent and poorly equipped. Both were often the object of public scorn. Moreover, the fact that the forces were independent of one another lead to rivalry, a lack of coordination and in some cases outright conflict.

Law and order in burgeoning American cities were not being well served by such a haphazard arrangement. Although the mayors of the large cities called attention to these inadequacies, their calls

[7] R. B. Fosdick, *American Police Systems* (New York: The Century Co., 1921), p. 60.

[8] F. J. Goodnow, *City Government in the United States* (New York: The Century Co., 1904), pp. 218-219.

went unheeded. It was a series of wild outbreaks in the major cities during the period 1838–1844 that underlined the urgency of the situation. The riots, touched off by the depression, unemployment, and by the antiforeign sentiment, caused huge damage to life and property. In these disturbances the police showed themselves completely incapable of maintaining law and order. In many instances the militia was called in to assist them.

The growth of a full-time police force. Out of these dramatic circumstances came the first fundamental police reforms. In 1844 the New York legislature, inspired by the Peel Reforms of 1820 in the London Metropolitan Police District, completely reorganized the police function of New York City. Both day and night watches were abolished, and in their stead an eight hundred man police force was established headed by a police chief appointed by the mayor and the governing body.[9] Thereafter, the New York example was widely copied by other cities: Chicago, in 1851; Cincinnati and New Orleans in 1852; Boston and Philadelphia in 1854; and Baltimore and Newark in 1857. The shift to an integrated full-time day and night force marked an historic change in the method for maintaining law and order.

While the step marked an advance, it was by no means a complete solution. As American cities grew, further changes would be needed. The New York experiment was only a beginning and it did not conform completely with the London police model which had inspired it. It is worthwhile to remember, in the light of later developments, the essentials of the English plan. These were: complete professionalization, the centralization of command, and finally, an organization that was paramilitary in character. To attain these goals required a sharp change in the thinking of the people and they were simply not ready for it.

Indeed, America at the mid-point of the last century was still in the throes of finding itself. The democracy of the village had not prepared it for the democracy of the city. The role of politics was not clearly understood and the people of the city had not learned, as yet, how to cope with the problems it faced. This was true of all levels of government and of course the city was no exception. Consequently, the police force suffered from short terms of office, frequent rotation and the persistent intrusion of politics. In such circum-

[9] Fosdick, *op. cit.*, pp. 65-67.

stances, the structure of police authority was undermined. Superiors found their orders defied by the rank and file who owed their appointments to "city hall." In some instances the rank and file attacked their officers. Indicative of the general temper of the police force was their resistance to uniforms which were characterized as, "Un-American," "undemocratic" and the "King's Livery." [10] Indeed, so great was the opposition that uniforms did not become standard until the Civil War.

The increased responsibility of the cities for the maintenance of the law and order was dramatized in the unruly decade before the Civil War. City after city was shaken with increasing disorder. Neighborhood gangs earned reputations for toughness by attacking citizen and police alike, and the latter seemed unable to cope with the situation. New York City furnishes an excellent example of what happened during this period. Gangs with such names as "the Bowery Boys" and the "Dead Rabbits," in a neighborhood called "Five Points," subjected the citizens to a veritable reign of terror without police interference. In 1858 gangs attacked and burned a hospital. By 1856 things had reached such a state of affairs that the New York Tribune was led to remark that "the police seem powerless for good . . ." [11] Other cities found themselves faced with similar conditions. The rising tide of immigration and the growth of neighborhoods threatened to make the situation more serious.

Police boards. As thinking citizens viewed with concern the gradual breakdown in law and order, they cast about for a solution. Control of the police by the city council on the theory that it would protect the citizen against the arbitrary powers of the police, it was evident, was not enough. Moreover, reliance upon the council could not take place at a time when its powers and prestige were on the decline. Finally, since the powers of the executive had not been developed, resort could not be had to him. The dilemma was resolved by the use of boards as administrative agents.

The rationale underlying the use of police boards was fairly simple. Their independence would assure the elimination of politics and result in the consequent increase in efficiency in place of the chaos and incompetence that prevailed. That multiple executives might cause indecision, inaction and avoidance of responsibility was

[10] Fosdick, *op. cit.*, p. 70.
[11] Quoted by Fosdick, *op. cit.*, p. 81.

either unthought of or largely ignored. Starting with the Philadelphia police board in 1850, the movement spread all over the country. Detroit, St. Louis, and Kansas City in 1861, New York in 1853, and Buffalo and Cleveland in 1866, are but a few of the many cities that experimented with the board type of administration. In the period 1850–1870 there was hardly a city that had not tried this experiment.[12]

Indicative of the level of administrative thinking were the method of choice and the composition of the boards. There was no uniform pattern. Some were popularly chosen. Others were selected by the governing body and the mayor. Boards were either bipartisan, partisan or nonpartisan in character. The range of board membership varied from two to a dozen. In some cities they were part of the government and subject to its control. In others they were independent of it. The experience of cities with the multiple executive was not a happy one. It has been ably summarized by Bruce Smith who stated that, under it, police protection "continued to founder in a morass of political uncertainty, intrigue, partisanship and corruption." [13] The strange almost crazy-quilt pattern of organization is mute testimony to the fact that the people in the cities were seeking solutions on an *ad hoc* basis.

The metropolitan police district. Side by side with this came another fundamental line of police development. The sad state of law and order in New York City in the fifties, which has previously been referred to, led to an investigation in 1856 by the state legislature. In the following year, a special act created a metropolitan police district for greater New York. State control of the local police function was vested in a board of police commissioners appointed by the governor. Despite the fact that partisan considerations were also involved in the change, the level of police administration was increased during the thirteen years of state control. In 1870 when control returned once more to the city, the New York Times, commenting on the "Tweed charter," predicted that "an independent police department which has given us a disciplined and uniformed force in place of a vagabond band of ragamuffins will yield obedience to that power which demands free rum and votes, and gives us police

[12] *Ibid.*, pp. 76-77.

[13] B. Smith, *Police Systems in the United States* (New York: Harper and Bros., 1949), pp. 207-208.

justices who regularly set free full half of all the villains the police properly arrest." [14]

The New York example coincided with the era of special legislation that prevailed during the period 1850–1870. In line with the general trend of the time, state after state assumed control of its local police force. Some were motivated by partisan considerations, particularly where a large city was involved. Others were genuinely desirous of cleaning up local conditions that constituted a threat to the life and property of the citizen. But, regardless of the motive, state-controlled local police appeared in Baltimore in 1860 and a year later in St. Louis, Kansas City, and Chicago. Later Detroit in 1865, Cleveland in 1866, New Orleans in 1868, Cincinnati and San Francisco in 1877 were the major cities subjected to state control of their police forces. Boston in 1885 was the last of the large cities to be affected by this trend.

The innovation of state administration of local police has had varying results. Not all of the cities had the happy experience of New York City, although even here the initiation of the new system provoked both discontent and bloodshed. More often the evils associated with special legislation were present in the state reorganization. There was a general lack of responsibility to the municipality. Police costs were rather high since the municipality had no authority to review police expenditures. Spoils and partisanship continued unabated, although it was the state house rather than city hall that benefited. State control only applied to selected cities, usually the larger ones, and was not uniform in its application. There was, as Fosdick has written, "little to choose between the state board and the municipal board." [15]

The growth of home rule, a general plea for local autonomy, was followed by a return to the traditional pattern for local police administration. Today, the vestigial remnants of state control exist in Kansas City and St. Louis, in Boston and Fall River, Massachusetts and in several of the New Hampshire cities.[16] The era of state control was noteworthy in its recognition that the police problem was a concern of more than just one city. In the present period when transportation and communication have made a virtual shambles of polit-

[14] Quoted by Fosdick, *op. cit.*, p. 97.

[15] *Ibid.*, p. 102.

[16] D. E. J. MacNamara, "American Police Administration at Mid-Century," *Public Administration Review*, X (1950), p. 182.

ical jurisdictions, its revival, provided that political traditions permit, may well hold the key to metropolitan police administration.

The growth of the single police executive. The recession in the tide of state control as a result of the general success of the home rule movement and the generally low level of civic morality led to many experiments in city government that were bound to have an important effect upon police organization. The need for more efficiency was highlighted by mass waves of immigration and the general state of lawlessness in most of the American cities. Out of these general trends was born a general belief in the need for more efficient government. Concentration of authority in a central executive as demonstrated by the business world was applied to the municipal executive. Commission government, the strong mayor, and the city manager emerged as administrative heads of the city. A general tightening of the apparatus of municipal direction occurred. The merit system gradually appeared and the police department shared in this development. One-man direction appeared in New York and Detroit in 1901 and it is now the most common form of police organization. The glimmerings of the merit system and professionalization became noticeable. In general, the first halting steps in the direction of improved police protection began at the turn of this century.

From the American police experience of the nineteenth century comes a legacy of attitudes that have had a continuous influence on police administration. Distrust of the police engendered by its excesses and inefficiencies and fostered by the growth of the police as a paramilitary organization led to the insistence upon popular control. Lay administrators with limited knowledge of the police function continue to direct the activities of the police force. The tradition of local responsibility has led to the insistence upon residence as an important qualification for police work. Limited tenure of office for the police administrator continues to a be a feature of our police systems. In general, the proper balance between the expert and the civilian head, a problem common to our government as a whole, has not been developed.

POLICE DEPARTMENT ORGANIZATION

The organization of a police department, like any other form of organization, seeks conformance with established principles of organization. It has a given set of objectives, a "chain of command," and a network of authority and responsibility. Its organization, however, is tailored to meet its specific needs.

The police are daily engaged in the protection of life and property. This entails the performance of three major tasks: law enforcement, traffic regulation and crime prevention. Normally these are carried out through units concerned with patrol, traffic regulation, criminal investigation (detectives), crime prevention and morals regulation. Supporting these are such central services as reports and records, personnel, property management and equipment maintenance. Many of these may be performed by the central units of the municipality. Where the area of the city is large further differentiation of functions occur in the form of field offices popularly called precincts. These police functions may vary in their degree of specialization in accordance with what the municipality can afford or is willing to spend. Fig. 8 gives an overall description of the organization of the department as a whole.

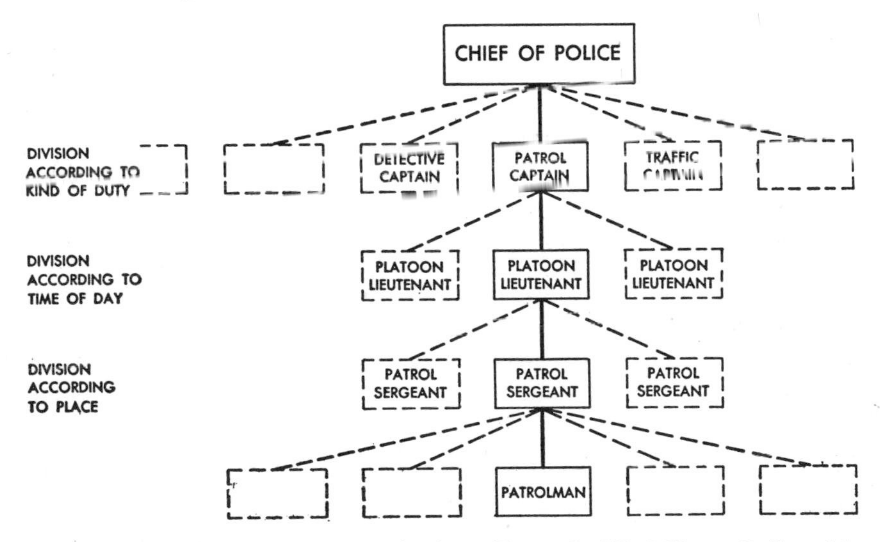

Fig. 8. Police Department Organization. (From O. W. Wilson, *Police Administration,* New York: McGraw-Hill Book Co., Inc., 1950.)

The supervisory structure. The supervisory structure of the police department as a minimum consists of a civilian head and a chief of police. The former is chosen in a variety of ways. In the weak-mayor plans he is usually the chairman of the councilmanic police committee and is designated as commissioner. In the commission governed cities, he is the head of the Department of Public Safety which also includes supervision of the fire function. In the strong-mayor cities, the department is headed by a lay person who is appointed by the mayor and responsible to him for the work of the department. In many council-manager cities, the head of the police force is a professional who reports directly to the manager. In general, in line with tradition the head of the department is a nonprofessional who is political in the sense that he is chosen by some elected officer. There is no discernible trend to leave the direction of the police force in the hands of an official who enjoys tenure during good behavior.

The professional head. Below the political head of the department is the professional police chief who is charged with the actual day-to-day direction of the department in line with the policy framework established by his superior. In a small department of eight men the chief usually is assisted by a lieutenant and a sergeant, the latter being responsible for the activities of the patrol force. As the department grows in size, the problem of supervision becomes greater and the organizational pattern begins to proliferate. In a fairly large department the chief is assisted by two lieutenants, one in charge of records and property the other in control of traffic; and two captains, one with primary responsibility for the patrol and the other charged with the supervision of detectives.

Still larger departments require further organization on an area basis. Captains are placed in charge of precincts and are made responsible to an intermediate level of supervision headed by an inspector. The twenty thousand man department of the city of New York consists of 84 precincts supervised by sixteen divisional inspectors. These precincts in turn are subject to control by deputy divisional inspectors. A chief inspector is responsible for the supervision of the entire field force. The detectives are organized on a similar basis. The levels of supervision and coordination are necessarily complex when one considers the number of men supervised and the area covered.[17]

Criterion of departmental structure. The structure of supervision has been the target of constant criticism by police experts. Distrust of the paramilitary character of police organization with its concomitant control by the lay administrator has led to uncertainty both in direction and control of policies. The average term of office

[17] Smith, *op. cit.*, pp. 235-242.

of the political head today is approximately four years, hardly enough time to gain even a minimal familiarity with the work of the department. Moreover, the very fact that the political head is not an expert often leads him into the error of by-passing the professional head of the department and dealing with the police and detectives as separate units when in fact they ought to be coordinated as one unit.

In many instances, the relationship between the political and professional head of the department has remained unclear and undefined. A strong political head may dominate the department while a weak one may allow the professional head to become the real police administrator. Where the latter occurs, the political control of the department is virtually nonexistent. Finally, the administrative head is seldom provided with the essential tools of administration. Organizational structure is often specified in ordinances; he is not given enough responsibility for planning and execution of departmental programs and he is not generally given the power to choose his subordinates. His staff assistants are not permitted to perform their true role.[18] "It is only when the administrative head has power to designate his deputy or assistant, and to remove him, that the essential administrative relationships are maintained with any consistency." [19]

THE WORK OF THE DEPARTMENT

Police work is concentrated mainly in large cities if one measures its activity by the number of employees on the force. About half of the total police force is found in cities with more than 250 thousand inhabitants.[20] For cities in this category there are about two and one-third police for every thousand of the population while in cities of 50 to 100 thousand class the ratio is one and two-thirds per thousand. Cities with a population of between 25 and 50 thousand have an even smaller proportion per thousand people. Country-wide as of 1954, the police in urban areas average about 1.8 employees per thousand of the population.[21] The average size of the police department for the 87 percent of the cities with less than 25,000 inhabitants is eight men. Ratios for municipalities will vary considerably in

---

18 W. H. Parker, "The Police Challenge in our Great Cities," *The Annals,* CCXCI (1954), pp. 9, 11-12.

19 Smith, *op. cit.,* p. 253.

20 U. S. Department of Commerce, *op. cit.,* p. 7.

21 *National Municipal Yearbook for 1955,* p. 405.

accordance with their size and financial capability. But, regardless of size or need, a major part of police expenditures is absorbed by personnel costs.

Uniformed and nonuniformed forces. The work of the department is carried on by two kinds of personnel; the uniformed and nonuniformed force. The former are popularly called the police and the latter the detectives, although many of the centralized services particularly of a clerical and fiscal nature are also performed by nonuniformed civil servants. The principal work of the department is carried out by the patrol, the unit that the public most often identifies as the police. Indeed, in the small department it is the only police force. It is only as specialization develops that criminal investigation, the function of the detective, appears on the scene. His relationship to the police has been aptly described in somewhat prosaic language, "The uniformed force is the infield and outfield on the home diamond. The detective force gets whatever the crooks bat over the fence." [22] In other words, continuous criminal investigation is carried out by the detectives.

The members of the detective force require a high degree of skill and ability. Generally they are considered the elite of the department, although their qualities on some police forces have often been the subject of criticism. Nonetheless, it is a post that is sought by the ambitious police officer. Detectives usually work in midafternoon and evening, although their tour of duty may be continuous where an important "break" in a case is about to occur. The organization of the detective force usually parallels that of the uniformed police. A small department may have a single detective. A larger one, a chief of detectives and finally, in the very large cities, a detectives' bureau or division headed by a captain and lieutenants is the usual method of organization.

The patrol. The patrol is the basic unit of police administration.[23] It has the principal task of maintaining law and order. Its constant presence in the city, operating as it does on a twenty-four hour, three shift basis, acts as a constant deterrent to crime since it increases the possibility of apprehension of the potential wrongdoer. The "cop on the beat" is a resort of first instance. He makes arrests, resolves minor disputes and constantly functions as the eyes and ears

---

[22] Quoted by Fosdick, *op. cit.*, p. 269.

[23] O. W. Wilson, *Police Administration* (New York: McGraw-Hill Book Co., Inc., 1952), p. 83.

of the department reporting on crime conditions in the neighborhood. These data, when properly employed, become the basis of preventive police action. So important are these functions that the noted police expert, Dean Wilson, feels that the other work of the department should be regarded as merely supplementary to the patrol. Indeed, he argues that other units should be created only when the outer limits of patrol usefulness has been reached.[24]

Originally, patrol was performed by foot police assigned to specified areas in pairs and later, singly, as crime conditions were stabilized and confidence in the ability of the policeman to take care of himself was increased. The justification of the foot patrol was relatively simple. His presence on an assigned beat meant that he could become fairly well-acquainted with the neighborhood and it, in turn, could learn to trust him. In this way a reservoir of mutual confidence could be created. When a dispute occurred, the people could turn to him as the symbol of authority. It was felt that a majority of the disturbances could be handled on the spot with a kind of rough and ready justice. Moreover, his location "on the beat" enabled him to get to the scene of the crime or dispute more readily. Later, in response to societal changes, foot patrols were supplemented by bicycle and horse patrols.

The coming of the motor car and the increased mobility of the people of the city, however, necessitated a drastic revision in patrol practice. The increase in the area of many cities weakened its effectiveness since there was just too much ground to be covered by the man on foot. Moreover, the automobile gave the criminal as well as the citizen greater freedom of movement. To apprehend the criminal required a police force improved to match the greater facility of the criminal to move around the city. Finally, advanced police thinking recognized that the foot patrol exposed the police officer to weather and fatigue.[25]

Since the foot patrol was merely a warning to the potential criminal, it was felt that the prowl car could be just as effective as the man on foot. As a consequence of both the changes in urban society and the theories of police administration, there has been a general shift to the motor patrol, particularly in the suburban cities. The motor patrol has the advantage of surprise. It can get to the scene of the crime just as quickly and it has the added advantage

24 *Idem.*

25 S. R. Schrotel, "Changing Patrol Methods," *The Annals,* CCXCI (1954), pp. 46-48.

that it can transport hospital cases and prisoners more easily.[26] Its effectiveness, however, depends upon the ability of its supporting units, the complaint center, the radio and communications system, and the relative degree of headquarters-field development.

The use of the motor patrol has been brought about at the expense of the foot patrol. The latter now consists of about one-third of the urban police distributed on a three-shift basis. The motor patrol reduces the number of police available because, to a considerable degree, it operates on the basis of practices that were accepted several generations ago. In many cities two men are assigned to a car on the theory that it is necessary for their protection. Except for especially dangerous neighborhoods, this practice has been discarded. Now the thinking is that one man will be more careful. There is a distinct trend now evident to use the one-man patrol car. In 1954, 767 muicipalities used them, either on a day or night basis. Two cities, Kansas City, Missouri and San Antonio, Texas employ them exclusively with a great saving in both man-power and money.[27]

Traffic control. Traffic control is another main function of the uniformed force. Cities are built around their roads. Access to and from the city and movement within it are a prime essential if the city is to exist. Almost from its very inception as an organized force, the police were engaged in traffic regulation. First it was horse-drawn traffic, and later it was motor transit that engaged the efforts of the police department. Today 60 million drivers and 50 million motor vehicles are on the roads. Top speeds of motor cars have increased from 20 to 70 miles per hour. The car in the hands of the careless or reckless driver has become a lethal weapon causing death and destruction of property. Small wonder, then, that traffic control has become a major concern of almost all police forces.

The rise in the number of fatalities in 1935 to 15.9 deaths per hundred million motor vehicle miles of travel and the killing of 40,-000 by automobiles in 1941 underline the herculean task faced by the police department. In its endeavor to reduce the toll of death and injury, it was largely responsible for the creation within many cities of specialized police divisions. Nationwide, the use of such units had the effect of halving the number of fatalities in 1952. It is the general

[26] *Ibid.*, p. 49.
[27] *National Municipal Yearbook for 1955*, pp. 404, 411.

consensus of all police experts that all cities, if they can afford it, can benefit by a specialized traffic division.[28]

The three "E's." In handling traffic, police follow the three "E's," education, enforcement, and engineering. One of the basic tools employed is accident investigation which is common to both enforcement and education. The police are trained to discover the causes of accidents and are required to make reports. Once this data is analyzed, a program of both enforcement and education is undertaken. The police try to educate all community groups who are interested in safety. Schools for the youthful driver are urged as part of their general education. Posters and programs emphasize the terrible toll of human suffering that results from failure to observe established safety rules. In some cities special squads are organized to patrol especially dangerous intersections. Unmarked cars may be used effectively, as was recently demonstrated in New York City.

Enforcement is designed to be strict but as Dean Wilson has remarked it must not "destroy the enforcement tolerance of the community." [29] In 1937 the city of Wichita, Kansas embarked upon an unusual experiment. Its police officers were forbidden to make arrests except for reckless driving or driving while intoxicated. While the program was launched with many misgivings, its results astonished everyone. Both the number of accidents and personal injuries were significantly reduced.[30]

It is obvious that the police cannot handle the entire traffic problem. Safety is a matter of roadway design. Traffic is also a function of land use. Building heights, businesses and multiple residences have a marked effect upon congestion. Street parking will often reduce traffic flow to about one-half of what it would be if parking were forbidden. Parking lots can remove cars from the street and thus improve traffic movement. Aside from stricter enforcement of traffic ordinances and more skilful direction of traffic the police have little or no control over these matters. They must either work with things as they are or seek the assistance of other departments of the city. Roadway design and signals are mainly the province of the public works department. Parking lots and land use are functions of the planning agency. Public cooperation with other municipal

---

[28] F. M. Kreml, "The Specialized Traffic Division," *The Annals,* CCXCI (1954), p. 66.
[29] Wilson, *op. cit.,* p. 159.
[30] *Ibid.,* p. 171.

agencies is a prime necessity. The police traffic personnel must work with the traffic engineers and planning experts and vice versa.[31]

Organized vice control. A primary function of the police department is the control of organized vice. Included in the meaning of this loosely defined term are such activities as the public has condemned as inimical to the welfare of society namely, prostitution, gambling, and illegal traffic in alcohol and narcotics. It is in the regulation of human behavior in these areas that the police face their greatest challenge. Americans seem to desire to regulate everything by law. Some of these are well conceived, but others rest upon the rather easy assumption that a law will readily cure any social ill. Morals legislation, furthermore, often represents a sharp conflict between public and private standards of morality. What the people are willing to put into law is not always what they are ready to observe in their private action. Consequently, the police are bedeviled by badly designed laws and either an uncooperative or an unwilling public.

Control of vice subjects the police to great pressure and temptation. Its enforcement poses a problem that is quite different from the ordinary supression of crime, although its consequences for society are just as great. Robbery and theft are largely an individual or group endeavor. Vice operations, however, are a different matter. The highly lucrative nature of the venture causes it to be organized on what is virtually a commercial basis. Police enforcement finds an enemy that is chameleon-like in character. It constantly changes its shape and form, and is ever present. It has "fronts" and seeks political influence. It buys "protection" by corrupting high and low alike. The difficulties inherent in morals regulation is evident in the daily headlines. Police alliances with vice rings and organized syndicates have occurred in the nation's capital as well as in almost every major city. A recently exposed example is the notorious Phenix City, Alabama. The process of infiltration and the presence of easy money constantly gnaw at the root of society.

Responsibility for the control of vice is vested in a centralized police division, variously called the vice squad, the morals division, or the vice division. Specialization of vice control is justified on the theory that it fixes responsibility and assures continuity of policy direction. All police units are, to some extent, engaged in morals

[31] W. S. Smith, "Widening the Traffic Enforcement," *The Annals,* CCXCI (1954), pp. 76-77.

regulation. The patrol forces handles vice complaints of a minor nature. It makes investigations and reports, and is expected to relieve the vice squad of some of its more onerous details. Only the detective force is relieved of its responsibility in this respect. The reason for this has been stated by Dean Wilson. "When detectives are also charged with the investigation of vice offenses, they either win the enmity of the vice operators and lose these sources of information or they effect an undesirable compromise. Detectives should not be required to prevent the illegal operations of persons from whom they must seek information useful in their investigations." [32]

Aside from the detectives, however, all other police units are expected to work closely with the vice squad. The operations of the latter are generally kept separate in order that "protection" will not go undetected. In its regulation of morals behavior, the vice unit performs several main functions. It is, first of all, concerned with the inspection of licensed establishments, although generally the patrol force is relied upon for preliminary investigation. It gathers information on vice operations through a rather elaborate system of records and reports. It handles complaints and where necessary it conducts raids to discourage and apprehend vice operators.[33]

The administration of vice control by a specialized division has been the subject of considerable criticism. Many argue that the function is one that should be carried out by the uniformed patrol force. Some cities, like Philadelphia, have put this theory into practice by the abolition of the vice division. Others argue that the vice squad is a necessary evil. Regardless of what stand one takes it is evident that the control of vice operations is the principal issue.

Whether performed by the uniformed force or the vice squad, the aim is better enforcement. Yet this is not always easy to obtain. Vice control is regarded as a "dirty business" by all who are engaged in its administration. The sordid aspects of human behavior produce cynicism and despair among those charged with its regulation. It requires a person of firm fiber to deal continuously with "fringe elements" and yet not to sink to their level. Often low pay combined with the constant intervention of "higher-ups" constitute further discouraging factors. Rotation of the work force and drastic reorgan-

---

[32] Wilson, *op. cit.*, p. 191.
[33] *Ibid.*, pp. 192-196.

ization of the vice squad seem to be the only remedies and these are at best temporary palliatives.[34]

In their efforts to deal with organized vice, police frequently are forced to contend with an uncooperative public that is seemingly unaware of the cancerous effects of organized crime upon society. In the minds of the latter, crime is identified with murder, robbery and theft rather than gambling and prostitution. All of the assorted vices of society rest upon its sufferance and if the public will not give the police its support, the work of the latter will be nullified to a large extent. At the most the police can only serve as gadflies for the organized criminal interests. That the path toward effective policing in the area of morals regulation is full of pitfalls has been ably summarized by Albert Deutsch in these words, "The problem of policing vice is inseparable from changing attitudes toward vice. The overhauling of our vice squad is undoubtedly a major issue in modern policing of American communities." [35]

The juvenile delinquent. Not all police activity is concerned with the detection and arrest of criminals. The police are acutely aware of the inherent limitation of these deterrents. They know full well that even the most efficient police force cannot eliminate crime within the community. Hence they are interested in crime prevention as well as law enforcement.

A major part of crime prevention is concerned with the juvenile delinquent. The disappearance of play space, the breakdown of the family under the stress of city life, and the general lack of an outlet for the energies of growing youth are reflected in the vast number of youngsters streaming through our courts. More and more crimes are being committed by the youthful offender. It is becoming increasingly evident that the child of today will be the criminal of tomorrow unless efforts are undertaken to reorient him.[36] To prevent crime necessitates a program that will deal with the juvenile.

That the police have not been too successful in combating juvenile crime is mute testimony to the fact that it is a larger social problem. Its causes are deeply rooted in the community. Of neces-

---

34 See the able discussion of A. Deutsch, *The Trouble With Cops* (New York: Crown Publishers, Inc., 1954, 1955), chs. 6-7.

35 *Ibid.*, p. 93.

36 The Federal Bureau of Investigation reports that in 1954, 63 percent of all robberies, 73 percent of the auto thefts and 55 percent of the larcenies were committed by youngsters under 21 years of age. See U. S. Department of Justice, *Uniform Crime Reports*, XXV, no. 2 (Washington, D. C.: U. S. Government Printing Office, 1955).

sity, corrective action must involve more than the efforts of the police. The police, however, have an important role. In their daily rounds they are the first to discover the evidence of wrongdoing. The presence of the juvenile has a marked effect upon their efforts to combat crime. Moreover, the experience gained by them furnishes them with an opportunity to give the community fruitful guidance on any program for the prevention of delinquency.

The patrol is the foundation of every juvenile program but a recognition of the special nature of the work has led its activities to be supplemented by specialists who seek to deal with the problem on a much wider front. Today almost every city has one or more juvenile officers. New York City with its imposing two hundred-man Juvenile Aid Bureau leads the way. On a smaller scale Los Angeles, Milwaukee, Minneapolis, Kansas City, Philadelphia and Detroit are but a few of the cities that are making a conscientious drive to meet the problem. A study of 611 cities in 1954 showed that 50 percent of the cities had juvenile specialists on their staffs.

In its daily rounds the patrol becomes aware of the breeding grounds of crime. In its enforcement of the law it discovers evidence of wrongdoing. How it handles the matter may have momentous consequences for the future of the delinquent. "That split-second decision by the cop with a child in his custody can make or break a human being." [37] It is here that the juvenile specialist comes into the picture. He can act as a "go between" with the patrol or where necessary, he can refer the child to the agency or agencies that can best supply corrective action.[38]

Intercession is only one of the many important activities entrusted to the juvenile specialist. In general, it is his duty to give leadership to the police department in all matters affecting the youthful offender. He is constantly educating his fellow officer in the importance of the first contact with the juvenile. On a wider front he seeks to assist the head of the department in mobilizing the community to the need for a program. Collaboration is sought with the courts, with the schools and with community agencies. Efforts are made to gain community sponsorship for such programs as will enlist the energies and interest of the growing youth. Vollmer's junior police, New York's million dollar Police Athletic League,

---

[37] Deutsch, *op. cit.*, p. 175.

[38] J. E. Rinck, "Supervising the Juvenile Delinquent," *The Annals*, CCXCI (1954), pp. 80-81.

the deputy auxiliary police of Los Angeles, and the vast network of little leagues are but a few of the useful by-products of such activity.

POLICE PERSONNEL ADMINISTRATION

The police have come a long way since the early days of the "watch." Urbanization has compelled the steady growth of the force and its transformation from a part-time, poorly organized group to a full-time highly disciplined unit. The complexity of urban life has been accomplished by better training and specialization of police personnel. Gradually a spirit of professionalization is being developed. Aside from an occasional outburst of public indignation, the police are no longer the object of ridicule and scorn. Their place in city government is secure. All of these trends signify progress but rapidly evolving urban society will continue to make further demands upon its protective force.

The police department is a costly operation. Aside from education, it is now the largest single municipal expenditure. Approximately nine-tenths of its budget is expended for salaries and wages, a factor which underlines the importance of personnel administration. The success of the police depends in large measure upon the extent to which it is able to enlist the energies and the talents of its personnel. This is the fundamental objective of the police administrator, as it is the head of any large enterprise; but its attainment involves a series of complex operations.

Recruitment and selection. The police head is interested in attracting and retaining the most capable people. To do this, he must not only develop adequate selection practices but more than this he must provide his force with a system of rewards and incentives that stimulate their best endeavor. Salaries and wage scales must be made attractive. Promotions and conditions of work must be constantly improved. Welfare benefits that will protect the individual during his days of service and thereafter must be provided.[39] Although personnel administration is basic to the morale and efficiency of the force, its principles are often shunted aside because of the preoccupation of the police with the detection and arrest of criminals.

But even the police chief who is aware of the importance of personnel administration finds that his efforts are constantly hampered by a series of obstacles. He is interested in getting the best man for

---

[39] O. W. Wilson, "Problems in Police Administration," *Journal of Criminal Law*, XLIII (1953), p. 840.

the job. Yet he finds that residence requirements limit his search to his own community. Most cities require that an applicant should be a resident of his community for terms of from one to two years, although in some instances the residence requirement is as high as ten years.[40] The justification of this practice rests upon the twin assumptions that it will guarantee a better knowledge of local conditions and will simplify character investigations. Neither of these are valid, but the police administrator must observe them if he is to conform with the law.

The poor quality of the police force is accentuated by the lack of adequate attention to the character of the prospective policeman. Investigations are quite routine, being limited mainly to fingerprinting and a check of references. The rather high rate of homicide in some police departments suggests that more attention should be paid to the emotional stability of the prospective applicant. Approximately 35 percent of the thousand candidates for jobs in two California cities were rejected as being emotionally immature and unstable.[41] Los Angeles, Berkley, Oakland, Philadelphia and Pasadena have adopted psychiatric examinations, but, on the whole, this is an innovation in police personnel practice.[42]

Finally, many police executives complain bitterly about the restrictions imposed by civil service systems. While they are agreed that insistence upon merit is a laudable objective, they nevertheless feel that the civil service agencies as presently constituted do not meet their needs. Civil service systems are remote from the day to day operations of the department. The sense of urgency that exists in the operating department is rarely felt by the civil service agency. Outmoded systems of recruitment and selection prevail. Examinations are routine. Reliance is placed mainly upon knowledge. The introduction of intelligence tests is a comparatively recent innovation, but, as yet, the real aptitude of the candidate for police work remains untested. All these criticisms have been uttered at one time or another by police executives, but their greatest complaint is reserved for the divided system of authority that civil service creates. The head of the police department, in the final analysis, is responsible for the work of his agency and this, in turn, depends

[40] Smith, *op. cit.*, p. 148.
[41] Deutsch, *op. cit.*, p. 51.
[42] *National Municipal Yearbook for 1955*, p. 427.

upon the quality of its personnel. Yet recruitment and selection in most jurisdictions belong to the civil service agency.[43]

Training. Police training is largely either of the pre-entry or post-entry variety. Both of these were hardly existent before 1920 when the era of the "strong back" prevailed. Today, however, effective training of both sorts is beginning to appear. The University of California, The University of Washington, San Diego State College, Michigan State University and several other schools are offering broad training for the aspiring patrolman. In the main the effort has been characterized by an attempt to give the individual a broad appreciation of the importance of police work. Courses are offered in such fields as public administration, criminology, parole, police science and related fields.[44] While these instances represent an advance, most of the pre-entry training is still of the "cram variety" designed to hurdle the immediate civil service barrier.[45]

Post-entry training is much more highly developed. The large cities with more than 500,000 people have their own police academies. The small cities may avail themselves of the opportunities afforded by state police schools. The National Police Academy of the Federal Bureau of Investigation annually gives two twelve-week courses to law enforcement officers, one-fourth of whom are heads of police departments.[46] The correspondence courses of the International City Managers' Association are also employed by the small jurisdictions.

Promotion and discipline. Promotion in the police department suffers from the same deficiencies as it does in other branches of the civil service. There is, as yet, no real test of supervisory ability. Consequently, reliance is again placed upon the written test to ascertain qualities of leadership. Reluctance to depart from this traditional practice rests mainly upon the fear that another system would introduce an element of favoritism. The written examination is also easier to rate. Police experts, however, feel that the defects of the

---

43 R. A. Lothian, "Operations of a Police Merit System," *The Annals,* CCXCI (1954), p. 97.

44 D. E. J. MacNamara, "Higher Police Training at the University Level," *Journal of Criminal Law,* XL (1950), pp. 657-658.

45 R. E. Clift, "Police Training," *The Annals,* CCXCI (1954), pp. 113-114.

46 J. E. Hoover, "The Basis of Sound Law Enforcement," *The Annals,* CCXCI (1954), p. 43. In the period July 1935–July 1955, 2666 police officers were graduated from the National Academy.

written examination should be modified by some form of oral test.[47]

Discipline is regarded by police authorities as a command prerogative. Yet the fact that the police can be a force for evil as well as good has led the public to hedge the authority of the police executive with civil service restrictions. In most cities the civil service commission has almost coequal authority with the police executive. Policemen are entitled to receive a departmental trial. Decisions of the department head are subject to review by the civil service agency and sometimes appeal may be made to the courts. There is, of course, the constant possibility that the police head may find that his decision has been overruled. It is this contingency that has led to a demand for a clarification of the respective responsibilities of the department and the civil service agency. The latter, it is argued, should not have the authority without the corresponding responsibility for its decisions.[48]

Compensation. Conditions of work also determine the relative effectiveness of the work force. An adequate pay scale and appropriate welfare benefits attract and retain the competent employee. In these respects, the police have not fared as well as other segments of the economy. Since World War II the police have shared in the general rise in salaries and wages but the progress has not been uniform. In 1954 median entrance salaries for patrolmen ranged from $3,212 for cities between 10 and 25 thousand people to $3,725 in the cities with more than 500,000 people. Median maximum salaries ranged from $3540 to $4500.[49] The median work week for cities with a population of less than 100,000 people is still 48 hours, although the larger cities have shifted to the 44 and 42 hour week.[50] In general, in all cities there is an increasing recognition of the need for sick leaves and pension plans for police department employees.[51]

POLICE PROBLEMS

Matters of administration are not the sole concern of the police executive. It can be taken for granted that most administrators will seek to raise the efficiency of the department to the highest possible

---

[47] O. W. Wilson, "Toward a Better Merit System," *The Annals*, CCXCI (1954), p. 91; Smith, *op. cit.*, pp. 153-154.

[48] G. D. Gourby, "Police Discipline," *Journal of Criminal Law*, XLI (1951), pp. 85-87.

[49] *National Municipal Yearbook for 1954*, p. 430.

[50] *Ibid.*, p. 428.

[51] B. Smith, Jr., "The Policeman's Hire," *The Annals*, CCXCI (1954), pp. 119-126.

level. But his ability to deal with crime and the maintenance of law and order is complicated by the rise of metropolitan areas, the increasingly polyglot character of the population, the group tensions and hatreds that it engenders and the persistent infiltration and pressure of the organized criminal element.

Metropolitan area law enforcement. One of the most persistent developments that complicate the problems of law enforcement is the rise of metropolitan areas. The coming of the automobile has caused the dispersion of vast numbers of people away from the large core cities. Suburbs and satellites ring the major cities. Varying standards of police administration and degrees of community morality exist. The automobile has also given the criminal a high degree of mobility. In a matter of minutes he may be out of the range of the police authority of the city. He may use the suburb as a base of operations to direct criminal activities in the central city. Police activity, like governmental authority, is divided and there is often a lack of uniform effort in dealing with crime.

Cook County, Illinois which embraces the nation's second largest city furnishes a representative illustration of the problems of law enforcement in a metropolitan community. Its four and one half million people are crowded into a 954 square mile area, and are distributed among ninety villages and cities, each of which has its own police. Chicago, which employs approximately four-fifths of the 8,100 police in the area, is itself divided into two police forces, the city police and the park police. Dispersion of police authority has its obvious consequences. Each municipality confines law enforcement largely to its own jurisdictional boundaries. There is a lack of coordination and a general failure among police to exchange information and reports. There is a duplication of overhead personnel and in general an overlapping of effort. In Chicago both the city police and the park police send cars whenever an accident occurs on a major boulevard. Both investigate major crimes that take place in parks. Similar instances could be cited in the surrounding areas.[52] Surrounding communities with lax standards of enforcement harbor criminals who prey upon the citizens of the central city. Only the voluntary cooperation of police officers prevents the almost complete breakdown of the law enforcement machinery. The difficulties faced by the police are inherent in the governmental problems of metro-

---

[52] G. Linkon, editor, "Disorganization of Metropolitan Law Enforcement and Some Proposed Solutions," *Journal of Criminal Law,* XLIII (1952), pp. 63-67.

politan areas. State police and perhaps the revival of the metropolitan police district are possible solutions.

Civil disturbances. Cities are often the focal point of riots and civilian disturbances. Since their net reproduction rate is low, they have generally relied upon the countryside and overseas to make up their population deficits. Separated by barriers of language, race, national origin, and creed, the newcomers have given the city a heterogeneous population. The existence of fairly well-defined neighborhoods and "little nations" produces tensions and distrust that sometimes burst forth with unaccustomed violence. The attitude of the police toward these minorities is an important factor in the handling of such disputes because, as has been so evident in the past, the use of force is not enough.

In 1943 the need for police training in this area was made patently evident. The war need for more manpower brought many new people to the city. The war for democracy gave a heightened sense of nationalism to racial, religious, and national-origin minorities. Under the quickened pace of city life, the interaction of the old and new brought rising tensions and often violent outbreaks. In that year, minorities in Los Angeles complained bitterly about the lack of adequate police protection. In Detroit racial tensions erupted into violence that caused the loss of thirty-five lives and many millions of man hours. New York City's Harlem area was the scene of a riot in which property damage mounted into millions of dollars, although prompt and effective action by the police prevented a loss of life. In the nation's capital Negro demonstrations for jobs in the transit system very nearly resulted in bloodshed. In war and in peace, the city's police are always faced with the need to deal with minorities.

These incidents, and many others, have led to a reassessment of the role of the police as a protective force. It is now agreed that proper police action can do much either to prevent or minimize the tensions and unrest of our urban communities. It has been shown that a thoughtful and perceptive approach has always been attended by a fair measure of success. When police understand the causes of unrest and respect the rights of minorities, and when they enlist the support of the leaders of the community, they generally are able to maintain order.[53]

---

[53] J. E. Weckler and T. E. Hall, *The Police and Minority Groups* (Chicago: The International City Managers' Association, 1944), pp. 3-4, 5-6.

It is now commonly agreed that improved police training and heightened community action are the best guarantees for meeting potential disorder in the area of inter-group relations. Police practice in the handling of disputes involving minorities has been greatly influenced by a pioneering study of the International City Managers' Association arising from its investigation of the 1943 outbreaks. There is hardly a city today that does not employ one or all of the corrective measures that it has suggested. The Association has recommended that the police should be given a thorough indoctrination in civil rights and group tensions. Police are to be taught to assess the meaning of rumors and grievances as a source of unrest. All police should be given a realization that prompt and proper action may well prevent serious disorders.[54] All of these points, it was suggested, should be incorporated in a "tactics manual" for in-service training purposes.

Police violence. Closely related to the handling of disputes involving minorities is the problem of police brutality. Police are a paramilitary force. They are given a monopoly of violence in order that they may protect the community against wrongdoing.

Yet there is much evidence to show that the police use their authority against the community. Indeed, in many cases they often ignore the law that they are supposed to guard. The reasons for such behavior are not too far to seek. The very nature of their work and organization create conditions that permit the unscrupulous to abuse the powers given to them. Police are subject to constant danger of attack from individuals and organized gangs of hoodlums. Many of them have been severely beaten and the spectacle of one man being hurt does not incline others to risk the same possibility. There is also a strong in-group feeling among police. They are taught to protect themselves and that it is the police against the "enemy" on the outside. There can be no scruples in dealing with the latter.

Moreover, police efficiency is often measured in terms of the number of arrests and convictions obtained. A constant temptation exists to use the "third degree" and protracted questioning to obtain confessions. This condition is intensified by the general failure of the police to restrain their fellow officers when acts of violence are committed. Thus the way is open for those who want to make their own immediate ends superior to law.[55]

---

[54] *Ibid.*, pp. 8-11.

[55] W. A. Westley, "Violence and Police," *American Journal of Sociology*, LIX (1953), p. 40.

The main justification for the illegal use of force is of course the protection of the members of the department. But one curious reason has also been given. Violence is justified on the ground that it will teach the public to respect the occupational status of the police. A study of a city of 150,000 people revealed that almost two-fifths of the police interviewed felt that it was legitimate to use force for this purpose.[56] There is considerable evidence that the police accept and justify the illegal use of violence as a necessary part of their activity.

In cities all over the country, north and south alike, the Negro and other minority groups have at one time or another been the victim of police brutality. In 1953 the behavior of the police in the city of New York evoked such a storm of disapproval that a grand jury was required to investigate the complaints. But New York is but one of the many cities where the constitutional rights of the citizen have been ignored.[57] Aside from the violation of constitutional guarantees, what makes the practice additionally reprehensible is the fact that not all individuals are treated alike by the police. The kind of treatment that a person receives at the hands of the police often depends upon his status within the society. The "big shot" criminal may be treated gingerly, while the poor and hapless representative of a minority may be given the "full treatment."

Police executives are not unaware of this condition. They have sought to meet it in many ways. Personnel have been screened more carefully for emotional instability. Departmental regulations are strictly enforced and in some instances the practice of referring civil rights violations to the federal Department of Justice is standard practice. Policemen are subject to instant dismissal where injustices are committed. The fact that more illegal violence has not occurred under conditions so replete with temptation is a tribute to the conscientious police administrator. Nevertheless, it is apparent that those who deal with violence are often corrupted by it. It will require constant vigilance before the illegal use of force is banished.

CONCLUSION

The rise of the city has conferred a key role upon the police department. The city is a mechanism for interdependence. It is

[56] *Ibid.*, p. 39.
[57] Deutsch, *op. cit.*, ch. 5, "What Price Brutality," cites numerous instances.

composed of many peoples with a variety of races, nationalities and religions. Its complex social structure is subject to constant onslaughts by changes in transportation and technology. The impersonality of city life and the increased mobility of the people when combined with the liberalizing effects of a democratic ideology often result in extremes of emotion and action. Social disorganization of the family and the home often weakens societal controls and places an inordinate reliance upon law. If the city is to function it is necessary that the behavior of the individual should be regulated in the greater interest of the municipality. It is the police who are charged largely with the maintenance of the intricate balance between the liberty of the individual and the authority of the community, at least as it is defined in law.[58]

As the cities have grown in numbers and size, there was a corresponding increase in the responsibilities of the police. To say the least, the duties of the police department have changed in the century or so of its existence as an organized force. To the primary duty of crime suppression has been grafted such functions as traffic control, maintenance of jails, control of organized crime, juvenile delinquency and even emergency welfare and relief activities. Often in the maintenance of peace within a community the police are forced into wider areas of social inquiry, such as the quest for an understanding of the meaning of group tensions and the causes of crime and delinquency.

Police organization, to meet its widened responsibilities, has made great strides over the past century. The force has become uniformed and disciplined. Its training has improved greatly, and even the glimmerings of professionalization are beginning to appear. Specialization in crime detection and criminal investigation has also been introduced. Although advances have been uneven, there has been on the whole an achievement of which the police can be reasonably proud.

Further progress, however, will depend upon the manner in which the police rise to the challenge of many persistent problems that face them. First, and perhaps most important, is the seemingly ever present tie-up of politics, organized crime and the police. Few

---

[58] W. H. Parker, "The Police Challenge in Our Great Cities," *The Annals,* CCXCI (1954), pp. 5-6.

police departments have escaped the toils of police-crime influence.[59] As Professor Goodnow has remarked, "There never has been invented so successful a get-rich-quick institution as is to be found in the control of the police force of a large American city." [60] As long as the police possess so much power, there will always be a temptation for the fringe elements to tamper with their operations either through the common bribe or indirectly through the use of political influence. Constant vigilance is needed if this pitfall is to be avoided.

This consideration highlights yet another need of the police department. Organized criminal infiltration cannot exist without at least the tacit consent of the public. Police executives have a chosen duty to educate the public to an awareness of the acuteness of the situation. In city after city this is an aspect that has been honored more in breach than in observance. Side by side with this must come a tightening of the methods of police administration. Proper selection and incentives must be given to the work force in order that the ethics of the police remain untouched. Respect for the law, surprisingly enough, must be constantly inculcated. More planning and control over the execution of plans are necessary.[61] Only an efficient police force can gain the respect and support of the public.

Finally, the problem of crime in metropolitan areas must be attacked more vigorously. The multiplicity of police units and the presence of divided effort in dealing with criminal elements who recognize no political boundaries constantly sap police effort. While the difficulties of police are inherent in the general problem of metropolitan government, much more can be done. The present informal cooperative relationships are inadequate. Because of their special problems, the police can take the lead in at least their particular area of the general problem.

Thus although many advances have been made, it would be idle to say that all is well in the police world. Critical self-analysis, however, is the touchstone of further improvements that have to be made.

---

[59] U. S. Senate, 82nd Cong. 1st. Sess., *Special Committee to Investigate Organized Crime, Second Interim Report* (Washington, D. C.: U. S. Government Printing Office, 1951); also N. Mockridge and R. H. Prall, *The Big Fix* (New York: Henry Holt and Co., 1954), especially pages 78-81.

[60] F. J. Goodnow, *City Government in the United States* (New York: The Century Co., 1904), p. 232.

[61] Parker, *op. cit.*, pp. 8-13.

BIBLIOGRAPHY

Books:

Deutsch, A. *The Trouble with Cops.* New York: Crown Publishers, Inc., 1954.

Fosdick, R. B. *American Police Systems.* New York: The Century Co., 1921.

——. *Crime in America and the Police.* New York: The Century Co., 1920.

Harrison, L. V. *Police Administration in Boston.* Cambridge, Massachusetts: Harvard University Press, 1943

Leonard, V. A. *Police Organization and Management.* Brooklyn, New York: Foundation Press, 1951.

Institute for Training in Municipal Administration. *Municipal Police Administration.* Chicago: International City Managers' Association, 1950.

Reynolds, Q. J. *Headquarters.* New York: Harper and Brothers, Publishers, 1955.

Smith, B. *Police Systems in the United States.* New York: Harper and Brothers, Publishers, 1949.

——. *The State Police: Organization and Administration.* New York: The Macmillan Co., 1925.

United States Senate, 82nd Congress, 1st Session. Special Senate Committee to Investigate Organized Crime in Interstate Commerce, *Second Interim Report.* Washington, D. C.: U. S. Government Printing Office, 1951.

Weckler, J. E. and Hall, T. E. *The Police and Minority Groups.* Chicago: International City Managers' Association, 1944.

Wilson, O. W. *Police Administration.* New York: McGraw-Hill Book Co., Inc., 1950.

Articles and Other Material:

Higgins, T. "Historical Background of Police-Women's Service," *Journal of Criminal Law,* XLI (1951), 822-833.

Lesher, E. W. "American Police Problems—Some Aspects," *Journal of Criminal Law,* XL (1950), 796-809.

Linkon, G. "Disorganization of Metropolitan Law Enforcement and Some Proposed Solutions," *Journal of Criminal Law,* XLIII (1952), 63-78.

MacNamara, D. E. J. *"American Police Administration at Mid-Century," Public Administration Review,* X (1950), 181-189.

"New Goals in Police Management," *The Annals* (edited by Bruce Smith), CXC, 1954.

Westley, W. A. "Violence and Police," *American Journal of Sociology,* LIX (1953), 34-41.

Wilson, O. W. "Can the State Help City Police Departments?," *Journal of Criminal Law,* XLV (1954), 102-109.

———. "Progress in Police Administration," *Journal of Criminal Law,* XLII (1951), 141-152.

Chapter Twenty-One

Municipal Fire Administration

Introduction

The danger of fire. Fire is both the friend and foe of man. Its discovery was a momentous milestone in the history of mankind. From that time onward man has employed fire to conquer the hazards of his environment. Fire has given man warmth and provided him with the means to surmount the rigors of cold climate. It has enabled him to unlock the secrets of nature and to build a civilization. With fire has come the exploitation of mineral resources and the creation of tools and implements that have built a better world. Fire has given man motive power and machinery. It has increased man's productivity a hundredfold. Physical and chemical processes, essentially heat reactions, have brought new methods and means for taming nature. So important was the discovery of fire that it is safe to say that no industrial civilization could endure without it.

But while fire has bettered man's condition, it also has often been an instrument of death and destruction. The same fire that warms a house may burn it down. Electricity, steam, the internal combustion engine and the miracle of chemistry have provided us with many creature comforts. Yet behind these essential processes lurks the constant element of danger. The forces of nature that have been tamed by man may also get out of hand and wreak terrible havoc. If fire has built civilization, it can end it. Today the dreadful energy release of the fusion bomb, fire in its ultimate form, holds forth the prospect that unless carefully used by man, fire may well become the absolute weapon of destruction.

Fire losses. Fire has always taken a toll of civilizations. The burning of Rome in 64 A.D., the great London fire of 1666, and our own Chicago fire of 1871 are examples. In our own country the advance in industrial development has been paralleled by increasing loss of life and property. In the period of 1865–1952 fire losses increased one thousand percent, reflecting the congestion in the cities and the dangers attendant upon the growth of industrial processes.[1]

Nor was this a temporary trend. In the two decades 1920–1940 aggregate property losses amounted to $8.5 billion or an average of $425 million annually.[2] In the first five years of this decade fire damage soared even higher. For this brief period property losses amounted to $3.9 billion.[3] The following table gives the nature of these losses in greater detail.

Table 6—FIRE LOSSES

Year	*Amount in thousands of dollars*	*Per capita loss in dollars*
1950	648,909	4.29
1951	730,084	4.76
1952	815,134	5.23
1953	864,863	5.46
1954	870,984	5.40

Source: *Statistical Abstract for 1955,* p. 482.

The perils that fire has for civilization were acutely demonstrated in 1954. In that year two million fires brought death to 12,-250 people. Of the 727,000 building fires that took place, more than half occurred in residential buildings.[4] The National Board of Fire Underwriters has estimated that each day the nation has 1500 fires and 30 deaths.[5] The most common causes of fire in the order of descending importance were: heating appliances, smoking and the use of matches, defective electrical equipment, rubbish, flammable liquids, and lightning.[6]

The cost of fire protection. That the people of the cities are not willing to accept the enormous toll of death and destruction as the price of civilization is evidenced by their efforts to protect themselves against the devastation of fires. Fire protection, next to education and police, is the third largest municipal expenditure. In the year 1954 fire protection cost the cities of the United States $473

[1] H. C. Brearley, *A Symbol of Safety* (Garden City, N. Y.: Doubleday, Page & Co., 1923), p. 6.

[2] National Board of Fire Underwriters, *Pioneers of Progress* (New York: 1941), p. 157. Statistics were adapted from the table on that page.

[3] *Statistical Abstract for 1955,* p. 482.

[4] *National Municipal Yearbook for 1955,* p. 359.

[5] National Board of Fire Underwriters, *op. cit.,* p. 159.

[6] *National Municipal Yearbook for 1955,* p. 359.

million or $7.63 per capita.[7] Statistics for October 1955 indicate a further rise in costs. In October of that year full-time city employees of the fire department numbered 116,000 with a monthly payroll of $42.1 million, approximately one-tenth of the city payroll.[8]

THE ORGANIZATION AND OPERATION OF THE FIRE FIGHTING FUNCTION

Historical development. The modern city fire department is the product of gradual evolution over the centuries. Minimal precautions against the hazards of fire have been observed in varying degrees by all societies. Fire fighting as a function can be traced to Rome and ancient Egypt where efforts of an exceedingly rudimentary nature were undertaken.[9] Attention to structural features of buildings date as far back as Babylonian times. Rome had structural regulations. London in the fourteenth century when it was beginning to experience revived urbanization required that all chimneys be made of stone.[10] Protection against fire, however, was mainly regarded as a private function.

In this country an almost similar evolution took place. The basis of fire protection was the "watch." It sounded the alert when fire was discovered and it mobilized the citizens to fight the fire. In a few communities regulations governing the storage of combustible materials were adopted but, in most, fire was considered a private matter. In some cases private insurance firms organized companies to protect their insured properties. Gradually, it was realized that fire was a danger to all and the beginnings of public concern appeared in the form of volunteer companies.[11]

Fire fighting was exceedingly primitive. Very little was known about the causes of fire. Equipment was limited very largely to the leather bucket. The volunteer character of fire fighting impeded the development of professionalization. A concentrated attack on the fire danger awaited changes in fire fighting equipment and greater public need. These were supplied by two developments that took place during the latter half of the nineteenth century. The appear-

[7] U. S. Department of Commerce, Bureau of Census, *City Government Finances in 1954* (Washington, D. C.: U. S. Government Printing Office, 1955), p. 11.

[8] U. S. Department of Commerce, Bureau of Census, *City Employment in 1955* (Washington, D. C.: U. S. Government Printing Office, 1956), pp. 2, 9.

[9] "Fire Protection," *Encyclopaedia of Social Sciences*, VI, p. 264.

[10] National Board of Fire Underwriters, *Building Codes, their scope and aims* (New York, undated), p. 1.

[11] National Fire Protection Association, *Fire Protection Engineering* (Boston, 1943), p. 117.

ance of first the steam driven and later the motor propelled pump with a capacity to deliver water under pressure revolutionized fire fighting tactics and brought about a specialization of the fire fighting function. The growth of cities brought congestion of population within relatively confined areas. The rapid evolution of industry, and processes associated with it, confronted people with constant hazards. It is significant to note that fire fighting became an exclusively municipal function, relatively unsupervised by the state. The danger to the public was local and had to be handled on that basis. The changes in equipment and heightened need resulted in the full-time paid department in many of our cities, especially the larger ones.

Fire fighting organization today. The organization of the fire department varies with both the size and the nature of the city. Residential areas obviously have different problems from those that confront industrial sections. There the presence of combustibles and the hazards of industrial processes compel a higher development of the fire fighting function. Size, too, is a constant factor in organization. A city with a relatively small area can concentrate its fire fighting efforts but a large one will have to decentralize its activities. The number of fires, too, will dictate whether a volunteer or full-time department is needed. As a general rule, cities with more than 25,000 people have a full-time paid department.

Nevertheless, despite the wide variety of conditions encountered, it is possible to isolate the common functions of fire protection. The two major purposes of all departments are fire extinction and fire prevention. Grouped around these are such subsidiary functions as the following: fire alarm systems, maintenance of fire fighting equipment, arson and fire investigation, inspection, training and personnel programs and rescue operations. In most instances, a medical person on either a full- or part-time basis is also attached to the department. In the small city there is usually very little specialization. But as the city grows in size or as the difficulty of the fire problem increases, differentiation and specialization takes place with each activity being given organizational status in the form of either bureaus or divisions. Where this occurs the problem of administration becomes similar to that of any large enterprise.[12]

The combat unit of the fire department is the engine company. In the small city this consists of a fire chief, an assistant fire chief

[12] See chapters 18 and 19.

and approximately twenty men. Work of the department is usually on a two-shift basis or a platoon system, although some cities operate on a three-shift, eight-hour basis. In either event, the department is on twenty-four-hour duty. The chief is responsible for the entire work of the department and his assistant is in charge of fire fighting. In the larger cities where fire fighting is decentralized on the basis of fire stations or districts, there is normally a battalion or district chief who supervises the work of the "districts."

For the very large city, an intermediate layer of command appears. Between the battalion chiefs and the headquarters are often found assistant or deputy chiefs who are the headquarters "contact" with the field. The headquarters office is concerned with the coordination of departmental activities. It performs such central services as purchasing, budgeting, the maintenance of equipment records and property management, communication, fire prevention and training. All of the common functions of the department are concentrated at the top of the organization. The morale, the discipline, and the facilities of the work force are its major concern. In the large city the head of the department may easily become remote from his personnel unless he is gifted in the arts of communication and command.[13]

Fire fighting equipment. Equipment is the main resource of those who fight fires. Here again differentiation takes place in accordance with the nature and the size of the problem encountered, although it can be safely said that American city fire companies are among the best-equipped in the world. Fire companies are provided with all of the essentials of fire fighting. Automobile trucks transport men to the scene of the blaze. The basic unit of all fire companies is the pumper truck which contains hose and pumps capable of delivering water in varying pressures together with a water reserve for handling small fires. For the more specialized fires, apparatus becomes more complex. "Hook and ladder" vehicles, water tower trucks, supply vehicles and squad wagons for specialized personnel and salvage operations are also employed. Seaport cities have fireboats to maintain a constant vigil over pier and wharf operations. In the large cities, the complexity of mechanisms and the nature of the conditions faced often dictate further specialization in organization. There are engine companies and ladder companies. There

---

[13] International City Managers' Association, *Municipal Fire Administration* (5th ed.; Chicago: The International City Managers' Association, 1950), pp. 66-68, 69.

are pumper-ladder and engine-ladder combinations. There are salvage squads and investigation personnel who are concerned with the causes of the fire.[14]

Fire fighting. The primary objective of fire fighting is to get to the scene of the fire and put it out as rapidly as possible. This is a function both of the location of fire stations and the adequacy of the alarm system. According to the standards established by the National Board of Fire Underwriters no point in a "high value" district should be located more than three-fourths of a mile from a pumper hose company or one mile from a ladder service. For closely built residential areas, companies should not be further than one and one half and two miles away for both types of equipment. Not more than three miles should separate scattered buildings from fire stations.[15] In general, the desired distribution of fire stations should be such that fires can be reached within two or three minutes. Whether this can be done will depend upon a number of factors, road access, traffic conditions and perhaps most of all, the efficiency of the alarm system. The standard fire alarm system is the "fire box" through which alarms are sent to the central station. This is usually supplemented by the telephone system which records calls and transmits them to the appropriate unit. Radio systems are often used to redirect the fire trucks to other fires and to issue additional commands.[16]

Training for fire fighting. The highly technical nature of fires and fire fighting equipment necessitates considerable training of fire personnel if they are to become proficient in fire fighting. Probationary firemen are given a fairly standardized program of instruction in fire fighting. Subjects covered include: fire department organization, drill work under simulated fire conditions, apparatus and tools, "ladder, hose and rope work," and safety precautions. In the larger cities more specialized training is given in fire extinguishing practice, in salvage operations and in the handling of special kinds of fires faced by the department. Schools for officers provide advanced training in fire fighting and administration. Most departments are guided in their training methods by the standards established by the Firemen's

---

14 *Ibid.*, pp. 63-65, 183-190.

15 National Board of Fire Underwriters, *Standard Schedule for Cities and Towns of the United States with Reference to their Fire Defenses and Physical Conditions* (New York: 1956), "Fire Companies," sec. 10.

16 International City Managers' Association, *op. cit.*, p. 191.

Training Committee of the National Fire Protection Association.[17] Post-entry training varies from twenty to twenty-four hours annually unless the fireman is willing to pursue additional training on his own.

Organization for training purposes varies considerably. In the small department reliance is placed mainly on its own resources. Training is generally on an apprentice basis with the deputy chief assuming responsibility for the training of his platoons. State-wide fire schools may give supplementary training although their use depends upon departmental policy. In the large cities, however, training is recognized as an important aspect of fire work. A high ranking officer of the department is given a full-time assignment to train both officers and men. Fire department schools are established and give detailed pre-entry and post-entry training. In the nation's largest city training is highly organized. It has a "fire college" (an officer school), a motor and pump operators' school and a school of instruction for probationary firemen.[18]

Cooperation with other city departments. Not all of the work of fire protection is located in the fire department, even though it is generally considered a major purpose department. For the effective performance of its functions it must rely upon the cooperation of other city departments. Water supply, for example, is a public works responsibility unless the water system is privately owned. In either event, the fire chief needs assurance that water in sufficient quantity will be available when fire occurs. Water pressures, hydrant service and water location are of more than casual interest to him.

Since fire conditions are closely related to the type of structures within the city, the fire chief will have to rely heavily upon the building department. The latter through its issuance of permits can supply essential data on the nature of occupancy, the kinds of fire hazards, the protective equipment and the building materials. Street widths, buffer zones, the segregation of buildings for different uses in separate districts, and the maintenance of an adequate distance between buildings are greatly influenced by zoning and planning agencies.[19] The right of way and access to fires, arson investigation, communications and rescue operations are activities of the police department that vitally affect the fire operation.

---

[17] International City Managers' Association, *op. cit.*, p. 98.

[18] R. B. Rankin, *Guide to the Municipal Government of the City of New York* (7th ed.; New York: Record Press, Inc., 1952), p. 121.

[19] National Fire Protection Association, *op. cit.*, p. 101.

From even this brief perusal of the activities of other city departments it is obvious that the fire protection function is as broad as city government. To gain the cooperation of other agencies it is necessary that they be brought into a cooperative relationship. In the cities where the power of the municipal executive is centralized, the activities of all agencies of government are brought into focus through conferences and discussions out of which emerge mutual understanding.

The measurement of fire fighting efficiency. Although the work of the fire department is of an exceedingly technical nature, the effectiveness of the fire fighting mechanism of the city is, surprisingly enough, susceptible of measurement. That this is so is due largely to the efforts of the National Board of Fire Underwriters, an association of fire stock companies that exist in every state of the union except Texas.[20] Its "Standard Schedule for Cities and Towns" assigns point values to various factors of fire protection and then rates cities into ten different classes. The "class" of the city becomes an important factor in the determination of fire insurance rates.

The relative importance of various "fighting factors" is contained in Table 7. Approximately two-thirds of the effectiveness of fire fighting resides in two factors, water supply and fire department organization. If one adds the adequacy of the fire alarm system, then three-quarters of the ability of a fire department to give its community protection is included. While it is true that the ratings of the National Board of Fire Underwriters have been criticized on

Table 7—FIRE FACTORS AND THEIR VALUES

Fire Factor	*Percent of the Total*	*Point Value*
Water supply	34	1,700
Fire department	30	1,500
Fire alarm system	11	550
Structural conditions	14	700
Fire prevention	6	300
Building laws	4	200
Police	1	50
Total	100	5,000

Source: National Board of Fire Underwriters, *Standard Schedule for Cities and Towns of the United States,* (1942), Introduction. See revised deficiency scale as shown in 1956 edition, p. 4.

[20] Texas has a state administered fire rating system.

the ground that it merely measures the conflagration factor, it is nevertheless a valuable index of measurement for the citizen, since the rating is done by experts for him.

From Table 7 it will be seen that the total number of deficiency points is a maximum of five thousand. A city is then rated by the underwriters on the basis of ten classes, each separated by intervals of five hundred points. The details of this are found in Table 8. As a result of the efforts of skilled engineers employed by the rating system many advances in fire fighting protection have been made.

Table 8—CLASSES OF CITIES ACCORDING TO THE DEFICIENCY POINTS

Class of City	*Number of Deficiency Points*
First	0–500
Second	501–1000
Third	1001–1500
Fourth	1501–2000
Fifth	2001–2500
Sixth	2501–3000
Seventh	3001–3500
Eighth	3501–4000
Ninth *	4001–4500
Tenth †	more than 5000

* A ninth-class municipality is one (a) receiving 4001 to 4500 points of deficiency, or (b) receiving less than 4001 points but having no recognized water supply.

† A tenth-class municipality is one (a) receiving more than 4500 points of deficiency, or (b) without a recognized water supply and having a fire department grading tenth-class, or (c) with a water supply and no fire department, or (d) with no fire protection.

Source: National Board of Fire Underwriters, *Standard Schedule for Cities and Towns of the United States* (1956), Grading of Cities and Towns Based upon Relative Points of Deficiency in Fire Defenses and Physical Conditions.

The integrated public safety department in small cities. Historically both the police and fire functions trace their origins to the early days of the "watch." In the years since then for a variety of reasons both have become separate city services. Lack of adequate communications fostered the police patrol. A similar necessity dictated that firemen be kept in a constant state of readiness. Technological advances in the nineteenth century brought a specialization in methods and equipment. Differences in the nature of the work widened the contrast in the attitude and interests of both services.

Finally, the growth of large cities with the complexity of their problems also contributed to the sharper delineation of their respective services.

In recent years the constant rise in the cost of city government has concentrated attention on the need to get the most mileage from the municipal tax dollar. Many experiments have been undertaken to increase municipal efficiency. Old patterns of administration have been re-examined and new departures have been undertaken. Equipment and labor-saving devices have been lavishly employed to effect economics. Organizational reins have been tightened through the use of improved management techniques. Through such measures many municipalities have been able to confine increased demand within the limits of available funds but the rigidity of municipal income, largely limited as it is to the property tax, will undoubtedly act as a continuous stimulus to further experimentation.

In the search for ways and means to "hold the line" on governmental expenditures, all city functions are now coming within the scrutiny of municipal authorities. Police and fire protection which in the past have enjoyed relative immunity from this trend, are now becoming the object of intensive investigation. This is due to a variety of factors. Public safety is now a major item of municipal expenditure and will undoubtedly continue to be so as cities multiply and become more complex. Police and fire, unlike other municipal activities, are exclusively local in character and must be financed out of the city budget. No relief through grant of assistance from other levels of government is in sight. Unless municipal revenues increase appreciably, the prospect exists that the growth of the protective services will have to be at the expense of other municipal functions, many of which are as vital to the welfare of the community.

In the large cities because of the highly specialized nature of the work and the problems encountered, it is taken for granted that the separation of the two functions is necessary. Whether similar considerations exist in the small municipality is at least open to question. There are some who urge the integration of both services in a department of public safety. Those who take this position argue that there is no real reason why the small city should ape the practices of its big brother. Its personnel and monetary resources are limited. Separation of the two departments often means that neither function can be administered adequately. Separate overhead services, purchasing budget, maintenance, records and communications are luxuries that no small city can afford.

An examination of both functions reveal many instances of potential waste and duplication. Both police and fire personnel respond to fire alarms. Indeed in many cases their duties overlap to the point where jurisdiction is often not clear. Police are concerned with arson investigation and the fire department is also interested in the suspicious origin of many fires. Both are semimilitary in character. Both respond in case of emergency. Moreover, a good part of the time of the fire department personnel is unproductive, since it is maintained upon a standby basis waiting for fires to occur. All of these considerations make feasible the combination of both elements in a single unit. Through the use of modern means of communication, fire personnel, if properly trained, can be employed to augment the police activity.[21]

Consolidation brings many advantages. A greater amount of manpower is available for the protective services. Duplication and overlap of functions are avoided. A single communication center and central stations serving both police and fire is more economical. From the standpoint of fire prevention, police trained in fire work will be more alert to the hazards of fire. If it be asserted that both functions require specialization, then it can also be said that the need exists within any department. Arrangements that serve for separate departments can also be applied to a single department. Finally, integration would provide for a coordinated public safety effort.[22]

Both Oakwood, Ohio and Sunnyvale, California have employed the integrated department with exceedingly favorable results. In the former the "experiment" is well established. In 1950 the latter adopted a public safety department. Its experience is worthy of summary since it demonstrates the fallacy of continuing things as they are without examining alternatives. At the time the new department was created, the city had a police department consisting of sixteen full-time people. Fire protection was in the charge of a fire chief and a volunteer company of twenty-nine men. To establish a full-time fire department would have meant additional expendi-

[21] H. G. Pope, "Organization of Fire and Police Services in Small Cities," *Public Management*, XXXIII (1951), pp. 98-104.

[22] *Idem.*

ture. Since the city could not afford a separate department, the merger took place.

After a year of operation, the city manager was able to report that extensive savings had been made. The city was raised from a class 6 to a class 5 rating and as a result fire insurance premiums for residential, and commercial and industrial areas were reduced respectively 8.5 to 10 percent and 6 to 22 percent. The total saving in fire premiums for the city amounted to $30,000 which was equivalent to 22.7 cents of the tax rate. Overhead costs were sharply reduced and traffic and disaster control greatly improved. It is interesting to note that the opposition to the merger had completely disappeared by the time a new council was elected.[23]

Personnel practices in the fire department. Personnel management in the fire department follows the pattern previously described in the chapter on personnel administration. (See Chapter XVIII.) Like any other municipal function, fire fighting has as its principal objectives the attraction and retention of capable people. Only a well-rounded merit system with a concern for all aspects of the individual's work status can achieve these aims.

Recruitment and selection. Fires are fought by both men and equipment. Although improved apparatus may extend man's ability to combat fires, in the final analysis it is the quality of the people who man the equipment that is the key to fire fighting efficiency. Indeed, with the present day emphasis on the use of fire apparatus, the ability of the personnel becomes an even more important consideration. Consequently attention to personnel practices is a necessary first step toward the eventual improvement of the fire fighting function.

No department can expect that capable people will automatically beat their way to its door to inquire about vacancies. It is necessary that those interested in fire fighting as a career be sought out. This is especially so in the present era where a high-level viable economy often places the fire department in a disadvantageous position with respect to the more highly paid occupations. Even with this disability, however, it is essential that the department should know the qualities of the personnel it is seeking if it is to undertake a successful recruitment and selection program.

In its search for capable personnel, the fire department is greatly

[23] H. K. Hunter, "An Integrated Public Safety Department," *Public Management,* XXIII (1951), pp. 105-107.

assisted by the existence of a position-classification system. The definition of the duties and responsibilities is a fairly accurate index of the qualities to be sought in the applicant. Desirable attributes in the prospective fire fighter generally are considered to be the following: physical strength, mental alertness, mechanical aptitude and cooperativeness.[24] The examination for prospective recruits is designed to test these qualities.

Written tests, usually of the short answer or multiple choice variety, are employed to eliminate those who are unable to meet defined standards of mental alertness and mechanical aptitude. Physical performance is measured by tests of strength, such as running, bar chinning and the like. Medical examinations also reveal physical handicaps and deficiencies. Oral interviews ascertain the ability of candidates to cooperate with one another, a factor of considerable importance in the fire service where men are kept together in a fire house in a constant state of readiness. Finally, a probationary period ranging from six months to a year enables the fire department to cull out those who are not successful in actual work situations.[25] In the large cities selection is carried out almost entirely by a central personnel office with the fire department in the role of technical adviser. In the smaller cities, however, selection and recruitment become a major responsibility of the fire department, although cooperative arrangements such as the Michigan Demonstration Project conceivably could be developed. (For a description of this plan see Chapter XVIII.)

Conditions of work. In its discharge of its part of the personnel process, the fire department is guided by the legal framework established by the council. The latter not only votes appropriations which determine the scope of the fire fighting activity but it also prescribes the policies to be followed in regard to wages, hours of work, promotion, discipline and other aspects of employment. The governing body also may define the relative responsibilities of the central personnel office and the department. It may grant the latter final authority subject to supervision by the personnel office, or it may assign a dominant role to the fire department.

Promotion, supervision and discipline are regarded as part of the command prerogative of the fire department. These are consid-

---

[24] Members of the Staff of the Public Administration Service, *The Selection of Fire Fighters* (Chicago: Public Administration Service, 1940), p. 4.

[25] *Ibid.*, pp. 9-20.

ered as necessary essentials in the direction of men to achieve the desired objective of fire fighting. Most authorities on fire administration feel that without these powers the department is denied its legitimate authority to properly carry out the mission assigned to it. It is rather common, therefore, to find that fire departments are subject to central personnel direction only when there is the necessity to have uniform standards of personnel administration throughout the municipality. In the interest of morale, the city cannot afford to allow one department to have advantages which are not enjoyed by others. In the matter of promotions the department makes recommendations that are reviewed by the central personnel agency. In many jurisdictions promotion is made on the basis of a written examination on the duties related to the work of the fire department. The preparation and administration of the test is usually undertaken by the central personnel office, although consultation with the department as to its content constantly takes place. Some cities follow the rule of seniority in advancing persons to higher rank. Promotion is a matter of great concern to members of the department since there is relatively little movement upward. Unless equity is achieved in this area, the morale of the department will be seriously impaired.

Supervision and discipline are regarded as primary line responsibilities. It is here that the head of the fire fighting team seeks to obtain a high level of performance from his men, and he can only do so if he is armed with sufficient authority. It is the task of the supervisor to instruct employees in their duties and responsibilities. A climate must be created where the expectation of obedience is obtained. In the fire department heavy emphasis is placed upon directives. The wishes of individuals are often made subordinate to the needs of the service. Nevertheless, despite the dependence upon orders, advanced fire departments do seek to enlist the cooperation of members through the use of both discussion and incentives.[26]

It is when orders and directives are disobeyed that the matter of discipline enters into the personnel picture. Violation of rules, insubordination, the taking of bribes and absence without leave must be checked not only in the interest of departmental morale but also to show the affected public that it can rely upon swift departmental

[26] International City Managers' Association, *Municipal Fire Administration* (5th ed.; Chicago: 1950), pp. 120-130.

response to infractions of regulations. Disciplinary action ranges from attempts to reform the individual when "salvaging" seems possible to outright dismissal from the service where remedial effort is impossible. Minor disobedience such as tardiness may be punished either by conference or oral warnings, or by the issuance of demerits. These are designed to effect a change of heart upon the part of the fireman.

Where more serious infractions of regulations occur, harsher methods are employed. A fireman may be demoted with his hope for promotion almost irrevocably destroyed. He may be transferred to a less desirable company or may be requested to perform more onerous duties. He may be suspended without pay, pending a departmental hearing to review the charges placed against him. Most drastic of all disciplinary action is separation from the service.

Because of its finality, the removal power of the head of the department is hedged in by various procedural restrictions. In most instances the supervisor must prefer charges before a civil service commission or an appeals board with the employee being given an opportunity to present his side of the case. The reviewing body either may make a recommendation regarding the disposition of the case or it may have the authority to make a final decision. In council-manager cities, the manager is frequently given final power in questions involving the removal of employees. In rare instances the head of the department is empowered to separate the employee from the service. Vesting final decision on removals in the department head would do much to stimulate the removal of "dead wood" from the department but, strangely enough, the fear of being overruled makes the department head reluctant to exercise this important command function.

In the administration of its functions in regard to personnel, the fire department, like other line agencies, is subjected constantly to a variety of checks imposed by the central personnel office. Frequently the "police attitude" of the latter results in an invasion of areas that are of primary concern to the head of the department without any corresponding assumption of responsibility by the personnel office for the decisions made by it. Where to draw the line between the needs of the line department and the personnel agency is one of the difficult questions in personnel administration. The recent development of the concept of the civil service commission as an aide to management represents one solution to the problem.

As it is more widely accepted it will do much to bring about a common approach to a problem in which both staff and line agencies are interested—the optimum utilization of personnel.

FIRE PREVENTION

Its importance. The staggering loss of life and property experienced annually by the nation has brought a realization that fire extinction is at most half of the battle of fire protection. Fire prevention, though less spectacular than the clang and whistle of the passing fire engine, is equally effective in combating fire loss and damage. Authorities are agreed that most fires can be prevented if proper precautions are taken.

"Fires," remarked DeWayne Nolting, "are fought with paper and pencil as well as with chemicals and water. . . ." [27] Analysis of fire data gathered by fire departments reveals the major causes of fire and at the same time furnishes a prescription for their elimination. In 1954, 480,000 of the 727,000 building fires occurred in residential buildings. The major causes of fire were the following: (1) heating appliances, 171,000 fires; (2) fires from smoking and matches, 144,000; (3) defective electrical equipment, 88,000; (4) accumulation of rubbish, 50,000; (5) flammable liquids, 40,000; and (6) lightning, 40,000.[28] The overwhelming number of fires resulted from carelessness, smoking and structural and electrical wiring deficiencies. It can be readily seen that most of these conflagrations could have been prevented.

Fire prevention methods. The heart of a fire prevention is contained in the three "E's," engineering, enforcement and education, used so effectively as a guide for the prevention of traffic fatalities.[29] Fire prevention begins with a recognition of the common fire hazards within the community. Every city, like the human organism, is in the constant process of change. Its homes and buildings age. Some reach a dangerous state of dilapidation. Blighted areas with rooming houses, the hot plate and the "octopus" outlet subject the city to risk daily. Electrical wiring systems, because of the greater use of electrical appliances, rapidly become outmoded. Building materials, particularly the use of wood in frame construction, are a constant

---

[27] D. E. Nolting, *A Model Records and Reporting System for Fire Departments* (Chicago: Public Administration Service, 1938), p. 1.

[28] *National Municipal Yearbook for 1955,* p. 359.

[29] See the remarks of Major General Fleming in *The President's Conference on Fire Prevention* (Washington, D. C.: U. S. Government Printing Office, 1947), pp. 11-12.

source of danger. Lumber yards, tire rebuilding plants, gasoline stations, dry cleaning establishments, piers and wharves and a host of other enterprises that together provide the basis of our civilization are also a peril to the safety of the community. With each new business or industrial process the need for fire prevention becomes more acute. Fire departments continually gather data showing the location of buildings, the nature and type of occupancy, the kinds of building materials employed, and the areas where fires begin.

The use of building codes. Familiarity with the causes of fire lead to corrective action. In most cities the knowledge gathered as a result of the extensive research and experience of fire protection engineers is embodied in local ordinances, popularly called building and fire codes. "Stripped of its legal and technical phraseology a building code is really a set of rules to keep people from getting hurt." [30] The code contains a series of regulations designed to achieve reasonable safety for the occupants of the building specifically and the citizens generally. The height of buildings, the materials used in their construction, the standards of electrical wiring, the exposure of adjoining buildings, and a host of other conditions that are necessary either to prevent or limit the fire hazard are normally the subject of regulation. In general it might be said that the design, construction, and the maintenance of buildings are covered by the building code. Where a code exists, building plans are reviewed by an appropriate official for conformance with the ordinance. The building code of the National Board of Fire Underwriters and the National Electrical Code are usually employed by city councils as models for their regulations.

The fire codes. Fire dangers that are not due to structural defects are generally included in a fire code. It is the content of the building as distinct from its structure that is regulated. Hazardous chemicals, combustible fibers, flammable finishes, rubbish and trash are controlled by municipal ordinance. For example, the code describes the type of refuse burners in lumber yards, forbids smoking and requires that the yard be weeded and that the dead weeds be removed. The fire code based upon the standards of the National Board of Fire Underwriters embodies the most effective means of preventing fires. When the code is adopted, it gives the fire department an opportunity to lessen the hazards within the community.

---

[30] National Board of Fire Underwriters, *Building Codes, their Scope and Aims* (New York: undated), p. 4.

Permits and licenses. The building and fire codes are enforced through the devices of permits and inspections. Through its building and electrical inspectors, the building department maintains a close watch over all types of construction within the community. It issues building permits which in ordinary practice means that the building plans have achieved conformity with the code. It checks the installation of electrical wiring systems to insure the observance of approved safety standards. Finally, when the buildings have been completed, it must issue a certificate of occupancy before the building can be legally occupied. The success of the building department depends upon the extent to which the code is kept up to date. An out-moded code has little or no value. Building inspection in general suffers from the fact that it rarely takes place after the completion of the structure, a fact that becomes significant when one realizes that more than half of the fires occur in residential dwellings.

Enforcement of the fire code follows a somewhat similar pattern. The fire department grants a variety of permits and certificates, all concerned with the elimination of fire hazards. Industrial processes and the use of dangerous materials are not permitted unless an appropriate permit is granted. Installation of electrical wiring, gas, and heating appliances must be done by persons whose qualifications are rated. Only licensed personnel can carry on such activities. Mechanical equipment that may imperil the life and safety of occupants of a building must receive a certificate of approval before it can be used. Normally an underwriters' label signifying approval is sufficient to establish the safety of the apparatus.[31]

Inspection. The standards of fire safety which have been set forth in the fire code are enforced through inspection. Almost all fire codes centralize this responsibility in an agency with the department. The National Board of Fire Underwriters has recommended that all fire prevention activity be centered in a fire prevention bureau. Large cities follow this practice and even in the smaller jurisdictions the task is assigned to a high ranking officer of the department.

Inspections are carried out in the main by fire companies. These have two main objectives: to see that the fire code is observed and to familiarize the personnel with the buildings and hazards they will encounter should fire break out. The officer in charge of the fire company schedules the inspections, although the work may be sub-

[31] Brearley, *op. cit.*, chs. 6-8.

ject to supervision by the fire prevention bureau. Where "high value" properties or complex operations are encountered, however, the work of the inspector is supplemented by a comprehensive engineering survey by a group of experts who are especially skilled in the task. Their recommendations form the basis of wholesale changes in the industry or operation surveyed.

Minor violations are handled by the fire inspector in the normal course of his work. Visits to buildings reveal violations. These are brought to the attention of the owner and through discussion an endeavor is made to obtain corrective action. Major violations, however, become the subject of formal complaints. Notices are issued ordering the elimination of the hazards within a specified period of time. Failure to comply results in legal action taken against the violator. The work of inspection in most municipalities is divided among two agencies, the building and fire departments. Coordinated effort is needed if there is to be an integrated attack upon all fire hazards. In most jurisdictions this is carried out through the periodic exchange of information. Conferences and discussion further this process. However, it is only when a fire prevention bureau is given the lead in such matters that concentrated action takes place.

Besides enforcing the code, the fire prevention bureau is required to investigate all fire damage in the community and to ascertain its nature and cause. Fires of suspicious origin are investigated. Fulfilment of this responsibility requires the attendance of the personnel of the bureau at all fires. It is their task to appraise the methods of fire fighting and to gather evidence if the nature of the fire seems suspicious. Fire prevention personnel, however, are not engaged in the extinction of fires.

Fire prevention education. Fire prevention is also concerned with the education of the public. Programs to alert the public to the dangers of fire are based upon the assumption that most fire hazards are easily recognized by almost anyone who will give a little thought and attention to the matter.[32] Fire education as an organized activity began in 1911 when the Fire Marshals' Association suggested that the fortieth anniversary of Chicago's great fire be used to publicize the dangers of fire. Since 1920 an annual proclamation of the President of the United States has been the basis of fire prevention weeks. In 1923 the fire waste council of the United States Chamber of Commerce sponsored fire prevention weeks and contests through the

[32] National Fire Protection Association, *op. cit.*, p. 57.

1,300 local affiliates of the Chamber. In 1947 a three day conference, called by the President of the United States, discussed ways and means by which communities could eliminate or reduce the loss of life and property. More recently in 1954, the Advertising Council with the cooperation of the National Fire Protection Association launched a most ambitious fire education program that blanketed the entire country.[33]

As a result of these efforts, it is now customary for all communities to have fire prevention weeks in the fall of each year. Through proclamations by leading public officials, speeches and communication media, the attention of the public is drawn to the need for fire prevention. Such occasions furnish the fire department with a rare opportunity both to build good will and to eliminate fire hazards. "Open house" at the fire station gives the people a chance to learn about the role of the fire department in the community. Fire prevention committees focus attention of the civic groups on many of the fire hazards that face the city. Inadequacies in the fire prevention code, or indeed its absence, may be brought to the attention of the city council. A favorable climate of opinion may enable the department to check on the violations in residential dwellings. Visits of fire department personnel to schools, headquarters of the Boy Scouts, and other community agencies, can mobilize these groups in the elimination of dangerous accumulations of rubbish and trash.

The importance of fire education can be demonstrated by several examples. Several years ago in the city of Los Angeles a visit of fire department personnel to the various schools resulted in a city-wide search to discover violations. In a four-year period school children discovered 387,000 hazards. It is estimated that if one out of ten of these had resulted in fires the loss to the city would have been about $7 million.[34] In Mansfield, Ohio, a concerted fire prevention campaign reduced the per capita loss from fires from $4 to $.80.[35] Obviously not all campaigns for fire prevention have had as spectacular results but the conclusion of one authority is worth remembering; "A study of the predominating cause of fire indicates that at least one-half of the property loss is from fires which might be prevented by the application of a reasonable degree of care and knowledge." [36]

33 *National Municipal Yearbook for 1955*, pp. 361-362.
34 The Encyclopedia Americana, XI (1953), p. 242.
35 *The President's Conference on Fire Prevention, op. cit.*, p. 22.
36 S. Inge, "Fire Protection," *Encyclopedia of Social Sciences*, VI, p. 264.

CONCLUSION

Fire, as we have noted, has given man civilization. Each step in the advance of mankind has been marked by a new application of the principle of fire. Fire has given us industry, and the latter has been mainly responsible for the rise of cities. But fire is also an awesome instrument of destruction. The same forces that have given rise to the city often peril its very existence. Industrial processes, hazardous machinery, the miracles of chemistry when combined with the close proximity of people are potential dangers which, if left unchecked, may destroy civilization as we know it.

Fire protection is closely related to the life of the city. When the nation was rural, fire fighting was rudimentary in nature. The fire "watch," the volunteer company and a handful of private fire fighters hired by insurance companies sufficed. When cities began to appear in increasing numbers in the post Civil War period, a parallel development took place in fire fighting. The fire function in larger cities shifted from a volunteer part-time activity to a full-time paid function. Although volunteer companies still exist, they remain only because the need for greater protection has not become fully evident to those who rely upon it. Industrialization and specialization in the city was accomplished by the increased use of highly technical fire equipment. At the same time the loss from fire led insurance companies to insist upon more adequate protection. The arrival of the National Board of Fire Underwriters, an association of private stock companies, led to the insistence upon more effective fire fighting measures. Under the stimulus of fire insurance rates and fire ratings of cities, fire protection achieved a new stature.

In the century or so of its organized existence the fire department has made great strides in fire fighting. Its record on fire prevention, however, is not equally good. European cities have done much more than our departments even though their fire equipment does not compare with ours. Part of our poor record of fire prevention is due to the prevalent use of wood and other combustible materials in the construction of our buildings. A part may also be charged to the higher unit value of our dwellings. Some of the blame may also be assigned to the lack of proper liability laws and "over insurance." But the overwhelming portion of the blame rests upon the inadequacies of fire prevention methods in this country. Inspection to eliminate potential hazards, in residential units, is hardly more than casual. Even in the case of industrial and commercial buildings, inspection methods have to be made more continuous if effective fire prevention is to take place.

It is thus in the area of fire prevention rather than fire fighting that the future course of fire development has to take place. There is more than a glimmering of hope in this connection. Fire education, alerting the public to the dangers of fire violations, is making some progress. Civic and community groups are being organized on a continuous basis. Recognition is needed, however, that fire education is more than a public relations job. Fire presents dangers every day of the week.

BIBLIOGRAPHY

Books:

Brearley, H. C. *A Symbol of Safety*. Garden City, New York: Doubleday, Page and Co., 1923.

International City Managers' Association, *Municipal Fire Administration,* Chicago: 1950. 5th edition.

James, C. S. *Police and Fire Integration in the Small City*. Chicago: Public Administration Service, 1955.

Kenlon, J. *Fires and Fire Fighters*. New York: George H. Doran Co., 1913.

National Board of Fire Underwriters. *Building Codes, Their Scope and Aims*. New York, undated.

National Board of Fire Underwriters. *Pioneers of Progress*. New York, 1941.

National Fire Protection Association, *Fire Protection Engineering*. Boston, 1943.

Nolting, D. E. *A Model Records and Reporting System for Fire Departments*. Chicago: Public Administration Service, 1938.

Public Administration Service. *The Selection of Fire Fighters*. Chicago: 1940.

Articles and Other Material:

Encyclopaedia of Social Sciences. 1st edition. Volume VI. Article. "Fire Protection."

Hunter, H. K. "An Integrated Public Safety Department," *Public Management,* XXXIII (1951), 105-107.

Pope, H. G. "Organization of Fire and Public Services in Small Cities," *Public Management*, XXXIII (1951), 98-104.

President's Conference on Fire Protection. Washington, D. C.: U. S. Government Printing Office, (1948).

Chapter Twenty-Two

Health and Welfare

City Life, Health and Welfare

The impact of technology. Technology and industry have profoundly altered the ways of life of our people. The widespread use of machines as a substitute for manpower has altered our occupational patterns. Less people are required on the farm. More are needed in manufacturing and service industries.[1] The fusion of the efforts of many people to produce or market a product or item has permitted specialization and a consequent increase in conveniences, luxuries, and leisure time. In the future it is reasonable to assume that even greater benefits are in the prospect.

At the same time, however, these marked advances are not without their drawbacks. Although much progress has been made in the application of the science of medicine, the massing of people in the city has subjected them to stresses and strains that are as yet unmeasurable. Traffic congestion, noxious fumes, the shock factor of noise and dirt, and the routine and monotony of the daily job combined with the general absence of organized recreation are an ever present threat to the city dweller. Fear and insecurity because of the primary dependence on wages and salaries are never entirely absent. Closeness of living and multiplicity of human contacts pose the possibility of the spread of communicable disease. Purity of water supply and the disposal of human and industrial wastes are constant problems. Over-refinement of foods for storage and use by the people of the city holds forth the prospect of malnutrition in the midst of plenty.[2]

Changes in industrial processes and a growing demand for new and different skills have placed a huge emphasis on education and a highly mobile work force. Finally, the aging of our population

[1] In 1950, 13 percent, 34 percent, and 50 percent of our people were engaged respectively in farming, manufacturing and service industries. See also chapter 1, The Changing City.

[2] J. Forman, "Biological Truths and Public Health," Elmer Peterson, ed., *Cities Are Abnormal* (Norman, Oklahoma: The University of Oklahoma Press, 1946), ch. 5.

has confronted us with many new problems: an increase in chronic diseases, health education, and the general need to protect people during their unproductive years. Thus the coming of the industrial revolution has been a mixed blessing. It has given us many comforts and conveniences but at the same time it has exposed our people to new hazards and dangers.

The changed governmental attitude. The shift from a rural to an urban situation has meant a drastic change in the role and attitude of government. In the past the maintenance of the health and welfare of the individual was only a limited societal responsibility. Safety of water supply and food, the condition of health and protection against sickness and old age were largely a matter of individual determination. What the individual did with his God-given attributes and resources were private matters.

During the more than a century and a half of our existence as a nation, however, this concept has been drastically altered. The individual is still on his own but it has daily become more apparent that there are factors beyond his immediate control. The pressure of circumstances led the citizens through social and political action to demand that the government supplement their efforts. In response to the need, the role of local government was heightened and, since 1932, it has been assisted by both the state and national governments. In the succeeding pages, an attempt will be made to portray the varied and multitudinous relationships that have been developed to protect the people from sickness and insecurity.

PUBLIC HEALTH

Health is the community's and the nation's greatest asset. A nation that is in poor health wastes its vitality and productivity. It suffers losses through sickness, disability, and death. Its manpower is depleted and the costs, in both human pain and misery, are incalculable. Both prosperity and security depend upon the maintenance of the nation's health at the highest possible level. Health, in the broad meaning of the term, may be defined as "more than freedom from disease, freedom from pain and untimely death. It means optimum physical, mental and social efficiency and well being." [3] Although the health of the citizen is a matter of national concern, the fulfilment of

[3] The President's Commission on the Health Needs of the Nation, *Building America's Health,* vol. 1, Findings and Recommendations (Washington, D. C.: U. S. Government Printing Office, 1952), p. 1. Public health as used in this chapter means the *public* measures to protect man against his environment.

the goal of better health is primarily the responsibility of state and local governments, voluntary agencies, and the citizens all working together.

Evolution of the health function. Public health measures are relatively recent in origin. The Greeks, almost instinctively, sought to practice the control of disease through isolation, but it was not because they understood the causes. In the medieval period, leprosy in the sixth century, the great plagues of the fourteenth century and the outbreak of syphilis a century later, the "three great teachers" as C.-E.A. Winslow has termed them, stressed the importance of quarantine. It was not until almost the middle of the nineteenth century, however, that the first fundamental steps were taken to control the adverse effects of man's environment. In England, Chadwick in 1842 was the first to suggest that there was a high correlation between disease and the presence of dirt and filth. His findings led to the general introduction of sanitary measures. The later discovery of the germ theory by Pasteur and the Englishmen, Snow and Budd, led to a whole new science of bacteriology.[4] The development of the microscope assisted in the identification of diseases, and their control was effected through vaccines and serums. By the end of the nineteenth century quarantine, sanitation and bacteriological methods as public health practices, were firmly established.

In the first decade of the twentieth century the campaign for the eradication of tuberculosis and the reduction of infant mortality resulted in health education as a further evolution of the public health function. Very little could be done to isolate those with tuberculosis since about 85 percent of the people were already infected. Infant mortality was largely a matter of understanding the principles of nutrition and health. It was necessary, therefore, to promote an understanding of healthful living habits and to foster the conscious desire to eliminate the causes of disease. In New York City in 1908 the creation of the first bureau of child hygiene, and six years later, a bureau of public health marks the beginning of organized effort in this area.[5]

Available data indicate dramatically the extent of success that has resulted from the application of medical principles. The greatest

[4] C.-E.A. Winslow, "The Evolution of Public Health and Its Objectives," in J. S. Simmons, ed., *Public Health in the World Today* (Cambridge, Massachusetts: Harvard University Press, 1949), pp. 20-21.

[5] Winslow, *op. cit.*, pp. 21-22; H. Emerson, "Essential Local Public Health Services," *The Annals,* CCLXXIII (1951), p. 22.

gains have been recorded in the area of infectious diseases. The death rate per 100,000 in the first half of this century for all such illnesses combined has dropped from 676 to 79, a decrease of approximately 90 percent. The rate for tuberculosis has dropped from

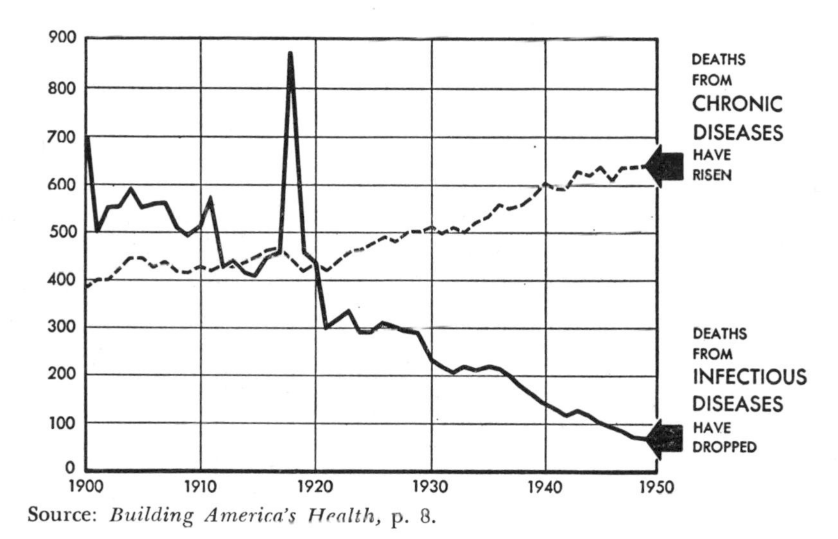

Source: *Building America's Health*, p. 8.

Fig. 9. Mortality Rate for U. S. Population, 1900-1950.

194 to 27; that of diptheria from 40 to less than 1; and that of influenza and pneumonia from 202 to 34. The death rates for children and young people have fallen 83 percent.[6]

The changes in the age character of our population has also beckoned the attention of the public health function. The spectacular advances in public health are reflected in the increased life expectancy from 47 years in 1900 to 68 in 1949. In 1948 there were 10 million people who were sixty-five years of age or older. By 1975 it is predicted that more than twice that number will be in that category. At that time more than one third of the nation will be forty-five years of age or older.[7] We are rapidly becoming a nation of older people. Chronic illness and disability are now our greatest health challenge. The health officer must now deal with people in their middle and older ages, an area where the high cost of medical

[6] The President's Commission on Health Needs of the Nation, *op. cit.*, pp. 8-9.

[7] O. R. Ewing, *The Nation's Health, a ten year program* (Washington. D. C.: U. S. Government Printing Office, 1948), p. 127. In 1800 the median life expectancy was 16 years.

care will necessitate an increasing resort to the public authorities.[8]

Health department functions. Broadly speaking, the functions of the health department are inherent in the methods employed to combat disease and promote a healthful environment for man. Acceptance of the germ theory has led to certain common measures: sanitation, the identification of disease, the use of serums and vaccines, and health education. Beyond these common aspects the activities of municipal health departments vary in accordance with local conditions, the demands for service and the relationship of the city to the state. A large city like New York with its great resources and large facilities enjoys relative freedom from state control. Its horizons are bounded only by the political decisions of the community. On the other hand, smaller cities are not only dependent upon the state for assistance but also are subjected to a considerable degree of state supervision. In some states cities do not possess the health function service since it is administered through the counties or health districts. Thus, despite the common acceptance of public health principles, there is a wide variation among cities in the scope and dimensions of public health work.

The services of a health department are highly responsive to the changing character of the health needs of the community. Traditionally, as we have seen, health activities were designed to minimize the day to day threats to health. At first, health authorities sought to control epidemic disease. Later, as considerable success was achieved, attention was centered on more specific programs, tuberculosis, venereal diseases, and the reduction of infant and maternal mortality. Now an attack is being made upon the diseases of an aging society, cancer, heart disease, and others that are a major cause of death.

Fulfilment of the role of the health department as the guardian of the community's health requires the performance of basic activities without which public health can only be an empty promise. These may be divided into two main categories: (1) services which are common to the department as a whole, such as the maintenance of vital and public health statistics, and the operation of a public health laboratory; and (2) programs with a concern for any or all of the following: (a) environmental health, (b) health education, (c) personal health services for the medically needy, and others, for

---

[8] L. I. Dublin, "Public Health and the Diseases of Old Age," Simmons, *op. cit.*, pp. 232-240.

whom the community has accepted responsibility and (d) the operation of health centers and hospitals. All of these are brought together to minister to the health needs of the community.

Vital statistics. Man fights disease with pen and pencil as well as with the scientific principles of medicine. Statistics on births, morbidity, communicable diseases and death are an important measure of the health of the community. These are usually obtained from physicians and hospitals on the basis of signed reports indicating the cause or origin of the ailment. Such data indicate the danger spots to health in the community. It charts the course of corrective action and measures the progress that has been made. In the hands of an enlightened executive it can point to the future course of public health activity. Without the proper analysis of public health and vital statistics, as Emerson has remarked, "neither the character nor the extent of preventable disease nor the results of measures for its control can be established." [9] Finally, the careful use of public health statistics has given the public an awareness of the health problem and as such has undoubtedly been a major factor in the expansion of public health work.

The public health laboratory. Another central service of great importance to the health department is the public health laboratory. The germ theory of disease led to the discovery of the causes of many infectious diseases and made the identification of the hostile organisms that invade the human body a necessity. In 1894 the first public health department was established in the city of New York.[10] Since that time it has become a standard asset of many health departments. It is in the laboratory that the science of bacteriology becomes a reality. Its facilities are employed by the practicing physician to aid him in his diagnosis of the cause of illness. Its analysis of food, water supply and other samplings assist enforcement units in the discovery of health violations.

Although all communities have the need for a laboratory, it is not generally considered practical for cities with a population of less than 50,000, primarily because of the difficulty in financing such an activity. In its stead, various *ad hoc* arrangements are made. Cooperative relationships have been established with other units of government and it has even been proposed that joint operation of a laboratory be established in connection with a hospital, if one

---

[9] Emerson, *op. cit.*, p. 22.
[10] Emerson, *op. cit.*, p. 21.

exists. The latter arrangement, as Smillie has suggested, is fraught with administrative difficulties.[11]

Maintenance of environmental health. Aside from these supporting services, the activities of the health department revolve about its primary objective—the maintenance of a healthful environment for all. This is truly a monumental undertaking, the full import of which is rarely realized unless one has had the occasion to live outside of the United States. It involves very largely an attempt to reduce the number of adjustments that man has to make to a hostile environment.

Most common among the many measures employed is community sanitation. Insects, flies, animals, and disease-bearing rodents are exterminated, although the latter is primarily the problem of a seaport city. Disposal of human and industrial wastes, an important source of contamination, is carefully regulated. In a city where contacts are multiplied, the dangers of infection from these sources are magnified. Consequently, the treatment of sewage, the use of septic tanks, and the dumping of raw sewage in surface waters are carefully watched. So great is the hazard to human life in this area that the health department is given summary powers to abate the nuisance.

The processing, handling, and distribution of foodstuffs, particularly milk and milk products, are carefully supervised. Eating establishments, hotels, bathing and recreation areas are licensed to meet appropriate health standards. Cleanliness and sanitary facilities are required for those handling food. Medical examinations for food handlers are made constantly. Because milk is such an important germ culture, special provisions are made to oversee its production and use. The model milk ordinance sponsored by the United States Public Health Service has been adopted by many municipalities. Inspection of dairy farms and herds is undertaken by the state, although in large cities, such as New York, city inspectors are also engaged in regulation. It is now standard practice in most cities to require the pasteurization of milk at plants located within the city limits. Laboratory tests of dealers' milk are made. Milk containers must show the date of processing.[12] More recently as our economy has begun to use more organic chemicals, air pollutants such as

[11] W. G. Smillie, *Public Health Administration in the United States* (New York: The Macmillan Company, 1949), pp. 400-401.

[12] Smillie, *op. cit.*, pp. 399-400.

sulphur dioxide and fluorine gases have posed the possibility of dangers to health and vegetation. Through smoke control measures an attempt is being made to abate this potential nuisance.[13] As a result of the labors of the health department, we are singularly free of water, liquid, insect and animal-borne diseases.

Control of communicable disease. Control of communicable disease is also a prime concern of the health department. This, too, is a difficult task involving the cooperation of the medical profession with health department personnel at the city, state, and national levels. Once the cause of disease is isolated, however, public controls go into operation, affecting both the sick and the well. Some departments quarantine the patient and seek to limit the contacts of his family with those on the outside. This is carried out either by sanitary or inspectional personnel, or by public health nurses. Smillie suggests that such action furnishes the occasion for the instruction of the family in the dangers of infection.

If the illness is especially severe, hospitalization is undertaken to prevent the further spread of the disease. Immunization measures such as vaccination and serums in the case of chicken pox, diptheria, smallpox, and now poliomyelitis, are employed to check the further spread of disease. Tuberculosis control requires early diagnosis and hospital care. Venereal disease is also handled in a similar fashion. Clinics often supplement hospitalization, although here, too, their use in areas with a population of less than 50,000 is considered impractical.[14] All infectious diseases, theoretically at least, can be eliminated or at least reduced. In 1948 it was estimated that 120,000 out of the 170,000 deaths from communicable diseases could have been prevented.[15] The fact that such a loss has occurred is an index of our failure to apply effectively the scientific principles of medicine.

Personal health services. In protecting the community's health, the health department also supplies personal health services to fill in the gaps that would otherwise exist for groups for which the community has accepted responsibility. Provision is made for the medically needy, for certain maternal and child welfare programs, for the treatment of chronic diseases and often for special diagnostic facilities. Hospitals and health centers are often operated by the depart-

---

[13] F. W. Went, "Air Pollution," *Scientific American*, CXCII (1955), pp. 62-73.

[14] Smillie, *op. cit.*, pp. 391-396.

[15] O. R. Ewing, *The Nation's Health, a ten year program* (Washington, D. C.: U. S. Government Printing Office, 1948), p. 9.

ment. Baby clinics and "kiddie keep well" stations provide the mother with instruction on the care of her child as well as herself. Although the physician is generally responsible for his patients, clinics provide medical services for those who cannot afford to pay for treatment.[16] To paraphrase Dr. Haven Emerson, the community is the patient of the department.

Health education. No review of the public health function can be considered complete without some reference to the role of health education. Alerting the public to the health facts of its environment is an important factor in combating disease and protecting the health of the community. It is in this area that the old adage, "An ounce of prevention is worth a pound of cure," has special relevance. The health department carries out the health education on its own and in conjunction with the school authorities. Each activity of the department furnishes the occasion for instruction and as each member of the department performs his daily tasks, he does, or at least should, consider himself a health educator. Aside from this continuous task, the health department through interpretive reports can analyze the community's health needs and enlist community support for the most pressing problems.

In its other educational activities the department has to draw a fine line between its own efforts and those of other agencies of city government and community organizations. Pre-school hygiene is normally the responsibility of the physician but clinics and baby stations also provide educational opportunities. School hygiene is the concern of school authorities but the health department can and does educate its personnel. Moreover, the conduct of medical examinations and health services for the children provide many opportunities for informal education. Community service organizations and the formation of health councils can be employed to assist the department in the education of the community to its health needs.

Most health departments operate within the above-mentioned spectrum of responsibility. Many often go beyond this. In some areas, the public health function includes nutrition, dentistry, accident prevention, bedside nursing, and a host of other health services. The problems at hand and the decisions of the community in response to these problems largely govern the scope and nature of the health function.

---

[16] Smillie, *op. cit.*, pp. 397-398.

HEALTH DEPARTMENT ORGANIZATION

Public health is one of the police powers that belong to the state under our federal system of government. It is applied at the local level by the municipality to the extent that the state considers it feasible. Consequently, the municipality as the recipient of state authority is subject to administrative supervision by the state, and in matters that are considered beyond its scope and competence the higher level of government generally assumes jurisdiction.

The board of health. Like its functions, the organization of the public health department varies with the city in which it is located. In commission-governed cities the common council is, to all intents and purposes, the board of health. In most mayor-council and council-manager cities, however, the board of health is composed of interested laymen who are appointed by the municipal executive. The boards of health vary in size from three to five members and are generally appointed for overlapping terms.[17] Health boards are generally entrusted with the administration of the health department. They choose the public health officer and formulate general policy for the guidance of the department. Through health rules and regulations they set the standards for water, milk and food supplies, sanitation of public places and the elimination of disease bearing insects and rodents. In special instances they also may hold hearings on special health problems as they arise.

The health officer. Below the board of health is the health officer who is its administrative agent. He is responsible for all of the details of personnel, budgeting and direction. He oversees the conduct of the many and varied functions noted above. For a city with a population of between 50,000 and 100,000 people, health activities are divided on the following basis: (1) the health officer, and (2) five divisions, concerned with the following: sanitation including food and milk inspection; public health laboratory; communicable disease; health education including child and school hygiene; and administration including vital statistics.[18] In support of the efforts of the health officer are personnel who are trained in inspection, sanitation, public health work and allied fields.

Adequacy of public health functions. It would be misleading to assume that the country is blanketed with adequately staffed public

---

[17] It is considered desirable to have one or two physicians on the board because of their acquaintance with the health of the community.

[18] Smillie, *op. cit.*, pp. 403-405.

health departments. Indeed, quite the contrary is the case. In 1955 only 22,385 full-time persons were directly engaged in health work in our cities. More than a quarter of these were located in cities with a population of 500,000 or more. A total of less than 1,500 persons were employed in cities of 25,000 or less people, the most numerous category of cities.[19] On a nation-wide basis, a report summarizing the nation's health pointed out that only 7 million people were being served by public health staffs that met acceptable minimum standards. At least 40 million people in 1,200 counties were either without a health department or had one that was operated on a part-time basis. Almost one hundred million people were denied the services of a health department.[20]

A variety of reasons may be advanced for these deficiencies: a lack of public understanding of the relationship of public health to their welfare; a severe shortage of trained personnel in almost every category of public health work; and finally, financial stringencies existent in the various communities. It is probable that many other factors could be cited, but more than anything else, it is apparent that most communities simply cannot afford to finance a full-time public health activity. The fragmentation of political authority into thousands of local units operates to prevent a concerted attack upon disease. In the final analysis, the gap in our public health services poses a basic question: how large does a community have to be before it can afford a full-time health department?

This question has been the subject of study by the American Medical Association and the American Public Health Association. It is now commonly agreed that a community of 50,000 people is needed to finance adequately a public health function. This is based upon an estimate of a minimum per capita cost of one dollar. Even this amount would not support more than the following: a full time medical officer, a sanitarian, ten public health nurses and three clerks. For the larger city, more personnel with a greater variety in talents, skills and training would be necessary with a much greater rise in expenditures. Since many communities are much smaller than the minimum standard size, it is obvious that a consolidation of health units is necessary. In 1945 a committee of the American Public Health Association recommended that the country, for health

[19] U. S. Department of Commerce, Bureau of Census, *City Employment in 1955* (Washington, D. C.: U. S. Government Printing Office, 1956), p. 7.

[20] Ewing, *op. cit.*, p. 163.

purposes, should be divided into 1,197 units. This would bring public health services within the reach of every person and family.[21] City-county consolidation and mergers of public health units seem to be the only solutions for the present inadequacies.

PUBLIC HEALTH PROBLEMS OF THE FUTURE

The health of our people in the cities is inseparable from the health of the entire nation. Very largely, the health problems encountered by the health department of the future will be governed by three factors, the age and character of our population, its income distribution and the kinds of medical services that can be mustered to meet the needs of the nation.

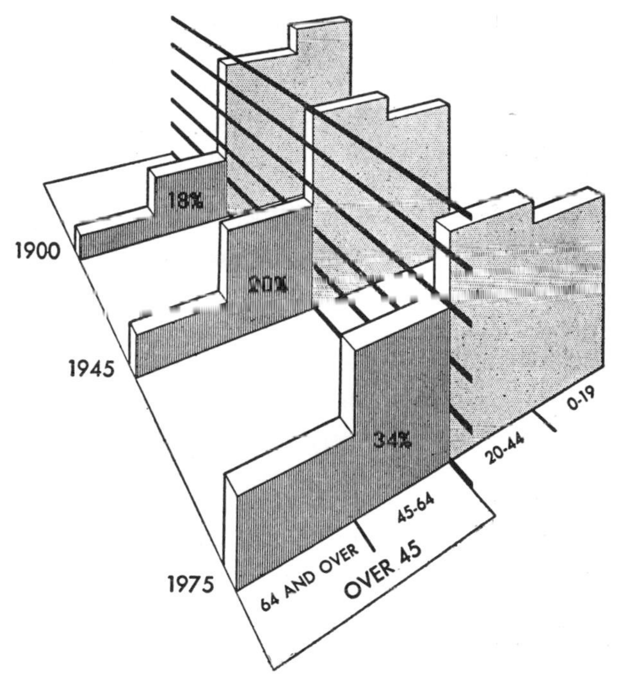

Fig. 10. Our Aging Population.

Chronic diseases. We are becoming a nation of older people. The very fact that public health measures have been so effectively employed has brought a longer life span for our people. But this trend has signalled the appearance of chronic diseases requiring the

21 H. Emerson and M. Luginbuhl, *Local Health Units for the Nation* (New York: The Commonwealth Fund, 1945), pp. 2-5.

most expensive type of medical care. Cancer, heart disease, mental illness and a number of other diseases can be treated by the physician but only with the assistance of public authorities. Long periods of hospitalization and expensive treatment are generally required.

Some measure of the problem in this area can be obtained by a brief review of the large amounts of data that have been accumulated. The aging of our population has intensified the need for more hospital beds for chronic illness. The days spent in a hospital for persons over 65 years of age are twice as many as for those under that age.[22] In 1952 more than one-half of the patients in our hospitals were victims of mental disease.[23] Two investigators report that the rate per thousand of the number of mental patients in hospitals has doubled in a half-century.[24] The greatest need today is for beds in mental and chronic disease hospitals.[25] It is estimated that public expenditures by states, counties and cities for their mental hospitals was $390 million.[26]

Cost of medical care. The ability of the city and the nation to deal with these problems must be related not only to the community effort but also to the ability of the individual to pay for medical care since his inability to do so often means a resort to public authorities. The average mean family income in terms of 1950 dollars is contained in table 9.

Although the average income of the American family has increased appreciably in the last two decades, one can assume, if the incidence of disease is roughly the same for all income groups, that the burden of medical care falls more heavily on the lower two-fifths of our population. Many cannot afford even routine medical care and it is certain that the large family with the single head of the household is at a serious disadvantage. Added to this is what seems to be a paradox: more effective health measures as a result of the advances in medicine operate so as to place them beyond the reach

---

22 U. S. Department of Health, Education and Welfare, *op. cit.*, pp. 130-131.

23 *Statistical Abstract of the United States* (1955), p. 81. The actual number of patients was 595,519. This does not include mental defectives and epileptics who numbered 128,431.

24 R. H. Felix and M. Kramer, "Extent of the Problem of Mental Disorders," *The Annals*, CCLXXXVI (1953), pp. 5-14, especially p. 9. In 1900 the rate was 1.9 patients per thousand people and fifty years later it was 3.8 per thousand. 577,000 people were in mental hospitals in 1950.

25 U. S. Department of Health, Education and Welfare, *op. cit.*, p. 130.

26 Felix and Kramer, *op. cit.*, p. 13.

Table 9—AVERAGE MEAN FAMILY INCOME IN THE UNITED STATES

Quintile	*Average Family Income in 1950 Dollars* [1]		*Percent Measure*
	1935–1936	1950	1935–1936 to 1950
All families	3,212	4,981	55
Lowest fifth	672	1,514	125
Next to lowest fifth	1,496	2,972	99
Middle fifth	2,281	4,063	78
Next to highest fifth	3,345	5,417	62
Highest fifth	8,263	10,941	32
Top five percent	17,180	19,545	14

[1] Excludes income of unattached individuals.

Source: U. S. Department of Labor, Bureau of Labor Statistics, *Economic Forces in the U. S. A. in Facts and Figures,* p. 52.

of those who probably need them most.[27] Particularly in the areas of mental and chronic diseases, it is probable that those who cannot afford to pay for medical care will require some other form of assistance. Regardless of whether such need is met by public support or by the action of voluntary agencies or groups, the horizons of public health will be broadened considerably.

Shortages in medical facilities. Finally there are extensive gaps in our health services such as a shortage of public health units, doctors, and hospital beds. In 1948 the status of these were summarized in Figure 11. These data have been confirmed by a 1952 study of the nation's health needs by a presidential commission.[28] There is an acute need for medical and dental personnel, more public health nurses and more hospital facilities.

There is considerable evidence that the nation is slowly becoming aware of the problems posed by our rapidly changing urban society. The Hill-Burton Act allocated $3 million for hospital surveys and authorized $75 million annually in the form of construction grants to assist the states and localities in building hospitals.[29]

[27] M. M. Davis, *Medical Care for Tomorrow* (New York: Harper and Bros., 1955), generally, and especially, pp. 23-31.

[28] The President's Committee on the Health Needs of the Nation, *op. cit.,* vol. 1.

[29] Public Law 275, 79th Cong. 2nd. Sess., (1946).

In seven years of operation, $1,849 million were spent on hospital construction, of which one-third was contributed by the federal government and the balance by the state and local units. Approximately 109,200 hospital beds and 483 health centers were added

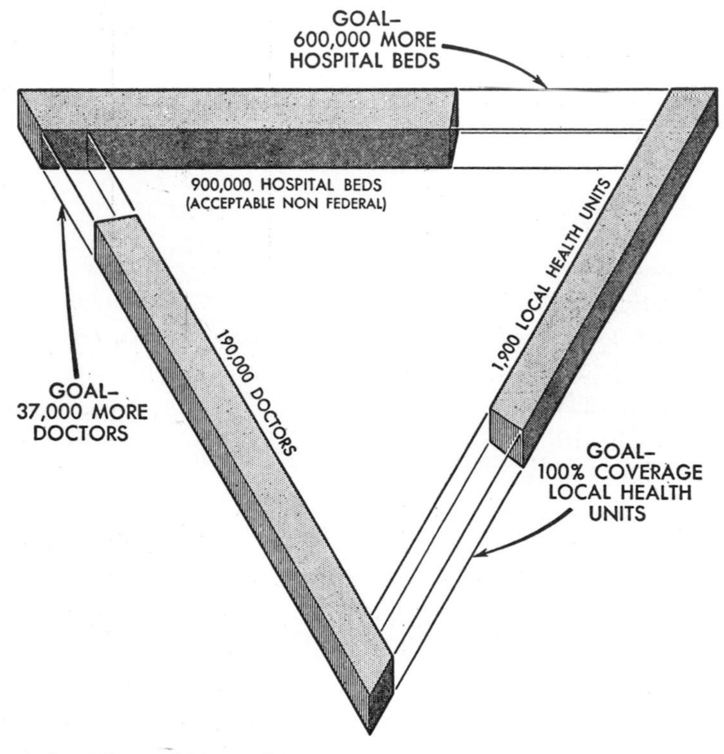

Source: See *The Nation's Health,* p. 16.

Fig. 11. Feasible Health Service Goals for 1960.

to the nation's health facilities.[30] The Truman health insurance program, while it aroused a storm of controversy, nevertheless focused public attention on the relationship of income distribution to health needs. The growth of voluntary health insurance plans has been stimulated. More recently in 1954 President Eisenhower's program for reinsurance of voluntary health and hospital plans, although rejected, has once again emphasized the need for more adequate health protection.

[30] U. S. Department of Health, Education and Welfare, *op. cit.,* p. 131.

WELFARE

The evolution of the welfare function. Welfare as a function is as old as government itself. The poor and needy, the orphaned child, the sick and disabled, the mentally defective and the aged have always been the subject of community concern. To a greater or lesser degree the vulnerable segments of our society have been the recipients of assistance from families and private individuals, and where these resources have been found to be inadequate, from the government. Welfare, broadly defined, embraces a variety of functions for the alleviation of poverty and distress. It seeks to minimize the hazards of economic insecurity. Obviously, this is an elastic term whose scope varies with the times and the degree of community political decision to assume responsibility for those who, for one reason or another, are not able to take care of themselves.

Welfare a local responsibility. At the present time the national government has assumed a very large measure of the responsibility for the welfare of our people. Its role is steadily increasing not only in matters of health but in almost all phases involving the security of the individual. This was not always so. Indeed, aside from a brief reference in the preamble and in article I section 8 of the Constitution, the federal government was not assumed to have any concern in this area. Welfare, or relief, as it was then termed, was regarded as a local function to be supplemented at most by state aid and assistance. The needy, aged and distressed were assisted by the community of which they were a part. The change in relationships that has taken place, primarily in the last two decades, reflects the operation of forces and factors that have been at work for at least a half-century. To understand the heightened role of the federal government, it is necessary to sketch the transformation of our society.

Reasons for federal interest. First and perhaps foremost among the reasons for federal interest is the drastic alteration in the pattern of our life. Science and invention have wrought many changes to which our society has not as yet adapted itself. The steady march of industrialization has rather sharply reduced the number and proportion of farmers and independent shopkeepers. Most of our population now resides in cities and towns. We have become primarily a nation of wage earners. We *buy* our living, that is we use our salaries to provide us with the necessities of living. Under such circumstances the individual is vitally affected by the vagaries of the business cycle, factors over which he has little or no control although they have a direct bearing on his welfare and happiness.

Secondly, dependence upon income and wages has important relevance for the welfare function. The ability of families to deal with adversity is directly related to their income and savings. Table 9 gives a percentage distribution of families by total income. In 1954, despite the rising level of income, there were 3.7 million families and 4.4 million individuals with money incomes under $1000; and 8.3 million families and 6.2 million individuals with incomes of less than $2000.[31] It is estimated that in 1950 the economic resources of over 6 million urban consumer units were too limited to provide an adequate standard of living. This total consisted of 19.5 million persons of whom more than 7 million were children under 18 years of age.[32]

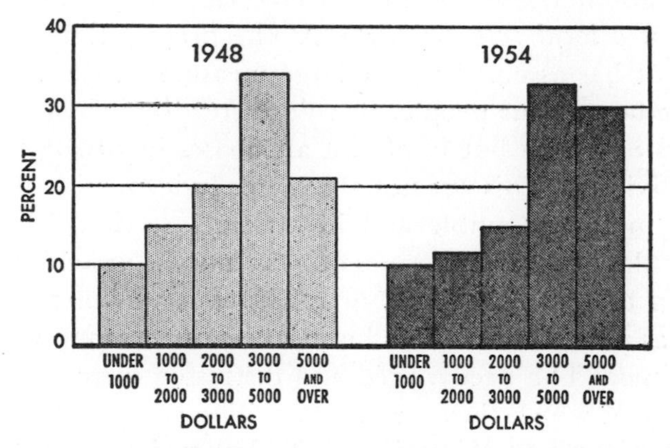

Fig. 12. Percentage Distribution of U. S. Families by Total Money Income (1948 Dollars); 1948 and 1954. (Source: Joint Committee for the Economic Report, 84th Congress.)

Reprinted in Joint Committee for the Economic Report, *Characteristics of the Low Income Population and Related Federal Programs,* 84th Cong. 1st Sess. (Washington, D. C.: U. S. Government Printing Office, 1955), p. 2.

These statistics point up the fact that the incomes of many low income families are inadequate as a bulwark against the insecurities of our modern urban and industrial life. The data gathered by the Joint Committee on the Economic Report in its comparison of low

[31] Joint Committee on the Economic Report, *Characteristics of the Low-Income Population and Related Federal Programs,* 84th Cong. 1st Sess. (Washington, D. C.: U. S. Government Printing Office, 1955), p. 1.

[32] *Ibid.,* p. 49.

and moderate income groups reveal the potential welfare problems inherent in the maldistribution of income. Broken families are more common in the low income group. The heads of such units, in general, tend to be older with less education. A majority of the low income units were headed by individuals who had either limited or no productive effort. Finally, low income units have very little savings. Less than one fourth of these units and individuals had savings of $500 or more.[33]

Lastly, our population is becoming older. For each person over 65 years of age in 1900 there are now approximately four people in the same category. There is a most striking increase in those who are 75 years of age or older. These now account for approximately four million people, a gain of 50 percent since 1940.[34] The contributions of better sanitation and nutrition, a higher standard of living and advances in medicine have already been noted. While these gains are gratifying, they have nevertheless brought a host of complex problems. Older people find it harder to get jobs. Because of technological progress they find it increasingly difficult to stand the pace of modern industry. Hiring practices show discrimination to the person over forty-five years of age. Even the person who is able to weather these challenges finds that when he has reached the age of sixty-five he is subject to mandatory retirement. A lifetime of productivity seems suddenly to have stopped.

Finally, changes in the pattern of family living have an important bearing on the problems of the aged. The "2 generation unit" under the impact of small homes and apartments does not leave much room for the older person. Even if he is made part of the household, he does not have the same sense of belonging as does the person in rural circumstances. Loneliness, frustration and fear of the future often gives rise to psychological problems and maladjustments. Lack of income upon the part of sons and daughters often leads to a dependence upon the organized welfare agencies for both advice and assistance.

These three factors—the changed pattern of living, the maldistribution of income, and the aging of our population—have been in operation for at least a half century. Side by side with these, how-

---

[33] *Ibid.*, p. 19.

[34] U. S. Department of Health, Education and Welfare, *Aging, a community responsibility and opportunity* (Washington, D. C.: U. S. Government Printing Office, 1955), pp. 1-10.

ever, there existed an attitude toward relief that seemed almost oblivious to the fundamental alteration in our way of life that was slowly but certainly taking place. For over a century relief was hardly more than rugged individualism tempered with mercy for those who were not clearly responsible for their state of need. The concept of relief stemmed from the early Elizabethan poor laws that the colonists had brought with them.

Local relief administration. From the founding of this country onward, relief was considered a local responsibility to be administered as the towns, cities and counties saw fit. Those who were at either end of the age spectrum, the young and the aged, the mentally defective and the physically incapacitated were given institutional assistance, sometimes termed indoor relief. These were generally the province of the county. The county "farm" or "poor house," or home for the aged, were common examples of this type of aid. Home relief in the form of grants for food, shelter, and clothing was generally a local responsibility. States and counties did not render assistance unless the applicant did not meet local requirements and was destitute.

State participation in providing assistance for the needy did not come about until approximately the turn of the century. The state boards of charity which until then had been only advisory, were given administrative power. In 1898 Ohio began a state program for the aid to the blind. By 1911 some states had begun to care for needy children. Old age assistance programs followed a decade later. It is a measure of the concern to note that by 1929 only 11 states had laws governing these activities and in most instances the programs were optional leaving their implementation to the wishes of the communities. Outdoor relief, that is, general assistance in the home, was a matter in which the state did not participate to any appreciable degree.[35]

Aside from relief to the helpless segments of our society, relief was administered on a parsimonious basis. Those who had lost their job or were destitute were regarded, in the main, as being lazy and shiftless. Their desperation was regarded as their own fault. Those who were given relief were made to understand this and were treated in such a fashion as to encourage them to leave the public

[35] Commission on Intergovernmental Relations, *Federal Aid to Welfare, a study committee report* (Washington, D. C.: U. S. Government Printing Office, 1955), pp. 6-7, 71.

assistance rolls as quickly as possible. The widespread unemployment of the 1930's exploded this myth. The large number of needy led to the imposition of a heavy burden upon both the states and the communities. Appeals by both units to the federal government led to emergency relief programs sponsored, and to a large extent financed, by the national government.[36] The turmoil of the depression years gave birth to a resolution that the despair and unhappiness that was the lot of so many Americans must not happen again. With the passage of the Social Security Act of 1935 protection against the hazards of insecurity and old age became a national responsibility, although the states and local units were not relieved of their share of concern for these matters.

Current welfare programs. The inability of the states and cities to cope with the problems of mass unemployment and relief led to a fundamental realignment of responsibility for the welfare of our people. The federal government took the lead in measures designed to prevent the recurrence of conditions that had led President Roosevelt to remind the American people that "the only thing they had to fear was fear itself." The passage of the Social Security Act of 1935 marks the beginning of a new concept of welfare. The individual is no longer held solely accountable for his inability to deal with the facts of his existence. Instead, it is recognized that dependence upon a money income for a livelihood subjects him to hazards that are often beyond his immediate control.

Old age and survivors insurance. One of the first fruits of this thinking was the federal old age and survivors insurance system, or as it was popularly termed, "social security." The program is nothing more than the application of the principle of insurance to the hazards of insecurity. Under its present provisions both the employers and employees are taxed by the federal government at the rate of 2 percent on all salaries and wages up to a maximum of $4200. Through their contributions the employed workers, during their working years, are able to build up a fund for the protection of themselves, their families, and their survivors.[37]

In June of 1954 6.6 million people, more than twice as many as in 1950, were receiving old age and survivors insurance. Roughly five out of six people, or 5.1 million of these, were sixty-

[36] See Chapter 16.

[37] Public Law 761, 83d Cong. 2nd Sess. (1954), also A. J. Altmeyer, *Your Stake in Social Security* (New York: The Public Affairs Committee, Inc., 1954).

five years of age or older.[38] In that year a far-reaching advance in social insurance was made. Ten million more people were added to the plan and it is estimated that the extension will provide coverage for 9 out of every 10 workers. The major provisions of the new amendments were: (1) increased payments from $5.00 to $13.50 per month for retired workers and proportionate increases for their dependents and survivors; (2) a higher earnings base, raised from $3600 to $4200, from which both the tax and the benefits are computed; (3) a new benefit formula that brought the monthly retirement benefits for the individual into a range that varied from $30 to $108.50, depending upon the individual contribution to the fund; (4) amended monthly family benefits were raised from $168.75 to $200; and (5) continuance of the retirement age at 65 but with the provision that beneficiaries may earn up to a maximum of $1200 annually without the suspension of benefits.[39] In July of 1956 widows were permitted to apply for benefits when they reached the age of 62. In the long run the extension of old age and survivors insurance is expected to reduce the case load of urban communities caring for the aged.[40]

Unemployment compensation and public assistance. Supplementing the system of social insurance are a series of complex federal-state programs designed to cover other aspects of security. Primarily these are of two kinds: those concerned with unemployment and those providing public assistance. Under the former, the federal government levies a tax of 3 percent on the payrolls of all employers who have eight or more employees. Nine tenths of this, however, is remitted to the states who have adopted a federally approved program. The states are responsible for the administration of the program, although unemployment accounts are maintained for them by the Treasury Department. While the benefits are not generally considered adequate, they do at least cushion the effects of unemployment while the worker is hunting for another job.[41]

Public assistance is also a joint federal-state venture. In meeting the needs of the blind, the needy aged, dependent children and the totally disabled the states are assured of contributions from the national government, provided their plans meet federally approved

[38] U. S. Department of Health, Education and Welfare, *op. cit.*, p. 18.

[39] *Ibid.*, pp. 31-33.

[40] Urban areas in contrast to rural communities have twice as many persons receiving old age and survivors insurance.

[41] See the criticism of Altmeyer, *op. cit.*, pp. 11-12.

standards. Grants-in-aid are usually on a matching or variable grant basis but the actual operation of the public assistance programs are the responsibility of the state and local units. In the fiscal year 1954 the federal government contributed $1,398 million for public assistance grants and an additional $30 million for maternal and child benefits. The total federal, state, and local expenditure in that year was $2,563 million.[42]

In summary, the responsibility for the maintenance of the welfare of our people is one in which the federal government shares very significantly. Old age and survivors insurance is a federal program but public assistance is a state and local affair subject to federal grant and supervision. Matters not covered by these categories are covered by the states and localities. The degree and kind of assistance given depends upon income ability and the community decision to assume the care for the unfortunates.

Welfare organization and administration. The broad outlines of welfare activity have already been sketched. Because of the provisions of the Social Security Act it can be expected that if the state has conformed with federal standards it will at least provide aid for the needy aged, the blind, the dependent child and the permanently disabled. Services for crippled children and maternal and child benefits will also be a part of the welfare function. Institutional care for the aged and infirm, the orphaned child, and the delinquent may also fall within the scope of welfare.

Supervision of probation, parole, and private charities may conceivably be within the province of the welfare department. In some instances, even jails may be under the jurisdiction of the welfare agency.[43] Within this broad spectrum, activities of the welfare department will vary to a greater or lesser degree in accordance with the community decision.

Welfare organization. Responsibility for welfare administration is rarely centralized. The handling of public welfare is carried out by the city, county, and sometimes by the state on a district basis. In Connecticut and Maine this system of administration is employed, the cities having only the responsibility for home relief. In most instances institutional care is undertaken either by the county or the

[42] U. S. Department of Health, Education and Welfare, *op. cit.*, pp. 41, 91.

[43] T. H. Reed, *Municipal Management* (New York: The McGraw-Hill Book Co., 1941), p. 482; R. C. White, *Administration of Public Welfare* (New York: The American Book Co., 1950), p. 482.

state or both. Large cities, like New York and Baltimore, have their own institutions but normally such a burden is too heavy for the average size city to shoulder. Assistance for those who are destitute is invariably an obligation of the city and usually takes the form of relief in the home. Regardless of where the function is lodged one must agree with White that "Contact with the individual and the family is local contact."[44] Administration by state, county or large city will therefore necessitate the use of district offices.

Welfare departments at the local level may be organized in one of three ways: (1) a director who is chosen by the head of the municipality; (2) a board of welfare or public assistance chosen in a similar fashion for overlapping terms varying in length from three to five years, very much like the local boards of health; and (3) a board of welfare that possesses direct administrative responsibility for the welfare program. Where the board does not have administrative authority it chooses a director of welfare who serves as the head of the department and acts as its administrative agent. The board type of organization, which seems to be preferred by most professional social workers, reflects the fear that politics will interfere with welfare administration. Where board administration does exist, the board meets monthly to lay down the broad policy lines for the guidance of its director.

Below the head of the department, the work is divided into two main categories, public assistance and institutions, both being guided by their defined responsibilities. Public assistance, child welfare and other functional activities are assigned to divisions and are staffed with social case workers. If the municipalities have institutions these are usually made the responsibility of a single official who is often called a superintendent. Reed recommends that institutions should be given divisional status within the department.[45]

Welfare administration. The work of the department revolves largely around case work. All welfare laws contain eligibility requirements and standards of assistance. Maintenance of these is the task of the social case worker. Necessarily, therefore, a determination must first be made whether or not the applicant is entitled to assistance. Investigation of the status of the applicant is the first step in case work. Data is gathered primarily through the interview

---

[44] White, *op. cit.,* p. 115.
[45] Reed, *op. cit.,* p. 488.

and then subsequent verification takes place by a search of all appropriate records. Following this, a diagnosis of the client's problem takes place. The aim is, or should be, to determine whether an individual can be rehabilitated as a useful citizen. His skills, his work habits and his family relationships may be the object of careful scrutiny. Following this, corrective action may be undertaken.[46]

Case work, as Reed has remarked, is the foundation of all public assistance. It requires a high degree of skill and training. Child welfare, for example, means not only foster homes but also a detailed knowledge of all aspects affecting his future life and development. Case work, in the final analysis, represents the individualized treatment of a person in need. The case load and the degree of supervision often determine the quality of welfare work.[47] The size of the case load will vary with the needs of a particular situation.[48] Supervision is undertaken by the case work supervisor and the head of the department. Since the welfare department is an agent of the state acting at the local level, it is subject to periodic administrative review by the state department of welfare.

CONCLUSION

The strength of our society rests upon the health and welfare of our people. These are our basic resources. How we utilize them will determine in large measure the future course of our society. As we look back over the years we can take pride in the many notable advances that have been made to banish sickness, poverty, and insecurity. These potential threats to our existence, however, have been minimized but not eliminated. The twin goals of better health and freedom from fear and want have not as yet become a reality for many Americans. To bring the benefits of our society to all of our people represents the challenge of the future.

Our efforts have not been decisive in this struggle largely because today we live in an urban society that is changing rapidly, and both people and government find it most difficult to comprehend what is happening. Yet a long look indicates the major trends. Technology and transportation, new forms of energy, and more complex industrial operations are constantly altering our way of life, bringing new problems and new challenges. The massing of

[46] White, *op. cit.*, pp. 140-149.
[47] Reed, *op. cit.*, pp. 493, 497.
[48] White, *op. cit.*, pp. 150-151.

people in the cities in response to the needs of the industrial machine has subjected them to stress and strains the full measure of which is as yet incalculable. Dirt, noise, congestion, and monotony have become the daily lot of many of our city dwellers. Fear and insecurity, arising out of dependence upon wages and salaries as the sole source of income, are ever present. The independence of farm life has yielded to the dependence of urban dwelling.

Although we have made marked progress in the application of the science of medicine, paradoxically medical care has been placed beyond the reach of many people because newly developed scientific techniques have become so expensive. Although we enjoy a high standard of living, the foundations of our prosperity, even with the presence of "built-in" stabilizers, have not as yet become firm. The vagaries of the business cycle have not been brought under control. Finally, a longer life span has brought with it a rising incidence of chronic disease and a greater need for protection for those who are in the shadow of life.

These broad trends were brought into sharp focus during the crisis-laden years of the 1930's when many Americans suddenly found themselves without a livelihood. Out of those dimly remembered times came unemployment relief, public works, and a broadly based system of social security. The inability of local units of government, particularly the cities, shattered the illusion of local responsibility for such matters as health and welfare. Out of those times of trouble emerged a new concept. The health and welfare of our people have become concerns of the national government. A framework of national assistance has been superimposed on the previously existing pattern of local effort. The fear and insecurity of city life are now problems for the nation as well as the municipality.

BIBLIOGRAPHY

Books:

Abbott, G. *From Relief to Security.* Chicago: University of Chicago Press, 1941.

Commission on Intergovernmental Relations, *Federal Aid to Welfare, A Study Committee Report.* Washington, D. C.: U. S. Government Printing Office, 1955.

Davis, M. M. *Medical Care for Tomorrow.* New York: Harper and Brothers Publishers, 1955.

Emerson, H. *Local Health Units for the Nation.* New York: The Commonwealth Fund, 1945.

Ewing, O. R. *The Nation's Health, A Ten Year Program.* Washington, D. C.: U. S. Government Printing Office, 1948.

Gagliardo, D. *American Social Insurance.* New York: Harper and Brothers Publishers, 1955. Rev. edition.

Mountin, J. W., Pennell, E. H. and Berger, A. G. *Health Service Areas.* Washington, D. C.: U. S. Government Printing Office, 1949.

President's Commission on the Health Needs of the Nation. *Building America's Health.* Vol. I. Washington, D. C.: U. S. Government Printing Office, 1952.

Simmons, J. S. (ed.), *Public Health in the World Today.* Cambridge, Massachusetts: Harvard University Press, 1949.

Smillie, W. G. *Public Health Administration in the United States.* New York: The Macmillan Co., 1949.

White, R. C. *Administration of Public Welfare.* New York: American Book Co., 1950. 2nd edition.

Articles and Other Material:

Felix, R. H. and Kramer, M. "Extent of the Problem of Mental Disorders," *The Annals,* CCLXXXVI (1953), 5-14.

Lawry, J. V. "Public Mental Health Agencies, State and Nation," *The Annals,* CCLXXXVI (1953), 100-106.

"Medical Care for Americans," *The Annals.* Edited by F. Goldman and H. R. Leavell. CCLXXIII (1951).

Chapter Twenty-Three

Education, Recreation, and Housing

Education

Evolution of the education function. Education has progressed a long way from the colonial days when Sir William Berkeley thanked God for the absence of free schools and printing presses. Today, despite his strictures and those of his followers, we have both, and apparently are none the worse for them. Indeed, quite the contrary is the case. Our educational system has given the individual an opportunity to develop his talents. It has provided the science and skills that have built our great industrial society. It has educated our people in the meaning and importance of democracy. Far from being the destructive force envisioned by Berkeley and others, it actually has given our people an understanding of the significance of the great issues that the nation has faced.

Education in the colonial period. The system of education that we have today is the product of approximately two centuries of development. In the beginning when society was relatively simple and occupations, aside from farming, were few in number, the school was hardly more than "a supplement to a way of life which was education in itself." [1] Education, in the main, was confined to reading, writing, and simple arithmetic. Most of it took place in the home. Formal schooling was provided by tutors, private and church schools, education overseas, and "charity schools" where deserving children of poor parents were given free tuition grants. In colonial times education was regarded as a private matter for which the individual, and not the community, was principally responsible.[2] Measured by our standards such education would be considered rude and almost primitive, and yet it was suited to the needs of an agricultural economy that did not put too much demand upon the skills of the individual.

[1] Frederick M. Raubinger, "Education at Mid-Century," *The First Annual Apgar Lecture* (New Brunswick, N. J.: Rutgers University, 1955 (pamphlet)), p. 3.

[2] E. P. Cubberly, *Public School Administration, Rev. Ed.,* (New York: Houghton Mifflin Co., 1929), pp. 8-9.

But even during this period the dim outlines of the future educational system were beginning to take shape in colonial New England. In Massachusetts as early as 1647 the towns were directed to establish and maintain a school system and its officials were faced with penalties for failure to comply. Later in the century, the towns were also requested to supervise the selection of teachers and to raise money for the support of schools. In the eighteenth century the responsibilities of towns for the education of the community were increased. School committees on an informal basis began to exercise a greater measure of concern over educational matters.[3] At the turn of the century in Delaware, New York, and a few other states, similar trends were evident. By the beginning of the 19th century the pattern of New England that education, even in its then minimal form, should be both public and secular was well on the road to acceptance.

Developments in the period 1800–1850. In the first half of the nineteenth century public education made further gains. The liberalizing impacts of the changes that were taking place in our society gradually were taking effect. New England people, migrating to the Northwest territory, brought with them their ideas of education and incorporated these within the laws of those states that became part of the territory. The dim stirrings of the industrial revolution that was yet to come resulted in the rise in the number of cities and towns. The increasing complexity of economic organization brought a recognition of the need for more and varied skills. The breakdown of property qualifications for voting led to the establishment of universal manhood suffrage. The tidal wave of Jacksonian democracy and the general political ferment of the times required a people who were more versed in the meaning of citizenship than those that had preceded them.

Public education reflected these changes in the character of our society. In the first quarter of the nineteenth century, New York, Delaware, Illinois and many other states enacted legislation permitting communities to carry out public education. Ohio in 1821 authorized localities to levy taxes for the support of free education. In the thirties and forties of the last century, the large cities, Cincinnati, Pittsburgh, Cleveland, Buffalo and New York, established free public school systems on their own initiative. The smaller

[3] *Ibid.*, pp. 149-151.

cities and towns, however, did not depart from the church and charity concept of education until forced to do so by mandatory action of the state.[4]

In this period further stones in the foundation of American education were laid. Perhaps because of the absence of state interference, education was made a community responsibility. Each community in the form of a district was given corporate authority to act as an agent of the state. Its resources were made the means of meeting its problem of education. School boards on a more formal basis gradually replaced the informal school committees in many areas. As early as 1838 Buffalo, New York and Louisville, Kentucky appointed superintendents of their schools.

Later changes. In the last half of the nineteenth century, education as we know it today became firmly established. Free public schools became universally accepted. The diversity in our society was accompanied by a further specialization in educational administration. Boards of education found it increasingly difficult to attend to school matters. Gradually their activities were restricted to the area of policymaking. The superintendent of schools became its executive officer carrying out its directives. He, in turn, found that it was necessary to delegate many of his responsibilities to subordinates. The business manager, the planning officer, and the directors of various aspects of public education, begin to appear as his assistants, a trend that was heightened during the twentieth century. Taxation for the support of education became an accepted community responsibility. Education as a state function at the municipal level received increasing autonomy, although it was carried out by local units in conjunction with their activities.

Side by side with the growth in local and city responsibility for education came an increasing measure of state control. At first the states limited themselves to matters of concern to the people of the state as a whole. Qualifications of teachers were examined and certifications were undertaken. Later this control was expanded to include compulsory attendance, the length of the school term, control of the curriculum to insure uniform standards of instruction, and generally the regulation of school finance. From 1920 onward the state through taxes and grants-in-aid sought to lighten the burden of the local property holder, a trend that was accelerated in the

[4] *Ibid.*, p. 10.

1930's when property as a source of municipal and local income was greatly diminished.[5] In all states of the union state control of education is now firmly entrenched. A state educational officer assisted by a state department of education supervises the standards of instruction and the operation of school plants in all communities.

Educational organization. These developments suggest the broad trends in educational organization. Education is, legally speaking, a state function. The community, however, has a different attitude. Opposition of the locality is strenuous when state intervention goes beyond the imposition of minimum standards. It is carried out by the county and local school district which for purposes of administration are subdivisions of the state. Where the area of the district coincides with the limits of the city, we have what is popularly termed the city school district. Local subdivisions, however, are agents of the state. The wide powers possessed by them are simply for convenience of administration, although it is true that they are a product of history and tradition. But at any time the state may either increase or decrease the size and area of the school district. Indeed, in the State of Delaware, except for the city of Wilmington, the state is, to all intents and purposes, the school district.

That the state can vary the size of the district enables it to expand the school function to meet the drift of population to the suburbs, provided that local traditions can be surmounted. The state exercises its powers through either mandatory or permissive legislation.[6] In the former category are those state endeavors that seek to establish uniform standards of instruction and education. Their enforcement is usually the province of a chief educational officer who is elected popularly in 31 of our states and appointed either by the governor or a board of education in the remainder.[7] Permissive legislation permits districts to develop extensions of the education function in accordance with their financial capacity and community decisions.

The school district. The basic unit of local school administration is the district. It is impossible to identify all of the types that exist because of the uneven pattern of educational development but roughly there are four main kinds: (1) the town district centering

[5] A. J. Burke, *Financing Public Schools in the United States* (New York: Harper and Brothers, 1951), pp. 120-121.

[6] H. L. Hagman, *The Administration of American Public Schools* (New York: McGraw-Hill Book Co., Inc., 1951), pp. 66-67.

[7] *Ibid.*, pp. 70-71.

primarily in New England; (2) the township district which is predominant in many middle western states; (3) the county which is the primary unit in many southern states; and (4) the city school district which exists in our cities.[8] In some states, the school district is independent of either the city, township or county. In cities, education is nominally a part of city government, although in many ways it is in fact separate from it. It has its own budget and tax resources, and its officials are not considered employees of the city, although the money for their salaries comes from the municipal treasury.

The districts, as we have noted, receive their authority from state law. Like municipalities, they operate within the confines of the general laws of the state exercising such powers as are delegated to them. The authority of the district is centered in a board of education chosen either by the mayor and council or by a vote of the people. Members of the boards of education are unsalaried laymen who are presumably chosen because of their interest in education.[9] There is no uniformity in either the number of board members or their term of office.[10]

The board of education. The board of education exercises the quasi-corporate powers of the school district of which it is a part. In effect it functions as the board of directors of a limited type of corporation. It has the power of eminent domain. It can buy and sell school sites and can contract for the construction of school plant facilities. It votes the budget for school expenditures. It can levy taxes or at least recommend a tax rate for the support of the schools.[11] It appoints the superintendent of schools and subordinate administrators, teachers, and employees. Finally it formulates, within the confines of state law, the general educational policy for the school system.[12] In brief, the district is a major purpose organi-

---

[8] A. B. Moehlman, *School Administration* (New York: Houghton Mifflin Co., 1940), pp. 208-209.

[9] In New Jersey, for example, the former method of appointment prevails in what is called the "chapter six" districts, whereas the latter is employed in the "chapter seven" districts. See S. H. Friedelbaum, *Municipal Government in New Jersey* (New Brunswick, N. J.: Rutgers University Press, 1954), p. 32.

[10] C. De Young, *Introduction to American Public Education* (New York: McGraw-Hill Book Co., Inc., 1942), p. 110.

[11] In New Jersey's "chapter seven" districts, the budget of the school board is submitted directly to the people and the governing body of the municipality must then vote the necessary funds.

[12] De Young, *op. cit.*, p. 113.

zation that has almost all the powers necessary to accomplish its objectives.

The board is assisted by a professionally trained educator who is termed the superintendent of schools. In practice he functions as the chief executive officer and in fact is the actual head of the school system. He furnishes the board with expert advice on school matters and directs the school enterprise. In the small cities he supervises almost all the operations, but as the city grows larger in size, his work is subdivided among his subordinates. Differentiation and specialization appear in the form of business managers, directors of elementary and secondary education, examiners and personnel experts, health educators, and a host of other specialists. Save for the fact that he is given tenure, the duties of the school superintendent in relation to the board of education and the public are analogous to the relationships that exist between the city manager and the council, although, of course, the superintendent functions in a much more limited area.

The anomalous governmental status of the school system. The traditional and legal fact that the city school system is not a part of city government raises some fundamental questions. The city administers a variety of functions—health, police, fire, sanitation, building codes and zoning regulations. It often has well-equipped architectural, legal, purchasing, and personnel services. It levies and collects taxes. A major part of its budget is devoted to school expenditures. Should the municipality insist that the schools employ many of its business services in order to avoid duplication of personnel and activity? Should it demand that the school system adopt its business practices? Should the school system have its own attorney, its own personnel system, its own health program? In brief, to what degree should it consider itself independent of the city government which provides it with the means for its existence?

Most school officers fear the intrusion of the city government into their activities and resist it strenuously. In the light of the misgovernment of many cities, particularly during the eighties of the last century, there is some justification for their stand. However, in an era of high costs, there is also considerable merit in the argument that waste and duplication must be cut to the bone. This can be done only by some kind of integration of those services that are common and those that do not affect educational policy.[13]

[13] See Reed, *op. cit.*, pp. 517-524, for an interesting discussion of these points.

Educational problems ahead. In the brief span of our national existence public education has made astonishing strides. In 1870, 57 percent of our children of ages 5-17 were enrolled in public schools with an average attendance of less than 80 days during the year. In 1952, scarcely a century later, 85 percent of our children were in public schools with an average yearly attendance of more than twice the number of days. In 1952, with a national population of over 160 million people, 33.5 million children were in the elementary and secondary schools.[14] In 1954 our cities spent more money for education than for any other single function at the municipal level.[15] Compared to most nations of the world this country enjoys a high level of education, but this should not blind us to the problems ahead.

The major problems facing the nation and the cities revolve around three main points: (1) mounting school enrollment; (2) shortages of plant and qualified teachers; and (3) methods of financing public education.

Mounting school enrollment. There are now approximately 11 million youngsters in the 15 to 19 year age group, about 16 million in the 5 to 9 year group, and almost 17 million in the 5 year or less category. By 1960 at least 46 million children will require education at all levels. Table 10 indicates the projection of school population to the year 1965. By that time we can expect increases in elementary and secondary enrollments of 28.6 and 60.2 percent respectively.[16]

Plant and teacher shortage. The present and forecasted rise in our school population is aggravated by a growing shortage of classroom and building facilities and teachers. The deferred building program as a result of the lack of materials, the rise in birth rates, and the fact that our present teachers are recruited primarily from the period when the nation's birth rate was lowest present added obstacles. It is estimated that there is now a shortage of 300,000 classrooms and 120,000 teachers. By 1960, assuming that our present rate of development continues, it will be necessary to add 565,000 classrooms and about twice as many teachers.[17] The growing de-

---

14 U. S. Department of Health, Education and Welfare, *op. cit.,* p. 9.

15 U. S. Department of Commerce, *Compendium of City Government Finances* (Washington, D. C.: U. S. Government Printing Office, 1955), p. 2. Cities over 25,000 in population spent $1,027 million, of which $985.6 millions were contributed by city school districts.

16 U. S. Department of Health, Education and Welfare, *op. cit.,* pp. 9, 175-176.

17 U. S. Department of Health, Education and Welfare, *op. cit.,* pp. 176-177.

ficiencies in our school system plague every community and city in their efforts to meet the increasing demands imposed upon their school systems.

Table 10—PROJECTION OF ELEMENTARY, SECONDARY AND HIGHER EDUCATION ENROLLMENTS, PUBLIC AND NONPUBLIC, 1954–55 TO 1964–65
(continental United States)

School year	Estimated total enrollment [1]			
	Elementary (grades K–8)	*Secondary (grades 9–12)*	*Higher education (regular session)*	*Total*
1954–55	27,738,000	7,422,000	2,740,000	37,900,000
1955–56	29,038,000	7,680,000	2,839,000	39,557,000
1956–57	30,231,000	8,006,000	2,949,000	41,186,000
1957–58	31,413,000	8,343,000	3,041,000	42,797,000
1958–59	32,568,000	8,762,000	3,119,000	44,449,000
1959–60	33,650,000	9,168,000	3,221,000	46,039,000
1960–61	34,482,000	9,485,000	3,349,000	47,316,000
1961–62	34,957,000	10,044,000	3,568,000	48,569,000
1962–63	35,226,000	10,731,000	3,726,000	49,683,000
1963–64	35,452,000	11,337,000	3,853,000	50,642,000
1964–65	35,659,000	11,890,000	3,953,000	51,502,000
Increase, 1955–65:				
Number ...	7,921,000	4,468,000	1,213,000	13,602,000
Percent	28.6	60.2	44.3	35.9

[1] Does not include private commercial schools or nurse training schools not affiliated with colleges and universities.

Source: Press release of Sept. 8, 1955, Office of Education, Department of Health, Education and Welfare. Reprinted in Joint Committee on the Economic Report Characteristics of the Low Income Population and Related Federal Programs, 84th Cong. 1st Sess. (1955), p. 165.

Finance. Finally, and perhaps most important, is the question of money: how can the school districts finance their heavy burden? In 1954, $10 billions were required to educate children in the 5 to 17 year group in our public, private, and parochial schools, nine-tenths of which was spent for public education.[18] By 1965 it is estimated

[18] Public school expenditures were $8.9 billions; private and parochial schools spent $1.1 billion.

that the present program will cost $13.5 billion, assuming that the average expenditure for each school child remains the same. However, if the salaries of teachers were lifted to the average spent in the State of New York for public education in 1954, then the total education outlay a decade later would be $17.1 billion. But if expenditures per school child, including an increase in teacher salaries, were raised to $400 a year to meet the standard prevailing in our better schools today, then our educational expenditures in 1965 would be $19.2 billion.[19]

These are enormous sums. Even the present expenditure of $10 billions is much larger than the national budget of 1933. Of course, national income has more than quadrupled since that time, but one must remember that school expenditures rely in the main on the real property tax which is highly inelastic and does not show much responsiveness to the changes in our economy. Harris, in a study of education approximately a decade ago, gives a graphic illustration of this inelasticity. In 1932 the real property tax yield was 4 billions; in 1945 it yielded 2 percent less. Yet during the same period the national income rose 300 percent. Moreover, the return from the real property tax in 1945 was worth only $3 billion in terms of purchasing power in 1932.[20] In the years after World War II states and cities have made strenuous efforts to revise their property taxes upward, but the forecast of still further rises in educational expenditures promises to vitiate these steps.

It is becoming increasingly apparent that new sources of revenue, other than the property tax, will be needed. Two schools of thought exist on the subject. One holds that the federal government, because of the greater flexibility of its taxing power, should provide for national minimum standards of education through a grant-in-aid system. This would enable many of the poorer states to improve their educational levels. However, there are many who fear federal interference in an area that has traditionally been considered the province of state and local units of government. This prospect of federal coercion, while it may occur, can nevertheless be avoided by the careful construction of a grant system. Perhaps the present welfare

[19] National Citizens' Commission for the Public Schools, *Financing Public Education in the Decade Ahead* (New York: 1954), p. 4.

[20] S. E. Harris, *How Shall We Pay For Education* (New York: Harper and Brothers, 1948), p. 13.

and health grant-in-aid programs are a pattern that can be usefully employed.[21]

Another view holds that the states and the cities can collect enough money through other kinds of taxes. The states have the means to provide for education. This is the conclusion of the Commission on Intergovernmental Relations: "*The Commission recommends that responsibility for providing public education continue to rest squarely upon the states and their political subdivisions. The Commission further recommends that the states act vigorously and promptly to discharge this responsibility. The Commission does not recommend a general program of federal financial assistance to elementary and secondary education, believing that the states have the capacity to meet their educational requirements.*"[22] Where it is clearly evident that the states do not have sufficient tax resources, "the National Government, through some appropriate means, would be justified in assisting such states temporarily in financing the construction of school facilities. . . ."[23]

The stimulation of both viewpoints, reinforced by the President's White House Conference on Education in 1955, resulted in a spate of measures introduced in Congress, designed to assist states in meeting their need for construction facilities. Some thought to aid local communities by the federal purchase of school bonds where rates of interest were unreasonable. Others tried to help the states by making grants to a state authority that would construct school buildings to be leased to local units. Precedents for state authorities in school construction already exist in Pennsylvania and Georgia. Still other proposals would provide outright construction grants to localities.[24] As of August 1956, Congress, despite the urgent need for financial assistance, had not taken any action. It is probable, however, that the causal factors of mounting enrollments and growing deficiencies in school facilities will bring federal action in the very near future.

---

21 National Citizens' Commission for the Public Schools, *op. cit.*, pp. 7-8. The opinion as to the feasibility of the use of the welfare and health grants is the author's.

22 Commission on Intergovernmental Relations, *A Report to the President for Transmittal to Congress* (Washington, D. C.: U. S. Government Printing Office, 1955), p. 194. Italics in the quotation.

23 *Ibid.*

24 See S. 968 and its companion measure H. R. 3770, and S. 5, 84th Cong. 1st Sess. (1955); and S. 2905 and H. R. 7535, 84th Cong. 2nd Sess. (1956).

RECREATION

Life in the city, even at its best, occurs under trying circumstances—noise, dirt, traffic, and congestion. Many city people live in crowded apartments and small homes on lots that are so close together that privacy is virtually impossible. Green space and open areas are disappearing constantly as more and more people congregate in the city. There is, in a sense, no place to hide. It is not entirely accidental that, with the coming of the motor car, a flight to the country and resort areas has taken place and highways leading from the city are crowded with automobiles. Unfortunately, so many like-minded persons create the very congestion that they have sought to avoid. It is evident that the home under urban conditions has lost much of its usefulness as a place for rest and relaxation.

These conditions make recreation on an organized basis the particular responsibility of urban areas. If the city is not livable, it is because municipal authorities have not taken the necessary steps to make it so. If green space is built over, it is because proper planning has not reserved areas for the recreation of the people. If housing is crowded and lots are small, it is a result primarily of the absence of effective building and zoning regulations. It is, of course, true that recreation is an individual responsibility, but providing recreational facilities on an organized basis are not within the individual's means. It is the city that must provide the parks, playgrounds, etc. Failure to do so often results in increased costs for health, welfare, and social services.

Evolution, recreation as a municipal function. Recreation as a municipal function grew rather slowly. At the turn of the century under the influence of the city planners' idea of the "city beautiful," green spaces were set aside, either in the heart of the city or in the outlying areas, to enable the citizen to gain momentary respite from the tensions of city life. But aside from benches and perhaps a band stand, the individual was left to his own resources. In a similar fashion, the youth of the city were often permitted to use the school grounds on an after-hour basis. But no directed program of recreation existed.

It was not until World War I that this development was to take place. The presence of army cantonments within close proximity of the community, the fact that the soldier came to the city for recreation, and, further, the increased opportunity for "harmful leisure" often evoked community protest and led to the creation of planned programs to occupy the soldier's time. Out of the joint community-army effort came many of the features that we presently associate with a recreation program. When the great depression of the 1930's made enforced idleness the lot of many Americans, the works program not only built community facilities but also reinforced the planned aspect of recreation. Today, to a greater or lesser degree depending upon the nature of the community, recreation has become accepted as a municipal function.

Recreation administration. Recreation in the modern city takes many forms. It begins first of all with the neighborhood. Play streets may be closed off for the use of children at stated periods of the year. Where space is available, a neighborhood playground may be established consisting of ball fields, tennis courts and skating rinks. Where the school facilities are employed, there may also be a swimming pool and a gymnasium. Generally, recreational programs begin with all those activities that engage the energies of the active child. Play is supervised by personnel in the employ of the recreation department. Reed believes that recreational programs at this level are the foundation of all other fields of recreation.[25]

Neighborhood facilities are often supplemented by parks. These are the modern version of the older concept of green spaces that were set aside for rest and relaxation. Play areas are much larger than those of the neighborhood and are designed to present a more balanced program for persons of all ages. Normally it may include a zoo, a lake for swimming and boating, play fields, golf courses, and outdoor eating facilities. Here, too, planned programs of the recreation department are also undertaken. The park is considered a community facility. Its use is open to community groups who may sponsor their own recreational activities. Parks are designed to facilitate a well-rounded recreation program.

Recreation administration varies with the degree and intensity of land use and the awareness of the city of the need for a recreational program. Because the function grew out of the original concern with parks, many recreational activities often are lodged in a parks department or parks board. In some communities a recreation commission, with an appointed director, is given responsibility for

25 Reed, *op. cit.*, p. 452.

the function. School boards, because of their control over neighborhood playground facilities, have also been charged with the supervision of recreation activities. Generally, the preferred type of administration seems to be the board with a professional director. Below the level of the head of the department, the recreation function is divided into four main segments; general programs, special programs, business management, and construction and maintenance. Funds for personnel and equipment are paid for out of the municipal budget.[26]

The importance of recreation for the health of our people and the economy of the nation was emphasized by recreation and park leaders during the Mid-Century Conference on the Resources for the Future held in Washington in December of 1953. The growth of juvenile delinquency, the steadily aging character of our population, and the increasing interdependence of our society presage the steady evolution of recreation as a municipal function.

HOUSING

Municipal activity in the field of housing is hardly more than thirty years old. It began with the pump-priming efforts of the 1930's and since that time the goal of a decent home for every American in a suitable environment has become the objective of both the national and the local governments.

Municipal interest in housing. The municipality had a definite interest in housing. This is evident not only from the building, fire, electrical and health codes that have been adopted, but also from its concern with the supply of housing. The condition of housing is a measure of our standard of living. It is also an index of land use, and since the municipality is dependent mainly on property taxes, the condition of housing has a direct bearing on the income of the municipality. The National Housing Agency estimated that housing constituted 40 percent of the developed urban areas, about 50 percent of the assessed value of urban property subject to local taxation, and about 60 percent of the total urban property valuation. Housing supplied 45 percent of local tax revenues.[27]

Poor housing in cities has a direct bearing on the health and

[26] Reed, *op. cit.*, pp. 459-471 has an extended discussion of this point.

[27] Testimony of John B. Blandford, Jr., Administrator of the National Housing Agency before the Senate Committee on Banking and Currency, *Hearings on the General Housing Act of 1945*, 79th Cong. 1st Sess. (Washington, D. C.: U. S. Government Printing Office, 1946), p. 44.

welfare of the people. Substandard areas, particularly under the congestion of city life, multiply the menace to health. Living conditions pose a threat to mental and emotional well-being and to the physical vigor of the individual. Slums are also the breeding grounds of crime, disease, and delinquency.

Dilapidated neighborhoods are a constant drain upon the city treasury. Not only do they provide the smallest amount of revenues, but also they cost the city most in the ratio of what they yield. In a small slum area in Cleveland with approximately 2.5 percent of the city's population, the city was forced to spend 6.5 percent of its expenditures for police protection, 7.3 percent for health, 12.3 percent for social services, and 14.4 percent for fire protection. Studies in slum areas in Indianapolis, Philadelphia, Birmingham, and Atlanta show roughly similar results. In Detroit, Cleveland, and many other cities, slum areas show excessive amounts of tuberculosis, pneumonia, infant mortality, delinquency, and crime.[28] Nearly every city of the country, despite the constant efforts of municipal officials, has slums. Some are in such a state of deterioration that, if nothing is done, they will become hopelessly blighted. Adequate housing is an important concern of the citizen as well as of the municipality.

Housing supply. In the past decade we have made great strides in our efforts to meet our housing needs. Starting with 1945 the

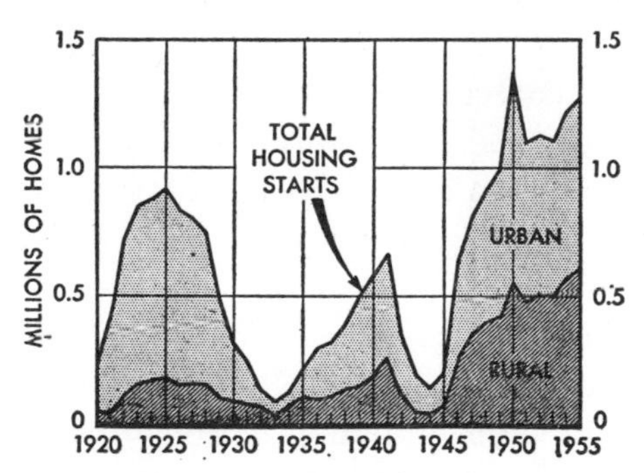

Source: *New York Times,* May 15, 1955, p. E7.

Fig. 13. The Trend in Home Building.

number of homes built each year has averaged well over a million. Figure 13 shows the long-term trend in construction. Our homes

[28] *Ibid.,* pp. 45-46.

have electricity, washers, ironers, modern stoves and a host of other conveniences.[29] There has been a marked shift to home ownership, with approximately 25 million persons owning their own homes.

Despite the recent additions to our housing plant, adequate supply of housing is beyond the reach of many Americans. Several reasons are responsible for this situation. The condition of our housing is such that a high rate of obsolescence and deterioration occurs. In terms of age almost half of our homes were built before 1920. Seventy percent of our housing is adequate, but 8 percent is considered dilapidated, and the balance is deficient in plumbing. Figure 14 gives a detailed explanation. In 1950 8.9 million urban housing units were considered substandard, 6.9 million of which were in such poor condition as to require replacement.[30]

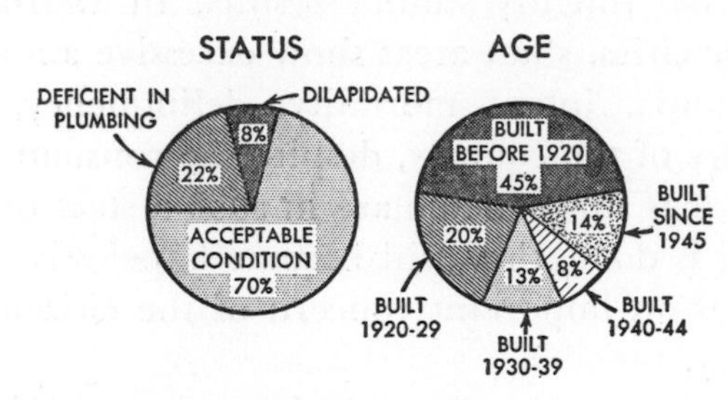

Source: *New York Times,* May 15, 1955, p. E7.

Fig. 14. The Condition of Our Homes.

It is estimated that replacement of current losses from all causes will in this decade require 1.1 million units, a rate equal to the number of dwellings presently being constructed.[31] For many of the people in the city this means that they will continue to have substandard housing.

Housing production and population growth. Not only is there a need for replacement but also the rate of housing production simply has not kept pace with population growth. Nonfarm housing construction for the years 1923–1927 averaged 872,000 housing starts annually. In the past three years it has averaged about 1.1 million starts annually, or a rate of about 14.6 percent above the

[29] U. S. Department of Labor, *op. cit.,* p. 79.

[30] Testimony of the officials of the National Housing Conference before House Committee on Banking and Currency, *Housing Act of 1954,* 83rd Cong. 1st. Sess. (1954), pp. 560-561.

[31] House Committee on Banking and Currency, *op. cit.,* pp. 559-561.

1923–1927 average. In the intervening period, however, our population has increased about 50 million or 45 percent. Our rate of housing production, although it is now at a peak, actually is not enough to keep pace with our population rise.

Housing costs and the availability of housing. But even if construction were to keep pace with our ever larger population, it still would not meet the needs of many people. Income levels simply do not permit them to obtain such housing. Census Bureau statistics indicate that 53.9 percent of the families have an income of $4000 or less.[32] The disparity in nonfarm income is somewhat less. Eighteen percent of the families have incomes of less than $4000 and 29 percent have less than $6000 in annual income.[33] Assuming that 20 percent of the family income represents an expenditure for housing, including maintenance, then the families in the $4000-$6000 group would have available for housing a monthly outlay of from $66 to $100.

A $10,000 mortgage at 4.5 percent interest with an F.H.A. insurance charge would bring monthly housing costs to approximately $82. There are few homes that can be obtained in this price range and, even if there were, they would still be available only to those in the upper bracket of the $4000-$6000 income level. Few of those in the lower income brackets, constituting the bulk of those in substandard housing, can take advantage of even the present high construction level. They are, as it were, priced out of the housing market. In the hearings on the Housing Act of 1954 it was suggested that a $7000 house with a lengthened forty-year mortgage was the answer for the low income groups. However, it is doubtful that present construction costs would permit any significant building at this price level; or even if such homes were built, it is doubtful that they would last the length of the mortgage period.[34]

Minorities and housing. Substandard housing and maldistribution of income, as Abrams has pointed out, are particularly marked in the case of housing for minorities. As a general rule, the income of the nonwhite is much lower than that of the white. Consequently,

---

[32] U. S. Department of Commerce, Bureau of Census, Series PC-60, no. 12., (1953). Income distribution was as follows: those with less than $2000, 25 percent; those between $2000-$3000, 15.4 percent; those between $3000-$4,000, 18.9 percent; and those between $4000-$6000 24.4 percent.

[33] House Committee on Banking and Currency, *op. cit.*, p. 569.

[34] See the exchanges between Congressman Multer and Messrs. Waltemade and Summer, House Committee on Banking and Currency, *op. cit.*, pp. 755-770.

a greater proportion of nonwhites are forced to live in slums. Overcrowding is much greater among the nonwhites and yet a greater proportion of their income goes for housing. Buildings are subject to greater deterioration because they are usually not worth repairing and lending agencies are hesitant to assume the risk. Even those nonwhites in the slums who can afford better housing are prevented from moving because of compulsions within the community.[35]

Mobility as a factor in housing supply. Aggravating these pressures upon housing supply is the phenomenon of migration and mobility. In 1954 approximately 29 million people changed their place of residence. Indeed, this rate has been remarkably constant since 1948.[36] Where in-migration is not balanced by out-migration, a need for new housing is created. In recent years a considerable part of the population movement has been to urban communities in the South and West. It is estimated that net migration will cause a 10 to 25 percent increase in our present new housing construction.[37]

Finally, modern urban highway construction and overcrowding have an impact upon the current supply of housing. A lineal mile of a superhighway in an urban area will result in the destruction of anywhere from 250 to 1000 homes. Displacements resulting from the construction of highways mean a net reduction in our housing supply.[38] The recently adopted federal highway aid program designed to stimulate new road construction will undoubtedly spur the demolition rate in many areas. The "doubling up" of many families as a result of the housing shortage after World War II will also have a continuing effect upon our housing needs. As late as 1950 1.7 million "social families" were still without separate housing. As these begin to separate, the pressure on our housing requirements may be expected to rise.[39]

In brief, then, present housing construction rates are high, but measured by population and income distribution they are inadequate. Low income groups, the bulk of our population, cannot afford adequate housing. The age of our housing structures and the mobility of our population are added elements in the demand pic-

---

[35] Charles Abrams, *Forbidden Neighbors* (New York: Harper and Brothers, 1955), pp. 73-77.

[36] U. S. Housing and Home Finance Agency, *8th Annual Report* (Washington, D. C.: U. S. Government Printing Office, 1955), p. 22.

[37] House Committee on Banking and Currency, *op. cit.*, p. 558.

[38] *Ibid.*, p. 559. Also pages 642-652 for the remarks of Monsignor John O'Grady.

[39] *Ibid.*, pp. 560-561.

ture. Greater production rates and lower housing costs seem to be the only answers, but whether they can be achieved is another matter.

Measures to improve housing. Federal, state and local officials have not been unaware of the reasons for the housing shortage. All have made strenuous efforts to eliminate substandard housing. The program that has emerged is an amalgam of cooperation at all governmental levels.

Traditional local efforts. Traditionally, municipalities have dealt with the housing problem through the exercise of their police powers. Planning and zoning regulations governed land use, building heights, occupancy, setbacks, and, generally, improvements on land. These have been employed to lay out carefully defined use districts and have prevented intrusions that would destroy the character of the neighborhood and bring blight and deterioration. Building, electrical, health, and fire codes have regulated the use of houses and buildings. Municipalities have endeavored to see not only that buildings were safe but also that they were fit to live in. Adequate ventilation was required and overcrowding was checked. Visitation and inspection frequently disclosed violations. When these were found, owners were directed to comply with the ordinances of the municipality. Unfortunately these measures often suffered from two fundamental weaknesses: codes were not kept up to date, and improvements in many instances were so costly that enforcement became almost meaningless.

Home ownership. To assist the home owner the federal government through its Federal Housing Administration made loans for property improvements through approved lending agencies for a three-year period. Money was made available to the property owner for such purposes as additions and alterations, plumbing, heating, roofing, interior and exterior finish, insulation, and a host of other miscellaneous items. The tremendous stimulus for property improvement can be readily understood if one realizes that, since the inception of the program in 1934, 18 million applications totaling $8.3 billions were approved. In 1954 88.4 percent of the loans were made to the possessors of single-family dwellings. Only 6.7 percent of the multi-dwelling units and 1.2 percent of the commercial and industrial property owners availed themselves of this opportunity. Two decades after the beginning of the program, Congress enacted legislation further stimulating property improvements. The F.H.A.

was empowered to finance on more liberal terms the rehabilitation of salvageable housing and new construction in slum areas for which urban renewal plans had been certified by the Housing and Home Finance Agency.[40]

The federal government is probably best known for its promotion of home ownership through its home mortgage insurance system. In the period 1935–1954 nearly 4 million homes were financed in this manner. The magnitude of this type of assistance can be appreciated only when one remembers that almost $23 billion in home mortgages were insured by the F.H.A.[41] In 1954 maximum mortgage amounts protected by the F.H.A. were liberalized still further.[42]

Low rent housing. Federal assistance to towns and cities to meet the problem of substandard housing has taken two other forms: (1) low rent public housing built under the provisions of the United States Housing Act and its amendments;[43] and (2) federal aid for urban renewal and slum clearance. The latter demonstrates present-day recognition of the premise that a piecemeal attack upon slums simply will not work. A thrust at one slum pocket merely results in its displacement to other areas. The city is like the proverbial dog that chases its tail. It simply never catches up.[44] Hence the acceptance of the view that slum prevention requires a coordinated program for launching an assault upon the entire problem of urban decay. Since 1937, therefore, our public housing program has come of age. Local responsibility for the elimination of slums has been continued, but the frontal attack upon the problem has been widened to include an amalgam of local police powers and federal assistance under the general heading of planning.

Low rent or public housing began with the passage of the United States Housing Act of 1937. The provisions of that law are of more than passing interest since they have served as the basic approach to federal-city relations in this area.[45] The United States Housing Authority was empowered to borrow $800 million for the purpose of making loans to local public agencies in order to assist the latter

[40] Public Law 345, 84th Cong. 1st Sess. (1955), sec. 220.

[41] Housing and Home Finance Agency, *op. cit.,* p. 115.

[42] Public Law 560, 83d Cong., 2nd Sess. (1954), especially section 203.

[43] Since 1947 the Statute has been administered by the Public Housing Administration of the Housing and Home Finance Agency.

[44] For example, New York City, since 1937 has build 70,000 low cost units at a cost of more than a billion dollars and yet today one out of five families in the city still live in slums. *New York Times,* March 15, 1954.

[45] See chapter 17.

in the building and administration of low rent and slum clearance projects. Loans to local agencies were not to exceed 90 percent of the cost of the project and were to be repaid in 60 years at the going federal interest rate plus one half percent.[46]

To foster local initiative, the federal government required the states to pass enabling legislation permitting local units, cities and towns, to create housing authorities. No loans were made available to low rent projects unless the city made a grant to the local agency in the form of cash, land, or community facilities equal to at least 20 percent of the development or acquisition cost of the project. This provision meant that the local governing body was required to approve all projects proposed by the local housing authority.[47] Finally the law contained a so-called equivalency requirement; the number of dilapidated and unsanitary dwellings closed or destroyed was to be equal in number to the low rent units to be built.

The local housing authority, usually a board, is responsible for the construction, operation, and maintenance of the project. In addition to the construction loans granted it by the federal government it also received an annual subsidy equal to the difference between the actual operating costs and the income it received from its tenants.[48] Dwelling accommodations were made available, to quote the law "only to families who lack sufficient income, without benefit of financial assistance, to enable them to live in decent, safe and sanitary dwellings . . ." [49] Federal law denies low rent housing to any tenant whose aggregate income is more than five times the annual rental charge.[50] Each year an inspection is made to enforce this low rent requirement.

Proposals for low rent public housing have always evoked a storm of controversy. The prevailing view seems to be that the government has no obligation to provide housing subsidies. This is the point often made by realty boards, mortgage and lending agencies who have always asked that private enterprise be "given a chance." This, despite the fact that the federal and local units have tried to meet only the needs of those who have been priced out of the hous-

46 Federal Code Annotated, *Low Rent Housing* (1956 supplement), Title 42, chapter 8, section 1409. After March 1, 1949 the maturity date on the loans was reduced to 40 years.

47 50 Stat. 888-889.

48 Federal Code Annotated, *op. cit.*, section 1410 (a) through (d).

49 49 Stat. section 4 (6). This provision was continued in all subsequent housing statutes.

50 *Idem.*

ing market. The so-called "Wet" bills sponsored by Wagner, Ellender and Taft in 1945 and 1946 were passed by the Senate and defeated in the House. In 1949 a program for 810,000 units to be built over a six year period was voted by Congress. In the first year of its enactment Congress sought to reduce the number of units to 5000 but public pressure succeeded in raising the number of units to 50,000, somewhat less than half of the originally proposed rate.

During the Korean war period, when national urgency resulted in a reduction in the amount of building materials available, the number of units was reduced to 20,000.[51] In 1956 Congress authorized the construction of 70,000 units for a two year span, or 35,000 annually. At the present time federally-aided low rent housing consists of those projects built by local housing authorities and those federally-owned projects that are being or were transferred to them. In December, 1954, 390,000 dwelling units in 2038 low rent housing projects were in operation.[52]

Urban redevelopment. The Housing Act of 1949 also contained a program for slum clearance and urban redevelopment in addition to its low rent housing features. Title I contained the so-called "write down" provisions. Municipalities desiring to redevelop an area could condemn the land and improvements on it and resell it to a private developer at a cost sufficient to permit him to make a profit on his investment. Two-thirds of this loss was borne by the federal government and the remainder by the municipality.[53] In 1954 a more comprehensive program for urban renewal was undertaken when Congress enacted a new housing law. The "write down" provision of the earlier law was continued but it was made part of a more concerted approach to the problem of urban blight and decay.

Three main objectives were contained in the new law: (1) prevention of the spread of blight through the enforcement of housing and occupancy controls; (2) rehabilitation of salvageable areas; and (3) clearance and redevelopment of nonsalvageable areas. The heart of the new program was contained in what is called its "workable program." Each community desiring federal assistance must prepare such a program whose main components are: adequate codes and ordinances, a comprehensive community plan, neighborhood

---

[51] Federal Code Annotated, *op. cit.*, section 1411.6.

[52] Housing and Home Finance Agency, *op. cit.*, 357.

[53] 63 Stat. 413-414 (1949).

analyses, proper administrative organization, provision for financing, housing for displaced families and community-wide citizen participation. Planning assistance is provided both by the Urban Renewal Service of the federal government and grants to municipalities and local bodies for planning efforts. Once a workable program has been certified to the federal government, the municipality becomes eligible for various kinds of grants: financial aid for physical clearance and redevelopment of slum areas; low rent housing projects; and assistance for displaced families. No aid, however, will be given unless the local agency has been authorized by state and local law. As of 1954 a total of 188 communities were in the process of developing "workable programs" for 279 renewal projects.[54]

The act of 1954 is notable for its departure from the previously segmented approach to housing. It recognizes urban blight and decay as symptoms and not causes. It focuses attention on the inadequacy of housing and occupancy codes, the lack of community-wide participation, and above all, on the need for a more comprehensive approach. The stimulus of federal funds for assistance to communities, cities and towns will undoubtedly result in great steps toward the goal of both federal and local governments—better housing for all Americans.

BIBLIOGRAPHY

Books:

Abrams, C. *Forbidden Neighbors.* New York: Harper and Brothers, Publishers, 1955.

———. *The Future of Housing.* New York: Harper and Brothers, Publishers, 1946.

Burke, A. J. *Financing Public Schools in the United States.* New York: Harper and Brothers, Publishers, 1951.

Cubberly, E. *Public School Administration.* New York: Houghton-Mifflin Co., 1929. Revised edition.

De Young, C. A. *Introduction to American Education.* New York: McGraw-Hill Book Co., Inc., 1942.

Hagman, H. L. *The Administration of American Public Schools.* New York: McGraw-Hill Book Co., Inc., 1951.

House Committee on Banking and Currency, 83rd Congress, 2nd Session. *Housing Act of 1954.* Washington, D. C.: U. S. Government Printing Office, 1954.

---

[54] Housing and Home Finance Agency, *op. cit.*, pp. 450-454.

Housing and Home Finance Agency. *8th Annual Report.* Washington, D. C.: U. S. Government Printing Office, 1955.

National Citizens' Commission for the Public Schools. *Financing Public Education in the Decade Ahead.* New York, 1954.

Senate Committee on Banking and Currency. 79th Congress, 1st Session. *General Housing Act of 1945.* Washington, D. C.: U. S. Government Printing Office, 1946.

U. S. Department of Health, Education and Welfare. *Annual Report for 1954.* Washington, D. C.: U. S. Government Printing Office, 1955.

PART
FIVE

Conclusion

The Future Development of the City

[illegible]

1. It is evident from what we have [illegible] ours is rapidly [illegible] [illegible] our national existence [illegible] [illegible] today [illegible] some [illegible] more intensified.

2. The [illegible] found [illegible] liberty, changed [illegible] the values of our society largely urban in [illegible]

In the city, division of labor and [illegible] of a machine civilization [illegible] and an unparalleled [illegible] At the same time, however, [illegible] confines of city life [illegible] community. The possibilities [illegible] the dangers of the [illegible] dwellers was [illegible] lived considerably [illegible] need of the entire [illegible] [illegible] in many areas [illegible] the [illegible] of the individual.

CHAPTER TWENTY-FOUR

The Future Development of the City

MAJOR TRENDS

An appraisal of municipal government at the mid-century necessarily involves an understanding of what has gone on before. A backward glance at the life cycle of the American city reveals many trends that are bound to affect its course of development in the years to come.

1. It is evident from what has been said in preceding pages that ours is a rapidly evolving urban economy, one in which the change to an urban circumstance is a dominant motif. In the brief span of our national existence, our society has been transformed from a nation of farmers to one of city dwellers. Whereas in 1790 approximately 95 percent of our population was engaged in agricultural pursuits, today three out of five people live in the city. In the decades ahead it is entirely probable that the urban trend will become even more intensified.

2. The shift from a rural to an urban condition has had profound consequences. It has altered our conception of individual liberty, changed our attitudes toward government, and has made the values of our society largely urban-oriented.

In the city, division of labor and specialization—the attributes of a machine civilization—brought the city dweller increased leisure and an unparalleled opportunity for the satisfaction of his wants. At the same time, however, his liberty of action within the close confines of city life represented a potential threat to the rest of the community. The possibilities for the violation of property rights and the dangers to the health of others were magnified. Thus the city dweller was confronted with a paradox: his range of choice was widened considerably, but his behavior was made subject to the greater need of the entire community. In brief, then, the shift from an independent to an interdependent society led the municipality to intervene in many areas which in a rural environment might properly be considered the province of the individual.

Urbanization has also had a marked effect upon the role of local government. Old problems were magnified and new ones appeared. The primary institutions of social control—family, church, and neighborhood—were subjected to increased stresses and strains. In such circumstances as these, traditional municipal functions such as sanitation, education, police and fire protection, were expanded. Health, welfare, recreation, housing and a host of other municipal activities were added. A greater reliance was placed upon law as an instrument of regulation. As a direct consequence of the closeness of city living, therefore, the contacts between the individual and his municipality have been increasing all of the time.

In slightly more than a century and a half urban values have gained increasing acceptance. Individualism, suspicion of government—the hallmarks of a rural society—have gradually yielded to the concept of the government as a guarantor of our rights. The welfare of the community has been placed above that of the individual. Today there is increasing recognition of the need for government when man lives in proximity to his fellow man. One can hazard the guess that in the years to come there will be a constant effort to redefine the relationship of the individual to his municipal government.

3. The rapid gravitation of people to the cities was accompanied by changes in governmental structure. Part-time government, the "impractical amateur," and the dispersal of governmental power among many agencies and boards were factors which left municipal government unable to cope with many of the immediate and pressing problems of urban America. Maladministration of city affairs became widespread and was the subject of frequent comment by both the reformer and the citizen.

The trials and tribulations experienced by many cities in the last quarter of the nineteenth century led to a search for more fundamental principles of government than those that had prevailed when the country was primarily a nation of farmers. The fruits of this effort appeared in the evolution of a strengthened municipal executive. The powers of the mayor were expanded, primarily at the expense of the council, and the council-manager with its separation of legislative and administrative power became an important part of the municipal scene. In more recent times the mayor-administrator plan, a union of political and managerial competence, has made considerable headway, especially in the large cities. With these changes came wide acceptance of professionalization, the merit system and full-time government in most of our larger cities and in many of the smaller ones. As the need for more technical and continuous administration makes itself felt, it can be expected that the tendency to concentrate authority and responsibility in the interest of efficiency and accountability to the people will be strengthened.

4. The enormous expansion of municipal power and the evils of city government portrayed so graphically by many of the muck-rackers led to many experiments designed to give the people a greater voice in their government. The direct primary, initiative, referendum and recall, proportional representation and preferential voting are but a few of the many attempts at "direct democracy" that have emerged. All of these were intended to counteract voter apathy by giving the people a greater share in the formulation of policies that affected them so vitally. Despite its laudable objectives, however, these efforts have largely failed, primarily because they overburdened the voter. There is no substitute for voter interest. The low rate of voter participation in elections at the city level continues. More civic effort rather than mechanical devices are needed if municipal government is to be made more responsive to the wishes of the people.

5. In the field of municipal politics, however, much progress can be reported. Here the efforts of the civic reformer have borne fruit. "Boodling" and the plundering of city treasuries have virtually ceased. Voting frauds have been almost eliminated. Political patronage is gradually being replaced by the merit system. In general, a better tone of political morality has emerged.[1]

The era of the boss is on the wane. Party politics have become more "free style" in many cities. Members of political parties have been given a greater voice in the formulation of party policies. Distribution of power within the party is much wider than was formerly the case. In response to this trend, the broadly based party has given rise to the leader, a party head who must win the acceptance of the rank and file to stay in power.

But it must also be noted that the complexity of modern urban government has made it increasingly difficult for the citizen to supervise his government. The regulatory and service functions of the city create new opportunities for those who would use govern-

[1] L. Gulick, "The Shame of the Cities—1946," *National Municipal Review*, XXXVI., (1947), pp. 18-25.

mental power for their own special interests.[2] As the city moves further in the twentieth century this will constitute a constant challenge to the citizens of our municipalities.

6. The administration of justice in the modern city has lagged far behind the needs of its people. Several weaknesses deserve to be noted. The courts of the city suffer from inadequate authority, low prestige and improper organization. Their jurisdiction is limited and often is insufficient to deal with many of the problems brought before them. County courts and higher courts of the state may have concurrent jurisdiction. In many instances it is difficult to discover where the authority of the city courts end and those on a higher level begin. Much of the failure in this area is a result of the inability of the state to comprehend fully the nature of the problems faced by our cities. But regardless of where the fault may lie, duplication, overlap and delay often bedevil the well-intentioned judge and the harassed citizen.

The agencies of the court also need modernization, and this becomes a fact of cardinal importance when one realizes that the court's work does not begin until law enforcement agencies have acted. The public prosecutor in most instances is an elected official. His office is staffed on a political or even a partisan basis. Organization on a professional and merit basis has made only halting steps. The continued use of the time-honored grand and petit juries has raised many doubts in the minds of the legal fraternity. The powers of the grand jury have been superseded largely by the prosecutor and whether the petit jury can properly decide complex questions of law that baffle even the highly trained lawyer is at least a debatable point.

Court procedures in many instances are archaic. The continued use of the adversary proceeding to solve such complex matters as family disputes, juvenile delinquency and a host of other social problems is open to question. Court fees, the printing of the record, the intricacies of legal procedure which only a lawyer can understand—in brief, the high cost of justice—operate to the disadvantage of the person without means.

Some progress has been made in this area. The short-lived unified municipal court system, the coming of the public defender, the rise of specialized courts such as the Small Claims court, and the

[2] *Ibid.*, p. 24.

legal aid effort of the American Bar Association are promising steps. More thought, however, will need to be given to the role of law in the cities as an instrument of control.

7. Rapid progress in the development of technology and transportation has made possible the dispersal of urban populations. This has an important bearing on the problem of intergovernmental relations since the city is highly responsive to the operation of these factors. The same forces that have brought about a concentration of people into closely congested areas have now made possible the dispersal of urban populations. The coming of electricity as a form of energy, the perfection of the internal combustion engine, and the development of a complex network of highways enabled both people and plants to flee the central city. The mushrooming of suburban and rururban areas has occurred at an unparalleled rate. In many instances, however, the economic nexus to the central city has been maintained.

This trend which promises to be a dominant one for many years to come poses many problems for the city. The mobility of plants and people influences land use and urban growth. The movement away from the city undermines its tax resource. Property values and the yield from property taxes may decline. Moreover, a city is vitally affected by factors beyond its borders over which it has little or no control. Fringe areas with a lower tax rate may attract industry. Suburban cities may depend upon the central city for water supply, schools, hospitals, police and fire protection, and a host of other services.

Above all, what we are witnessing is the growth of economic regions in which political authority is fragmented among many political units. Common problems must be handled by divided political authority. There is no single government for the area as a whole. In brief, the technological forces that have given rise to the city are no respecters of political boundaries. They have made existing legal lines obsolete. The powers of our municipalities no longer coincide with economic and social fact. Thus the persistent outward movement is forcing us to think more and more in terms of metropolitan areas rather than cities. Yet thus far no form of government has been devised that has either the power or the authority to deal with the problems of the entire metropolitan community.

8. State-city relationships are now in a period of readjustment. Indeed, the process has been a continuing one for more than half

a century. Here too, technology, because it has brought about an interdependence among the people of the state, has had a significant impact.

For almost a century after the founding of the republic, the towns and, later, the cities enjoyed a large measure of self-government, even though legally they were considered creatures of the state. The rapid spurt of industrial development in the last half of the nineteenth century, however, brought renewed state interest in the city. Part of this was due to a growing realization that the activities of the cities had an effect not only upon their own people but also upon those outside of their borders. Communicable diseases, for example, were not confined to legal boundaries. Unsanitary conditions in one municipality could spread to another or to the rest of the state. State interference in local affairs was also motivated by maladministration in city government, by partisan politics, and by rural fear of the growing urban majorities.

In the period 1850–1870 a rash of special legislation was passed by the state legislatures. The nature and extent of state control have been described in prior pages. Here it is merely necessary to note that city after city lost control over many vital aspects of its internal affairs. City hall was replaced by the state house often with drastic consequences for the people of the city. The many disastrous experiences of our cities provoked resistance and ultimately caused the rise of the home rule movement, essentially a plea for greater municipal autonomy. A large number of our states today permit their cities to determine their own governmental structure. Special legislation has been eliminated.

While this may be considered a gain, it is also true that the powers of the city vis-a-vis the state are in a continuous state of flux. In a sense this was almost inevitable since the only constant was change itself. The states cannot and apparently will not ignore the growing need for uniform standards for all its citizens. The wide variation in financial resources and administrative capacities of its municipalities and the aforementioned growth of metropolitan areas have compelled them to intervene. General legislation applying to a class of cities instead of to a single city has been passed. State administrative supervision of cities is on the increase precisely because the activities of local governments often have a direct bearing on the welfare of the people of the state. Frustrated city officials may fulminate against state interference, but it cannot be denied that the states have a legitimate interest in the government of the city. Consequently, the powers of the city are more and more becoming a matter of state definition. It is in this connection that rural dominance of state legislatures acquires new significance. The real issue is not state legislation but rather the passage of laws that will reflect an appreciation of the needs of the cities. This can come about only when the voting strength of urban majorities is reflected more fully in the formulation of state policies.

9. The factors of technology have also been responsible for the growth of federal-city relationships. Just as the city became an interdependent community, so was the nation bound together in an intricate maze of relationships. The health, education, and welfare of our people according to the Constitution are matters of concern to the state and local governments. Yet the national government cannot afford to ignore the widely varying standards in these areas since they do have an important bearing on the welfare of the nation.

Perhaps this was nowhere more dramatically made evident than in the depression of the thirties. In that era of desperation the cities faced the hard reality of many millions of people who were destitute and unemployed. Frantic appeals to the states were followed by resorts to federal assistance when the resources of the former were exhausted. Federal-city relations were born in the time of the city's greatest trial. Welfare programs, public assistance, housing and health, to mention but a few areas, came within the purview of federal authority.

Today the purse strings of the federal government have enabled it to extend its authority into that domain that was reserved to the states under the Constitution. One can speculate on the consequences of such action for our society, but for the cities the crucial question is whether aid shall come to it directly from the federal government or whether it shall come through the states. Here again rural dominance of the state legislature is a matter of significance. The cities can gain a greater measure of autonomy either by breaking the hold of the rural elements on the instrument that defines the scope and extent of their powers, or it can look to the national government where in the past it has received somewhat more sympathetic consideration.[3]

[3] D. W. Hanks, Jr., "Neglected Cities Turn to U.S.," *National Municipal Review*, XXXV., (1946), pp. 172-173.

THE ROLE OF THE PLANNING INSTRUMENT IN URBAN GOVERNMENT

A broad review of the development of the American city, therefore, reveals much evidence of astonishing growth and ferment. Many governmental changes have been made in response to the needs of people living in close proximity to one another. Many more are needed. In many instances the evolution of our society has been so rapid that a lag in our municipal political institutions has occurred. More change and further adjustment can be forecast for the future.

In the government of urban communities much more is needed than immediate attention to pressing problems. It is essential that we gain an understanding of our present circumstances in order that we may deal more effectively with them. More than this, it is necessary to think of future problems in order that we may anticipate them before they become acute. Above all, a knowledge of the factors affecting city development will enable us to chart their future course. It is in this connection that the use of the planning instrument by city governments, already given tremendous impetus by the Housing Act of 1954, assumes particular importance.

The formulation of a master plan is a complex task, but it is the key to the present and future course of city growth. It involves the gathering of data on land use, population growth, economic trends, traffic, congestion, and a host of other factors that affect the life cycle of the city. These data can be employed in innumerable ways to guide the physical development of the city. They are the basis of adequate zoning. They highlight the persistent needs of the city, present and future, permitting the budgeting of city expenditures in the light of fiscal capacity and community decision. They permit the delineation of both the public and the private areas of responsibility. Housing, traffic, street widths, and parking are all dependent upon the wise use of planning based on accurate data. Planning, in brief, furnishes the basis for informed judgment by members of the council and the executive officers of the city. It is the starting point for community action. Once planning is under way, the efforts of elected officials can be synchronized with the various elements of power within the community. With this kind of implementation, planning becomes a working reality. Without it, it is hardly more than an empty gesture. Finally, the planning instrument permits the hurdling of outmoded legal and jurisdictional lines by linking the efforts of citizens, urban planners, and the city upon the basis of area rather than governmental jurisdiction.

The American city, as we have previously noted, is the workshop of the nation. It produces the goods and services upon which most of our people depend. Within its borders are to be found a major part of our communication and educational facilities, and indeed, most of our people. The city not only produces the goods that make our civilization what it is today but it also molds our viewpoints. City attitudes toward individual liberty and government are fast becoming national attitudes. How the city meets its problems will determine in large measure the future of our society.

Index